THE HOLIDAY WHICH?
GUIDE TO ITALY

GW00319539

THE HOLIDAY WHICH?
GUIDE TO
ITALY

Edited by Ingrid Morgan

Published by
Consumers' Association and Hodder & Stoughton

Acknowledgements to: **Susie Boulton**, **Val Campbell**, **Frances Roxburgh**, **Adam Ruck**; **Anne Rook** (Art and Architecture)

Tony Garrett, Text design
Ray Evans, Illustrations
David Perrott Cartographics, Maps

Which? Books are commissioned and researched by The Association for Consumer Research and published by Consumers' Association, 14 Buckingham Street, London WC2N 6DS and Hodder & Stoughton, 47 Bedford Square, London WC1B 3DP

British Library Cataloguing in Publication Data
The Holiday Which? Guide to Italy.
1. Italy — Description and travel 1975-
—Guide-books
I. Boulton, Susie II. Morgan, Ingrid
914.5'04928   DG416
ISBN 0-340-39966-X

Typeset by Marlin Graphics Ltd
Printed and bound in England by
Hazell, Watson & Viney Limited
Member of the BPCC Group
Aylesbury, Bucks

CONTENTS

INTRODUCTION

*❝A man who has not
been in Italy is always
conscious of an inferiority❞*
DR JOHNSON

ORENRINCIPISAPOST CAVIVSVSI

Italy has pulled in the crowds for almost as long as the human race can remember. Throughout modern history the faithful have travelled there in pilgrimage and the most ambitious political rulers, from Charlemagne to Napoleon, have looked to Rome for the ultimate legitimacy. Artists and those aspiring to an understanding of arty matters have made the same journey as an essential part of their training and education, the northern barbarian's bid to acquire civilisation. If it had not been so obvious, Goethe would have said not that Italy without Sicily makes no sense, but that Europe without Italy makes no sense. Our civilisation has its roots there.

In the Age of Reason when the fashion for the Grand Tour was at its height, its impetus was not simply the desire to educate the eye and furnish the ancestral pile with souvenir views of Venice and oddments of classical statuary; nor even the urge to sow a few wild aristocratic oats, although this was certainly one of the attractions. Italy was also a lesson in history for the young empire builders from wave-ruling Britain. For having been all-powerful, Italy had fallen right to the bottom of the heap: disunited, subjugated, dilapidated, backward, in Byron's words "the Niobe of nations..... childless and crownless in her voiceless woe; an empty urn within her withered hands, whose holy dust was scattered long ago." Gibbon and his fellows sifted sherds among the cow pats in the Roman forum and thought how transitory are the works of man, how trifling his most noble efforts; how easily and how surely do the structures of the most solid empires crumble.

We no longer visit Italy for food for thought about the fate of empires, but continue to visit the country for its civilisation. It is said that in the western world two thirds of the historic monuments and works of art are Italian. Plundered as the country has been down the centuries, it has not surrendered more than a small part of its heritage, and remains in places – Rome, Florence, Venice, Naples and Sicily – almost indigestibly rich in historic and art historic interest. In Venice the digestion problem is worse for the city than the visitor: so great is the number of visitors that the precariously floating museum city now has to close its gates at ten in the morning on busy days. And in Florence sensitive sightseers have been going down with Stendhal's syndrome – fainting fits brought on by hyper-sensitivity to beauty – in the Uffizi. Unhealthy as it may be, people are increasingly interested in the past and its monuments. For such people there is nowhere more rewarding than Italy, and we make no apology for the fact that much of this guide is devoted to sightseeing. Many cities have the added attraction of living culture in the form of internationally famous music and film festivals.

As if the art were not enough, Italy is also a country of legendary natural beauty. It may come as a surprise that, with the broad exception of the Po Valley in the north, the peninsula is mostly mountainous – there are ski resorts just outside Rome and Florence, in Calabria and in Sicily – and most of its scenic spectacles involve mountains. Italy can claim Europe's most famous lake district and long stretches of magnificent mountainous coastline, with pastel-painted villages clinging to fertile volcanic slopes high above the sea.

Many regular visitors and expatriate residents choose Italy not for the art but because of the beauty of the land that gave birth to it and the balmy Mediterranean climate of a land of olive and citrus groves extending south to within sight of Africa, on a clear day. Perhaps the best-loved of all Italian landscapes is an inland one: the Tuscan and Umbrian hills so familiar from the background of Renaissance paintings, decorated with quiet old villages, cypresses and vines. In this classically balanced, civilised landscape it is easy to feel at peace with the world.

Even for the most devoted sightseer, the zest of an Italian holiday is being among Italians and their way of life, so refreshingly unlike us and ours, so Latin. If their art is part of our culture, it is an even bigger part of theirs, and the truism that culture is part of life is truer of Italy than anywhere. Professors are two a penny, taxi drivers talk opera and the erudition required to qualify as an official tourist guide is staggering. The Italians are demonstrative, histrionic, colourful, noisy, tactile. "They pour themselves one over the other like so much melted butter over parsnips," wrote DH Lawrence, who loved the Italian's freedom from inhibitions but, British after all, tired of the exaggerated emotionalism and the tenderness, "the macaroni slithery slobbery mess." In the homeland of opera, we see the natives as a race of lyric tenors, passionate hot and cold romantics, their feet way off the ground, a hand on the heart, a tear always at the ready.

Everyone agrees that Italians have style, and that the "Made in Italy" ticket means made well. They move with a natural grace, they are insufferably good-looking, and until a diet of pasta, oil and ice cream takes its toll in middle age they are the sort of shape that Italian clothes fit. They seem to know instinctively what looks good, and they care about how they look apparently more than anything else. They love to make a display of themselves and, better still, their children, and the spirit of peacock nation finds what we imagine to be its full expression in the evening promenade (*passeggiata*) when the entire population goes public.

Lawrence reflected on the contrast between this aspect of the Italian temperament and the spirit of ancient Rome, and concluded that in their unimaginative steamrolling efficiency the Romans were the least Italian of people. Yet the memory of Rome is part of the Italian temperament, another aspect of its romanticism which resurfaces from time to time in fits of grandiose revivalism, the role of the heroic tenor. One such revival was the Renaissance. Another was Fascism, short-lived and hollow in its pretension but very important, beyond the punctuality of trains, in its effect on the face of modern Italy. Resorts, both along the coasts and in the mountains, were conceived on a grand scale, and are now showing their age.

We tend to assume that romanticism is a luxury for the idle and that the Italian is more interested in frittering away the day in talk about art, revolution or sex than in doing an honest day's work. The political system is so paralytic that a government's life expectancy is counted in months. The economy we consider a joke: the land where modern financial methods were invented, now a *baci* republic where they give you sweets for small change. Other cherished notions are that Italians are corrupt, argumentative, shallow, capricious, violent without being strong, the most reckless of drivers and passionate of football supporters, incapable of making the distinction between sport and real life. Or perhaps they do make the distinction, but treat life as a game and only games as truly serious.

These are the modern myths of Italy. Despite the grains of truth they paint a misleading picture. Italians are not idle and the economy defies analysis and a lack of management by proving astonishingly resilient; vigorous growth at a time of international recession has been one of the main problems. We are told that they have more cars and washing machines than we do and that they have overtaken us in terms of economic importance in the world. The Italians have made a better job of dealing with industrial unrest and terrorism than many nations, bombs on the beach in other parts of the Mediterranean have distracted attention from Italian violence and there are reports that even street crime is on the wane.

At the heart of the Italian way of life and behind its strength lies the tradition of individual resourcefulness and expert craftsmanship, whether it be Florentine leather, Pininfarina design, manufacturing fake works of art or smuggling real ones. The streets may be inches deep in litter, Venice may be encrusted by corrosive filth, the sea water may be dangerously polluted, but the individual is immaculate, cutting a *"bella figura"*. His salary may be low, but somehow he prospers. There may be no government, but family life and town life go on. The state is a relative novelty in Italy and there is no trust in its benevolence and no respect for it, as you will discover if you wait obediently at a red traffic light in Naples.

Because it has communists we tend to think of Italy as a left-wing country, but at heart it is deeply conservative, a society run by the family, the church and vested interest. Economic progress has brought social change and challenge to traditional values and prejudices, but Italy retains the forms of a strict and hidebound Catholic country. In some areas topless bathing is still a punishable and punished offence, and in many churches you will physically be refused entry if not properly clothed, which means covering knees and shoulders.

The post-war economic boom has also changed the face of the country. After the Second World War nearly half the working population was engaged in agriculture; three decades later the figure was 11%. Remote regions have been civilised and now lack the appeal of being picturesquely primitive. TV and migration are blurring the once sharply-drawn lines of regional character in a country which despite its clear geographic unity has spent most of history politically fragmented and subject to foreign powers, and where the native blood of different regions has been diluted by infusions from all corners of the Mediterranean world. Italians cling tenaciously to their fierce local patriotism and especially the contempt felt by the urbane northerner for the uncultured native of the God-forsaken south.

For all its beauty, colour and vitality, Italy is not always an easy country to enjoy. It was relatively cheap ten years ago, but is no longer so. Many of its most beautiful monuments are in the middle of noisy modern cities which many of us go on holiday to escape. Much of the beauty of its most famous coastal scenery – the Bay of Naples, Taormina, the Bay of Palermo – has been squandered in an uncontrolled rash of shoddy building of new suburbs and concrete-block resorts. Most of the long sandy Adriatic coast has suffered the same ugly fate, and the coastal drive to Bari is the most effective antidote to romantic ideas about the style and elegance of everyone and everything Italian. Equally unworthy things, although on a smaller scale, have been perpetrated in the Alps.

Perhaps with reason, the Italians do not always feel the need to put themselves out greatly for the tourist. Towns close down for several hours in the middle of the day. You may have no appetite for a three-hour lunch, nowhere to go for a siesta, and a keen desire to visit the museums: so much the worse for you. Famous buildings are closed for long years of restoration. Museums are short-staffed and only partially open, and almost nowhere do you find explanatory notices or guided tours in English. Paintings in museums are poorly displayed. Country churches are almost invariably closed and the man with the key puts in an appearance when it suits him.

Eating out enjoyably is a problem. In both town and country you will eat your dullest meals in the smartest-looking restaurants and hotel dining rooms, and your most memorable ones in the discreetly advertised places round the corner, which you came upon by chance. The best sign is usually not being offered a menu or a wine list, but simply being asked what you want, or told what's on – a daunting experience for the first-time visitor worried about being taken for a ride and without much Italian on the tip of the tongue. Breakfast is not so much a problem as a non-event. The Italian is not interested in it, and the only concession he will make to your national routine is the ironic offering of watery coffee to accompany your papery roll.

All these things contribute to the robust flavour of Italian life and the challenge of a country that demands to be taken on its own terms, and richly rewards those who make the effort. The country's rough edges make a guidebook all the more valuable, potentially anyway. Italy's roughest edge is hotel accommodation. Outside Tuscany, the South Tyrol and the most exclusive coastal precincts few hotels contribute anything to the enjoyment of an Italian holiday and the few tend to be extremely expensive. The welcoming, cared-for family hotel and restaurant, which lies at the heart of provincial French life and tourism, is not an Italian phenomenon. All too often the tourist has the choice between the run-down pre-war relic of Mussolini's bold bid to create a tourist infrastructure and the equally impersonal modern airport-lounge business or package holiday hotel.

"But what of that? Comfort must not be expected by folks that go a pleasuring," wrote Byron. When in Italy, follow the Italian (if not the Byronic) example. Enjoy Life.

ABOUT THIS GUIDE

This is an all-in-one, a body-stocking guide designed not to take up much room but to cover just about everything and not leave you exposed. Our aim has been to produce a guide that you won't need to supplement except with road maps and city plans. The other exception would be a restaurant guide, but if there is one worth using we have not discovered it.

We have carved the country up in what we hope is a logical and useful way, with separate chapters for the big three city destinations (Florence, Venice and Rome), for the two big Italian islands, and a split for the rest of the country broadly following administrative regional boundaries except in the north where these make no sense for holidaymaking purposes. On page 66, our key map shows the chapter boundaries.

The introduction to each chapter is intended to give a flavour of what the region or city or island is like, what it has to offer whom, in fact whether or not you are likely to want to visit it. We have included summaries of local historical and art historical background in those chapters where such information is most likely to be of interest and relevant. Each introduction is followed by a separate section ("Visiting ....") with more detailed practical information about how and when to arrange and set about a holiday in the region, and specific recommendations of resorts and areas within the region. In all but the city chapters there follow descriptions of the region's towns, resorts, monuments and places of scenic interest, in alphabetical order. Inevitably, some villages and monuments are included in the entry of a nearby town or, in a few cases, country area. Those that are not cross-referenced can be found via the index. We have included addresses and/or directions only for sights likely to be difficult to find. We have not resorted to any device other than adjectives to convey degrees of beauty or interest. If this means you have to read the guide to extract information from it, we are not sorry.

The city chapters are structured differently, with brief descriptions of the city's areas, sightseeing descriptions divided by category, and separate sections on shopping and nearby excursions. Many chapters include separate features on themes of specific regional interest, varying from the *Mafia* in Sicily and the *Renaissance* in Florence to *Self-Catering Holidays* in Tuscany and Umbria and *Opera* in northern Italy.

Each chapter includes hotel recommendations, the result of first-hand inspections by us. As already indicated, our experience of Italian hotels is that most of them are either very expensive or dull or shoddy, and many are at least two of these three things. You will find the happy exceptions to this rule recommended here, along with some of the best in the expensive category and a number of hotels which we recommend, or rather suggest, not because they are excellent but because they seem to us to be the best there is in a place where you are likely to want to spend the night on a touring holiday.

If it is rare to find a good hotel in Italy, it is rarer still to find a good hotel with a good restaurant. We have eaten at many of the hotels in the guide, and in these cases include comments on the food where it is recommendable. We have found that a good, often relatively inexpensive, option is to stay at a restaurant which has bedrooms; we include several among our hotel recommendations.

We find accents useful as an aid to pronunciation and have included them, accentuating the stressed syllable of an Italian word whenever it deviates from the normal rule that the penultimate syllable carries the emphasis. "I" before another vowel counts as a syllable, so *trattoria* is normal and does not need the accent on the stressed 'i'. There is great flexibility in the use of accents and they are usually omitted from well-known words – Venézia, Caravággio – but a wrongly stressed word may well mean nothing, or the wrong thing, to an Italian. A cheese merchant may not be impressed if you ask him for a dung heap (*meta*) instead of half (*metà*) a cheese. Different accents also indicate how a vowel is pronounced, but this is of little importance to the tourist.

If this guide adds to the enjoyment of your holiday, please help us to improve it in future editions. We should be particularly grateful for reports on hotels you stay and/or eat in, whether it be to recommend the inclusion of hotels not in the guide, the exclusion of hotels currently included, or the amendment of existing entries. A hotel report form is included at the back of the book.

Hotel recommendations: explanation of symbols

Under each entry, we list the hotel's main facilities, including restaurant, swimming pool and sports on the premises. We indicate whether there's a lift, and a private parking area or garage. 'AC' means that most of the bedrooms have air-conditioning; it's wise to stipulate clearly in advance if you want this facility, and establish whether there's a supplement payable. All hotels have bedrooms with bath or shower unless we say otherwise. Our closing dates are inclusive.

Our £ symbols represent the maximum cost of a double or twin-bedded room with bath or shower, including breakfast for two people. In some areas – particularly coastal resorts, a minimum stay of 3 nights and half-board are obligatory in high season. As any hotel's stipulation of such requirements and indeed its observance of the area's "high season" dates – which can be June to September or only July and August – may depend on whether it has rooms to spare at a given moment, we have not indicated these terms unless they are an unexpected departure from the norm in an area (obligatory half-board in Florence or Venice, for instance). For more details, see the section on Accommodation, page 511 in our General Information chapter.

£	= you can expect to find a room for under £35
££	= you can expect to find a room for under £55
£££	= you can expect to find a room for under £75
££££	= you can expect to find a room for under £125
£££££	= you should expect to pay over £125 for a room

HISTORY

❝ *The ancient world ran down into the completed Roman Empire as into a reservoir... the modern world has flowed outward from that reservoir* ❞

HILAIRE BELLOC

ROME AND EMPIRE

A weighty overture to a lively opera, the centuries of Rome open yet hardly introduce the history of Italy. The Romans were one among several Latin peoples on the western plain of central Italy, who in the 6th century BC exhibited organisational virtues which were to outstrip the old Greek communities on the south coast, the Phoeniceans in Sicily, assorted mountain tribes and the elusive Etruscans, who dominated and civilised Rome for two centuries. Etruscan remnants suggest a lifestyle both highly cultured and fun; contemporary Romans were solid citizens who developed, ungratefully, in more political ways. In 510BC they threw out the royal Etruscan dynasty to become a republic. After a prolonged period of class struggle which strengthened and stabilised the relations of consuls, senate and plebs, Romans systematically conquered and colonised the Italian peninsula. By the middle of the 3rd century BC they had a wide web of municipal government, semi-autonomous but centralised by military commitments and varying degrees of citizenship. The formula proved exportable.

Roman possessions overseas began with Sicily, where a small-scale intervention sparked off the first long Punic War. Military and political impetus and an absolute faith in Roman values accumulated a vast and ultimately unwieldy empire. Continuous war produced military colossi – Sulla, Pompey, Julius Caesar – until in 27BC republic gave way to the personal rule of the overall winner: Octavius was hailed as the Emperor Augustus.

For two centuries the Pax Romana endured more or less intact. Italy was the privileged heart of the Empire where enormous wealth, unevenly distributed, sustained an elaborate economy that came to depend on imports of corn, oil and wine. Rome absorbed the customs and cults of many lands, though not the Christians whose habits of secrecy and flat refusal to recognise state gods were seen as threatening state authority. Christians were persecuted with increasing savagery as the later Empire began to disintegrate round its beleaguered borders and Rome itself came under threat; yet martyrdom under Diocletian around 300AD was followed under Constantine by Christianity's establishment as state religion. The bishops of Alexandria, Antioch and Constantinople were designated "patriarchs"; Rome's preferred the title "Papa".

The decline of the empire, Gibbon's "natural and inevitable effect of immoderate greatness", was swiftest in the west. During the 4th century the centre of power shifted eastwards to the security of Constantinople; in 395 the two sons of Theodosius divided their inheritance. The Western Empire, governed from Ravenna, was successively invaded by Visigoths, Vandals and Ostrogoths and in 476 formally ceased to exist. In Rome the popes, increasingly the agents of Imperial administration, were left as sole negotiators with the conquerors of Italy.

EARLY INVADERS

Not all barbarians proved barbarous: Theodoric for one ruled tolerantly over his Goths and Italians, Catholic Christians and heretical varieties, with the help of the Roman Senate. In the sixth century an attempt to revive the Western Empire died with Justinian, who left Byzantine art at Ravenna, considerable land in the hands of the pope, and a codified version of Roman law. Italy was an undefended Imperial outpost when the Lombards arrived; for two centuries they preserved the Roman language and culture by adoption and intermarriage, dividing Italy into dukedoms. The south they failed to conquer – Arab invaders had settled in – and Rome they left to the popes. Gregory the Great not only dissuaded them from siege but converted them from Arian heresy.

The fall of Imperial Ravenna to the Lombards in 751 finally broke all links with Constantinople: the pope appealed for aid to western Christendom in the person of Pepin, king of the Franks, who drove the Lombards out of Ravenna and handed the old Imperial lands to the pope. Pepin's son Charlemagne completed the Lombards' defeat, and on Christmas Day 800 the pope crowned the Frankish war leader "Emperor of the Romans", a ceremony reviving the powerful idea of a supreme western ruler, now allied with a supreme spiritual authority. But Charlemagne's heirs divided his empire; it was a single northern nation which later dominated Italy by right of the Imperial title.

After the break-up of the Carolingian empire Italy fragmented. Nothing hindered a proliferation of sparring feudal regimes. In the south, Lombard barons skirmished with the Saracens for two centuries before the Normans, land-hungry ex-Crusaders, forged a united Kingdom of Sicily on the feudal pattern. In the north, Magyar raids until the mid-10th century sent rural refugees to enlarge the towns, each governed by a count or bishop representing former Imperial authority. Strengthened and turning increasingly to commerce, towns by means of charters, agreements or simple revolt won the right to self-government. During the 11th century the northern cities of Italy were acquiring European pre-eminence as traders and bankers; overlordship within Italy they could resist.

POPE AND EMPEROR

The "Holy Roman Empire" was reinvented in 962 by Otto I of Germany and a pope whose influence was in eclipse; for several centuries after, a ruler elected by the German magnates had a legitimate title to Italy. Otto III was expelled by the Romans for his grandiose dreams – a precedent for lay and civic opposition. In the undignified power struggles of the 11th century the big issue was investiture: were bishops created by emperor or pope? Moral victories won by the papacy as it fought to keep the Church from lay control had to be backed up by someone else's army. The Norman kingdom in the south, originally "legitimised" by papal sanction, was the mighty ally; to keep Sicily and Empire well apart was obvious papal policy. It was therefore disastrous when the Hohenstaufen dynasty married into the Norman house and produced Frederick II, born and bred in Sicily, an emperor with comprehensive plans for Italy and many supporters. Three successive popes rallied the opposition and the struggle between

Guelfs (the papal party) and Ghibellines (pro-emperor) became part of every quarrel. In Guelf Florence, the party was itself split into Blacks and Whites, hardliners and moderates. Dante, who venerated the papacy but deplored its degradation, was a White exile.

When Frederick died in 1250 his son could not prevent the papacy offering his Sicilian kingdom round the courts of Europe, inviting its conquest. A French pope finally secured a French champion: Charles of Anjou defeated and killed the Hohenstaufen heirs. His rule was resented. On Easter Monday 1282 some insolent French soldiers in Palermo were the first victims of the Sicilian Vespers, an island-wide massacre whose leaders had Spanish allies. Anjou lost the island to Aragon and Spain acquired a lasting interest in Italy. The next German emperor however had none, and the papacy indulged unchecked in temporal intrigues. Boniface VIII, condemned with hatred in Dante's *Divine Comedy*, proclaimed "It is necessary for salvation that every human being should be subject to the Roman Pontiff" and treated as sinners all opponents to his ambitions. He antagonised the powerful religious orders, the Ghibelline nobles of Rome and the Guelf magistrates of Florence, the Aragonese in Sicily and finally the king of France who arranged his downfall. The papacy was removed for nearly a century to Avignon, whence it was unable to prevent its cities in central Italy being ruled by independent princes. One more emperor, Henry VII, came south in 1310 with hopes of unifying Italy. He died of fever, no match for the resistance of 14th-century Italians to any such idea.

THE CITY-STATES

The separate growth of the city-states, so out of step with the centralisation under a monarchy of most European nations, kept Italy fragmented. A handful of wealthy republics – maritime Venice and Genoa, academic Bologna, mercantile Florence, Siena and Lucca – held out against the 14th-century drift toward government by despot. In other towns all over Italy conflicts of parties and factions led to the dominance of a single family, reinforced by the confiscated assets of exiled rivals, who became dynastic *signorie*. Secure in their own domains, they battled for regional domination with the aid of mercenary troops – mostly foreign adventurers like Sir John Hawkwood's famous White Company. At home, the *signorie* kept order, collected taxes and added style to the municipality. The greater families – Este in Ferrara, Della Scala in Verona – established brilliant civilised courts; the Visconti of Milan concentrated on agressive expansion over the greater part of northern Italy.

By the 15th century five chief city-states had become established among a few small independent duchies and republics. The Kingdom of Naples had one huge city and a feudal peasant population; in the papal states, Rome had a pope again whose task was to reclaim authority after years of absence and schism. The powerful Venetian republic had acquired mainland possessions as well as her maritime empire, and petty warfare continued as she and

Florence resisted the encroachment of Milan. Mercenaries were Italian now: this was the era of the *condottieri*, proud professionals highly trained in all military arts who took their troops to the highest bidder. The greatest was Francesco Sforza, who made himself indispensable to Milan and after the last Visconti died became its ruler, founding a dynasty of his own.

In mid-century the formation of the Italian League ended hostilities. Nearly fifty years of peace and increasing prosperity saw in the Italian Renaissance, that extraordinary revel of talent in art and thought spreading from Florence – in her golden age, under the Medicis – to Milan, Venice, Rome, Ferrara, Verona, Urbino, Siena, Mantua, Verona; giving Italy a self-esteem unknown since classical times; continuing to flourish though the political climate changed.

FOREIGN DOMINATION

The 16th-century "calamities of Italy" began with French invasions of Naples and Milan, each with support from an Italian state playing the game of foreign intervention for domestic ends. Lodovico Sforza boasted in 1496 that the pope Alexander was his chaplain, the emperor Maximilian his *condottiere*, Venice his chamberlain and the king of France his courier who must come and go at his bidding; a few years later he was ending his days in a French prison, and no combination of Italian states had much effect on further events. Francis I of France and the new emperor Charles V, ruler of Spain, the Netherlands, Austria and Italy, fought their battles for supremacy on Italian soil. In 1527 Habsburg troops out of control sacked Rome – the barbarians had come again. Between wars, Charles distributed titles and Habsburg marriages among Medicis, Sforzas, Estes, Gonzagas and lesser houses. He transferred imperial rights in Italy to his son Philip II of Spain, and by the settlement of Câteau-Cambrésis in 1559 a Spanish peace descended on Milan, Naples and a patchwork of affiliated autocracies – including the Duchy of Savoy, in due course to make modern Italian history.

For a century and a half, while Spain, France, England and the brand-new Dutch republic matured through religious wars, political struggles and world exploration, very little happened to Italy except economic decline. Spanish taxation and corrupt officialdom lay heavy; Jesuits, the Index and the Inquisition arrived; intellect and creativity were increasingly stifled and there was a considerable exodus to France and England. The astronomer Galileo was tried, and the philosopher Bruno burned. Music, less controversial, was much developed.

Savoy was the exception in Italy's stagnation. Not really an Italian state in the 15th century and an anonymously strategic battleground for much of the 16th, it emerged as a diplomatic buffer zone between Spanish Milan and France. Its reinstated duke efficiently rebuilt a modern state, and successive rulers played intricate politics, winning and losing fortresses and Alpine passes, until 1713. The Treaty of Utrecht, which ended the War of the Spanish Succession and put Italy under Austrian domination, gave Sicily to Savoy. This arrangement was rapidly corrected and Sardinia handed over instead, with the consolatory title king of Sardinia.

Grand Tourists in 18th-century Italy relished the surface opulence of Rome, Venice, Florence, Milan, even Naples, ignoring their poverty and crime. To correct the tragic social and economic imbalances by rational reform was the aim of the century's benevolent despots: "Enlightenment" methods were attempted first in Naples and Sicily by the Bourbon Charles III (Don Carlos) who regained the kingdom in 1734. He made little headway against the numbers and privileges of the clergy and the feudal excesses of the nobility. But in Tuscany, Austrian since the last Medici died, grand-duke Leopold introduced vaccination, free trade, equality of taxes, considerable reform of the Church and abolition of torture, of the death penalty and most of the armed forces. In Milan the sweeping reforms of Maria Teresa and Joseph II led to Lombardy's lasting economic success.

The French Revolution in 1789 nevertheless revealed the existence in Italy of agents, extremist groups and Jacobin clubs. The royal army of Sardinia and Piedmont (Savoy's territory was extended eastward in 1748) fought the French alone from 1793 to 1796, when Napoleon swept across the country sowing republics behind him. By 1799 every part of the mainland except Venice (presented to Austria) had experienced a French republican constitution. Napoleon's eventual arrangements strikingly simplified Italy into three – imperial France, the kingdom of Italy and the kingdom of Naples. The local complexities of centuries were replaced by a single system of administration and the Code Napoleon.

RISORGIMENTO

After Napoleon's downfall the 1815 Congress of Vienna, determined to prevent any future French domination, put back the clock in Italy. Absolutist regimes, restored, were under repressive Austrian control. "Italian affairs do not exist" declared Metternich, ensuring he be informed of any by planting an espionage network. The Italian response, a ferment of secret societies, conspiracies and local rebellions, was presently given national expression through patriotic literature and journalism. Plays and operas illustrated the overthrow of oppression; inspirational-historical novels became popular after Manzoni's splendid *I Promessi Sposi*. Journals were more overtly revolutionary but lacked a common aim – the liberated republican unity urged by the influential Giuseppe Mazzini was countered by monarchist schemes and non-agressive federations under the pope.

The monarchists' white hope was Charles Albert (1831-49) of Sardinia and Piedmont, his kingdom further extended by the Congress of Vienna to reach from the Alps to the Genoa coast. Charles Albert was a romantic, most untypical of the tough dynasty of Savoy; he had nationalist sympathies and an army. In 1848-9, responding to successful revolts in Venice and Milan and promised support from all over Italy, he twice went to war with Austria and was twice defeated. It took Austria a few weeks longer to dislodge the republics set up in Venice and – by Mazzini and his guerilla disciple Garibaldi – in Rome.

Charles Albert abdicated in favour of Victor Emmanuel, who in honouring the constitution granted by his father preserved the only liberal element in a subjugated Italy. Piedmont, meeting-place for exiles from other states, became more Italian. Her prime minister from 1852, Camillo di Cavour, proved to have a talent for practical diplomacy unknown in Italy since the Medicis. Grasping the need for international negotiation rather than domestic upheaval, he sent troops to the Crimean War and was present – without specific hopes – at the ensuing Congress of Paris. There resulted an extraordinary conspiratorial meeting between Cavour and Napoleon III of France, who wanted Victor Emmanuel's daughter to marry his cousin and in return was prepared to help in a manipulated war between Piedmont and Austria.

This he did; during 1859 the French drove Austria out of Lombardy. Subsequent arrangements, not entirely smooth, were still being negotiated when Garibaldi and his Thousand, all red shirts and fervour, sailed from Genoa for Sicily. Their four-month epic enthralled Europe. From Sicily Garibaldi advanced north toward Naples; Victor Emmanuel and the royal army hastened south to take the papal states and meet the hero. Plebiscites ratified Piedmont's victories and the kingdom of Italy was proclaimed in 1861. Cavour, its chief begetter, died the same year. Venetia was added in 1866, spoils of participation in the Austro-Prussian war, but the question of Rome remained an embarrassment. In 1870 the diversion of Europe's attention by the Franco-Prussian war gave the new state the opportunity to seize Rome from the pope and complete the unification of the country.

POLITICS AND WARS

The right-wing ministers who succeeded Cavour proceeded to "Piedmontise" an Italy largely illiterate, where outside Rome and Tuscany only a minute percentage spoke Italian rather than a dialect. The south was subject to uniform heavy taxes and agriculturally inappropriate laws; the north was where the taxes were chiefly spent – on towns, communications, schools, industry – as Italy scrambled to become a modern nation. The state had to deal with brigands, rioting, anarchists, strikes and the thriving Sicilian mafia. When a Liberal regime took over in 1876 the need for stability was arguably paramount: Depretis maintained his ministries by *trasformismo*, "transforming" opposition into support by bribery, a process which undermined both party politics and the confidence of the electorate. Socialist groups spread, cohering by the 1890s into the legal opposition of the Italian Socialist Party. This decade saw the major scandal of the banks' collapse, the humiliating defeat of colonial hopes in Abyssinia and the assassination of the king.

Italy entered the 20th century under Giolitti, master of the "absorption" process by which subversive Radicals, Republicans, Socialists – and Catholics since the Pope now allowed them to vote – were all "reconciled" in pursuit of stability and economic growth. Great advances, particularly in engineering, were made with the introduction of hydro-electric power; Fiat and others led a developing car craze. In 1911 Italy expunged the shame of Abyssinia by winning Libya for a colony, though few wanted to go and live there even in an era of massive emigration. The successful war roused tremendous patriotism. Votes for soldiers – virtually universal male suffrage – doubled the electorate, and the Giolitti system failed to contain the resulting mass parties.

A year into the First World War, Italy abandoned a 30-year-old alliance with Austria and Germany to join in on the side of Britain and France, who offered a discreet understanding about territorial gains. By the armistice, the entire economy was geared to the war, and 5,000,000 men had won more battles than they had lost. The peace brought Trieste and the Trentino to complete Italy's frontier, but no prestigious colonies. Postwar exhaustion, inflation and unemployment exacerbated all divisions; extreme Socialists adopted the hammer and sickle and helped multiply riots, strikes and sit-ins; weak coalition governments failed to halt a slide toward total chaos. It was hardly surprising that when something did, it attracted support.

Benito Mussolini, editor of a pro-war, pro-revolution journal, formed his *Fascisti di Combattimento* (Battle Groups) in 1919. Para-military squads of students and ex-officers burned down Socialist party offices all over central Italy and "purged" union leaders with castor oil and bludgeons, winning the approval of landowners, industrialists, police and respectable Liberals for rescuing the country from tyranny. Recruits flooded in. Mussolini found himself leader of a mass movement which won 35 seats in the 1921 elections; he rapidly formalised the National Fascist Party and announced a confident programme. A disastrous general strike allowed the takeover of towns and communications and the "march on Rome". Martial law might have stopped the Fascists and was at this point requested by the Liberals in office, but king Victor Emmanuel III refused and instead invited Mussolini to form a cabinet. After his first low-key coalition, the power of the *squadristi* and new militia carried the Duce through a brutally rigged election and the murder of Socialist leader Matteotti. Attempts to assassinate him thereafter served as "provocation" for press censorship, political police, repressive laws and a re-jigged administration. State machinery rather than the bully-boys supported his grandiose, flat-footed dictatorship. Even the Church settled for peaceful co-existence; the pope finally accepted the limitation to the Vatican City of his secular powers.

Mussolini's foreign manoeuvring, culminating in the conquest of Ethiopia, completely alienated Britain and France. His intervention in Spain impressed nobody and the resulting involvement with Hitler trapped him in the Second World War. For Italy it proved ignominious: the army, overstretched and out of date, failed in every campaign. At home the realities of bombs and hunger made nonsense of Fascist propaganda. In 1943 as the Allies landed in Sicily Mussolini, aged and apathetic, was deposed by a consensus of king, army and politicians. The new government then so bungled their armistice that German troops had time to occupy most of Italy, planting Mussolini in a puppet regime in the north. The Allies spent a year and a half fighting their way up the battered peninsula to a weary and expensive victory.

POST-WAR ITALY

Anti-Fascist movements long exiled or underground had swelled the vigorous Resistance in northern and central Italy. The partisans who shot Mussolini and liberated Milan, Turin and Genoa belonged to half a dozen political groups, of which by far the most effective was the wide network of the Communists. In 1946 the northern vote carried the referendum which exiled the monarchy and made Italy a republic, and three mass parties emerged from the pack – Christian Democrats, Communists and Socialists. Then cold war and Red Threat irretrievably split the Socialists, and put American influence as well as the Church urgently behind the Christian Democrats. This gave them a central domination over all parties, since diminished to necessary coalitions but never lost. Boosted by Marshall Aid and purged of nationalism, Italy in the 1950s and early 1960s achieved her "economic miracle". She had, to begin with, a huge supply of cheap labour – between 1954 and 1962, Fiat never had a strike; she discovered natural gas in the Po valley and oil in Sicily; and she acquired up-to-date technology. The problem of the South was tackled, first by pouring capital into roads and services, later by investment in new industry. The Fund for the South was one of many powerful Italian "quangos": the Christian Democrats, permanently in power, tended to bypass the cumbersome Civil Service and make use of national agencies whose staffing and policies often coincided with party support. "*Sottogoverno*" improved efficiency. It also kept the press busy with tales of scandal and corruption.

In 1968-69, the stresses of major, rapid change erupted in violence. There were demonstrations, wildcat strikes and factory occupations by workers objecting to programmes of "rationalisation", and riots by a generation of surplus students from the overcrowded universities. The first terrorist acts were a neo-Fascist response that died away in the 1970s, but left-wing terrorism became thoroughly established – scores of separate groups operated with international links and covert public sympathy. Terrorist activities became commonplace, a national melodrama of bullets, bombs, kidnappings and communiqués. The hard line taken by the authorities in 1978 over the kidnapping and murder of ex-Prime Minister Aldo Moro by the Red Brigade was something of a watershed, and Italian terrorist acts diminished to the level of a nuisance rather than a threat.

In 1971, the State decentralised itself, creating 15 semi-autonomous regions in addition to the five established in the 1940s and 60s. Italy's structure of municipality, province and region is now that proposed in the 19th century by Cavour. Its aims were to reform central bureaucracy and release local energies; its opponents saw it as the opportunity for multiple Communist takeovers. Neither highest hopes nor worst fears have yet been justified.

ART &
ARCHITECTURE

❛ *Travellers do nothing else but run up and downe to see sights, that come into Italy* ❜
JOHN EVELYN

THE ANCIENT WORLD

The Etruscans

Who the Etruscans were and whence they came is uncertain but
from the 8th century BC until the 1st century BC, when they were
absorbed within the Roman civilisation, they dominated the area
between the Po, the Tiber and the Arno in northern and central
Italy. Etruscan art was strongly influenced by Archaic Greek art but
evolved its own vigorous expression. Most of what has survived
comes from tombs or temples. As in most ancient and medieval
cultures Etruscan life and art revolved around religion and the
problems of death and immortality. Although no temple survives
we know that they were not unlike Greek ones with a colonnaded
portico in the front but smaller, squarer and with a superstructure
made of wood rather than stone or marble. Tiles and sculptural
decorations for the roof, often statues of gods, were made of
terracotta. These cult statues stood either inside the three inner
chambers (cella) of the temple or on its roof. Many of the Etruscan
gods were borrowed and adapted from Greek ones. Whole cities of
underground tombs (necropolises) have yielded paintings,
terracotta and bronze sculpture, metalwork and painted vases. The
wall paintings usually depicted scenes of pleasurable activity,
banquets, dance and games in a flat but lively and expressive style
related to Greek vase painting. The most important examples are at
Tarquínia, north of Rome.

Sculpture (stone and terracotta, not marble) survives in the form
of sarcophagi; reliefs on the sides or reclining figures on the lid,
often of startling realism, were motifs later used by the Romans.
High quality of craftsmanship can be admired in small bronze
statuary, objects such as engraved mirrors, elaborate jewellery and
pottery fired in blackish grey and often decorated with figures. In
Etruscan art, vitality and realism were sometimes allied to a brutish
quality which reflected a culture in which human sacrifice was not
uncommon and in which fear of death led to elaborate funerary
artefacts and the practice of divination.

The Greeks in Italy

As early as the 8th century BC, Greek settlements appeared in Sicily
and the south of Italy. The ruins of several monumental temples,
mainly from the 6th and 5th centuries BC, testify to the importance
of these settlements which modelled themselves on the great cities
of Greece such as Athens. This Greek colony of southern Italy – later
called Magna Graecia, Greater Greece – and its art, architecture and
culture had much impact on the Romans.

Temples were built in the Doric, Ionic or Corinthian styles, or
"orders". The Doric was the earliest and the Corinthian the latest,
although the adoption of one order or another was partly dependent
on the area of mainland Greece from which the building community
came. The plan of the temples however varied little. On a stepped
base stood the rectangular sacred chamber (cella) completely
surrounded by a colonnade (peristyle) which was often double at

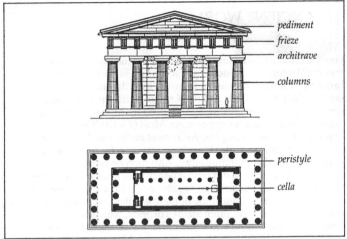

the front and back of the temple. The columns supported an architrave, a frieze and eventually a triangular pediment. Marble was the material used for the whole structure, including the tiles, although terracotta was also employed especially for roofline decoration. The pediment, and often the frieze, were decorated in honour of the gods with relief sculptures telling their story. Many works of art were looted by the Romans when they took over southern Italy in the 3rd century BC. But with the looting came also a whole-hearted admiration and the adoption of a complex culture with its mythology and colourful gods.

The Romans

In the 8th and 7th centuries BC early Romans established themselves around the seven hills of what was to become Rome. The position was strategically sound for defence and trade. In the early years of its history Roman art showed little imagination and creativity. The military and economic building of the Republic was paramount and much of the artistic production was borrowed from the Etruscans and, increasingly, from the Greeks. The Romans' domination over Magna Graecia brought them into direct and plentiful contact with Greek art and the wide variety of styles which had evolved over several centuries. Archaic, severely classical or, later, more emotive and softer (Hellenistic) sculptures and paintings were in turn admired, adopted or abandoned to suit Republican or Imperial taste and need.

The design, type and architectural vocabulary of buildings were derived from Etruscan and especially Greek architecture but the Romans made imaginative and technical contributions in their use of the arch, of lime-based concrete and of brick. These design and technical innovations revolutionised the concept and practice of building by making the spanning of enormous spaces possible and by allowing lighter constructions. It led to the erection of several-storeyed buildings, aqueducts, grandiose baths and theatres and the architectural feat of the Pantheon (Rome) with its domed ceiling. The principal buildings were not only temples but also civic ones. The forum – not unlike the modern Italian *piazza* – served as a meeting place, a market and an administrative, legal and religious centre. All towns had their forum but the best surviving examples are in Rome and Pompeii. In the Forum of Trajan (Rome) colonnaded areas enclosed porticoed temples, basilicas (justice and trade halls), the tabularium (state archives), libraries, arcaded markets and columns of victory (Trajan's Column). In other parts of the town, palatial public baths (thermae) were erected. They performed the social function of a lavishly decorated meeting place as well as providing a hot and cold bath system of great sophistication. The vastness of the Baths of Caracalla (Rome) which could accommodate some 1,600 people gives some indication of the architectural skills of the Roman architects. Amphitheatres rather than theatres provided for the type of entertainment the Romans preferred – games and gladiatorial contests. Elliptical or round, they were built as a series of superimposed arcaded openings. The Colosseum in Rome has three storeys of 80 openings each linked by vaulted corridors. Triumphal arches were erected to commemorate the military victories of generals and emperors and, like much of Roman art or architecture, were examples of art at the service of the state. Their decoration consisted not only of applied Greek orders, but also of reliefs or monumental sculptures which celebrated the victory and the men responsible for it.

Their deep admiration for Greek art led the Romans to copy and emulate; their sculpture is often thought, sometimes unfairly, to be derivative. Copies of famous Greek statues of athletes, philosophers, heros and gods abound in Italian museums. Much of Roman sculpture either in relief or in the round was executed as state propaganda. The large standing portrait of Augustus (Vatican, Rome) celebrates him as a great general and his presence, with his family, on the reliefs of the altar, the Ara Pacis (Rome), shows the increasing involvement of the state in religious affairs. Later, emperors saw themselves as gods and were depicted as such. Portraiture in the form of busts reflects a general interest in the individual. Busts of ancestors placed in the home protected it and busts of great men in public places were an inspiration to all. The decoration of sarcophagi (tombs) sometimes included portraits as well as mythological or historical themes. Public buildings and private houses had rich decoration; the surviving wall-paintings of Pompeii and Herculaneum give some idea of its variety, with illusionistic architectural vistas, landscapes, stories from classical myths and scenes of daily life.

BYZANTINE AND EARLY CHRISTIAN ART

In 313 the Emperor Constantine gave Christians the freedom to worship unmolested and the earliest examples of Christian art date from around that time. The Roman basilica, a central rectangular space framed by colonnaded aisles, was converted into a church, setting down the traditional plan of later churches with nave and aisles. Many of the symbols expressing the Christian faith were borrowed from either Jewish or Roman imagery (Christ as the Good Shepherd). Painted examples can be seen in the Catacombs (Rome) which were both cemeteries and meeting places at times of persecution. From the 5th century some of the fundamental Christian sacraments and devotions were represented in paintings or mosaics on the walls of churches: the Baptism, the Eucharist, the Madonna and Child and the four Evangelists and their symbols (St Mark, the lion; St Luke, the ox; St Matthew, the angel; St John, the eagle) are commonly seen. Santa Maria Maggiore (Rome, 5th century) even has a mosaic cycle of the Infancy of Christ.

With the decline of the Roman Empire the political and religious centre moved from Rome to Byzantium (Constantinople). The influence of Byzantine art in Italy was felt more specifically at certain periods and in certain centres. Byzantine artists were most prolific under Justinian in the 6th century and under the Macedonian emperors in the 9th. Byzantine churches were built on a central (cruciform or polygonal) rather than a longitudinal (basilican) plan and roofed with domes. Outstanding examples, dating from the 6th century, can be seen in Ravenna, then the western capital of the Byzantine empire. San Vitale and Sant' Apollinare Nuovo (Ravenna) were also wonderfully embellished with mosaics (small fragments of stone or glass, tesserae, set in mortar to form pictures), a medium much employed in Byzantine art. From the 9th century to the 13th Venice was the centre of Byzantine culture and influence in the peninsula, as the church of St Mark attests. The domes of Byzantine churches were usually dominated by a monumental image of Christ Pantocrator (the Almighty) with a cruciform halo. Lower down, scenes illustrating the festivals of the church (Christmas, the Nativity; Ephiphany, the Adoration of the Magi, etc) were often illustrated. Saints identified by inscriptions in Greek, and the Virgin and Child were also traditional subjects. The style of paintings and mosaics was characterised by clear contours, stylised forms and the use of repetitive lines to create decorative patterns. It was a style well suited to the didactic purpose of the Church at the time and to the easy reading of narratives, even at a distance. It was influential throughout Italy up to the 13th century.

THE MIDDLE AGES: ROMANESQUE AND GOTHIC

Romanesque architecture and sculpture

In the 11th and 12th centuries the regional character of Italian art began to be more marked. The north of Italy was susceptible to Germanic and French forms while in the south, Byzantium, Arabia and the remains of Magna Graecia were important sources of inspiration. Relatively typical of Italian architecture, however, was the fact that the bell-tower (campanile) was not an integral part of the church, as in buildings north of the Alps, but was built separately. Quite often the baptistery (round or polygonal) was also independent. The complex of two or three distinct buildings can still be seen in several towns: at Pisa in Tuscany or at Verona in the Veneto (both 12th-century) for instance. Churches were usually basilican in plan (with or without transepts) and often roofed in wood. Italian Romanesque façades were broad and screen-like with superimposed rows of arcading, occasionally embellished by sculpture (San Michele, Pavia, 12th-century). In Lombardy brick was the usual building material; in Tuscany, stone and marble were easily available and therefore more usual (cathedral, Pisa, 12th-century). Facing walls in marble was also quite common and in Florence (San Miniato, 11th-century) and Siena (cathedral, late 12th- to early 13th-century) a colouristic effect was achieved by combining two different kinds of marble. In the south, mosaic decoration and stilted arches indicate Byzantine and Muslim influences as at Monreale in Sicily (cathedral, 12th-century).

The earliest architectural sculpture was ornamental in character, decorating capitals and the lintels of portals. Its imagery consisted mainly of foliage and monster-like forms; Lombardy is particularly rich in examples (San Michele in Pavia, 12th-century). In the south (Apulia) classical remains promoted a more naturalistic treatment of forms. **Wiligelmo**, the great sculptor of Modena cathedral, may have trained there. He carved, for the cathedral façade, lively and expressive reliefs (early 12th-century) with Old Testament stories (Genesis). At Ferrara and Verona another sculptor, Niccolò (c1130-1140) executed reliefs in a more delicate style. In Tuscany sculpture was sparingly used on exteriors and was more usually seen in the interior of churches on furniture such as pulpits. In Pisa, Guglielmo carved a pulpit (1162), now in Cagliari, in an ornate style which had much impact around Pisa. Bonanno da Pisa made unusual bronze doors (cathedral, Pisa, c1180) with narrative reliefs of the New Testament in a style still dependent on Byzantine art and its motifs. In Parma, **Benedetto Antelami** and his workshop carved a complex iconographical programme in clear, rhythmic forms on the baptistery (late 12th-, early 13th-century).

Gothic architecture

The reception of the Gothic style in architecture was spasmodic and patchy in Italy and, with the exception of Milan cathedral (begun late 14th century), no building was whole-heartedly Gothic. The style was characterised by the use of a system of ribs, shafts and pointed arches (as opposed to Roman or Romanesque round ones) which allowed walls and vaulting to be lighter. The problem of sideways thrust which had led earlier masons to build very thick walls was thus reduced. Lofty churches with large expanse of glass and exterior buttresses were erected in northern Europe. Beyond the system of ribbed vaulting and shafts and an emphasis on airiness and slightly larger windows, Italian masons took little from this. Walls remained fairly solid, left bare of tracery decoration and instead painted with frescoes. Gothic architecture varied much according to regions and the domes of San Antonio in Padua (13th-century) revealed a latent Byzantine element in the Veneto. But many churches like Santi Giovanni e Paolo (Venice, 1260-1385) and Santa Croce in Florence (late 13th-century) shared the characteristics of widely placed columns and of uncluttered spaciousness. This was due to the rise and rapid spread of the mendicant religious orders in the early 13th century. Dominicans and Franciscans were preachers first of all and the design of the churches allowed unimpeded seeing and hearing. City-states erected magnificent, sometimes fortified town-halls (Siena and Florence, early 14th-century) often in widely differing style (Doges' Palace, Venice, 14th- to 16th-centuries) while fortified palaces in Milan, Ferrara and Mantua testify to the importance of princely courts in northern Italy.

Gothic painting and sculpture

The preaching of the mendicant orders promoted an increasing demand for devotional images. The visual arts were the teaching books of the time and even when commissioned by lay patrons, works of art were essentially religious in character. Relief sculpture, painted altar-pieces (wood panels) and wall frescoes (paint applied on wet plaster) told stories from the Old and New Testaments and the Apocrypha. The lives and sufferings of Christ and the Virgin inspired some outstanding works of art as did the lives of favourite saints such as saint Francis, the founder of the Franciscan order who died in 1226.

With **Nicola Pisano** Italian sculpture entered a new era. Classical elements gave his first pulpit a new solidity and vocabulary of forms (baptistery, Pisa, 1260) while the softness and slenderness of his second pulpit for Siena cathedral (1265) derived from French Gothic sculpture. His gifted pupil **Arnolfo di Cambio** was also an architect of talent (Florence cathedral) and the range of commissions he received shows a new impetus given to the role of sculpture: large scale figures for the façade of Florence cathedral, a fountain for Perugia and monumental tombs. Arnolfo is one of the first of these great artists able to rise to the challenge presented by different media. Another of Nicola's pupils, and possibly the greatest sculptor of the period, was his son, **Giovanni Pisano**. Whether in large scale figure sculpture (Siena cathedral, façade, late 13th century) or in reliefs (pulpits, Pistoia 1301 and Pisa 1311) Giovanni explored the human and dramatic element of each subject, often creating images of great poignancy. Many of his interpretations were quite new and very influential. A notable example was his rethinking of the Madonna and Child group; no longer a frontal, austere and formalised image, it expressed a loving relationship.

The Sienese **Tino da Camaino** (splendid tombs in Siena and Naples) may have trained with Giovanni but worked in a gentler style. The Pisani's clear and exciting story-telling capacity was followed up in softer forms by another Sienese, **Lorenzo Maitani** (façade of Orvieto cathedral). Maitani was also the architect responsible for the design of its façade. **Andrea Pisano**, another Pisan though not from the same family, modelled and had the first set of doors for the Florence baptistery cast (between 1329 and 1336). A technical feat, the gilt bronze reliefs tell the story of saint John the

Baptist in a delicate, rhythmic style.

The ability of sculptors to represent increasingly complex stories was soon matched by painters. Rome was one of the centres where the stylised Byzantine manner was gradually rejected. Roman painters also worked at Assisi on the early decoration of the church erected in honour of saint Francis. From c1270 for some 80 years Assisi became a training ground for artists from all over Italy. The Florentine Cimabue (1240-1302) decorated the apse of the church with a cycle of the Life of the Virgin. **Giotto** (c1266-1337), who may have been his pupil, probably worked there, benefitting not only from contacts with other artists but also from the variety of challenging subjects which were depicted for the first time (Life of St Francis). Giotto's own first masterpiece, the frescoes of the Arena chapel at Padua (c1305), reveal him as an artist of intense imagination, a pithy story-teller inventing new ways of depicting space, time and motion for greater expression. His solid figures and his forceful interpretation of subjects had an immense impact on his native city, Florence. His frescoes in the new Franciscan church of Santa Croce (Bardi and Peruzzi chapels) influenced a whole generation of painters (Taddeo Gaddi, Maso di Banco), most of whom were also involved in the decoration of that building. It was customary for wealthy families to undertake the decoration of a whole chapel (or even its actual building). In that way they acquired a family chapel and contributed to the overall ornamentation of the church at the same time. Santa Croce had several such chapels provided by prominent Florentine families. It is a pattern of patronage which recurred throughout this period, the Renaissance and later.

In Siena, **Duccio**, apparently still under the sway of brilliant Byzantine colours, motifs and stylised drapery, was nevertheless outstandingly inventive. Like Giotto, he was the initiator of a whole school of painting which flourished in the first half of the 14th century. He painted in tempera (pigment mixed with an egg medium) on panels, rather than *buon fresco* (true fresco) on walls, and his more delicate and elegant style reflects the smaller scale of his works and the very different medium. Duccio was a story-teller first of all. The lucidity and logic of Giotto's spatial organisation were often ignored but never to the detriment of the story. Duccio's wish to convince led him to paint delightful details: coloured and intricate buildings, trees and occasional homely objects were lovingly painted in his masterpiece, the Maestà (Museo dell' Opera del Duomo, Siena, 1311). Whether painting in tempera or in fresco **Simone Martini** (c1284-1344) kept Duccio's jewel-like colours and elegance of line. His understanding of the expressive power of linear rhythm and abstract shapes was outstanding and he created an art at once lyrical and visually rich. He worked in Siena, Assisi, Naples and Avignon. His exact contemporaries, the Sienese **Lorenzetti** brothers **Pietro** (active c1306-45) and **Ambrogio** (active 1319-1347) shared with him a sense of the decorative and rich Ducciesque colours but both were fascinated by the way in which the clear and logical organisation of buildings and landscape could help the reading of a story. In that sense they were influenced by Giotto. Ambrogio surpassed all other painters of his time in his magnificent panoramic landscape of Siena, and its surrounding countryside executed as an allegory of the Good Government of Siena in the Palazzo Pubblico (1337-39). The skill with which both Pietro and Ambrogio were able to convey a convincing sense of perspective on the flat surfaces of frescoes and panels was not equalled until the early 15th century. The Black Death of 1348 took its toll of artists and patrons alike but, in Florence, **Andrea Orcagna**, painter and sculptor, carved an impressive tabernacle dedicated to the Virgin for Orsan Michele (1350s), and large scale decorative schemes in Santa Maria Novella (Spanish chapel, 1360s) and Santa Croce (choir, c1380) were undertaken. Similar projects in northern Italy (Padua, Santo and Oratorio di San Giorgio; Verona, Sant' Anastasia) show that neither the spirit of the church nor of the artists had been extinguished by the catastrophic pestilence.

Towards the end of the 14th century close links between the courts of northern Italy and the very splendid ones of Bohemia and France brought to that region the International Gothic style. Essentially created under the patronage of kings and princes, it was an elegant and refined style suited to small precious-looking objects (ivories, metalwork, small paintings and manuscript illuminations). Beyond its appearance of refinement, however, it explored the natural world: delightful studies of plants, animals and buildings abound amid the graceful forms and rich materials. **Gentile da Fabriano** (c1370-1427) brought these aspects to Florence (Uffizi, Adoration of the Magi altarpiece, 1423) from northern Italy and the precise and elaborate drawings and paintings of Pisanello (c1395-1457) which include so many nature studies may be seen to have derived from this earlier International Gothic style.

THE EARLY RENAISSANCE – FLORENCE

Against a background of political instability caused by episodes of fighting with Milan, a new intellectual assertiveness seems to have pervaded the city of Florence at the beginning of the 15th century. Scholars contributed to the changes about to take place by the re-evaluation or rediscovery of classical texts and history. Artists and patrons alike began to look afresh at classical remains as sources of inspiration. It is possibly no accident that the new developments in the visual arts should have originated within the democracy of a city-state and not in a court environment.

Architecture

Visits to Rome and careful study of its Roman buildings and their methods of construction spurred the sculptor and architect **Filippo Brunelleschi** (1377-1446) to rethink traditional Tuscan architecture. Strict proportions governed the plan and elevation of his loggia, chapels and churches in Florence. Arches and Corinthian capitals were inspired by antique buildings but the use of a dark grey stone, *pietra serena*, to stress details and the structure of the building was a traditionally Tuscan element. His greatest claim to fame is the technical feat of spanning the vast crossing of Florence cathedral which had remained unfinished for more than a century. His knowledge of Roman building methods helped him considerably in the construction of the dome. Its imposing yet elegant design is testimony to Brunelleschi's genius and to the determination and pride of the Florentines to embellish their city. **Michelozzo** (1396-1472) built for the Medici family what was possibly the most influential palace of the time – the Palazzo Medici-Riccardi. Cosimo de' Medici also commissioned him to build the Dominican convent of San Marco, the decoration of which was entrusted to Fra Angelico. The architect and humanist writer **Leon Battista Alberti** (1404-72) was an antiquarian and his own buildings emulated Roman design and vocabulary more closely. What characterises his churches (Mantua; Rimini) or his domestic architecture (Rucellai Palace, Florence) is clarity of forms and imposing appearance. He established rules and models which were of fundamental importance for later architects. Alberti wrote a treatise on the art of painting in which he codified a system of geometric perspective probably devised by Brunelleschi; his thoughtful advice to painters and sculptors on organisation, study of forms and representation of subjects and stories derived from the achievements of some of his greatest contemporaries but also provided useful concepts for artists throughout the century.

Painting and sculpture

A major feature of the Early, and indeed of the High Renaissance, is the intimate relationship between the two arts: painters learned from and emulated the qualities of volume and mass inherent in scupture, while sculptors of reliefs wanted to rival the complexity of painted scenes suggestive of city or landscape settings. Many artists were both painter and sculptor.

The most inventive sculptor of the century was **Donatello** (1386-1466) whose work, mainly in Florence, Siena and Padua, encompassed a variety of styles and materials (marble, bronze, wood, terracotta). Like his friends Brunelleschi and Alberti, Donatello studied the Antique and the poise and massiveness of his earliest large-scale marble figures for the church of Orsan Michele and the cathedral in Florence are evidence of his knowledge of classical sculpture. Donatello constantly challenged traditional forms and in every work a new and more vivid interpretation signalled his genius. His was a sensitive, intensely human approach which explored every facet of divine and human love and suffering. The bronze pulpits in San Lorenzo and the painted wood Mary Magdalen in the Museo dell' Opera del Duomo (Florence) are outstanding examples of the way in which he manipulated materials for expressive effect. A very different personality was the sculptor **Lorenzo Ghiberti** (1378-1455), rightly famed in his own time for the two sets of doors he cast in bronze for the Florentine baptistery. A superb craftsman, Ghiberti was also an inventive story-teller whose reliefs on the doors provided generations of painters and sculptors with motifs and ideas.

The short-lived painter **Masaccio** (1401-28) shared with the young Donatello a concern for clarity and solidity. Aware of Brunelleschian perspective Masaccio was the first to represent figures, forcefully modelled by means of a consistent light, within a credibly spacious setting. Masaccio's frescoes in the Brancacci chapel (Florence, church of the Carmine, 1420s) are expressive and deeply serious. Perspective also fascinated the painter **Paolo Uccello** (1396-1475) and his fresco of the Flood (Santa Maria Novella, 1430s) organised a chaotic scene within a deep space. By temperament more gentle and essentially concerned with the expression of sincere devotion, the painter **Fra Angelico** (c1400-55) worked almost exclusively for the order of the Dominicans (Convent and Museum of San Marco); clearly aware of the simple grandeur of Masaccio and of new architectural forms, he painted with simplicity in fairy-tale vibrant or pastel colours. More mysterious were the colours and compositions of the defrocked monk **Fra Filippo Lippi** (1406-69) whose inventiveness in figure groupings and interpretations of traditional religious subjects is a constant source of pleasure. The frescoes of **Andrea Castagno** (1421-57) suggest a more tortured spirit. They portrayed tense figures drawn in nervous outlines and deep colours (Convent of Santa Apollonia). The sculptor **Luca della Robbia** (1400-82) was a more joyful personality and his invention of the polychromed and glazed terracotta technique created a whole new range of colourful and weather-proof relief sculptures which adorned the façades of buildings or brightened up the gloom of church interiors (Pazzi Chapel, Santa Croce). The sober and restrained style of Luca was popularised and made more elaborate later by a large family workshop. Working in mid century, the brothers Bernardo and Antonio Rossellino (1409-64, 1427-79) and Desiderio da Settignano (1428-64) produced some magnificent tombs (Santa Croce, San Miniato) and sensitive portrait busts which stressed the uniqueness of the individual: a sentiment which characterised the 15th century and which heralded the beginning of the genre of portraiture. Two major workshops, that of **Antonio Pollaiuolo** (c1432-98) and **Andrea Verrocchio** (c1435-88) produced a wide range of bronze and marble sculptures and paintings. Both were concerned with the representation of movement and both undertook an amazing variety of different commissions (portraits, altarpieces, tombs, bronze statuettes, fresco decorations, equestrian monuments), dealing equally with religious and mythological subject matters. Their output exemplifies the widening range of interests of enlightened patrons (Medici) in the late 15th century. The sensitive and intellectual approach of **Botticelli** (1445-1510) was particularly well suited to the painting of complex mythological allegories (Birth of Venus, Primavera, both in the Uffizi). Botticelli's intensely emotional late paintings coincided with the new mood of religious fanaticism created by the preaching of the Dominican Savonarola in Florence at the end of the century. A similar intensity pervades the paintings of his pupil Filippino Lippi (1457-1504) whose fantastic imagination drew upon recently rediscovered Roman wall decorations (Santa Maria Novella, Strozzi chapel).

Leonardo da Vinci (1452-1519), who trained in Verrochio's workshop, represents the paragon of the Florentine Quattrocento artist, proficient in all the arts. He sought employment from Ludovico Sforza in Milan, claiming great skills as a military engineer, architect and sculptor as well as painter; it was there that one of his masterpieces, the Last Supper, was painted (Santa Maria delle Grazie, Milan). His obsessive studies of natural phenomena and his theoretical writings took much of his time and he finished few paintings. In the handful that have survived a new attention to the effects of light can be observed. His study of light led him to evolve a new *sfumato* technique (very gradual transition of tones from light to dark) which, eventually, revolutionised the way painters thought and used colour and tone.

THE EARLY RENAISSANCE – OUTSIDE FLORENCE

From Florence many artists were called to other centres and brought with them the new style (Donatello to Padua, Fra Angelico and Botticelli to Rome for instance). Others flocked to Florence itself to admire and learn. **Piero della Francesca** (c1415-92) trained in Florence but took back to his native Umbria and to Urbino, in the Marches, the monumental style of early Florentine painters and the clarity of the new perspective system. Piero's serene style relied on forms of mathematical proportions and a superb sense of balance.

In Siena the sculptors **Jacopo della Quercia** (1374-1438) and later Vecchietta (1412-80) showed awareness of Florentine ideas but retained essentially individual styles. Painters (Sassetta, Giovanni di Paolo) were building upon the rich Sienese tradition and were concerned with the clear and somewhat naïve representation of narratives, paying relatively little attention to Florentine spatial experiments. In Rome the popes and other patrons called artists from Florence for most major commissions, initiating a pattern of prestigious patronage which would eventually turn Rome into the artistic centre of Italy in the 16th century.

In the Veneto **Andrea Mantegna** (1431-1506) was a painter of outstanding stature. Although he trained in Padua he had a sound knowledge of Florentine artistic developments, possibly through his father-in-law, the Venetian painter Jacopo Bellini (c1400-71). A deep love and understanding of antique remains pervades his works in which skilful manipulation of illusionistic effects is combined with forceful linear drawing (St Zeno, Verona; Eremitani church, Padua). His employment as a court artist in Mantua resulted in imaginative secular decoration which foreshadows much later illusionistic ceiling decoration (Castello, Mantua, Camera degli Sposi).

In Venice the early part of the 15th century was still dominated by Gothic and Byzantine influences. The first major artist to give Venice an artistic identity was Jacopo's son **Giovanni Bellini** (c1435-1516). Deeply influenced at first by both his father and by Mantegna, Bellini produced a multitude of Madonna and Child groups of great originality. These and his portraits were in great demand. His monumental altar-pieces (Accademia, Venice) set new standards of composition and size. Bellini's most important contribution, however, was his study of light and the soft, poetic luminosity which pervades his paintings. Carpaccio (c1470-1523) was a painter of large narrative scenes in which the Venetian scene is carefully depicted.

At the court of Ferrara the painter **Cosme Tura** (c1430-95) displayed some affinity with Mantegna's linear and tense drawing. His work often appears tortuous yet has an intensity and tautness which lifts him above the simply mannered. Cossa (1435-77) and Ercole di Roberti (c1448-96) followed this distinctive style (Schifanoia palace, Ferraca, 1470). North Italian sculptors working in the late 1440s (Quattrocento) were consciously emulating the Antique. Piero Buonacolsi, called Antico, (small bronze figures) and Tullio Lombardo (monumental marble tombs, Venice) both showed a sensitive assimilation of Antique sculpture.

HIGH RENAISSANCE AND MANNERISM

Florence and Rome

For a few years after 1500 Florence retained its artistic primacy with Leonardo da Vinci and the young Michelangelo as the great figure-heads, but the imposing personalities of Julius II, Leo X and Clement VII gradually drew major artists to the papal court in Rome. The architect Bramante, Michelangelo and Raphael are the three giants of the first half of the 16th century. The versatility of their talents is a measure of their outstanding abilities and of the demands of contemporary patronage; the painter Raphael also worked as an architect and Michelangelo was sculptor, painter and architect.

From Milan **Bramante** (1445-1514) arrived in Rome in 1499 where he studied Roman remains and was given papal patronage. His works may be seen as typifying the architecture of the High Renaissance: grandiose plan and a clear structure were matched by appropriate decorative features (Rome, Tempietto, 1502). Many of his projects were never executed but his ideas and designs were broadly adopted by Antonio Sangallo (1473-1546), among others, for the Palazzo Farnese (Rome), the façade of which was partly designed by Michelangelo. Like all the above architects (and many others including Raphael) **Michelangelo** (1475-1564) was also involved in the gigantic task of redesigning old St Peter's, essentially going back to Bramante's design. New St Peter's was not however finished until the 17th century and after many more alterations, and Michelangelo's inventive architecture is best appreciated in Florence (Medici chapel, San Lorenzo and Biblioteca Laurenziana, designed 1520s). The concept of the "villa" is essentially a 16th-century one and **Raphael** (1483-1520) and **Giulio Romano** (1492-1546), his pupil and assistant, were responsible for some of the earliest examples (Villa Madama, begun c1516). Romano's Palazzo del Te in Mantua, which he built and decorated in the 1520s and 1530s for the Gonzagas, was a bold and imposing extension of the ancient Roman concept of the *villa suburbana*, a pleasurable living space for the summer. In Verona and Venice the High Renaissance style initiated by Bramante was implemented by two great architects and engineers, Michele Sanmicheli (1484-1559) and Jacopo Sansovino (1486-1570). Palaces in Verona and the Venetian Mint are respective examples of their work.

Michelangelo is more familiar now as sculptor and painter, Raphael as painter. **Michelangelo** was primarily concerned with heroic figures and, whether nude or draped, these were expressive of his deeper concerns. His almost exclusive dependence on the nude figure as the principle vehicle for the expression of all emotions had an immense influence on contemporary and later artists and was instrumental in formulating the Mannerist style. Trained as a sculptor and preferring to work in that medium he was often frustrated in the execution of the large projects he undertook (tomb of Julius II); many of his surviving works are unfinished, providing the modern onlooker with an understanding of the technical and conceptual process involved in the carving of these figures but obscuring his final intentions (Accademia, Florence). A large proportion of his early (David) or later sculptures (Medici chapel tombs, San Lorenzo) are in Florence but his major pictorial undertaking, the ceiling of the Sistine Chapel, is to be seen in Rome. The painting of the Old Testament scenes for the ceiling was completed in 1512 while the Last Judgement of the altar wall was not painted until much later (1536-1541). The stories were told with a boldness of conception and a richness of forms which inspired artists for centuries. **Raphael**'s paintings were no less influential but for different reasons. It was the sense of order, the carefully thought-out compositions and the softness of light derived from Leonardo which were admired. His groups of Madonna and Child, his portraits and the grandiose compositions for the fresco decoration of the Vatican Stanze were sources of inspiration for countless artists over the centuries. From Tuscany the sculptor and architect Jacopo Sansovino went to Rome where Raphael's sensitivity and Michelangelo's energy had a formative impact. He moved to Venice to become the major sculptor and architect of that city. In Florence **Andrea del Sarto** (1486-1531) and **Jacopo Pontormo** (1494-1556) also integrated the new ideas from Rome but were principally superb, and very different, colourists. Pontormo's bright and acid colours reinforced the disturbing and agitated forms of his masterpiece, the Deposition (Santa Felicita, Florence, c1525), a work of great importance for the development of Mannerism. In the frescoes which he painted to decorate the Palazzo del Te, **Giulio Romano** proved himself the heir to both Raphael and Michelangelo and the violent illusionism found there can also be seen to herald the Mannerist style.

The unease created by the sack of Rome in 1527, the subsequent transformation of the city-states into principalities or duchies by the end of the Italian Wars in 1559, and the incipient Reformation (Luther) can be seen as the background to Mannerism. It was a style in which the figure, often distorted or elongated, dominated but was placed within a setting where the rules of perspective set by the Renaissance artists were deliberately falsified. It aimed at surprise, even shock. Colours were often harsh and contributed to a general feeling of disquiet. Rosso Fiorentino (1495-1540) and Francesco Primaticcio (1504-70) were part of this development. They promoted the spread of Mannerism abroad by going to France and working on the decoration of the palace of Francis I at Fontainebleau. The court painter of Cosimo I de' Medici, **Bronzino** (1503-72), was a superb portrait painter, combining suggestion of the sitters' status with richness of lines and colours. Grand-duke Cosimo encouraged the creation of academies where the importance of drawing and design was stressed. Bronzino and the painter, writer and historian **Vasari**, were two of the personalities involved. Mannerist sculpture could be extraordinarily refined and elegant, stressing graceful and mannered forms verging on the bizarre (the goldsmith Cellini, 1500-71), yet also explored exaggerated movements or, in the case of Baccio Bandinelli (1493-1560), the display of powerful musculature. The sculpture of Giovanni di Bologna (Giambologna, 1529-1608) portrayed a subtle, slightly decadent voluptuousness.

In northern Italy the painter **Correggio** (1489-1534) may well have trained in Mantua where the illusionistic ceiling of Mantegna had a lasting effect on his decorative works (San Giovanni Evangelista and cathedral, Parma, 1520s). His paintings have a shimmering voluptuousness which has fascinated ever since. The style of his pupil Parmigianino (1503-40) was more tense with elongated, refined figures which had much influence on other Mannerist artists.

Venice

Geographically isolated from the main artistic developments of Florence and Rome and politically independent, the city of Venice retained an artistic integrity throughout the 16th century. The emphasis on design and draughtsmanship which characterised the early 1500s (Cinquecento) in Florence and Rome (Michelangelo) and was a dominant aspect of Mannerism later, was not the concern of Venetian artists. They were aware of Tuscan and central Italian achievements and began to assimilate Mannerism from c1540. They were however far more interested in the study of colour, tone and luminosity. The manipulation of surface by means of contrasts of light and shade was one of the features of the architecture of **Palladio** (1508-80). The rhythmic façades of his Venetian churches (San Giorgio Maggiore) rising above the lagoon, the rusticated texture of his Palazzo Thiene in Vicenza or the classical elegance of his numerous villas in the Veneto are enhanced by the light and dark accents created by columns and porticoes. Palladio's architecture was strictly based on harmonious proportions derived from Vitruvius, the theoretician and architect of Ancient Rome. Like him Palladio wrote a very influential treatise setting out principles of proportion and plan which were subjected to a system of strict order and practicality. His own buildings exemplified his writings, especially in his development of the villa-palace. What made these villas so utterly compelling was their imaginative structure and the awareness and use of their setting to enhance their beauty.

The luminosity of **Giovanni Bellini's** late works in the early years of the 16th century was of fundamental importance for Venetian painters of that century. **Giorgione** (1477-1510) had a short but dazzling career. His paintings expressed a mood of melancholy and established new themes of pastoral landscape, feminine beauty, music and lyricism. A suffused yet dramatic light bathes the soft tones of the Tempesta in the Accademia in Venice. What characterises his work, and Venetian Cinquecento painting in general, is the building-up of forms through gradation of tones instead of lines and volumetric shapes as in Florentine or Roman painting.

Titian's longevity (c1485-1576), and the admiration in which he was held throughout Europe, assured his immense influence on Venetian and North Italian painters. A large workshop and extraordinary vitality allowed him to explore and rethink most Christian and mythological themes and to transform them into magnificent chromatic epics. He achieved an imposing grandeur through balanced composition and careful controlling of large masses of colour. Intensity of tones, loose, liquid brushwork and a sense of pathos are characteristic of his late works. His impact was enormous. Lorenzo Lotto (c1480-1556) retained an independence of spirit visible in the sombre mood of his paintings and their cool colours; he was, however, not really appreciated in Venice. Unlike Titian, **Tintoretto** (1518-94) was little interested in the world outside Venice. A tense and determined personality, he evolved a style of great dramatic force through the manipulation of elongated figures, deep space and a changeable, pathos-creating light. A cooler, more detached mood, well suited to the essentially decorative intent of his paintings, pervaded the work of **Veronese** (1528-88). The decoration of the Villa Barbaro at Maser with its bright and light colours and its play of architectural illusionistic elements framing charming landscape views seems to epitomise his style. Grandiose scale, illusionism and *trompe l'oeil* effects, allegorical subject matter – for which the study of male nudes and of feminine beauty played an important part – and the increasingly important genre of portraiture were some of the characteristics of the 16th century which became features of the arts of later centuries.

THE BAROQUE

In the wake of the Counter-Reformation the Catholic church, with militant optimism, promoted a more exalted faith and the cult of saints and martyrs. The religious fervour of the Jesuits and the rule of wealthy and luxury-minded popes helped to shape the arts from the early 17th century to the mid-18th century. Papal patronage on a grand scale meant that although regional centres were unusually active and productive, Rome attracted major artists and architects.

Architecture

The interest in town planning and the organisation of areas (piazzas) around which key buildings were placed originated in the Early Renaissance, in the writings of the architects Alberti, Filarete and many others and in the efforts of popes including Sixtus IV and Pius II (Pienza). But this interest was put into practice and brought to stunning fruition in the Baroque period. Theatres and magnificent gardens of huge and sometimes complex proportions were built everywhere in Italy. Large and magnificent fountains were erected as the centre-pieces of redesigned piazzas. One of the most exciting was the Fountain of the Four Rivers by the sculptor and architect Gian Lorenzo Bernini (Piazza Navona, Rome, 1647-52). Bernini's remodelling, into a large colonnaded piazza, of the area in front of St Peter's in Rome may be seen to epitomise the Baroque concept of the grandiose restructuring of space.

From the second quarter of the 17th century three outstanding architects dominated the scene: the painter Cortona, the sculptor Bernini and the architect Borromini. All three combined traditional architectural vocabulary derived from the Antique, as their predecessors had done, but in a new inventive and plastic way. **Pietro da Cortona** (1596-1669) for instance allowed the façades of his churches to swell forward or shrink backward in an interplay of convex and concave forms (Santa Maria della Pace, Rome, 1656). **Gian Lorenzo Bernini** (1598-1680) experimented with complex ways of enclosing space in his centrally planned churches (San Andrea al Quirinale, Rome, 1658), often using columns and colonnades to create rich and sculptural effects. His Baldacchino (1624) for St Peter's imaginatively integrated sculptural effects to architectural forms and luxuriously combined marbles of different colours, bronze and gold into a dazzling whole. Concave and convex forms, deliberately truncated traditional features and undulating walls (San Ivo della Sapienza, Rome, 1642-50) were exploited inventively by the great architect **Borromini** (1619-1667). Most of these new Roman churches were domed and many had splendidly decorated ceilings. One of the most impressive, showing off the way in which skilful illusionism could be used to dramatise a religious concept, was the Apotheosis of the Name of Jesus painted for the Jesuit mother church (Gesù, Rome, 1672-79).

Painting and sculpture

The painted ceilings for the Palazzo Farnese (Rome, from 1595) by **Annibale Carracci** (1560-1609) initiated the vast decorative schemes of the 17th and 18th centuries. Planned aroud a strict architectural framework the decorative scenes nevertheless had amazing vitality and played on *trompe l'oeil* effects. The later ceiling decorations of **Pietro da Cortona** (Palazzo Barberini, Rome, 1640) or of the Neapolitan **Luca Giordano** (Palazzo Medici-Riccardi, Florence, 1682-83) which respectively glorify the Barberini and Medici families displayed an astounding exuberance and dazzling virtuosity. Besides Annibale, two other Carracci (Ludovico and Agostino) were instrumental in forming, in Bologna, a school of painting of which **Guido Reni** (1575-1642) and **Domenichino** (1581-1641) were the more talented, the former often preferring dark, mysterious lighting and typically Baroque diagonal compositions, the latter more classical and subdued representations in lighter tones.

Michelangelo da Caravaggio (1573-1610) was, besides Annibale, the other painter who greatly influenced 17th-century painting. A difficult, tense personality who fled Rome under suspicion of murder, his early paintings portrayed ambiguous youths. Later, religious themes were not idealised but treated with dramatic empathy. Strong colours and a deep chiaroscuro in which light became powerful spotlights enhancing the drama gave his works an unforgettable poignancy and theatricality not always appreciated by his patrons (Conversion of St Paul, 1600-01, Santa Maria del Popolo, Cerasi chapel, Rome). His influence throughout Italy was, however, all-pervasive and reached many of the major artistic personalities north of the Alps – the Dutch painter Rembrandt, the Flemish Rubens and the French Georges de la Tour, for instance. Caravaggio's stark realism had great impact on the Spaniard **Ribera** (1591-1652) who settled in Naples for most of his working life. Through him the chiaroscuro and sympathetic realism of Caravaggism reached Spain and the painter Velasquez. The Neapolitan **Salvator Rosa** (1615-1675) was an altogether more grandiloquent painter whose sombre and romantic mood pervaded his picturesque landscapes or sweeping battle-scenes, foreshadowing the Romantic movement of the 19th century.

Something of the theatrical quality of Caravaggio's art appeared in the religious sculpture of **Bernini**. One of his masterpieces, the Ecstacy of St Teresa (1645-52, Santa Maria della Vittoria, Cornaro chapel, Rome) made use of mixed media (architecture, sculpture, painting) to convey a visionary recreation of ecstatic mysticism. Visionary experience and near-hysterical ecstacy corresponded closely to the Counter-Reformation militancy of the church and to the teaching of the Jesuits. When representing saints, such inspired moments were often chosen (Ecstacy of St Margaret of Cortona by Lanfrano, c1620, Palazzo Pitti, Florence). The marble sculpture of Bernini also excitingly portrayed movement as well as feelings and a whole range of dynamic poses and groupings was explored (Rape of Proserpina, 1621-22; Apollo and Daphne, 1622-24, Borghese Gallery, Rome). The taste of cultivated patrons promoted these mythological subjects and also the oustanding portrait busts of some of the foremost statesmen of the day. Bernini's inventive and dynamic works, constant sources of surprise and pleasure, were enhanced by the supreme skill with which he handled marble suggesting the smoothest or roughest of textures.

FROM ROCOCO TO THE TWENTIETH CENTURY

Venetian painting of the 17th century had been less than brilliant but in the 18th century it was in Venice that the genius of Italian painting expressed itself most forcefully, not to say exclusively. The magnificent decorative schemes of Baroque Rome and Florence did not, however, find any counterpart in that city until the first quarter of the 18th century. The only great Venetian building of the 17th, the church of Santa Maria della Salute by Longhena, had been decorated by the peripatetic Neapolitan painter, Luca Giordano (c1685) who brought to that city large compositions of architectural settings and light, bright colours. Their brilliance and airiness anticipated that of later artists and especially of Tiepolo. The lightness of touch and airy appearance of the paintings of Sebastiano Ricci (1659-1734) and Pelligrini (1675-1741), who both visited and worked in England, were partly due to Luca's influence. A far greater painter was **Giovanni Battista Piazzetta** (1682-1754). Unlike Giordano he worked slowly and eschewed facile effects. A powerful sense of design, a concentration on the essential rather than the trivial and the use of a strong chiaroscuro gave his paintings concentration and unity. Although many of his works were religious commissions (Glory of St Dominic, Santi Giovanni e Paolo, Venice), a relatively new type of genre subjects were increasingly in demand, and paintings of idyllic peasant girls and boys are part of the range of subjects he tackled.

Pietro Longhi (1702-85), on the other hand, devoted himself exclusively to genre painting and the depiction of certain aspects of his city and his age: music making and social occasions of all sorts were the themes of his competent if uninspired paintings. More inventive were the landscapes of Sebastiano and Marco (1676-1729) Ricci in which ruined architecture made a picturesque appearance. Sometimes seasonal and weather changes were studied with stunning effects. Francesco Zuccarelli (1702-88) painted charming landscapes with figures, mainly for English patrons. Also greatly appreciated by English patrons, though even more humble in the contemporary hierarchy than landscape painters, were the painters of views of Venice. The "Veduta" painters worked for the delight of the onlooker and made no attempt at social comment. **Giovanni Antonio Canaletto** (1697-1768) was trained as a stage designer and brought the skill of that trade to Veduta painting. Interesting angles diagonal compositions and a clear, sunny luminosity gave his Venetian scenes an immediate appeal beside their obvious topographical interest. The success of Canaletto attracted other artists to the genre. The most talented and inventive of these was **Francesco Guardi** (1712-93). With him views of Venice and imaginative landscapes with picturesque features (caprice landscape) took on another dimension. Looser brushstrokes, informal compositions and shimmering effects of light gave his paintings a poetical and lyrical quality far removed from the precision of the more famous Canaletto.

If landscape was regarded by contemporaries as one of the lowest categories of painting, portraits were more highly esteemed and the pastel portrait painter **Rosalba Carriera** (1675-1757) enjoyed a fame at home and abroad hardly matched by any other artist of her time beside Tiepolo. The dominating genius was indeed **Giambattista Tiepolo** (1696-1770) who represents the purest expression of Rococo in Italy. A style originally evolved in France, Rococo was characterised by the use of decorative curves and scrolls, light, pretty colours and gay, lighthearted subject matter. Tiepolo adapted this to the grander decorative tradition of Veronese, Giordano and Piazzetta. Working mainly in fresco Tiepolo's virtuosity of handling was expressed in light, unreal colours and lofty compositions in which an easy illusionism added to the dazzling effect. He worked widely in Venice (Palazzo Labia), the Veneto (Archbiship's palace, Udine; Villa Valmarana, Vicenza) and abroad in Bavaria and Spain. After Tiepolo the international role of Italian art declined. In his later years he saw the advent of Neo-Classicism which opposed to the excesses and lightheartness of Rococo the restrained and severe forms of classical Antiquity. Only one artist may be said to have risen to the challenge of the new style, the sculptor **Canova** (1757-1822) whose smooth, cool style gained him a well deserved international reputation. One of his most famous works is a portrait of Napoleon's sister (1808, Borghese Gallery, Rome).

Italian art remained on the periphery of European development until the early 20th century. Even the monument to Victor Emmanuel (1885-1911, Rome) built in honour of the unification of Italy was more impressive as a major landmark than as a building. The classical, monumental but ugly architectural style of Fascist Germany filtered through into the Italy of Mussolini where it was used slightly more sympathetically; commercial buildings and blocks of flats (tower, Brescia; Palazzo Littorio, Rome) display shiny marbles within rectangular forms. Far more exciting and ranking with the greatest buildings of the pre-war era were the designs of Pier Luigi Nervi whose stadium in Florence (1930-32) and aircraft hangar at Orbetello (1938) utilised modern engineering technology and the possibilities of concrete to the full.

In painting the early years of the 20th century saw an influential movement, Futurism. Launched at first (1909) as a literary and political declaration, it was quickly (1911-12) expanded by a group of painters, Boccioni, Carra, Balla, Severini and Russolo. The impact of contemporary technology led them to regard the machine as the new inspiring muse. Photographic records of real and mechanical motion provided them with a basis for the representation of the continuum of movement. Works by the imaginative **Umberto Boccioni** (1882-1916) and others sought to portray the force-lines of figures in action, the components of movements and the emotional response which they engendered. These ideas resulted visually in the fragmentation of objects and forms. Reality was challenged and this probably contributed to the other revolutionary movement initiated by **Giorgio de Chirico** (c1911-12) – *Pittura Metafisica* (Metaphysical Painting). Imaginary classical-looking figures were meant to express the "states of mind" created by dreams. In many ways the intent was close to that of Surrealism and the Futurist painter Carrà joined Chirico in the exploration of dream and mood equivalence. The remarkable personality **Giorgio Morandi** (1890-1964) confined his search for metaphysical moods within still-life painting. **Amedeo Modigliani** (1884-1920), a more tragic figure, was acutely sensitive to suffering and he expressed his response in taut compositions in which lyrical lines and distorted forms wrote the sadness he felt and saw. The feeling for design and purity of forms found in Morandi and Modigliani may well be seen as epitomising the particular genius of much of Italian art.

FOOD & WINE

❝ *All Italy, apart from the plains, is a hanging garden… Man, feeling his way sensitively to the fruitfulness of the earth, has moulded the earth to his necessity* ❞

DH LAWRENCE

Buying food and eating out

Eating in Italy is about nourishment and enjoyment, not about elevated gastronomic experiences. At its best, Italian cooking is a question of fresh ingredients, be they sun-ripened vegetables and fruit or fish caught that morning, lovingly prepared in time-honoured fashion. And if restaurants sometimes disappoint, you can at least be assured of one truly fresh meal every day: the one you prepare yourself with a few *etti* of Parma ham, some tomatoes, some ricotta cheese, and a juicy peach, washed down with local wine.

FOOD SHOPPING

Italian housewives buy their food fresh daily from markets. Nearly every town has its market square (a *piazza delle erbe*, or *della frutta* in the north) selling primarily fruit and vegetables in season, plus local cheeses and salamis. Fish, shellfish, poultry and game may be sold too. Stalls will often specialise in just one product, like peaches "*nostrano*" (home-grown) or tomatoes for bottling, and competition is fierce. Roadside fruit stalls are a common sight; particularly popular are watermelon stalls where you can ask for a slice for immediate consumption.

Bakeries (*panificio/panettiera*) normally sell a range of bread, not necessarily local, from the small round rolls, *michette*, used for *panini* (filled rolls), to the large loaves such as *pane toscano* or *pane pugliese*. Bread is invariably white and goes stale fast. Some bakers now sell *gnocchi*, small pizzas and fruit tarts.

Pasticcerie (equivalent to the French *pâtisseries*) sell *brioches*, *cannoli alla siciliana* and other ricotta-filled pastries, open fruit tarts and macaroons, fruit breads and fritters. *Gelaterie* are ice-cream parlours, often attached to bars, and invariably offering a mouth-watering selection of flavours, usually "*artigianale*" (home-made).

Salumerie offer sausages and salamis and often cheese. In addition, you can usually buy ready-made salads and *delicatessen* food such as stuffed aubergines, home-made *gnocchi*, and freshly stuffed pasta. Almost anything, in fact, that might be served as a first course, plus main course dishes such as vol-au-vents, quiches, pies, cooked chicken and fish, delicacies in tins and jars. These shops are usually expensive.

The traditional *alimentari* (small family-run grocers and mini-supermarkets) usually sell a selection of local dairy products, salamis and wine in addition to staple store-cupboard food. Their fruit and vegetables are noticeably poorer than those in markets. *Alimentari* are small, inefficient and expensive, but friendly and very much a part of local Italian life.

Greengrocers and fishmongers are rare but most towns have a *macelleria* (butcher's shop). Poultry and game are sometimes sold (often ready jointed, by the kilo) and offal is popular although some is intended for pet, rather than human, consumption.

Shops usually close for a few hours at lunchtime, sometimes until late afternoon – worth remembering if you're planning a picnic.

CAFÉS AND BARS

Fare uno spuntino, to take a snack, is in all the Italian phrasebooks. It's part of Italian life, particularly in the south. A glass of wine and a slice of pizza, indispensable to the labourer who has been up since dawn, adapts well to the needs of footsore tourists. The average bar offers *panini* (dry rolls) with ham or cheese and *tramezzini* (sandwiches made with crustless white bread), slices of pizza and sometimes hard-boiled eggs. Bars come into their own at breakfast – in summer the perfect outdoor meal. There are usually *bomboloni* (sugared doughnuts), *croissants* and *brioches* (the Italians have adopted the French terminology), often "*ripieni*" (filled) with a slightly sweet custard, the ideal accompaniment to *cappuccino* or *caffelatte*. Sicilians are said to be partial to a *brioche* filled with ice-cream for breakfast.

Italians normally drink their coffee *espresso*: small, black and very strong. Milky coffee is considered to be for breakfast – and children and tourists – only. A *caffelatte* is a large cup of coffee with hot milk while a *cappuccino* is strong with a spurt of foaming hot milk and a sprinkling of grated chocolate (more often cocoa powder). There are a number of variations. *Caffe doppio* is simply a double measure of *espresso*, *caffe ristretto* is extra strong, while *caffe lungo* or *caffe alto* is a weaker black coffee. Ask for *caffe macchiato* and you will get a cup of black coffee with just a splash of milk, ask for *latte macchiato* and proportions will be reversed. *Caffe montata* is with whipped cream, *caffe freddo* is cold, unsweetened black coffee (there's no equivalent to a creamy iced coffee). Finally *caffe corretto* has a drop of brandy or *grappa* in (there's often just a charge for "*correzione*" – the dose of alcoholic improvement – on the bar list). Tea comes without milk.

Bars serve wine by the glass or *caraffa*; beer, bottled or draught (*alla spina*); *spremute*, freshly squeezed fruit juices; soft drinks and mineral water (ask for *con gas* or *gassata* if you want it fizzy, *senza gas* if not). There's a formidable range of whiskies in many bars, but Campari Soda remains the classic *aperitivo*, and a liqueur (*digestivo*) is a very popular aid to digestion.

It's cheaper to take a drink at the bar than to sit outside with waiter service. In most bars and some *gelaterie* you pay first and present the till receipt with your order. This system doubles the queuing at busy times. If you opt for waiter service, it is quite in order to accumulate chits for as long as you choose to stay and to leave payment (plus a small tip) on the table. Most bars sell tobacco, cigarettes and chocolates and some sell stamps.

RESTAURANTS

Only the most tourist-orientated restaurants offer set-price meals and they're not usually the bargain they might seem. The humblest *trattoria*, usually family-run, may not have a menu at all – this is invariably a good sign.

Menus normally offer two kinds of first course – both *antipasto* and a *pasta* course, sometimes combined under the title "*primi piatti*" (first courses). The *antipasto* is often a buffet selection of fish and salads with stuffed or marinated vegetables, salads and some local salamis, cheeses and seafoods. Parma ham with melon or figs finds its way onto most menus. Next come *minestre* (soups) into which category *gnocchi*, risottos and even pasta somewhat confusingly fall. Main courses, *"secondi piatti"*, are normally plainly cooked and simply garnished; vegetables (*contorni* or *verdure*) must be ordered separately (in the south, they're served cold). *Dolci* (desserts) may appear on the menu but often the choice is offered verbally. It is frequently restricted to fruit or ice-cream but a smarter *ristorante* may produce a dessert trolley. Similarly, the most sophisticated restaurants produce lengthy international wine lists while middle-of-the-road *trattorie* offer national or regional wines and the simplest *osteria* will unceremoniously deposit a *caraffa* of the local product at your table.

For snacks and light meals, a *tavola calda* (self-service restaurant) has a selection of hot and cold dishes; a *rosticceria* (mainly found in towns) specialises in spit roasts, and a *pizzeria* can provide you with a substantial meal or simply a slice of pizza to take away.

For most Italians, especially outside the larger cities, lunch is the main meal of the day, and a family affair. Shops and offices close down for a couple of hours and town restaurants fill up by 12.30pm. In country *trattorie* however you can usually get lunch as late as 2pm. Sundays and public holidays are days for large family outings, so booking a table is advisable. Dinner is eaten at around 8pm.

Regional food specialities

It is less than thirty years since Italy celebrated the centenary of Unification. So it is hardly surprising that the blanket term "Italian cooking" is misleading, if not inaccurate. Historical and geographic factors as well as local traditions and availability of ingredients have played a part in ensuring regional differences. Broadly speaking, the north is a country of rice, dairy products and meat, the south of pasta, olive oil and fish. But it's not as simple as that. While many dishes have become national, even international, there are rivalries between towns in the same province as to who can claim the best *tagliatelle* or a superior *bollito misto*.

At first sight it may appear that regional differences have disappeared for ever. Menus all over the country offer dishes with identical names. However, a *fritto misto* will have completely different ingredients in different areas. A *cassola* is a fish stew in Sardinia but a pork stew in Milan. On the other hand the same cuts of meat have different names in different cities. To compound the confusion many fish and shellfish have at least two names and there are dialect versions, particularly in Venice, Sardinia and Sicily. There are said to be over 600 names for pasta (from "angels' hair" and "silk handkerchiefs" to "priest stranglers") and 200 types.

However much the boundaries may have blurred, the most satisfactory – and challenging – solution to eating out in Italy is to look for local specialities on the menu. The cook's pride and reputation are at stake.

THE NORTH

The Veneto

Sopa coada, a pigeon soup originally from Treviso; game and poultry, notably *pollo alla padovana*, a chicken fricassee; *pastizzada*, meat stew; *baccalà*, a salt cod dish from Vicenza; *polenta*, corn maize pudding; vegetables including *funghi porcini* and other distinctive mushrooms, and *radicchio*, a wild red chicory; *peperata* and *peará*, sauces from Verona, the latter a delicate blend of breadcrumbs and bone marrow; *tiramisu*, literally "pick-me-up", an alcoholic chocolate and coffee gâteau from Treviso; Asiago cheese.

Venice

Risottos such as *risotto alla sbiragglia* (with chicken) or *in Capro Roman* (with mutton); *baccalà Mantecato*, creamed salt cod with olive oil; *bigoli in salsa*, spaghetti with an onion and anchovy sauce; *pasta e fagioli* (pasta and bean soup) and *brodetto* (fish soup); fish and shellfish from the Adriatic, especially *San Pietro* (John Dory), *bisato* (eel) and *seppie* (cuttlefish), the last often *in saor*, in a sweet and sour sauce; *fegato alla veneziana* (liver and onions).

Trentino Alto Adige

Austrian-style sausages and smoked hams such as *speck*, and dishes like *crauti* (sauerkraut) and *gulasch*; potato and polenta based pies; *minestra di frittata*, pancake soup; game; *canederli* or *knödel*, dumplings; *gnocchi*; "piatto elefante", a gargantuan meat and vegetable dish served in Bressanone; berry fruits and apples, often used as a filling for sweet omelettes or *strudel*.

Friuli-Venezia Giulia

Fish, especially sardines, anchovies and shellfish; hams, notably *prosciutto di San Daniele* from north of Udine; *gnocchi*; *paparot*, spinach soup; "la Jota", a beans and sauerkraut soup; *fagioli*, beans; *cialzons*, a type of ravioli with meat and herb filling; veal; *brovada* (marinated turnips) with *musetto*, a herb-flavoured pork sausage; Slav dishes around Trieste; pastries with chocolate, nut and candied fruit and grape fillings; Liptauer cheese from Trieste.

Piedmont

Risottos; *sciule piene*, stuffed onions – or stuffed *zucchini*; *peperoni*, sweet peppers; white truffles from Alba; cardoons; river and lake fish; *tajarin*, a type of taglierini, and *agnolotti*, ravioli stuffed with truffles, spinach or veal; *pollo alla marengo*, chicken with white wine, mushrooms, tomatoes and garlic; veal from the Langhe; *vitello tonnato*, veal with a tunny sauce; *carbonata* or *brasato al Barolo*, beef in red wine from the Barolo area; *bolliti*, boiled meats with vegetables and a *salsa verde*, green sauce. Other sauces are *bagna cauda*, a hot anchovy dip with garlic, and *finanziera*, with truffles, Marsala and sweetbreads. From the Valdostana area hare, chamois and *vitello valdostano*, breadcrumbed veal topped with mountain ham and Fontina cheese; other cheeses including *tomini del Talucco* from

Pinado (goats' milk), *paglierino* and *pannerone*, a white Gorgonzola. *Gianduia* (chocolate pudding), *zabaglione* (whipped egg yolks and Marsala) and *grissini* (breadsticks) all originated in Turin.

Liguria

Fish and shellfish, particularly in soups such as *burrida* (similar to the French *bouillabaisse*), *zuppa di datteri* (shellfish soup) and *zimino*, a Genoese fish stew; *cappon magro*, a traditional fish and vegetable salad from Genoa; *antipasto* of raw broad beans, salami and Sardo cheese; savoury pies, notably the *torta pasqualina*; omelettes and fritters; pasta including *pansoti*, a kind of ravioli stuffed with herbs, ricotta and walnuts and *trenette al pesto*, pasta with a sauce of pinenut, garlic and basil; light potato dumplings; *focaccia*, a savoury bread with olive oil and sage; *sardenara*, a type of pizza with onions, olives and anchovies; sauces, including *pesto* and *agliata*, a garlic sauce (equivalent to Provençal *aïoli*); *cima*, stuffed veal roll from Genoa; *condiggion*, a salad (similar to *salade niçoise*); pastries and biscuits.

Lombardy

Zuppa pavese, a clear soup with egg and bread; risottos; *carpaccio*, thinly sliced raw beef, and *bresaola della Valtellina*, smoked beef – both served with oil, lemon, parsley and pepper; *casoncelli alla bergamasca*, ravioli stuffed with butter and sage (especially in Bergamo and Brescia); pasta stuffed with pumpkin or chestnuts, a speciality of Mantua; *insalata di nerv(ett)i*, calf's foot with oil, capers and onion; *polenta*, maize pudding, especially with small roasted birds (*uccelletti*) in Bergamo; fish from the Lakes, often "*in carpione*", marinated with herbs and fried; *mostarda di Cremona*, fruit chutney served with boiled meats; *torta paradiso*, sponge cake from Pavia: *sbrisolana*, a crumbly cake from Cremona and Mantua; dairy products including creamy cows' milk cheeses used in almost all dishes from the Valtellina and *grana* from Lodi, a Parmesan-like cheese.

Milan

Minestrone, served cold in summer; *busecca*, a soup with tripe and white beans; *risotto alla milanese*, creamy saffron rice; breadcrumbed dishes such as *costoletta milanese*, veal, and *fritto misto*, here with veal, calf's liver, sweetbreads and vegetables; *ossobuco*, a stew of veal marrowbone; *cassoeula*, pork and vegetable stew; *mondeghili*, beef and ricotta rissoles; *busecchina*, chestnuts stewed in white wine, milk and cream; *panettone*, a spiced cake with sultanas.

Emilia Romagna

Divers salamis, hams and sausages, notably those from Parma, Langhirano and Felino, and the Modenese speciality *zampone*, stuffed pigs' trotters; stuffed pastas in broth; *passatelli* (Parmesan and breadcrumbs) in broth; *portafoglio*, meat with asparagus and Parmesan; mixed boiled meats; plaited breads from Ferrara; white truffles from the hills round Parma and the pinewoods near

Ravenna; fish on the coast, especially in *fritti misti*; *brodetto*, fish soup with tomatoes, red mullet, eels, monkfish, turbot and sole; cherries from Vignola; *zuppa inglese* ("English soup"), trifle. From Bologna: pasta, particularly *tagliatelle*, usually *alla bolognese* (with traditional meat sauce or *ragù*), *lasagne*, and *tortellini*; chicken and veal *alla bolognese*, with ham and cheese; *pan speziale*, a rich cake with honey, nuts, raisins and spices. From Parma: *anolini*, stuffed pasta served in broth, and *tortelli di erbette*, stuffed with ricotta and Parmesan; *bomba di riso*, classic rice dish with pigeons; Parmesan cheese.

THE CENTRE

Tuscany

Soups, such as *acquacotta* (of tomatoes and peppers); mountain hams; *cinghiale*, wild boar salami (from the Maremma region) and *finocchiona*, a garlic and fennel-flavoured salami; spinach *gnocchi*; white beans, especially served in soups and *all' uccelletto* (with tomato, garlic and sage) to accompany spit-roasted meats; *uccelletti*, small birds; beef from the Val di Chiana; the Livorno version of *baccalà*, salt cod with tomatoes, garlic and black olives; *triglie alla Livornese*, red mullet with tomato, garlic and parsley, and *cacciucco alla Livornese*, a spicy fish stew; *pappardelle alla lepre*, tagliatelle in rich hare sauce; tripe with onions and tomatoes; chicken, often charcoal-grilled (*alla diavola*) or *in porchetta*, stuffed with ham; meat stews; *tortino di carciofi*, baked artichoke pie from Siena; *panzanella*, a bread salad with tomato and onion; sweetmeats such as *panforte*, a spicy cake, and *ricciarelli*, honey and almond biscuits, both from Siena; *castagnaccio*, a chestnut-flour pie with pinenuts and sultanas from the Apennines near Pistoia.

Florence

Soups such as *minestrone* and *ribollita*, a bread-based vegetable soup; *crostini*, rounds of fried or baked bread spread with chicken livers; *bruschetta*, a sort of garlic bread with olive oil; *fritto misto*, here a mix of frittered artichoke hearts, calf's brains, mozzarella and zucchini; grilled and roasted meats such as the very large *bistecca alla fiorentina*, and *àrista*, loin of pork roasted with garlic and rosemary; tripe with tomato sauce and marjoram; sauces *alla fiorentina*, often with cheese and spinach; *zuccotto*, a chilled pudding of liqueur-soaked sponge and chocolate; *bongo-bongo*, profiteroles.

Umbria

Black truffles from Norcia, served with spaghetti ("*al tartufo*") or on *crostini*, croutons; *pan 'unto*, garlic bread with olive oil; *cappeletti*, stuffed pasta in broth; spinach and ricotta *gnocchi*; chicken livers, on *crostini* and with veal escalopes ("*alla perugina*"); spit-roasted meat, especially *porchetta*, suckling pig, cooked with wild fennel and herbs and *palombacce*, wood pigeons, basted with a vegetable and herb sauce; *spezzato di tacchino*, turkey casserole with olives; freshwater fish from the river (mainly trout) and from Lake Trasimeno (roach, trout, mullet, perch, carp and eel); mountain hams and various sausages and salamis from Norcia, eaten with *torta sul testo*, unleavened bread; wild asparagus and mushrooms.

The Marches

Fish dishes: *brodetto*, fish soup, and *garagoli in porchetta*, shellfish with garlic, rosemary and wild fennel; *Vincisgrassi*, a lasagne dish; stuffed olives from Ascoli; spit roasts, especially pork; lamb, chicken or rabbit cooked *"in potacchio"*, with oil, white wine, garlic, rosemary and parsley; *stoccafisso all' anconetana*, dried cod, also with garlic and rosemary; *salame* from Fabriano, hams from Montefeltro; vegetables including mushrooms and white truffles; fruit (apples, peaches, figs, cherries); cheeses such as *pecorino* and *caciotto*, *ricotta* from Amandola and Urbino, *bazzott* from Fano.

Rome and Lazio

Pasta: often *fettuccine* (the Roman equivalent of *tagliatelle*) or *bucatini* (spaghetti) *all' amatriciana*, with a bacon and tomato sauce, *alla carbonara* with cream, bacon and egg, and *alla gorgonzola*; *rigatoni con la pajata* (with veal offal). *Gnocchi*, traditionally eaten on Thursdays with meat or tomato sauce and savoury rice croquettes called *suppli al telefono*; fish soups and *stracciatella*, a clear broth with egg; baby lamb roasted with rosemary; pork from Arpino; beef stews usually with celery; *coda alla vaccinara*, oxtail stuffed with celery, onions and carrots; *saltimbocca alla romana*, escalopes of veal with ham and sage. Vegetable-based dishes such as wild asparagus; *fave al guanciale*, broad beans with onion and bacon; *carciofi alla Giudea*, fried artichokes; *piselli al prosciutto*, peas with Parma ham and bacon; broccoli; white olives from Gaeta. *Pecorino romano* cheese from Moliterna; *ricotta*; *crostata di ricotta*, cheesecake.

Abruzzi

Fish from the Adriatic, used in *fritti misti*; *brodetto* (fish soup) with *peperoncini*, fiery red peppers, and *scapece di vasto*, marinaded skate; *scrippelle m'busse*, pancakes; *maccheroni alla chitarra*, pasta made using a special guitar-like wooden frame, with a sauce of tomato, bacon and *pecorino* cheese; local hams, sausages and cheeses, especially *scamorza*, *pecorino* (sometimes served with pears) and the mountain cheese *littecini*; *cassata abruzzese*, a creamy dessert from Sulmona.

Molise

Fish; mountain hams, sausages and salamis used in *affettati misti*, mixed cold cuts; *maccheroni alla chitarra*; kid, rabbit and lamb *alla brace*, cooked over embers; *pezzatto*, lamb stew; lentils from Capracolta; trout from the River Biferno and mountain streams.

THE SOUTH

Basilicata

Salamis, smoked hams and sausages; *mandorlata di peperoni*, peppers cooked with sugar and almonds; various kinds of pasta (*orecchiette, fusilli, strascinati*); game; lamb, kid, pork; *pollo alla lucana*, chicken

stuffed with chicken livers, eggs and *pecorino* cheese; trout from
Lake Sirino; olives; chestnuts; beans; lentils; peppers from Senise;
mushrooms; *casiddi*, ewes' milk cheeses.

Campania

Fish, especially *alici*, anchovies, *sarde*, sardines and *sgombro*,
mackerel; *zuppa di pesce*, fish soup; *impepata di cozze*, mussels with
garlic, parsley and pepper; the original pizzas; *zite*, pasta, often
covered simply in oil and garlic, or with tomato and basil; various
dishes "*alla napoletana*", usually with capers, tomatoes, black olives
and garlic; snacks such as *calzoni*, crescent-shaped pizza envelopes
with ham and cheese, *mozzarella in carrozza*, a fried "sandwich" of
cheese; veal escalope or steak *alla pizzaiola*, with tomatoes, garlic and
oregano; vegetable dishes made with potatoes (*gattò di patate*),
aubergines (*Parmigiana*) or zucchini (*a scapace*, with tomato sauce);
Genovese, a beef stew with onions and tomato sauce. Peaches;
pastiera, a *ricotta* pie with candied fruit and spices; *sfogliatelle*, sweet
ricotta turnovers; *mozzarella*, *provola* and *scamorza* cheeses.

Apulia

Antipasti di mare with octopus and shellfish; *zuppa di cozze*, mussel
soup; *ostriche*, oysters from Taranto; salamis; varied vegetable dishes
including stuffed tomatoes and aubergines, cardoons with olives
and anchovies, *n'capriata* or *fave e cicoria*, a bean soup. *Orecchiette*,
ear-shaped pasta; *friselle* or *frisedde*, bread with oil, tomatoes and
peppers; *pizza rustica*, a version of the Neapolitan *calzone*, with a
richer filling. *Cerignola*, giant green olives; *cima di rape*, turnip tips.
Lamb and kid, usually spit-roasted with herbs ("*allo spiedo*") or
casseroled with herbs and *gnummeriddu*, lamb sausages from Bari;
tortiera (tiella) alla barese, a pie with rice, mussels, potato and
zucchini; cheeses including *caciotta*, *caciocavallo* and *burrata* from
Andria; breads from Altamura and Gravina; cakes made with
almonds and honey; *carteddate*, pastries with honey or wine
characteristic of Bari; sweet *calzoni*, ricotta pasties.

Calabria

Antipasto calabrese consisting of local salamis (often flavoured with
peppers and fennel seed), cheeses, olives, mushrooms and
melanzane (aubergines), *sott' olio*, marinaded with oil, garlic and
peppers; fish, particularly tuna and *pescespada*, swordfish; also
sardines, anchovies and *aguglie*, garfish. *Sagne chine*, lasagne with
cheese, meatballs and artichoke hearts; *morseddu*, pitta bread stuffed
with cooked giblets, tomatoes and peppers; *mustica*, baby eels or
anchovies dried in the sun with peppers and preserved in oil; lamb
and kid; sweet red onions from Tropea; *mostaccioli* and *cannariculi*
biscuits and *torrone gelato*, chocolate-covered nougat.

Sicily

Antipasti of seafood and cold stuffed vegetables ("*alla siciliana*", with
capers, anchovies, tomatoes and olives); *caponata*, dish of capers,
aubergines, tomatoes, olives and oil (similar to French *ratatouille*).

Pasta *con le sarde*, with sardines, pinenuts and sultanas or *"alla Norma"*, with aubergines (speciality of Catania). Fish: *pescespada*, swordfish and *triglia*, red mullet; *tonno*, tuna from the Egadi islands. *Farsumagru*, veal with eggs, ham and cheese cooked in oil and served with a tomato sauce; *cuscus* (couscous), in Trapani; *arancini*, rice balls with meat and peas in breadcrumbs; *salmoriglio* (*salamurigghiu*), sauce of oil, lemon and garlic. Ice-cream; pastries and desserts such as *cannoli* and *cassata siciliana*, both traditionally made with ricotta and candied fruit (although cassata is now usually simply ice-cream); marzipan fruits.

Sardinia

Roast meats from the mountain areas; *cassola*, fish stew; *porceddu*, road suckling pig; *malloreddus*, dumplings; *carta da musica*, wafer-thin bread eaten with oil and salt; *pane frattau*, softened *carta da musica* with tomato sauce and a poached egg; *zuppa quata*, a savoury bread dish baked with cheese and tomato sauce.

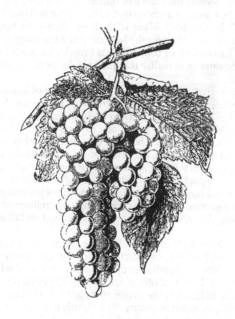

Buying and tasting wine

For centuries wine has been the standard drink of Italy. The Etruscans tended vines 3,000 years ago; the Greeks called Italy *Oenotria Tellus*, the immemorial land of wine; and the Romans revelled in wine and revered it with poem and song. Today Italy is the largest wine producing country in the world. Only Portugal has a higher consumption per capita and only France exports a greater quantity. Vines are grown in every province, from the foothills of the northern Alps to the lower slopes of Mount Etna in Sicily. No one knows exactly how many individual wines there are, but reliable sources suggest several thousand.

But familiarity with cheap (and not always cheerful) Valpolicella and Soave has given Italy a reputation as a poor relation of France. Although it is true that Italian wines rarely match the French top *crus*, this reputation is largely undeserved. Italy is now producing more and more top quality wines, many of which are much better value than better-known wines from France.

Until quite recently the choice of Italian wine on the shelves of English shops was no real indication of the range and quality of wines that Italy produced. Many of the best wines were kept for home consumption. But over the last few years the range of wines exported to this and other countries has broadened considerably and people are beginning to realise that Italy produces much good quality wine.

Even wine experts are bewildered by the variety of Italian wines – very few would recognise all the wine names and know which varieties and methods went to make them. The Italians themselves – including wine lovers and experts – tend to know and drink only their local wines. There are over 80 types of grape, a variety of soils and climates, and methods of production which range from peasants tending small plots for their own casual consumption to spacious vineyards, big efficient modern cooperatives and huge private cellars. Some vines grow among crops or olive groves, others are trained high on trellises or sprawled over lofty pergolas, and others are neatly groomed on hillside terraces.

Adding to the complexity of it all are the anomalies of Italian wine law (see below), and the unpredictability of any given wine type. Hundreds of different producers make Valpolicella, and while some Valpolicellas are delicious, others are mouth-strippers. Just like anywhere else in Europe, the producer's name on the bottle is the only ultimate guarantee of quality. You simply can't rely on a renowned name such as Valpolicella, Barola and Chianti.

Unlike France, Italy is not really in the business of catering for foreigners who want to visit vineyards and taste wines on the premises. Although there are well-established wine routes in Piedmont. Chianti and the Castelli Romani south of Rome, there are relatively few vineyards where you are welcome without prior and preferably written notice. Vines grow two a penny in Italy, and most

Italians can't really appreciate the British interest in vineyards and cellars. There are, however, plenty of *enoteche* (in theory wine museums, but many are more akin to shops) with a wide range of wines for tasting and buying.

THE SYSTEM OF CONTROL

DOC *Denominazione di Origine Controllata* is a system of governmental control similar to the French *Appellation Contrôlée* system – a guarantee of origin, not necessarily of quality. It applies only to about 12% of the wine in Italy. The term guarantees place of production, type of grape or grapes used, alcoholic strength, and countless traditional techniques of cultivation, vinification and ageing. Although there is no doubt that in general the quality of wines has improved since its introduction, in the case of some wines the EEC rules have stultified progress. In some regions there are producers who rightly feel that there is too much emphasis on the traditional system of ageing red wines for several years in old wooden barrels. As a result the wine loses all its fruity flavour and becomes heavy and hard-hitting, out of line with the modern preference for young, fruity wines. Some of the producers are steering away from the old methods and bottling earlier – but thus sacrificing DOC status.

   Another of many complaints against the system is the fact that so many good wines fail to qualify for DOC merely because the grapes used are not officially accepted in that particular zone; for instance the excellent Sassicia from Tuscany is made from the Cabernet Sauvignon grape, which is not recognised for DOC Tuscan wines. This and various other fine wines are therefore classified merely as *Vini da Tavola* (see below).

DOCG Since 1983 the theoretically higher title of *Denominazione di Origine Controllata e Garantita* has been awarded to Barolo, Barbaresco, Brunello di Montalcino, Vino Nobile de Montepulciano and Chianti. Although the wine is tasted by a specially selected panel in Rome and approved by the government, DOCG is not always a guarantee of top quality. Vino Nobile di Montepulciano, for example, varies from excellent quality to mediocre.

Vino di Tavola This designation applies to any other wine, but does not necessarily denote poor quality. Some excellent wines fall into this category merely because they don't abide by all the DOC regulations of their region (see under DOC). But if it's cheap, it's likely to be very poor.

Vino da Tavola con Indicazione Geografica and **Vino Tipico** These supposedly superior examples of Vini da Tavola are similar to French *Vins de Pays*. The first designation relates to the colour and place of origin (eg Bianco di Assisi) and sometimes to the grape variety and place (eg Sangiovese dei Colli Pesaresi). Vino Tipico is a loosely defined term guaranteeing only origin.

ITALIAN WINE LABELS

The labelling of all wines is now controlled by EEC regulations.
Every label must state the name of its wine, its categorisation, the
producer or bottler, the place of bottling, alcoholic strength and
volume of contents. Unlike France – where wines are named after
the regions, villages or vineyards where their grapes are grown – in
Italy the naming of wines follows no general pattern. It may be the
name of a place (Orvieto, Elba, etc), a wine region (Valpolicella,
Chianti, etc), a grape variety with no link with village or brand
name, (Barbera, Pinot, etc), a place and grape variety (Nebbiolo del
Piemonte, Moscato d'Asti) or merely fanciful (Est! Est!! Est!!!,
Lacrima Cristi, Sangue di Giuda).

Terms on a bottle include:

classico – from the historic heartland (for a DOC wine)

superiore – denotes extra alcohol, longer ageing, but not necessarily a
superior quality

riserva – aged for a specified period and normally better quality than
a non-*riserva* wine

Qualitätswein – Alto Adige equivalent of DOC

Consorzio – voluntary association of growers and producers who
organise analytical and tasting tests; each one has a seal, for example
Chianti Classico (a black cockerel) and Chianti Putto (a cherub)

VIDE (as collar label) – the winery belongs to an association of
quality producers and this particular wine has passed genuinely
stringent tests.

secco – dry; *amaro* – very dry or bitter; *amabile* or *abboccato* – medium
sweet; *dolce* – sweet and rich; *spumante* – sparkling; *frizzante* – semi-
sparkling; *vin santo* – sweet dessert wine made from dried grapes;
rosato – rosé; *vecchio* – old.

VINTAGES

Many Italian wines, especially whites, don't improve with age, so
much is consumed within a year of bottling. Beware bottles that do
not state their vintage – there's no way of knowing whether they are
too old, and any producer or merchant who cares about quality will
tell you the vintage. However, many red wines do improve with
ageing – and indeed some are much too tough to drink in their
youth. Some types of Italian red wine are renowned for their
keeping ability – Barolo and Barbaresco, for instance. But whether
they really taste good after long ageing depends entirely on the
methods of the individual producer; some Barolos taste as hard and
bitter at 10 or 20 years old as when they are first bottled. The longest
keepers, if well made, are the reds of the north-west – Barolo,
Barbaresco, Ghemme, Gattinara, Valtellina and a few more, all made
from the Nebbiolo grape, which sometimes appears on the label.
The best Chiantis, Vino Nobile di Montepulciano and Brunello di
Montalcino, all from Tuscany, will age for up to eight years – look
out for the name of an estate, and expect to pay quite a high price for
a Tuscan wine that will age well. Most of the expensive DOC-

defying *vini da tavola* age well, too. But most Valpolicella and Bardolino and many other Italian reds need drinking young.

The wine areas

Vines cover the whole country, but the north and centre, with favourable climates and often progressive techniques, produce the best wines. The best whites come from the cooler north, especially the Alto Adige up near the Austrian border, known locally as the Südtirol. In the south, fierce sun, hot soil and backward methods of production produce stronger, coarser wines; although methods of vinification have made great headway in recent years (particularly in Sicily), most of these wines are consumed locally, blended with other wines or poured into the EEC wine lake.

Below we divide the country into four main wine-growing regions: the North-West, which to most wine lovers means Piedmont; the North-East, which includes the three major wine-growing regions of Trentino Alto-Adige, Veneto and Friuli-Venezia Giulia; the Centre, an area of huge production covering the well-known Chiantis from Tuscany, Orvietos from Umbria and Frascatis from Latium, plus some DOCs from the Adriatic; and the South (including Sardinia and Sicily).

At the end of the regional sections we list the names of the best wine producers, those to look out for in shops and restaurants.

THE NORTH-WEST

The north-west's fame as a wine producing region rests mainly on Piedmont. Valle d'Aosta in the north and Liguria in the south are very modest producers in comparison.

Piedmont

Regarded by many as the home of the greatest Italian wines, Piedmont specialises in deep, robust reds. Barolo – "King of wine and wine of kings", as it is proudly entitled by the Piemontesi – is a big, heavy red which has traditionally ranked among the best wines of Europe. It is a highly complex wine, made entirely from the great black Nebbiolo grape. More often than not it is extremely tough, and rather short of fruitiness, so it needs robust food. Experts say it evokes comparisons with truffles, tar and violets or raspberries, dead leaves and mushrooms; no two comparisons seem to coincide, which is hardly surprising since one Barolo is rarely like the next.

The Nebbiolo (sometimes called Spanna) grape is used for all Piedmont's well-known wines: the DOCG Barbaresco, neighbour and cousin of Barolo, and other reds like Freisa, Gattinara, Ghemme and the slightly lighter Nebbiolo d'Alba. The Dolcetto is another major grape of Piedmont, producing fresh, fruity and easy-to-drink wines, sometimes compared to Beaujolais.

Traditionally the greatest wines of Italy, Barolo and Barbaresco have been going out of fashion over the last few years. Their deep flavour, high alchoholic strength and austere character make them an acquired taste, and the modern trend is for lighter wines.

For wine touring, Piedmont is the best organised region in Italy. The core of the wine country lies east and south of Turin, in the Langhe and Monferrato hills and the towns of Alba and Asti. There are well marked wine routes; from Alba for instance you can follow signs to the cellars of some of the great wines of Piedmont. There are small family businesses, some of whom welcome tasters, castle estates (sometimes with a restaurant serving local specialities) and *enoteche* where you can drink and buy. One of the main detours for wine buffs is the castle at Grinzane Cavour (in the Barolo region) with its museum, restaurant and Piemontesi wines.

The town of Alba is something of a gastronomic centre, lying in the heart of the vineyards and renowned for prized white truffles. To the north, the hills around Asti produce the well known sparkling white Asti Spumante and Moscato d'Asti, both made from the sweet Moscato grape. Traditionally scorned in the UK as sweet and cheap, the wines have greatly improved over recent years and are today the finest and most refreshing sparkling whites in Italy, and very reliable. Further to the north, the villages in and around Gattinara and Ghemme are less commercial, and produce red wines which are mellower, more fruity and less demanding than Barolo and Barbaresco.

Apart from Asti Spumante, white wine is not very big business in Piedmont. The leading still white of the region is the dry and light Cortese. Piedmont is also the native region of vermouth – a blend of wines (most of which come from Sicily and southern Italy) flavoured with numerous herbs from the aromatic plants of Alpine pastures and lightly fortified with local brandy. It was first made in Turin in the 19th century and the name comes from the wormwood plant which was known as *Wermut* in German and featured in most of the original recipes. The two main types, *Bianco* and *Rosso*, are both sweet, *secco* or *bianco secco* are dry. Some of the big vermouth houses open their doors freely to visitors. At Martini e Rosso in Pessione, 25km south of Turin, an English guide will show you round – there is no admission charge and you are free to taste but not to buy. There's also an impressive History of Wine Making Museum.

Wine producers in Piedmont:
Altresino, Duca d'Asti, Produttori del Barbaresco, Fattoria dei Barbi, Marchese di Barolo, Terre Di Barolo, Biondi-Santi, Bologna, Giacomo Borgogno e Figli, Caparzo, Fratelli Cavallotto, Ceretto, Pio Cesare, Aldo Conterno, Gioacomo Conterno, Guiseppe Contratto, Fontanafredda, Franco-Fiorina, Gaja, Gancia, Bruno Giacosa, Mascarello, Castello di Neive, Oddero, Poggio, Alfredo Prunotto, Ratti.

Valle d'Aosta and Liguria

The diminutive northern border region of Valle d'Aosta is more famous for ski slopes than vineyards, but it does produce modest quantities of wine – all of which is kept for home consumption. The vines are some of the highest in Europe, reaching 2,000-3,000ft above sea level. Liguria produces more wine, most of which is drunk in the cities and resorts along the coast, but the vineyards are gradually being taken over for the more profitable industry of flower growing. While whites are more prominent than reds, the region's best wine is probably the red Rossese di Dolceacqua, from vines close to the French border. Cinqueterre wine, praised and romanticised for centuries, is still grown on the vertiginous slopes of the five remote villages north of La Spezia; but nowadays the wine is less distinguished and hard to come by.

THE NORTH-EAST

This is one of the most innovative regions of Italy and a major producer of good wines. Vineyards are professionally run, a host of different grapes are grown (including French and German varieties) and more wine is exported than from any other region in Italy.

Trentino Alto-Adige

The northern section of the Alto Adige valley north and south of Bolzano produces the best wines of the region. Known locally as the Südtirol, it was ceded to Italy by the Austrians in 1919 and still owes much of its character and culture to its Austrian neighbours. German is widely spoken, vineyards are tended with German precision, bottles are labelled in German and the wine is drunk with sausages and *sauerkraut*.

This is one of the most delightful wine touring areas of Italy. Added to the attraction of the wines and vineyards are the towering mountains, green hillsides, lakes and forests. Most towns have a winery, ranging from castle cellars to large modern cooperatives, known locally as *Kellereigenossenschaften*.

The white wines are excellent and include Sylvaner, Riesling, Pinot Bianco, Pinot Grigio, Müller-Thurgau, Gewürztraminer, Sauvignon and Chardonnay (the wines are usually named after the grape in the German tradition). The Schiava (Vernatsch) is the most common red wine grape, producing the full bodied, ruby-red Santa Maddalena, acclaimed (with extraordinary over-enthusiasm) by Mussolini as one of the three greatest wines of Italy. The Schiava is also the source of the popular everyday drinking wine, Lago di Caldaro, known in German and locally as Kalterersee – a light, fresh, grapey wine with a hint of almonds. The Lagrein (or Lagrein-Kretzer) grape, a little of which goes into Caldaro and Santa Maddalena, is used mainly on its own to make really excellent, flavoursome reds and good dark, dry *rosés*.

Trentino, to the south, is far more Italian in character than Bolzano; it produces Cabernets, Merlots and Pinots in abundance, but in comparison with the Alto-Adige, most of the wines are uninspiring. The robust Teroldego is the main red wine, made largely for local consumption and drunk liberally in the city of Trento.

Wine producers in Trentino-Alto Adige:
Arunda, Ferrari, J Hofstätter, Istituto Agrario Provinciale San Michele all' Adige, Alois Lageder, Pojer e Sandri, J Tiefenbrunner,

Viticoltori Alto Adige, Roberto Zeni.

Veneto

The Verona hills, stretching east from the shores of Lake Garda to beyond the walled city of Soave, are thick with vines. Wines include the familiar names of Valpolicella, Bardolino and Soave, the lesser known but top quality Recioto and a variety of table wines. The whites range from fairly good to awful.

Soave is produced in huge quantities, mainly in big cooperative cellars. It's Italy's best selling DOC wine – at worst dull and industrial, at best bright and firm. The Recioto di Soave, very rarely seen, is a rich, golden and raisiny wine, up to 14% in alcohol. But for best buys in ordinary Soave, look for a vineyard name (often Cru something) on the label. Often better value than Soaves are the slightly more flavoursome dry whites of Bianco di Custoza, a zone bordering Lake Garda and Lombardy.

The large area between the town of Soave and the Adige river is Valpolicella country – a pretty region of vineyards in terraced valleys. Like Soave for white wine, Valpolicella is the market leader among north-eastern reds. Despite huge quantities of cheap, poor quality stuff arriving on supermarket shelves, good Valpolicella is having something of a revival. Much of the wine is made by small family producers and some will be proud to give you a tasting, particularly of their Recioto della Valpolicella, a sweet, rather port-like strong dessert wine, or Valpolicella Amarone – a highly regarded heavy, dry and bitter red wine. As in Soave, the best Valpolicellas come from named vineyards.

Bardolino, made from the same grapes as Valpolicella, comes from the south-eastern shores of Lake Garda. It should be a light, fresh, fruity wine, best drunk young. Quality, however, is nearly as variable as in Valpolicella; look for vineyard names again, and pay a little more than the basic prices.

The dramatic steep hills south of Padua produce wines from grapes as varied as the Cabernet Sauvignon, the Moscato, the Tocai (not to be confused with the Tokay of other regions) and the local Durello with its strong scent and high acidity. Closer to Venice it's worth trying the white Verduzzo di Piave and the refreshing, sparkling Prosecco.

Wine producers in Veneto:
Allegrini, Bertani, Bolla, Boscaini, Conte Arvedi d'Emilei, La Fattoria, Guerrieri-Rizzardi, Lamberti, Maculan, Masi, Pieropan, Fratelli Portalupi, Giuseppe Quintarelli, Tedeschi, Le Tende, Venegazzù-Conte Loredan-Gasparini.

Friuli-Venezia Giulia

The main wine producing area of Friuli straddles the eastern border of Veneto occupying the southern half of Friuli-Venezia Giulia. After a sluggish few years the area is undergoing something of a revival with good wines in the lower and middle price range. The three DOC areas to look out for are Collio Goriziano, Colli Orientali del Friuli and Grave del Friuli. More reds are made here than whites – some good, light Cabernet and Merlot for drinking young. Perhaps best of the local white grapes is the Tocai. Other popular grapes include the Riesling Italico, Gewürztraminer, Müller-Thurgau, Pinot Grigio, Pinot Bianco and the latest additions of Sauvignon and Rhine Riesling. The rare Picolit grape produces a rich, flowery dessert wine, once drunk by the Hapsburgs and optimistically put on a par with Château d'Yquem – but it is extremely rare and expensive since yields are low owing to the variety's susceptibility to 'floral abortion', a failure of the fruit to set.

Friuli is a popular area for winelovers. It's a relatively short drive from Venice; there are wine routes through the vineyards, and wineries and bars which welcome tourists.

Wine producers in Friuli-Venezia Giulia:
Collavini, Fratelli Pighin, Pittaro, Villa Ronche.

Lombardy

Despite substantial home production of wine, Lombardians seem to look elsewhere to satisfy their vinous taste. This is not through any lack of decent local wine. There are some excellent reds with plenty of character – many of them underrated.

Best of all are the red wines from Valtellina on the Swiss/Italian border. The vines are grown on amazingly steep walled terraces, and cables are used to bring the grapes down to the valleys at harvest time. The wines are not unlike those from Piedmont and generally better value. Those from the evocatively named vineyards of Inferno, Brunello and Sassella in the *superiore* zone are reckoned to be the best, but a large proportion are sold across the border to Switzerland or taken across duty-free by Swiss proprietors of the Italian vineyards.

The Oltrepo Pavese zone, in the Po valley south of Pavia, produces a broad range of wines, both through large modern cooperatives and small-scale growers. Three of the best are Barbacarlo, Buttafuoco and Sangue di Giuda – all high-class reds best known in a *frizzante* form. But such are the anomalies of the DOC system that all ten wines of this area come under the one sole *denominazione*.

The lake shores of Lombardy produce some attractive wines, many of them consumed liberally by tourists in the lakeside resorts. Francia Corta, from the banks of Lake Iseo, is a fragrant, mellow wine made from an unusual marriage of four red grapes including about half Cabernet, plus Barbera, Nebbiolo and Merlot. Lugana wine, from the south-western shores of Lake Garda is becoming increasingly popular; and there are some very attractive wines from around Lakes Maggiore, Varese and Como, though these are rarely seen in anything but carafes in local restaurants.

Wine producers in Lombardy:
Ca' del Bosco, La Castellina, Castello di Grumello, Longhi-de Carli, Castello di Luzzano, Nera, Rainoldi, Tona, Enologica Valtellinese.

Emilia Romagna

The well deserved reputation for good living in Emilia Romagna is based more on food than wine. Huge amounts of wine are produced – in 1980 the harvest was greater than the whole of West Germany's – but the quantity far outweighs the quality.

The controversial Lambrusco is the overwhelming wine of the region. Described by one pundit as "thin, tart and perilously close to vinegar" it rarely appeals to serious wine lovers let alone experts. The red cherry-like alcoholic "pop" is nevertheless very serious business. It is produced by a number of giant wineries and the export trade flourishes, especially to the United States. Famed as a frothy sweet red drink, it can in fact range from dry to medium sweet and from pink to ruby – but it almost always *frizzante*.

Wine producers in Emilia-Romagna:
Cavicchioli, Fattoria Paradiso, Pasolini, Zerioli.

THE CENTRE

Central Italy encompases Chianti, Orvieto, Frascati and Verdicchio, and much much more besides. The dominant red grape is the Sangiovese, mainstay of Chianti and most other Tuscan wines. The whites of the region, based on the Trebbiano grape, have improved considerably over recent years, though they can never be exciting from this basically dull grape.

Tuscany

This is perhaps the most beautiful of Italy's winegrowing regions, and the combination of scenery, oustanding sights and fine wine draws increasing numbers of British holidaymakers. It's also an attractive region for wine touring, with routes winding through a romantic landscape of vineyards, olive groves and hills dotted with country houses and great estates.

For centuries wine has been made in Tuscany. But Chianti as we know it today was created just over 100 years ago in the Castello di Brolio, a castle in the hills north-west of Siena. It was owned by an Italian baron called Bettino Ricasoli, one-time prime minister of Italy, but probably best known as the inventor of modern Chianti. By combining San Gioveto and Cannaiolo grapes, plus a little white Malvasia and Trebbiano, he gave birth to the basic formula that was used to make Chianti Classico. It was not until recently that the recipe changed – now very little or no Trebbiano is added.

To the uninitiated Chianti is synonymous with Italian wine and its popularity (at least among foreigners) has tended to overshadow other Italian wines. It is certainly the most important wine in Tuscany and it can vary widely – from a light, refreshing, inexpensive drink labelled simply Chianti to the fully flavoured, deep red, estate-bottled, barrel-aged reserve wines. Between the two extremes come thousands of different wines, varying in quality, colour, strength and character, but all based on the Sangiovese grape. Wines are produced by both large and small estates, some of them run by Tuscan aristocrats who give their names to their finest wines. The descendants of Baron Ricasoli, who still live in Castello di Brolio, produce a fine Chianti under the name of Brolio.

Of the seven different Chianti zones, Chianti Classico is the most important. Wines produced here usually bear the symbol of a black cockerel on their labels and they, along with Chianti Rufina (not to be confused with the firm of Ruffino) and Chianti dei Colli Fiorentini, stick to stricter regulations and are often of better quality than the other Chianti sub-divisions. Some Chiantis bear a cherub or *putto* seal on the label, a sign of membership of the Chianti Putto Consortium, but this is no particular assurance of quality. The cheapest category is ordinary Chianti, which you find on supermarket shelves and in cheap restaurants, sometimes in the traditional raffia covered *fiaschi*; they are for drinking young. Superior Chiantis are sold in straight claret-shaped bottles, and may keep and improve for several years.

There are other reds of distinction in Tuscany, though fundamentally they are close in character to Chianti. Best known is the lofty-sounding Vino Nobile di Montepulciano from the hills surrounding the old picturesque town of Montepulciano. This was Italy's first DOCG wine but until recently most experts agreed that its quality was unreliable. Now the standard is improving and some of it ranks among the finest wines of Italy (it came top in a recent *Which? Wine Monthly* tasting session). The hill town of Montalcino, 37km west of Montepulciano, produces the complex, powerful and very expensive Brunello, a wine which needs to be matured for four years in barrel under DOC rules and sometimes suffers from too woody a flavour. Rosso di Montalcino is generally a better bet – lighter, fruitier, and much cheaper. Carmignano, from a tiny zone west of Florence, is a soft, smooth and fragrant wine made from the basic Chianti formula with a little Cabernet added.

Chianti is at present going through a massive trauma. The price has sunk, stocks are accumulating fast, many producers have gone out of business and there's a huge surplus of wine. The year DOCG status was granted – 1984 – was a disastrous vintage. Nevertheless the introduction of DOCG should eventually mean higher standards.

Tuscany has some excellent unclassified wines. Sassicaia was once described by Hugh Johnson as "perhaps Italy's best red wine", but since it uses Cabernet Sauvignon grapes, which are not recognised in its zone, the wine is not entitled to DOC (or DOCG) status. Some other top-class *vini da tavola* are Coltassala, I Sodi, Prima Vigna, Sangioveto di Coltibuono, Solaia and Tignanello.

Traditionally white wines are not big business in Tuscany but as methods of vinification improve they are making some headway. Of the DOC whites, the ancient Vernaccia di San Gimignano (served and sold everywhere in the town) is worth trying as is the recently developed fresh, pale DOC Galestro; among the unclassified wines, the elegant Torricella from Brolio stands out. Chardonnay wines are also worth looking out for, particularly Tenuta di Pomino of Frescobaldi.

Vin Santo is (or rather can be) one of Italy's great dessert wines. The origin of the name ("holy wine") is still something of a mystery though it's generally believed that it was drunk at religious rites and ceremonies. The wine is golden in colour, strong, smooth and usually quite sweet, though it varies greatly from area to area and some experts insist it should be dry. The grapes of the true Vin Santo are semi-dried on beams or racks, then pressed and fermented and sealed in small barrels for at least three years. It's made by thousands of Tuscan families, often just for home consumption – as a guest you may well be offered a glass.

The best known wine route in Tuscany is the Chiantigiana (SS222), cutting through the Chianti Classico zone from Florence to Siena. Most estates in Chianti welcome visitors although it's wise either to write or telephone at least 24 hours in advance. There are various *enoteche* open to the public – the Enoteca del Gallo Nero in the delightful little town of Greve sells a complete range of Chianti Classico; there's also a Bottega del Chianti Classico in the same town. Siena has Italy's national wine library and a sample of every good Italian wine is stored in the hall of the 16th-century Medici fortress. Theoretically you can taste any of the wines but advance notice may be needed for some.

Two of the most important estates – Castello di Brolio and Marchesi Antinori – both have English-speaking guides but visits are by appointment only. Ruffino is also well equipped for English visitors. For those who want to combine visiting an estate with eating out, Castello Vicchiomaggio has a restaurant.

Wine producers in Tuscany:
Antinori, Badia a Coltibuono, Biondi-Santi (Il Greppo), Tenuta di Capezzana, Castelgiocondo, Castellare, Melini, Castello di Fonterutoli, Frescobaldi, Isole e Olena, Marchesi Incisa della Rocchetta, Fattoria Montagliani, Pagliarese, Poggio Reale, Rocca delle Macie, Castella di Rompolla, Ruffino, Castello di San Polo in Rosso, Conti Serristori, La Torre, Fattoria dell' Ugo, Castello Vicchiomaggio, Castell' in Villa, Villa di Vetrice, Castello di Volpaia.

Umbria and Lazio

Scenically and culturally Umbria is generally linked with Tuscany, but as far as wines are concerned it has far more in common with Lazio. Orvieto, Frascati and Est! Est!! Est!!! from Umbria and Lazio are mostly the products of the ubiquitous Trebbiano, a sound but undistinguished grape.

Orvieto comes from the ancient vineyards on the steep rocky terraces around the old cathedral town of Orvieto in Umbria. Traditionally it is a medium-sweet wine, but in response to popular taste an increasing amount of dry wine was produced – much of it rather dull. However the recent re-introduction of the Grechetto grape, the original source of Orvieto, has improved the quality of the wine considerably.

The great entrepreneur producer of Umbria is Lungarotti, a name inextricably linked with Torgiano wines. Their red Rubesco – not unlike a Chianti – is one of Italy's finest wines, and the whites are light, dry and fresh. The vineyards lie in the hills between Perugia and Assisi, close to the town of Torgiano. This is one of the few places in Tuscany and Umbria where no introduction is necessary: there's a warm welcome, English is spoken and there is liberal tasting. Lungarotti also run the excellent wine museum in Torgiano; and if you're planning on staying the night, the Tre Vaselle Hotel in town has wine tasting rooms and a well stocked cellar.

Other Umbrian wines include some sound DOCS (Colli del Trasimeno, red and white, and Colli Altotiberini, white) and a host of local wines, some of which are produced from vines strung haphazardly over pergolas and even interplanted with potatoes – known in Italy as *coltura promiscua*.

Est! Est! Est!!!, from close to Lake Bolsena just across the border in Lazio, is one of the crisper white wines of the area, but its reputation rests mainly on its name and the well-known story behind it. Legend goes that a bibulous German bishop travelling to Rome sent his servant ahead of him to chalk the word *Est!* (short for *vinum bonum est*) on the walls of the inns where the wine was good. At Montefiascone, near Lake Bolsena, he was so impressed by the wines that he wrote the word three times, which led to the bishop drinking himself to his grave.

Frascati is the most famous wine of Rome, drunk liberally in the city and surrounds, and exported worldwide in vast quantities. It is naturally dry, with a straw-gold hue. But most of the Frascati that finds its way to foreign shelves is dull and industrial. The best are made not from Trebbiano, but from the fragrant local Malgasia, or a blend of the two grapes. Unfortunately the label gives no clues. The best is probably Colli di Catone – the version in the frosted bottle. In the town of Frascati itself there is a suprising lack of inviting bars and cafés for tasting wine, though you can visit some of the cellars of the local vineyards – not all need prior booking. The main wine routes from Rome include Frascati and the other towns and villages of the Alban Hills or *Castelli Romani*.

Wine producers in Umbria:
Antinori, Decugnano dei Barbi, Barberani, Luigi Bigi, Lungarotti, Torricello.

Wine producers in Lazio:
Bruno Calacicchi produces the sought-after Torre Ercolana, a blend of Cabernet, Merlot and Cesanese grapes (only about 200 cases are made a year); Colli di Catone.

The Marches, Abruzzi and Molise

Legend goes that when Alaric the Visigoth set forth from Ravenna to sack Rome in 410AD, he took a large supply of wine from the Adriatic for the sustenance of his army. At least 300 years before that we know the Romans were fermenting wine at Piceno. Today a lot of the land is still under the vine, but there are few wines that would satisfy an army of northerners. The pale dry Verdicchio, in its distinctive green amphora-shaped bottle and pseudo-Greek lettering, has the widest repute; and some of the better Verdicchio is now bottled in non-gimmicky burgundy-style bottles. The Verdicchio dei Castelli di Jesi is the best-known zone, although the Matelica is said by many of the locals to be the best.

Rosso Piceno, a good ruby coloured wine from the Sangiovese Tuscan grape, is the most plentiful wine of the Marches; Rosso

Cónero, made largely from the Montepulciano grape, is a fine, rich, fruity red from the Monte Cónero Massif south of Ancona.

The commonest white of Abruzzi is the DOC Trebbiano d'Abruzzo, which can be rather bland but at best is a simple, dry but fruity wine. The main grape of Abruzzi is the Montepulciano (not to be confused with Vino Nobile di Montepulciano of Tuscany) which produces wines which can be rich, robust, soft and yet quite dry. Look for the labels Montepulciano d'Abruzzo, delle Marche and del Molise, depending on which region you're in.

Wine producers in the Marches and Abruzzi:
Fratelli Bucci, Fazi-Battaglia, Umani Ronchi (Marches); Barone Cornacchia, Tenuta del Priore, Cantina Sociale di Tollo, Colle Secco, Illuminati, Pepe, Edoardo Valentini (Abruzzi).

THE SOUTH

The Mezzogiorno, stretching from south of Rome and the Abruzzi to Sicily, produces huge quantities of wine, a lot of which ends up in the European wine lake. Apulia, an almost uninterrupted vineyard, is the biggest producer.

The Greeks introduced vines to the south and their Krimisa wine, the ancient counterpart of the modern Ciro of Calabria, was so highly esteemed that it was offered to winners of the Olympic Games – or so the story goes. The full-bodied Falerno from Campania was the most celebrated wine of ancient Rome, praised by Pliny and Horace.

Today a good deal of wine from the south is exported for blending or used to make vermouth. For a long time the south has had a reputation for poor-quality wines and primitive methods of production, but things are changing fast and the quality is improving right across the region. Sicily is the area that has advanced most dramatically over the past few years and many of the other areas are gradually moving over from the old peasant traditions to more efficient cooperatives.

Campania, Basilicata, Apulia and Calabria

In Campania the wine best known to tourists is the romantically named Lacrima Cristi, grown on the slopes of Mount Vesuvius. (The story goes that on the seventh day God looked down on the world He had created and was so moved by the beauty of the Bay of Naples that He shed a tear; from the tear came the first vine, and from the vine Lacrima Cristi). The first Lacrima Cristi DOC was introduced only very recently – and none too soon.

The consistently best whites are the Greco di Tufo and the Fiano di Avellino. The region's best red is Taurasi – dark, deep and always improving with age.

Other wines worth looking out for in the south are the red Aglianico del Vulture, the only DOC of Basilicata (d'Angelo is the only really good producer); the Calabrian Ciro; and the reds and, perhaps even more, the rosés of Castel del Monte near Bari. There are also a few good *vini da tavola* in Apulia – generally those that are more expensive than the average.

Ischia produces light red and white wines and has been awarded its own DOC.

Wine producers in the south:
Episcopio, Mastroberardino, Saviano (Campania); Leone de Castris, Rivera, Torre Quarto (Apulia); Fratelli d'Angelo (Basilicata); Librandi (Calabria).

Sicily

Of all the southern regions, Sicily has made the greatest headway in improving its wines. There are now several DOCs although the best wines are in fact *vini da tavola*, using grapes which do not come from any one region. The unclassified Corvo and Regaleali wines, for example, are very successful and are now exported to the United States and to the UK.

Marsala is still the best-known wine of Sicily. It was first made in the late 18th century when an English family living in western Sicily began making a wine fortified with brandy to compete with the wines of Spain and Portugal which were then popular in England. The result was Marsala. Today it varies from a sweet, gooey liquid (usually used for Zabaglione) to the long lasting Marsala Superiore or, best of all, Marsala Virgine – a finely perfumed aperitif. Stronger still are some of the local dessert wines, produced both in Sicily and its offshore islands. Look out for the delicious, often complex, grapey Moscato Passito di Pantelleria from the island of Pantelleria way off the Sicilian coast, not far from North Africa.

Wine producers in Sicily:
De Bartoli, Corvo, Duca di Salaparuta; Rallo; Rapitalà; Regaleali; Samperi; Settesoli

Sardinia

In Sardinia, as in Sicily, producers traditionally make sweet or fortified wines. The best-known is Vernaccia, a dry aromatic wine, high in alcohol. Sardinia is now also producing better table wines, thanks to improved methods of vinification. The entrepreneurs are Sella e Mosca at Alghero, whose cultivation and wine-making techniques owe much to Piedmont. They produce a range of wines including Torbato di Alghero, Sardinia's finest white, and a good red table wine from Cannonau.

Wine producers in Sardinia
Cantina Sociale di Dolianova, Marmilla, Sella e Mosca.

Twelve pages of maps appear at the back of the book (page 538); they are designed to help situate most of the places mentioned in the text. This key map shows how we have divided the country for our area chapters.

1 **Lakes and Mountains**
2 **Venice**
3 **Northern Cities**
4 **Liguria**
5 **Florence**
6 **Tuscany and Umbria**
7 **Rome**
8 **Central Italy**
9 **Naples and Campania**
10 **The South**
11 **Sicily**
12 **Sardinia**

LAKES &
MOUNTAINS

*❝How can one ignore these conspicuous actors,
the half-wild mountains where man has taken
root like a hardy plant; always semi-deserted
for man is constantly leaving them?❞*
FERNAND BRAUDEL

Gardone Riviera

Introduction

Italy, a geographical expression to borrow Metternich's phrase, has two boundaries: the Mediterranean and the Alps. A glance at a map shows the mountains to be a formidable natural barrier, a 1,300-mile wall rising abruptly from the sea coast and the plains of Piedmont, Lombardy and Venetia, closing the peninsula off from all its neighbours. This barrier has done little either to keep intruders out, so great has been the temptation posed by Italy's rich and often poorly defended pickings, or to foster national unity. Not only has the frontier been highly mobile in the short history of the Italian nation but the human boundary coincides neither with the mountain barrier nor the current political frontier. Italy has fringe zones inhabited by people who do not appear or consider themselves to be Italian, and there are fringe zones outside Italy (in Switzerland, mainly) that the Italians consider to be theirs by natural right. The natural boundary is defined by watershed: the Italian side drains into the Po or the Adriatic near the Po delta.

Historians tell us that the reason for all the confusion is the strange fact that there has in the past been more communication within the Alps than between the plains and the high mountain valleys. Alpine tribes migrated, resulting in the colonisation of southern valleys by northern people, and these peoples have not been Italianised. For centuries much of the western Alps formed an independent state (Savoy) straddling the highest peaks in the Alps on both French and Italian sides of the range. The Italian Valle d'Aosta has more in common with the French Savoie than either has with Italy or France.

Because of their location and the busy through traffic into Italy of invading armies, pilgrims and curious travellers, not to mention heavy lorries and freight trains, the Italian Alps have been and remain more of a thoroughfare than most high mountain regions. Seventeen out of the 23 main passes across the chain were regularly used in Roman times and most of the ones now closed for five, six or even seven months of the year were regularly used in winter. Villages of waggoners and porters grew up at the foot of the passes and made a living out of their jealously guarded monopolies of the passing trade. The mountains concentrate the traffic and the region is an exaggerated version of the pattern of many rural areas, with a few very heavily-used routes taking travellers to Milan, Turin and Verona via the main passes (Mont Cenis and the St Bernards in the west, the Simplon and St Gotthard in the centre, and the Brenner and Tarvis in the east), with large remote areas between them. Tunnels through the mountain barrier have not changed the old routes much but have made them practicable all the year round and have made crossing the high passes in summer much more enjoyable for motorists, as the heavy traffic now passes below ground. These days the great trunk routes, heavy with juggernauts, are the Mont Blanc tunnel and the great breach that is the Brenner Pass, the lowest of the natural gateways into Italy.

In the western (Piedmont) Alps there are no road communications other than along the valleys and distances are long: getting by car from one place to its neighbour on the other side of the hill can be a matter of many hours and touring the mountains is more or less impossible. The most inaccessible area of all is that between the Valle d'Aosta and the lakes north of Milan, where narrow and steep-sided valleys wind tortuously down from the southern walls of some of the highest and most celebrated of all Alpine peaks, including the Matterhorn and Monte Rosa. There are hiking trails linking the heads of these valleys but for the motorist the distances between them are enormous.

These remote valleys were havens for medieval heretical sects and the setting for fierce campaigns of repression, notably in the Valsesia which runs down from the foot of the Monte Rosa to Vercelli. Admirers of Umberto Eco's *The Name of The Rose* will find their curiosity aroused by such names on the map as Campodolcino (near the Swiss border north of Lake Como) and seek out mountain monasteries or memorials to the heretics and to those who battled and preached to bring them back into the orthodox fold. Except in a couple of valleys west of Turin, they will be disappointed: the sects were not favourably inclined towards works of art or great building projects, and repression was all too effective.

Of less academic interest is the way a few valleys have kept their own individual ethnic character (costumes, language, domestic architecture) at a time when mass communications have gone most of the way to relegate folklore to museums and festivals, at least in most European countries. There are high villages founded by migrants from the Swiss Valais in the 13th century where a German dialect is still spoken and colourful costumes still worn. The Valle d'Aosta's dialect is a French one, and place names (such as Courmayeur and Pré-St-Didier) have a very French ring. The two influences coexist most confusingly in the Val de Lys where the place names (such as Gressoney-St-Jean) are French but the local people speak German, and this in Italy.

Throughout the Valle d'Aosta, one of several semi-autonomous corners of the far north, the local building style is very attractive wood and rough-stone chalets (known as *rascards*) which gives the Italian mountain landscape an unfamiliar picturesque look. Provided you do not expect too much of the main road drive down from the Mont Blanc Tunnel to Aosta and Turin, the scenery is spectacular, dominated by the highest of all Alpine peaks along the French and Swiss borders and several very beautiful ones inside Italy, notably the Gran Paradiso, the only all-Italian 4,000-metre mountain. In the Valle d'Aosta there are resorts large and small with a mixture of summer and winter tourism. Far and away the most important is Courmayeur, at heart a delightful old village in a magnificent setting at the foot of the Mont Blanc massif. Courmayeur was a famous mountaineering village and developed into an elegant year-round resort long before the Mont Blanc Tunnel put it on one of the main roads of Europe. This takes the edge off the charm of the place, to put it mildly, but Courmayeur is still the best holiday base in a region with plenty of historical interest as well as natural beauty. Aosta is an attractive old town with impressively preserved Roman buildings and walls, and there are medieval fortresses to admire, and in a few cases visit, along the main valley. The Valle d'Aosta used to be duty-free but with the opening of the tunnel the privilege was withdrawn.

Piedmont, it does not take a great linguistic genius to work out, means the area at the foot of the mountains. Although about a third of the region is actually mountainous, most of its population and wealth is indeed concentrated at the foot of the mountains. Turin (*see later chapter on Northern Cities*) is the regional capital, a dignified city most famous for its motor industry. But this is no Birmingham, and it is typical of the high-falutin' tone of the place that its great mogul, Fiat's Giovanni Agnelli, cuts a dashing princely figure, a merchant adventurer among car manufacturers.

In the 11th century Piedmont came by marriage into the possession of the House of Savoy, and refined Turin continued to speak French well into the 19th century despite an increasingly Italian outlook and a growing role as the unifying power in Italy. Cavour, subtle architect of Italian unity, was more at home writing and speaking French than Italian. In the 18th century the dukes of Savoy gained royal status with the kingdom of Sardinia, and after the defeat of Napoleon they were granted Liguria as well as Piedmont. Steadily the Piedmontese consolidated their power in the peninsula at the expense of the Austrian empire, while renouncing territorial claims west of the Alpine barrier except for a small neighbourhood around Tende, one of Victor Emmanuel's favourite hunting grounds which Napoleon III generously allowed him to keep. In 1861 Victor Emmanuel became the first king of an Italy united except for a small papal state in the centre, and Turin was briefly its capital. The present frontier was fixed in 1947 when a few border posts at the high passes were moved, and the inhabitants of Tende voted to become French. The last king of Italy, called Humbert like so many of his predecessors in Europe's most durable ruling dynasty, died in 1983.

Lombardy is the heartland of industrial Italy, and Milan the nation's economic and cultural capital. Lombardy is also Italy's Lake District. Touring the mountains in the north of the region is more practical than in Piedmont and there are important wintersports resorts, but it is the lakes not the mountains that pull in the tourists from all over the world and especially Britain. The ebb and flow of glaciers has left lakes in all the Alpine countries as well as in England. The Italian lakes became most fashionable at the same time as our own lakes, when mountains in general thrilled the Romantics and mountain lakes in particular provided their blend of picturesque and sublime beauty, to use the aesthetic jargon of the time.

The basic ingredients and the appeal of a mountain lakescape are pretty much the same in Italy, Alberta and Westmoreland: an unusually satisfying, perhaps comforting, prospect of an enclosed landscape with a symmetry of colours and patterns mirrored in the water, so much more like a work of art than nature usually is.

Turner looked no further than the landscape of Lake Lucerne for his inspiration, Lamartine found the Lac du Bourget more than sufficiently moving for one over-sensitive Romantic soul. Wainwright and many others before him have been content with our own lakes. Wordsworth and Shelley, on the other hand, thought the Italian lakes altogether enchanted. Was it just because they were in love with the idea of Italy, or is there something special about the Italian lakes? It is tempting to say that what is indeed special about the lakes is that they are in Italy. Unfortunately they aren't: the top of Lake Maggiore is in Switzerland and so is most of Lake Lugano, which lies on the most confusing stretch of this highly indecisive national frontier. There are no less than six border crossings along the banks of little Ceresio (to give Lake Lugano its alternative name), two of them being the edges of Campione d'Italia, a tiny Italian enclave surrounded by Swiss territory.

Be that as it may, the lakes are distinctively Italian. They lie close to the important historic cities of Milan, Bergamo, Brescia and Verona, and the delights of the lakeside were known to the citizens of these places long before the Romantic poets moved in. The result is that the lakes, and especially Como, are more than just a pretty view. Shelley, who thought that Lake Como exceeded in beauty any thing he had ever beheld except the arbutus islands of Killarney, found that "the union of culture and the untameable profusion and loveliness of nature is here so close that the line where they are divided can hardly be discovered". Grand and sumptuously decorated villas and medieval castles are surrounded by rich and even exotic vegetation that flourishes in the lakes' sheltered position on the south side of the mountains. Como itself was an important and powerful medieval city and would be worth visiting even if it were not set on one of the world's most beautiful lakes. The mild winter temperatures allow figs, olives, citrus fruit (notably on Garda) and even palms to thrive along with camelias and azaleas in the gardens along the lakes' shores. Snowy peaks, rocky cliffs, glassy waters, lush gardens and elegant palaces, little islands popping up from the deep: paradise indeed.

There are at least a dozen of these Italian Lakes, and their varying dimensions are a statistician's dream. Garda is the largest (370 sq km) and lowest (65m), Maggiore the longest (65km) and Como the deepest (410m), its bottom some 200 metres below sea level. Idro is the highest (368m), but despite this is surrounded by some of the least interesting country. Excluding Lake Lugano, the most interesting parts of which are Swiss, five of the lakes – Como, Maggiore, Garda, Iseo and Orta – are worth bothering with. Como and Maggiore are two of a kind: close neighbours, both long and narrow and surrounded by a landscape that varies from high mountains in the north to the edge of the urban plain in the south. Their main resorts have a comfortable, old-fashioned charm and attract large numbers of not very energetic visitors, many of them elderly and many of them British. The hills and mountains around the lakes are not ideal for gentle walks and most visitors content themselves with pottering around enjoying the scenery, taking funicular rides and boat trips round the lakes and visiting islands, gardens and lakeside villas. More ambitious sightseeing excursions to Milan and other northern cities are easily arranged.

Long stretches of the lakeside, including all of Como's eastern shore and much of Lake Maggiore's western one, are spoilt by heavy traffic on narrow and tortuous roads that serve inadequately as the main access routes from the cities to the Italian and Swiss mountain resorts. Given the north Italian's impatience at the wheel and his blind confidence in the benevolent power of St Christopher, these roads can be nightmarish, especially at weekends. The village of Bellagio enjoys the dual blessing of being set in a spectacular position on a promontory in the middle of Lake Como and in being free from through traffic, although in high season plenty of tourist coaches and cars use the beautiful road which goes around the peninsula.

There are various styles of resort: rows of grand-ish hotels along the prom at Stresa, Cadenabbia, Menaggio; town hotels of all standards at Como; old lakeside palaces and parks transformed into luxurious hotels at Cernobbio and Bellagio. Little Lake Orta (the only one of the lakes in Piedmontese territory) is less celebrated as a beauty spot and its surroundings are less mountainous, but it offers much the same style of holiday without the faded grandeur. Its single resort, Orta San-Giulio, is one of the most picturesque of all the lakeside villages, along with Bellagio. Lake Iseo does not have a resort to rival Orta but is otherwise similar.

Lake Garda also stretches south from mountains to plain but is as different from the other main lakes as the Adriatic coast is from the Riviera, and for the same reason: Garda is on the route south from Bavaria and the Brenner Pass and is overwhelmingly the domain of German tourists. Restaurants and hotels advertise and speak to foreign visitors in German. Nor is its custom elderly and sedate: windsurfers will tell you that the steeply enclosed narrow northern half of the lake is exceptionally suitable for their purposes, and around the main northern resort of Riva there is plenty of nightlife to keep the young and energetic entertained in the evening. Nothing could be more different from the gentility of Lakes Como, Maggiore and Orta.

Not all of Lake Garda is like Riva. The southern half of the lake is so broad and the surrounding landscape so flat that the shore could be a coast. On the tip of a long peninsula in the south, the fortified old village of Sirmione is a famous beauty spot and spa in a similar situation to Bellagio's although it is more of a tourist trap. Between Riva and Sirmione there are quieter resorts (Salò, Gardone, Fasano, Limone) at the foot of green and fruitful hills, mainly on the Lombard west bank.

In a large area of the eastern Italian Alps the German voices you hear are those of locals as well as tourists. This is Bolzano province, known officially in Italy as Alto Adige, but South Tyrol to its friends, who believe the area to be neither Italian nor Austrian, but simply that part of the Tyrol (which takes its name from a castle above Merano) lying south of the Alpine barrier. Unhistorical though it may be to do so, most of us think of the Tyrol as being the essence of Austria, and Alto Adige seems like a large chunk of Austria where the currency in circulation happens to be the lira. The valleys are green, the villages colourful, the chalet balconies heavy with winter firewood and brimming over with flowers. On Sunday mornings the village band of ruddy musicians turns out in *lederhosen* and embroidered waistcoats to play in the local beer garden. In the restaurants they serve up sausage and dumplings, and the villagers take people into their spotless homes for B&B. Hotels tend to be smart and carefully rustic with dark wood, bright white duvets and saunas in the basement. In Tyrolean style, the local people take the business of being welcoming to tourists very seriously.

That the south Tyrol belongs to Italy is usually blamed on President Wilson who, in 1919, conceded to Italian demands for a defensible frontier. Mussolini tried to suppress German names and language but in 1946 the Italians were made to promise that the south Tyroleans would be granted a large measure of autonomy. Cunningly, the government joined Alto Adige to the neighbouring thoroughly Italian province of Trentino in its autonomy, so the Tyroleans are still effectively subject to Italian control.

Obviously, if what you like about Italy is the Italian style of life, the south Tyrol is not an ideal choice. Otherwise it is a delightful area, more rural than much of the Italian Alps (where the divide between remote mountains and built-up plain is very abrupt), and very popular with hikers. The charming old town of Merano is one of Italy's big resorts and in its old-fashioned way is the mountain equivalent of the main resorts on the lakes, except in being more suitable as a touring base and also a very good resort for walkers.

There are a few interesting old towns in the north-east, mainly along the Adige valley between Trento and the Brenner pass, but the area's great beauty is the scenery, and most spectacularly the scenery of the Dolomites, which is quite unlike the rest of the Alps. Named after an 18th-century French geologist (a M. de Dolomieu) who first analysed their cristalline limestone, the Dolomites soar in jagged pinnacles, towers and walls of rusty rock which catch fire in the oblique light of dawn and dusk. Roads are good and cross very high passes at the foot of massive fortifications of these castles in the sky, and there are cable-cars lifting tourists from car park to dizzy clifftop perch in a matter of minutes. If you want to enjoy mountain scenery from a car and cable-car, the Dolomites is without doubt the best place in Europe to do it. The area, which mostly falls east of the main Adige valley, is also a celebrated playground for rock climbers, hikers who have a taste for exposed ledges with flimsy ropes to grasp and iron staircases on the edge of cliff faces, and sane people who stick to the green pastures at the foot of the rocky peaks. All in all, the Dolomites is one of the busiest holiday areas of the Alps, with a very important tourist season in winter as well as summer. Cortina d'Ampezzo, self-styled queen of the Dolomites, is Italy's smartest wintersports resort, and although much quieter in summer it is still an excellent place for a comfortable mountain holiday, which is more than can be said for most ski resorts. Cortina is at the

Visiting the Lakes and Mountains

There are regular scheduled and charter flights from London and some regional airports to Milan, plus seasonal charters to Verona – the best airports for the lakes. By train you could go to Stresa (for Lake Maggiore) or Desenzano (for Lake Garda) in 21 to 23 hours; allow 26 hours for Bolzano, 28 for Merano. The journey by coach from London to Milan via Turin takes over 24 hours; you can stop at Aosta (22 hours). For a holiday in the Mont Blanc area it is normally more convenient to fly to Geneva than Milan; for the Dolomites, to Zurich (or by charter flight to Treviso). If taking your own car you should anticipate an overnight stop and allow for frontier delays and tolls for mountain passes. You might consider using Motorail: Boulogne to Milan, May to mid-September, 15 hours.

The lakes are less suitable for a touring holiday than for a comfortable, relaxing stay in one place with excursions on the boats that cruise round all the main lakes. Driving can be slow and tiring with endless tunnels often blocking the views and narrow twisting roads. However, there are car ferries across the three major lakes. Excursions to interesting towns and sights are organised from almost all resorts.

Lake Garda is the most popular of the lakes, especially with German tourists. It is the only lake that attracts many bathers and watersports people (Riva is the main resort for this). It is also a good base for visits to Brescia, Mantua and Verona. Lake Como is the most beautiful and least spoilt of the major lakes, with Bellagio easily the most civilised resort. Resorts on the smaller lakes (Orta, Iseo and Lugano) fill up at weekends but see little international tourism and can seem very lacklustre during the week; there is little comfortable hotel accommodation.

Even the mountains are within weekend range of the 14 million Italians who live in Lombardy, Piedmont and Venetia. As with the lakes, there are a number of small local resorts with little to offer the visitor from farther afield. The exceptions in the western Alps are the Upper Susa valley and the Valle d'Aosta, the most beautiful and varied part. The eastern Alps are much more suitable for motoring tours, and the spectacular Dolomite scenery between Bolzano and Cortina is a powerful magnet in high summer to motorists, climbers and walkers, most of them German. For panoramic drives and exciting cable-car ascents, this area is unrivalled in the Alps. The passes are high and the roads, although well-engineered, are hard work on car and driver. In summer impatient local bus drivers and tourist coaches add to the hazards. In the very attractive western part of the south Tyrol, Merano, a charming old town, is the main resort. Cervinia and the Stelvio pass (near Bormio) are the main Italian summer ski areas.

The lakes are a favourite destination for British package tour operators, who offer one- or two-week holidays by air, rail or coach – the greatest number to Lake Garda. Most hotels on the lakes have succumbed to package tours, so there is usually little advantage in booking independently. A few specialist companies offer art tours with visits to villas and gardens.

By contrast, very few operators offer flight and hotel packages to the mountains in summer. There are some coach holidays and a few companies organise summer skiing, mountaineering and walking holidays. Agents can arrange self-catering chalets.

The main season for the lakes is late spring (when many of the beautiful lakeside gardens are at their best and the mountain peaks are snowy) and summer. Some resorts on Maggiore and Garda still claim to be winter resorts thanks to their mild climate but the fashion for wintering in these parts has passed. Summer visitors should be warned that while there are small beaches round all the lakes, most of them shelve steeply and the water is never very warm. The main cultural attractions are the festival of early music on Lake Orta in June and the Verona Opera festival from July to September, when it may be difficult to find accommodation on Lake Garda.

eastern end of the Dolomites and is much more Italian in atmosphere than the German-speaking valleys to the west and north. The border of south Tyrol runs through the heart of the Dolomites, and the contrast in the styles of village when you cross the border is as sharp as if it were still a national frontier.

Of all the troubled periods of its history, the south Tyrol has known none more remarkable than the First World War, when the Austro-Italian front line extended for hundreds of miles across the mountain region, most of it above the summer snow line, without any significant movement for two and a half years. Gun emplacements were set up on the highest peaks including the Ortler (3,905m) and the highest Dolomite, the Marmolada (3,344m). Electrically-lit ice tunnels were carved out of the glaciers, cable-cars were constructed and war was waged in conditions of almost unimaginable hardship, summer and winter. The winter of 1915/6 saw heavier snowfalls than any skier could dream up, and over 10,000 soldiers died in avalanches. Commanders soon learnt that the most effective way to attack the enemy was to aim at the snowy slopes above him, and a conservative estimate of the avalanche toll for the war is 50,000.

To the east of the Dolomites another semi-autonomous region, Friuli-Venezia Giulia, is also a post-war creation. After bitter fighting in the First World War the area passed from Austrian to Italian control along with much of what is now Yugoslavia (Istria). The poet and patriot Gabriele d'Annúnzio led a proto-Fascist freelance expedition to establish personal rule in Fiume. At the end of the Second World War Yugoslavian forces under Marshal Tito reclaimed the lost territory except for the coastal area around Trieste which was declared neutral and governed initially by an Allied military force. The present frontier dates from 1954, when Trieste became Italian. The most recent troubles to beset this eastern fringe zone have been earthquakes, which claimed some 1,000 lives over a period of months in 1976 and reduced several towns north of Udine to a state of desolation. It is not a busy tourist region, but there are some quiet resorts in the wooded mountains of the north, near the Austrian and Yugoslavian frontiers.

Places to visit

ALAGNA

Remote climbing resort in an enclosed setting at the head of the Valsesia and at the foot of the Monte Rosa, second peak in the Alps (4,633m). A 17th-century chalet houses a small local folk museum (Museo Walser) devoted to the Valaisan migrant people who colonised this high valley and several of its neighbours. A long three-stage cable-car to Punta Indren at the foot of the glaciers on the southern shoulders of Monte Rosa is a favourite starting point for climbers and also speeds the hiking trail over to Gressoney in the Val de Lys. (*See also Macugnaga*)

AMPEZZO

A small village and modest resort on the main east-west road in the north-eastern corner of the country, between Tolmezzo, the main town in the Carnic Alps, and Pieve di Cadore (*see separate entry*). A minor road leads up the narrow Lumiei valley to the peaceful resort of **Sauris**, made up of several hamlets above a large reservoir. The road to Vigo is very rough and wild.

AOSTA

The capital of the semi-autonomous Valle d'Aosta region is now a sizeable town which has far outgrown its old centre, with some industry and supermarkets lining the main valley road south of town. Although the region is no longer duty-free, these still flourish on the sale of cheap clothes, shoes, souvenirs and alcohol. Aosta is a very ancient city at a valley junction where the roads down from both St Bernard Passes meet. The occupying tribe of Salassi resisted Roman domination until 25BC when 36,000 of them were auctioned into slavery on the market square in Ivrea. The city was renamed Augusta Pretoria and later became subject to Burgundy and Savoy. The present town retains not only a derivative of its Roman name but also the clear rectilinear plan of the ancient city, and extensive monumental remains from the Roman period and Middle Ages. Apart from the rather lifeless main square, the old grey town is handsome and harmonious, with attractive pedestrian shopping streets.

☛ **Cathedral** The main interest is mosaic pavements from the 12th to 14th centuries and choir stalls from the late 15th century.

☛ **Collegiate church of Sant' Orso** Founded by Anselm, 11th-century Archbishop of Canterbury and a native of Aosta. The handsome campanile dates from the 12th century and the wooden stalls inside the church from the late 15th century. The crypt has a dozen Roman pillars and may have been a very early Christian basilica. The cloister is surrounded by beautiful marble capitals, one of them dated 1133. It is well worth inspecting the nearby priory building with its graceful octagonal tower and Renaissance decoration.

☛ **Roman remains** Long stretches of the Roman **city walls** are still intact, especially in the south and west of the town, and include the massive Porta Pretoria (1st century BC) – a triple-arched gateway flanked by a medieval tower, one of many that were incorporated into and added onto the old walls in the Middle Ages by rival factions. Near the gateway is the Roman theatre, complete with its 60ft buttressed rear wall. To the east of the city walls, the triumphal **Arch of Augustus** was erected at the time of the city's foundation in 25BC. The pitched roof dates from the 18th century. There's a well-preserved single arched **bridge**, no longer spanning the River Buthier which changed its course in the 17th century.

(*See also Gran Paradiso National Park, and Valle d'Aosta*)

AVIGLIANA

Small old town on a hill not far from Turin, now a fashionable residential area for commuters. Avigliana was the birthplace of Savoy's Red Count Amadeus VII, and a favourite residence of the principality's medieval rulers. Their castle was demolished in the 17th century, but its remains still stand above the town. In the centre of the old town, around the arcaded Piazza Conte Rosso are numerous 15th-century houses and old towers. The two lakes on the edge of town are popular among Torinese watersports enthusiasts at weekends, but at other times are peaceful. There is some lakeside accommodation. Nearby sights include:

☛ **Sacra di San Michele** An important medieval fortified abbey spectacularly perched on a spur nearly 600m above the Dora Riparia and commanding the entrance to the Susa Valley. First founded in the 10th century, the abbey became a popular halt on pilgrimages to Rome and a rich and powerful centre of learning until coming under Savoyard control in the 14th century. The valley is a major international thoroughfare and, if you're passing through, it is well worth not only looking out for the abbey's dark silhouette high above the road, but also making time to drive up through the woods from Avigliana to visit it. This is no Mont St Michel, but the setting is most impressive, the views from the church terrace are magnificent and there is good relief carving in the 11th- to 13th-century church and round the Zodiac door at the top of the long Scalone dei Morti (the abbey's restorers found some mummified bodies there). Frescoes near the church entrance date from the early 16th century.

☛ **San Antonio di Ranverso** An elegant 13th-century abbey church in a quiet farmyard setting to the south of the main road about half way between Avigliana and Rivoli. Works of art inside (guided tours) include a series of 15th-century frescoes. The doorway and windows of the old hospital can be seen in the structure of farm building opposite the church.

BARDONECCHIA

(See Upper Susa Valley)

BELLAGIO

The pick of the lakeside resorts, a quiet and very picturesque old village enjoying an unrivalled setting on the wooded tip of the hilly triangle that divides the Lecco and Como branches of Lake Como. There is very little to the village apart from a colourful group of small hotels lining the waterfront and quay and a few steep streets around the restored 12th-century church. The village looks out over the Como side of the promontory but there are walks round the cape giving marvellous views in all directions, notably north to the mountains along the Swiss border; even in summer this backdrop is often snowy after a spell of bad weather. The hill immediately behind the village is occupied by the magnificent gardens of the 17th-century **Villa Serbelloni** (guided tours morning and afternoon), on a site previously occupied by a medieval castle and, perhaps, by a villa belonging to Pliny the Younger. The villa (not the same as the Grand Hotel of the same name at the foot of the hill, which is also worth a visit if only for a musically accompanied evening drink) now belongs to the Rockefeller Foundation and is used for medical conventions. Near the lido at the Como end of the village, the neo-classical **Villa Melzi** and its gardens are also open to visitors.

BELLUNO

Lively provincial capital in a splendid position at a river junction on
the southern edge of the Dolomites. The old centre of town is set on
a spur overlooking the two rivers (Piave and Ardo) and mainly dates
from the 15th and 16th centuries when the town was under Venetian
control. The most interesting building, on the Piazza del Duomo, is
the late 15th-century **Palazzo dei Rettori**, now the prefecture. The
tower at the east end of it is all that remains of the 12th-century
bishop's palace. The cathedral dates mostly from the 16th century
except for the Baroque campanile (18th-century). The nearby market
square, Piazza delle Erbe, is surrounded by porticoed Renaissance
buildings.

Excursion from Belluno
☞ **Mel** (*16km south-west*)
On the beautiful left bank of the Piave, this small town has
numerous late Renaissance and Baroque houses around the Piazza
Umberto I and interesting paintings in the 18th-century Parrocchiale
church.

BOLZANO (BOZEN)

Capital of the south Tyrol and centre of its wine industry, this is a
busy market town on one of the main routes into Italy and at the
confluence of the rivers Talvera and Isarco. Bolzano is more of a
bustling town and less of a sedate resort than Merano but the style
of the centre is similar, with very charming, colourful, narrow old
shopping and market streets, notably the **Via dei Portici** or
Laubengasse, lined with elaborately decorated 16th- to 18th-century
houses. On the south-western side of the wide central square is the
very northern-looking Gothic **cathedral** (14th- and 15th-century)
with a Renaissance campanile and colourfully tiled roof. There is an
interesting **folklore museum** near the Ponte della Vittoria and
splendid walks in the gardens on both banks of the Talvera, as well
as on the slopes above the town. Mountain transport includes the
world's first cable-car (to Colle), constructed in 1908. The original
was destroyed in the Second World War and the present lift is only
about 20 years old.

Bolzano is near the southern limit of the south Tyrol and was for
centuries disputed between the bishops of Trento and the rulers of
Tyrol. Its style of life is less thoroughly Tyrolean than many towns
and villages further north, but the old centre has a distinctly
northern look about it and in the restaurants you should expect to be
confronted with *speck*, *gulasch* and *knödel*.

➤ **Castel Roncolo**   Of all the many castles overlooking the valleys around
Bolzano the most interesting is Castel Roncolo (or Runkelstein) on a rock
above the Talvera and within walking distance of Bolzano. The interior is
decorated with a remarkable and very extensive series of non-religious
frescoes giving a vivid picture of courtly life (people bathing, hunting,
dancing etc). The castle itself was first built in the 13th century, but often
altered. The paintings date from the 14th and early 16th centuries.

➤ **Parrocchiale** (parish church)   In the comfortable garden suburb of Gries, on the right bank of the Talvere, the Parrocchiale (not the large Baroque church on the main square) has a beautiful altarpiece by Michael Pacher (late 15th-century).

Excursions from Bolzano

☞ **Great Dolomite Road**

Bolzano is a convenient base for exploring both sides of the Adige Valley by car and a good starting point for a tour of the most famous Dolomite scenery. The most celebrated route – the Great Dolomite Road – is from Bolzano to Cortina via the passes of Costalungo, Pordoi and Falzarego. The entrance to the Val d'Ega through a tight gorge of porphyry makes a dramatic gateway to some of Europe's finest mountain scenery. On the Bolzano side of the Costalungo Pass, the wooded **Lago di Carezza** (Karersee) is a popular beauty spot, the peaks of the Latemar reflected in its waters. The most attractive of the possible variants of the return trip from Cortina is via the passes of Valparola and Gardena into the Val Gardena. (*See also Cortina and Val Gardena*)

☞ **Passo della Mendola** (*25km south-west*)

On the other side of the Adige Valley it is well worth making the steep drive up through woods south-west from Bolzano to this pass (1,363m) for the views across the main valley to the Dolomites.

BORMIO

A busy year-round resort and small town at the head of the Valtellina in a vast theatre of mountains. Although best known for its skiing (it hosted the 1985 World Skiing Championships), the character of what is a very old village has not been lost and Bormio has far more ordinary Italian charm than most ski resorts and indeed than most spa resorts, of which it is also one. The saving grace is that the new crop of skiing hotels has grown up at some distance from the old town (across the river) as has the spa establishment, a short distance up the Stelvio road. Bormio and its healing waters were known and used by the Romans, but the town's period of greatest prosperity was the 15th and 16th centuries, thanks to its trading monopoly over north-south traffic which was then considerable, although this corner of the Alps now seems decidedly remote. At the time there were 32 towers; not many remain but the narrow cobbled streets still have a medieval look about them. There are several very appetising shops selling Valtellina wines and food specialities.

Bormio is an excellent place for an active holiday in summer as well as winter – good riding, mountain walks, climbing, eagle spotting in the Stelvio National Park (there is a National Park exhibition centre in the resort) and one of Europe's biggest summer skiing areas on the glaciers above the very high Stelvio pass. There are also plenty of organised excursions from Bormio to Livigno (*see separate entry*), St Moritz and Innsbruck.

Excursions from Bormio

☞ **The Gávia and Stelvio Passes**

The **Gávia Pass** (2,621m), south of the relatively quiet resort of Santa Caterina, is steep, high, narrow and exposed, although scenically not particularly beautiful. The **Stelvio Pass** road is higher (2,758m) but easier and an important link between Valtellina and the south Tyrol. To the north of the pass is the so-called Dreisprachenspitze, the point of division between Italian, Romansch and German languages. There are a few hotels and some ski equipment shops at the pass, making the Stelvio a particularly suitable summer skiing place for people who just want to do an hour or two on their way through. Serious summer skiers should stay in Bormio (daily transport up to the Stelvio). From the pass and ski area there are magnificent views of the glaciers of the Ortler, one of the most beautiful and highest of Italian Alpine peaks (3,905m), its slopes the chilly theatre of prolonged fighting in the First World War. From the Stelvio there are roads down into Switzerland (over the Passo Santa Maria) and, in a splendid sequence of 48 hairpins for a descent of 1,215 metres in 13km, down to the woods of the south Tyrol. The colourful, neat and tidy villages at the foot of the road (such as Trafoi) could be in another country.

BRESSANONE (BRIXEN)

A very interesting small Tyrolean town-half way between Bolzano and the Brenner, well worth a pause if you're passing through and a good base for excursions into the Dolomites and the mountains around Merano. In the Middle Ages and Renaissance the prince bishops of Brixen were powerful landowners, controlling a vast area including much of what is now Austrian Tyrol. The town has an attractive leafy riverside and a picturesque old centre, with arcaded shopping streets around the colourful cathedral square. A long series of cable-cars and other lifts starts at the south-east edge of town, and Bressanone is also a popular base for mountain walks.

☛ **Cathedral** The twin-towered façade and most of the interior of the cathedral are unremarkable Baroque, but the cloister is much older (13th- to 14th-century) and has some interesting early Renaissance frescoes, as does the small baptistery, accessible from the cloister. A very lively series of funerary relief portraits of local churchmen adorns the walls of cloisters and the cathedral façade.

Excursions from Bressanone

☞ **Novacella** (*3km north*)

Although hardly one of the wonders of the world, as is suggested by an amusing series of paintings in the courtyard, this is an impressive, still partly walled abbey with an extravagantly ornate 18th-century church, set beside the Brunico road a mile or two north of town, in the middle of vineyards. Local wine is on sale at the entrance. There are guided tours a few times a day: frescoes and tombs in the 14th-century cloister, and an altarpiece by Michael Pacher in the sacristy.

☞ **Chiusa** (*11km south*)

For those prepared to walk uphill as well as down, a very beautiful excursion is to walk to or from Chiusa (Klausen) on the western slopes of the main valley, passing through Velturno and the old monastery of Sabiona, the original seat of the local bishop. The trip takes about 3 to 4 hours. A minor road closely follows the path as far as Velturno, but then drops down to the valley. Chiusa itself is very picturesque, with medieval and Renaissance houses and a 13th-century tower.

BRUNICO
(*See Pusteria*)

CERVINIA
One of the highest and most celebrated of Italian ski resorts, dominated by the Matterhorn (4,478m) – known in Italian as Il Cervino – with cable-cars linking up over the glaciers with Zermatt in Switzerland. In pre-skiing times Cervinia, or Breuil as it then was, amounted to no more than a cluster of buildings on the gentle slopes at the foot of a severe amphitheatre of rock and glacier dominated by the massive pillar of the Matterhorn, which is very much more elegant when seen from Zermatt. The Matterhorn was thought to be a castle inhabited by devils and Breuil did not develop as a climbing resort as Zermatt did in the Victorian period, although a few local guides did take up the challenge. They were Edward Whymper's opposition in the Boy's Own story of the conquest of the Matterhorn, which ended in victory for Whymper by a couple of days in July 1865. Contrary to received wisdom at the time, Whymper had guessed that the route from Zermatt was in fact much easier than the ascent from Italy.

Cervinia got its own back on Zermatt in the early days of skiing when it became one of the smartest and most modern of pre-war resorts, with cable-cars up to unprecedented heights (3,500m) long before similar installations sprung up on the Swiss side of the mountain. Now Cervinia has lost most of its cachet – the surroundings are severe and the village itself a monumental eyesore. The cable-cars will take you up to Europe's highest ski fields – a vast area of glacier on the Swiss side of the border ridge, and from the top of the lifts it is scarcely more than a walk to the top of the easiest of the local 4,000m peaks, the Breithorn. Because of the international dimension of the lift system, summer skiing from Cervinia is even more expensive than in other places.

For those not requiring the sports facilities, there are more attractive and older villages lower down the **Valtournenche** valley, notably Valtournenche itself. The valley specialises in the production of elaborate wooden loving cups (*grolla*, meaning grail) filled with sweet alcoholic coffee. You find these in souvenir shops throughout the Valle d'Aosta.

CHAMPOLUC
(*See Val d'Ayas*)

CHIAVENNA
A small and, in the centre, picturesque old town north of Lake

Como in a strategic position (whence the name, which means key) at the foot of two passes across the Alps, the more important of which is the Maloja to St Moritz and the Inn Valley. Steep rocky vineyard slopes surround the town. The border is only a few miles up the Maloja road and the Val Bragaglia between the frontier and the pass is an Italian-speaking part of Switzerland.

CHIUSA
(*See Bressanone*)

COMO
A busy city of some 100,000 inhabitants at the south-west end of Lake Como, an important Roman town and independent commune until the mid-14th century when it came under Milanese control. Como stands on a busy road and rail thoroughfare between Milan and the north (Zurich) and covers a large built-up area with some industry (the traditional one is silk weaving). As such it is hardly the natural choice for a lakeside holiday, but it is worth visiting. There are regular ferry services to other towns and resorts round the lake. The old centre, with pedestrian-only arcaded shopping streets around the cathedral, is set back only a little way from the gardens along the lakeside where the busy 19th-century Piazza Cavour is open to the lake.

The main sight in the old part of town is the splendid group of medieval buildings consisting of marble **cathedral** (the late Gothic façade decorated with Renaissance sculpture) and 13th-century town hall and communal tower. The statues on either side of the central doorway of the cathedral are of the elder and younger Pliny who were natives of the city. Works of art inside the cathedral include paintings by Gaudenzio Ferrari and Luini. The other church to visit is the beautiful Romanesque **Sant' Abbondio**, not shown off to its best in a gloomy quarter on the south-west edge of town beside the railway. There is a funicular from near the lake to the village of **Brunate**, a good viewpoint high above the lake.

Excursion from Como
☞ **Cernobbio** (*5km north on west bank*)
A lakeside village on the outskirts of Como famous for the 16th-century Villa d'Este and its park. Now a luxurious and extremely expensive hotel, the villa was inhabited from 1815 to 1817 by the forsaken and voluntarily exiled Caroline of Brunswick, Princess of Wales, whose retinue included the person and family of Bartolomeo Bergami, said to have been "her equerry, her chamberlain, her constant companion even at dinner" and honoured by her with a barony in Sicily, a knighthood in Malta and the Order of Saint Caroline, which was instituted for him.
(*See also Lake Como*)

CORTINA D'AMPEZZO
The undisputed queen of Italian wintersports resorts, a small and thoroughly Italian town spread widely across a busy junction of

valleys and surrounded by Dolomite peaks of celebrated beauty, notably the Sorapis to the south-east. Not much of Cortina pre-dates this century, and a noisy one-way system takes traffic on a circuit round the centre which consists of little more than a single long street of shops and hotels with an undistinguished 18th-century church in the middle. Despite this, Cortina is not an ugly place. There are attractive small hotels as well as the palaces in their parks on the edge of the resort, and cable-cars provide plenty of variety of panorama and long walks back to the resort.

Excursions from Cortina
☞ **Mountain tour**
Cortina is also a very good base for Dolomite motoring tours, and lies at one end of the so-called Great Dolomite Road (to Bolzano via Pordoi and Costalungo passes – *see Bolzano*). A more suitable round trip is the tour of the mighty **Sella Group** (Falzarego, Gardena, Sella and Pordoi passes), a circuit well known to skiers. Of the numerous lifts climbing from the roadside, the Pordoi cable-car and the Col Rodella and Sassolungo lifts from near the Sella pass are the most exciting. One of the most striking aspects of the tour of the Sella is the contrast between the styles of village in the different valleys: Cortina itself and the valleys to south and east of the mountain are Italian, those to the north and west Tyrolean.

The **Pordoi Pass** is the highest in the Dolomites (2,239m) and was the scene of bitter fighting in the First World War. There is a war memorial near the pass and a crater on the grimly-named Col di Sangue (Blutberg) where Italians, frustrated after a fruitless year of attacking the Austrian position, blasted it sky high with 5,000kg of explosive. From points along the road near the pass, as well as from the cable-car top station, there are splendid views of the Marmolada (3,344m), the highest Dolomite and the only one covered by a large area of glacier.
(*See also Misurina and Sella Pass*)

COURMAYEUR
A very busy old village and year-round resort in a beautiful situation beside the Dora Baltea at the foot of the massive wall of Mont Blanc, fortified with toothy, jagged peaks. Courmayeur is one of the most accessible and busiest of Italian ski resorts and an excellent summer base for excursions by car, on foot and by cable-car. It is the only true mountain resort in the main valley and the best place for exploring the whole region although, inevitably, noisy and touristy. Once quietly set at the head of the dead-end valley, Courmayeur has been transformed by the opening of the Mont Blanc road tunnel twenty years ago. The main road bypasses the old village, but only just, and along it have sprung up souvenir supermarkets, exchange offices and garages, as well as a large amount of new hotel building. Despite this, the tortuous heart of the old village is delightful with dark cobbled streets around the old church. The resort is surrounded by, and is beginning to merge with, a number of picturesque old hamlets, notably **Entrèves** and **Verrand**. There are

beautiful walks along the two quiet valleys at the foot of the Mont Blanc glaciers – Val Veny and Val Ferret – both of which form part of the famous walking tour of Mont Blanc.

☛ **Alpine Museum** Courmayeur has an illustrious tradition of mountaineering to rival that of Chamonix at the other end of the tunnel and the museum is full of fascinating tributes to the local heroes and mementoes of their world-wide mountaineering and exploratory exploits.

Excursions from Courmayeur

☞ **Mont Blanc massif**

The most spectacular cable-car ride in the Alps crosses the Mont Blanc massif from La Palud (3 ½km *north-west*) to the edge of Chamonix on the French side of the mountain via Punta Heilbronner (the frontier) and the Aiguille du Midi (3,795m). The excursion is expensive and rather than do the same journey twice you can catch a bus back through the tunnel. Even in warm summer weather, it is advisable to take extra clothes for the high altitude part of the trip. There are viewing terraces at both top stations on the Italian and French sides of the massif, and climbers use the lifts to start them off on more adventurous journeys. But for anyone not equipped for exploring glaciers there is no question of venturing beyond the lifts and lift stations. The 11 ½km road tunnel through the mountain was opened in 1965, nearly 180 years after the Genevois scientist Horace de Saussure sat on top of Mont Blanc and foresaw the event.

CRISSOLO

(*See Saluzzo*)

CÚNEO

A dull town at the foot of the southern Alps with a grid of streets around a wide and usually empty square. The choice of routes over to France includes the Col di Limone above the long-established mountain resort of **Limone Piemonte**, a picturesque old village which fills up at weekends. The road tunnel below the pass leads into a corner of France which remained part of Italy until its inhabitants voted to change nationality in 1947. The road follows the beautiful narrow Roya Valley past the suspended cliffside village of Saorge before crossing back into Italy near Ventimiglia.

DOMODÓSSOLA

Main town on the road up from Milan and Lake Maggiore to the Simplon (Sempione) pass and rail tunnel where cars can be put on the train. The main attraction is the old market square (instituted, according to a tablet, on 19th December 917 by king Berengar) surrounded by houses with arched porticos and loggias. A detour up the long Val Anzasca to Macugnaga (*see separate entry*) is recommended.

FÉNIS

(*See Valle d'Aosta*)

FELTRE

A sizeable town between Trento and Belluno with 16th-century gateways and many beautiful Renaissance houses in the upper town, mostly along the main street (**Via Mezzaterra**) and around the Piazza Maggiore. The collection of paintings in the museum (**Museo Civico**) includes works by Gentile Bellini, Cima di Conegliano and Morto di Feltre. Morto (nicknamed because of his pale complexion) was a local artist whose work is closely related to that of the mysterious Giorgione, said to have been Morto's rival in love. Morto's masterpiece is the fresco in the sacristy of the **Ognissanti** church (Borgo Ruga, east of the Porta Oria gateway).

Between Feltre and Bassano rises the tall, isolated **Monte Grappa** (1,775m), a battlefield in 1917/18 and now a war memorial with some 25,000 soldiers commemorated in the two cemeteries near the summit, which is accessible by car and commands a vast panorama.

GRAN PARADISO NATIONAL PARK

Of all the 4,000m peaks in the Alps, the Gran Paradiso is the only one entirely in Italy and is said to be the easiest to climb. The mountain stands at the heart of Italy's oldest National Park, once a royal hunting domain and now linking up with the Vanoise National Park across the French border. Pride of place in the park goes to the ibex which survived nowhere else in the Alps. During the Second World War numbers declined to a few hundred, but careful protection has subsequently allowed a recovery to several thousand and the ibex has been recently reintroduced from the Gran Paradiso to other areas of the Alps. Even here you need to be lucky or very patient to see the shy animal which spends most of its time well above the treeline. The ibex is very hardy and lives for up to 20 years but its frugal reproductive habits – about one offspring every two years – have made it very vulnerable to hunting. A much more reliable sight is that of furry marmots playing on the lower grassy slopes.

Flowers are at their best in early summer. There is a botanical garden at **Valnontey**, a few kilometres from the old mining village of **Cogne**, now the main resort on the Aosta side of the park and a good place for excursions on foot into the high mountains. For the ascent of the Gran Paradiso itself, the usual starting point is **Pont** at the head of the neighbouring Valsavarenche via the Rifugio Victor Emanuel II, which is used for ski touring in spring, as well as in summer for climbers. Some maps mark a road up from Pont over the Col de Nivolet to join up with the main valley on the southern side of the park where **Ceresole Reale** is the main resort. The northern half of this road does not exist but it is possible to drive up from Ceresole past a series of lakes to a high plateau at about 2,500m where there is a small café.

GRESSONEY
(*See Val de Lys*)

ISSOGNE
(*See Valle d'Aosta*)

IVREA

Gateway town on the Dora Baltea at the entrance to the Valle d'Aosta. Its riverside setting is a fine one and there are several small lakes to the north of town. A 14th-century castle and cathedral (which retains some part of its original 11th-century structure) make a handsome group at the centre of town. Ivrea's February carnival celebrations are famous, re-enacting the heroic deeds of a miller woman who avenged her honour by murdering a marquess of Monferrato, thereby freeing Ivrea from tyranny.

LAKE COMO (LÁRIO)

The deepest of the Italian Lakes and the one with the longest shoreline (over 100 miles). The three legs of the lake, which is shaped like an inverted Y, are known after the towns at their extremities: Como in the south-west, Lecco in the south-east, Cólico in the north. The lake is flanked by mountains all along its length and the landscape is more impressively rocky than the wooded slopes beside Lake Maggiore. The most beautiful part of the lake, and the most popular resort area, is the central section with **Bellagio** (*see separate entry*) supremely privileged in its situation. Frequent boats cross the lake (some of them taking cars) between Cadenabbia, Bellagio and Varenna, and there are services along the lake linking the resorts with the main towns. Quite apart from the pleasure of the ride, taking the boat from one side to the other saves a lot of driving. The road along the east bank is busy and often slow.

Apart from Bellagio the main resort is **Menaggio** (west bank). It has no great character, but its large and comfortable hotels are quietly set (by no means common along either bank of the lake) along the waterfront. There is plenty of scope for boat trips and long walks in the hills behind the resort.

Between the roadside resorts of Tremezzo and Cadenabbia is the 18th-century **Villa Carlotta**, with beautiful gardens (at their most spectacular in spring) and sculptures by Canova inside the house.

Lecco is a large and unprepossessing town at the point where the Adda flows out of the lake, beneath the steep, dolomitic Grigna massif, a popular climbing area. Lecco's greatest fame is as the setting for much of Alessandro Manzoni's famous novel *I Promessi Sposi*, one of the most important works of modern Italian literature. There is a small museum in the 18th-century Villa Manzoni where the author spent time in his youth.

The list of composers inspired by (or at least beside) Lake Como is a long one: Verdi (who composed *La Traviata* in a villa near Cadenabbia), Bellini, Rossini, Donizetti, Liszt. Winston Churchill claimed to have painted never so well as when staying beside the lake in late 1945. Apart from Manzoni and the Plinys (natives of Como) the main literary connection is with the English Romantics, notably Wordsworth and Shelley.
(*See also Bellagio and Como*).

Villa Carlotta, Lake Como

LAKE GARDA (BENACO)

The largest of the Italian lakes, shared by the regions of Trentino, Lombardy and Venezia, Garda presents a great variety of landscape: narrow, rocky and steeply enclosed in the north, broad and flat in the south, hilly and pleasantly fertile in the middle and known for its citrus and olive groves. The busiest resorts are at the two ends. **Riva**, in the north, is the main town on the lake and has developed a long, modern, anonymous resort sprawl along the eastern shore south of the old town centre. Riva is a lively place, full of young people and watersports enthusiasts. Because of its position it is the best base on the lake if you want to make daytrips into the Dolomites.

At the end of a long sandy isthmus dividing the two halves of the southern section of the lake, **Sirmione** lies only a few minutes from the main Milan-Venice motorway, very much on the beaten track of north Italian communications. Being a highly picturesque place it suffers from this, filling up with coachloads of people disgorged at its gateway for their statutory 20-minute walkabout beside Garda before moving on to gasp beneath Juliet's balcony in Verona. If you find wandering around the tourist shopping streets of Sirmione a claustrophobic experience it may be some consolation to observe the infinitely more cramped conditions tolerated by bloated fish in the moat of the 13th-century fortified town gateway (or Rocca) built by Sirmione's Veronese rulers (the Scaligers) in the 13th century. Sirmione has hot springs and has been a spa since Roman times. Beyond the town and thermal establishment the promontory comes to a hilly and much less crowded end, with gardens and olive groves and some ruins of the largest Roman villa in northern Italy, known as the Grottoes of Catullus. From the top of the hill there are wonderful views over the lake; at its foot on the eastern side is a small lido.

Apart from Riva and Sirmione the main resort area on the lake is between Salò and Gargnano on the western shore, known as the Riviera Bresciana which sums up its main role as weekend outlet for this nearby city. **Gardone** is the main centre on this section of the lake. Among beautiful gardens above the resort stands the **Vittoriale,** built for the poet Gabriele D'Annúnzio (d1938). The numerous buildings have been preserved as a museum and make an interesting period piece (*see also page 355*). Further north beneath steeper mountains **Limone Sul Garda**, named after its citrus groves, is one of the most attractive and quietest resorts on the lake, bypassed by the road (Gardesana) which cuts through one of the many tunnels along this stretch of shore.

LAKE ISEO (SEBINO)

The natural beauty of mountainous hills surrounding water surrounding a mountainous island can scarcely be dismissed as uninteresting, but apart from these natural advantages Iseo has little to be said for it. The best scenery and the least busy lakeside road is between Lóvere and **Riva di Solto**, a picturesque old village on the north-west side of the lake among vineyards and olives. There is also a cement factory and marble quarries which supplied the columns for St Mark's in Venice.

The island (**Monte Isola**) is the largest in the Italian lakes, 9km round and rising over a thousand feet from the waters to its summit. There is a small fishing village on the southern tip of the island opposite Sulzano. There are boats between Sulzano and the island (no cars allowed) and other ferry services between the main towns around the lake.

LAKE LUGANO (CERÉSIO)

A spindly, many-fingered lake deep in the mountains between Lakes Como and Maggiore. Just over a third of its 94 kilometres of shore belong to Italy, the rest to the Italian-speaking Swiss canton Ticino. Much of the lake is very steeply enclosed, notably the eastern part, well seen from the beautiful corniche road from Swiss Lugano to Menaggio on Lake Como. The main road north from Milan to the St Gotthard Pass crosses the Swiss part of the lake, most of which is barely wider than a broad river, near the little enclave of **Campione**, a tiny patch of Italy surrounded by Swiss land and water (Swiss francs prevail).

Lugano (just over the border in Switzerland) is the capital of the Canton Ticino and the only big town on the lake. Like many international lakes, Cerésio is a busy smuggling area and Lugano prospers greatly from the periodic flight of Italian capital. The Lugano banking community has seen more than its fair share of financial scandal as has the town's most famous resident, the super-rich baron Thyssen. The previous baron Thyssen accumulated one of the world's greatest private collections of (mostly Renaissance) paintings on display (on Fridays, Saturdays and Sundays) in the **Villa Favorita** overlooking the lake at **Castagnola**. If you're interested in art, this museum will be right at the top of the list of sightseeing priorities in the region.

LAKE MAGGIORE (VERBANO)

A long narrow lake, its west bank in Piedmont, the east in Lombardy and its northern tip and the resort of Locarno in Swiss territory. The main tourist area is the gulf half-way up the western side where Maggiore's main resort, **Stresa**, looks northwards to high mountain peaks over waters dotted with small islands. As on Lake Como, there are plenty of ferry services across and along the lake and to the islands. The main car ferry service links Laveno on the east bank with Intra, part of the conglomeration of Verbania. There are huge old-fashioned hotels all along Stresa's wide promenade, a busy terminal for boat trips to the islands and round the lake and a long funicular up to the Mottarone – a splendid viewpoint high above the lake.

Except in the north, Lake Maggiore is less steeply enclosed than Como and the scenery of its southern part, especially on the east side, is not particularly interesting. The main road runs along the more beautiful western shore. Apart from Stresa, the main resorts are nearby **Baveno**, **Cannobio** on the road north towards Locarno, and **Pallanza** which faces Stresa across the gulf and merges with Intra. Here it's well worth visiting the beautiful gardens of the Villa Táranto. The tiny **Borromean islands** are accessible from Stresa, Baveno and Verbania. **Isola Bella** is occupied by the sumptuously decorated 17th-century Palazzo Borromeo and its beautiful terraced gardens, complete with urns and peacocks (open from March to October, guided tours available). **Isola Madre** has a botanical garden, also open from mid-March to October. Unlike the others, the **Isola dei Pescatori** is not owned by the Borromeo family and lives up to its name, with a single very picturesque fishing village.

LAKE ORTA
(*See Orta San Giulio*)

LA THUILE
(*See Little St Bernard Pass*)

LECCO
(*See Lake Como*)

LIMONE PIEMONTE
(*See Cúneo*)

LIVIGNO

One of the more remote corners of the Alps, a high lost valley, often referred to locally as "Piccolo Tibet", between Bormio and Switzerland and on the northern side of the Alpine watershed (the waters of the Spöl flow into the Inn). The people of Livigno fiercely defended their independence down the centuries and joined Italy only in 1911. To save anyone the trouble of having to visit Livigno in a probably fruitless attempt to collect taxes, the valley was granted duty-free status, which has fuelled its recent growth as a popular wintersports area. The après-ski is notoriously liquid, and the single road is lined with supermarkets, garages (petrol is half the normal Italian price) and new hotels. This has done much to spoil the beauty of the community with its old chalets made of tree-trunks split down the middle, although many of these survive. The village is so remote that defence was clearly never a priority; the locals spread themselves along the valley to reduce the risk of fire, and the village stretches for several miles without any real focus.

Easiest access is from Switzerland via a toll road tunnel (closed at night) and from Bormio over the Foscagno pass. On this road, the small village of **Trepalle** is the highest in Italy to be inhabited all the year round. There is a summer road over the head of the valley to St Moritz via the Bernina pass and Pontresina.

MADONNA DI CAMPIGLIO

One of Italy's smartest winter sports resorts, whose great attraction to summer visitors is the isolated beauty of the Brenta massif, the only part of the Dolomites on the western side of the main Adige/Isarco valley. Its cliffs and pinnacles are much favoured by climbers and there are also vertiginous ledge walks with iron staircases on the rock and a vast network of paths in the thick pinewoods around Madonna and on the open slopes above, where there are lifts and welcoming mountain restaurants. At the pass above Madonna (Campo Carlo Magno) is a golf course. Madonna itself has grown up this century, but it has done so in an unusually harmonious style with wood more in evidence than concrete in the building style.

Excursion from Madonna

☞ **Pinzolo** (*16km south*)

The larger and quieter resort of Pinzolo has two churches with beautiful frescoes of the Dance of Death, by the same early 16th-century artist. San Vigilio on the edge of the village has the finer of the paintings. Santo Stefano is a short distance up the narrow and very beautiful wooded **Val di Génova** which divides two of the highest local mountain massifs, the Adamello (3,554m) and Presanella (3,556m). The valley is now a conservation area and is popular with both walkers and climbers setting out for the high peaks.

MACUGNAGA

A popular summer and winter resort made up of two neighbouring beautiful old hamlets (Staffa and Pecetto) in a magnificent setting beneath the towering east wall of the Monte Rosa which climbs over 3,000m above the village. The tallest rock face in the Alps is a notorious place for avalanches and ice falls and an almost constant background noise of the roar and clatter of snow and stones makes a rather sinister contrast with the usual Alpine muzak of cowbells. A cable-car will take you to the Passo del Monte Moro (2,868m), the old route over to the Swiss valley of Saas. There are splendid views, as there are from the chair-lift to the foot of the Monte Rosa glaciers, a better starting point for walks.

The Italian side of the majestic chain of peaks from Monte Rosa to the Matterhorn is ideal hiking territory with paths of varying arduousness crossing high passes linking the heads of the five main valleys from Macugnaga to Valtournenche (via Valsesia, Val de Lys and Val d'Ayas), each valley crossing making a full day's walking of at least four hours.

MALLES VENOSTA (MALS)
(See Val Venosta)

MEL
(See Belluno)

MENAGGIO
(See Lake Como)

MERANO

An old south Tyrolean town on the banks of the Passirio near its confluence with the Adige, one of the largest and most famous of Italian Alpine resorts, known for its mild climate, its beautiful open but sheltered setting and its spa waters. Merano now spreads for a long way round the fruitful slopes of the valley and forms a large garden suburb area with scores of large, comfortable and peaceful hotels. There are good bus services and plenty of mountain transport from the edge and outskirts of the town to sunny pastures and winter ski fields with beautiful walks down from them through the vineyards and orchards around the town. The most popular walks of all are on the banks of the river, the sunny and shady *passeggiate d'Inverno* and *d'Estate* (winter and summer promenades).

There is plenty to do in Merano apart from walk: concerts, organised excursions throughout north-eastern Italy and a racecourse. The old centre of town is full of charm and bustle for a long summer season which peaks in spring and late summer. There are leafy squares with fruit stalls and *wurst* sellers, old bookshops, cafés with beer gardens, and *weinstuben* down tiny alleys. The most picturesque street is the long arcaded **Via dei Portici**. At the end of it stands the 15th-century cathedral, its campanile spanning a street. The 15th-century **castle** and local **art museum**, both in the centre of town, are also open to visitors.

Excursions from Merano
☞ **Dorf Tyrol** (*5km north*)

An almost prohibitively popular excursion in the immediate
neighbourhood is the tourist village of Dorf Tirol, about an hour's
walk or a short drive from Merano at the foot of the 12th-century
Castel Tirolo (Schloss Tirol), home of the rulers of the Val Venosta
who adopted the name of the castle for their whole region. In the
late 14th century the Tyrol came under Hapsburg control and
Innsbruck came to be preferred as the regional capital. The main
attraction of the castle is its splendid setting and the beautiful views
over the Adige and Venosta valleys, but there is good Romanesque
carving around the doorways in the hall and chapel.

☞ **Passirio Valley**

From Merano it is a very pretty drive up the Passirio Valley to the
little resort of **San Leonardo** (*20km north*), very German and full of
walkers, and from there over the high Passo Monte Giovo
(Jaufenpass; 2,099m) to Vipiteno (*58km north-east, see separate entry*).

MISURINA

A small resort beside a picturesque round lake surrounded by
woods and beautiful Dolomite scenery near Cortina d'Ampezzo.
The most spectacular local peaks are the Sorapis (to the south of the
lake) and the famous **Tre Cime di Lavaredo** (to the north), equally
popular with mountaineers, sightseers and postcard sellers all over
the region. You have to pay a sizeable toll for the last few steep miles
of the road up to the base of the pillars of rock, where there is a
clapped-out refuge building and café. There is a path round the base
of the peaks.

MONDOVI

Market town east of Cúneo, in two parts – Mondovi Breo is the
modern town by the river, Mondovi Piazza the mostly Baroque old
town climbing steeply to the east. There are fine views from the
gardens behind the Baroque cathedral and an imposing *trompe l'oeil*
painted architecture in the church of La Missione. The vast nearby
pilgrimage church of Vicoforte boasts the fifth largest dome in Italy.

MONTE GRAPPA
(*See Feltre*)

ORTA SAN GIULIO

Very picturesque old village on a small promontory just off the main
road which runs along the eastern bank of Lake Orta, and the main
resort on what is the only one of the famous Italian pre-Alpine lakes
in Piedmont territory. The lake is small and surrounded by pretty
although unspectacular hill country. The village itself is full of
charm, especially the central square with its 16th-century town hall
on one side and the other open to the lake, with views from
vine-covered café terraces out to the tiny island of San Giulio, less
than half a mile in circumference. There are boats for hire and

regular ferry trips round the lake and to the island, which has an
elegant waterside with villas and boathouses, and a basilica said to
have been founded after the island was cleared of snakes in the 4th
century. It was much reworked and impressively redecorated in the
17th and 18th centuries but has kept its richly carved, black marble
11th-century altar. On a hill outside Orta St Giulio is a Sacro Monte
similar to the one in Varallo, although less impressive in scale (there
are some 20 chapels with 17th- and 18th-century frescoes and
painted groups of terracotta statuary) and quality.

ORTISEI
(See Val Gardena)

PIEVE DI CADORE
Main town of the Cadore region of the Dolomites, known mainly as
the home town of Titian (Tiziano Vecellio), greatest of all Venetian
painters. Of all the "Titians" in the otherwise uninteresting main
church (Parrocchiale), the one most widely accepted as autograph is
the Madonna and Saints in the third chapel on the left. There is a
bronze statue of the artist on the square and a small museum of
memorabilia (but not paintings by the master) nearby.

PONT-ST-MARTIN
(See Val de Lys)

PORDOI PASS
(See Cortina d'Ampezzo)

PUSTERIA (PUSTERTAL)
To the north of the finest area of Dolomite mountain scenery is this
wide east-west valley of the Rienza, a busy through route to and
from Eastern Austria. It is a clean and tidy, colourful rural landscape
with onion-domed churches and pretty, very Austrian looking
villages. **Brunico** (Bruneck) is the main town, pleasant without being
particularly interesting. The high open slopes about it (Riscone) are
popular walking territory with clean new hotels and small ski areas.
The main points of interest in the valley are the beautiful collegiate
church at **San Cándido** (Innichen) with a fresco by the famous local
artist Michael Pacher (late 15th century) over the south doorway;
and the little **Lago di Braies** (Prags), a popular beauty spot among
the woods beneath the tall cliffs of the Croda del Becco (2,810m).
There are cafés and boating.

RIVA
(See Lake Garda)

SACRA DI SAN MICHELE
(See Avigliana)

GREAT ST BERNARD PASS
This 2,472m pass links Aosta and Martigny in the Swiss Valais. The

road closes with the first snowfall, but a road toll tunnel is open all the year round. The drive up from Aosta climbs steeply through woods to a peaceful rural Alpine landscape with old rough grey villages (**Étroubles** and **St-Oyen**) and cow fields. There is some accommodation, mainly in Étroubles where Napoleon spent the night on 20th May 1800. **St-Rhémy**, above the division of the pass and tunnel roads, is now a village in decline. In the past its inhabitants and those of Étroubles shared the monopoly of transporting goods over the St Bernard, a right granted them in the 13th century. These *marroniers*, as they were inexplicably known, gained exemption from military service in the 17th century and assumed the grand title of Soldats de la Neige.

The pass itself divides the massifs of Grand Combin and Mont Blanc, and stands above a small lake. It is known to have been used in the Bronze Age and was called by the Romans Mons Jovis or Poenine after a temple which stood at the pass. Saint Bernard of Menthon may have built the first medieval hospice at the pass in the 11th century, but the present building dates from the 19th century. For the last 300 years at least, the hospice's Augustinian monks have been assisted by the famous breed of rescue dogs, which are credited with saving 2,500 lives.

LITTLE ST BERNARD PASS

This lower (2,188m) pass, one of the many claimed to have been used by Hannibal, links Pré-St-Didier with Bourg-St-Maurice (France) and is closed in winter. The drive up through woods from Pré-St-Didier gives some splendid glimpses of the Mont Blanc massif. For the classic view of its Italian side a path climbs to the Tête de Crammont (2,737m), several hours' walk from the St Bernard road starting from near the first tunnel entrance.

La Thuile is a large and long-established winter and summer resort in a wide, rather severe bowl of mountains. There is some modern ski-related development but the old centre of the resort by the river is run down and has no great charm. The pass itself is a long high marshy plateau, the watershed between the Isère and Dora Baltea. It was the main road from Rome to Lyon and beside the pass itself are the remains of a small Roman temple and a prehistoric burial circle. The old hospice building, now inside French territory, was heavily shelled in 1940 and 1944 and stands today, desolate and derelict, a melancholy monument to the war. A 19th-century rector of the hospice created a botanical garden for high-altitude flora which is being reconstituted.

Not far below the plateau on the west-facing French side is the small ski resort of **La Rosière** where a small troop of St Bernards is on display in roadside kennels. They are brought out for exercise twice a day and dog owners are advised to lock up their pets at these times.

ST-VINCENT

A comfortable spa with mineral-rich spring water (the *fons salutis*), a large casino and conference centre in the main Dora Baltea valley

below Aosta near the bottom of the **Valtournenche**, the long valley most famous for the Matterhorn.
(*See Cervinia*).

SALUZZO

One of the few towns worth visiting at the foot of the Alps between Turin and the Mediterranean. Saluzzo flourished as the brilliant capital of an independent ruling family of marquesses from the 12th to the mid-16th century, before coming under French and then Savoyard control. The old part of town, with its narrow cobbled streets and warm brick buildings, is very unspoilt and delightful to explore. The most notable individual buildings are the Casa Cavassa (a Renaissance town house with a small museum) and the church of San Giovanni (13th- to 15th-century), both near the castle. San Giovanni has some interesting tombs including that of Ludovico II (d1505), the most famous of the marquesses of Saluzzo.

Excursions from Saluzzo

☞ **Staffardia** (*10km north*)
A Cistercian monastery founded in the 12th century, much damaged in 1690 during the course of the battle between French and Austro-Piedmontese forces, but well restored.

☞ **Crissolo** (*33km west*)
The long valleys into the high mountains on the French border include the upper valley of the Po, where the main resort is Crissolo at the foot of the isolated pyramid of the Monte Viso (or Monviso), one of the most famous peaks of the southern Alps and at 3,814m one of the highest. Crissolo lies a short steep drive below the source of the Po at Piano del Re (2,020m). High above Piano del Re, about 100m below the Col de la Traversette (2,950m), is a tunnel dug by Ludovico II in the late 15th century to make it easier to cross over into the Guil Valley on the French side of the mountain. The tunnel has been opened and shut several times in its history but is currently impassable. The Col de la Traversette is another of the many passes claimed to have been used by Hannibal.

SAN MARTINO DI CASTROZZA

A large and comfortable climbing and skiing resort in a beautiful south-facing position among thick woods at the foot of Passo di Rolle, and overlooked by the magnificent jagged peaks of the Pale di San Martino. Most of the peaks are very serious mountaineering propositions but you can take a spectacular cable-car ride to a station just below the peak of the Rosetta, high up among them and on the edge of a remarkable rocky wasteland plateau, the Alti Piano delle Palle. The paths down from here to San Martino are said to be easily manageable. The gentler mountains on the other side of the valley are more suitable for walking and skiing and give fine views of the Pale.

SAPPADA

A quiet and very spread-out mountain resort near the Austrian
border in a German-speaking corner of the mountains on the
western side of the pass separating the regions of Cadore and
Carnia. There are some attractive simple hotels and chair-lift rides
on the slopes of Sappada's modest skiing area.

SAUZE D'OULX

(See Upper Susa Valley)

SELLA PASS

Just above Selva (see Val Gardena) the roads up to the Gardena and
Sella passes divide. Of these two, the Sella (2,213m) gives the more
spectacular view, over the green flanks of the Val di Fassa to the
brilliant white Marmolada. The drive between the Sella and Pordoi
passes is perhaps the most beautiful section of all the Dolomite
roads, with all the scenic ingredients for which the region is famous:
dark green pinewoods, massive cliff faces of orangey grey, open
pastures, long views and jagged rocky peaks.
(See also Cortina)

Refuge in the Dolomites

SESTRIERE
(See Upper Susa Valley)

SIRMIONE
(See Lake Garda)

SOLDA (SULDEN)
A very high resort spread round an open grassy bowl at the foot of the Ortler and Cevedale, a popular place for climbers and walkers in summer and skiers in winter. There are several typically Tyrolean, new, comfortable chalet-style hotels.
(See also Bormio for description of the Stelvio Pass)

SONDRIO
Main town in the important wine-growing Valtellina, as the long west-flowing upper valley of the Adda, one of the largest Italian Alpine valleys, is known. Sondrio has a small regional museum but is otherwise uninteresting.

In 1512 the region and the area around Chiavenna came under the control of the Swiss Grisons, but the Valtellinese rose up in bloody revolt in 1620 against the Swiss reformers. Seven hundred Protestants were killed in what is known as the Holy Massacre of the Valtellina. After 20 years of war between the major continental powers (Spain, France, Switzerland and Germany) the area reverted to Swiss control until 1797. Unlike many Italian Alpine valleys, the Valtellina is not a dead end – several passes lead over to eastern Italy as well as into Switzerland and the route is a useful tourist one. Unfortunately it is not strikingly beautiful by Alpine standards. There are several narrow tributary valleys running down to the Adda from the north with climbing base villages at their heads, notably the Val Masino. The main local peak is the jagged Monte Disgrazia (3,678m).

STELVIO
(See Bormio)

STRESA
(See Lake Maggiore)

SUSA
An interesting and lively old town at the foot of the Mont Cenis and Montgenèvre pass roads, historically two of the most important routes into Italy, now supplemented by the Frejus rail and, since 1980, road tunnels. In its setting, history and sightseeing interest Susa is similar to Aosta, but is in all respects more ordinary. The sights to see are all on the western side of town, near the Piazza Savoia. The **cathedral** is a splendid 11th-century building, with 13th-century choir stalls. **Roman remains** include some towers and a gateway of the town walls and an arch raised in 8BC for Augustus by the local Celtic ruler Cottius, whom Augustus had made prefect.

This part of the French and Italian Alps is known as the Cottian Alps.
(*See also Upper Susa Valley*)

TARVISIO

A small border town and year-round resort on a junction of important transalpine routes in the extreme north-eastern corner of the country. Main roads to Austria (Villach) and Yugoslavia are low and open all year. Beauty spots on the Italian side of the frontiers include several very picturesque mountain lakes, notably the **Laghi di Fusine** near the road to Yugoslavia, beneath the towering walls of Monte Mangant (2,678m).

The main Tarvisio to Udine road, much of it now relieved by a motorway, runs through the heart of the area devastated by earthquake in summer 1976. **Venzone** and **Gemona** are two formerly beautiful old towns that still show all too clearly the extent of the damage, which claimed hundreds of lives.

LA THUILE

(*See Little St Bernard Pass*)

TIRANO

A small town at the foot of the Bernina Pass road and railway over to St Moritz and the Swiss Engadin. Here, as at Chiavenna, the border is a long way (over 20 miles) on the Italian side of the watershed and language frontier at the pass. Just outside Tirano, at the main road junction, is the graceful **Madonna di Tirano** basilica built in 1505 after the appearance of the Virgin to a local man. Rich stucco work decorates the interior.

TORRE PÉLLICE

A small town near Pinerolo and the main community of the Waldensian church which survives in this valley and its northern neighbour, the Val Germanasca. There is a small museum devoted to the church and its history (it descends from a medieval heretical sect once widely spread throughout Europe) of persecution and stubborn local resistance. The annual ruling council of the church convenes at Torre Péllice.

TRENTO

Capital of the semi-autonomous Trentino-Alto Adige region in the main valley north of Lake Garda. Trento lacks the colourful charm of the Tyrolean towns to its north and is now Italian-speaking, although the 16th-century traveller Thomas Whythorne described how "the langwages indifferent are to all, both alman and Italien, eevn az on toong doth fall". The prince bishops of Trento were powerful and independent actors in the turbulent history of north-east Italy from the 11th to the 19th centuries and their city on the Italian borders of the Empire was the chosen site for the Council of Trent, convened to reform the Catholic church, unify and bolster it against the rising tide of Protestant reform. The council lasted in three sessions from 1545-63 and was of enormous importance for the development of the Catholic church both in settling important doctrinal issues and in reinforcing papal authority; less was done about reform of abuse. The greatest of the prince bishops was the early 16th-century humanist Bernardo Cles who commissioned the splendid and beautifully decorated Castel del Buon Consiglio and modernised the face of the city, enlarging and straightening streets, classicising palaces, painting the outsides of houses with fresco and replacing wood with stone.

☛ **Castel del Buon Consiglio** A fortified bishops' palace built in several stages from the 13th to the 16th centuries. The fortifications are medieval, but the palace is the great legacy of Bernardo Cles who in the early 1530s invited the two Dossi brothers and Romanino to decorate the interior, which has recently been restored to brilliant effect. Romanino's magnificent frescoes include a portrait of his patron in one of the rooms on the ground floor. As well as Renaissance decoration, there is a very interesting series of 15th-century frescoes in the Torre dell' Aquila illustrating the different tasks of the months of the year. The castle also houses a museum devoted to the Risorgimento and the Liberation of the Trentino, where Austrian control from 1813 to 1918 was much resented.

☛ **Cathedral** (San Vigilio) An impressively beautiful 12th- to 16th-century church with bishops' tombs and some remains of 13th- and 15th-century frescoes in the transept. It is well worth walking round the south side of the building to admire the east end, joined to the fortified 12th-century Palazzo Pretorio. The north flank of the cathedral forms one side of the picturesque Piazza Duomo, with an 18th-century Neptune fountain. The **Via Belenzani** runs north from the square through the most beautiful part of the old town and is lined with many painted Renaissance façades.

UPPER SUSA VALLEY

Since the opening of the Frejus road tunnel the slow road between Susa and Bardonecchia has been massively overburdened with heavy lorries. The snail's pace, the state of the road and the work in progress on improvements to it combine to make about 15 miles of this road extremely tiresome. The long narrow valley between Susa and Oulx was a strategic one and above Chiomonte belonged to the French Dauphiné until the treaty of Utrecht in 1713. A massive frontier fortress and prison plugs the valley at **Exilles**; the mysterious Man of the Iron Mask was an inmate.

The upper valleys which converge at Oulx have been popular skiing grounds for the Torinese since the beginning of the century, and now make up one of Italy's most developed skiing areas. **Sauze d'Oulx**, on a sunny ledge above the shabby old town of Oulx, is now the main British haunt. Most of the old village's charm has been sacrificed and this is scarcely a place for a summer holiday, but there are several peaceful simple hotels in the woods above the resort which are open in summer as well as winter. There is an old centre to the village and the small hamlet of **Jouvenceaux**, just below Sauze d'Oulx, has also kept some of its old tumbledown charm despite the development of the skiing. From Sauze d'Oulx it is a long but not difficult walk or a short bumpy drive over the Col Basset to

Sestriere, a desolate ski resort at a high pass (2,000m), built from almost nothing in the 1930s on the initiative of the Agnelli family and once the high spot, as it were, of winter sporting fashion.

Bardonecchia is a large and characterless resort town at the end of the first trans-Alpine rail tunnel, opened in 1871. There are ski slopes on several sides and plenty of mountains to climb for summer visitors, of whom there are many. A beautiful excursion for motorists is the narrow road over the **Col della Scala** (Col de l'Échelle) – another of the many Alpine passes said to have been the one used by Hannibal – to Névache near Briançon (France). The main road over to Briançon is the wide **Montgenèvre**, the lowest and easiest pass in the western Alps and open all the year round. The pass itself is in France and the village beside it is a ski resort.

In July 1747 the local mountains provided the setting for one of the decisive battles in the war of Austrian Succession when French troops, under the glory-seeking Chevalier de Belle-Isle, invaded Italy and attacked impregnable Piedmontese defences around the Col dell' Assietta above Exilles. In the course of the encounter, the French distinguished themselves more by their courage than common-sense and lost over 5,000 men to 200 Piedmontese. One of the victims was Belle-Isle himself, who is said to have received the fatal wound while attempting to dismantle the palisades with his teeth, both arms having been incapacitated by previous wounds. The leaderless French withdrew over the Montgenèvre whence they had come and buried many of their dead, including Belle-Isle, at Sauze d'Oulx.

VALLE D'AOSTA

This valley is famous for its fortresses, most of them built by the Challant family, the most powerful in the region for many centuries. The most impressive of these fortresses, especially when lit up at night, is **Fénis**, between St-Vincent and Aosta. At **Verrés** the valley is controlled by a massive square castle on a spur above the river. The nearby late 15th-century castle of **Issogne** is a gracious Renaissance dwelling, beautifully restored and refurnished in the original style: this is the most interesting of the castles to tour. There are colourful fresco scenes of everyday life and heraldic paintings around the courtyard. The Challant's home territory was the long **Val d'Ayas** (*see next entry*), which runs down from the Monte Rosa to Verres.

(*See also Aosta*)

VAL D'AYAS

A beautiful open valley with quiet village resorts and a tradition of making wooden clogs. **Champoluc** is the main resort in a fine setting beneath the glaciers of Monte Rosa and has some skiing facilities. **St-Jacques**, at the head of the valley, is a base for climbers. **Antagnod** is one of the most picturesque of the many attractive hamlets along the sides of the valley, which as a whole is noted for its splendid stone and wood chalets.

VAL DE LYS

The Val de Lys is long and beautiful and its main community,
Gressoney, is much used by climbers aiming for the numerous
peaks that together make up Monte Rosa, named not after its colour
but from the local word for glacier. Of the two Gressoneys at the
head of the valley, St-Jean is much the more attractive as a village.
Beyond Gressoney-La-Trinité there are lifts up to the high pass, the
hiking trail east to Alagna. At the bottom of the Val de Lys,
Pont-St-Martin is a small town with a well preserved single-arched
Roman bridge over the rocky torrent.

Local dialect is of more than passing interest around here, for
there survive in the Val de Lys colonies of early medieval settlers
from the Swiss Valais whose German (or Walser) dialects differ from
village to village which, confusingly, have French names. **Issime**,
the lowest of these colonies, has a very colourful fresco of the Last
Judgement on the church façade.

VAL GARDENA (GRÖDEN)

One of the busiest and most interesting of the Dolomite valleys
where the original Ladin dialect has survived what the Italians
describe as invasions of barbarians from the north. This adds a third
element of confusion to the two official languages and place names
in the south Tyrol. The locals are very proud of their cultural identity
and traditional crafts. The most important of these is woodcarving
(mainly of devotional objects and church furniture) which still
employs some 3,000 people in the valley. A number of craftsmen
have shops with displays of their work and there is a gallery of the
local talent in the tourist office at **Ortisei** (Sankt Ulrich in German,
Urtiji in Ladin), a small and lively town at the entrance to the high
part of the valley. Ortisei's other great pride is what is claimed to be
the largest alp (in the sense of high pasture) in the Alps: the Alpe di
Siusi (Seiseralm), a vast grassy plateau high above the valley
reached by cable-car from the village or by road from Castelrotto
(Castelruth). This broad plateau, impressively overlooked by the
three towers of the Sassolungo (3,181m), is a celebrated beauty spot
and now a nature reserve banned to traffic. Throughout the summer
you are likely to have to queue for space in the car park and shuffle
along the walking paths with crowds of others. There are more
peaceful places to walk elsewhere in the valley and no shortage of
lifts to take you quickly up to the higher slopes.

At the head of the valley, **Selva** (Wolkenstein) is the main skiing
resort and has recently grown into a straggling modern place along
the road at the foot of the cliffs of the Sella group, which catch fire in
the evening light. The **Vallunga** is a beautiful and secluded side
valley near Selva.

(*See also Sella Pass*)

VALTELLINA

(*See Sondrio*)

VAL VENOSTA (VINSCHGAU)

The main community in this wide open and fruitful valley is **Malles Venosta** (Mals), one of the most attractive corners of the Italian Alps at the head of the Adige valley between Merano and the Austrian border at Passo Resia (Reschen Pass). Malles has kept five medieval towers including a 12th-century one from the old castle and a Romanesque campanile of a destroyed church. There are 9th-century frescoes inside the church of San Benedetto on the northern edge of town (ask around for a key).

Glorenza (Glurns), a tiny town enclosed by 16th-century walls and gateways at the foot of the Ofenpass road into Switzerland, is the most picturesque of a number of unspoilt old villages nearby. Other sights include the abbey of **Monte Maria** which looks down on the valley from a wooded hillside above Burgusio. Most of the abbey dates from the 18th century but there are 12th-century frescoes in the crypt. In the Middle Ages the Val Venosta belonged to the bishops of Chur who built themselves a castle (**Castel Coira** or Churburg), a splendid medieval and Renaissance building originally constructed in the 13th century. Guided tours include an interesting collection of armoury.

If staying in the Val Venosta, it is well worth making the round trip to the **Stelvio Pass** (*see Bormio*) via the Swiss Munstertal, over the **Umbrail Pass** (2,502m) and back down via the very pretty resort village of **Trafoi** at the foot of the Stelvio road.

VARALLO

A small town and capital of the Upper Valsesia and a good place to admire the work of Gaudenzio Ferrari (1480-1546), born locally and one of the leading north Italian artists of the early 16th century. There is a fine altarpiece in the church of **San Gaudenzio** which stands on a rock above the main square, and frescoes in the church of **Santa Maria della Grazie**, but Gaudenzio's most remarkable work and Varallo's great distinction is the **Sacro Monte**, a collection of some 45 chapels with 900 statues and over 4,000 fresco figures on a hill above the town, reached on foot, by funicular or by road. The Sacro Monte was the idea of a Friar Minor who returned from Jerusalem in 1488 with a desire to rebuild the holy places of Jerusalem, decorating the chapels with scenes of the Life of Christ and the Passion as a way to reinforce the orthodox faith of the local people, in a region notoriously plagued by heresy. In the interests of maximum realistic effect, Gaudenzio and the other artists combined fresco painting with coloured terracotta statues to create entire theatrical scenes; work went on well into the 17th century and the style varies from chapel to chapel. Gaudenzio's most striking work is the one devoted to the Crucifixion.

VARESE

A large and prosperous modern town, near but not beside the eponymous lake. There isn't much to see in town except for the 18th-century **Palazzo Estense** and its park, now public gardens. A few miles to the north is the Sacro Monte, a pilgrimage hill with fourteen 17th-century chapels along the road up to the summit, each one decorated with frescoes and groups of terracotta statues illustrating the mysteries of the Rosary.

Excursions from Varese
☞ **Towns between Varese and Milan**
Several otherwise unappealing towns beside the road from Milan to Varese are well worth visiting for their individual works of art. **Castiglione Olona** (*10km south-east*) is a small town beautified in the early 15th century by a cardinal who had spent time in Florence and returned, bringing with him Masolino, master of Masaccio. The frescoes in the Collegiata and nearby baptistery are among Masolino's greatest works. The exquisite Brunelleschian Chiesa di Villa on the main square dates from the same period, also commissioned by the cardinal. In **Castel Seprio** (*14km south-east*), the early 8th-century chapel of Santa Maria Foris Portas is shoddily built but decorated with a remarkable and equally ancient series of frescoes, the work of a Byzantine artist. **Saronno** (*27km south-east*) is best known for its treacly almond-flavoured liqueur or Amaretto; the sanctuary of the Madonna dei Miracoli has frescoes by Gaudenzio Ferrari in the dome, and Luini in the Madonna's chapel. The domed 16th-century church of Santa Maria di Piazza at **Busto Arsizio** (*25km south, and west of the direct Varese to Milan road*) also has frescoes by Gaudenzio Ferrari and Luini.

VERCELLI

A large town on the Sesia in the Piedmontese plains, at the centre of a vast area of rice-growing. The most interesting buildings are the 13th-century basilica of **Sant' Andrea** (near the station) and the church of **San Cristoforo**, with frescoes and an altarpiece by the local master, Gaudenzio Ferrari (16th-century). The **Museo Borgogna** (open Sunday mornings and Tuesday and Thursday afternoons) has a fine collection of Piedmontese paintings.

VERRÉS

(*See Valle d'Aosta*)

VIPITENO (STERZING)

A picturesque and thoroughly Tyrolean old town beside the river Isarco at the foot of the Brenner pass, a position which makes it a prime target for day-trips organised for tourists based in and around Innsbruck. The most powerful attraction is neither the delightful and colourful main street with its old shop signs and a handsome 15th-century **gateway** at the end of it, nor the famous altarpiece by Hans Multscher of Ulm (1458), most of which is in the **museum** on the main square, but the Italian shopping facilities. There is uphill transport on the nearby Monte Cavallo (Rosskopf).

VITTORIO VÉNETO

The area between two old towns (Céneda and Serravalle) is now built-up and the whole forms Vittorio Véneto, site of the decisive battle (October-November 1918) on the Italian front. Apart from the interesting war museum on the main square in Céneda, **Serravalle** is the more appealing of the two old communities, well-preserved with many medieval and Renaissance houses along the via Martiri della Libertá and on Piazza Flaminio. The painting over the high altar in the 18th-century **cathedral** is by Titian. Several other interesting churches include **Santa Giustina** (Via Marconi outside the centre) with the beautiful carved tomb of one Riccardo da Camino.

Hotels

Alpe di Siusi (Seiseralm) ££
FLORALPINA *Closed Easter to May, Oct to Christmas*
39040 Bolzano *Tel: (0471) 72907*

The most secluded and comfortable of the hotels dotted around this vast high plateau, the biggest alp in the Alps and a paradise for walking, riding and sitting in deck chairs soaking up the sunshine and spectacular Dolomite scenery. The hotel is a big, fairly modern chalet-style building in standard bright and wholesome Tyrolean mountain style–duvets, balconies, lots of wood and pot plants–and has a pool, tennis court, sauna and a ski-lift nearby. You will be humming "doe–a deer" before you can say Julie Andrews and if you wander out by moonlight you may well see one. Approach from Santa Cristina in the Val Gardena (private road).

Facilities: *48 bedrooms; restaurant; lift; swimming pool; tennis court; garage*
Credit/charge cards accepted: *none*

Avigliana £
CHALET DEL LAGO *Open all year*
Via Monginevro 26, 10051 Torino *Tel: (011) 938691*

Avigliana is a handsome old town between Susa and Turin, one of the beaten tracks into Italy, and its small lakes are a popular weekend bolt-hole for city dwellers. At other times they are very quiet and this is a very basic but adequate, cheap and peaceful lakeside stopover close to Sacra San Michele. Bedrooms, in a separate building from the restaurant/discothèque, are reasonably spacious and have balconies looking out over the water. If tempted you can swim and feed the ducks. You are not expected to eat in, and we didn't.

Facilities: *16 bedrooms; restaurant; disco; swimming pool; garage* **Credit/charge cards accepted:** *none*

Bellagio   ££
DU LAC   *Closed-mid Oct to Easter*
22021 Como   *Tel: (031) 950320*

One of the three hotels sharing the privileged situation of Bellagio's small arcaded prom, where ferries moor. The Du Lac is run by an Italo-British couple and offers a happy marriage of qualities: good Italian food (especially the ices) in the cramped but panoramic dining room and outdoor terrace, and many touches elsewhere betraying the foreign influence: real towels and soap in the bathrooms, and breakfast with genuine orange juice, croissants and Frank Cooper's. The views and boat-spotting are even better from the 5th-floor roof terrace. Bedrooms are mostly simple and there is no real sitting room apart from the café at ground level. British visitors are numerous, and the atmosphere is quietly friendly.

Facilities: *48 bedrooms; restaurant; lift; parking*   **Credit/charge cards accepted:**
Amex, Diners, Eurocard, Visa

Bellagio   ££
FLORENCE   *Closed mid-Oct to mid-Apr*
22021 Como   *Tel: (031) 950342*

An attractive hotel in Como's loveliest resort, the Florence is an 18th-century villa (with a later extension) but has none of the dreary faded grandeur of so many lakes hotels, although it has been a hotel for 150 years. The decoration and furnishing of most rooms is appealing: whitewashed walls, beams and traditional dark wood rustic furniture, enlivened with bright upholstery. The back bedrooms (about 40%) are old fashioned and simply furnished although not without charm; and all are due for gradual renovation. There's no garden but an attractive lakeside terrace for drinks and summer dining opposite the hotel. Food is adequate rather than inspired.

Facilities: *75 bedrooms; restaurant; lift*   **Credit/charge cards accepted:** *Amex, Diners, Eurocard, Visa*

Bormio   ££
NAZIONALE
Via al Forte 14, 23032 Sondrio   *Tel: (0342) 903361*

A large modern chalet-style building quietly set off the road on the edge of the old town centre. For skiers' purposes it is the wrong edge, in winter anyway, but the hotel has its own ski bus, as it has in summer, when teams of young racers shuttle up to their training fields above the Stelvio pass. Even if you don't want to ski, Bormio has lots to offer as a summer resort and is a natural staging post on a mountain tour. Widespread use of pine in public rooms and bedrooms is about the extent of the hotel's style, but it is reasonably comfortable and lively. There is a sun terrace and a small amount of garden.

Facilities: *48 bedrooms; restaurant; lift; parking*   **Credit/charge cards accepted:** *Amex, Diners*

Bressanone (Brixen)
ELEFANT
Via Rio Bianco 4, 39042 Bolzano

£££
Closed mid-Nov to Feb
Tel: (0472) 32750

In December 1550 an Indian elephant, a Portuguese gift to emperor
Ferdinand, broke his journey from Genoa to Vienna to spend a fortnight in
the only stable in town large enough to accommodate him, in what was then
the High Field Inn. Modern Bressanone is as busy a thoroughfare as ever and
an excellent holiday base, and the now famous, smart and serious hotel has
much more to offer passing travellers than big stables. Dining rooms (2 old, 1
new) serve the same excellent south Tyrolean food and wine, including lots
of home produce; the hotel is a splendid old building, full of delightful
elephant-related decorative detail inside and out, and beautifully furnished;
and it is also no doubt a very comfortable place to stay (we were unable to see
any bedrooms). There are attractive gardens and a small pool across the road.

Facilities: *42 bedrooms (14 in garden annexe); restaurants (closed Mon); swimming
pool (heated); garage* **Credit/charge cards accepted:** *none*

Cannobbio
PIRONI
Via Marconi 35, 28052 Novara

££
Closed Jan, Feb and Nov
Tel: (0323) 70624

You would not go to the Pironi for a summer holiday; it has no garden or
pool and it is set back from the lake (Maggiore). But you might well choose it
for a night or two on a touring holiday. It is situated in one of the most
appealing and least touristy resorts on Lake Maggiore, well off the main
road. The hotel is an unspoilt medieval building (dating from around 1400)
and bedrooms are decorated with solid rustic furniture. Bathrooms have
pretty brightly coloured trellis-effect tiles. Public rooms are decorated and
furnished in keeping with the building; the restaurant retains charming
frescoes on ceilings and walls. There is also a piano bar and taverna.

Facilities: *10 bedrooms; restaurant (closed Mon); lift; parking* **Credit/charge
cards accepted:** none

Cernobbio
MIRALAGO
22012 Como

££
Closed Nov to Apr
Tel: (031) 510125

An old-fashioned hotel which has not lapsed into faded gentility and
mediocrity. The Miramare was redecorated a few years ago and some effort
has gone in to modernising it without destroying its character; fresh cotton
upholstery and curtains, new carpets and a few new brass fittings here and
there have smartened it up. The restaurant is largely unchanged but the ugly
old windows have been disguised with elegant cream blinds. The food is way
above average for hotels in the area. Ideal for a short stay, the Miramare does
not offer enough comforts for a complete lakeside holiday.

Facilities: *30 bedrooms (all with shower only); restaurant (closed Mon); lift*
Credit/charge cards accepted: *Amex, Diners, Eurocard, Visa*

Cortina d'Ampezzo   £££
MENARDI   *Closed April to mid-June, mid-Sept to Christmas*
Via Maion 110/112, 32043 Belluno   *Tel: (0436) 2400 2480*

Here is a rarity: a comfortable, friendly, warmly traditional, family-run hotel
in an Italian ski resort as attractive in summer as it is in winter. An old
coaching inn on the edge of town beside the Dobbiaco road, it has been in the
proud hands of the Menardi family since the turn of the century and is very
well looked after, with colourful window boxes, handsome old rustic
furniture and *objets d'art*, bright and comfortable bedrooms, and several cosy
public rooms. The food is not at all institutional and board menus give plenty
of choice. There is a large sunny garden at the back with good views of the
surrounding mountains and (under construction) an annexe with
apartments, sauna and a garage. Cortina is Italy's smartest ski resort;
although the Menardi is not one of its grand hotels, it is by no means cheap.

Facilities: *49 bedrooms; restaurant; lift; parking*   **Credit/charge cards accepted:**
none

Fasano di Gardone Riviera   £££
VILLA DEL SOGNO   *Closed mid-Oct to Mar*
Via Zanardelli 107, 25083 Brescia   *Tel: (0365) 20228*

A comfortable hotel overlooking Lake Garda, set back from the bustle of the
resort. The villa is quiet and self-contained, with an excellent pool and close
to the most beautiful part of the lake (the north-west) as well as being within
a half hour's drive of Brescia. Most rooms are old-fashioned without being
drab. You do need fine weather though; the pool and terrace are easily the
most attractive features. The restaurant is traditional, the food average.

Facilities: *25 bedrooms; restaurant; lift; swimming pool; tennis court; parking*
Credit/charge cards accepted: *Amex, Diners, Eurocard, Visa*

Merano   £££
SCHLOSS LABERS   *Closed Nov to Mar*
Via Labers 25, 39012 Bolzano   *Tel: (0473) 34484*

Not so much a castle as a rambling turreted mansion beautifully set among
orchards and vineyards high above Merano, with splendid views over the
town and surrounding mountains. Labers was converted just over a century
ago and is still in the hands of the same family, whose present friendly
representatives have been careful to preserve the traditional style of the old
building. They have succeeded without too much baronial gimmickry,
despite the armour and a moose's head over the stone staircase, and without
discomfort. Bedrooms have double doors, old beds and rugs, and good
bathrooms. The menu offers little choice but you can put in special requests
at breakfast, which is a good Germanic buffet. There is a shady terrace and
rose garden, clay tennis court, and solar-heated pool.

Facilities: *32 bedrooms; restaurant; swimming pool; tennis court; lift; garage*
Credit/charge cards accepted: *Amex, Diners, Eurocard, Visa*

San Mamete
STELLA D'ITALIA
Piazza Roma 1, 22010 Valsolda (Como)

££
Closed Nov to Mar
Tel: (0344) 68139

A popular hotel with its mainly English clientele, the Stella d'Italia has a friendly, homely atmosphere and is reasonably priced. It is within a short (approximately 20 minute) drive or bus ride of the Villa Favorita near Lugano in Switzerland. The chief attractions are the picturesque location right on the lake and the little terraces which overlook it. There are no signs of Swiss neatness here; everything is slightly run-down. The rooms are 1950s in style with wing chairs, reproduction paintings and houseplants; in the sitting rooms is a bookcase full of English books. A disadvantage for some is the enforced mealtime of 7.30pm and the dull set menus – less careful than the à la carte.

Facilities: *36 bedrooms; restaurant (closed Weds); lift; parking (for 14 cars)*
Credit/charge cards accepted: *Amex, Diners, Visa*

Solda (Sulden)
ZEBRU
39029 Bolzano

£
Closed May to June and Oct to Christmas
Tel: (0473) 75425

A typically smart, comfortable and predictable modern south Tyrolean ski hotel in a magnificent sunny position at the top of the road that climbs through this peaceful and spread-out mountain resort, popular with hikers and climbers in summer. At this altitude (about 6,000 feet) few will regret that the pool is enclosed. A chair-lift runs from beside the hotel up the slopes facing the Ortler; many bedrooms have views of the same beautiful peak, and most have balconies.

Facilities: *45 bedrooms; restaurant; swimming pool; garage* **Credit/charge cards accepted:** *Diners*

Stresa
VERBANO
Isola Pescatori, 28049 Novara

££
Closed Nov to mid-Mar
Tel:(0323) 30408

A delightful alternative to the grand old hotels of Stresa itself, the Verbano is a five-minute boat ride away, on a tiny island. The hotel is a simple villa of no architectural distinction. A gravelled terrace overlooks the supremely romantic Isola Bella, another, under a canopy of oleanders, the Isola Madre. Bedrooms are quite large, typically with old-fashioned embossed wallpaper, pretty new carpets and attractive hand-painted furniture. Bathrooms retain the original plumbing. Downstairs there is a simple bar, a lounge with traditional floral sofas and a vast restaurant. None of these is used much in fine weather when you can eat or relax with a drink on the terrace. Cooking is gastronomically undistinguished, but most ingredients are at least fresh. Lemon puddings are made with lemons from their own trees.

Facilities: *12 bedrooms; restaurant (closed Wed)* **Credit/charge cards accepted:** *Amex, Diners, Visa*

VENICE

❛Nothing is like it, nothing to equal it, not a second Venice in the world❜
ELIZABETH BARRETT BROWNING

Grand Canal

Introduction

"Originality of attitude is utterly impossible" complained Henry
James, "Venice has been painted and described many thousand
times, and of all the cities in the world it is the easiest to visit without
going there." It is Ocean's nursling, phantom city, a dream come
true, the world's unconscious; the revel of the earth, a great genre
picture; latterly a drawing room in a gas station, and a Renaissance
Disneyland. Those streets not full of water are paved with purple
passages. Nor is this merely a modern reaction: Venice has been a
much-reported marvel since the Middle Ages. Her history, like her
geography, is unique.

When the disintegrating Roman Empire divided east and west as
barbarians swept down the middle, Christian communities around
the north-west corner of the Adriatic withdrew to island refuges in
its lagoon. "In the midst of the waters, free, indigent, laborious and
inaccessible, they gradually coalesced into a republic" wrote Gibbon,
ineffably summing up three centuries and all the circumstances.
While many towns reached the point of rejecting the provincial
authority of the distant Byzantine emperor, Venice alone achieved
lasting independence. In 726 she elected her first *dux*, or doge, and
inaugurated a tradition of a thousand years. Imperial usages,
Byzantine ceremonial and practical links with Constantinople
remained strong, surviving the prudent homage paid to
Charlemagne by the doge of 805: Venice never became embroiled in
the feudal upheavals of the rest of Italy. Her only Roman legacy was
her aversion to kingship–dynastic-minded doges were thrown out.
So that neither individual charisma nor mob rule should disrupt the
State, Venice gradually perfected a system of government whose
stability was the envy of medieval Europe. The doge, elected by
incorruptibly intricate ballots, was hemmed in by his *Signoria* of six,
and their decisions were ratified by a self-electing Great Council
which in practice excluded the general populace. In 1297 the Council
became by law a closed society: eligibility was restricted to Venetians
whose paternal ancestors had been members. A long list of those
eligible was the basis of the *Libro d'Oro*, the Golden Book of patrician
birth and marriage records. Venice's state security–fearsome
intelligence networks, streamlined powers over life and death–was
administered by the famous Council of Ten.

Peace and efficiency at home were essential to Venetian
enterprise; battles she fought (like England) on others' territory.
Until she began to acquire an eastward empire of ports and islands
her chief asset had been salt. For growth and for survival she traded,
and her resources were in constant deployment on the high seas.
Venetians believed in prestige abroad, pride in their city, and the
profit-motive elevated to a principle. They were *"Veneziani, poi
Cristiani"* ("Venetians first, then Christians") but nonetheless well
provided with saints and symbols. Their early patron saint Theodore
and his obscure dragon were abandoned for saint Mark and his
winged lion: the 9th-century theft from an Alexandrian tomb of the

body of the Evangelist brought profitable pilgrims and a spiritual prestige second only to Rome's. There was a convenient legend which described saint Mark in the vicinity of Venice being blessed by an angel in the words *"Pax tibi Marce, evangelista meus. Hic requiescat corpus tuum"*; Venice built him a basilica, the most magnificent resting-place in the world. Many of the city's carved lions clamp a paw on a book open at the angel's first five words.

The only animals of equal esteem to Venetians are the four great bronze horses they set above the main door of St Mark's Basilica, whose provenance is worse than body-snatching: they came from the fourth crusade. The Republic went crusading chiefly for profit. In the first (1095) she acquired Tripoli and what she claimed to be the body of saint Nicholas; in the second she managed to make war on Norman Sicily; the third she all but ignored, and the fourth (1202) made her fortune. Venice alone had the ships to transport the crusading army to its destination, and she required both considerable cash in advance and a proportionate share of the profits. At point of departure, the assembled Franks and Flemings couldn't pay. Doge Enrico Dandolo – an energetic octogenarian, stone blind – "had the cross sewn on to his great cotton hat" and proceeded to exploit the situation. Debt and crusade were postponed while the army first liberated a Dalmatian port in Venice's commercial interests, and were then persuaded to Constantinople where the Byzantine emperor had recently been deposed. Their siege was epic, not least for the exploits of the old blind doge; their subsequent sack of Constantinople was the worst in history. Let loose among the treasures of nine centuries the Franks smashed them up, but the Venetians sent their loot home intact, beginning with the four Roman horses from the Hippodrome. By the terms of her contract with the crusaders, the Republic gained control of the eastern Mediterranean and was thereafter self-styled "Ruler of a Quarter and Half a Quarter of the Roman Empire".

In the centuries of her commercial supremacy the Most Serene Republic made her capital a showcase and shop window. She had no need of fortifications – the lagoon was her security – and the doges' palace, unlike most contemporary seats of power, was no stronghold: its Gothic grace is airy and accessible. Venetian architects have rebuilt and remodelled and filled gaps in all the European styles of Renaissance and Baroque, but the city's essence remains an oriental extravagance. St Mark's, encrusted with spoils from Constantinople, was embellished over six centuries; no city is so full of carved detail – not only the schematic decoration of palaces and churches, but an incidental abundance of heads and beasts, symbols and emblems, the charming and the grotesque.

Early tourists (Venice had a form of tourist police as early as the 14th century) were dazzled by the display of luxury – silken embroideries, scarlet and gold, jewels and perfumes – on the Venetian person and premises, and on their graceful town carriages, the gondolas. Sumptuary laws classifying and regulating rich apparel were often disregarded, but since 1562 all workaday gondolas have been by statute painted black. Their familar, traditional shape is today a much-refined model, its precise measurements, asymmetrical curve and many different component woods perfectly adapted to swift passage through the canals. A gondola needs scraping and re-varnishing every few weeks, and its proud six-pronged *ferro* a housewifely polish every day. The little square cabin (the *felze*) which reminded so many writers of a coffin is seldom seen now: gondolas are summer affairs, their numbers dwindled to a few hundred, their gondoliers mostly out of work in winter. Gondola fares are necessarily high, and *vaporetti* have taken over for practical transport. Horatio Brown's "dear and lovely feature, the most familiar in the city of the sea" has survived as a romantic extravagance, uncompromising in craftsmanship and careful of tradition. In the summer of 1986, gondoliers were rebuked once again by the Venetian municipality for singing Neapolitan arias.

In the heyday of her success, Venice had routed her rivals in sea power the Genoese, and added to her empire those mainland territories which controlled trade routes through the Alps. But in 1453 the Turks took Constantinople, and by the 16th century Venetian prosperity was seriously threatened by the twin disasters of an expanding Ottoman Empire and Vasco da Gama's new sea route for the spice trade. Venice stepped up her showmanship. Feasts and ceremonies filled her calendar, spectacular set pieces greeted visiting dignitaries. Henri III of France came in 1574 to be enthralled for a week by actors, dancers, acrobats, floating glassblowers, a galley built and launched between sunrise and sunset, a banquet of 1,200 dishes and the attentions of Veronica Franco, most celebrated of courtesans. Venetians are credited with inventing mirrorglass, easel painting, the opera, the weathercone and the ships' biscuit. Their more serious institutions included income tax, quarantine, an early form of national health service and the ghetto. Venetian Jews enjoyed a higher degree of tolerance than elsewhere and indeed rights – for which they paid – on the basis summed up by Shakespeare's merchant: "For the commodity that strangers have/ With us in Venice if it be denied'/ Will much impeach the justice of this state,/ Since that the trade and profit of this city/ Consisteth of all nations."

The Jews had a synagogue, the Muslims a mosque and the Greek Orthodox community its own church; as the Reformation spread over Europe and the papacy demanded counter-measures, Venice was equally tolerant towards Lutheran or Calvinist merchants and foreign diplomats – like England's Henry Wotton, who imported Protestant prayerbooks and held Anglican services. Her stance led to a papal interdict against the Republic in 1606: not her first state excommunication, but the last anywhere in the history of the church. The doge told the legate "We ignore your excommunication: it is nothing to us. Think now where this resolution would lead, if our example were to be followed by others." Through the brilliant advocacy of Paolo Sarpi – friar, scholar and scientist friend of Galileo – Venice outfaced the ban. Mass continued to be said in her churches, all Europe took sides, and France was mediator in negotiations which humiliated papal authority. Sarpi, recorded by Wotton as "fenced in with a castle of paper about his chair and over his head when he was reading or writing alone", achieved a personal fame far beyond his desires and survived an assassination attempt which left a dagger embedded in his cheekbone. Nothing was provable, but he remarked afterwards that he recognised the "style" of Rome.

This Venetian cause had done no harm to her reputation in Europe, which mattered the more as her eastern empire dwindled. She had acquired a western one, taking untyrannical charge of north-east Italy to a border with Milan, and in the early 16th century surviving the League of Cambrai, an alliance against her of pope, emperor, France and Spain. She had become the free intellectual centre of Europe, publishing more books than Rome, Milan, Naples and Florence combined, and her greatest artists were flourishing. As her independent power diminished her renowned diplomatic skills were used to preserve peace where possible, but in any event her own neutrality, leaving her free to fight her Turkish battles. During a campaign in 1687 she had the guilty misfortune of demolishing most of the Parthenon, which the Turks were using as a powder magazine.

The 18th century saw the end of battles, east or west. For eighty years Venice was a pleasure ground, offering the comedies of Goldoni, the music of Vivaldi and Albinoni, the paintings of Guardi and Canaletto. A score of hotels received rich foreign visitors and Grand Tourists bought "views" as souvenirs: most of Canaletto's best work ended up in England. Europe had reached the Age of Reason, to find Venice still more godless in a hedonistic Age of Carnival, full of courtesans and licentious convents, *cicisbei* and Casanova. Those of the ruling families who still had money to burn gambled, masked, at the *ridotti* (or openly held the bank). Impoverished nobles living on poor relief were still obliged to wear silk. Seats on the Great Council were offered for sale, to attract new blood. The emperor Joseph II was aghast at the extravagant plans for his reception, the grand duke of Russia approved the good behaviour of the crowds at his; in 1782 even the pope came. The doge that died in February 1789 was buried secretly at night so as not to stop the carnival.

Venetians took small heed of the French Revolution, though the French representative was duly authorised to fly his Republican flag. Spoilt, sapped and politically inert, the *Serenissima* dithered with diplomatic incompetence as France and Austria once again fought across Italy. Napoleon Bonaparte's famous diatribe ("I shall be an Attila to the State of Venice") breathes irritation. He never set foot in the city, but in 1797 his written requirements dismantled the Republic in complete and undignified detail. The absence of any Venetian resistance at least ensured that Napoleon's looting – including St Mark's bronze horses – was carried out methodically by his agents instead of brutally by his troops.

The horses were returned at the fall of the French Empire, but

Napoleon's inroads on Venetian institutions were continued by the Austrian regime that followed. Monastic foundations were suppressed, their islands used as isolation hospitals and military depots, their city churches as store houses. Employment dwindled. By 1817 it was estimated that a quarter of the city's population lived by begging. In 1848, in a phoenix-flame of the old Venetian spirit, Daniele Manin's Republic of St Mark threw out the Austrians, to be bombarded into surrender after a heroic summer of siege and cholera. They had tried, among other things, to demolish the new railway causeway which linked Venice with the mainland. By 1866, however, she was willy-nilly part of a united Italy. Sympathy with the Risorgimento brought some philanthropic foreign investment – a short-lived grain mill on the Giudecca island, revived glassworks on

Visiting Venice

There are regular scheduled flights from London and charter flights from London and regional airports to Venice. The most glamorous and dramatic entrance to the city is by water and it's well worth the expense of taking the comfortable public *Motoscafo San Marco* launch service from the airport across the lagoon (but beware touting watertaxi drivers who charge over three times as much). If your hotel is closer to the city terminal at Piazzale Roma than to Piazzo San Marco it is more convenient, as well as cheaper, to take the bus or a land taxi to the terminal.

The most romantic way to get to Venice is by the Venice Simplon Orient Express. An ordinary second-class rail return costs about the same as a typical charter flight. The worst way to arrive in Venice, from a practical point of view, is by car; parking at Piazzale Roma is expensive and space is at a premium. There are cheaper car parks at Isola del Tronchetto, Fusina, San Giuliano and Mestre, with boat or bus connection to Venice; and there is free parking at the airport.

Porters are expensive; unless your hotel is very close to your arrival point, they will take your luggage on water and charge for the boat fare as well as each item. They can be booked by telephone – 715272 (railway station), 5223590 (Piazzale Roma) or 5200545 (Piazza San Marco).

The most practical way of getting around the city is by waterbus. The *motoscafi* are the fastest but *vaporetti* are more comfortable and provide better views. The no. 1 (confusingly called *accelerato*) stops at virtually every landing stage along the Grand Canal, taking about 35 minutes to do so; no. 5 is the scenic line, going right round Venice, including Murano. Other lines worth knowing about are no. 2, a short cut from Piazzale Roma to San Marco, and no. 4 (summer only), a faster version of no. 1. The no. 34 (*espresso*) runs from Tronchetto (car park), Piazzale Roma and the railway station to Piazza San Marco. *Un Ospite di Venezia*, a booklet provided free by most hotels, gives very useful waterbus information and nearly all city maps mark routes and landing stages. Tickets can be bought at the main landing stages and at some bars and tobacconists; you can pay on board but it's more expensive to do so. A suitcase costs the same as a passenger but children under a metre tall go free. You save nothing (except, possibly, time) by buying books of tickets, and tickets for 24 hours' unlimited travel are only a good deal if you're on a whistlestop tour. Tickets should be punched at the automatic machines on the landing stages. Watertaxis are small, fast and comfortable – but exorbitantly priced – launches. Fares are regulated and published in the booklet *Un Ospite di Venezia*; it's essential to establish the price before setting off. The most luxurious way of seeing the city is by gondola. Serenaded group tours are much cheaper than hiring by the hour.

Murano – but by comparison with Milan and Turin *fin-de-siècle* Venice was desperately poor, a city of melancholy beauty preserved by sheer neglect.

Reclamation of the marshlands at mainland Marghera and use of the deep channels for a port serviced by industry was the profitable conception of count Giuseppe Volpi at the end of the First World War. By 1933, a year when Mussolini welcomed Hitler in Venice, count Volpi was Minister of Finance and his new road bridge carried busloads of Venetian commuters. Marghera, and neighbouring villages, were put under Venice's municipal jurisdiction and the city itself known from then on as "the historic centre". The Second World War, like the First, left Venetian fabric almost unscathed, but after it Venetian life was fundamentally different. As Italy's

---

Most of Venice's main sights are within fairly easy walking distance of the hotels and you can cross the city from north to south in about half an hour. If you keep to the main thoroughfares the distinctive yellow signs pointing the way to Piazza San Marco, Ferrovia (railway station) and Piazzale Roma will keep you more or less on course. Tracking down an address can be extremely confusing. Venetian addresses usually consist of no more than the name of the *sestiere* and its number (eg Dorsoduro 4789).

Several local companies organise excursions and prices vary little. Walking tours are usually poor value; better value is the launch trip down the Grand Canal, with a commentary. There are serenaded group tours by gondola, and boat and bus trips down the Brenta canal to Padua (*see Northern Cities chapter*). The most popular excursions are to the three main islands in the lagoon, with visits to glassmaking centres; but independent visits using public transport cost about half the price.

Advance booking of hotels is essential, particularly in the spring and summer; in winter some hotels close. At certain times it's virtually impossible to find a room at all: during the Carnival (week before Lent), the International Film Festival (late August, early September) and the Biennale modern art exhibition (June to October, even years). Venice's luxury hotels charge a good deal more than a 5-star hotel in London, and a simple hotel will charge about the same as a 3-star hotel elsewhere in Italy. Generally the further you go from San Marco, the less costly the hotels; the cheapest ones are in the station area. Small rooms and noise are the main drawbacks of Venetian hotels; for a traffic-free city there is a surprising amount of disturbance at night.

There are no campsites in Venice itself, or on the Lido. Those around Mestre and Marghera on the mainland are generally noisy and basic; the best bets are the beach sites at Punta Sabbioni, 45mins by ferry from San Marco.

Tour operators arrange holidays by air, for a week or long weekend, all year round. They use grand hotels and *pensioni* as well as standard middle-sized, medium-priced ones. However, it can be cheaper to go independently if you use a charter flight.

There is a good case for going to Venice at any time of year, depending on your priorities. Early summer is perhaps ideal; before May it can be rather cool. The peak tourist season is from June to September; July and August are the worst months for heat, crowds (including hordes of daytrippers), mosquitoes and smells, but there is always plenty going on – several major international cultural festivals and some traditional ones. Autumn is a good season for music-lovers, with concerts in many churches; the opera season does not start until November. Winter is relatively uncrowded and a few hotels offer cheaper rates; but although mists can be romantic, it is often just foggy and cold. The Carnival in the week before Lent has become a major attraction.

"economic miracle" got under way the industrial zone expanded and workers' apartment blocks sprang up round nearby Mestre. Central heating and sanitation were more attractive than life in a decaying Historical Monument, a category for which 95 per cent of Venice's buildings qualify and to which any alteration is prohibited except through vast expense of money and red tape. By the 1950s Venice was suffering from both pollution and depopulation.

Since the big flood of November 1966 much has been done to preserve the beauty and restore the treasures of Venice. Her livelihood, as in other centuries, is tourism; at Easter and in the summer the city is packed to capacity and the spontaneous revival of the carnival – by the visiting youth of Padua, Treviso and Vicenza who arrived in homemade fancy dress on the traditional weekend in 1975 – has become a winter boom, backed by fashion, public relations and the municipal authorities. Palaces still stand empty, but the market in smaller properties has soared since rich Italians from Rome and Milan have come to appreciate the attractions of Venice for a holiday home or a *pied à terre*. Venice does not have kidnappings or muggings; what crime exists is petty. Getaway is too much of a problem. She was always beautiful; now she is also exclusive, and above all she is safe.

Area by area guide

THE GRAND CANAL

Not, of course, an area, but Venice's most ubiquitous feature, sweeping in an inverted "S" shape through the heart of the city. The "finest street in the world", the Grand Canal is the main thoroughfare of Venice and teems with the traffic of small motor boats, launches, barges and gondolas. Ideally, a slow journey down the canal should be your first introduction to the city: if not in a gondola, in the No. 1 waterbus from the station or from St Mark's square (this, despite being marked *accelerato*, stops at virtually every landing stage along the canal so you'll have time to take in at least some of the architectural masterpieces that line the two miles of its banks). There are over a hundred *palazzi*, providing a grand parade of mellow-tinted façades, flamboyant or stately, restored or sadly dilapidated.

SAN MARCO

As far as many tourists are concerned, San Marco is the only *sestiere* (one of the six administrative areas into which Venice is divided) in Venice. It contains the city's two top sights (the basilica of St Mark and the Doges' Palace), the widest variety of hotels, shops and restaurants, and sufficient quaint canals and alleyways to convince first-time visitors that they have seen the entire city.

Piazza San Marco, perennially lauded and romanticised, is arguably the most beautiful square in the world and certainly the most famous. Strictly speaking it is the only "piazza" in Venice.

Piazza San Marco

There are, of course, other beautiful squares but no other could rival San Marco for size and splendour, so the others were called *campi* (fields) or *campielli* (little fields) and San Marco's was – and still is – simply "the Piazza".

This great stage setting, coveted even by Napoleon as the most elegant salon in Europe, is an intriguing scene of exotic east merging with classical Christian west. Three of its sides are enclosed by the grandiose façades of public buildings, but the eye is invariably drawn towards the bubbling domes of the sumptuous basilica of St Mark, which has attracted much written comment – from the wildest eulogies to the less flattering "tawdry", "a hodge-podge" or "a vast warty bug taking a meditative walk" (Mark Twain's affectionate description). Beside it stands the campanile, a massive brick tower, in sober contrast to the voluptuous façade of St Mark's. On 14th July 1902 the tower collapsed, crushing Sansovino's Loggetta (a former meeting place of patricians) below but causing no other casualties. By popular demand an exact replica was built. A fast lift takes you to the top for a splendid panorama of the city (queues tend to subside at lunchtime). For grand views of the piazza, you can also go up the ornately sculptured clock tower (Torre dell'Orologio), where a famous pair of giant bronze moors strike the hours. The grandiose 16th-century galleried buildings which form the north side of the piazza are the Procuratie Vecchie (procurators' offices); opposite are the complementary Procuratie Nuove, completed a century later and now housing the Correr Museum of art and history and the archaeological museum. For those who can afford it the square is best admired from one of the elegant cafés under the arcades. Florian's, which opened in 1720, is an ex-haunt of the *literati*; Quadri's opposite was patronised by those supporting the régime in the 18th century; it was subsequently shunned by Italians. Black-tied waiters serve drinks on silver plates while five-piece orchestras strike up Viennese waltzes and other romantic strains.

For most of the year the square is a Mecca for tourists but commercialism and crowds are nothing new. In 1751 John Moore wrote "In the evening there generally is, on St Mark's Place, such a mixed multitude of Jews , Turks, and Christians; lawyers, knaves, and pick-pockets; mountebanks, old women, and physicians; women of quality, with masks; strumpets barefaced; and, in short, such a jumble of... people of every character and condition,... that you can think, or reflect, on nothing...". In 1882 Henry James described Venice as "a great bazaar" and San Marco as a scandalous square of pedlars plying their trade. Pigeons are an integral part of the scene, penetrating every nook, fed and loved by overindulgent tourists, merely tolerated by the Venetians.

To the south side the square opens on to the Grand Canal through the Piazzetta, a dignified square bounded on one side by the lacy loggia of the Doges' Palace and on the other by the Libreria Marciana, designed by Sansovino and considered by Palladio the finest building since ancient times; it is still the main public library of the city. The busy waterfront of the Molo provides a glorious panorama across the lagoon.

The triangle formed by Piazza San Marco, the Rialto Bridge and the Accademia gallery contains the main shopping area of Venice. The busiest street, the Merceria, starts at the clock tower and leads up as far as the Rialto Bridge. This surprisingly narrow street has always been the chief thoroughfare of the city and was once lined with the shops of merchants selling fine fabrics. Today it's a bustling street of boutiques and souvenir shops with the occasional grocer's.

West of Piazza San Marco the busy Calle Frezzeria is lined with fashionable boutiques, and the Calle Larga 22 Marzo has some of the most exclusive shops and galleries in Venice. It's also an area of luxury hotels, several of which occupy *palazzi* in prime locations on the Grand Canal. But this part of San Marco also has its more modest aspects: tiny quaint alleys, bridges with pretty wrought-iron parapets and quiet quaysides where gondolas are moored. There are plenty of small, second class hotels and local *trattorie*. The squares have none of the grandeur of Piazza San Marco but plenty of local charm: the quiet Campo Maurizio, the large and rambling Campo Santo Stefano (otherwise known as Campo Francesco Morosini), and the pretty Campo Sant' Angelo with open-air cinema in summer, and fine views of Santo Stefano's acutely leaning tower. On the Campo San Fantin, the opulent Fenice Theatre – a splendid setting for 19th-century operas – is well worth visiting when rehearsals are not taking place.

Churches
San Marco

Galleries, museums and palaces
Correr Museum
Doges' Palace
Fortuny Museum

Hotels
La Fenice et Des Artistes
Flora
Gritti Palace
Kette
Monaco and Grand Canal
Do Pozzi
Santo Stefano
Saturnia e International

DORSODURO

This is the most southerly section of the historic centre and among its many attractions are the panoramas across the lagoon to the island of Giudecca which is part of the same *sestiere (see below)*. From the Zattere, the broad stoneflagged quay skirting the wide canal, you can watch the *vaporetti* plying across the water or the incongruously large ocean-going liners that dwarf the local vessels. *Zattere* means rafts and refers to the timber which was brought down the rivers and moored here. Today it has something of a seaside atmosphere with open-air cafés and ice-cream parlours overlooking a large expanse of choppy, blue water. Ruskin stayed in one of the two *pensioni* on the front, approving the view – though it included the Redentore, one of the Venetian churches he most despised.

Dorsoduro can be divided into two areas. East of the Accademia gallery lies a quiet neighbourhood of artisan shops, *alimentari*, galleries and picturesque residences of wealthy Venetians and foreigners. In the early 1900s it was a quarter popular with English expatriates, who attended the Anglican church of St George. Frederick Rolfe ("Baron Corvo") lampooned them in *The Desire and Pursuit of the Whole*, his scandalous "Romance of Modern Venice" written in 1909 but unpublished until 1934. The area remains quiet and relatively undisturbed by tourism despite its delightful streets, beautiful canals and sunlit squares. Particularly pretty are the Rio San Vio, the Fondamenta Bragadin and the shady little square, Campiello Barbaro. The most familiar landmark is the soaring Baroque dome of Santa Maria della Salute, marking the very eastern tip of Dorsoduro and the entrance to the Grand Canal.

Going west from the Accademia, the Dorsoduro becomes gradually more shabby, culminating in the working-class quarter around the charming Romanesque church of San Nicolò dei Mendicoli, traditionally an area inhabited by fishermen and sailors. Going north-west from the Accademia you pass the quiet, unspoilt area around San Barnaba – traditionally the area for poor Venetian

Santa Maria della Salute

nobility. On the canal beside the church of San Barnaba you can see one of the last surviving floating vegetable shops and to the north the Campo di Santa Margherita – a large beautiful square of bustling local life, with fish market and fine cake shops.

The Dorsoduro is an important sightseeing area: the Accademia gallery has the most important collection of Venetian art in the world, the church of San Sebastiano has paintings by Veronese, the Sculoa Grande dei Carmini and the Church of the Gesuati have Tiepolo ceilings. And in the quiet square of San Trovaso you can see one of the last surviving gondola shipyards.

Dorsoduro is an excellent area to stay if you're looking for a quiet, reasonably priced *pensione* in a convenient area. Apart from the two on the Zattere, there are several charming small hotels close to the Accademia.

Churches
Santa Maria del Rosario (Gesuati)
Santa Maria della Salute
San Sebastiano

Galleries and museums
Accademia
Ca' Rezzonico (Museum of the Venetian 18th century)
Guggenheim Collection
Scuola Grande dei Carmini

Hotels
Accademia
Alboretti
Seguso

THE GIUDECCA AND SAN GIORGIO MAGGIORE

Facing the Dorsoduro, and part of that *sestiere*, lies the **Giudecca**, a quiet island possibly named after the Jews who settled here at the end of the 13th century. A five-minute ferry ride from the Zattere takes you to the quayside which stretches almost the entire length of the island. The views of Venice from here are magnificent, particularly from the eastern tip which overlooks St Mark's.

In the early Renaissance the Giudecca became the home of rich Venetians who built elegant villas here; today it's essentially a quiet working- and middle-class district of fishermen's houses and apartment blocks. The main reason for a visit is to see Palladio's Redentore church whose dome is the prominent feature of the waterfront. Set inconspicuously in lush gardens at the eastern end of the island is the modern Hotel Cipriani and its private yacht harbour.

San Giorgio Maggiore is a tiny island once occupied by a Benedictine monastery, and now the site of Palladio's church of San Giorgio Maggiore – one of the most familiar and noble landmarks at the entrance to the city.

Churches
Redentore
San Giorgio Maggiore

Hotels
Casa Frollo
Cipriani

SAN POLO

This is the smallest of the city's *sestieri*, lying to the north-west of San Marco and west of the Rialto bridge, and includes a number of Venice's less important (but nonetheless interesting) churches, as well as one of her greatest, the Frari. The Rialto bridge, a beloved if inelegant landmark of the Grand Canal, marks the geographic centre of the city and until 1854, when the first Accademia bridge was built, it was the only means of crossing the Grand Canal by foot. Despite competition from such eminent architects as Michelangelo, Palladio and Sansovino, Antonio da Ponte was granted the commission to design it. It was built in stone (the previous wooden bridges had collapsed) and 28m high, to make way for the great galleys. Today the bridge is tightly packed with souvenirs and stalls, and the views from it are rather more impressive than the bridge itself.

Officially "the Rialto" is the quarter around the bridge where the first inhabitants of the lagoon are said to have settled. It became the commercial hub of the city, venue of the early traders and merchants from the east. Markets were established here in the 11th century and today they are still very much part of the Rialto scene. North of the bridge stalls are piled high with gleaming fruits and vegetables and tiny grocery shops are stacked with pasta, cheese and coffee beans. On the site of the 14th-century fish market stands the modern Pescheria, with its astounding selection of fresh fish and live eels, all displayed until evening in an early 20th-century open stone loggia overlooking the Grand Canal.

The northern area of San Polo is a quiet and relatively poor neighbourhood where washing hangs from windows and dark alleys lead off ramshackle squares. Tourists tend to keep to the main Rialto/Railway thoroughfare passing through the southern part of San Polo, which links the most attractive of San Polo's squares and takes you along a series of quaint and sometimes rather chic alleyways. Campo di San Polo, largest square in Venice after San Marco, at one time witnessed bullfights, tournaments and masked balls. Nowadays it serves as a playground for noisy Venetian children. There are several patrician mansions around the church of San Polo; in one of them – the Palazzo Corner-Mocenigo – Frederick Rolfe was a guest while writing *The Desire and Pursuit of the Whole*. When his hostess read some of this ungrateful *roman à clef* he was promptly turned out.

The soaring Gothic façade of the Frari church dwarfs the eastern section of San Polo. It was built for Franciscan friars in a suitably severe and simple style and its plain red brick façade makes a striking impact in a city with so many elaborate and exotic monuments.

The only places in which to stay in San Polo are a handful of basic *pensioni* in the southern part of the area and a couple of simple hotels on the Grand Canal.

Churches
Santa Maria Gloriosa dei Frari (Frari)

Galleries and museums
Scuola Grande di San Rocco

SANTA CROCE

Tourists rarely penetrate the heart of Santa Croce. There are no major sights or thoroughfares, few hotels and the only familiar buildings are the venerable palaces that line the northern arc of the Grand Canal. The sole concession to tourism is the Piazzale Roma at the western end – a dreary modern car and coach park which makes an unsightly introduction to Venice for those who arrive by road. Elsewhere Santa Croce is a quiet, residential area where the houses and *palazzi* are distinctly more decayed than those of the areas to the south.

The core of Santa Croce is a labyrinth of covered alleyways, lined by peeling façades and crossed by canals – some so narrow that delivery barges can barely squeeze past each other under the humpbacked bridges. As you approach the Grand Canal quays (*fondamente*) there are fine views of the splendid palaces across the water. Santa Croce's squares are pleasantly run-down, frequently flanked by dilapidated Gothic houses where dusty geraniums and aspidistras sit on crumbling ledges. The largest square is Campo San Giacomo dell' Orio, a homely scene of local working-class life, dominated by a suitably shabby church and its tall campanile. Another unspoilt square is the Campo Santa Maria Mater Domini with a fine 14th-century wellhead, a little Renaissance church and picturesque early *palazzi*.

Churches
San Stae

Galleries and museums
Ca' Pesaro (Gallery of Modern Art)
Natural History Museum

Hotels
Al Sole Palace

CANNAREGIO

Cannaregio forms the northern arc of the historic centre, stretching from the sleek 20th-century railway station in the west to the part furthest east which is generally regarded as the oldest quarter of the city. The name Cannaregio comes from *canne* (reeds), dating from the time when the whole area was marshland. Today it's a quiet area of wide canals, secluded squares, churches, minor *palazzi* and hidden gardens. The only tourist thoroughfares are the Lista di Spagna and the Strada Nuova which together form the main route running north of the Grand Canal.

More or less in the centre of Cannaregio lies the world's oldest "ghetto", a grey and melancholy area of huddled houses and washing strung across streets. The word derives from the Italian word for foundry – *getto* – and dates back to very early times when there was an iron foundry here for making cannons. The oldest settlement, confusingly called Ghetto Nuovo, was the area where Jews were permitted to live after the early 16th century (before that they had been confined to the Giudecca or Mestre). The name "ghetto" was subsequently applied to isolated Jewish communities all over the world. It was not until 1797, when Napoleon had the gates torn down, that Venetian Jews were able to choose where to live. Some stayed put; tall tenements, old synagogues, a kosher restaurant and some antiholocaust sculpture all give the quarter a distinctly ethnic air.

Northern Cannaregio is quiet and remote. One of the more charming areas to explore is around the lovely church of Madonna dell' Orto, whose domed campanile provides a prominent landmark. Eastern Cannaregio, beyond the Canale delle Misericordia, is a warren of alleys and canals. On the north it's bounded by the Fondamente Nuove (New Quays). Steamers from here ply to and from the outlying islands (*see Excursions*).

But most tourists don't stray far from the well-trodden route from the Rialto to the station. The Strada Nuova, which was knocked through Venice in the 19th century, is an area of tourist shops and reasonably priced cheerful *trattorie*. The Lista di Spagna, close to the station, is an unattractive street of *pensioni* and hotels; some of the better hotels have sites on the Grand Canal. The advantages of staying close to the station are lower prices and a hassle-free journey (without expensive porters) to your hotel – worth considering if you're staying only for a night or two and arriving at the station or Piazzale Roma.

Churches
Madonna dell' Orto
San Giovanni Cristostomo
Santa Maria Assunta (Gesuiti)
Santa Maria dei Miracoli

Galleries and museums
Ca' d'Oro (Franchetti Gallery)

Hotels
Giorgione

CASTELLO
Castello is an area of contrasts, from the wide, bustling waterfront in the south to the quiet, humble quarters in the north. From Piazza San Marco it's only a couple of minutes' walk to the Riva degli Schiavoni, the wide curving waterfront which, with the Piazza San Marco, is the busiest and most solidly commercial area of Venice. Apart from a large concentration of hotels, cafés and restaurants, there are souvenir kiosks, lightning portraitists, touting gondoliers and a host of excursion boats. But nothing destroys the glorious panorama across the shimmering lagoon, to the islands of San Giorgio Maggiore (with its grandly conspicuous church) and the Giudecca.

Of the hotels along the Riva degli Schiavoni, the Danieli is something of an institution, renowned for the illustrious guests who have stayed here, among them Alfred de Musset and George Sand.

The quarter behind the Riva degli Schiavoni is worth exploring for its quaint quaysides flanked by elegant but dilapidated palaces, tucked away *trattorie*, secluded squares and its churches and works of art – particularly San Zaccaria and the Scuola di San Giorgio degli Schiavoni. The Campo Santa Maria Formosa is a pleasantly rambling market square of handsome palaces with a buxom (*formosa*) Renaissance church. Just to the north-east is the Campo Santi Giovanni e Paolo (locally referred to as San Zanipolo), a grand ceremonial square. Here is the Scuola Grande di San Marco (today the civic hospital), with a Lombard Renaissance façade, the gaunt and grandiose Gothic church of Santi Giovanni e Paolo, and Verrocchio's vigorous equestrian monument to Bartolomeo Colleone,

considered by some to be the finest equestrian statue in the world.

Northern Castello has unspoilt squares and alleys and quays providing a broad view of the Venetian lagoon.

Much of eastern Castello is occupied by the Arsenal, once the shipyard of Venice's great maritime republic. During its heyday 16,000 men were employed to build, equip and refurbish the great galleys of the Republic and there was a time when an entire galley could be churned out in a day – built in a conveyor belt system, passed from warehouse to warehouse. Today the walled docklands are desolate reminders of that splendid era (the No 5 waterbus will take you right through but there is no access on foot). The residential area south of the Arsenal is aesthetically dull, except during the Biennale art exhibition in alternate years; but keen sightseers might get as far as San Pietro in Castello, former cathedral of Venice, which stands in a positively un-Venetian grassy tree-lined square.

Churches
San Giorgio dei Greci
Santi Giovanni e Paolo (San Zanipolo)
Santa Maria Formosa
San Zaccaria

Galleries and Museums
Naval Museum
Palazzo Querini-Stampalia
Scuola di San Giorgio degli Schiavoni

Hotels
Danieli
Paganelli

Shopping

Like most Italian cities, Venice has a large number of stylish,
enticing windowfronts but – apart from some leather items –
bargains here are virtually non-existent. There's also the inevitable
abundance of souvenirs, including coloured glass animals,
miniature gondoliers and lace placemats. Most shops are
concentrated in the San Marco area: expensive lace, jewellery and
glass boutiques under the arcades of the Piazza, the lively and more
informal Merceria running north from the Clock Tower as far as the
Rialto, and the streets west of the Piazza. This is where you'll find all
the big names in Italian fashion, though you could find most of the
items in London for around the same price. Only if you make a big
purchase – particularly with items like glass or lace – is it worth
bargaining. Most shopkeepers speak English.

Books　Three of the best shops are Libreria Internazionale
Sangiorgio in Calle Larga XXII Marzo, Libreria Sansovino at 84
Bacino Orseolo (just off Piazza San Marco), and Il Libraio a San
Barnaba, off Campo San Barnaba; all have a good selection of
English books on Venice (and Venetian art). Alberto Bertoni, in Calle
della Mandola (San Marco), sells second-hand art books with a 40%
to 50% discount.

Clothes　The top names are concentrated in the San Marco area,
either west of the Piazza – Valaressa is very smart, Frezzeria is
trendy – or along the Merceria. The two department stores are Coin,
off Campo San Bartolomeo, which has a large selection of clothes
and accessories, and Standa (several branches). Cheapest of all are
the stalls on the northern side of, or actually on, the Rialto
Bridge – silk scarves and ties and very reasonably priced lambswool
and angora sweaters.

Glass　For centuries Venice (actually Murano) has been a glassmaking centre. Glass goods can be seen everywhere, ranging from
garish kitsch to beautiful crystal glasses. There are various places
where you can watch the glass being blown: Calle Cappello Nero
just behind Piazza San Marco, Calle San Gregorio in eastern
Dorsoduro and several of the workshops in Murano. Don't assume
cheaper prices in Murano than in central Venice – it's often the
contrary; but try bargaining here.

Jewellery　The shops surrounding Piazza San Marco are the most
reliable, but there are dozens of jewellers selling gold and silver (and
imitations), on and north of the Rialto Bridge, and in San Polo.

Lace This is traditionally made in Burano and you can still buy it there from the women who make it. Lace sold in Venice varies enormously in quality and price, and it's not always easy to pick out the local hand-made article from the imitations from Taiwan or Korea. Demonstrations of lacemaking are held at the Lace School, 'il Merletto', in San Marco 95-96 close to the Piazza, or at the lace school in Burano.

Leather Shoes are probably the best bargain in Venice. A pair of fine quality hand-made shoes costs considerably less than the Bond Street equivalent and there are bargains in the middle range too. Leather goods generally are usually cheaper than in the UK, but more expensive than in other Italian cities. The cheapest place for handbags, gloves, belts and so on is the Rialto Bridge.

Masks For centuries masks have been part of the culture of Venice, frequently imitating the faces of notorious doges. The 18th century was the great age of masked balls and carnivals, and masks were frequently worn by nobles and servants alike. This came to an abrupt halt when Napoleon gave the order for all masks to be burnt, and the Fascists went even further with a death penalty for the making of masks. But since the reinstitution of the Venice carnival in 1980, masks have again become all the rage. They vary from poor papier mâché imitations from Taiwan to beautifully crafted leather masks sold from workshops.

Prints Small shops all over the city sell prints of 18th- and 19th-century Venice, ranging from high priced original engravings to the cheaper reproductions which make excellent souvenirs.

Markets The daily food market, just north of the Rialto Bridge, is one of the most colourful sights in Venice. Go early in the morning and you'll see all the locals here doing their shopping.

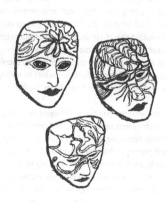

VENICE IN PERIL

The slight but regular tides of the upper Adriatic have always cleansed the canals of Venice and given the Venetian lagoon its ecological balance. The big tide called *acqua alta* is a recurrent but irregular phenomenon requiring a combination of low pressure and a strong bout of the sirocco, the prevailing wind. Even at spring or autumn equinox, no sirocco means no *acqua alta*. But once flood conditions have built up, the sirocco can counteract the ebb of the tide, the *acqua* remaining *alta* until the wind drops. This happened on the 4th November 1966, and the second tide into Venice that day reached an unprecedented six feet above normal high level.

Nobody drowned and no work of art was damaged in this flood. Florence, inundated by the river Arno the same stormy day, had much the more tragic emergency. Her massive rescue operation produced techniques of repair and restoration which were immeasurably useful in Venice later, when – after another exceptional *acqua alta* in November 1967 suggested that major floods might now be annual events – international attention turned to Venetian problems. In the intervening year the dire state of the city had been discovered. Impoverishment and neglect had left the art and monuments at risk throughout the 19th century, and in the 20th the industrial zones of the mainland had greatly increased pollution. UNESCO declared Venice "a moral obligation on the international community", and soon over thirty organisations in fourteen countries had responded with private fund-raising for the retrieval of Venice as a work of art. Britain's was the "Italian Art and Archives Rescue Fund", reorganised in 1971 as "Venice in Peril".

The majority of buildings in Venice are of brick, faced with stone, resting on wooden piles sunk into the clay (underwater the wood petrifies rock-hard; only exposed to air can it weaken and rot). The Venetians knew the value of a damp course, and used a layer of Istrian marble, impervious to water and salt air. But big waves from motor boats, let alone an *acqua alta*, can bring the canal water above the damp course so that moisture repeatedly reaches the brick. Even if the perennial damp problem fluctuates, apparently dried-out walls can be so penetrated by salt in a capillary action that brick is reduced to the consistency of powdered sugar. Porous stone, once inundated by salt water, is not only corroded by salt but vulnerable to other pollution. The industries at Marghera used to discharge a long list of chemicals into air and water, and Venetian flues emitted the residue of oil-fired central heating. (Pigeons were also blamed by some, but experiment revealed that their droppings were protective, not corrosive.) Not only do stone sculptures crumble: whole buildings are in danger of collapse as floor timbers and iron tie rods are exposed to the atmosphere. Frescoes, mosaics, and paintings whether attached to walls or (a Venetian habit) to ceilings, deteriorate with the surface behind them and to some extent also from the frontal attack of the atmosphere.

Action after 1966 began with the paintings. Canvases were typically enormous, and the first restoration laboratory was set up in the chill space of an abbey church disused since Napoleon. Apart from restoring its backing, each painting presented individual problems of chemical and photographic analysis, cleaning solvents and aesthetic judgement. Considerably less was known about rescuing stonework; experimental techniques such as consolidation with silicone resins were on occasion unsatisfactory. British experts developed a safe method of cleaning intricate carving by bombardment with high-velocity glass particles – with infinite patience, through a tool like a dentist's drill. On a larger scale, damp-proofing and stabilisation of whole buildings proceeded with success. All projects were undertaken with the guidance and permission of Venice's twin authorities for Galleries and Monuments – since 1978 given unwieldy

VENICE IN PERIL

titles (the Superintendent of the Artistic and Historic Heritage, and the Superintendent of the Architectural Heritage and the Environment) which reflect the complexities of Italian bureaucracy.

Other levels of it, Italian national and regional bodies funded by the government, confronted vast engineering and ecological problems. To control the *acqua alta* and protect Venice from flooding, moveable barriers were envisaged across the three sea entrances of the lagoon (opposition from shipping companies produced an interesting but fortunately temporary stipulation that the sea should be kept out at only two). A competition for this *Progettone* held in 1970 produced various designs, all feasible, all astronomically expensive. In 1975 a consortium including the Pirelli company proposed a cheaper scheme involving inflatable tubes, which caught international interest, but failed to survive bureaucratic procedures and commercial rivalry. The Italian government also seemed to favour a substantial permanent narrowing of the entrances, something which alarmed every expert trying to predict the effect on the lagoon. More than a decade later, with the Thames barrier at Woolwich as an achieved point of reference, experts are yet again studying the feasibility and possible consequences of the *Progettone*. Conservationists welcome the delay, convinced that the huge permanent structures necessary to position moveable barriers would incalculably change the flow of tides and currents.

One question – was Venice sinking? – found a solution. Much more relevant than the rising of a land mass and the melting of polar ice was the human interference in and around the lagoon. Twentieth-century Venice was subsiding at an accelerated rate, as a result of removing fresh water from beneath the bed of the lagoon, for use in the industrial zone. When instead of artesian wells a new aqueduct began to supply the needs, the water table rapidly recovered. Venice is no longer sinking: in 1986 it was reported that since 1970 the city has risen, by three-quarters of an inch.

There can be no such elegant answer to the internal problem of the lagoon. The necessary equilibrium between too much water and too little was a matter of checks and balances vigilantly enforced by the Venetian Republic, who in 1553 inscribed in marble (and in Latin) that "whoever in any way dares damage the public waters shall be declared an enemy of the State". Now, conflicting interests produce expensive mistakes. Alarmed at the potential dangers of modern cargo shipping passing through Venice, the authorities dredged a long new channel straight across two tidal basins to the mainland, ignoring the pattern of currents. Ships had trouble staying in its narrow course and heavier vessels had to be towed; costs soared, even before it silted up. Dredging continues but shipping has returned to the Giudecca Canal.

The ebb and flow of Adriatic tides are as essential as ever, for the health of canals and the shallow lagoon's ecology. It has to cope with discharge still from the petro-chemical industries, with fertilisers and pesticides drained from farmland, with household pollution from Venice. In recent years there have been some ominous accumulations of thick green algae, stinking itself in summer and suffocating small fish which putrefy in turn. Land reclamation, dredging, even the substitution of more solid barriers for the traditional nets of the fishing nurseries, all affect the working of the lagoon – about which, conclude the experts, almost nothing is known for certain.

Sightseeing

Galleries, museums and palaces

Opening hours in Venice are even more baffling than those of the average Italian city and they change about four times a year according to the season. The main closing day for museums is Monday. A few sights, including the Guggenheim collection, are closed in winter, and open only in the afternoon; the Accademia is open only in the morning (9am to 2pm). The tourist office can usually provide an up-to-date list of opening hours.

☛ Accademia

A rich and definitive collection of Venetian masterpieces spanning five centuries, starting from the early Venetian/Byzantine school. The order – subject to changes at all times – is more or less chronological with the exception of rooms 20 and 21 which jump back a couple of centuries. The worst rooms for crowding are 4 and 5 where the concentration of small masterpieces includes the legendary Tempest by Giorgione (the only painting behind glass) and the most beautiful of Giovanni Bellini's paintings. Lighting leaves a lot to be desired in places and since the galleries depend on natural light it's wise to go on a bright morning.

There are too many masterpieces to take in in one visit; for those with only an hour or two to spare, we list below the greatest treasures, which can be seen comfortably in a couple of hours.

Selected masterpieces:

Room 2: an outstanding group of altar-pieces of which the finest is Giovanni Bellini's majestic Madonna with Saints (or San Giobbe altarpiece, c1487); Carpaccio's Presentation of Jesus in the Temple, painted for the same church; Cima da Conegliano's serenely poetic Madonna of the Orange Tree

Room 4: a group of beautiful Madonnas by Giovanni Bellini of which the supreme example is the Madonna and Child with St Catherine and St Mary Magdalene. Notable works by non-Venetian artists are the St George by Mantegna and the contemplative Portrait of a Young Man by Memling

Room 5: more masterpieces by Bellini, notably the Madonna of the Little Trees and the Pietà. However, the painting that draws the greatest crowds here is Giorgione's enigmatic and evocative Tempest, one of the very few works definitely attributable to the artist – though its date and exact significance remain a mystery. Also by Giorgione is the extraordinarily realistic portrait of the Old Woman

Room 6: Titian's St John the Baptist (c1530), with the saint boldly presented as a muscular athlete in a theatrical pose

Room 7: Lorenzo Lotto's characteristically penetrating Portrait of a Young Man (c1524)

Room 8: Palma Vecchio's sumptuous and richly coloured Sacra Conversazione, heavily influenced by Titian – some believe that the landscape was finished by Titian himself when Palma Vecchio died

Room 10: Veronese's grandiose Feast in the House of Levi, covering an entire wall of this magnificent room. It was painted as the Last Supper in 1573 but the sensual realism and pagan pursuits in the painting (dogs, drunkards, dwarfs and so on) brought Veronese before a tribunal of the Inquisition, accused of heresy. Reluctant to eliminate the details which offended their religious sensibilities, Veronese did nothing more than change the title of the painting. In the same room Tintoretto's first great painting, the Miracle of St Mark (1548), creates a dramatic impact. In contrast Titian's Pietà is dark and sober; it was the artist's last work and was finished in 1576 by Palma Giovane who added the cherub with the torch

Room 11: radiant, richly coloured works by Veronese – the Marriage of St Catherine is an exquisite example of his use of sparkling colour; several Tintorettos; Bernardo Strozzi's exuberant baroque Banquet at the House of Simon; and the surviving fragment of Tiepolo's ceiling from the Scalzi church which was bombed in 1915

Room 16a: Piazzetta's Gypsy (or Soothsayer) c1740, distinctive for intense chiaroscuro – densely laid-on paint and dazzling luminosity

Room 17: a view by Canaletto, typical in its precision of detail and accuracy of perspective. Guardi's views of Venice are far more romantic and loosely handled

Room 20: faithfully recorded scenes of Venice by Gentile Bellini, Carpaccio and others, painted for the Scuola di San Giovanni Evangelista between 1494 and 1501. The scenes are painted in minute, colourful detail, providing a brilliant kaleidoscope of Venetian views. Gentile Bellini's Procession of the Cross in the Piazza San Marco shows how little has changed in the square since 1496, while Carpaccio's Healing of the Madman illustrates one of the earlier Rialto bridges, built of wood, with gondolas (like the ones you see today) passing below

Room 21: The Legend of St Ursula by Carpaccio, which was painted for the Scuola di Sant' Orsola, originally at the church of Santi Giovanni e Paolo. The cycle of large narrative canvases (begun 1490) illustrates the story of the daughter of a Christian King of Brittany who agreed to marry the son of a pagan king of England on condition that there would be two years before the marriage was consummated, during which time they would make a long pilgrimage accompanied by 10,000 virgins. The scenes are full of endearing detail and give a good insight into the life and customs of the time

Room 24: Titian's Presentation of the Virgin in the Temple (1538), still occupying its original position on the entrance wall of the gallery (once a charitable hostel). It is a complex and unusual composition worked in characteristically rich colours and subtle tones

☛ **Ca d'Oro** (Franchetti Gallery)
A very fine Venetian palace which, despite vandalism and heavy-handed alterations (notably by the ballet dancer Marie Taglioni, who was given the palace by a Russian prince), is again very beautiful. This is largely thanks to Baron Franchetti who in 1894 restored the palace and later bequeathed it – along with his impressive collection of paintings, sculpture and tapestries – to the state. Further renovated after the floods of 1966, the museum reopened in 1984. It includes works by Carpaccio, Mantegna, Titian, Guardi and Van Dyck plus interesting remnants of frescoes by Giorgione and Titian, and a fine collection of small bronzes. There is a fine courtyard and lovely views of the Grand Canal from the first floor loggia.

☛ **Ca' Pesaro** (Gallery of Modern Art)
A flamboyant palace designed by Longhena – a Baroque variation of Sansovino's Palazzo Corner. Its huge rooms house the Gallery of Modern Art (presently undergoing restoration), a large and varied collection of 19th- and

20th-century paintings and sculpture by Italian and other artists – among them Rodin, Chagall, Klee and Kandinsky. The palace also contains the rather mediocre Oriental Museum.

☞ Ca' Rezzonico (Museum of the Venetian 18th century)

A large stately palace designed and begun by Longhena in the 1660s (but completed long after his death) and similar in style to Ca' Pesaro. Robert Browning died here in December 1889 while staying with his son, Pen. The inside is well preserved and gives a very good idea of the affluent style of 18th-century Venetian life. Large rather grand rooms are decorated with painted ceilings (some by Tiepolo), suitably Rococo canvases and period furniture.

☞ Correr Museum

The Civic Museum of Venice, on the south side of Piazza San Marco. The first floor is devoted to detailed historic documentation, the second to a picture gallery. The art collection as a whole gives a good idea of the transition of Venetian art from early Gothic to 17th century, and there are excellent introductions to each room in English. Highlights include two masterpieces by Giovanni Bellini – the Crucifixion (1460) and the Transfiguration (1465); Carpaccio's famous Two Courtesans (c1500); and the damaged Dead Christ and Angels by the Sicilian artist Antonello da Messina.

☞ Doges' Palace (Palazzo Ducale)

The residence of the Venetian doges and seat of the Government from the 9th century to the fall of the Venetian Republic in the late 18th century. The interior of the palace, which is more or less as it was 400 years ago, has none of the light and airy quality of its pink-shimmering façade. The rooms are large and rather gloomy, decorated by dimly lit canvases of monumental proportions – some great works of art, others no more than historical documentation. The magnificent 15th-century gateway, courtyard and staircase make a fitting introduction.

A visit to the interior covers the well-displayed armoury and various stately meeting rooms. The doges' private apartments can only be seen when they are used for special exhibitions (for which you have to buy a ticket).

The **Sala del Collegio** has an opulent ceiling by Veronese, glorifying Venice, but the most important room is the massive **Sala del Maggior Consiglio** which accommodated 3,000 guests when Henry III was entertained there in 1574. It was here that the doges were elected and where the last doge abdicated in 1797, marking the end of the Venetian Republic. Covering the entire eastern wall is Tintoretto's Paradise, painted in 1588 when the artist was 70 and said to be the largest oil painting in the world. Cold, dark corridors lead past former prison cells to the notorious Bridge of Sighs – named, according to anti-Venetian writers, after the lamentations of prisoners who crossed it (although only one is recorded to have done so).

☞ Fortuny Museum

Turn-of-the-century house which belonged to the Spanish artist Mariano Fortuny, famed for Fortuny silks. There are paintings (of dubious quality) by the man himself, silk dresses and Fortuny textiles. Temporary photographic exhibitions are held on the second floor.

☞ Guggenheim Collection

An outstanding collection of modern art, housed in the late Peggy Guggenheim's home on the Grand Canal. The neoclassical *palazzo* was begun in 1749 and was never finished – hence its alternative name "Palazzo Non

Finito." Cubist, Abstract and Surrealist paintings and sculpture are beautifully displayed in light airy rooms, and the garden is the setting for sculpture. Artists represented include Picasso, Mondrian, de Chirico, Max Ernst, Magritte, Bacon, Brancusi, Dali and Moore. The best collection of modern art in Venice, but with few Venetian works of art.

☛ Natural History Museum
Venice's zoological and botanical collections are housed in the Fondaco dei Turchi, the former warehouse of the Turkish merchants, standing right on the Grand Canal. In 1853 Ruskin found the palace "a ghastly ruin", but it was almost entirely rebuilt after 1858. Exhibits include one of the biggest dinosaur skeletons in existence and a giant crocodile, both found in the Sahara in 1973.

☛ Naval Museum
A large collection of models of 17th- to 19th-century boats including galleys and gondolas, housed in a former granary near the Arsenal.

☛ Palazzo Querini-Stampalia
A pretty Renaissance *palazzo* close to Campo Santa Maria Formosa, bequeathed with its contents to the city by Count Giovanni Querini, and housing an interesting and varied collection of 14th- to 18th-century paintings, mainly Venetian. Tucked behind the church, it's missed by most tourists.

☛ Scuola Grande dei Carmini
Headquarters of the Carmelite confraternity, built in 1663 and partly designed by Longhena. The highlight is Tiepolo's ceiling (1739-44) representing St Simon Stock receiving the scapular of the Carmelite order from the Virgin – a typically hedonistic and carefree work of art where the architecture recedes into dizzy distances; it was such a success that Tiepolo was made an honorary member of the confraternity.

☛ Scuola di San Giorgio degli Schiavoni
Tiny *scuola* founded in 1451 by the Slavs (or Dalmatians) to protect their colony of merchants in Venice. It houses one of the most exquisite collections of paintings in Venice – a frieze by Carpaccio of episodes from the lives of the three Dalmatian patron saints, St George, St Tryphon and St Jerome. The scenes are vivid, exotic and full of graphic detail; several are set in Venice or Venetia, and give a very realistic insight into life in the early 16th century.

☛ Scuola Grande di San Rocco
A vast monument to the work of Tintoretto. This is the most important single collection of paintings by him, commissioned by the *scuola* and painted between 1564 and 1588. There are 24 scenes of the life of Christ, almost all of them vast, theatrical canvases displaying in different ways Tintoretto's unique ability to convey a dramatic effect by the use of intricate composition, movement and most of all light. The Crucifixion, an immensely powerful work of art, is worth singling out.

RENAISSANCE ART IN VENICE

Venice itself is a supremely picturesque work of art, and one does not visit it primarily to spend time in museums. Besides, Venetian masterpieces are so widely spread round the great museums of the world and the country houses of Britain that the need to go to Venice to enjoy its art is not compelling. Which is not to say that the art is not there, nor to deny its historical importance. The Renaissance in Rome ended abruptly with the sack in 1527, and the importance of Florence as a creative centre declined rapidly under the Medici dukes. Only Venice came through the 16th century with its political independence inviolate and the fire of its artistic genius alight. The torch was picked up not by local artists (Venetian 17th-century art is thoroughly undistinguished) but by the foreign creators of the Baroque, who inherited more from Venice than they did from Florence or Rome.

"Florence for line, Venice for colour" runs a traditional summary of Renaissance painting. In a country dominated by inter-city rivalries, local styles were perceived in terms of polarisation and opposition. Vasari records the expatriate Venetian artist Sebastiano del Piombo's view of Titian, namely that if he had studied design he would have done stupendous things considering his mastery of colour, and might have equalled Raphael and Michelangelo. A similar remark is attributed to Michelangelo himself ("if only the Venetians learnt to draw at a young age... "), the point of the stories being more to prove Florentine superiority than to shed light on the art of Titian. You would be forgiven for imagining that Florentine paintings are dry and drab, Venetian ones brilliantly colourful but sloppy and without design. The surprising truth is that Florentine Renaissance paintings look brighter and more colourful than Venetian ones.

The difference is one of method. Influenced by Michelangelo, a sculptor first and a fresco-painter second, Vasari defined a painting as a plane with patches of colour filling spaces circumscribed by clear outlines; painting, as we would say, by numbers. The Venetian practice was quite different: drawing did not become a self-sufficient art form as it did in Florence, and neither complexity and refinement of gesture and pose nor virtuoso anatomising were Venetian preoccupations. Venetians drew to take notes and work out ideas and compositions. On the canvas forms were built up with masses of colour, the drawing was done with the brush not the pen. Put in such terms, it is not surprising that the more painterly Venetian manner had more to offer artists of future generations, from Rubens and Van Dyck to Manet and Cézanne (who summed up his own approach with the statement that colour and form could not be separated).

The idea of ideological opposition between regional styles of painting is not a great aid to understanding how they evolved. Far from occupying entrenched positions, artists travelled and studied widely and carefully, picking up and passing on ideas. Prints were even more influential in disseminating art across Europe. The ideas of humanist Florence did not find a natural welcome in the conservative city of Venice, but in the third quarter of the 15th century the Venetian artist Giovanni Bellini could study the work of Donatello (in the antiquarian city of Padua) and that of Andrea Mantegna, his brother-in-law and one of the most seriously archaeological of Renaissance artists in his attitude to the art of Antiquity.

To Mantegna's often harsh realism Bellini added humanity. His paintings of religious subjects have a depth of feeling that is almost unbearably moving and the same quality produced some outstanding portraits. Equally open to influences from the north (perhaps via the art of Antonello da Messina, who is said to have taught him the

RENAISSANCE ART IN VENICE

northern technique of painting in oil), Bellini mastered the depiction of light and atmosphere to create an utterly convincing ideal world of perfect calm and naturalness. Figures fit immovably into a lovingly painted landscape or the painted architecture of a chapel extending the space where the viewer stands. The altarpieces in Venetian churches (the Frari, San Zaccaria, and San Giovanni Crisostomo) and the Accademia are among Bellini's greatest masterpieces.

Whereas Florentine humanists had studied the ancient philosophers, the Renaissance in Venice meant a revival of interest in classical lyric poetry. At the turn of the century a new Romanticism suddenly became fashionable in Venice and a new secular art was part of the movement. Although the form was new, it was only a short step (and one that the old master was himself able to take) from Bellini's serene Madonnas to paintings of naked women in Arcadian landscapes and from his music-making angels to idealised portraits of effeminate lutanists. And although the art is distinctively Venetian, local artists did not work in a vacuum: such diverse artists as Perugino, Dürer and Leonardo da Vinci spent time in Venice, and contributed in different ways to the style known as Giorgionismo, after the artist credited with inventing it.

Giorgione is said by Vasari to have given the "dry, crude and stiff Venetian manner" (not the biographer's fairest judgement) "new softness and relief", using light and shade to create a mood no doubt under the influence of Leonardo. Giorgione himself is an irresistibly romantic figure – an accomplished musician and incurable womaniser who died young in 1510, having caught the plague from his girlfriend. To complete the chiaroscuro image, Giorgione's work is shrouded in mystery. Contemporaries could not tell it apart from that of two other former pupils of Bellini, Titian and Sebastiano del Piombo, so it is hardly surprising that art historians are still arguing about the authorship of key works of the first decade of the 16th century. One of these works is the famous Concert Champêtre (in the Louvre), a scene where musicians and naked women picnic in an ideal landscape. Try as we may to read eroticism into the painting, it is not there. This is the Venetian counterpart of a Florentine façade or painting of an ideal city: a representation of total harmony which the Florentines sought in intellectual theories of proportion, the Venetians in a visual poem of concerted sensual delight.

Paintings such as the Concert invite complicated allegorical interpretation, and many Venetian romantic paintings and portraits, such as Giorgione's famous Tempesta (in the Accademia), probably refer to specific literary texts. But on the whole the attitude of Venetian patrons to art seems to have been refreshingly unintellectual and Venetian painting, like Venice, is primarily a visual feast. If the Tempesta has an obscure specific meaning, this was lost on a highly cultivated collector who described the painting not long after Giorgione's death. And if Giorgione's Venus and the naked women in the Concert Champêtre express a lofty idea of beauty, patrons soon developed a more basic appreciation of paintings of beautiful naked women. Palma Vecchio (c1480-1528), painter of countless voluptuous bedclothed La Bellas, is the great master of the Page Three school of Venetian art, but Titian also catered for the same taste, dressing up the subject matter (if not the model) in the clothing of ancient mythology when required, as in a series of paintings (which he called poems) for Philip II of Spain. Titian's Venus of Urbino (1538; in the Uffizi, Florence) was described by its first owner simply as "the naked woman" and by a recent critic as "pure hedonism... an invitation to love" (Michael Levey). In the less liberal climate of the end of the century the painting's

RENAISSANCE ART IN VENICE

owner described it as a lascivious work which he kept only because it was by Titian, an interesting early contribution to the "porn or art?" debate.

During the course of a very long career Titian (c1485-1576) became the most sought-after painter in Europe, courted by royalty mainly for his portraits. Charles V, who in a famous and probably apocryphal story stoops to pick up the artist's brush, joked that Titian's portraits made him look even uglier than he was, so that people who met the Emperor were pleasantly surprised. In reality Titian's achievement in his portraits (especially those of Charles V) was quite the opposite: abandoning the portraitist's traditional concern for the minutiae of physical detail, he consistently succeeded in endowing his sitters with great nobility of face and bearing (they were nearly all men and women of wealth and high social standing) without any loss of vitality and character.

Titian never allowed the demand for portraits to dominate his work. Visiting Venice and other nearby cities gives the chance to see some of his greatest religious paintings, including the glorious Assumption (1516/19) over the high altar of the Frari in Venice, Titian's first public commission and the painting that established his leading position in Venice after the deaths of Bellini and Giorgione. There is no question of deficient drawing or design here, as Titian takes on Raphael at his own heroic game, and wins. More than his portraits, these works show how attentively Titian studied the work of other artists (notably Michelangelo and Raphael) and classical sculpture throughout his life. But ready as he was to dip into this rich image bank, Titian did not attempt a more Florentine/Roman style, and in later life moved instead towards freer handling and an increasingly expressive use of colour. Sebastiano del Piombo took the other course, leaving Venice for Rome soon after Giorgione's death and attaching himself to Michelangelo.

Although active like Titian in all the branches of painting, Veronese (1528-88) was essentially a wonderfully inventive, hugely influential and thoroughly enjoyable decorator in what became a great Venetian tradition. A well-known story no doubt exaggerates his nonchalant approach to subject matter: Veronese filled a huge painting of the Last Supper with all sorts of richly-attired figures and such off-the-ball incidents as an apostle picking his teeth with a fork. Hauled up before angry inquisitors, Veronese pleaded artistic licence but wisely admitted that perhaps it was not fitting to treat the Last Supper in such a way. He was given a month to make the necessary changes, and did so, coolly renaming the painting Feast in the House of Levi. It is now in the Accademia. Veronese's decorative art can be seen at its best in the Villa Maser (*see under Ásolo in Northern Cities chapter*).

Tintoretto (1518-94) was an artist more in tune with the spirit of the Counter-Reformation, and devoted much of his time to the task of decorating walls and ceilings of Venetian palaces (notably the Scuola di San Rocco) with religious compositions. He covered vast areas with great speed, fluency and a dynamic energy which is the greatest quality of his art, together with dramatic light effects. At the age of 70 he painted a 10 by 30 yard Paradise for the council chamber of the doges' palace. On his studio wall Tintoretto pinned his motto, or perhaps his aim, "colour of Titian, drawing of Michelangelo". Fortunately this by now familiar impossible dream did not come between Tintoretto and originality. "Clouds and whirlwinds and fire and infinity of earth and sea", wrote Ruskin, who felt that he didn't know what painting was until he discovered Tintoretto.

Churches

Paintings and frescoes in Venetian churches are frequently hard to see, either because of poor or non-existent lighting or because they're hidden away in some obscure corner. Even in a relatively unknown church you may find a Titian or a Tintoretto tucked away in a side chapel or sacristy, and sometimes the only way to get access is to bribe the custodian. Take 100L and 200L coins for possible slot-machine lighting, and for ceiling paintings ask for a mirror (specchio) which will magnify the frescoes and relieve neck-ache.

Churches in Venice have erratic opening hours – most close for lunch and some are also closed in the afternoon.

☛ Basilica di San Marco
The sumptuous symbol of Venetian glory, dominating Piazza San Marco, built to enshrine the body of saint Mark which was smuggled from Alexandria in 828 (legend goes that the body was buried under slices of pork to keep away the Moslems). Saint Mark became not only the patron saint of the city (usurping saint Theodore) but a major figurehead of Venetian power and justice. The basilica came to be the private chapel of the doges and the civic centre and church of the Venetian state. The building you see today is essentially the 11th-century basilica rebuilt after a fire in the 10th century, and enriched throughout the centuries. This "treasure heap", as Ruskin called it, is a bizarre museum, where every niche is lavishly decorated. The dazzling mosaics are Byzantine and Renaissance; some of the finest examples are in the first two cupolas, and on the walls of the aisles.

The richest contents of all are the **Pala d'Oro**, a beautiful golden altar-piece encrusted with jewels, and the **Treasury**, a hoard of silver and gold, precious stones and glass looted during the Crusaders' conquest of Constantinople. The gallery (*loggia*) above gives you close-up views of some of the mosaics (and also of the swarming hordes of tourists who do much to destroy the aura of magic and mysticism with which the basilica is often credited). Near the gallery exit are the famous Roman bronze horses (another conquest from Constantinople), which once adorned the façade but are now kept inside to protect them from pollution. They have been replaced by copies.

☛ Madonna dell' Orto
A beautiful Gothic church painstakingly restored by the British Venice in Peril Fund after the 1966 floods. This was Tintoretto's parish church and he is buried here. There are several important paintings by him in the church.

☛ Redentore
The apogee of Palladian religious architecture, its great dome one of the most conspicuous landmarks of Venice. In 1577 the Venetian Senate swore to build a church to Christ the Redeemer (*Redentore*) in gratitude for the deliverance of Venice from the plague which had ravaged the city; Palladio was chosen to design it. Every year the doge visited the church, via a bridge of boats built over the Giudecca Canal, and the tradition is still carried on every third Sunday in July. Some find the classic perfection of the facade and interior rather stark and aseptic.

☛ San Giorgio dei Greci
A church with a leaning tower, built for the Greek community in the 16th century. The interior is ornately decorated and it contains Byzantine works. The neighbouring **Scuola di San Nicolò dei Greci** houses the Museum of

Icons, a comprehensive collection of paintings combining local and Byzantine style, by Greek artists who worked in Venice. (If the church is locked asked the custodian of the museum to open it).

☛ San Giorgio Maggiore

The red brick and marble façade and towering campanile of Palladio's church, set on its own island, form one of the most popular perspectives in Venice. The interior is cold, white and classical and, like the Redentore, gives a remarkable effect of expansion as you approach the altar. The church houses Tintoretto's Last Supper and Gathering of the Manna (1592-94), on either side of the choir, and several other works of art in the side chapels. There are excellent views from the top of the campanile (you can go up by lift). Behind the church are fine cloisters and a staircase by Longhena (now belonging to the Cini foundation).

☛ San Giovanni Crisostomo

The last and probably the most restrained work of Mauro Coducci, leading architect of late 15th-century Venice. The beautiful Renaissance interior contains paintings which include Sebastiano del Piombo's Seven Saints (1510; over the altar) and Giovanni Bellini's Saints Jerome, Christopher and Augustine (1513).

☛ Santi Giovanni e Paolo (San Zanipolo)

Huge brick edifice dominating one of Venice's finest squares and rivalling the Frari as the city's greatest Gothic church. The Pantheon of Venice, it is dominated by the tombs of 46 doges and other dignatories. A fire in 1867 destroyed altar-pieces by Titian and Giovanni Bellini. Surviving works of art include ceiling paintings by Veronese in the Rosary Chapel and an early polyptych by Giovanni Bellini in the right hand nave.

☛ Santa Maria Assunta (Gesuiti)

Uncompromisingly Baroque church rebuilt by the Jesuits in the early 18th century. The first altar on the left has a fascinating, grim night scene by Titian of The Martyrdom of St Lawrence (c1557).

☛ Santa Maria Formosa

Fine Renaissance church dominating a lively local square. The interior is plain and restful to the eye; paintings include Palma Vecchio's St Barbara altar-piece and Vivarini's Madonna of Mercy (1473).

☛ Santa Maria Gloriosa dei Frari (Frari)

Vast Gothic church and convent built by Franciscan friars (*frari*) in typically austere style (completed in the 15th century). The interior is a gallery of masterpieces. Titian's Assumption of the Virgin (1518) crowning the main altar is a gloriously rich work of art; and his Madonna di Ca' Pésaro (1519-26; commissioned by the Pésaro family, various members of which feature in the lower half) is another masterpiece of light, colour and composition. Both paintings are major landmarks of High Renaissance art in Venice. Another very fine work is Giovanni Bellini's Madonna and Child with Saints (1488; in the sacristy). Sculptures include Donatello's St John the Baptist, in wood (1439), and the somewhat incongruous monument to the sculptor Antonio Canova after a design by Canova himself for a monument to Titian. The outstanding interior feature of the church itself is the beautifully carved marble choir screen, dating from the 15th century.

☛ Santa Maria dei Miracoli

A little Renaissance gem built by Pietro Lombardo to enshrine a miraculous image of the Virgin. The façade is exquisitely carved and inlaid with marble.

The interior is also beautiful, its walls decorated with rose and grey marble and its ceiling covered with portraits of saints and prophets. Not surprisingly this is one of the most popular churches for Venetian marriages.

☞ Santa Maria del Rosario (Gesuati)

A rococo prettification of Palladio's Redentore across the Giudecca canal, echoing its dome and twin campanile. The spacious, radiant interior has a ceiling frescoed with early works by Tiepolo, already illustrating his mastery of colour, light and ingenious perspective. Altar-pieces in the chapels include Tiepolo's lovely Virgin and Saints (c1740), a powerful Crucifixion by Tintoretto, and works by Piazzetta and Sebastiano Ricci.

☞ Santa Maria della Salute

This Baroque masterpiece by Longhena, built on more than a million piles at the entrance to the Grand Canal, was compared by Henry James to "some great lady on the threshold of her salon. She is more ample and serene, more seated at her door, than all the copyists have told us, with her domes and scrolls, her scolloped buttresses and statues forming a pompous crown, and her wide steps disposed on the ground like the train of a robe." The interior of monumental proportions and dramatic vistas is as theatrical as the exterior.

The church was built to commemorate the deliverence of Venice from the plague of 1630 although it was not finally consecrated until after Longhena's death, in 1687. Every year in November a commemorative procession takes place from San Marco, and a bridge of boats is built across the Grand Canal from Santa Maria del Giglio.

☞ San Sebastiano

A church that is rarely accessible (open some mornings only) but one which is worth seeing for the works of Veronese – who took refuge here when he fled from Verona in 1556 having allegedly committed murder. There are striking ceiling paintings with brilliant colours and masterly foreshortening (ask the custodian to switch on lights and give you a magnifying mirror) and superb scenes from the Life of St Sebastian in the chancel. Veronese was buried near the organ in 1588.

☞ San Stae

Recently restored Baroque church on the Grand Canal, used now for concerts and exhibitions. Lively statues embellish the façade while the interior is decorated with paintings by leading 18th-century Venetian artists, among them Tiepolo and Piazzetta.

☞ San Zaccaria

Unusual church built in a successful compromise of flamboyant Gothic and classical Renaissance styles. One of Giovanni Bellini's first altar-pieces, Madonna with Saints (1505), dominates the left wall. Don't miss the frescoes in the Cappella di San Tarasio, by the Florentine artist Andrea Castagno.

☞ Scalzi

An elaborate and imposing Baroque church at the railway station end of the Grand Canal, described by Henry James as "all marble and malachite, all a cold, hard glitter and a costly, curly ugliness…". The interior is profusely decorated with marble and sculpture but the finest work of art, the ceiling by Tiepolo, was destroyed by a bomb in 1915. The sketch and some fragments are now in the Accademia gallery.

Excursions from Venice

SAN MICHELE

One of the small islands nearest to Venice (10 mins on waterbus 5),
whose pristine white Renaissance church, and cemetery studded
with pines, are clearly visible from the Fondamente Nuove, Venice's
northern quays. Napoleon, who banned burials in the city,
established the cemetery in the early 18th century; among the
eminent visitors to Venice who are buried here are Ezra Pound, Igor
Stravinsky and Frederick Rolfe (Baron Corvo).

MURANO

One of the larger islands of the lagoon, best known for its
glassworks. The furnaces were first set up in the 13th century and
Murano became a prosperous island exporting fine crystal ware.
Today it's sprawling and slightly melancholy, usually inundated
with tourists on organised sightseeing trips who see no more than a
glassblowing display and showrooms with the finished products.
It's far more interesting to take a ferry independently (it takes 15
mins on waterbus 5 or 12) and see the main sights which are
evidence of its former splendour.

☛ **Glassmaking museum** (Museo dell' Arte Vetraria)   About 4,000 glass
pieces, many of them rare and dating back to the 15th century.

☛ **Santi Maria e Donato**   Much restored, this is one of the most important
Veneto-Byzantine buildings of the 7th-century. Inside there's a magnificent
mosaic floor and above the apse a Byzantine mosaic of the Madonna.

VENICE LIDO

Venice's beach resort, on a seven-mile strip of land separating the
Venetian lagoon from the Adriatic (reached in 10 to 20 mins on
waterbus 1, 2, 6 or 11). Indeed the beach is the only real attraction
and even that has its drawbacks, particularly if you're imagining
something out of the film of *Death in Venice*. The water is polluted by
the industry at Mestre and – apart from two scruffy public sections at
either end – the beach is organised by hotels which levy exorbitant
charges for the use of facilities. Plentiful activities include sports.
There's a summer casino and an International Film Festival.

BURANO

An appealing little island (reached in 35 mins on waterbus 12) of
brightly painted houses and friendly fish restaurants. In the 16th
century Burano made famous lace; in the 19th the industry was
revived; today lace is on sale everywhere, though not much of the
modern stuff is made by the traditional methods on show in the
Scuola dei Merletti (Lace School).

TORCELLO

A tiny forlorn island lying in a desolate part of the lagoon (45 mins on waterbus 12). When you arrive on its shores it's hard to believe that Torcello and its neighbour islet was once the most prosperous outpost in the lagoon with 20,000 inhabitants. From the 7th century it was the home of refugees from Altinum on the mainland, driven out by the Barbarians. Decay set in in the 14th century with the rise of Venice and the spread of malaria. The only evidence today of its most splendid era is the **cathedral** (rebuilt in the 11th century) with its outstanding Byzantine mosaics, heavily restored. The other attractions of Torcello are the two *locande* (inns), one of which is the famous and expensive Locanda Cipriani.

Hotels

ACCADEMIA   **£££**
Fondamenta Maravegie
Dorsoduro 1058   *Open all year*
30123 Venezia   *Tel: (041) 710188*

A delightful *pensione* which is so popular with British regulars that you may need to book a year ahead. The charming 17th-century villa is set well back from the Grand Canal, close to the Accademia, only about 10 minutes on foot from Piazza San Marco and a short walk from the prettiest parts of Dorsoduro. If you're lucky, you'll hear little more than the occasional delivery barge or launch, the distant chug of waterbuses, and the birds in the back garden; but rooms are not always quiet. The *pensione* feels like a relaxed private home. There is an unpretentious medley of antiques and paintings, with occasional modern touches. Bedrooms (6 without private facilities) are pleasantly old-fashioned, but not always well co-ordinated or spacious. In fine weather breakfast is served in the front garden which overlooks the narrow San Trovaso canal. There's a grassy garden at the back.

Facilities: *26 bedrooms (AC)*   **Credit/charge cards accepted:** *Amex, Diners, Eurocard, Visa*   **Landing stage:** *Accademia*

AGLI ALBORETTI   **££**
Rio Terrà Sant' Agnese
Dorsoduro 882/4   *Open all year*
30123 Venezia   *Tel: (041) 5230058*

A delightful little family-run *pensione* facing the back of the Accademia in an unspoilt area of Dorsoduro. The reception is a cosy wood-panelled room with a 17th-century hand-made model galleon in its streetside window; the sitting room and restaurant are homely, with a mixed collection of paintings. Bedrooms are modern, spotlessly clean and simple with plain white walls. Behind the hotel there's a pretty trellised courtyard for breakfast.

Facilities: *19 bedrooms*   **Credit/charge cards accepted:** *Amex*   **Landing stage:** *Accademia*

CASA FROLLO ££
Fondamenta Zitelle
Giudecca 50   *Closed end Nov to mid-Mar*
30123 Venezia   *Tel: (041) 5222723*

There is nothing to tell you this fine old mansion on the waterfront is a hotel, and once inside you could well be in a private home. The main room is a large, rather grand drawing room with large bowls of flowers on antique tables, a superb collection of paintings, from old masters to modern art, and stunning views across the lagoon to Santa Maria della Salute and the domes of San Marco and the Campanile. Bedrooms don't all live up to the splendour of the public rooms and there are very few private bathrooms.

Facilities: *26 bedrooms*   **Credit/charge cards accepted:** *none*   **Landing stage:** *Zitelle*

CIPRIANI £££££
Giudecca 10   *Closed end Nov to mid-Mar*
30123 Venezia   *Tel: (041) 5207744*

This is one of the most famous hotels in Europe, under the management of the Venice Simplon Orient-Express. The modern building occupies three lush acres at the eastern tip of Giudecca – a little oasis at the otherwise suburban end of the island. Guests are transported across the lagoon from the city by private launch and delivered at the banks of the Cipriani's immaculate gardens; and such is the luxury of the hotel that the great temptation is to stay put. There are creamy bedrooms overlooking the gardens or the lagoon behind Giudecca (there are no views across to Venice), and impeccable marble bathrooms. Public areas are elegant and comfortable. In summer lunch is served by the pool, dinner outside or in the stylish dining room which has lovely views of the lagoon. After a long day's sightseeing you can swim in the Olympic pool, have a sauna or Turkish bath, play tennis or get your hair done. If these extras are not important to you, the Cipriani is a very extravagant choice.

Facilities: *98 bedrooms; restaurant; lift; swimming pool (covered and heated in winter); tennis court; fitness centre; private yacht harbour; private motorboat service to San Marco*   **Credit/charge cards accepted:** *Amex, Diners, Eurocard, Visa*   **Landing stage:** *Zitelle*

DANIELI £££££
Riva degli Schiavoni
Castello 4196   *Open all year*
30122 Venezia   *Tel: (041) 5226480*

This fine Gothic palace has been a hotel since 1822 and has had its fair share of famous visitors – Georges Sand and Alfred de Musset among them. It has always ranked among the finest hotels in Venice, although over the last few years it appears to have been resting too much on its laurels and losing regulars to other hotels. But whatever the complaints (usually about service), the Danieli is unlikely to lose its two best assets: the stunning views across the lagoon, and the Gothic foyer built around a courtyard. Bedrooms are luxuriously furnished and there's a choice of traditional or new styles. In the late '50s the hotel was expanded and an annexe built beside it in stark, unsightly contrast; however the rooftop restaurant has glorious views.

Facilities: *236 bedrooms (AC); restaurant; lift; private launch service to airport and Lido* **Credit/charge cards accepted:** *Amex, Diners, Eurocard, Visa* **Landing stage:** *San Zaccaria*

DO POZZI   £££
Calle Larga XXII Marzo
San Marco 2373   *Open all year*
30124 Venezia   *Tel: (041) 707855*

Tucked away in a tiny alleyway close to Piazza San Marco, the do Pozzi is quiet and central. It is not perhaps as immediately appealing as the nearby Flora although it does have its own quiet, leafy courtyard and bedrooms are comfortable and reliable, albeit on the small side. Furnishings are well co-ordinated in browns and beiges, and there's a large collection of modern art. Breakfast is taken in the courtyard, weather permitting; otherwise, there is normally a fight for the few tables in the breakfast room. There is no bar. For lunch and dinner guests are often cajoled into patronising the adjoining Raffaele restaurant (closed Thurs) under the same ownership; this has the advantage of a pretty quayside terrace but prices are steep for the quality of food.

Facilities: *35 bedrooms (AC); lift* **Credit/charge cards accepted:** *Amex, Diners, Eurocard, Visa* **Landing stage:** *San Marco/Santa Maria del Giglio*

LA FENICE ET DES ARTISTES   ££££
Campiello de la Fenice
San Marco 1936   *Open all year*
30124 Venezia   *Tel: (041) 5232333*

The Fenice is right by the opera house and the hotel has a regular clientèle of actors, musicians and artists, as well as tourists. It stands in a quiet square ten minutes from Piazza San Marco and the only noise at night is from the taverna below (under separate management). Downstairs the hotel offers either the civilised comfort of its various salons where marble, velvet and antiques merge successfully with modern art, or the bright, inviting atmosphere of two patios, the larger of which is used for breakfast. Upstairs there are marble corridors and staircases, high quality carpeting and a variety of rooms ranging from very elegant to simple. There is no restaurant and the taverna beside the hotel is overpriced; but there are plenty of inviting and cheaper places to eat in the neighbourhood. Good value for a comfortable central hotel.

Facilities: *68 bedrooms (AC); lift to some rooms only* **Credit/charge cards accepted:** *none* **Landing stage:** *San Marco*

FLORA ££££

Calle Larga XXII Marzo
San Marco 2283a *Closed mid-Nov to end Jan*
30124 Venezia *Tel: (041) 5225324*

This favourite little haunt of English and Americans lies five minutes from
Piazza San Marco, in a quiet cul-de-sac off a smart shopping street. The
garden gives it immediate appeal: stone fountains, shrubs in urns, creepers
and flower beds. The reception area is small and welcoming, with velvet
armchairs, prints of Venice and views through an arch to the garden.
Breakfasts (which are unusually generous) are served in the pink salon or,
weather permitting, outside. Bedrooms range from spacious and elegant
(with brocaded walls and traditional Venetian furniture) to cramped and
un-coordinated (some doubles are adequate only as singles). Overall,
however, this delightful little hotel rarely disappoints. It is one of the few
Venetian hotels which refuses package tours and as a result the atmosphere
is rather more exclusive and intimate than many other hotels in Venice.

Facilities: *44 bedrooms (AC on request); lift;* **Credit/charge cards accepted:**
Amex, Diners, Eurocard, Visa **Landing stage:** *San Marco*

GIORGIONE £££

SS. Apostoli
Cannaregio 4587 *Open all year*
30121 Venezia *Tel: (041) 5289332*

A quiet hotel in one of the prettiest and least spoilt parts of Cannaregio, just
off Campo Santi Apostoli. Although slightly faded outside and in, this is
nevertheless a civilised and spacious hotel with character. Meals are taken in
a creeper-covered courtyard or in the informal restaurant. Bedrooms are well
cared for and prettily furnished with Venetian carved and painted bedheads.

Facilities: *56 bedrooms; restaurant; lift* **Credit/charge cards accepted:** *Amex,*
Eurocard, Visa **Landing stage:** *Cà d'Oro*

GRITTI PALACE £££££

Campo Santa Maria del Giglio
San Marco 2467 *Open all year*
30124 Venezia *Tel: (041) 794611*

Here – for those who can afford it – is the ultimate in formal luxury in one of
the most exclusive locations in Venice, praised by many for its setting,
elegance and exquisite attention to detail. The *palazzo* once belonged to the
doge Andrea Gritti, whose portrait you can see in one of the salons. It stands
on the Grand Canal with superb views. Since it opened in 1948 its clients
have included Somerset Maugham, Graham Greene and Ernest Hemingway.
Today the majority of guests are Americans. Public rooms are furnished with
fine antiques, oil paintings, mirrors, huge crystal chandeliers, and Persian
rugs on marble floors. Bedrooms are the height of luxury: either traditional
with wood floors, chandeliers and brocade curtains, or newer with mock
marble wall panels, wall-to-wall carpeting, matching fabrics and antiques.

The cheapest are the internal rooms. The waterside restaurant terrace is one of the most delightful spots in Venice.

Facilities: *90 bedrooms (AC); restaurant; lift; private launch service to airport and Lido* **Credit/charge cards accepted:** *Amex, Diners, Eurocard, Visa* **Landing stage:** *Santa Maria del Giglio*

KETTE ££££
Piscina San Moisè
San Marco 2053 *Open all year*
30124 Venezia *Tel: (041) 5222730*

A charming small hotel in a quiet, narrow street close to the Fenice Theatre. The whole hotel was carefully refurbished a few years ago and it's still looking new and spruce. Rooms are in traditional Venetian style and there's an interesting collection of art.

Facilities: *50 bedrooms (AC); lift* **Credit/charge cards accepted:** *Amex, Diners, Eurocard, Visa* **Landing stage:** *San Marco*

MONACO AND GRAND CANAL £££££
Calle Vallaresso
San Marco 1325 *Open all year*
30124 Venezia *Tel: (041) 700211*

A prime location on the Grand Canal and an intimacy rarely found in luxury hotels makes this one of the most desirable hotels in Venice. The San Marco landing stage at the doorstep is convenient for *vaporetti* rides down the Grand Canal, and there's a row of gondolas beside mooring poles just in front of the hotel, too. Several elegant little salons with canopied terraces look out across the lagoon to Giudecca, as do the equally elegant terrace restaurant and the best of the bedrooms. The smaller, cheaper bedrooms (more than half are singles) surround a quiet, leafy courtyard.

Facilities: *75 bedrooms (AC); restaurant; lift* **Credit/charge cards accepted:** *Amex, Visa* **Landing stage:** *San Marco*

PAGANELLI ££
Riva degli Schiavoni
Castello 4182 and 4687 *Open all year*
30122 Venezia *Tel: (041) 5224324*

This small, unpretentious hotel lies on the Riva degli Schiavoni waterfront, close to the Danieli. A few of the rooms look out over the lagoon and these are the prettiest and most Venetian in character. Most rooms are smaller and simpler, some in '60s style, others refurnished over the last few years. The annexe down a side street houses the simple, modern restaurant and some of the hotel's bedrooms. Not expensive considering the position.

Facilities: *23 bedrooms (AC in 4); restaurant* **Credit/charge cards accepted:** *Amex, Eurocard* **Landing stage:** *San Zaccaria*

SANTO STEFANO   ££
Campo Santo Stefano
San Marco 2957   *Closed Jan*
30124 Venezia   *Tel: (041) 5224460*

An immaculate little hotel standing in a large, lively square, close to the
Fenice theatre and the Accademia. Space is at a premium but the lack of it is
more than compensated for by the delightful décor. Bedrooms are
exceptionally pretty with painted furniture and feminine fabrics.

Facilities: *14 bedrooms (AC on request); lift*   **Credit/charge cards accepted:**
none   **Landing stage:** *San Samuele*

SATURNIA E INTERNATIONAL   ££££
Calle Larga XXII Marzo
San Marco 2398   *Open all year*
30124 Venezia   *Tel: (041) 708377*

A converted *palazzo* in a smart shopping street, five minutes from Piazza San
Marco. The foyer is the most striking part of the hotel with its Gothic patio,
intricate inlaid ceiling and creepers trailing over a central well. There are two
restaurants: the candlelit Caravella, with a marine theme, and the cheaper
Cortile which has tables laid out in the courtyard. Bedrooms can be grand
and baronial or compact and modern. Unlike most 4-star hotels in Venice,
there are no rooms with a view of the Grand Canal.

Facilities: *97 bedrooms (AC); restaurants (closed Wed low season); lift*   **Credit/**
charge cards accepted: *Amex, Diners, Eurocard, Visa*   **Landing stage:** *San*
Marco/Santa Maria del Giglio

SEGUSO   ££
Zattere
Dorsoduro 779   *Closed Dec to Feb*
30123 Venezia   *Tel: (041) 5222340*

This is an ideal location if you want to escape the madding crowds of the San
Marco area and enjoy stunning views across the lagoon. It is an old-
fashioned *pensione* on the Zattere quayside, facing the island of Giudecca.
Inside there are antiques, leather seats, plants in battered copper pots and
outdated guidebooks on Italy. The dining room is delightful: pretty grey silky
walls, antique-style seats, mirrored wall lamps, geraniums on window
ledges and the soporific sound of lapping water from the canal below. The
best bedrooms (half without bathrooms) are large and handsome,
overlooking the lagoon; rooms further back are smaller and simpler.
Washing facilities range from a basin in the room to marble splendour. Half
board is obligatory.

Facilities: *36 bedrooms; restaurant (closed Wed); lift*   **Credit/charge cards**
accepted: *Amex, Eurocard, Visa*   **Landing stage:** *Zattere*

AL SOLE PALACE   £££
Fondamenta Minotto
Santa Croce 136   *Closed Nov to Mar*
30125 Venezia   *Tel: (041) 32144*

Although close to the Piazzale Roma, this 14th-century converted palace
stands in one of the prettiest parts of Venice. Low beamed ceilings, rustic
tables and rugs on marble floors give the place a distinct old world charm,
which is frequently disturbed by the groups of tourists that come and go. The
restaurant is modern and cheerful, and there's a delightful trellised courtyard
with a central well and huge urns of laurel. Bedrooms are a blend of modern
and antique, a few of them quite grand.

Facilities: *80 bedrooms; restaurant; lift*   **Credit/charge cards accepted:** *Amex,
Eurocard, Visa*   **Landing stage:** *Piazzale Roma*

VENICE LIDO

DES BAINS   £££
Lungomare Marconi 17   *Closed Nov to Mar*
30126 Venezia Lido   *Tel: (041) 765921*

This grand old hotel occupies one of the prime positions on the Lido, across
the road from the best part of the beach. Although it's lost a lot of cachet
since the days when it featured in Thomas Mann's *Death in Venice* and the
atmosphere is slightly sedate, it is still a very comfortable and civilised place
to stay. There are spacious elegant public rooms with high stucco ceilings,
crystal chandeliers, and Persian carpets. Bedrooms vary from comfortable
and modern to solid and traditional. Exorbitantly-priced cabins are available
on the Des Bains beach – the cost is not included in the room rate.

Facilities: *268 bedrooms (AC); restaurants; lift; swimming pool (heated); tennis
courts; boat service to and from Venice; parking*   **Credit/charge cards accepted:**
Amex, Diners, Eurocard, Visa   **Landing stage:** *Casinò*

VILLA PARCO   £
Via Rodi 1   *Closed Nov to Feb*
30126 Venezia Lido   *Tel: (041) 5260015*

This quiet villa in a residential area about six minutes from the beach and
casino is one of the cheapest places to stay on the Lido. It is a small
pensione – family-run and very friendly. Breakfast in summer is taken in the
garden. Bedrooms are quite simple and modern with the exception of one or
two with handsome antiques.

Facilities: *22 bedrooms*   **Credit/charge cards accepted:** *Amex, Diners,
Eurocard*   **Landing stage:** *Casinò*

QUATTRO FONTANE
Via 4 Fontane 16
30126 Venezia Lido

££££
Closed mid-Oct to mid-Apr
Tel: (041) 5260227

This charming hotel lies three minutes' from the beach, close to the casino and the venue of the Venice International Film Festival – which takes place annually in late August/early September. It's a rustic-style, creeper-covered building standing in a large and flowery garden; there's a terrace with wicker chairs where drinks and meals are taken in summer, and a tennis court. The public rooms are well decorated and furnished with antiques, and the bedrooms are comfortable – some with ornate metal beds. It's a peaceful and charming base.

Facilities: *70 bedrooms; restaurant; tennis court; parking*   **Credit/charge cards accepted:** *Amex, Visa*   **Landing stage:** *Casinò*

NORTHERN CITIES

*❝ For you have thus beneath you . . . the
birth-place of the highest art; for among these
hills, or by this very Adige bank, were born
Mantegna, Titian, Correggio and Veronese❞*
JOHN RUSKIN

Verona, Roman arena

Introduction

The flat triangle of land stretching between the Alps, the Apennines and the Adriatic, and bisected by the River Po is not, scenically, good touring country. Agriculture – for this is one of Italy's richest farming areas – is fast losing out to industry and the crops that are left, mostly maize and sugar beet, have none of the visual appeal of the vine or the olive. The characteristic trembling poplars that you might expect in Lombardy are indeed a feature of the landscape but so is the fog, and not only in winter. This dreary picture is true at least of much of Lombardy (Shakespeare's "pleasant garden of great Italy") and neighbouring Emilia Romagna, south of the Po, which stretches to the Adriatic. From Venice to Ravenna the coast is characterised by the desolate lagoons of the Po delta, with the odd old fishing town of some interest and charm (notably Chioggia and Comacchio). South of Ravenna are miles of sandy beaches with a string of popular, overcrowded and hectic resorts. Parts of Venetia, to the north, offer some relief from the dreary flatness of it all, with hills and vineyards and fine country villas but much of the coastline is marshy and the waters are muddied by the industry at Mestre. It is not surprising that the cities of the north are by-passed by so many tourists, eager for the sunny delights of centre and south, or at least for the more romantic mists of Venice itself.

Yet within this triangle are some of Italy's most venerable cities, conveniently linked by motorway. They are all within easy striking distance of more appealing countryside: the Lakes from Milan, Bergamo, Brescia and Verona, the Apennines from Bologna, Parma or any of the other cities along the Via Emilia (the old Roman trading route which runs straight for about 250km from Piacenza to the sea at Rimini), the Alps from Piedmont and the Dolomites from the Veneto. So a carefully planned holiday need not be an entirely urban affair. Still, unless you want to bask on a beach, the main point of a holiday here is to visit the historic cities and see some of the major works of art, particularly of the Renaissance. No other area of Italy provides such a rich variety of architecture. You can follow developments from the Roman remains at Verona through the early Christian churches of Ravenna and Milan to the Lombard Romanesque cathedrals of Modena and Parma; and from the civic Gothic architecture of Verona to the Renaissance architecture of Mantua or Brescia, the Baroque of Turin and the pioneering 20th-century blocks of modern Milan. Some of the finest and most original buildings are outside the cities.

Another major attraction of the area is the high quality of restaurants, not only in the towns but also (and especially) outside them. Quantity is as prodigious as quality; there is a saying that Emilians eat in a day what Romans eat in a week and the Genoese in a month. Certainly Emilia-Romagna, known as the Red Belt of Italy because of the political domination of the Left, enjoys a bourgeois lifestyle. An advantage of the Veneto area is the handful of civilised hotels in converted country villas, some with swimming pools.

You may well find that the cities are more varied than you expected. As elsewhere in Italy, though possibly more so, the cities have a well-developed sense of identity and independence; a man's home-town is more important than his region or even his country. Milan, Turin and Bologna print their own daily newspapers with international coverage. There is a historical reason for this traditional rivalry and insularity. Most of the cities had Roman, or earlier, origins (Ravenna, Aquileia and Verona bear the most traces of this) and then became separate city states, with their own methods of government, in the Middle Ages before succumbing to the territorial ambitions first of pope or emperor, later the French and the Austrians. As in Tuscany and Umbria the medieval communes were constantly bickering, among and within themselves; the famous vendetta in Verona between Montagues and Capulets is but one, typical, example. The tower houses at Bologna were built by rival clans in the same town. Occasionally the cities banded together against a common enemy; in the 12th century the Lombard League (Milan, Bérgamo, Brescia, Cremona, Mantua, Bologna) united against the emperor Barbarossa and later Verona, Vicenza, Padua and Treviso formed the Veronese League, also in an attempt to curb imperial power.

The 13th century began an era of greater stability with the firm establishment of family rule in some of the key cities: the Visconti in Milan (and later neighbouring towns such as Bérgamo and Pavia), the d'Este's in Ferrara and Modena, the della Scala family (or Scaligers) in Verona and later Vicenza. Government was despotic – unlike in republican Florence – but the often cruel and ruthless rulers of the 14th and 15th centuries, men like Gian Galeazzo Visconti, Nicolo III d'Este and Sigismondo Malatesta (of Rimini), were invariably able administrators and enthusiastic patrons of the arts.

Towards the end of the 14th century, Venice began to extend her net, moving westwards from Treviso (1389) to Bérgamo (1428). Vicenza, Padua, Verona and smaller townships were obliged (not always by force) to take refuge under the great Venetian umbrella, a more comfortable fate than rule by Visconti or d'Este. In these cities you still hear Venetian dialects, eat typically Venetian dishes (usually better than in Venice itself) and see the symbol of the Lion of St Mark on public buildings. The cities were ruled by councils of aristocrats and artists were often imported from Venice.

The great Venetian painters Titian and Veronese were born and often worked outside Venice itself, and their works can be seen in churches, villas and museums formed from aristocratic collections. However, lesser figures including Cima da Conegliano, Jacopo Bassano and Pordenone who lived and worked in the provinces are also of more than local interest. Individual schools of art evolved and flourished; Padua, for instance, cherished its antiquity and, far from being swamped by Venice, began a classical revival, encouraged by the arrival of Donatello from Florence in 1443 (for a ten-year stay) and continued by Andrea Mantegna, the leading north Italian painter of his day. By the 16th century, the golden age of Venetian painting, there was considerable cultural give and take between Venetian dominions and Venice itself; most provincial artists of any stature spent some time in Venice or at least absorbed ideas from Giorgione, Titian and Veronese. A concrete (as it were) example of the effect of Venetian protection on art was that Palladio was able to build his unfortified country villas in the countryside of the Veneto; visiting these is now one of the most enjoyable aspects of touring the area around Vicenza.

By the mid 1400s the great families of Milan, Ferrara and Mantua had established civilised Renaissance courts which drew the great artists, poets and scholars of the time. All the families were related by marriage so there was a continual interchange of artists and ideas between the courts (portraits were often exchanged as keepsakes). The greatest patrons and collectors also had agents in Florence, Venice and Rome to keep them abreast of artistic developments. But in many ways the courts themselves were trendsetters: for instance the fashion for scholarly collectors was to have a study (*studiolo*) decorated *all' antica* in both style and content and this phenomenon was to encourage a return to classical subject matter in Venetian painting.

In 1450 the Sforza family inherited Milan from the Visconti and continued the glorification of the city begun by the tyrant/aesthete Gian Galeazzo Visconti; Lodovico il Moro (who married Beatrice d'Este) was their greatest patron of the arts, attracting Bramante and Leonardo da Vinci to the city. The arrival of Leonardo was a turning point in north Italian art; he was to influence a whole generation of Milanese painters. Mantua, too, had become a major focus for artists and architects. Ludovico II encouraged Alberti, the great Florentine architect, and made Andrea Mantegna his court painter. One of the greatest patrons of the arts (and certainly the most famous) was his daughter-in-law Isabella d'Este, who came to Mantua as a young bride in 1470. She was a passionate collector of books, jewellery, coins and antiquities and desired "the most outstanding masters in Italy" to decorate her apartments. Isabella's son Federico was a major patron of Titian, Correggio and Giulio Romano (who built the famous Palazzo del Tè); Vincenzo I recruited the Flemish Pourbus (as court painter) and Rubens whom he used for diplomatic missions; and the intellectual cardinal duke Ferdinando employed the Baroque Bolognese artists Guercino and Guido Reni. The princely d'Estes made of Ferrara a great city (as large as Milan) and attracted poets and artists including Ariosto and Torquato Tasso, Roger van der Weyden and Titian, who painted his great series of Bacchanals for Alfonso d'Este's study from 1518-25. The claustrophobic court of Ferrara seemed to breed intellectuals and eccentrics like Cosimo Tura (1430-1495), strongly influenced by the harsh, linear, classicising influence of Padua.

This Renaissance glory was short-lived. By the end of the 16th century Milan had already succumbed to Charles V, and Ferrara fell to the popes. In 1630 Mantua was crippled by the plague, a siege and a succession crisis and the ducal collections (some 2,000 paintings) were ignominiously sold off, partly to Charles I of England. The power of Venice declined sharply too and the republic was extinct by 1797. From the 17th century travellers consistently remarked that cities of northern Italy were decayed and lifeless. "'Tis in a word a durty Towne, & though the Streetes be large they remain illpav'd" (John Evelyn of Ferrara); "The most melancholy city of Europe" (William Lithgow of Padua); "an ill-built, melancholy place" (Thomas Gray of Modena); "a black, dirty, stinking dismal place" (Arthur Young of Bergamo); "A brown, decayed old town, deserted, solitary, grass-grown" (Charles Dickens of Piacenza).

Despite these depressing reports, the average Grand Tourist continued to be sufficiently tempted by the cities, particularly Verona with its Roman amphitheatre, and Vicenza with its Palladian villas. Bologna's Baroque school of art put it firmly on the map: Goethe, for instance, spent several days in Bologna though he "did not wish to stay long" in Florence. It is often forgotten that until the 19th century Bolognese art was considered more important than Florentine. In the late 16th century the Carracci family led a revival of the classical tradition in painting based on an idealisation of nature. With their followers Guido Reni, Domenichino and Guercino they had a far-reaching effect on the development of the Baroque style in Rome and, ultimately, beyond. Another draw was Turin (the gateway to Italy for many early tourists); much of it was rebuilt by the Baroque architects of the 17th and 18th centuries, and it was usually pronounced clean, beautiful and lively. Milan was little visited until the 19th century when the post-Napoleonic, aristocratic, opera-going society was the main attraction.

Ironically, it was after the widespread destruction of the Second World War that the cities of northern Italy rose from the ashes. Now they are once again prosperous and thriving. But for the tourist this often means penetrating grim industrial outskirts to reach the historic centres and staying in hotels designed for businessmen rather than holidaymakers. What, then, remains to attract the tourist today?

Although there are excellent restaurants and stylish shops in even the most provincial towns, and most can provide reasonable accommodation for an overnight stop in transit, there is little point in touring the area unless you are interested in art and architecture (or opera, *see page 168*). A few towns, including Bérgamo, Ásolo and Verona, could exist on charm alone but most are an acquired taste. They don't fit our preconceptions as neatly as Venice, Florence, Rome or Naples. Milan is the supreme example of the city of surprises. It has become the financial and economic nerve centre of Italy and an international banking centre, with a population (including suburbs) of some three million people and a work ethic which is almost Swiss. Yet to bypass Milan is to miss Leonardo's Last Supper (alone worth a special detour), the only High Gothic cathedral in Italy, several rich art collections and the famous opera house, La Scala. As an international fashion capital, Milan also has that magic ingredient, style. Turin, similarly, though renowned as the headquarters of the Fiat factory, cannot be simply dismissed as an industrial city of no interest or beauty. Several cities have little to

Visiting Northern Cities

There are regular direct scheduled flights from London and some regional airports to Turin, Milan and (from London only) Bologna. There are also direct charter flights to Bergamo, Verona, Treviso, Trieste and Rimini. A train or coach from London to Milan takes around 24 hours; you could also take the Orient Express to Verona. If you take your own car, you could consider Motorail from Boulogne to Milan.

The cities are conveniently spaced, and the area defined by the triangle Padua/Milan/Bologna makes a good touring circuit, with a possible extension to Turin, Ravenna, or the area north-east of Venice. You would need two or three weeks for a comprehensive itinerary. The main cities are linked by motorway (some only two-lane). But parking in all the cities is a problem and the historic centres are usually closed to traffic.

This is one area of Italy where a touring holiday by train is worth considering; there are regular rail services between all the cities. Stations are usually fairly central, and reasonable hotels within a short taxi ride. A 15-day rover ticket is valid on *rapido* (fast) trains without payment of the usual 30% supplement. In all the cities there is a bus service; Milan has an efficient underground system.

If you do have a car, there are good opportunities for excursions to the lakes and mountains (within an hour's drive of most of the cities), plus the chance to sample some attractive country hotels and restaurants. The Veneto is the most rewarding area to explore; there's scenic variety, and the Palladian villas and the vineyards provide a contrast to the attractions of the cities.

The range of hotels varies a great deal from city to city but most cater for the needs of travelling businessmen rather than holiday-makers. Milan, and to a lesser extent Bologna, have plenty of large, modern purpose-built hotels; Verona is better geared to tourists than most of the other cities; Padua and Vicenza have simple accommodation only; Ferrara and Modena each have an attractive old mansion hotel, but little else. However, one of the attractions of a touring holiday in the area is that there are some appealing hotels in the countryside between the towns; restaurants with bedrooms around Mantua and Parma, and Palladian villas with swimming pools in the Veneto, can make a good base for seeing several cities. It's also a good area for eating out.

A few tour operators offer package holidays by air to the various cities of Lombardy, Emilia Romagna and the Veneto. Milan, Bologna and Verona are the most popular (apart, of course, from Venice). A typical stay is from three to seven nights, with winter prices comparable to those of the previous summer. A few companies specialising in Italy organise tours of a week or so staying overnight in two or three places, but these normally include a night on the lakes or time spent in Venice, and cover the other cities only superficially. The Veneto is the most popular touring area and some specialised tours include visits to museums and art galleries, villas and gardens. Some operators offer package deals to Verona during the opera season, often with accommodation on the lakes rather than in the city itself.

The Po valley is notorious for fog; in winter it can be grey and very cold, in summer overcast and humid. Early summer and early autumn are probably the best times to choose; the weather is reliably warm and you can find accommodation fairly easily (from mid-September until May there are trade fairs and conferences in many cities). May is generally slightly cooler and wetter than September; by October it can be quite cold. August is a bad month as cities are virtually closed down for the summer holidays but July is fine if you choose a country hotel with a swimming pool. Summer is a good time for music-lovers; in addition to the Verona opera season there are concerts in churches, villas and in the open air. Museum- and opera-goers could consider a spring break: the opera season begins in December and lasts until April or May.

offer apart from one or two, admittedly great, artistic experiences:
Ravenna (the best early Christian mosaics west of Istanbul); Parma
(the frescoes of Correggio, *in situ*); Módena (the superb Lombard
Romanesque cathedral); and Vicenza (the buildings of Palladio).
Others, especially the historic centres of the ducal cities of Mantua,
Ferrara and the little town of Sabbioneta, are rather like ghost towns;
here you need a bit of history and a lot of imagination to make sense
of a visit.

Places to visit

ADRIATIC COASTAL RESORTS

The Adriatic coast between the Yugoslav border near Trieste and
Rimini, south of Ravenna, is characterised by broad gently-sloping
beaches of fine sand, and a flat and fertile hinterland with marshy
lagoons (many with abundant wildlife). Some of the coastal resorts
grew up around old and charming towns (Grado, Cáorle, Chióggia);
some (including Lido di Jésolo) were purpose-built in the '60s and
are now beginning to show their age; and others are brand new or
are still being developed. All offer a similar style of holiday, mainly
beach based, with ample opportunities for watersports, evening
activities (generally of a fairly unsophisticated kind) and interesting
day excursions inland – to Ravenna, Venice, Verona and San
Marino. Beaches are usually well kept, gently-sloping and safe for
children, with bars and cafés, changing rooms, mattresses or
deckchairs and sunshades. Most tourists are on a half- or full-board
package, so there's little need for restaurants other than simple
snack bars or pizzerias.

   Grado is an island reached by a causeway, with a sandy beach and
a network of quaint old streets around an interesting cathedral.
There are several hotels left over from Austrian imperial days and
the resort has a certain *fin-de-siècle* atmosphere; it's popular with
Austrian and German tourists. To the west of the Marano lagoon lies
a peninsula with the new resort area and spa of **Lignano
Sabbiadoro**, with hotels, villa developments and campsites.
Sabbiadoro is the built-up centre, Lignano is quieter, with
accommodation scattered among pinewoods. To the west lies the
old fishing village and resort of **Cáorle**, with an 11th-century
cathedral.

   Lido di Jésolo is a post-war resort which boomed in the mid
'sixties; it's one of the leading resorts of Italy. The clean sandy beach
stretches for ten miles – in places 200 yards deep – and is lined with a
continuous ribbon of hotels, apartment blocks and souvenir shops.
Hotels generally have pools, but there's little space for gardens.
There's no seaside promenade, and most hotels are in side streets or
squares; at night the ample pedestrian precincts are lively. There are
plenty of activities, watersports and nightlife, but there's little style.

   Chióggia, at the southern end of the Venetian lagoon, is one of
Italy's largest fishing ports. It's an attractive and bustling old town

with narrow streets, canals, a fine old market hall and some interesting churches. The rather dull resort extension of **Sottomarina** has a gently-sloping beach, with pine trees and car parks behind. South of Chióggia and east of Ferrara, backed by marshes, rice fields and main road, lies a series of developing resorts known as the Lidi Ferraresi. **Comácchio**, slightly inland, is an eel-curing centre, with canal-lined streets.

South of Ravenna, **Cérvia** is a small late 17th-century town built on a grid plan, which has been adopted in the modern resort suburb of **Milano Marittima**, a pleasant area with private villas among trees, visited almost exclusively by Italian families.

Rimini is the leading resort of the Adriatic, stretching for ten miles along the coast. It's brash and noisy, with juke boxes in cafés and megaphone announcements to keep you abreast of local boat excursions and the evening's disco activities; there's open-air dancing, British-style pubs, bingo and slot machines. The beach is excellent, with pale, velvety and neatly-raked sands, almost obliterated by densely-packed sunbeds and parasols.

The old city of Rimini, which merges with the resort, has a Roman bridge and triumphal arch, several churches, a good museum and the famous **Tempio Malatestiano**, a key building of the Renaissance. It's a Gothic church completely transformed into a classical temple to the designs of Leon Battista Alberti, the Florentine Renaissance architect. The façade, based on a Roman triumphal arch, is a model of harmonious, mathematical proportions. The interior is decorated with sculptures by Agostino di Duccio and contains a portrait of Sigismondo by Piero della Francesca (1451).

To the north, **Cesenático** is another large resort with a good beach and a colourful canal port; it's also lively but less brash than Rimini.

AQUILEIA

On the extreme east of the Venetian plain, close to the Yugoslav border, Aquileia was once a great Roman port and still has considerable remains, both outdoors and in the Archaeological Museum.

☛ **Basilica** (Santa Maria)   A lovely Romanesque cathedral with a remarkable mosaic pavement (4th-century) with lively naturalistic detail. The crypt is decorated with Romanesque frescoes and there are more mosaics in the Cripta degli Scavi.

ÁSOLO

A romantic hill town, beloved of Robert Browning and the Italian actress Eleonora Duse who both had villas here. Its lively cultural traditions and its popularity with poets, painters and musicians have their roots in the 15th century when Caterina Cornaro, the Venetian-born queen of Cyprus, was exiled here and established a splendid court. Pietro Bembo, the poet and scholar at Caterina Cornaro's court, invented the verb *asolare*, meaning to idle away time; nearly 500 years later this still seems to be the chief pleasure of Ásolo.

Excursions from Ásolo

☞ **Possagno** (*9km north*)
The birthplace of the neo-classical sculptor, Antonio Canova
(1757-1822); his house contains a museum of casts and the temple he
designed (now the village church) contains his tomb.

☞ **Palladian Villas**
Villa Maser (*6km east*) The splendid Villa Barbaro-Volpi,
commonly called Maser, after the village it dominates, is the product
of the combined efforts of Palladio and Veronese in the 1560s.
Veronese's enchanting frescoes make bold use of *trompe-l'oeil* with
figures appearing from balconies and half-opened doors. They are
also important in the history of Venetian landscape painting.
Villa Emo (*12km south-east*) This villa, at Fanzolo di Vedelago, is
also worth seeing. It was built 1550-60 and frescoed by GB Zelotti.
(*See also Castelfranco Véneto*)

ASTI

An attractive old city beside river and motorway east of Turin,
celebrated for its wines (not only *spumante*) and its 600 year-old Palio
festival (3rd Sunday in September) which includes horse races on
the vast Campo del Palio, and coincides with the local wine festival.
The most interesting monuments, all close to the main axis Corso
Vittorio Alfieri, are the 12th-century baptistery, the 14th-century
church of San Secondo and the cathedral. The most picturesque and
medieval looking part of town is its northern side, where there are
remains of old town walls.

BASSANO DEL GRAPPA

A small town worth a visit for the paintings of the Bassano family,
notably Jacopo (c1510-92), mostly in the museum. An elegant
covered wooden bridge designed by Palladio spans the river Brenta.

BÉRGAMO

A pretty old hill city, relatively unknown and quite unspoilt. Almost
all the interest is concentrated in the old **Città Alta** (upper town)
whose fortified walls are one of few external reminders of the long
period of Venetian rule (1428-1797). The narrow cobbled streets with
their tall shuttered houses and small squares and courtyards are
miraculously peaceful; only the chimes from the belltowers and the
splashing of fountains seem to disturb the tranquillity. The main
street, Via Gómbito, is closed to through traffic and lined with
attractive shops. At the heart of old Bérgamo is the beautiful **Piazza
Vecchia**, a haphazard but harmonious grouping of medieval and
Renaissance buildings round a Venetian fountain. Through the
arcades of the Palazzo della Ragione there is a tantalising glimpse of
the adjacent Piazza del Duomo. Small bars and restaurants line the
Piazza Vecchia; sitting here in the evening when the buildings are lit
you may even be inclined to agree with Stendhal who thought it
"the most beautiful place on earth, and the prettiest I have ever

seen". In the daytime you can take a lift up the clock tower (Torre del Comune) for a fine panorama of the plains and a bird's-eye view of the intricate façade of the Colleoni chapel. In the old town there are several good restaurants with bedrooms.

The business and shopping areas and larger hotels are in the newer **Città Bassa** (lower town) which was laid out with broad avenues and spacious squares early this century. The chestnut-lined Sentierone is the scene of the evening *passeggiata*. There are altarpieces by Lorenzo Lotto (c1480-1556/7) in the churches of **San Bartolomeo** (opposite the Sentierone), and **Santo Spírito** and **San Bernardino** on the winding Via Pignolo, lined with noble old palaces, which leads up to the old city.

The composer Donizetti was born in Bérgamo in 1798 and is commemorated by a street, a theatre and an excellent small museum with memorabilia and his two pianos. A Donizetti festival is held in April and June.

A funicular from the lower to the upper town operates daily every 10 to 15 minutes until about 11.30pm.

☛ **Accademia Carrara**   The collection of count Giacomo Carrara (1714-95), housed in his neo-classical mansion. There are works by the highly individual Bergamasque school of painting, which reached its full glory in the 16th century, including masterpieces by artists such as Lorenzo Lotto and Giambattista Moroni (1523-1578). Pisanello's portrait of Lionello d'Este is among the other treasures; the Venetian school, not surprisingly, is well represented, with paintings by Bellini, Titian and Tiépolo.

☛ **Piazza del Duomo**   The **cathedral** is the poor relation in a remarkable group of buildings which includes the basilica of Santa Maria Maggiore and the Colleoni chapel (see below). The cathedral has been largely rebuilt but the Baroque interior contains 18th-century paintings, notably The Martyrdom of St John by Tiépolo. Opposite is the **baptistery**, a 19th-century copy of the original by Giovanni da Campione, built in 1340.

☛ **Colleoni chapel**   A masterpiece of the early Lombard Renaissance by Amadeo, architect of the Certosa at Pavia. More sculpture than architecture, the intricate façade of inlaid marble is a visual feast. The magnificent interior contains the tombs of Colleoni, the Venetian *condottiere* or soldier of fortune who commissioned the chapel, and his daughter, Medea; the vault is decorated with frescoes by Tiépolo.

☛ **Santa Maria Maggiore**   A Romanesque church with fine carved porches, and a florid Baroque interior adorned with Flemish and Florentine tapestries, frescoes and 16th- and 17th-century paintings. On the neo-classical tomb of Donizetti, children carved in bas-relief tearfully break musical instruments and the figure of Music bows her head. Ask the guide to light the exquisite marquetry choir-stalls (some designed by Lorenzo Lotto).

☛ **San Michele al Pozzo Bianco**   In one of Bérgamo's most picturesque streets, the Via Porta Dipinta, this medieval church contains frescoes, notably in the chapel decorated by Lorenzo Lotto (c1523).

BOLOGNA

The capital of Emilia-Romagna is an active industrial and business centre, with a reputation for gastronomy and for its politics which has earned it the nickname Bologna La Rossa (The Red). But it's also an exceptionally fine example of Roman and medieval town planning, with its ancient town gates, radial plan and long straight streets. Characteristic are the arcades which in the Middle Ages provided cover for furtive assassinations and the amorous assignments of, among others, Boccaccio and the Marquis de Sade. Another feature of Bologna is its brick towers (the city once bristled with them), built for defence and as status symbols by warring medieval families who ruled Bologna until it became part of the papal states in 1506; there's a splendid bird's-eye view of the city with its red brick and terracotta roofscape from the top of the (slightly leaning) Torre degli Asinelli.

At the heart of the city is the **Piazza Maggiore**, surrounded by impressive medieval buildings, notably the Palazzo Comunale and the church of San Petronio. The slightly raised part in the middle of the square is called the *crescentone* after a local type of bread which it resembles in shape. Adjacent is the **Piazza Nettuno** dominated by Giambologna's striking bronze statue of Neptune (1568). On the east side of the piazza is the Palazzo di Re Enzo, built in 1246 but much restored.

Europe's first university is still famed for law and medicine and celebrates its 900th anniversary in 1988. Some 60,000 students are registered here. Also surviving from the Middle Ages is Bologna's great mercantile tradition (the arcades encouraged stallholders as well as ne'er-do-wells) and many shops have preserved their original façades and signs; you can still buy cheese at the oldest shop in Bologna (1273), on the Piazza della Mercanzia. Travellers in the 17th century knew Bologna as the place to buy sausages and "little dogges for Ladyes"; it is now famous for its food shops and restaurants. The main shopping streets are Via d'Azeglio, a short, smart pedestrians-only street, and Via Rizzoli.

In addition to the main sights listed below there are many interesting churches and palaces and a number of small museums; the tourist office can supply detailed lists, and also suggests walks and organises free guided tours in English on Sunday mornings.

Main sights

☛ **Art Gallery** (Pinacoteca Nazionale)   A fine collection of works by artists of the Bolognese school, including some exquisite 14th-century altarpieces and several rooms devoted to the Carracci family and their pupils. A cool and spacious gallery with well-displayed paintings, though labels are irritatingly small and low.

☛ **Palazzo Comunale**   The local government offices since the end of the 13th century, but much rebuilt, with Gothic, Renaissance, Baroque and 20th-century alterations. On the balcony is a statue of pope Gregory XIII, reformer of the calendar, who came from Bologna. The interior contains opulent 17th- and 18th-century rooms with furniture and paintings of the Bolognese school.

☛ **San Giacomo Maggiore**   In the Bentivoglio chapel and the adjacent oratory of St Cecilia are remarkable Renaissance frescoes by painters from Ferrara, notably Francia and Lorenzo Costa, commissioned by the powerful Bentivoglio family. Other paintings in the church include part of a polyptych

Bologna, Neptune statue

by Lorenzo Veneziano (1368).

☛ **San Petronio**   The immense church of San Petronio (almost legendary bishop and protector of the city) was begun in 1390 but the façade was never finished and the main external feature is the doorway carved by the Sienese Jacopo della Quercia. Charles V was crowned Holy Roman Emperor here in 1530.

Inside there are some finely frescoed – but poorly lit – side chapels, an unusual 17th-century sundial set into the floor and a small museum which includes a number of projects for the completion of the façade and a treasury with illuminated manuscripts and reliquaries.

☛ **Santo Stefano**   A lovely group of ancient and medieval churches (originally seven, as at Jerusalem), of which the oldest is the early Christian church of Santi Vitale e Agricola. Off the peaceful Romanesque cloister, part of a Benedictine monastery, is a one-room museum of early Bolognese paintings.

Other sights

☛ **Davia-Bargellina Gallery**   A small collection of Bolognese art in one of the fine old palaces of the Strada Maggiore (number 44).

☛ **Palazzo Magnani**   Now the headquarters of the Credito Romagnolo, this palace, opposite San Giacomo Maggiore at Via Zamboni 20, has a hall of honour with a frieze depicting the story of Romulus and Remus frescoed by the Carracci family, which can be seen on request.

☛ **San Doménico**   A much altered church worth visiting chiefly for the tomb of St Dominic by Nicola Pisano (1237) with three small statues by the young Michelangelo. The 16th-century marquetry choirstalls are remarkable.

Excursions from Bologna

☞ **Churches outside the city walls** (*about 3km south-west*)
Two churches just outside Bologna are famous for their panoramic views over the city. Linked to a city gate, the Porta Saragozza, by a portico over 3km long, the majestic sanctuary of the **Madonna di San Luca** houses a Byzantine image of the Madonna. **San Michele in Bosco**, a fine 16th-century church, is also a popular destination for a walk (or take bus 28).

☞ **Apennine hills**
The spectacular scenery of the Apennine hills (on the way to Florence) is the setting for many a summer picnic, and roads are crowded at weekends.

BRESCIA

An ancient town which, like its neighbour Bérgamo, came under the rule of Venice for nearly 400 years. Although much spoilt by the proliferation of the steel industry, Brescia has an interesting old centre with Renaissance palaces and churches with some marvellous works by painters of the local school (notably Girolamo Romanino and Moretto.) Life revolves around three squares at the centre of the city. The charming **Piazza della Loggia** is distinctly Venetian in contrast to the Mussolini-style **Piazza della Vittória**. Nearby is the rectangular **Piazza del Duomo** with the medieval town hall (Broletto), the circular Romanesque **Duomo Vecchio** and the 17th-century **Duomo Nuovo**, plus several pavement cafés. The sights can be covered in a day and Brescia can be visited as an excursion from Bérgamo or Lake Garda.

☞ **Art Gallery** (Pinacoteca Tosio Martinengo) A fine collection consisting primarily of Brescian paintings of the 15th and 16th centuries, characterised by their gentle mood, influenced by Venetian colour and composition.

☞ **Roman Museum** The remains of a Capitoline temple erected by Vespasian (AD73) houses a small museum whose most outstanding exhibit is a Winged Victory, discovered here in 1826.

☞ **Santi Nazaro e Celso** An 18th-century church with Titian's altarpiece of the Risen Christ (1522) and paintings by Moretto.

BUSSETO

A small town with some fine buildings including the Villa Pallavicino, a castle and several churches. Nearby, at Róncole Verdi, is the humble cottage where the composer Verdi was born (admission fee includes the G Verdi theatre at Busseto). At Sant' Agata di Villanova is the Villa Verdi, built, and lived in, by Verdi.

CASTELFRANCO VÉNETO

A quiet fortified town, the birthplace of the painter Giorgione.

☞ **Cathedral** This contains Giorgione's marvellous Madonna and Saints (1504), where the landscape echoes the mood.

CENTO

The birthplace of the Baroque painter Guercino has an art gallery and church containing his works but is otherwise uninteresting.

CERVIA, CESENÁTICO AND CHIOGGIA

(See Adriatic Coastal Resorts)

CIVIDALE DEL FRIULI

One of the most interesting towns in the Friuli area, Cividale was an important centre of the medieval patriarchate of Aquileia. Despite earthquake damage in 1976, there are interesting sights.

☛ **Archaeological Museum**   Local Roman finds, and a rich collection of early medieval artefacts.

☛ **Cathedral**   An elegant Gothic/Renaissance cathedral whose museum contains the "Baptistery" of Callixtus and the "Altar" of Ratchis, both superb examples of Lombard stonemasonry.

☛ **Santa Maria in Valle** (Il Tempietto)   This intriguing 8th-century church has beautiful stucco decoration inside.

CONEGLIANO

A wine-growing town, the birthplace of the painter Cima da Conegliano. Cima's house has been restored with reproductions of his paintings; his altarpiece of 1492 is in the cathedral.

CREMONA

Home of the great Stradivarius and still a centre for violin-making, Cremona is something of a backwater for tourists. Its main attraction is the piazza, focal point of life in Cremona; as Edith Templeton noted "Here in Cremona [people] work like a stage crowd: they appear, walk across the square, disappear, walk round the back of the cathedral and emerge again from the other side". The Romanesque cathedral boasts a splendid brick belltower, the tallest in Italy, known as the *torrazzo*.

☛ **Cathedral** (Duomo)   The beautiful façade of the cathedral is an ornate amalgam of Romanesque and Gothic styles, with a Renaissance loggia. The dark interior has some fine frescoes, notably Pordenone's powerful frescoes of The Passion (1520), influenced by Raphael and Michelangelo (he probably visited Rome in 1516).

FAENZA

An old walled town famous for the fine collection of majolica (also known as *faience* after the town), in the Museum of Ceramics.

FERRARA

An important centre of the Renaissance under the d'Este family, who patronised artists, scholars and poets. The heart of the town, locked in a time warp, is still dominated by the vast moated castle of the d'Estes. But its artistic heritage is sadly depleted. Most of the great works of the Ferrarese school are dispersed in public collections, notably the National Gallery of London. Titian's great

Bacchanals are in the Prado, Madrid. Ferrara was virtually abandoned around 1600 after the departure of the last duke to Módena. Already earthquakes and the burden of taxation imposed on the inhabitants to finance the d'Estes' projects of self-glorification had taken their toll. From the 17th to the 19th century, travellers found Ferrara something of a ghost town, where the inhabitants were few and grass grew in the streets. However, since disastrous bombing in the last war, the city has revived; it is now a busy market town with a far larger population than comparable Mantua.

☛ **Cathedral** (Duomo) The vast Romanesque cathedral (begun in 1135) has a later interior containing works by the local school of painters. In the small museum is a pair of organ shutters (St George and the Annunciation, 1469) by Cosimo Tura, first Court Painter to the d'Estes.

☛ **Palazzo dei Diamanti** The palace of Sigismondo d'Este with a façade of some 12,000 pointed blocks (hence the name), built by Biagio Rossetti, the chief Renaissance architect of Ferrara. It contains a well laid-out **picture gallery** devoted to the Ferrara school whose artists produced tautly drawn, intense images which are highly original (and often rather eccentric). Outstanding works include a Deposition by Ercole de' Roberti, a polyptych by Dosso Dossi and several paintings by Garófalo. There are 13th-century frescoes in the Great Hall, which has a superb wooden ceiling.

☛ **Palazzo Schifanoia** Summer residence of Borso d'Este, designed by Biagio Rossetti, in a sad state of repair. The charming frescoes in the Hall of the Months (Sala dei Mesi) are mostly by Francesco del Cossa and are the artist's best-known works, probably influenced by Piero della Francesca's work in Ferrara, now lost. Ercole de' Roberti, possibly his pupil, painted September, in which the influence of Bellini is clear.

☛ **Palazzina di Marfisa d'Este** (Civic Museum) Close to the Palazzo Schifanoia, a charming small palace with 16th-century furniture and art.

☛ **Palazzini Cavalieri di Malta** Now a museum for Giovanni Boldini who was born in Ferrara in 1845, but achieved fame as a fashionable portrait painter in Belle Époque Paris.

FIDENZA

A small industrial town which has a remarkable Lombard Romanesque cathedral with a richly decorated façade.

FORLÌ

A provincial capital worth visiting for the Basilica of San Mercuriale and the good collection of Renaissance and Baroque art in the picture gallery, including works by Guercino and Fra Angelico.

GRADO

(*See Adriatic Coastal Resorts*)

ÍMOLA

A small commercial town, with an imposing castle, a picture gallery, several churches and some good restaurants.

LIDO DI JÉSOLO

(*See Adriatic Coastal Resorts*)

MANTUA (MÁNTOVA)

Once one of the greatest Renaissance courts in Europe and one third the size of London, Mantua is now a provincial town with unprepossessing outskirts and a population only half the size of Bergamo's. It is best approached from the north whence you can appreciate its unusual setting, surrounded by lakes on three sides. Ruled by the Gonzaga family from 1328-1708, the city enjoyed its heyday in the 16th and early 17th centuries when travellers described its magnificent palaces and spacious streets.

The historic and artistic centre of Mantua, concentrated around the three interlinked squares at the heart of the town, has changed little, and the vast Ducal Palace still gives a vivid idea of the brilliance of the Gonzaga court. Hotels are run-of-the-mill, but it's worth staying overnight so that you can dine out by candlelight on the Piazza Erbe (by day the market square), in front of the arcades of the **Palazzo della Ragione**, built in 1250, and the rotunda church of **San Lorenzo** (1082).

☛ **Ducal Palace**   A complex of several buildings dating from different periods, containing some 500 rooms and 15 courtyards and gardens, and covering an area of 34,000 square metres. Check that the highlights aren't closed for restoration before embarking on the two-hour guided tour in Italian.

The most important galleries and apartments include the Sala di Pisanello, re-named after the discovery in 1967 of fragments of frescoes by the first Court Painter to the Gonzagas; the Hall of Mirrors (Sala degli Specchi); and the apartments of Isabella d'Este (the paintings she commissioned, by Mantegna, Correggio, Perugino and others, now hang in the Louvre). Curiosities include the labyrinth decoration on the ceiling of Vincenzo I's room (the Renaissance equivalent of the crossword, perhaps), the staircase for horses, and the scaled-down apartments of the court dwarves. But the real *pièce de résistance* is Mantegna's lively group portrait of the Gonzaga family in the so-called Camera degli Sposi (Bridal chamber) in the Castello di San Georgio. There are often queues to be squeezed in to see it. There are also rooms decorated by Giulio Romano and paintings by various court artists, including Rubens. The Gonzaga collection of antique sculpture is distributed through the palace.

☛ **Palazzo del Tè**   An extraordinary summer palace built for the Gonzagas by Giulio Romano and decorated by his pupils. The exterior is rather dilapidated but some of the frescoes inside are being restored. Life-size portraits of the favourite Gonzaga horses, mythological scenes inspired by Federico Gonzaga's passion for Isabella Boschetti, and stuccoes by Primaticcio (of Fontainebleau fame but Bolognese birth) adorn the walls. Most imaginative of the rooms is the overwhelming Hall of Giants (Sala dei Giganti) where the walls seem to be collapsing around the spectator. Aggressive over-restoration doesn't add to the comfort. Jove punishing the giants for daring to scale Olympus would have been read as a caveat to the enemies of Charles V, a guest of the Gonzagas here in 1530. Concerts are held in the Sala dei Cavalli.

☛ **Sant' Andrea**   An important landmark in Renaissance architecture, designed by the great theorist Alberti in 1470. The façade is inspired by the

Mantua, Ducal Palace

classical triumphal arch. The harmonious interior contains frescoes by
Correggio, *trompe-l'oeil* vaulting and Mantegna's funerary chapel, with a
bronze bust, thought to be a self-portrait.

Excursions from Mantua
☞ **Sabbioneta** (*34km south-west*)
The tiny town of Sabbioneta was built in the 16th century by
Vespasiano Gonzaga, a cousin of the duke of Mantua, as an ideal
Renaissance city. Today it is something of a ghost town but,
mid-way between Mantua and Parma, it makes a good overnight
base for unhurried motorists. The fine Renaissance buildings of this
small-scale city include Scamozzi's Teatro Olimpico (based on
Palladio's at Vicenza), the Palazzo Ducale and the frescoed Palazzo
del Giardino. In the church of the Incoronata is the tomb of
Vespasiano, who died in 1591. Apply to the tourist office for a
guided tour of the buildings (normally locked).

MARÓSTICA
A pleasant medieval town, famed for the giant chess board on the
castle square. The game of human chess has been played, with
much pageantry, every other September since 1454.

MILAN (MILANO)

Henry James once described Milan as "prosaic and winterish, as if it were on the wrong side of the Alps" and indeed the city does have a certain sobriety untypical of Italian cities, and a greyness often attributable to its misty northern climate. But despite its rather dull image (mainly to those who don't know the city) Milan has a lot to offer the tourist. The industrial zones, the residential suburbs and the modern business quarter form concentric circles around a compact historic heart.

The cosmopolitan character of Milan is due in part to foreign rule (it has belonged to France, Spain and Austria), in part to its 20th-century role as Italy's real economic capital. Imposing 19th-century buildings and wide boulevards give Milan a stately, almost Parisian, elegance. The café society of the glass-vaulted Galleria Vittório Emanuele (said to have been inspired by the Crystal Palace) where people meet, read their *Corriere della Sera* at pavement bars, or go shopping is rather different from the *dolce vita* of Rome; here the world goes by rather more purposefully than in the average Italian city. It is a sophisticated, cultured place, renowned for its opera house and its fashion shows. The most elegant shopping street is the Via Montenapoleone, lined with designer boutiques.

The focal point of the centre of Milan is the gigantic Gothic cathedral. The city has several other remarkable churches, and more than its fair share of art collections, and it has Leonardo's Last Supper, alone worth a major detour. It is essential to stay at least two nights here to see all the sights; there are plenty of good hotels and with its two international airports Milan makes a natural starting point for a tour of the northern cities.

☛ **Ambrosiana Gallery** (Pinacoteca Ambrosiana)   A private collection whose nucleus belonged to cardinal Federico Borromeo in the 17th century. There are rooms dedicated to Raphael, Titian and the school of Leonardo da Vinci as well as to Venetian and Flemish painting.

☛ **Brera Art Gallery**   The finest existing collection of north Italian painting. Masterpieces include Giovanni Bellini's Pietà, Caravággio's Supper at Emmaus and Tintoretto's Finding of the Body of St Mark (c1565). Two of the most famous pictures are from central Italy (Room 22): Piero della Francesca's last known work, a beautiful Madonna and Child with Saints (c1475), and Raphael's Betrothal of the Virgin (1504), an early work still influenced by Perugino.

☛ **Castello Sforzesco**   Huge castle of the Sforza family who ruled Milan from 1450 to 1533. It contains several historic collections, notably the well laid-out Municipal Museum of Art which covers the decorative as well as the fine arts with an exceptional collection of furniture and musical instruments. Michelangelo's Rondanini Pietà, his unfinished last work, is displayed in the Sala degli Scarlioni.

☛ **Cathedral** (Duomo)   Begun in 1387, Milan cathedral, which took nearly 500 years to realise, is the only full-blown Gothic cathedral in Italy. The exterior, a marvel of complexity with hundreds of marble pinnacles and spires, has invoked the derision of purists. The sombre interior has little of great interest, but the museum has a collection of Lombard sculpture. On a clear day it's worth taking a lift to the roof for panoramic views.

☞ **Poldi Pezzoli Museum**   A delightful and varied private collection of paintings, armour, bronzes, solar clocks, ceramics and Persian carpets, housed in a charming palace.

☞ **Sant' Ambrogio**   On the site of an earlier basilica, where saint Ambrose baptised saint Augustine, this church is the prototype of Lombard Romanesque architecture. It dates mainly from the 11th and 12th centuries. Parts of the church, including Bramante's portico (1495), were rebuilt after considerable damage in the war. The interior contains 4th-century Byzantine mosaics, a richly-decorated altar and paintings by Luini and Bergognone.

☞ **Sant' Eustorgio**   A much restored Romanesque basilica. Its chief glory is the Renaissance Portinari chapel, designed by the Florentine Michelozzo and decorated with frescoes by Vincenzo Foppa, leading painter in Milan before the arrival of Leonardo. There are some fine tombs.

☞ **Santa Maria delle Grazie**   Bramante's cloisters and dome are worth seeing but it's Leonardo da Vinci's The Last Supper in the adjacent refectory that really pulls the crowds. Leonardo arrived in Milan in 1482-3 and was working on The Last Supper in 1497. The remarkable subtle undercurrents of tension ("one of you will betray me") mark it as the first great work of the High Renaissance. But Leonardo's technique – working in oil rather than fresco – resulted in almost immediate deterioration. The painting is now half-obscured by scaffolding in another desperate bid to save it from disintegration.

☞ **La Scala**   The world's most famous opera house has a rather unassuming neo-classical exterior, an opulent auditorium (which you can see if there's no rehearsal in progress) and a theatre museum with a fascinating collection of operatic memorabilia.

☞ **Other churches**   San Simpliciano and San Lorenzo (with an early Christian basilica, rebuilt in 1573 but retaining its original quatrefoil plan) both date from the 4th century. Renaissance churches worth seeing include Santa Maria presso San Celso, Santa Maria della Passione (both with many works by painters of the 17th-century Milanese school), San Maurizio (with frescoes by Bernadino Luini) and San Satiro, which has behind the altar an early masterpiece by Bramante, with a bold use of false perspective.

Excursions from Milan

☞ **Certosa di Pavia** (*about 30km south*)
This famous Carthusian monastery, built for the Visconti of Milan, is one of the most elaborate buildings in Italy. The intricately sculpted façade of coloured marble (which was to influence the architects of many of the châteaux of the Loire valley) is its chief glory and dates from the 16th century. The church is mainly Gothic, with some fine tombs and paintings by Milanese artists.

Public transport is available from Milan, via Pavia, but it's easier to make a detour by car on the way to Turin or Parma.

☞ **Monza** (*15km north*)
Merging with the outskirts of Milan, Monza is not a prepossessing place. Its only attractions are the **cathedral**, with an exceptionally rich treasury, and the **Villa Reale**, a grand neo-classical villa with a landscaped park and an art gallery. The famous motor-racing track is within the grounds.

OPERA IN NORTHERN ITALY

The North Italian cities are strongly linked with the history of opera, and there are few that cannot boast a musical contribution of some kind, whether past or present. Claudio Monteverdi, born at Cremona in 1567, was for 22 years attached to the Gonzaga court at Mantua where his *Orfeo*, produced in 1607, was one of the first operas ever performed. Monteverdi later became the first *Maestro di cappella* at St Mark's in Venice, where he earned the reputation of 'Il Divino Claudio', the most admired vocal composer in Europe. In 1637 the first public opera house opened in Venice; the horseshoe shape with box tiers was soon the model for opera houses all over Europe. Monteverdi's masterpiece *The Coronation of Poppaea* was first performed in Venice in 1642.

Bérgamo was the birthplace of Gaetano Donizetti (1797-1848), who was to become one of the greatest Italian composers of Romantic opera (the other being his predecessor, Vincenzo Bellini, a Sicilian whose *Zaira* was the first opera performed in Parma's Teatro Regio in 1829 and whose greatest triumphs, including *Norma* in 1842, were scored in Milan). Donizetti studied at the Bologna conservatory and produced the first of some 70 operas in Venice at the age of 21. Although he later settled in Naples, he had his first success in Milan in 1830 with *Anna Bolena* (English history provided suitably melodramatic plots).

By the time of Donizetti's death, Giuseppe Verdi had established himself as the most popular composer in Italy, a status he retained throughout his long life. Verdi was born at Le Róncole (now Róncole Verdi), near Busseto in the province of Parma, in 1813. His humble birthplace can still be visited, as can his home, Villa Sant' Agata, still privately owned with its original furnishings. Some of Verdi's greatest operas first went on the boards at La Scala: *Rigoletto* (set in Mantua) in 1851, *La Traviata* in 1853, and his last operas *Otello* (1887) and *Falstaff* (1893 – when Verdi was 90). *Aida*, his most spectacular work, is a regular favourite in the dramatic setting of the Arena at Verona where it was first performed in 1913. With his patriotic themes, Verdi became a national hero and in 1861 Cavour persuaded him to take part in the new government of a united Italy. He died in Milan in 1901.

Other north Italian composers of opera include Salieri, Mozart's rival (born near Verona in 1750); Amilcare Ponchielli, born near Cremona in 1834, who taught Puccini at the Milan Conservatory and whose *La Gioconda* was first performed at Milan in 1876; and Ottorino Respighi (1879-1936), a Bolognese whose *Lucrezia* was premiered at Milan in 1937. Among the Venetians were Ermanno Wolf-Ferrari (1876-1948) who composed a number of comic operas and Francesco Malipieri (1882-1973) who, in addition to composing, edited the complete works of Monteverdi.

☞ **Opera performances**

The opera season in Italy lasts from December to April or May (early July to September in Verona). If booking independently, write for programme details early in September, using an international reply-paid coupon. Bookings are made by post and money is refunded if seats you have requested are not available. Write to the *Botteghino* (Box Office) at the following addresses: Bérgamo: Teatro Donizetti, Piazza Cavour; Bologna: Teatro Comunale; Milan: La Scala, Via dei Filodrammatici 2; Parma: Teatro Regio, Via Garibaldi; Turin: Teatro Regio, Piazza Castello; Venice: Teatro La Fenice, San Fantin 2549; Verona: Teatro Arena di Verona, Piazza Bra 28. Programmes for La Scala and the Arena at Verona (available in January) can also be obtained through C.I.T. in London (tel: 01-434 3844); they will book tickets for a fee of £10. The Italian State Tourist Office can supply names of tour operators specialising in opera trips.

MÓDENA

A busy town on the ancient Roman Via Emilia which crosses the province and bisects the town. The quiet centre is dominated by the majestic cathedral, the piazza usually peopled by groups of old men. There is a friendly atmosphere and chic shops line the main street. There are surprisingly few traces of the d'Este family who controlled the city for 500 years; the immense Ducal Palace (where Mary of Módena, wife of James II of England, was born) is now an academy and closed to the general public. Módena is worth a stop on the way to Bologna, the town's traditional enemy, especially if you acquire the taste for *zampone* (stuffed pigs' trotters), the local speciality.

☛ **Cathedral** (Duomo)   An exceptionally fine Romanesque building, recently restored to reveal the carvings of Lombard sculptors in their pristine beauty. In a tribute rare for the 12th century, the names of both the architect, Lanfranco, and the master sculptor, Wiligelmo, are recorded on tablets on the outside of the cathedral. The sinuous, finely-chiseled carving of the façade shows the hand of the maestro, while the south door (facing the

Modena, cathedral

square), of lesser craftsmanship, is decorated with scenes from Arthurian legend, an unusual subject for the time and place. The pale brick interior contains various works of art including a finely carved pulpit and rood-screen by north Italian masters. The adjacent bell-tower, known as La Ghirlandina, was completed in 1310.

☛ **Palazzo dei Musei**   Several museums including the Galleria Estense, the exceptionally rich collection of the d'Este family. They were prodigious patrons and the collection includes Flemish as well as Venetian and Ferrarese works of art, and also busts, ivories, ceramics and medals.

PADUA (PÁDOVA)

The "mart town of learning", as Thomas Coryate described Padua in 1611, is still very much a university town, with lots of bookshops and bicycles. The old part of the city, which became part of the Venetian empire in 1405, is little altered; narrow, cobbled streets with arcades lead to three adjacent market squares, lined with some fine medieval buildings. The neo-classical Caffè Pedrocchi, once the meeting place for intellectuals and political activists, is now a rather tarnished venue for shoppers and students. There's an ugly post-war business and shopping district.

Pilgrims come from all over the Catholic world to see the shrine of St Anthony. Cultural pilgrims come to admire Giotto's frescoes and Donatello's sculptures. There are other (scattered) attractions, including the oldest Botanic Gardens in Europe and a civic museum with a fairly good collection of paintings, poorly displayed. Hotel accommodation is geared to businessmen and generally fairly basic.

☛ **Basilica of Sant' Antonio** (Il Santo)   The vast basilica, reminiscent with its domes and minarets of St Mark's in Venice, was built between 1232 and 1307. The mortal remains of saint Anthony, patron saint of lost property, are still much revered. Numerous works of art include the bronzes by Donatello on the high altar.

Donatello's famous equestrian statue of the Venetian *condottiere*, Erasmo da Narni, known as Gattamelata, stands outside the Basilica. It was the first great Renaissance bronze to be cast in Italy.

Next to the Basilica are the Oratorio di San Giorgio and the Scuola di Sant' Antonio, decorated with frescoes by artists including Titian.

☛ **Church of the Eremitani**   Bomb damage in the last war all but obliterated Mantegna's celebrated frescoes depicting the Martyrdom of St Christopher. Fragments are worth seeing.

☛ **Scrovegni Chapel**   This is decorated with superb frescoes by Giotto, begun in 1303, illustrating the life of Christ and the Virgin. They were completed by 1313, probably after the (now disputed) Assisi frescoes. You read each scene in sequence, rather like a strip cartoon, so it's important to start at the beginning, endure the crick in the neck and ignore (if possible avoid) the crowds.

☛ **University**   A tedious tour of the halls of the university yields a few curiosities: the *cattedra* (professor's chair) from which Galileo lectured, the medicine hall, where skulls of teachers are still displayed, and the tiny and perfectly preserved anatomical theatre (1594) whose ingenious design enabled 250 students to watch dissections performed. Apply at the *Direzione Amministrativo*.

Excursions from Padua
☞ **Brenta Canal**
In summer you can take a boat trip along the Brenta Canal to Venice.
If you go by car (the road follows the canal) you can visit some of the
nearby villas; most impressive are the 18th-century Villa Nazionale
(Pisana) at Strà and Palladio's Villa Fóscari (La Malcontenta) with
16th-century frescoes, within sight of the oil refineries of Mestre.

☞ **Euganean Hills**
Owing to the volcanic origin of the hills with their numerous hot
springs there are several spa towns (Ábano Terme being the most
flourishing with a wide range of hotels); there have also been fertile
vineyards since Roman times. For a day trip the attractions of the
area include plenty of *trattorie* and opportunities to taste and buy the
local wine. The most attractive places to visit are the lovely
Benedictine abbey at **Praglia** (afternoon tours; the monks sell wine
and honey), the **Villa Barbarigo** at Valsanzibio (splendid gardens)
and Petrarch's house at the medieval hamlet of **Arquà Petrarca**. The
Euganean hills inspired some of Shelley's less felicitous lines:
"Beneath is spread like a green sea/The waveless plains of
Lombardy, Bounded by the vaporous air/Islanded by cities fair".

☞ **Monsélice, Este and Montagnana**
Three small towns on the edge of the Euganean hills are worth
visiting although the drive which links them is dreary. **Monsélice**
(*23km south*) is a charming town, with some attractive villas and a
castle containing a fine collection of furniture. **Este** (*32km south-west*),
less picturesque, has an interesting archaeological museum and,
nearby, the villas where Byron and Shelley lived. **Montagnana** (*48km
south-west*), encircled by impressive medieval walls and a moat, has a
spacious central piazza. Outside the eastern gate is the Villa Pisani
by Palladio (1553) and, 7km north, his Villa Poiana (1547) at Poiana
Maggiore.

PARMA
A prosperous but rather austere city, much of it 19th-century and
post-war, but dominated by the forbidding bulk of the Palazzo della
Pilotta, headquarters of the Farnese family who ruled Parma from
1545 till 1731. Life revolves around the large and busy Piazza
Garibaldi with pavement cafés and some fine 17th-century
municipal buildings. The square is bisected by the main shopping
street which crosses the town. At the heart of Parma, a network of
quiet old streets opens into the harmonious Piazza Duomo where
the cathedral and the graceful pink marble baptistery form a lovely
ensemble, often the setting for concerts in summer. On the far side
of the tree-lined river Parma, a tributary of the Po which dries up in
summer, is a residential district with the vast Ducal Park.
  Parma is traditionally associated with dried ham, sugared violets
and Parmesan cheese, and with Stendhal's famous novel *The
Charterhouse of Parma* (though he visited the city only briefly). The
main reason for visiting Parma is to see the paintings of Correggio,

in the cathedral and elsewhere, and the Lombard Romanesque architecture of the *centro episcopale*, which includes the cathedral, baptistery and church of San Giovanni.

☞ **Camera di San Paolo** A room in the former Benedictine Convent of St Paul, frescoed (c1518) by Correggio for the abbess. These are Correggio's earliest frescoes in Parma and show the influence of Mantegna in the use of perspective and classical themes, which Correggio treats more light-heartedly than Mantegna.

☞ **Glauco-Lombardi Museum** A collection devoted to Napoleon's wife Marie-Louise of Austria, who became ruler of Parma in 1815. It contains her jewels and nightgowns, her letters and accounts, and French 18th-century water-colours and drawings.

☞ **Madonna della Steccata** A Renaissance church with frescoes by Parmigianino (and others), painted from 1530-1535.

☞ **Palazzo della Pilotta** This contains two museums. The National Gallery has a superb collection, recently re-organised. Masterpieces by Correggio inevitably dominate, but there are also fine pictures by Parmigianino, Cima da Conegliano and the Bolognese school, among others. Ask the custodian to show you the remarkable Farnese theatre, built entirely of wood in 1615 in imitation of the Teatro Olimpico at Vicenza, and restored after bomb damage. The National Museum of Antiquities has a collection of finds from nearby Velleia.

☞ **Piazza Duomo** The large and very fine 11th-century **cathedral** is in typical Lombard Romanesque style – pink brick, a projecting porch supported by lions, and elaborate carving both inside and out. The interior of the cathedral dome is a stupendous triumph of *trompe-l'oeil* by Correggio, depicting the Assumption of the Virgin (1526-30). A contemporary criticised it as "a hash of frogs' legs", but Titian, recognising its artistic achievement, said that if the dome were turned upside down and filled with gold it would not be as valuable as Correggio's frescoes.

The neighbouring **baptistery** is a good example of the transition from the Romanesque to the Gothic style. It's a very beautiful octagonal building, built of rose coloured Verona marble, with superbly carved galleries and portal (the work of the great local 12th-century sculptor Benedetto Antelami). The rib-vaulted interior, decorated with 13th-century frescoes of biblical and legendary scenes, contains a series of sculptures by Antelami.

☞ **San Giovanni Evangelista** A Renaissance church with a Baroque façade, just behind the cathedral. In the dome Correggio's Vision of St John on Patmos (1520-23) is brought to the spectator with a directness and realism previously unknown (though it is unsophisticated compared with the later Assumption, in the cathedral).

Excursions from Parma

☞ **Castles**

In the countryside around Parma, particularly in the lovely hilly area to the south, are a number of fine castles, built for feudal families. Some are open to the public; worth visiting are Bardi, Felino (now a restaurant), Fontanellato (*20km north-west*) with a fresco by Parmigianino, San Secondo (*25km north-west*), Soragna (*28km north-west*) and Torrechiara (*20km south*).

☞ **Colorno** (*15km north*)
The ducal palace of the Farnese set in an English-style park. The side
facing the river is picturesque, but in a poor state of repair. There are
fine 18th-century rooms, currently under restoration (although
much of the furniture is now in the Palazzo Reale in Turin). "This is
the Versailles of the Princes of Parma" wrote Stendhal, without
much conviction.
(*See also Fidenza*)

PAVIA

An old town with fine Romanesque and medieval buildings. Ten
kilometres north is the famous Carthusian monastery, the Certosa di
Pavia (*see excursions from Milan*).

PIACENZA

A fine old town with "streets of stern houses, moodily frowning at
the other houses over the way" (Dickens) and a central square, the
Piazza dei Cavalli, dominated by the equestrian statues of Farnese
rulers and the fine old palace known as Il Gotico. There are several
churches worth seeing, and most contain some interesting
paintings.
☛ **Alberoni Gallery** (Collegio Alberoni)   An interesting art collection on the
outskirts of the city (2½km from the centre, towards Parma), with works by
important Italian and Flemish artists (including a masterpiece by Antonello
da Messina). Opening hours are very restricted.
☛ **Cathedral** (Duomo)   A fine but much-restored Lombard Romanesque
cathedral, with dome frescoes by Guercino and other works of art.
☛ **Civic Museum**   A picture collection and archaeological museum, housed
in the 16th-century Palazzo Farnese. An Etruscan bronze, known as the
Piacenza liver, is the rarest exhibit.
☛ **Madonna di Campagna**   A Renaissance church with frescoes by
Pordenone (c1530).

POMPOSA

An isolated Benedictine abbey which takes its style from the early
Christian churches of Ravenna. 14th-century frescoes adorn the
interior of the church and the refectory of the monastery.

PORDENONE

Chief town of the province of Friuli, and the birthplace of the painter
Giovanni Antonio de' Sacchis, known as Pordenone (1483-1589).
The town suffered in the 1976 earthquake and there is little of
interest except the cathedral, with a Romanesque campanile, and
the small museum with works by local painters including
Pordenone. There is adequate hotel accommodation.

RAVENNA

A thriving Roman port and great imperial capital, Ravenna was
more or less history by the Middle Ages. The magnificent Byzantine
mosaics, a legacy of Eastern influence from the 5th century to the 8th

century AD, are generally considered the finest in Europe.

The streets of old Ravenna are eerily quiet with sleepy old palaces, courtyards and cloisters and overgrown gardens. The heart of the city is the small Piazza del Popolo, now closed to traffic, described by Edith Templeton as "a pretty little reception room, well furnished with a medieval palace, a Baroque palace or two, a church with a clock that lights up at night, arcades along two walls, and two Renaissance columns with saints on them" (the columns are Venetian, symbolising dominion by that city from 1441 to 1509). Apart from the sights, which can be seen in a day, Ravenna has few attractions. It is a tangle of one-way systems and the business and residential areas are of no great interest or beauty. Oil and petro-chemical industries have all but destroyed the beauty of the surroundings, including the pinewoods beloved of Dante and Byron. Ravenna is on the day-trip programme of the big Adriatic resorts.

☛ **Archbishops' Museum** This contains the intricate ivory throne of the archbishop Maximian, carved in the 6th century, and a small chapel, the oratory of St Andrew, with a barrel-vaulted vestibule decorated with a charming mosaic of birds.

☛ **Art Gallery** (Pinacoteca Comunale) The art gallery is housed in a converted monastery with glassed-in cloisters and peacocks on the lawn. Many north Italian artists are represented, and there's a modern section of landscapes and portraits. Tullio Lombardo's finely-chiselled effigy of a young prince killed in battle is his masterpiece.

☛ **Basilica Sant' Apollinare Nuovo** A vast, bare church, echoing with antiquity. The mosaics – depicting 22 virgins leaving the port of Classis to follow the Three Magi and, opposite, a solemn procession of 26 martyrs – are wonderfully naturalistic, despite a traditional format. Clearly depicted is the palace of Theodoric (who ruled Ravenna 493-526) which he regarded as "the fine façade of government and a witness to kingship, which is displayed to the admiration of ambassadors, so that they can see from his dwelling what its master is like." The putative remains of this palace are adjacent to the Basilica.

☛ **Basilica di San Vitale** A simple octagonal-plan brick church, consecrated in 547. The interior is decorated with superb mosaics, remarkable for their clarity of design and colour, and comparable with those of Santa Sophia in Istanbul.

☛ **Mausoleum of Galla Placidia** Next to San Vitale, this tiny cross-shaped mausoleum with its starry dome is decorated with mosaics of religious-pastoral subjects. More Roman than Byzantine, they are probably the oldest mosaics in Ravenna (5th-century).

Excursions from Ravenna

☞ **Basilica di Sant' Apollinare in Classe** (2km south)
This is almost all that's left of the 6th-century port of Classis (which first flourished nearly 2,000 years ago). The plan is similar to that of Sant' Apollinare Nuovo: a main aisle with great arches supported by marble columns. Here the focus of attention is the apse and choir with breathtaking mosaics, full of lovely landscape details.
(See also Pomposa)

REGGIO NELL' EMILIA

An industrial city with little charm but some interest for art-lovers. The cathedral and several other churches are rich in works of art and the Civic Museum and Parmeggiani Gallery are worth visiting; the latter has a collection of Spanish art.

RIMINI

(See Adriatic Coastal Resorts)

ROVIGO

A dull provincial capital between Padua and Ferrara. The art gallery, with paintings by Giovanni Bellini, Dosso Dossi, Tiépolo and the Flemish painter Mabuse, is, however, worth visiting.

At Fratta Polesine *(18km south-west)* is Palladio's Villa Badoer.

SPILIMBERGO

An attractive small town, with a fine Gothic cathedral (restored after the 1976 earthquake), containing organ shutters painted by Pordenone. It has a mosaic school.

TREVISO

An attractive old town whose medieval centre was much damaged in the Second World War; many of the arcades have been rebuilt. The canals are a very faint reminder of Treviso's neighbour and protectress, Venice. On the main square, Piazza dei Signori, concert and theatre performances are held in summer. The cathedral and other churches and the civic museum contain paintings by local artists.

☛ **Cathedral** (Duomo)   The cathedral contains an Annunciation by Titian and frescoes by Pordenone.

☛ **Santa Caterina**   The chapel of the Innocents contains an impressive series of frescoes by the 14th-century artist, Tommaso da Modena. You can see them only by going to the Museo L. Bailo (1km away) first, and asking the custodian to unlock the convent.

☛ **San Nicolò**   A fine Gothic church, with lots of interesting paintings, particularly the frescoes on the columns by Tommaso da Modena and an altarpiece by Lorenzo Lotto. There is an enormous fresco of St Christopher, attributed to Antonio da Treviso.

In the province of Treviso are several country villas, converted to luxurious hotels (antique furniture, swimming pools and tennis courts).

Excursions from Treviso

(See Ásolo; Conegliano)

TRIESTE

A major port and capital of the province of Friuli-Venezia Giulia. Under Austrian rule from 1382 until 1918, it preserves some superb 19th-century architecture. The main sight is the fine cathedral of San Giusto (mostly 14th-century).

Excursions from Trieste

☞ **Miramare** (*7km north-west*)
This summer palace was built for the archduke Maximilian of
Austria (shot in Mexico in 1867) and is a popular excursion,
especially by boat. There is a small museum and gallery.
☞ **Istria**
There are organised excursions to the Istrian peninsula, just over the
Yugoslav border, where many towns still preserve reminders of
Venetian rule.

TURIN (TORINO)

The elegance of Turin may come as a surprise to those who associate
it with industry in general and the Fiat factory in particular. It's still
visited more by businessmen than by tourists and the lack of
appealing hotels reflects this. Still, the keen Italophile should relish
the sense of discovery in exploring the fine old centre of the capital
of Piedmont and one-time capital – of Savoy (16th century), Sardinia
(18th century) and, briefly, of a united Italy (1861-1865).

Many English travellers visited Turin as part of their Grand Tour
in the 18th and 19th centuries; they remarked on the fine layout of
the city with its regular streets, but also on the fact that many
buildings were left unfinished or in a poor state of repair. The
English-born Signora Piozzi, whose *Observations* reveal a
housewifely distaste for dirt and drains, accorded Turin high praise:
"Model of elegance, exact Turin!…This charming town is the *salon* of
Italy." The arcaded Piazza Carlo Felice, with its sumptuous old
cafés, retains the atmosphere of this drawing-room age, but the
superb Baroque architecture of Guarino Guarini and Filippo Juvarra
is perhaps the main reason for visiting Turin. Almost everything
worth seeing (except churches) is closed on Mondays.

Main sights

☛ **Palazzo dell' Accademia delle Scienze** (Egyptian Museum and Sabauda
Gallery) Two important museums housed in a dour palace built by Guarini.
The large **Egyptian Museum** is the oldest of its kind in Europe and ranks
third in importance to those of Cairo and London. A black granite statue of
Rameses II dating from c1200BC, a series of wall paintings from the XI
dynasty (2122-1991BC) discovered in a tomb in 1911 and a rock-cut temple
built in the 15th century BC are among the treasures.

The **Galleria Sabauda** is an outstandingly fine picture collection started by
the princes of Savoy. The Italian section includes works by Tuscan, Lombard
and Venetian artists, with separate rooms devoted to Piedmontese painting.
Masterpieces include Veronese's Supper in the House of Simon. The Flemish
and Dutch collection is possibly the best in Italy, with works by Van Eyck,
Memling and Rembrandt. Van Dyck's portrait of the children of Charles I is
one of the highlights of the collection. The small Gualino collection is worth
seeing too; here pictures are hung in the context of furniture and *objets d'art*.
☛ **Palazzo Madama** Juvarra's superb Baroque façade with its sweeping
double staircase is a front for a medieval castle. The palace contains a
museum of "ancient" art (mostly Gothic and Renaissance sculpture and
paintings) and richly furnished state apartments.

☛ **Palazzo Reale**   The princes of the House of Savoy moved their capital from Chambéry to Turin in 1573 and built this brick castle some 80 years later. The splendid staircase designed by Juvarra leads to state rooms, many in Frenchified taste. See the sumptuous Great Gallery with frescoes by the Austrian artist Daniel Seyter (1690), the Chinese room by Juvarra and the exquisite apartments of Queen Maria Teresa. There's also a Royal Armoury.

Other sights

☛ **Borgo Medioevale**   A bogus medieval castle, where furnishing and the way of life of a feudal estate have been recreated for visitors.
☛ **Cathedral** (Duomo)   A Renaissance building mainly of interest for Guarini's chapel of the Holy Shroud (Cappella della Santa Sindone), containing the famous relic, which has been described as "the oldest photograph in the world." It is not on general view but there is a life-sized reproduction.
☛ **Palazzo Carignano**   A fine villa by Guarini where Victor Emmanuel II, first king of Italy, was born (1820) and the Unification of Italy was proclaimed (1861).

Excursions from Turin

☞ **Basilica of Superga** (*10km east*)
A masterpiece by Juvarra, on a hill with splendid views of Turin. In the crypt are the grandiose tombs of the kings of Savoy.

☞ **Stupinigi** (*10km south-west*)
A vast hunting lodge built by Juvarra for Victor Amadeus II of Savoy in 1729-30, and topped with a statue of a stag. In a sad state of decay, the palace has a rather feeble furniture museum but is worth a visit for the decoration of its huge, echoing rooms. Fiat is financing a restoration project, expected to take three years.

☞ **Sacra di San Michele** (*25km west*)
Ancient Benedictine monastery, superbly sited.
(*See Avigliana, Lakes and Mountains chapter*)

UDINE

The main town of Friuli is an attractive medieval hill-town with the stamp of Venetian culture (it belonged to the republic of Venice from 1420). The lovely Piazza della Libertà is surrounded by distinctive Venetian Gothic and Renaissance buildings, and the town is rich in paintings by Tiépolo, the great Venetian painter of decorative Rococo schemes (1696-1770).
☛ **Archbishops' Palace**   Tiépolo's first fresco commission (1725); the grand staircase and apartments are decorated with frescoes of subjects such as the Fall of the Rebel Angels and the Judgement of Solomon.
☛ **Castle**   An impressive 16th-century Venetian fortress, with a museum and art gallery, closed for restoration since the 1976 earthquake.
☛ **Cathedral** (Duomo)   The Gothic cathedral contains paintings by Tiépolo, notably the Assumption (1757) in the oratory.

Excursions from Udine

☞ **Palmanova** (*17km south*)

A remarkable star-shaped fortress city, built by the Venetians at the
end of the 16th century and added to by Napoleon in 1806. Radial
streets converge on the hexagonal central piazza and 17th-century
cathedral.

VERONA

Famous for its Roman remains and for Shakespearean associations,
Verona is steeped in the past. But the heart of the city is very much
alive, especially during the opera season (early July until the
beginning of September). Life still revolves around the market
square (Piazza Erbe, once the Roman forum), the vast Piazza Bra,
dominated by the Arena, and the elegant pedestrians-only shopping
street Via Manzoni which links the two squares. Apart from the
Arena, there are other, less spectacular, **Roman remains** including
city gates (the Porta Borsari is notable), the remains of roads and
walls, and, reached via the reconstructed Ponte Pietra, the theatre.

However, the centre of Verona, bounded by a loop of the River
Adige and by medieval walls, is predominantly Gothic in aspect;
many of its buildings of matt pinkish marble have pointed-arch
windows and fish-tailed battlements. Most of it dates from the rule
of the della Scala (Scaliger) and Visconti families or from the period
of Venetian domination after 1405. **Churches** are chiefly worth
visiting for the paintings they contain: the cathedral (Titian's
Assumption), Sant' Anastasia (pale fragment of Pisanello's St
George and the Dragon), San Fermo Maggiore (Pisanello's
Annunciation). Concerts are often held in the churches in summer.

Hotel accommodation is plentiful and varied, but gets booked up
well in advance, particularly during the summer opera season.
Many people stay on Lake Garda and go into Verona by bus or car in
the evenings.

☛ **The Arena**   One of the largest and best-preserved Roman amphitheatres
in the world, used for opera and ballet (it was previously used for gladiatorial
combats and executions).

☛ **Castelvecchio**   The former stronghold of the della Scala family has been
beautifully converted to a museum and art gallery with good examples of
Venetian art, and fine views from the battlements over the Ponte Scaligero.

☛ **Juliet's Balcony**   The balcony from which Shakespeare's Juliet cries
"Romeo, Romeo! wherefore art thou Romeo?" is surprisingly small and
surprisingly accessible. The little courtyard is – not surprisingly – usually
crammed with tourists.

☛ **Piazza dei Signori**   The centre of civic life until the 16th century is rather
like a stage set and you half expect Shakespeare's two gentlemen to stroll by.
The medieval **Torre dei Lamberti** offers a magnificent view of the city and of
the **Piazza delle Erbe** with its rows of giant mushroom-like sunshades.
Nearby are the elaborate tombs of the Scaliger family.

☛ **San Zeno Maggiore**   On the outskirts of the town, an exceptional
Romanesque church. There's a superb bronze doorway with biblical scenes,
a charming cloister and works of art including a marvellous triptych by
Mantegna above the main altar.

Vizenza, Villa Rotonda

VICENZA

Vicenza's fame rests solely on Andrea Palladio (1508-88), last great architect of the Renaissance, whose style, backed up by his study of classical antiquity, echoed ancient Rome. The town is something of a backwater, little geared to tourists, but a fascinating architectural showcase, with some interesting churches. Vicenza was part of the Venetian republic from 1404-1813; many of the streets are called *contra* or *contrada* (Venetian dialect for alley). The main street, which runs the length of the old part of the city, is named after Palladio and contains some of his *palazzi* and the house where he lived. Behind The Piazza dei Signori, dominated by Palladio's vast green-domed basilica, is the main square. The classic villas of Palladio and his followers are dotted around the countryside (*see Palladian Villas on the following page*).

☞ **Basilica of Monte Bérico**   The church contains Veronese's Supper of Saint Gregory the Great and a good Pietà by Bartolomeo Montagna, principal artist of Vicenza in the late 15th century. On a clear day Venice and the Alps can be seen from the belvedere opposite the church.

☞ **Palazzo Chiericati** (Museo Civico)   One of Palladio's best villas (1550-57) which was to be the model and inspiration for two of Inigo Jones' buildings in London about 70 years later (the Queen's House at Greenwich and the Banqueting House in Whitehall). It now houses the **Municipal Museum** notable for works by artists of the Veneto, especially Bartolomeo Montagna. There are also works by the major Venetian artists including Tintoretto, Veronese and Tiépolo.

PALLADIAN VILLAS

Strictly speaking, Palladio (whose real name was Andrea di Pietro della Gondola) was a Paduan, but he is always associated with Vicenza where he spent his early working years as an apprentice stonemason and carver and later designed some of his greatest public buildings. In the 1540s he designed his first "villas". The secure protection of the Venetian republic had made it possible to have unfortified villas outside the towns for the first time since the Romans. Instead of castles, Palladio designed working farms, with wings called *barchesse* where farm labourers could be housed ("a villa", he later wrote, "is no more than a small town"). He usually incorporated stables, granaries and pigeon lofts or dovecotes. But the villas were also grand country houses, their interiors elaborately frescoed to recreate the atmosphere of a Roman villa. The adjectives most often used to describe Palladio's villas are "serene" and "civilised". The classic 18th-century English country house tradition is an almost direct result of Palladio's villas in the countryside of the Veneto: he set both the style and the standard.

In 1570 Palladio published his *Four Books of Architecture*, a detailed exposition of his architectural principles. In 1716 it was translated into English and helped start the vogue for "Palladian" architecture, which lasted for over fifty years and is reflected in the buildings of London and in many country houses of the period.

The villas mentioned below are not necessarily by Palladio himself, but most are influenced by him; some are included because the interior decoration is worth seeing. Many villas are privately owned and not open to the public; they are listed only where it is possible to get a good view of the exterior. It is unlikely that either of the two suggested itineraries from Vicenza could include visiting all the villas as most have very restricted opening hours with complicated seasonal variations; it is essential to get the latest list published by the Tourist Office in Vicenza before setting out (they also publish an illustrated leaflet suggesting several more detailed itineraries).

☞ **South of Vicenza** (*round trip via Noventa, 100km*)
After visiting Palladio's Villa Rotonda and Villa Valmarana ai Nani in Vicenza, continue via Longare (17th-century villas at Custozza, one now a restaurant) and Noventa (Villa Barbarigo, a 17th-century villa, now the town hall, can be visited) to Villa Poiana at Poiana Maggiore. Continue to Villa Pisani (an early villa by Palladio) at Bagnolo di Lonigo and then to Villa Pisani (designed by Scamozzi, 1576) at Lonigo. Villa Cordellina-Lombardi (Palladian-type 18th-century villa with frescoes by Tiépolo), near Montecchio Maggiore, can occasionally be visited.

☞ **North of Vicenza** (*round trip via Lugo, 55km*)
Passing the Villa Caldogno (built in 1570 after a design by Palladio; not open to the public) near Caldogno, proceed to Thiene (*20km*). Here is the Castello Colleoni, a castellated villa dating from 1476 (guided tours of frescoed rooms; pretty Venetian chapel). Continue to Villa Godi near Lugo, the first country house designed by Palladio (1540-1542) with frescoes by Zelotti (plus small museums of fossils and 19th-century pictures). Nearby is Villa Piovene, attributed to Palladio but with additions. Return direct or via Sarcedo, Montecchio Precalcino and Dueville, all with villas in Palladian style.

Palladio's more important country villas are most easily visited from Ásolo (Villa Maser) and Padua (Villa Malcontenta), with the notable exception of the Villa Rotonda on the outskirts of Vicenza. His two great churches are in Venice.

☛ **Santa Corona** An early Gothic church containing Giovanni Bellini's beautiful Baptism of Christ.

☛ **Teatro Olimpico** Palladio's last work (1580), once again on the antique model, completed by Scamozzi who designed the stunning stage sets in illusionistic perspective. Outside the entrance is a floral clock and calendar, replanted daily in summer.

☛ **Villa Rotonda** Palladio's most famous villa, inspired by a classical temple, is a masterpiece of symmetry whose simplicity prevents it from being pompous. It was copied in England at Chiswick and Mereworth, and also in America, notably by president Thomas Jefferson at Monticello. Only the grounds are open to the public (there's also a good glimpse from the road).

☛ **Villa Valmarana ai Nani** This villa, near the Villa Rotonda, is worth visiting for the superb frescoes by Tiépolo (1757) and his son Gian Domenico.

Excursions from Vicenza
☞ **Palladian villas**
(See opposite page, and Ásolo)

VIGÉVANO

For centuries a small market town under the dominion of the Milanese Sforza and Visconti families, Vigévano is now an important centre for the shoe-making industry. However the heart of the town is relatively unspoilt, with some lovely 15th-century buildings. The focal point is the beautiful arcaded piazza, designed (possibly by Leonardo da Vinci) for Ludovico il Moro in 1494, as an approach to the vast castle of the Sforzas (now awaiting restoration). The approach was later blocked by the concave Baroque façade of the cathedral (with Lombard paintings and a rich treasury).

Hotels

Ásolo	£££££
VILLA CIPRIANI	Open all year
Via Canova 298, 31011 Treviso	Tel: (0423) 55444

The most charming hotel in the CIGA chain, and one of the loveliest anywhere. Owned briefly by Robert Browning, the 16th-century Villa Galanti then passed to the Guinness family who enlisted the services of Giuseppe Cipriani to transform it into a hotel. It remains remarkably unspoilt; public rooms are small, intimate and beautifully furnished with antiques, traditional bedrooms (in three grades of luxury) are welcoming and attractive, always with fresh flowers and fruit. All rooms focus on the glorious hills around Ásolo and the Dolomites in the distance and there's a lovely terraced garden where meals are often taken. The manager, Giuseppe Kamenar, is holding out (against all the odds) against the building of a swimming pool which might commercialise and spoil this seductive retreat.

Facilities: *32 bedrooms (AC); restaurant; lift; garage* **Credit/charge cards accepted:** *Amex, Diners, Eurocard, Visa*

Barbiano di Cotignola ££
VILLA BOLIS *Open all year*
Via Corriera 5, 48010 Ravenna Tel: (0545) 79347

A fine 17th-century mansion set in dull, flat countryside about 30km from
Ravenna. Bought in a state of ruin, it was expertly restored in 1983 and
converted into a hotel. Bedrooms are very large (except the attic singles) and
elegantly decorated to complement the style of the house; original
architectural features have been preserved and antique furniture and oil
paintings abound. Guests may use the facilities (swimming pools, tennis
courts) of a local sports club in the grounds. Exceptionally good value.

Facilities: *14 bedrooms; restaurant (closed Mon); parking* **Credit/charge cards
accepted:** *Amex, Diners*

Bergamo £
AGNELLO D'ORO *Open all year*
Via Gombito 22, 24100 Bergamo Tel: (035) 249883

A tall, narrow, shuttered building, tucked away off the main pedestrian
street of the old town. Bedrooms are simple but cheerful, some with
traditionally painted bedheads and tables. Only the splashing of the fountain
below and the dawn chorus from the bell-tower disturb the peace. In the cosy
bistro-like restaurant, festooned with copper pots and pans, hand-painted
plates, and framed gastronomic awards, you can sample produce from the
valleys, woods and lakes – like quails on a mound of fluffy golden *polenta* (not
the usual coagulated slab) and *funghi porcini* – and choose from a selection of
Tuscan and Piedmontese wines displayed on shelves. In fine weather there
are tables outside on the little piazza.

Facilities: *20 bedrooms; restaurant (closed Mon); lift* **Credit/charge cards
accepted:** *Amex, Diners, Visa*

Bergamo ££
GOURMET *Open all year*
Via San Vigilio 1, 24100 Bergamo Tel: (035) 256110

On the road to the summit of San Vigilio, but only a short walk from the
Piazza Vecchia of the old town, this is a restaurant with rooms, with the
emphasis (as the name suggests) on the restaurant part. Cooking is
inventive, with an excellent range of desserts and a good wine list; you dine
in a bright and airy room or on the shady terrace. Bedrooms are of a high
standard, neat, modern and well-equipped, but lacking in atmosphere.

Facilities: *10 bedrooms; restaurant (closed Tues); parking* **Credit/charge cards
accepted:** *Amex, Eurocard, Visa*

Bologna ££
DEI COMMERCIANTI *Closed Aug*
Via de' Pignattari 11, 40100 Bologna Tel: (051) 233052

In a side street off the main Piazza, a small, central hotel under the same
management as the nearby *Orologio* (see below). At the time of inspection,
bedrooms were basic but clean, mostly with showers only, but a complete
overhaul was due for completion to the standard of the *Orologio*.

Facilities: *35 bedrooms; garage* **Credit/charge cards accepted:** *Amex, Diners,
Eurocard, Visa*

Bologna ££££
CORONA D'ORO *Closed Aug*
Via Oberdan 12, 40100 Bologna Tel: (051) 236456

Well-situated near the Piazza Maggiore, the Corona d'Oro (Golden Crown)
has been a hotel since 1890. Antique features (like the 16th-century painted
beamed ceiling and the wrought-iron staircase) are successfully combined
with sophisticated contemporary furnishings and pale shades of pale.
There's no lounge or restaurant but a Liberty-style extension to the hall and a
small, bright (but not very comfortable or cosy) bar.

Facilities: *35 bedrooms; lift; garage service* **Credit/charge cards accepted:**
Amex, Diners, Eurocard, Visa

Bologna £
OROLOGIO *Open all year*
Via IV Novembre 10, 40100 Bologna Tel: (051) 231253

A small hotel right by the clock tower of the town hall after which it is
named. Recently completely renovated, the hotel is simply decorated and
furnished as a convenient base for tourists and businessmen. The bright
white breakfast room doubles as a coffee bar and lounge.

Facilities: *32 bedrooms; lift; garage* **Credit/charge cards accepted:** *Amex,
Diners, Eurocard, Visa*

Bologna ££
ROMA *Open all year*
Via Massimo d'Azeglio 9, 40100 Bologna Tel: (051) 274400

A civilised, traditional hotel on the smartest shopping street in Bologna.
There's a variety of very individually decorated bedrooms, mostly in a floral,
chintzy English-country-house style. Public rooms are on the fusty side of
formal, though, and the management a little starchy.

Facilities: *85 bedrooms (AC); restaurant (closed Aug); lift; garage* **Credit/charge
cards accepted:** *Amex, Diners, Eurocard, Visa*

Brisighella   £
GIGIOLÉ   *Closed Feb*
Piazza Carducci 5, 48013 Ravenna   *Tel: (0546) 81209*

A simple family-run hotel on the market square, in the centre of this
attractive old village, 45km from Ravenna. Bedrooms are basic but
reasonably cheerful. Downstairs the emphasis is on the restaurant which is
surprisingly sophisticated and attracts a cliéntèle from quite far afield.
There's an interesting menu of local specialities; if you have *spoja lorda*, a kind
of soup, you are awarded a hand-painted plate.

Facilities: *17 bedrooms; restaurant (closed Sun dinner, Mon); lift*   **Credit/charge
cards accepted:** *Amex, Diners*

Busseto   £
I DUE FOSCARI   *Open all year*
Piazza Carlo Rossi 15, 43011 Parma   *Tel: (0524) 92337*

In Verdi country, 40km from Parma, a detached villa in the style of the local
castles (although less than thirty years old). Bedrooms are spacious and
comfortable, individually decorated with traditional furniture, some antique.
Each has its own portrait of Verdi, the local hero, born at nearby Roncole.
There's a rustic, medieval-style bar and restaurant, a taverna, and a terrace
for summer meals. The young manager and his staff are helpful and friendly.

Facilities: *20 bedrooms; restaurant (closed Mon); parking*   **Credit/charge cards
accepted:** *Amex, Eurocard, Visa*

Cavasagra di Vedelago   ££££
VILLA CORNER DELLA REGINA   *Open all year*
Via Corriva 10, 31050 Treviso   *Tel: (0423) 481481*

A beautiful villa, dating from 1500 but remodelled by a pupil of Palladio in
1700 and transformed into a luxurious country hotel in 1983. The original
villa belonged to Catherine Cornaro, ex-Queen of Cyprus who was given
nearby Ásolo and Castelfranco in exchange for her dominion. There's an
elegant restaurant occupying several rooms overlooking the park (Venetian
and international cooking) and a summery pink-and-white drawing room.
Bedrooms are cool and spacious, some with beautiful stuccoed walls and
ceilings, most with grand but graceful Empire furniture. There are 12
simpler, modern bedrooms in the annexe, the old *barchesse* (tenants'
quarters). One of the glories of the Villa Corner is its fine formal park, with
an attractive pool near the former orangery which is now an airy second
restaurant. There are also 11 hectares of vineyards, producing a *spumante*
served in the hotel.

Facilities: *23 bedrooms; restaurant; swimming pool; tennis courts; parking*   **Credit/
charge cards accepted:** *Amex, Diners, Eurocard, Visa*

Ferrara £££
RIPAGRANDE *Open all year*
Via Ripagrande 21, 44100 Ferrara *Tel: (0532) 34733*

The solemn façade of a Renaissance mansion (Palazzo Beccari-Freguglia) conceals an unusual hotel. Expert restoration and antique furniture and tapestries have preserved the atmosphere in the hall but duplex-style bedrooms with unit furniture (and some kitchen facilities) come as a shock. The restaurant, serving regional food, is lacking in atmosphere but in summer drinks and meals are served in the charming rosy-bricked courtyard.

Facilities: *40 bedrooms (AC); restaurant (closed Mon and Aug); lift; parking* **Credit/charge cards accepted:** *Amex, Diners, Eurocard, Visa*

Mantua ££
BROLETTO *Closed Dec to mid-Jan*
Via Accademia 1, 46100 Mantova *Tel: (0376) 326784*

In an old inn near the Piazza Erbe, this small hotel was opened in 1984. The bedrooms and breakfast room are clean and neat, with no frills. There's no lounge or restaurant, but the Broletto is fine for a short stay.

Facilities: *16 bedrooms (AC); lift* **Credit/charge cards accepted:** *Amex, Diners, Eurocard, Visa*

Mantua £££
SAN LORENZO *Open all year*
Piazza Concordia 14, 46100 Mantova *Tel: (0376) 327044*

A traditional hotel, well-placed for seeing the historic nucleus of Mantua. Comfortable, old-fashioned bedrooms, some overlooking the 12th-century rotunda church of San Lorenzo and the market square. A small roof terrace provides some relief from the rather dowdy public areas.

Facilities: *42 bedrooms (AC); lift; garage* **Credit/charge cards accepted:** *Amex, Eurocard*

Milan ££
ANTICA LOCANDA SOLFERINO *Closed two weeks in Aug*
Via Castelfidardo 2, 20100 Milano *Tel: (02) 6599886*

Close to the Brera gallery, a charming small hotel with the atmosphere of an old country inn. Bedrooms, on the first floor, vary in size and shape but have pretty pieces of old furniture, faded flowery curtains, whitewashed walls and uneven wooden floors. Modernisation is confined to the plumbing, with bathrooms in fresh cottagey style. An equal delight is the adjacent old-fashioned bistro-type restaurant, of the sort more usually found in Paris. The Milanese love it, and the food is delicious, so be sure to book a table.

Facilities: *11 bedrooms; restaurant (closed Sat lunch and Sun)* **Credit/charge cards accepted:** *none*

Milan   £££
GRAN DUCA DI YORK   *Closed Aug*
Via Moneta 1a, 20100 Milano   *Tel: (02) 874863*

Near the Ambrosiana gallery, a 19th-century *palazzo* which is fairly quiet for
such a central location. Bedrooms and bathrooms are rather spartan but large
and clean. There's a bright breakfast area and a separate bar.

Facilities: 33 *bedrooms (AC); lift*   **Credit/charge cards accepted:** *none*

Milan   £££
MANZONI   *Open all year*
Via Santo Spirito 20, 20100 Milano   *Tel: (02) 705700*

A civilised hotel just off the most elegant shopping street, the Via
Montenapoleone. Bedrooms are plain but comfortable and public rooms (a
bar and basement breakfast room) have been smartly redecorated.

Facilities: 52 *bedrooms; lift*   **Credit/charge cards accepted:** *none*

Modena   ££££
CANALGRANDE   *Open all year*
Corso Canal Grande 6, 41100 Modena   *Tel: (059) 217160*

The Canalgrande, once a noble patrician villa, is close to the centre of
Modena but is quiet, with a lovely garden and terrace. Much of the original
17th-century decoration survives in the ground floor rooms, notably the
splendid neo-classical entrance hall. In the comfortable old-fashioned salons
there are stuccoes, frescoed ceilings and full-length portraits of members of
the European royal families including Louis XIV of France and Maria Teresa
of Austria (most, but not all, of the dukes of Modena are relegated to
head-and-shoulders). Bedrooms have been modernised and are comfortable
with well co-ordinated decoration, some with smart marble bathrooms. The
adjacent basement restaurant, called *La Secchia Rapita*, is a simple trattoria.
The best place to stay in Modena, if you can afford it.

Facilities: 80 *bedrooms (AC); restaurant (closed Tues and Aug); lift*   **Credit/
charge cards accepted:** *Amex, Diners, Eurocard, Visa*

Modena   £
IL CASTELLO   *Open all year*
Via Curtatone 321, 41100 Modena   *Tel: (059) 361033*

A mock castle in a semi-rural situation about 5km out of town. Bedrooms are
basic but quite spacious. The restaurant offers honest home cooking with a
minimal choice of dishes. A modest alternative to the Canalgrande, best
suited to people on a touring holiday who want to avoid staying in town
centres.

Facilities: 30 *bedrooms; restaurant (closed lunch); parking*   **Credit/charge cards
accepted:** *none*

Mogliano Veneto   **£££**
VILLA CONDULMER   *Closed Nov to March*
Zerman, 31020 Treviso   *Tel: (041) 457100*

Seven km from Treviso, 20km from Venice, the Villa Condulmer is a faded
18th-century villa set in lovely gardens with a particularly pretty pool area.
The interior is grand, with impressive stucco ceilings, splendid Murano glass
chandeliers and 19th-century frescoes in the hall and main restaurant.
Bedrooms vary in comfort and atmosphere from old-fashioned, slightly
faded grandeur in the main villa to modern luxury in a new annexe (with 32
bedrooms). There are simpler rooms in the converted stable wing at lower
prices. A good choice for a comfortable country hotel holiday with plenty of
sightseeing opportunities, for the price of a modest hotel in Venice.

Facilities: *45 bedrooms; restaurants; swimming pool; tennis court; golf course;
riding; parking* **Credit/charge cards accepted:** *Amex, Diners, Eurocard, Visa*

Padua   **£**
CASA DEL PELLEGRINO   *Closed mid-Dec to Jan*
Via Cesarotti 21, 35100 Padova   *Tel: (049) 27801*

An old building on the Piazza del Santo, with a modern extension at the back
which includes an institutional restaurant and bar. The Casa del Pellegrino is
used by pilgrims and bedrooms are suitably ascetic, less than half with
private bathrooms. A good choice for budget travellers.

Facilities: *183 bedrooms; restaurant* **Credit/charge cards accepted:** *none*

Padua   **££**
DONATELLO   *Closed mid-Dec to mid-Jan*
Via del Santo 102-4, 35100 Padova   *Tel: (049) 36515*

Directly opposite St Anthony's basilica, this is a modern hotel in a much
renovated old shell. Bedrooms are spacious, furniture strictly utilitarian. The
Sant' Antonio restaurant, under the same management, offers reasonable
plain food, and summer dining on the pavement overlooking the basilica.
There's a bright breakfast café, used by passers-by as well as hotel guests.

Facilities: *42 bedrooms (AC); restaurant (closed Fri except mid-July to end Sept); lift;
garage* **Credit/charge cards accepted:** *Amex, Diners, Eurocard, Visa*

Our price symbols

£   = you can expect to find a room for under £35
££   = you can expect to find a room for under £55
£££   = you can expect to find a room for under £75
££££ = you can expect to find a room for under £125
£££££ = you should expect to pay over £125 for a room

Parma ££
TORINO *Closed 3 weeks Aug, Christmas*
Via A. Mazza 7, 43100 Parma *Tel: (0521) 281046*

A small, welcoming hotel in the centre of Parma. The ground floor consists of a lounge area, bar and breakfast room, all pretty, light and comfortable. Bedrooms are no more than adequate with some bathrooms (mostly showers only) in need of modernisation. But the saving grace is the peace and quiet; the hotel is in a pedestrian zone, although hotel guests may drive to the private garage. The lack of restaurant is not a drawback – there are several good ones within walking distance of the hotel.

Facilities: *33 bedrooms; lift; garage* **Credit/charge cards accepted:** *Amex, Diners, Eurocard, Visa*

Pomponesco £
IL LEONE *Closed Jan*
Piazza IV Martiri 2, 46030 Mantova *Tel: (0375) 86077*

A 16th-century summer house of the Gonzaga family, in the large deserted square of a small town on the Po. The gracious dining room has the original frescoed ceiling (depicting an allegory of four of the Continents) and tables are laden with heavy silver and cut glass. At dinner, the younger members of the family (Mori, not Gonzaga), formally dressed, offer friendly but slick service. The main courses can be daunting to all but the most adventurous palate and you may yearn for a safe *cotoletta milanese*. At any rate, try to leave room for their *dolce dei Gonzaga*, an exquisite concoction of sponge, biscuit and chocolate. After the visual and gastronomic feast of the dining-room you retire to a spartan bedroom. The swimming pool, in a pretty courtyard, is an unexpected luxury.

Facilities: *8 bedrooms; restaurant (closed Sun dinner and Mon); swimming pool* **Credit/charge cards accepted:** *Amex, Visa*

Ravenna £
CENTRALE BYRON *Open all year*
Via IV Novembre 14, 48100 Ravenna *Tel: (0544) 22225*

A well-located hotel, close to the main square. Unfortunately the rather basic bedrooms don't live up to the promise of the smart mirror and brass entrance hall and bar. However convenience may overcome considerations of comfort.

Facilities: *56 bedrooms (AC); lift* **Credit/charge cards accepted:** *Amex, Diners, Eurocard, Visa*

Sabbioneta   £
AL DUCA   *Closed Jan*
Via della Stamperia 18, 46018 Mantova   *Tel: (0375) 52474*

A good place for an overnight stay, in the Renaissance ghost town of
Sabbioneta, half-way between Mantua and Parma. In a town house dating
from the time of Vespasiano Gonzaga (after whom the hotel is named) this is
a simple hotel with cool, spacious bedrooms, cheaply but adequately
furnished, and a trattoria restaurant, serving good food and local and
national wines.

Facilities: *10 bedrooms; restaurant (closed Mon); parking*   **Credit/charge cards
accepted:** *Amex, Diners, Visa*

Sabbioneta   £
CA' D'AMICI   *Open all year*
Via Anna d' Aragona 2, 46018 Mantova   *Tel: (0375) 52318*

A restaurant with rooms on the Mantua/Parma road, just outside the town
walls of Sabbioneta. The restaurant is chalet-style, with French windows
overlooking a small garden area where you can sit for drinks or breakfast.
The bedrooms, whitewashed and tiled, have a rustic feel and are surprisingly
quiet. The Ca' d'Amici is run by an enthusiastic and friendly young couple.
Their American-speaking chef produces fairly standard Italian food, perhaps
not quite up to the expectations engendered by the handwritten menu.
There's an interesting wine list, with a range of local products.

Facilities: *9 bedrooms; restaurant (closed Tues); parking*   **Credit/charge cards
accepted:** *none*

Turin   ££££
VILLA SASSI   *Closed Aug*
Strada al Traforo del Pino 47, 10132 Torino   *Tel: (011) 890556*

Turin has no shortage of standard hotels for businessmen. But if comfort and
good food are a high priority then Villa Sassi is an experience worth paying
for. It is an aristocratic 17th-century villa set in a lovely park on the edge of
the city. It does not feel like a hotel; there are just 12 bedrooms (none with
numbers), all spacious and tranquil with parquet floors and antique
furniture. Public rooms are equally civilised and the restaurant – El Toulà – is
suitably serious. The chef, Antonio Ibba, favours the freshest, simplest
dishes: asparagus, salmon or *funghi porcini* in season as well as regional
specialities like *agnolotti alla piemontese* and a wide range of meat courses. The
wine list is prodigious, and not overpriced, but I Sassi is an expensive treat.

Facilities: *12 bedrooms; restaurant (closed Sun); parking*   **Credit/charge cards
accepted:** *Amex, Diners, Eurocard, Visa*

Verona   £££
COLOMBA D'ORO   Open all year
Via Cattaneo 10, 37100 Verona   Tel: (045) 595300

A comfortable hotel in a quietish street close to the Arena, the Colomba
d'Oro is a favourite haunt of opera goers (but charges a high commission for
getting tickets). There are no frills; bedrooms are plain and public rooms
rather club-like – hushed, with leather sofas and seating units. A fair choice
for people who want to try Verona's various good restaurants, and for those
with cars.

Facilities: 51 bedrooms (AC); lift; garage   **Credit/charge cards accepted:** Amex,
Diners, Eurocard, Visa

Verona   £££££
I DUE TORRI   Open all year
Piazza Sant' Anastasia 4, 37100 Verona   Tel: (045) 595044

Well-situated in a quiet square near the river, an imposing villa rebuilt in the
1950s along the lines of the original hotel which closed in 1882. Rooms are
decorated in different 18th- and 19th-century styles to remind the guest (as
he selects from an antiquated slide show of those available) that he is in the
company of Mozart, the archduke Maximilian, Garibaldi, Charles II of
England, Napoleon, Joseph II of Austria, Goethe, Victor Emmanuel II and
others. An exceptional collection of European porcelain is displayed in the
lounge and there's an Empire-style writing room. Nearly all the decoration
dates from the 1950s and the atmosphere is fusty. Still, it's one of the most
extraordinary hotels in Italy.

Facilities: 100 bedrooms (AC); restaurant; lift   **Credit/charge cards accepted:**
Amex, Diners, Eurocard, Visa

Verona   ££
IL TORCOLO   Open all year
Vicolo Listone 3, 37100 Verona   Tel: (045) 21512

Very close to the Arena (at the time of inspection the hotel employed a
chambermaid called Tosca!), and popular with the cognoscenti who book their
favourite rooms a year in advance of the opera season. The somewhat
dilapidated exterior gives no indication of the charm of the interior, each
bedroom individually decorated by the owner, Silvia Pomari, who has
collected the furniture and paintings. The attic bedrooms are modern, the
rest more traditional, some with antique country furniture. You can take
breakfast in the tiny modern breakfast room, in your bedroom, or on the
terrace outside, shared with the restaurant next door.

Facilities: 19 bedrooms (AC); lift   **Credit/charge cards accepted:** none

LIGURIA

*❛Look landwards from the water – purple
Apennines are ever in sight❜*
NORMAN DOUGLAS

Portovenere

Introduction

A narrow arc of beautiful mountainous coastline stretching from France to the Tuscan border, Liguria is the smallest of the old Italian provinces. The region (officially designated as such in 1970) takes its name from the earliest inhabitants of the area – tribes isolated by the Alps and the Apennines from their nearest neighbours, distinct and independent. The Ligurians were known to the Phoenicians and to the ancient Greeks for their piracy as well as their trading posts, and proved impervious to influences of classical culture, even when the Romans' Via Aurelia made their territory the land route between Italy and Roman France. Roman remnants in Liguria are scanty: a few inland bridges, some fragmented tombs. After the Empire collapsed Liguria reverted for a time to inaccessible independence – many barbarian raids of Italy's Dark Ages never reached this corner – but Lombards and Franks successively divided it into feudal domains.

Saracen pirates constantly threatened this coast and in 934 sacked its biggest port, Genoa. The Genoese raised money to build an independent war fleet and began to retaliate. Over the next three centuries they routed the Saracens, taking the strongholds of Sardinia and Corsica with the help of Pisa; they then fought the Pisans until their former allies ceased all maritime ambitions, and established a Genoese ascendancy in the Mediterranean. Profiting from the crusades they went on to acquire trading colonies extending to Constantinople, Syria and Crete. "*Genuensis, ergo mercator*" (from Genoa, so in trade) was a reputation they accepted with pride. There were less flattering descriptions; Dante declared them "eaten with rapacity" and wished them expunged from the world, a proverb (possibly Pisan) linked *Genoa Superba* (The Proud) with "men without faith, women without shame", and an English traveller reported from Florence in 1645 that "the Genowaies have not the Fortune to be so well belov'd as other People in Italy; which proceeds, I believe, from their Cunningness and Overreachings in bargaining, wherein they have something of the Jew". The reputation for miserliness (or, at best, thrift) has stuck.

By the end of the 14th century Genoese rule stretched the length of Liguria. The city was rich and splendid, and commercial affairs abroad were excellently managed by Genoese bankers and creditors in a remarkable institution later known as the Office or Bank of St George, which inspired Machiavelli's phrase "a State within a State". But the turbulence of political factions and families at home was extreme, even by the standards of medieval Italy. Jacob Burkhardt's famous account of the 15th-century Italian Renaissance dismisses Genoa in a paragraph: "The inhabitant of the Riviera was proverbial among Italians for his contempt of all higher culture. Party conflicts here assumed so fierce a character, and disturbed so violently the whole course of life, that we can hardly understand how, after so many revolutions and invasions, the Genoese ever contrived to return to an endurable condition"

Genoa's greatest naval commander Andrea Doria gave her stability and a constitution in 1528, but by then her heyday abroad was over. Venice had won another long war for Mediterranean supremacy; the Turkish Empire was wiping out the eastern colonies; and Genoa's own Christopher Columbus by reaching America had altered the whole pattern of world trade.

Liguria shared the Spanish-dominated stagnation of all Italy, but evidently kept the regional combination of seamanship and business acumen. A popular story concerns the captain from Bordighera who was in St Peter's Square in 1586, watching its great obelisk being erected in the presence of the pope, who had decreed silence on pain of death. He saved the operation from disaster, by crying out at a critical point *"Acqua alla corde!"* ("water on the ropes!"). Hastily soaked, the ropes gained enough tension to bring the obelisk vertical. The captain was rewarded by a grateful pope; he requested, and got, an exclusive contract for his native Bordighera to supply Rome with all her palms for Holy Week, for ever.

Liguria's trade in out-of-season flowers is documented since the 16th century; in 1565 masses of roses and carnations were required for the December wedding of a d'Este duke and Hapsburg princess. Nowadays market gardens and greenhouses are a major part of the landscape of Liguria, especially on the so-called Riviera of Flowers, from San Remo to the French border. Not only does the area produce tons of cut carnations for export all over Europe, it also has several botanical gardens, international trade fairs and research institutes dedicated to the science of floriculture.

The year-round sheltered warmth that permits such abundance (even on slopes and terraces too rugged for agriculture) became a major tourist asset to the region from the 18th century on. The travels of the valetudinarian Tobias Smollett in the 1760s introduced British Grand Tourists to the calmer pleasures of wintering on both French and Italian Rivieras. Voyaging toward Genoa he reported: "There is very little plain ground in this neighbourhood; but the hills are covered with oranges, lemons, pomegranates, and olives, which produce a considerable traffic in fine fruit and excellent oil. The women of St Remo are much more handsome and better tempered than those of Provence." The French Revolution and subsequent upheavals interrupted the travel habit; Genoa was much beleaguered, but the rest of the region, historically inured to foreign takeovers, came to little harm. Napoleon revived its old name in his Ligurian Republic, and later made it part of a French province governed by his relatives. After his final defeat, the Congress of Vienna gave it to Piedmont. In its 19th-century poverty, Genoa made a gloomy first impression on Charles Dickens (though later he loved it) – "I thought that of all the mouldy, dreary, sleepy, dirty, lagging, halting, God-forgotten towns in the wide world, it surely must be the very uttermost superlative". Appearances were deceptive: Genoa, always Radical, was secretly seething with the early stages of the Risorgimento.

Foreign visitors soon returned, and recorded their approval. "Never have I been more struck or enchanted" enthused Lord

Macaulay of Genoa in 1838. Mark Twain, Herman Melville, Gustave Flaubert and Henry James were among the more literary visitors who came to love Genoa. The German philosopher Nietsche owned a house there and found it ennobling to the soul. Byron and Shelley are forever linked with Lerici and the Bay of Poets, while the Bay of Fables at Sestri Levante is said to be so-called in honour of Hans Christian Andersen. A number of musicians lived parts of the year in Liguria; Tchaikovsky finished *Eugen Onegin* in the Russian colony at San Remo, Verdi wrote *Aida* in Genoa and Wagner also found inspiration there, while dreaming 'one divine night' in his hotel room. Not everyone was highbrow; in the 1890s the English introduced soccer and tennis to Italy, in Genoa and Bordighera respectively.

As a winter retreat for the wealthy Liguria began the 20th century with almost all the cachet of the South of France. The '20s brought a surge of visitors – the British escaped to the Mediterranean after the rigours of war, and Americans swelled a summer season. A casino was built at San Remo and it seemed as if the party would go on indefinitely. But during the Second World War the Rivieras were very vulnerable – Genoa was bombed 85 times.

Italy's rapid economic recovery after the war gave Liguria – as elsewhere – an uncontrolled building boom and expanded industries. Genoa, the biggest port in the country, still has its densely atmospheric old quarter, but visitors must negotiate miles of unlovely development and fearsome traffic to reach it. West of Genoa the Riviera di Ponente (the sunset Riviera) no longer has the groomed sophistication of the French Riviera, even at its Alpine end, though the scenery is as beautiful and the gardens as lush. Beaches are sandy but over-crowded and highly organised. All-out modern tourism swamps the resorts and chokes the roads, though escape to little inland villages is still possible. Between Spotorno and Genoa the coastline is dominated by industry. East of Genoa is the so-called Riviera del Levante (the sunrise Riviera), with more spectacular, and less spoilt, scenery but fewer good beaches. Fishing villages retain their charm, although none has totally escaped the onslaught of tourism. The heart of the Riviera di Levante is the Portofino peninsula, still on the itinerary of the rich and fashionable. Further round, the villages of the precipitous stretch called Cinque Terre are no longer inaccessible, and indeed much visited, but offer the last glimpse of unspoilt Liguria.

Visiting Liguria

Direct scheduled (and regular charter) flights are available from London to Genoa and Pisa; for resorts on the western part of the coast you could fly (more expensively) to Nice. The train from London to Nice takes 20 hours and from London to Genoa (via Basel) about 21 hours. Calais to Nice is about 1,220km (760 miles) of driving; you might consider the French Motorail service from Calais to Nice (14 hours overnight).

Road and rail links along the coast are good, although this is something of a mixed blessing, particularly in those resorts where the beach is separated from the town not only by the Via Aurelia 1 which runs right along the coast but also by the main Nice-Rome railway line. The motorway, with many spectacular viaducts, also runs very close to the coast. Using the motorway is a good way of covering longer stretches of coast quickly, but driving through the frequent tunnels cut into the rock is tiring. Public transport is plentiful and cheap. Several companies run bus services along the coast, notably between Genoa and Alassio. A train linking Sestri Levante to La Spezia stops at the remote villages of the Cinque Terre, only three of which are accessible by car. Roads to the inland villages are often narrow, twisting and steep. Much of the Portofino peninsula can be explored only by boat or on foot. Genoa has a funicular railway in addition to a city bus service.

Most resorts offer at least a small selection of excursions, and in a region where the most spectacular feature is the scenery it is worth trying to cover at least part of the coast whether by road or sea. From the western half there are day trips by coach to Monte Carlo and the fashionable resorts of the South of France, and to the Toirano grottoes; and there are boat trips to the tiny Gallinara island between Albenga and Alassio. From the eastern half there are day trips to Pisa or other parts of Tuscany. Otherwise excursions take you to other resorts along the coast, to the port at Genoa, or occasionally to the medieval hamlets of the Ligurian hinterland.

If you have to make the choice between the Riviera di Levante (east of Genoa) and the Riviera di Ponente (west of Genoa) the former, favoured by Shelley and Byron, is still the loveliest and the resorts are more appealing than those west of Genoa. Although you can find a choice of luxury hotels in places like San Remo and Santa Margherita Ligure, the majority are fairly modern, unsophisticated and informal. A large number of hotels suffer from the noise of the main road or railway (and Italian train drivers hoot their horns almost as frequently as motorists). There are campsites in batches along the coast, most of them well-organised and well-equipped. Hostels are housed in some of the watchtowers and castles along the coast.

Very few British tour operators organise package holidays by air to Liguria; those that do invariably offer a stay of either 7 or 14 nights, and the majority of resorts are on the (cheaper) Riviera di Ponente. Genoa (by air) is occasionally offered. However a number of coach companies arrange holidays, nearly all in Diano Marina and Alassio; and it is also possible to take a package holiday by train. A few companies arrange self-catering accommodation, sometimes as part of a motoring package; villas are bookable by the week.

The earliest tourists were attracted by the mild climate of Liguria and it originally became known as a winter destination; it's protected by the Alps and the Apennines, ensuring a temperate climate almost all year round. Now the majority of tourists come from May to the end of September, July and August being the busiest and hottest months. June is a particularly good month for the flowers. Art lovers might consider Genoa for an unusual off-season break, ideally not over a weekend when some of the palaces are shut on Saturday and/or Sunday afternoons.

Places to visit

ALASSIO

Deservedly one of the most popular resorts of Liguria, Alassio is large and lively with an air of affluence and excellent beaches which stretch the entire length of the resort. There are over 100 concession areas with soft, well-manicured sands which are undoubtedly the best in Liguria. The fact that there are virtually no public beaches is an indication that Alassio caters for wealthier Italian families and foreigners. The centre is suitably smart with shady squares and gardens and dignified buildings; the more unsightly modern development being restricted to the outskirts. The shops are among the best in Liguria and the most popular area is a traffic-free alleyway running parallel to the beach, commonly known to the English as "The Drain". The cafés, bars and boutiques all open late for the benefit of evening strollers.

Alassio has had a succession of famous visitors and the *muretto*, or little wall, has countless ceramic tiles reproducing the signatures of well known names including Winston Churchill and Sophia Loren. In 1922 Ernest Hemingway stayed for some time in Alassio and made fond acquaintance with a parrot in a café that he used to frequent. "Hemingway's parrot" died quite recently, having become something of a celebrity.

Excursions from Alassio

☞ **Gallinara** (3km north-east)

There are regular boat trips in summer to this small island between Alassio and Albenga. There's nothing to see but the waters are good for skin-diving. (See also excursions from Albenga)

ALBENGA

The resort is little more than a soulless conglomeration of scruffy apartment blocks running parallel to the beach, but for sightseers there's a surprisingly rich concentration of well-preserved Romanesque, Gothic and even Baroque architecture in the walled medieval town a short distance inland.

➡ **Cathedral quarter** The picturesque old town of Albenga is concentrated around the 13th-century cathedral and the polygonal baptistry which dates from the 5th century. Medieval palaces include the old town hall (Palazzo Vecchio) which contains an archaeological museum (Museo Civico), and the nearby Palazzo Peloso-Cepolla housing a Roman naval museum.

Excursions from Albenga

☞ **Grotte di Toirano** (15km north)

A huge network of caves with remarkable stalactites and stalagmites in the mountains beyond the medieval hamlet of Toirano.

☞ **Loano** (11km north-east)

A small resort with an interesting old town. The Palazzo Doria (now

the town hall) is a Renaissance building with a mosaic from an old
Roman villa and there are paintings of the Genoese School in the
church of San Giovanni Battista.

BORDIGHERA

An all-year resort, famed for its flora and the fact that it has the
exclusive right of supplying the Vatican with palm-fronds in Holy
Week. There are few signs now of the large English colony that
occupied the resort in the 1920s and it is primarily a beach resort for
Italian families – or, out of season, the elderly. As in so many
Ligurian resorts, the beach is backed by a tree-lined promenade with
the railway and main road immediately behind. The quietest and
most civilised area lies at the back of the resort, with hotels and
grandiose villas set among lush gardens. The old town of Bordighera
stands high up above the coastal bustle, its quiet alleys, arcades and
tiny sunlit squares commanding good views below.

CAMOGLI

An attractive little port on the edge of the unspoilt Portofino
promontory. Pastel-washed, six-storey stucco houses, many of them
decorated with a very convincing *trompe-l'oeil* effect, cluster around a
cobbled seafront of art galleries and cafés. In front is a steeply
shelving pebble beach. The name Camogli is an abbreviation of *Casa
Moglie* (House of Wives), originally referring to the houses where
the wives were left alone while the men went out to fish. To a large
extent this is still the pattern of life today and the town's activities
continue to revolve around fishing. At the fish festival, held on the
second Sunday in May, the day's catch is fried in two 12-foot pans
and distributed free on the quays.
(See Portofino for excursions)

CINQUE TERRE

The "Five Lands" is a collection of remote fishing villages forming a
distinct coastal district near La Spezia. The cliffs drop so
precipitously that the construction of a coast road has had to
progress at a remarkably slow pace – even by Italian standards – with
the result that the area remains relatively unspoilt. Of the five
coastal villages, three are now accessible by car but the drive down
on the twisting secondary roads is arduous, and the magnificent
views are small compensation for the long queues in high season
(the distance seems short on the map but takes far longer than you
might imagine). However, a train service runs between Sestri
Levante and La Spezia stopping at all five villages. The most
pleasant alternative is to take a summer boat trip from Portovenere
or La Spezia.

The Cinque Terre area is famous for its wines and vines are
planted in terraces over the hills and cliffs (in parts so steep that they
can be reached only by ladders from terraces below). Cliff paths link

the villages and command fine views of the jagged and exposed rocky coastline. **Monterosso** is the largest village and the only one that has really succumbed to tourism but it is still picturesque with pink, peeling houses and arched twisting alleys. A rough two-hour hike through vineyards and olive groves brings you to **Vernazza**, by far the prettiest of the villages with its tightly packed houses and imposing church clustering around the small harbour. **Corniglia** to the east (1 ½ hours' walk) is the least interesting of the villages and also the least accessible, being a steep climb up from the cliff path and railway station. **Manarola**, seen from the cliff path below Corniglia, is a delightful conglomeration of multi-coloured houses hugging the rockface; but the village is spoilt by unsightly apartment blocks and a network of TV aerials. **Riomaggiore**, now linked to Manarola by road as well as a path (the so-called Via dell'Amore), has a certain shabby charm, with dilapidated houses built vertically up the cliff and a tiny marina crammed with fishing smacks. It takes a further 1 ½ hours to walk from Corniglia to Riomaggiore, via Manarola. All the villages have interesting 14th-century churches.

DIANO MARINA

Of all the Ligurian resorts, this one has the most solidly commercial holiday atmosphere. The old town was virtually demolished in an earthquake in 1887 and the modern town is a purpose-built resort entirely geared to tourism. The British come here on package holidays to find something of a home-from-home atmosphere with English beer and tea "like mother makes it" served in the local cafés.

The resort lies in a wide bay, backed by gentle green hills and olive groves. Behind it is the remains of the medieval hamlet, **Diano Castello**. The beach is a long stretch of sand, divided by stone jetties and blanketed by ranks of green and blue parasols. The main road runs behind, separating the beach from the package hotels and souvenir shops. The best area to stay is the western end, where the beach has finely groomed sands and the hotels have more character than the modern blocks in the residential eastern section. **San Bartolomeo al Mare**, more or less a continuation of Diano Marina, is a dull conglomeration of hotels, apartments and beaches with ugly breakwaters.

Excursions from Diano Marina
☞ **Cervo** (*4km north-east*)
This picturesque and unspoilt medieval village, clinging to the steep hillside above the coast, offers a peaceful contrast to the modern resorts below. There is a 13th-century castle, a Baroque church and the remains of Genoese walls.

FINALE LIGURE

On a splendid coastline of craggy cliffs and wooded mountain backdrop, this is the exception in a string of fairly scruffy resorts – a civilised town with a good beach, pretty seafront gardens, fashionable cafés and a distinct air of prosperity. The resort comprises Finale Marina and Finale Pia and extends to **Varigotti**, a simple resort with old houses below a steep headland.

Excursions from Finale Ligure
☞ **Finalborgo** (2km north, frequent buses)
Behind the marina is the old town (borgo), dominated by a ruined castle. The Gothic church of San Biagio has a pretty octagonal campanile. In the cloister of the Renaissance convent of Santa Caterina there is a museum with finds from the local prehistoric caves.

☞ **Roman remains**
On the old Roman road (Via Julia Augusta) behind Finale Pia are five Roman bridges, crossing the Ponci valley.
(See also Noli)

GENOA

Genoa is largely neglected by tourists and is generally regarded as a raucous city of ships, factories and refineries. It is after all the greatest seaport of Italy, with miles of docks sprawling along the seafront and skyscrapers, towers and new suburbs climbing up the amphitheatre of hills behind. But there is more to Genoa than first meets the eye. Behind the industrial sprawl and screen of modern blocks lies what is at least in parts a civilised city of palaces, churches, parks and handsome piazzas.

For centuries Genoa was a major maritime port with so powerful a fleet that it earned the title of *Genoa La Superba* (The Proud). By the Middle Ages it had become one of Europe's largest and most affluent cities. Its colonial Empire extended as far as the Crimea, Syria and North Africa and might have ruled the Mediterranean were it not for the intense rivalry with Venice and the consequent defeat of the Genoese by the Venetians in a sea battle of 1380. From then on internal disorder led to repeated submission to foreign rule and rising military powers – kings of France and Naples, counts of Monferrat and dukes of Milan. Ironically it was a Genoese who was partially responsible for the greatest decline in the city's prosperity; after Christopher Colombus discovered America, the Mediterranean became an economic backwater, and it was not until the opening of the Suez Canal that the city resumed its importance as a major maritime port.

Ever since Chaucer visited Genoa in 1372, it seems to have attracted the comments of literary figures. Thomas Gray wrote in 1739 "We find this place so fine, that we are in fear of finding nothing finer". In the 19th century Smollett and Dickens recorded mixed impressions, and Leigh Hunt and Thomas Hardy wrote poems bewailing Genoa's loss of greatness. Flaubert was unequivocal, describing Genoa as "a city all in marble with gardens full of roses"; Henry James wrote "Genoa is the queerest place in the world and even a second visit helps you little to straighten it out". Mark Twain was captivated by its women whom he described as "enchanting and clothed in white clouds from head to foot" (but

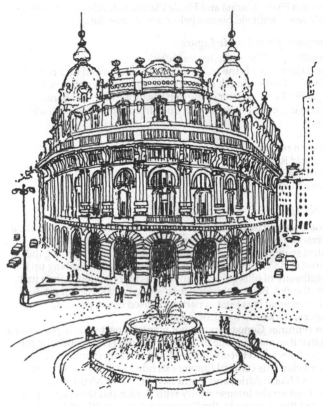

Genoa, Piazza de Ferrari

Leigh Hunt, under a similar apprehension, was accused by an Englishwoman of "short sight").

The architecture of Genoa is predominantly solid and commercial. Stately mercantile mansions line its streets, notably Via Garibaldi and Via Balbi. Some of these old *palazzi* are sumptuously decorated by Genoese painters, influenced by Florentine art and, particularly, by the Flemish artists brought to the city to work for rich merchant families. Rubens was in Genoa in 1607 and Van Dyck started his great career as a portrait painter here in the 1620s. The most important names in Genoese art are Luca Cambiaso (16th century); Bernardo Strozzi, known as *"Il Prete Genovese"* (the Genoese priest) and profoundly influenced by Rubens (17th century); and Valerio Castello and Alessandro Magnasco (17th-18th centuries).

The port, frequently romanticised in guide books, is in fact no more than extensive warehouses, funnels and factories, stretching alongside oily waters. More interesting are the steep and crooked lanes *(carrugi)* which wind behind the port, many so narrow that they are barely wide enough for a couple of Vespas. These alleys, which early travellers found dark and claustrophobic, are now lined with elegant shops.

The one-way streets and chaotic traffic jams of Genoa and its suburbs understandably deter foreigners from penetrating its centre. Drivers need as much nerve as they do in Rome or Naples, and for those unfamiliar with the town it is wiser to go by bus, train or organised excursion. The most interesting parts of the city can be seen in one day, although you will need longer to visit all the palaces.

Main sights

☛ **Cathedral** (San Lorenzo) In a curious fusion of styles, the façade of San Lorenzo is striped black-and-white marble (Pisan Romanesque) with French Gothic portals. The austere interior has some richly decorated chapels, notably the Cappella Senarega, with a beautiful Vision of Saint Sebastian by Federico Barocci (1595) and the Renaissance Cappella di San Giovanni Battista. The treasury (in the vaults of the sacristy) is spectacular.

☛ **Palazzo Bianco** (Via Garibaldi 11) An important collection of Flemish paintings with works by Jan Provost, Hugo Van der Goes, Van Dyck and Rubens. There are also works by the local school (mainly 15th-17th centuries) showing the influence of Flemish art on Ligurian and Genoese painters.

☛ **Palazzo Reale** (Palazzo Balbi Durazzo, Via Balbi 10) A splendid palace, built for the wealthy Balbi family, which became a royal residence in 1824. The lavishly decorated but rather empty rooms include a glittering Hall of Mirrors (Galleria degli Specchi) with Baroque sculptures. The (unlabelled) paintings include works by Guido Reni, Guercino and Van Dyck.

☛ **Palazzo Rosso** (Via Garibaldi 18) A magnificent 17th-century mansion. On the first floor are displayed paintings from various North Italian schools, with good Venetian and Genoese pictures. The upstairs apartments, with exuberant frescoes of the Seasons on the ceiling, contain some of Van Dyck's brilliant portraits of the Genoese aristocracy.

☛ **Palazzo Spinola** (Galleria Nazionale, Piazza Pellicceria 1) A 16th-century mansion of rather faded splendour, with good frescoes and furnishings. There are paintings by Antonello da Messina (Ecce Homo), Joos Van Cleve (Adoration of the Magi), Rubens and Van Dyck as well as the Genoese artists Bernardo Strozzi and Valerio Castello.

☛ **Santi Ambrogio e Andrea** (Il Gesù) A Baroque church opposite the cathedral. The sumptuous interior contains several paintings by Rubens, notably the Circumcision (1605) over the main altar, and an Assumption by Guido Reni (third chapel on right).

Other sights

☛ **Churches** Sant' Agostino (archaeological museum in the cloister) and the nearby Romanesque church of San Donato; San Matteo (typically Genoese striped façade dating from the 13th century, and the tomb of Andrea Doria); and, at opposite ends of the town, Santissima Annunziata and Santa Maria Assunta di Carignano (both with Baroque paintings).

☛ **Edoardo Chiossone Museum of Oriental Art** Probably the best collection of oriental art in Italy, housed in an appropriate modern building outside the centre.

IMPERIA

This mainly industrial provincial capital was formed by the joining (in 1923) of two towns: **Oneglia**, centre of olive oil and pasta production and **Porto Maurizio**, the more interesting medieval quarter standing back from a sheltered harbour. Imperia is the chief town of the so-called Riviera del Ponente.

LAIGUEGLIA

On the same huge sweeping bay as Alassio, Laigueglia is neither as large nor as smart as its neighbour; but it is one of the more pleasant resorts west of Genoa, and is particularly well suited to families. There are nearly two miles of narrow sands. Between the beach and the main road is the old fishing quarter of arcaded passageways now lined with shops and stalls. The Baroque church of San Matteo dates from 1754.

LAVAGNA

(See excursions from Rapallo)

LERICI

Lerici was originally a Pisan stronghold and the town still nestles below the Pisan castle which dates from the early 13th century (extended and altered by the Genoese who conquered Lerici in 1256). The area appealed to the Romantic poets of the 19th century (Leigh Hunt called Lerici "wild and retired") and it is still known as the Golfo dei Poeti. The resort lies at the head of a sheltered cove, surrounded by steep, terraced slopes; there is no beach but the seafront with pines and palms is popular for promenades. The only swimming is from the shingle to the north and south of the town.

Excursions from Lerici

☞ **San Terenzo** *(2km north)*
A small and unspoilt fishing village, where Shelley rented a house (Casa Magni) the summer he died (1822).

LOANO

(See excursions from Albenga)

NERVI

A small resort, now part of the city of Genoa, and geared mainly to locals. The main attractions are the long promenade, gardens and cliff walks; but the resort is somewhat spoilt by the railway line running right behind the beach. Nervi is the venue of Liguria's biggest summer event, a festival of ballet, music and opera held from the end of June to the second week of August.
☛ **Villa Luxor** (Museo Giannettino Luxoro, Via Aurelia 29)   Museum of Genoese decorative arts and painting.

NOLI

A small resort and fishing village with picturesque old houses, arcaded streets and brick towers dating back to the Middle Ages when it was a major port and mini-republic. It is still guarded by the ruins of a castle on Monte Orsino. The cathedral (with a rich treasury) and the Romanesque church of San Paragorio are worth visiting. There is a sandy beach at Spotorno, 3km away.

PORTOFINO

Portofino is a very chic resort, and one of the most fashionable of the whole Italian coast. The setting, in a sheltered natural harbour at the base of a wooded promontory, is quite beautiful. In the 1930s Portofino was a popular haunt for artists; then the fashionable set moved in and built luxury villas on the hillsides. Yachts are gradually outnumbering the coloured fishing smacks and Portofino has become the Italian St-Tropez.

The resort is really no more than a few pink and ochre shuttered houses and cafés with awnings and tables on the cobbled piazza around the waterfront. Behind is a shopping street of expensive Paris-Rome boutiques. Despite a daily influx of tourists, Portofino is undeniably picturesque and still surprisingly unspoilt. If you arrive early you can still see fishermen mending tackle and nets; but by mid-morning tourists throng the harbour and the jet-set arrive in yachts for lunch at the restaurants on the waterfront. To escape the crowds you can walk, via the church of San Giorgio and the medieval castle (with a picture gallery), to the lighthouse (20 mins).

Excursions from Portofino

There are several walks on the Portofino peninsula; the tourist office can provide a list and maps.
☞ **San Fruttuoso**
A tiny fishing hamlet, with a ruined monastery, reached on foot by a cliff path (about 1½ hours). There are also regular boat trips from Portofino (and Camogli and Santa Margherita).

PORTOVENERE

A fishing village of singular charm , preserving something of the character of the original fortified outpost, with tall old narrow houses wedged along the seafront and main street. Steep stairways lead up from the port to the cobbled streets and alleyways of the old town and to the charming Romanesque church of San Lorenzo and the ruined Genoese castle above. From Portovenere Byron is said to have swum across the gulf to visit Shelley at San Terenzo in 1822.

Excursions from Portovenere

☞ **Islands**
There are boat trips to the offshore islands, Isola **Palmaria** (with a Blue Grotto) Isola del **Tino** (with a ruined Romanesque abbey) and Isola del **Tinetto**.
(See also Cinque Terre)

RAPALLO

The name of this resort is associated (like Portofino and Santa Margherita) with the rich and titled. Rapallo has long been popular with the English and in the 1920s it was a well known meeting place for the literary set, among them Sir Max Beerbohm and Ezra Pound (who produced many of his cantos here). Today the atmosphere is distinctly passé with sadly faded Edwardian hotels and a rather sedate palm-lined promenade. Unchecked development resulted in the coining of a new word, *rapalizzare*, to spoil. Rapallo's most appealing feature remains its situation, at the end of a deep narrow bay at the foot of steep sheltering mountains and beautiful wooded scenery.

Excursions from Rapallo

☞ **Chiavari** (*12km south-east*)

A modern ship-building town, worth a passing visit for its arcaded old street, called the *carruggio drittu*, and the gallery in the Palazzo Torriglia (Baroque and 18th-century paintings). About half an hour's drive inland from the neighbouring resort of **Lavagna** is the remarkable Gothic basilica of San Salvatore dei Fieschi.

SAN REMO

The first resort to be established on the Italian Riviera, San Remo had become a playground for high society and royalty by the early 19th century. It provided a welcome retreat from harsh Northern European winters, and enjoyed all the cachet of the resorts of the French Riviera. There were two Anglican churches and as many as five resident British physicians to meet the needs of the British colony, and the Corso degli Inglesi still recalls its fashionable and glamorous heyday. It also became an expatriate Russian enclave especially after the Revolution when Russian aristocrats built themselves large villas and a Russian church with a handsome onion dome. The Corso Imperatrice was named after the wife of Tsar Alexander II who lived here from 1874. There is a handful of grand hotels and the famous casino, which dates from 1920, but much of San Remo's Edwardian elegance has given way to the trappings of modern day tourism. San Remo now offers more hotels and entertainment than any other resort along the Ligurian coast. The centre is commercial and chaotic, with cars roaring by close to the harbour and a main street choked by traffic and trams. In contrast, in the old town, La Pigna, local life carries on unperturbed by the frenzy below. There are very few good beaches in San Remo; the most attractive are man-made and belong to hotels, while the public stretches are made up of grey sand, shingle and rocks, backed in parts by the road and railway. The quietest places to stay are the villas and hotels in the wooded hills behind the resort.

San Remo (and the surrounding area) is famous for its luxuriant gardens and for a thriving industry in floriculture which produces thousands of tons of cut flowers for export and sale within Italy. The daily flower market, held from October to June, is a glorious sight, but to see it you must arrive early – it's almost over by 8am.

☛ **La Pigna** A cluster of small houses on the hillside, with a maze of quiet stepped alleyways, tiny dark bars and bistros, and fine views of the town and coast from the Baroque church at the top. The great collegiate church of **San Siro**, in Lombard Romanesque style (now stripped of Baroque additions) is worth visiting.

Excursions from San Remo

☞ **Bussana Vecchia** *(8km east)*
Ruined by an earthquake in 1887 and partially restored, this village
is now an artists' colony with galleries lining cobbled alleys, quiet
sunlit squares, dozing doorstep cats and ruins sprouting wild
flowers and roses. You could continue to Taggia (see below).

☞ **Taggia** *(7km east)*
A well-preserved medieval village with several interesting churches,
notably San Domenico (part of the Dominican convent) with
excellent sculptures by the Ligurian artist, Lodovico Brea (1443-c1523).

☞ **Monte Bignone** *(15km north)*
For really stunning views of coast and country, you can take the
cable car from the Corso degli Inglesi (45 mins one way) up this, the
highest of the surrounding hills. Alternatively, take the panoramic
drive (25km) up through Poggio to the picturesque medieval villages
of **Ceriana** and **Baiardo**, both with Romanesque churches.

SANTA MARGHERITA LIGURE

A well-established resort, which owes much of its appeal to the
setting on one of the most beautiful bays of the coast (the Gulf of
Tigullio), and on the edge of the Portofino peninsula, a hilly
hinterland carpeted by lush semi-tropical vegetation. This is one of
the most fashionable resorts in Liguria with a harbour of luxury
yachts, streets of elegant shops and several smart hotels of
Edwardian elegance. The beaches however are no more than
concrete platforms or narrow stretches of shingle with occasional
man-made sandy concession areas.
(For excursions see Portofino)

SAVONA

A major seaport. Although parts of the old town have been preserved, the overriding features are industrial chimneys, cranes and oil tankers. The churches, cathedral and art gallery (pinacoteca civica, with paintings by North Italian artists) are probably not worth a detour.

SESTRI LEVANTE

Lauded by poets from Dante to Byron, this resort may not live up to romantic expectations but is nevertheless a pretty little place, enjoying a serene setting on a natural isthmus with a wooded promontory (L'Isola) jutting into the sea. However, neither of the two crescent-shaped bays provides ideal bathing. Tourism is concentrated on the western side, romantically called the Baia delle Favole (Bay of Fables) somewhat spoilt by development. The seafront with its palm trees and gardens retains its charm. The other side, known as the Baia di Silenzio, provides a more local scene with fishermen mending nets and women knitting in doorways.

☛ **Rizzi Art Gallery** *(Via Cappuccini 10)*   A private collection with works by Raphael, Tiepolo, El Greco and Rubens. Open summer only, restricted hours.

LA SPEZIA

A busy port and naval base, much rebuilt since heavy bombing in the Second World War, La Spezia is superbly sited at the base of two long peninsulas enclosing a deep sound. There is an archaeological museum and a naval museum but little to merit a detour from the other attractions of this beautiful part of the coast.
(*See also Cinque Terre, Lerici, Portovenere*)

SPOTORNO

(*See Noli*)

VENTIMIGLIA

The gateway from southern France to Italy is not a promising introduction to the Italian Riviera; after the pristine, pastel-washed villas of the French coast, this resort looks distinctly scruffy. The streets are traffic-choked and the beach is cut off from the centre by a railway line. If there is a redeeming feature, it is the old quarter, lying to the west of the modern town, with steep covered alleys and crumbling houses linked by lines of laundry. The cathedral, built in the 11th-12th centuries, has been restored.

Excursions from Ventimiglia

☞ **Hanbury Gardens** *(at Mortola Inferiore, 5km west)*
A large botanical garden which spreads down to the sea from the slopes of the wooded promontory of Capo Mortola. It was founded in 1867 by an Englishman, Thomas Hanbury, and remained in the family until 1960. The garden was badly damaged and neglected in the Second World War, but it is gradually being restored; meanwhile it still boasts many exotic plants and over 200 flowers in bloom on New Year's Day. An interesting feature is the narrow sunken lane

which goes through the garden and is all that remains of the ancient Via Aurelia from Rome to Gaul.

☞ **Balzi Rossi Caves** (*7km west*)
Palaeolithic caves with paintings of hunting scenes and a museum with excavated relics, including the remains of Cro Magnon man.

☞ **Dolceacqua** (*9km north*)
A medieval hill village with a picturesque old bridge and the shell of a 15th-century castle of the Doria family above.

Hotels

Bordighera   ££
VILLA ELISA   *Closed Nov to Christmas*
Via Romana 70, 18012 Imperia   *Tel: (0184) 261313*

Lying well back from the noisy centre of town a 10 minute walk from the sea, Villa Elisa is a quiet family-run hotel surrounded by lush gardens of citrus trees, oleander and roses. There are civilised old-fashioned salons with oils and watercolours, parquet floors and chandeliers; and there's a spacious restaurant with an airy terrace protected by an awning, overlooking the garden. Bedrooms are solidly traditional but plainer than public rooms.

Facilities: *34 bedrooms; restaurant; lift; parking*   **Credit/charge cards accepted:** *Amex, Visa*

Finale Ligure   ££
PUNTA EST   *Closed Oct to mid-April*
Via Aurelia 1, 17024 Savona   *Tel: (019) 600611*

Converted from an 18th-century villa, with stunning sea views and quiet rooms, this is one of the most desirable places to stay along the coast; it is at the eastern end of this cheerful resort, a long walk to the centre. Drystone walls, arches, beams and original fireplaces have been preserved in the public rooms and the bedrooms are exceptionally attractive (old-fashioned in the main villa, modern in the annexe). Breakfasts are taken off Staffordshire china in a light and airy outbuilding, other meals in a medieval style restaurant. There's a pebble beach across the main road.

Facilities: *40 bedrooms; restaurant; lift; swimming pool; parking*   **Credit/charge cards accepted:** *Amex, Visa*

Laigueglia   ££
SPLENDID   *Closed Oct to Easter*
Piazza Badarò, 17020 Savona   *Tel: (0182) 49325*

This pink, shuttered building in the old centre dates back at least four centuries and a story goes that the two skeletons discovered here in relatively recent excavations belonged to a British officer and his *aide-de-camp* who had been captured and imprisoned during the coastal invasions by the British in c1800. There is still a lot of old world charm about the building and the rooms are prettily furnished in rustic style. Bedrooms are cool and inviting, with good bathrooms. The beach is only 50 metres away and the hotel has its own small pool, garden and terrace for tea and drinks.

Facilities: *50 bedrooms; restaurant; lift; swimming pool; parking* **Credit/charge cards accepted:** *Amex, Diners, Visa*

Portofino ££
EDEN *Closed Dec*
Vico Dritto 18, 16034 Genova *Tel: (0185) 69091*

This tiny hotel is tucked away in a side street close to the harbour and the building is practically hidden behind a garden of palms and shrubs. The main public areas are the restaurant and the shady terrace where meals are served in summer. Bedrooms are simple and modern. This is one of the few hotels in the centre of Portofino, so it's wise to book well ahead.

Facilities: *12 bedrooms, restaurant* **Credit/charge cards accepted:** *Amex, Eurocard, Visa*

Portofino £££££
SPLENDIDO *Closed Nov to March*
Viale Baratta 13, 16034 Genova *Tel: (0185) 69551*

No expense has been spared in this luxury hotel perched in wooded hills high above the port. Originally an aristocratic 17th-century villa, it was converted to a hotel in 1901. Rooms are refined, quiet and elegant. The salons are furnished with antiques and the restaurant and pool terraces make the most of the glorious views of the bay. Bedrooms are exceptionally comfortable; some now have a jacuzzi. Facilities include sauna and beauty parlour; excursions and various sports – golf, riding – can be arranged.

Facilities: *65 bedrooms; restaurant; lift; swimming pool (heated); tennis court; garage* **Credit/charge cards accepted:** *Amex, Diners, Eurocard, Visa*

Sestri Levante ££
HELVETIA *Closed Nov to mid-March*
Via Cappuccini 43, 16039 Genova *Tel: (0185) 41175*

A simple but casually stylish little hotel tucked away on the quiet old fishing port side of Sestri Levante's promontory. There are few more charming views than the one you can enjoy over a drink or a meal on the Helvetia's terrace, looking out over the so-called Bay of Silence where colourful old houses drop down to a small strip of beach. The interior of the hotel is a bit cramped and dark, but the rooms are reasonably comfortable and, except for the dull dining room, attractively furnished. There is a small garden, a roof terrace, and a small enclosure on the rocks at the end of the beach.

Facilities: *28 bedrooms; restaurant; lift; garage* **Credit/charge cards accepted:** *none*

FLORENCE

❛Florence is no more: there remains beside the
Arno between the hills where once Florence
stood, the most beautiful museum in the world,
the one city in Italy that seems to have lost all
character, to be at various seasons almost
English or German or American, and, save in
the dog-days perhaps, never really Tuscan at all❜

EDWARD HUTTON

Duomo

Introduction

Florence is the capital of Tuscany, a thriving city of about half a million notoriously noisy, argumentative and arrogant inhabitants. It is famous for its crafts – fashion, leather, metalwork, furniture – its culture and its antique business. Above all though it is famous for the Renaissance. Florence is not so much its cradle as the crucible where a ferment of new ideas produced an explosion of creativity in all directions, an extraordinary flowering of urban culture. For the tourist, the blooms from that flowering are the paintings, sculptures and buildings of a relatively brief period between about 1400 and about 1550. They fill Florence almost to the exclusion of works from other periods and they are the reason for visiting the city. If you go to Florence you may enjoy other aspects of the city than the contents of its churches and museums (although plenty of visitors find that they don't), but if you don't enjoy the art you won't enjoy Florence.

Florence is set beside the river Arno some fifty miles from the sea, in a broad basin framed by the hills of Careggi, Fiésole, and Settignano on the right bank (north) with the higher peaks of the Apennines behind them; and, to the south, by Belvedere, Bellosguardo and the beautiful region of Chianti, the heart of rural Tuscany. Lately Florence has spread along the main roads out of town in an unattractive way, and the by-passing motorway forms an abrupt southern and western perimeter; but the hills themselves are not unduly built up and as well as offering magnificent views over the city's famous skyline they provide a welcome and very nearby rural retreat from the noisy city centre, ignored by too many hurried visitors. The hills account for a somewhat oppressive summer climate in the city and for wet winters. The Arno is a fickle mountain torrent subject to frequent drought (it is rarely more than a muddy trickle in summer) and flooding. In November 1966 the waters rose to five metres in parts of the city, causing widespread and in many cases irreparable damage to the city and its heritage.

The historic centre of the city is extremely compact, not even filling the partly preserved enclosure of medieval walls. Very few monuments are not within easy walking distance of all the others and there is no real need to use public transport except for excursions and travelling between the centre and outlying accommodation. North of the Arno the walls were replaced in the 19th century by a ring-road boulevard (the Viali) punctuated by a few medieval gateways left standing. These are worth looking out for if you're passing, but scarcely worth a pilgrimage. The equivalent sequence of roads to the south, known collectively as the Viale dei Colli, runs across the hillsides above the city outside the line of walls, and gives beautiful views.

Florence grew prodigiously in the 13th century and in the 15th was greatly embellished with imposing town houses, called palaces after the Italian habit but many of them hardly matching up to our idea of a palace. In Florentine palace architecture of the Renaissance the fortifying mentality of the Middle Ages has not been entirely forgotten and the façades with their massive rough-hewn (or rusticated, to use the technical term) blocks are more solid than decorative. A common feature is a bench running along the lower storey, a condition of planning permission typically Florentine in its public-spiritedness.

Since the Renaissance Florence has changed relatively little apart from the widening of some of the main streets in the centre and the creation of the Piazza della Repubblica in place of the old market at the end of the 19th century. In August 1944 the retreating German army destroyed all the bridges over the Arno except for the 14th-century Ponte Vecchio, and that was spared only at the cost of an area of devastation at each end of the bridge to block the passage.

Unspoilt though it is, Florence fails to inspire affection in many disappointed visitors. There are several reasons for this, the main one (apart from the hordes of tourists) being the fact that it is a modern city, albeit in the ancient costume of its Renaissance buildings. The shops are up to date, the traffic is noisy and some of the squares are used as car parks. In its bustling way Florence today must be much closer in spirit to the Florence of 500 years ago than Venice is, for example. But it is much less picturesque and there are countless small Italian towns that seem more appealing in the way time seems to have left them behind. Unlike Florence they nourish our fantasy of a time when life in town was as peaceful as in a monastery.

Another reason is the austere, forbidding architectural style of the Renaissance buildings. It can come as a surprise to find that at street level the city looks rather different from the lovely warm views of rust-coloured roofs, towers and gracious cathedral dome that are so familiar from film and brochure. There are areas of colour (notably the cathedral square with its great buildings of coloured marble), but as a whole central Florence does not charm in the way fountain-filled Rome and watery Venice do. Unlike these two cities, indeed to a greater extent than any other city, Florence is not a place for the casual stroller with no great interest in studying great works of sculpture and painting. The streets are narrow and lined by churches with blank, unfinished façades and tall, stern-faced palaces looming oppressively and amplifying the noise of all the traffic. Pavements are a rare luxury. There are cafés, but few spacious, quiet places for taking a break from all the sightseeing to observe Florentine life. This makes the nearby hills all the more appealing, and means that for those who don't have the time to take their sightseeing at a leisurely pace, the experience of the city is thoroughly exhausting; leaving it comes as a relief for many visitors, although few admit it. There is no solution, except not to try to cram too much sightseeing into a short time.

Although for tourist purposes Florence is divided simply into two unequal halves on this and that side of the Arno, for the Florentines it is more regional than this. The notoriously brutal free-for-all football games held at the end of June are disputed between the four teams of the different quarters: San Giovanni (central), Santa Croce (east), Santa Maria Novella (west) and Santo Spirito (the Oltrarno, or left bank dwellers). Within these broad sectors there are minor parish distinctions which may have some meaning for the Florentines. The wool industry, on which medieval and Renaissance Florence depended, was decentralised like an urban cottage industry, most of the work being done in people's homes throughout the city. The main working class quarters were Santa

Visiting Florence

Florence's nearest airport is Pisa *(see Tuscany and Umbria chapter)* – 80km away. There is no bus or coach service to the city; the train takes about an hour, and you may have to wait that long at Pisa airport station. The taxi alternative is very expensive.

Florence is not a good place to take your car: driving around the city is complicated and parking difficult. If visiting Florence from outside the city the best policy may be to leave the car at the big car park at the Fortezza da Basso north-east of the station, and walk or take the free bus service into the centre. Tourists staying in very central hotels are allowed to drive into the blue zone, which is reserved for pedestrians on weekdays from 8.30am to 7.30pm; but, as few hotels have garages, parking remains a problem. In the surrounding green zone parking is not allowed from 8am to 10am and 3pm to 5pm. They do tow cars away, a long way.

Noise, traffic, cobbles and narrow pavements mean that Florence is not always pleasant for the casual stroller. The centre of Florence is based on a grid-like pattern of streets and, with the River Arno as a reference point, you are unlikely to get lost. However, the dual system of street numbering, with all commercial premises numbered in red, indicated by "r" after the number, can cause some confusion.

The bus system is efficient but rather complicated by the one-way system. Maps and timetables are available from the ATAF office (Piazza del Duomo 57r). Tickets have to be bought from bars or tobacconists and fed into automatic punching machines on the bus. Taxis wait in ranks on the main squares. If tempted to take a ride in a horse-drawn cab, be sure to establish the fare before embarking.

Various companies, including CIT (Piazza Stazione 51) operate bus tours of the Tuscan countryside and historic cities: detailed information is available from the tourist office or the local newspaper La Nazione. Use public transport rather than an organised excursion to visit Siena (bus) and Pisa (train).

There is plentiful and varied accommodation in the centre but prices are high, rooms are mostly dark and without a view, and there are enough exceptions to the traffic ban for many streets to be noisy (buses, motor bikes and delivery vans). A feature of Florence is the old-fashioned *pensione*, often several floors up and usually close to the Arno. There is cheap accommodation around the station, but few places with any charm or character and not many that are comfortable. The Ognissanti area has a number of comfortable hotels, several with pools, and is fairly convenient for sightseeing; riverside rooms tend to be very noisy. The Oltrarno has one or two attractive exceptions to a general lack of hotels. Outside the built-up area there are comfortable and expensive hotels along the Viale dei Colli and peaceful accommodation of varying degrees of comfort in and around Fiesole. These two areas also have the best campsites in the immediate neighbourhood of Florence.

The best food is invariably found in small backstreet *trattorie*, often cramped and inconspicuous. Fixed-price tourist menus are rarely good value. There are cheap self-service restaurants around the cathedral and San Lorenzo; Santa Croce and the Oltrarno offer more characteristic local eating places, often good value.

Lots of tour operators offer package holidays to Florence on its own or as part of two- or three-centre holiday. If you want simply to stay in Florence for a week or two,

Croce and Ognissanti on the right bank and San Frediano on the left, access to the Arno for washing the dyed cloth being a vital part of the manufacturing process. Nowadays Florence's crafts are localised up to a point – leather around San Lorenzo, antiques and furniture in the Oltrarno, metalwork and jewellery on the Ponte Vecchio. The river itself does not add greatly to the beauty of Florence.

Ponte Vecchio

you will probably be able to beat package prices by arranging your own charter flight and accommodation. If you arrive on spec the tourist office at the railway station may be able to fix you up with a room. This is not recommended in summer when there are long queues.

You need to be in a fairly robust mood to take on Florence and come out of the encounter, if not the winner, a contented loser; the heat and crowds of midsummer will put most people at an immediate disadvantage. But in the evenings you could escape the heat by going to the music and drama festival at Fiesole (June to August). In August many Florentines leave town and some shops and restaurants are closed. April, May, and September and October are obvious months to choose for a fair chance of good weather with temperatures that are not too sapping. The *Maggio Musicale*, an important classical music festival, takes place in May and June. There is no particular reason not to prefer winter, except that many of the works of art in churches are difficult to appreciate in poor light and excursions to the countryside are less appealing. There are concerts in November and early December and opera in December and January. In October and March fashion shows mean that the city is packed and hotel rooms as hard to come by as in summer.

THE FLORENTINE RENAISSANCE

The Why, When and How of the Renaissance – and even the What and So What of it – are questions that have much exercised historians and art historians. Because of the justly famous writings (a history of art in the form of artists' biographies) of a Florentine painter and architect of the late 16th century, Giorgio Vasari, there is a tendency to overstate the importance of Florence in the history of the Renaissance and that of the visual arts in the history of the Florentine Renaissance. Nevertheless, there certainly was a new art, it was most definitely Florentine and the Florentines were acutely conscious of it as their own achievement. It was (and remains) a banner they carried before them, a proof of their superiority.

By the end of the 13th century, a time of economic boom throughout Europe, Florence had become one of its richest and largest cities, with a population of about 100,000 of which a third was dependent on the manufacture of an international trade in woollen cloth. Florentine merchants acted as bankers all over Europe and the florin was international currency. In Tuscany they built up landed estates at the expense of improvident churchmen and members of the old nobility, forming the territorial basis for a powerful Florentine state which later conquered and absorbed other independent cities in the region (Pisa was the great rival). The city was independent, its government based on an electorate of professional guild members who appointed short-term executives ("priors") to run the city's affairs as a group. The nobility was excluded from government unless they stooped to trade and became guild members. Not all the guilds had equal electoral power, and in practice an oligarchy of the most powerful merchant families vied for control of the city government, managing their clans of supporters like Mafia bosses. Faction was constant and those temporarily in the ascendant habitually exiled their rivals in a bid to consolidate their position. Dante (d1321) spent the last twenty years of his life in exile from the native city he loved to hate. Florence bristled with over 150 of the tall towers (of the kind still standing at San Gimignano) that accompanied civic discord. With a stable régime in the 15th century they were demolished.

At the end of the 13th century Florence embarked on an ambitious programme of new buildings, including a new cathedral, a new town hall (the Palazzo Vecchio) and a new set of walls to accommodate the expanding population. It seems fitting that the cathedral project, the great expression of Florentine wealth and pride, came briefly under the control of the artist who is the acknowledged father, or perhaps grandfather, of the Renaissance in Italian painting, Giotto (d1337). In Giotto's art the unapproachable became human. His surviving masterpieces are sequences, or cycles, of paintings telling stories on the walls of churches. The technique used was fresco, painting with water-based pigment on small areas of fresh plaster applied daily, so that the colour sank into the plaster and was fixed in it.

For us Giotto's greatest qualities are his narrative skill of reducing scenes to their essential elements of human drama and stripping out the distractions of incidental and decorative detail, and his mastery of composition not just of individual scenes but of entire walls filled with scenes. For his contemporaries what mattered was that the figures seemed to be alive; they have weight, volume and space in which to move. It is difficult not to see a parallel between the down-to-earth vitality of Giotto's art and the spirit of the hard-headed businessmen in charge of Florentine affairs.

Throughout Europe the 14th century was a time of natural disaster, social crisis and economic depression from which the 15th saw only a limited recovery. Plague (of which there were about ten prolonged epidemics between 1348 and the end of the next century) and war hindered travel and damaged trade as well as collective

THE FLORENTINE RENAISSANCE

psychology. The population of Florence declined by about half and its cloth output by about three quarters; the space enclosed by the new city walls remained unfilled until this century. Aggressive Florentine bankers lent Edward III of England far more than they could afford to lose and when he casually defaulted to the tune of some 1 ½ million florins they crashed. As in all periods of depression wealth came to be concentrated in fewer hands and social tensions became acute; Florence had its proletarian revolt in 1378. The lowest class of cloth workers demanded a say in the conduct of communal affairs and forced new democratic procedures, but these soon lapsed and the powerful merchants consolidated their position as the city's bosses. In the arts little happened to add to Giotto's achievement; the spirit of the late 14th-century frescoes in Santa Maria Novella is one of turmoil and pessimism.

In the last quarter of the 14th century the Florentine mood changed, although not as a result of any very obvious improvement in the fortunes of the republic. On the contrary its survival was repeatedly threatened by other predatory powers, mainly the Visconti rulers of Milan. In the face of the threat the Florentines, who had in earlier crises placed themselves in the hands of the military leaders from outside with disastrous results, appointed a succession of outstanding classical scholars as chancellors of Florence, from 1375 to 1459. These men, mostly lawyers, defended Florence with the power of their Ciceronian rhetoric. The great enemy Giangaleazzo Visconti, himself not short of a rhetorical flourish, reckoned that one letter by the first of the humanist chancellors, Coluccio Salutati, was worth a troop of cavalry.

In the ideological warfare Salutati and his successors (two of whom are commemorated by magnificent tombs in Santa Croce) built up a case for Florence as the true defender of liberty and the values of republican Rome against the imperial forces of Milan, and they wrote histories of Florence tracing its foundation back to the time of the Republic. Florentines were encouraged to think of themselves as new Romans and behave accordingly. More important than this for the Renaissance as a whole, the humanists championed learning and a classical education (in what came to be known as the humanities) as the only path to virtue and self-fulfilment, not just for aspiring lawyers and scholars, but for everyone with any aspirations in any field of activity. There is no finer image of a Renaissance man than the portrait in Urbino of Duke Federico da Montefeltro, a great general in full armour in his study, intently studying a book from his famous collection of previous manuscripts.

Themselves scholars in public service, the chancellors argued that an active life was as sure a route to salvation as a life spent in contemplation and prayer. The possession of wealth they defended as a means of improving the lot of one's fellow men and of glorifying God by commissioning beautiful works of art and architecture. The change in attitude is a bit like the contrast between the public attitudes to business in Britain and America. Before, people who made good had been encouraged by churchmen to feel guilty about it; now, they could take pride in themselves and their mercantile city. The spirit of the time in Florence was heroic, positive, and confident.

In the arts, a practical boost to Florentine sculpture came from the remarkable decision of the guilds to commission a lavish new set of doors for the baptistery in 1401, at a time when the Milanese threat to the city's independent survival was particularly menacing. Whereas in the past the Florentines had looked to Pisa for the most excellent sculptors, they now offered the commission out to tender among local artists. The door-building project, which occupied Ghiberti and a large workshop of assistants for half a century, turned Florence, previously famous for its painters, into an equally important centre for sculpture.

THE FLORENTINE RENAISSANCE

In a more general sense the attitude to learning had a profound effect on the visual arts. To study was to earn respect and develop powers of expression; the artist, if he wanted to be taken seriously as more than a craftsman, took pains to master the theoretical side of his art and show off his mastery of it. The Florentines developed a passion for mathematics as the key to a true understanding of the world and a truthful representation of it in art. This was not a matter of pure scientific interest: to understand the truth about the world was to understand the work of God and to come as close as possible to understanding the ultimate, unknowable Truth.

The first artist to take a close scientific interest in the application of optics to art was Filippo Brunelleschi (1377-1446), a well-educated notary's son turned goldsmith who demonstrated his discoveries with an illusionistic painting of the baptistery and cathedral square as seen through the door of the cathedral, which he displayed in that same doorway. Brunelleschi was mainly interested in the application of perspective and ideal proportion to architecture and created a new style based on classical theory, direct inspiration from local Romanesque architecture (notably the baptistery and San Miniato, which were thought to be classical buildings) and, not least, his own invention. Brunelleschi's most famous achievement was as much a feat of engineering as one of art – erecting the cathedral dome, which had been on the drawing board defying construction for over a half a century before he devised a solution. The Florentine ambition came first, the means to realise it followed. His own churches and chapels (Santo Spirito, San Lorenzo, the Pazzi chapel at Santa Croce) are composed of varied harmonies of the ideal forms of square and circle, with a sober, elegant decorative scheme of grey sandstone and white plaster, perhaps inspired by the coloured marble of the Romanesque façades. Colour and figurative decoration are supplied by the glazed terracotta medallions that were a speciality of the period.

Brunelleschi's ideas were developed by Alberti and Piero della Francesca, and perspective became a major interest for Florentine artists in the middle years of the 15th century. Masaccio combined the new ideas with a grave and monumental figure style, at last building on Giotto's achievement, with a result which like Brunelleschi's architecture is genuinely classical in spirit rather than specific imitation. Ghiberti and Donatello introduced perspective to relief sculpture and their followers in paint Paolo Uccello and Andrea del Castagno went further in their exploration of the dramatic potential of using perspective construction to foreshorten human and animal forms.

The Florentine Renaissance is inseparably linked with the name of Medici. The family had banking and trading companies with branches all over Europe and by the early 15th century had established a position of great wealth and influence over city affairs based on the loyal support of the Florentine populace, which made it difficult for the Medici's rivals to exclude them for long. Recalled after a brief period of exile, Cosimo de' Medici (Cosimo il Vecchio) became the accepted ruler of the city from 1434 until his death in 1464. Although posthumously awarded the title Pater Patriae, Cosimo had no official ruling position in the city, never failed to respect the forms of republican government and lived in fairly modest style. The family's business interests (the Medici were bankers to the papacy) gave Cosimo's outlook on politics an international dimension and led him naturally to favour peaceful over military solutions, even when this meant alliance with Milan. Foreigners looked to him as the man in charge and the Florentines, traditionally suspicious of anyone in power, gradually came to appreciate that with Cosimo at the helm the ship of state was sailing comfortably and in a direction that suited Florence as much as it suited the Medici. The family's pre-eminent position survived Cosimo's death and in 1469 that of his gouty son Piero who was succeeded by

THE FLORENTINE RENAISSANCE

the young Lorenzo, known to posterity as Il Magnifico, who died in 1492.

Cosimo, Piero and Lorenzo presided over a rare period of peace which, apart from anything else, liberated huge amounts of money to be spent on things other than war: art and gracious living. To judge from the Florentine art of the second half of the 15th century the proud republican spirit gave way to one increasingly epicurean. Artists flattered their patrons with the depiction of expensive clothes and furnishings of comfortable household interiors decorated with elegant classical friezes according to the current fashion. In about 1460 the palace chapel of the Medici was decorated with frescoes nominally depicting a procession of the Magi towards Bethlehem but whose real subject appears to be the sumptuous pageantry attending the leading members of the Medici family. The sweet Madonnas of Fra Filippo Lippi (1406-1469), a notoriously naughty friar who ran off with a nun, betray a not wholly spiritual sensitivity to womanly beauty. There were signs that the patrician Florentines, relaxing on soft pillows of material well-being, were themselves going soft and becoming more interested in trappings than essentials. That at least was how it seemed to Girolamo Savonarola, a severe Dominican preacher who became prior of the Florentine monastery of San Marco in 1490.

There had always been a certain tension, to say the least, between Christianity and the humanists' interest in pagan moral philosophy and an increasingly empirical approach to life, encouraging belief only in what could be demonstrated to be true. Much erudite humanistic energy was devoted to establishing the compatibility of Christianity and the Classics, but for Savonarola no clever neo-Platonic argument could disguise the fact that the Florentines had strayed far from the path of humility and true religion; their pride was vanity, their carnivals were shameless orgies, they had instated Aristotle and Plato on the lectern in place of the Bible, they made the Virgin Mary look like a harlot. "Your life is spent in bed, gossiping, promenading and debauchery" he stormed at his Florentine congregation. If they did not mend their ways retribution would not be long delayed.

The impact of Savonarola's call to repentance was enormous. His message struck a chord in a city where the culture of a sophisticated intellectual minority had become increasingly estranged from the preoccupations of the masses. Suddenly the joyous carnival atmosphere of city life was transformed. Hair was cut short and gaily-coloured clothes were thrown away along with mirrors, wigs, chessboards and other "vanities" which were burnt in ceremonial public bonfires. Hymn-singing vigilante groups patrolled the streets for signs of moral laxity.

Savonarola ran Florence for a few years before public opinion turned against him. The new democracy lasted only 14 years after he was hanged and burnt on the main square in 1488. It is easy to dismiss the Savonarola episode as a short-lived outburst of hysteria, a throwback to the Middle Ages against the historical trend and of little importance in the longer run of things. But the terrifying apocalyptic sermons made a lasting impression on the hearts and minds of the Florentines and, even when the great milestone of 1500 was passed and it was possible once again to look forward with hope, the joyous mood of confident materialism was never recaptured. The late paintings of Botticelli (1444-1510) most specifically illustrate the spiritual crisis of the last years of the century, reaching the court circle of the Medici. The early years of the 16th century saw a new, soberly classical style, led by a disciple of Savonarola from San Marco, Fra Bartolommeo (1472-1517), and brought to perfection in the graceful work of Andrea del Sarto (1486-1530). Like the democratic government, it did not last: the art of the 1520s was increasingly personal in its means of expression, and took an

THE FLORENTINE RENAISSANCE

almost neurotic form in some of the work of Pontormo, a man obsessed by fear of death. As the century progressed and Medici dukes (and soon grand dukes) consolidated their power in Florence and Tuscany, Florentine art became court art, the portraitist Bronzino its most polished exponent in the mid-16th century.

All the different strains of the Florentine Renaissance found their full expression in the life and work of two artists, Leonardo da Vinci (1452-1519) and Michelangelo (1475-1564). The older man, already mature by the time of Lorenzo the Magnificent's death, is the supreme Renaissance intellectual artist-scientist, with less interest in learning from the antique than from nature, which he observed with sharper eyes and intelligence than anyone before or since. His naturalism led him to explore not only the question of how to paint a material object but an idea, an atmosphere, a storm. Leonardo was for long periods a court artist (in Milan and France) and spent much of his time in the service of his princely patrons (and on occasions Florence) engaged on ambitious engineering projects or designing costumes and stage sets for festive processions. His flying machine was a device for mechanical angels at some such event. It makes no sense to draw lines between Leonardo's activities or around his apparently limitless interests. They are all part of his art at a time aptly described as "that one magic moment in the history of western civilisation when art was at the forefront of the move into the modern scientific world and budding science was the catalyst for supreme artistic achievement" (John White).

Michelangelo, an impressionable young man in the 1490s, said in his very old age that the voice of Savonarola continued to ring loud, clear and terrible in his ears. In the Renaissance language of ideal beauty Michelangelo expressed a view of the material world which is more reminiscent of the Middle Ages. He was not remotely interested in landscape. Despite using the human form as his sole expressive vehicle, he scorned portraiture except, as he put it, in cases of extreme beauty.

Michelangelo's outlook was not made more optimistic by the decline into servitude of the proud, republican Florence of his youth. Unlike Leonardo, who sailed under his own flag wherever the wind of fortune blew him, Michelangelo was a devoted and fiercely patriotic Florentine. Perhaps the most famous and characteristic image of the Florentine Renaissance is his giant marble statue of David (1501-4), commissioned for public display and placed on completion in front of the Palazzo della Signoria, where a copy still stands. The sculptor suppressed all narrative and used the form of an enormous nude male to express the subject's heroic moral quality, not simply anatomical beauty and not simply the artist's virtuosity in the representation of it. David's alertness to danger is the vigilance of the ever-ready Florentines.

Michelangelo's next major commission was for a battle scene to decorate a wall of the Great Council chamber in the same palace, an even more specific illustration of Florentine triumph. In the event the public theme seems to have been subordinated to a private competition between two rival artists (Leonardo had already begun work on his part of the commission, another battle scene). Michelangelo chose a subject (Florentine soldiers surprised while bathing in the Arno) which was scarcely more than a pretext for a virtuoso display of nude males in a variety of complicated postures as they haul themselves out of the water, drag on their clothes and leap to battle stations; an artist's manifesto. The subject of the decorative scheme of the chamber was not Florence v Pisa (or Milan, in Leonardo's case) but Michelangelo v Leonardo. That transformation, not simply an upset in the balance between form and content but also the logical conclusion of the new self-importance among artists, seems to announce the passing of the classical phase of the Renaissance.

Area by area guide

THE CENTRE

The heart of the city is the area between the cathedral and the Arno with its three great public spaces; much of it is a pedestrian precinct, in theory anyway.

The Piazza della Signoria, dominated by the medieval town hall, the Palazzo Vecchio, is the forum of civic life where since the 13th century Florentines have gathered at times of crisis and celebration or simply, as they do now when the torrent of tourism is at its low winter ebb, to discuss their business. The square (which it isn't) is an open-air gallery of Renaissance and Antique sculptures, exemplifying the importance and public status of art in the Florentine state. Michelangelo's David, set up here in 1504, invites political interpretation (the original is now in the Accademia). The Neptune fountain, by Bandinelli and Ammannati, may relate to duke Cosimo I's ambition to establish Florence as a naval power (the bronze figures disporting themselves around the edge are more successful than the marble Neptune). The graceful Gothic Loggia dei Lanzi shelters Cellini's magnificent bronze Perseus (1545-54) and Giambologna's marble Rape of a Sabine (1583), a celebrated masterpiece of Mannerist sculpture.

In the narrow space between the Piazza della Signoria and the river lies the building which housed duke Cosimo's administration and which now contains one of the world's most famous art galleries – the Uffizi. The long arcades shelter scores of stalls piled high with souvenirs, bags and straw hats.

A monumental traffic island at the heart of the city, the Piazza del Duomo is almost entirely taken up by the cathedral and the adjacent campanile and baptistery. The decorative 19th-century façade of pink, green and white Tuscan marble, though dirty, provides visual relief from the overall brownness of Florence, but the people, the postcard stalls and the endlessly swirling traffic can mar the experience. Crowds of tourists make it difficult to get a good sighting of the baptistery's famous east doors, facing the cathedral. Sitting on the cathedral steps is now discouraged by some rather municipal terracotta flowerpots and makeshift covered entrance.

The Piazza della Repubblica is one of the most unanimously deplored parts of the city. The inscription on the pompous triumphal arch states with pride that the square was built over an "unworthy" medieval district. Despite the discordant note struck by its buildings and advertisement hoardings the square does have one attractive feature – outdoor café tables – and is a busy centre of everyday activity, with a flower market on Thursday mornings. Nearby is the arcaded Mercato Nuovo selling leather and straw bags, linen and souvenirs. It dates from the 16th century (the "old" market having been destroyed to make way for the Piazza della Repubblica), and is still sometimes called Il Porcellino after the splendid bronze boar which used to stand here but has recently been moved to the Uffizi. Many of the surrounding streets are lined by elegant shop windows of Florentine fashion houses and boutiques; if you can tear yourself away the exterior of the church of Orsanmichele provides a fascinating guide to the development of Renaissance sculpture.

Easily the smartest shopping street is the Via dei Tornabuoni which forms the western boundary of the city centre; shops include, among other internationally famous names, the HQ of Gucci. There are also some beautiful buildings to admire: Palazzo Strozzi, built at the end of the 15th century as a town house for Florence's second banking dynasty, is the most impressive with its uncompromising façade of massive rough blocks. At the river end of Via Tornabuoni, Palazzo Spini Feroni (opposite the church of Santa Trínita) preserves in its façade some of the medieval fortifications that flanked the river, with just a few gaps for wharves, until the 15th century. The beautiful Ponte Santa Trínita, designed by Ammannati, was painstakingly rebuilt after the War using as many of the old stones as possible. The old Bóboli quarries were reopened for the new stone needed and the new blocks were cut with old-fashioned tools to ensure the right effect.

The Arno itself marks the southern boundary of the city centre, and the old walls have been replaced by embankment streets (*lungarni*) which are busy thoroughfares of no particular interest. The main appeal of the Arno is the Ponte Vecchio, itself a bustling and very touristy shopping street with poky old shops hanging out over the river. When duke Cosimo de' Medici moved across the river at the end of the 16th century he ordered the building of a private corridor running between the Pitti and the Palazzo Vecchio, over the Ponte Vecchio, and decreed that the shops on the bridge itself should for the sake of propriety be limited to goldsmiths and jewellers, as they have been ever since. There are beautiful views over the city from the open arches in the middle of the bridge, a favourite spot for snap-happy tourists and loving couples.

Churches
Badia
Duomo and Baptistery
Orsanmichele
Santa Trínita

Galleries, museums and palaces
Cathedral Museum
Palazzo Davanzati
Palazzo Vecchio
Uffizi

Hotels
Hermitage
La Residenza
Tornabuoni Beacci

NORTH AND NORTH-EAST OF THE CATHEDRAL

Although not a very picturesque part of town this is an important one for tourists with some of the city's greatest Renaissance treasures, both artistic and architectural, many of them closely connected with the Medici family. Their family palace (Palazzo Medici-Riccardi), the work of Michelozzo in the 1440s, is on busy Via Cavour; nearby is their local church, San Lorenzo, whose blank façade looks out over a dull statue of duke Cosimo I's father, Giovanni delle Bande Nere.

The area is one of long straight streets with narrow pavements, punctuated by squares. There's a good cross-section of attractions with several interesting churches, plenty of shops and a couple of the city's most civilised small hotels. To the north, west of Borgo Pinti, the area is mainly residential, with some old palaces and gardens.

Piazza San Lorenzo is the scene of one of the city's busiest street markets with stall after stall of bags, belts and other products of Florence's thriving leather industry. The stalls fill the Via dell' Ariento which leads to the city's main food market.

Piazza San Marco is a lively square usually full of university students, people queuing for buses, and tourists flocking to the Accademia and San Marco museums. The neighbouring square to the east, Piazza Santissima Annunziata, the most beautiful square in Florence, has been released from its undignified role as a parking lot. The elegant colonnaded porticoes of the Ospedale degli Innocenti (Foundlings' Hospital, on the east side of the square), one of Brunelleschi's first architectural works, are echoed opposite; the original side is instantly recognisable by the swathed infants depicted on the terracotta medallions (by Andrea della Robbia). The equestrian statue of Cosimo I's son, grand duke Ferdinando I de' Medici, is by Giambologna.

Churches
Santissima Annunziata
Sant' Apollonia
San Lorenzo
Santa Maria Maddalena dei Pazzi
San Marco
San Michele Visdomini
Lo Scalzo

Galleries, museums and palaces
Accademia
Archaeological Museum
Innocenti Museum
Medici-Riccardi Palace

Hotels
Loggiata dei Serviti
Monna Lisa

NORTH-WEST AND WEST OF THE CENTRE

The best thing about the station is that it is very central, although outside the original city walls. The building is a functional one (1930s') and so is the surrounding area, with plenty of cheap accommodation and backpacks propped up against café tables. But nearby Santa Maria Novella is one of the great churches of Florence and one of the few whose façade was completed in the Renaissance. To the north of the station is the Fortezza da Basso, a powerful fortress built in the 1530s by the first Medici duke, the loathed Alessandro, killed by his cousin Lorenzino in 1537. The fortress turned out to be something of a white elephant, and is now used for craft and fashion exhibitions.

The Ognissanti area, between the station and the Arno, is neither picturesque nor very interesting for sightseers, although it is within easy walking distance of the centre and the Oltrarno. It is a reasonably quiet area to stay in and there are hotels at various price levels, including several with swimming pools. Several noble families built palaces in the area: the Palazzo Rucellai, built by Alberti in the mid-15th century, features an early use of the classical orders on different storeys (it was Giovanni Rucellai, a wealthy merchant, who commissioned Alberti to complete the façade of Santa Maria Novella). To the west of Ognissanti, along the river, are the Cascine gardens with a zoo, a race course, tennis courts and swimming pool, and a general market on Tuesday mornings. Originally a farm and hunting ground for the Medici dukes, in the 19th century the Cascine was the fashionable place to be seen. Now the gardens are rather neglected, by tourists and gardeners.

Churches
Ognissanti
Sansepolcro (see Palazzo Rucellai)
Santa Maria Novella

Galleries, museums and palaces
Palazzo Rucellai

Hotels
Aprile
Ariele
Kraft

EAST OF THE CENTRE: SANTA CROCE

The narrow streets and dark alleys around the medieval Bargello and between the Piazza della Signoria and Piazza Santa Croce form the most characteristic part of old Florence, traditionally the working class and artisans' area. Since the Renaissance artists and craftsmen have had their workshops here although many of the premises are now being given over to tourist shops. There are few places to stay, but plenty of good places to eat, from unpretentious *trattorie* to the most expensive (and arguably the best) restaurant in Florence – the Enoteca Pinchiorri – and Vivoli's, legendary for ice creams.

The main tourist attraction is the outwardly undistinguished church of Santa Croce, and, beside it, Brunelleschi's tiny Pazzi chapel. The spacious (but not particularly beautiful) square, once focal point of the area and used for public occasions like the burning of heretics and jousting tournaments, is now rather lifeless. Some of the houses still have their overhanging upper-storey rooms (*sporti*), once a common architectural feature in a city cramped for space.

To the north of Santa Croce the Piazza San Pier Maggiore is a lively square with fruit stalls under the arches; the Borgo degli Albizi, lined with fine palaces, leads back towards the cathedral. Apart from one or two small churches and the city's flea market there is little to entice the visitor to the ill-reputed quarter east of Santa Croce. The market takes place around the Piazza dei Ciompi, named after the lowest of the low labourers in the wool industry who revolted in 1378, demanding a piece of the democratic action in republican Florence.

Churches
Santa Croce

Galleries, museums and palaces
Bargello
Horne Museum
Michelangelo Museum (*Casa Buonarroti*)

Hotels
Rigatti

OLTRARNO

The Oltrarno is all of Florence south of the Arno, a much smaller area than the right bank part of town. As its name suggests it was regarded as suburban until the 16th century when fashion followed the Medici dukes who installed themselves in the Pitti Palace, now the Oltrarno's main tourist attraction. The inhabitants, or San Fredianini, are said to have their own dialect and slang, rather like the Trasteverini in Rome, and most of the Oltrarno is a lively popular quarter busy with street markets and craftsmen's shops. Shady Piazza Santo Spirito is the heart of the Oltrarno, in the mornings scene of a local market, at night a hangout for students, trendies and drug addicts. Just round the corner from the workshops of furniture restorers (and fakers) are the elegant antique shops of Via Maggio, with its fine old palaces (a natural extension of the elegant Via Tornabuoni on the other side of Ponte Santa Trínita). There are also smart shops and restaurants on Borgo San Jacopo, which runs parallel to the river.

Hills climb from close to the river on this side, and from the heart of the city you can walk easily up into the Tuscan countryside, within half an hour of the Ponte Vecchio. One of the most beautiful walks is through the Bóboli gardens from the Pitti Palace entrance up to the Belvedere fortress (part of the city walls), and from there up the Via di San Leonardo, flanked by dry-stone walls and

Renaissance villas with olives, cypresses and sweet-smelling, colourful gardens. Turn right along the Via Galileo (part of the Viale dei Colli) which leads round to the great Romanesque church of San Miniato, the most lovable of all Florentine churches, and the Piazzale Michelangelo, a celebrated belvedere over the city and northern hills behind. The monument to Michelangelo, with reproductions of his most famous works in Florence, dates from 1875 (the 400th anniversary of his birth). The Piazzale, lit at night, is a very popular destination for a romantic evening stroll (but there's also a bus service).

Churches
(Santa Maria del) Carmine
Santa Felicita
San Miniato
San Salvatore al Monte
Santo Spirito

Galleries, museums and palaces
Bardini Museum
Pitti Palace, and Bóboli gardens

Hotels
Annalena
Pitti Palace
Silla

Shopping

Florentine craftsmanship is legendary; all over the city are little workshops where picture frames are being carved, leather tooled or fashioned into bags or belts, books beautifully bound with marbled endpapers. Since the Renaissance (at least) the Florentines have excelled in the production of gorgeously embroidered fabrics and finely wrought jewellery.

Antiques   The vast majority of antique dealers are concentrated in the Ognissanti area around Via dei Fossi and Borgo Ognissanti, and in the Oltrarno along Via Maggio and Borgo San Jacopo. There is a flea market at Piazza dei Ciompi.

Books   There are several good bookshops, usually selling guidebooks to the museums and galleries of the city. Seebers in Via Tornabuoni meets most needs; Centro Di on Piazza de' Mozzi is a specialist art bookshop with old exhibition catalogues.

Clothes   The centre of Florence is full of clothes shops; the smartest shopping street is Via Tornabuoni. For bargains, try the department stores and the markets (recently the fashion for leather clothing has produced a glut of jackets and skirts, not always particularly good value). For shoes, try the Borgo San Lorenzo (cheap) and the Via dei Calzaiuoli (expensive).

Food The main market for food is the covered Mercato Centrale, near San Lorenzo; there are smaller local ones such as that on Piazza Santo Spirito, with fresh fruit and vegetables from the Tuscan countryside.

Jewellery Florence is full of jewellers, often with tiny one-room shops. The Florentines have a reputation as excellent goldsmiths which dates back to the 15th century and some shops still have workrooms behind. The greatest concentration of jewellers is on the Ponte Vecchio. Costume jewellery can be found at the market stalls at San Lorenzo (good paste) and in *profumerie*.

Leather The 'Made in Italy' label on handbags bought all over the world usually denotes Florentine origins, the city being famous for its craftsmanship in this field for hundreds of years. Most of the workshops are around San Lorenzo and Santa Croce, but a lot of them now turn out poor merchandise for the tourist market. For real quality you will have to go to the smartest shops, but there are always some good bargains at the San Lorenzo market. There is a leather school in the monastery adjoining the church of Santa Croce.

Linen Embroidered linen and lingerie, particularly silk, is a good thing to buy in Florence, and Ognissanti a good area to try. There are some stalls selling cheaper linen at the Mercato Nouvo.

Paper A Florentine speciality is marbled paper (Florentine paper shops have now opened up in London and elsewhere). You can buy endpapers for bookbinding, desk sets, photograph albums and frames and pretty boxes, notebooks and pencils. The best shop is Giulio Giannini e Figlio, opposite the Palazzo Pitti; a close second is Il Papiro with branches in the Piazza del Duomo and Via Cavour.

Wool Yet another traditional Florentine industry. Cheap jerseys and scarves (mostly lambswool) can be found at San Lorenzo and other markets. In shops prices are slightly lower than in the UK.

Sightseeing

Churches

*Most churches are open from about 7.30am to noon and from about 3.30pm
to 6.30pm (earlier in winter). The Medici chapels in San Lorenzo are open
on weekdays, except Monday, until 7pm. The cloisters and Spanish chapel of
Santa Maria Novella are also open late on weekdays (except Friday but
including Saturday).*

*Many Florentine churches are not oriented. For simplicity we refer in
these cases to the two sides of churches as left and right (looking towards the
main altar). Some guidebooks use south (right) and north (left) even in
churches that are not oriented.*

*When visiting churches take plenty of 100 lire coins to light the works of
art.*

☛ Badia

Important Benedictine abbey church first built in the 10th century, enlarged
in the late 13th and completely reoriented in the 17th when the original
church, built on a conventional east/west axis, became the transept of the
new one. The outstanding work of art in the church is on the left of the
entrance, Filippino Lippi's delightful Vision of St Bernard (c1480), including a
portrait of the donor and his family. There are several interesting funerary
monuments in both the church and its very charming cloister.

☛ Baptistery (Battistero)

In many ways a more important building for the Florentines (whose main
patron saint is the Baptist) than the cathedral, and one of enormous influence
on Florentine Renaissance architecture. The original building dates from the
7th century but during the Renaissance it was traditionally assumed to be a
converted Roman Temple of Mars, and contemporary architects who drew
on the colourful and elegant design and centralised plan for inspiration
imagined that their source was Antiquity. The building, with its beautiful
green-and-white marble exterior, was actually completed in the 12th century.

The most famous features of the exterior are the bronze doors on south,
east and north sides, each set made up of relief panels framed with elaborate
decorative motifs. The earliest are Andrea Pisano's south doors (1330-9). The
reliefs illustrate the Life of the Baptist in a clear and vigorous style
reminiscent of Giotto, but with great delicacy of detail. The group above the
door (the Beheading of the Baptist) is by Vincenzo Danti (1570).

In 1401 the wool guild organised a competition to design a new set of
doors. The young goldsmith Lorenzo Ghiberti's version of the test subject,
the Sacrifice of Isaac, was preferred to Brunelleschi's (both panels are on
display in the Bargello) and Ghiberti spent over 20 years on the work, now
the north doorway. The panels (New Testament scenes, evangelists and
church fathers) retain the basic format of Pisano's doors with a new technical
refinement and variations of depth of relief giving a much richer, pictorial
effect. Among the heads poking out of the framework is Ghiberti's own,
sporting an elegant turban (centre left, five rows down). The group above the
door (the Baptist, a Pharisee and a Levite) is by Rustici (1506-11), perhaps

assisted by Leonardo da Vinci.

Ghiberti's east doors (1425-52) known, after a remark by Michelangelo, as the Gates of Paradise, represent a further development in the new style. The Old Testament scenes fill larger, square panels, and are full of elegance and incident with elaborate effects of landscape and, in the later central panels, architectural perspective. Each panel contains several separate scenes. Ghiberti's self-portrait (centre left), is now bald.

The interior of the building is dominated by the sumptuous mosaics of the vault, mostly 13th-century and influenced by St Mark's in Venice. Narrative cycles in four bands depict the Creation (the inner ring), the Story of Joseph, the Life of Christ and the Life of the Baptist. They are not easy to study in detail, except for the Last Judgement with its 25ft Christ above the apse. The mosaics in the small vault over the main altar are the earliest and signed by a Franciscan monk "Jacobus". To the right of the altar is the tomb of anti-pope John XXIII, designed by Donatello but executed by his assistants with the possible exception of the bronze effigy. The beautiful mosaic pavement with geometric patterns and signs of the zodiac dates from the 12th to 14th centuries.

☛ Campanile

The campanile was designed and begun under Giotto, who was in charge of the cathedral work from 1331 until his death in 1337. Some of the lower relief panels decorating the exterior may have been designed by Giotto. The originals are in the cathedral museum (Museo dell' Opera del Duomo). It is a long, steep staircase to the top (but less unnerving than the climb to the cathedral dome) for very fine views, especially down over the baptistery.

☛ Duomo (Santa Maria del Fiore)

Although there is no connection between the words, in Florence more than anywhere else the Duomo is the dome, the crowning centrepiece of the skyscape and the symbol of Florence. The project of a new cathedral was part of the building boom at the end of the 13th century, a period of expanding population and growing wealth. Like other prosperous cities, Florence decided that its cathedral would be bigger and more beautiful than any other. Work went on throughout the 14th century under a succession of chief architects (including Giotto). After half a century of worry about the problem of how to construct a dome over the enormous crossing, a competition was held in 1418. The winning scheme was Brunelleschi's, which had the great merit of ingeniously dispensing with the need for very expensive wooden scaffolding. The cathedral was consecrated in 1436, but the lantern was not completed until 1467. The present façade dates from the 19th century, with white marble from Carrara, pink from the Tuscan Maremma, and green from Prato. Over the Porta della Mandorla, the north side door, is a beautiful relief of the Assumption of the Virgin by Nanni di Banco (1414-21).

Most of the works of art have been removed to the cathedral museum (Museo dell' Opera del Duomo) and the interior gives an impression of cold and emptiness.

On the left side are the famous equestrian monuments to Sir John Hawkwood (by Uccello, 1436) and Niccolò da Tolentino (by Andrea del Castagno, 1456). Both paintings (fresco transposed onto canvas) imitate sculpture and are often cited as examples of Florentine thrift in honouring outsiders. The painting of Dante holding up his *Divine Comedy* in front of Florence (with the unfinished Duomo), Heaven and Hell, was painted by

Domenico di Michelino in 1465 for the bicentenary of Dante's birth. The nearby door gives access to the dome.

The 463-step climb to the dome is not recommended for the unfit or those without a good head for heights. It follows a tortuous course up to the drum and on up between the two shells of the dome to the lantern and gives a fascinating opportunity to study Brunelleschi's constructional techniques as well as magnificent views. Half way up there is a splendid bird's-eye view of the church (the lurid paintings of the Last Judgement by Zuccari and Vasari inside the dome are temporarily veiled for restoration) and close-up views of the stained glass windows in the drum, designed by the leading artists of the 15th century (Uccello, Resurrection and Nativity; Castagno, Deposition; Donatello, Coronation of the Virgin; Ghiberti, the other three scenes).

Along the right side are various monuments to famous Florentines including a bust of Giotto by Benedetto da Maiano (c1490), with an inscription by the leading Florentine Renaissance poet, Politian. Beneath the altar in the central chapel of the main apse, a beautiful urn, by Ghiberti (1432-42), contains the relics of Saint Zenobius, first bishop of Florence.

Steps lead down to extensive excavations of several earlier buildings (including Roman ones) on the site of the present cathedral, and Brunelleschi's tomb, a simple slab.

☛ Ognissanti

An originally 13th-century church (for whose high altar Giotto painted the famous Maesta now in the Uffizi) mostly submerged beneath Baroque decoration. Works of art in the church include (2nd altar on right) Ghirlandaio's Madonna of Mercy with the Vespucci family (c1470), said to include portraits of Amerigo, the navigator who gave his name to America and Simonetta, favourite of Giuliano de' Medici, and traditionally the model for Botticelli's Venus in the Uffizi. Ghirlandaio's reflective St Jerome faces Botticelli's more intense St Augustine. In the old refectory (*cenacolo*) is Ghirlandaio's typically charming fresco of the Last Supper.

☛ Orsanmichele

A massive square 14th-century cornmarket later consecrated as a church on account of the miraculous image of the Virgin on one of the pillars. A unique and yet typically Florentine mixture of business and devotion, Orsanmichele is the clearest embodiment of the competitive spirit between the different guilds in the city, each trying to outdo the others in the magnificence of its own altar. The most interesting feature of the interior is Orcagna's richly decorated tabernacle (1359) for the sacred painting of the Virgin, by Bernardo Daddi.

Outside, elaborately decorated niches were filled with statues of the guilds' patrons, making a celebrated ensemble of Florentine Renaissance sculpture: *East side* (Via dei Calzaiuoli), *left to right*: Ghiberti's Baptist (1414), the first life size bronze statue to be cast since ancient times, but still in the Gothic idiom; Verrocchio's Doubting Thomas (1466-83); Giambologna's St Luke (c1600). *North side* (Via Orsanmichele), *2nd niche from right*: Nanni di Banco's four Christian sculptors (martyred for refusing to make a profane image for Diocletian), modelled on classical art, for the masons' and carpenters' guild (c1413). *Right hand niche*: bronze copy of Donatello's marble St George (now in the Bargello) for the armourers' guild. The relief of St George killing the Dragon is the original (c1417) and famous as perhaps the earliest example of illusionistic perspective, ten years before Masaccio.

West side (Via dell' Arte della Lana), *left to right*: Ghiberti's St Matthew (1419-23) and more classical St Stephen (1425-9); Nanni di Banco's St Eligius (c1410) – the decorative detail round the tabernacle relates it to the smiths' guild.

South side (Via dei Lamberti), *left hand niche*: Donatello's St Mark (1411-12), one of the earliest works to embody the heroic ideal of the Renaissance.

☛ Santissima Annunziata

The church, on the north side of Brunelleschi's graceful square, is named after a fresco of the Annunciation said to have been started by a monk in 1252 and completed by an angel. The miraculous powers of the shrine called for repeated enlargement of the building, in the last instance by Michelozzo in the mid-15th century. The new design included classical features such as a circular choir (Rotonda) and an entrance cloister like an atrium. The entrance cloister, known as the Chiostro dei Voti after the votive offerings left by pilgrims which once filled it, is now bare and covered by a glass canopy. The early 16th-century frescoes on the walls are very faint. Andrea del Sarto's marvellously domestic Birth of the Virgin (1514) and Pontormo's Visitation (1516) are among the finest examples of Florentine painting of the period. The Assumption is an uneven early work by Rosso Fiorentino (1517). Sarto was also responsible for all but one of the scenes illustrating the Life of St Filippo Benizzi. The earliest of the frescoes is Baldovinetti's Nativity (1460-62), a beautiful landscape.

The interior of the church is Baroque at its heaviest and darkest. Michelozzo's tabernacle encloses the sacred image of the Annunciation, rarely visible, and there are works by Andrea del Castagno, The Vision of St Julian and St Jerome praying to the Trinity (both c 1455), in the first two chapels on the left (lights inside on left). A separate entrance at the side of the church leads to the main cloister (Chiostro dei Morti) where Andrea del Sarto's famous Madonna del Sacco (c1525) is painted over the door leading into the church.

☛ Sant' Apollonia (*Via XXVII Aprile 1*)

The refectory of a former Benedictine convent decorated by Andrea del Castagno with a powerfully dramatic fresco of the Last Supper, beneath the scenes of Crucifixion, Entombment and Resurrection (c1450). Other paintings by Castagno have been assembled in the same place.

☛ Santa Croce

A vast and beautiful Franciscan church full of tombs and monuments and other important works of art. The present building was started in 1295 and finished in 1385 except for the façade, completed in the 19th century. Vasari's alterations to the interior in the late 16th century included the demolition of the monk's choir and screen, a coat of whitewash over the frescoes that originally covered most of the interior and a series of painted altarpieces illustrating The Passion, by the leading Florentine artists of the time (including Vasari himself). He also designed the monumental tomb for Michelangelo (right of the entrance) with three figures representing Architecture, Sculpture and Painting, the last holding a statuette signifying the influence of sculpture, and Michelangelo's sculpture in particular, on painting.

Beyond monuments to Dante and Machiavelli is a beautiful relief of the Annunciation by Donatello (c1430). The famous tomb of Leonardo Bruni by Rossellino (1444) is very classical in spirit and detail, as befitted one of the

Santa Croce

most distinguished of Florentine humanist chancellors. Bruni is portrayed, as he was buried, with his *History of Florence* on his chest. On the opposite side of the church is the tomb of another of the famous chancellors, Carlo Marsuppini, by Desiderio da Settignano (1455). The work is sweeter in sentiment and richer in delicate ornament, but clearly influenced by the Bruni tomb.

The most important frescoes in the transept chapels are: scenes from the Life of the Virgin by Taddeo Gaddi, a pupil of Giotto (the Baroncelli chapel, right transept); Lives of St John and John the Baptist, late works by Giotto (the Peruzzi chapel, 2nd to right of the chancel); Life of St Francis, slightly earlier works by Giotto and painted in true fresco technique (on wet plaster) unlike the Peruzzi chapel paintings (the Bardi chapel, between chancel and Peruzzi chapel). In the vault are the figures of Poverty, Obedience and Chastity, the Franciscan vows. The 13th-century altarpiece also depicts scenes from the Life of St Francis.

Another Bardi chapel at the end of the left transept contains a wooden crucifix by Donatello, thought to be the one Brunelleschi dismissed as being the portrayal of a peasant.

Next to the church stands a modest little edifice which is one of the most famous monuments of the Renaissance, Brunelleschi's **Pazzi Chapel**. It was begun in 1430 as a family chapel and chapter house for the monks, and decorated with terracotta medallions by Luca della Robbia. The wonderfully clear, balanced and uncluttered design, based on harmonies of square and circle, is a perfect expression of the spirit of an age of confidence in the supreme power of human intelligence. A doorway in the right-hand corner of the first cloister gives access to another, more beautiful, also designed by Brunelleschi.

The old refectory, flanking the main cloister, houses the **Museo dell' Opera di Santa Croce**. Its contents, severely damaged by the 1966 flood, include a Crucifix by Cimabue, fragments of a fresco of the Triumph of Death by Orcagna, Taddeo Gaddi's fresco of the Last Supper (c1330) – the earliest example of this subject being used for a refectory decoration, Donatello's St Louis of Toulouse (c1423) originally outside the church of Orsanmichele, and Domenico Veneziano's fresco of St John and St Francis (c1460).

☛ **Santa Felicità**

A small church, worth visiting for Pontormo's painting of the Entombment (first chapel on right). In the astonishingly complicated composition the figures come together in a ghostly dance of death rotating around a hub of linked hands, the whole group supported by three toes of one of the bearers of Christ. Colours and lighting are arbitrary. There is no tomb in the painting: the chapel floor, with funerary vault below, completes the composition. On the window wall Pontormo painted the Annunciation with the Virgin looking across to the Entombment, hauntingly depicted not as a real event but as a vision revealed to her at the moment of Annunciation.

☛ **San Lorenzo**

The leading Florentine artists of the time were employed to work on the Medici family's parish church. In 1419 Brunelleschi was commissioned to build a new sacristy (now called the Old Sacristy), one of his first architectural projects. So remarkable was his plan that Giovanni de' Medici handed over the rebuilding of the entire church to Brunelleschi. The interior was not finished until over 20 years after his death in 1446. Michelangelo was later engaged to design the façade, but the work was not carried out and the exterior remains to this day in a rough, unfinished state.

The interior of the church is a cool and spacious grey-and-white harmony of clearly ordered geometry, the Renaissance mathematical ideal of beauty born mature, classical in spirit although not in direct inspiration. Although the church is fairly bright the detail of some of the individual works is hard to appreciate. Under the dome a round composition of coloured marbles marks the place where Cosimo il Vecchio lies buried in the crypt; Donatello, who enjoyed a particular place of friendship in the heart of his great patron, lies here too. Donatello's famous bronze pulpits, decorated with reliefs of scenes leading up to and following the Crucifixion, are intensely emotional late works of the 1460s. Donatello himself chased some of the panels on the right hand pulpit (Descent into Hell, Resurrection and Ascension) but most of the execution was the work of his pupils. On the wall by the right-hand pulpit is

Desiderio da Settignano's beautifully carved altar tabernacle (1461).

The most important paintings in the church are Filippo Lippi's Annunciation (Martelli chapel, west wall of right transept) dating from c1440 and Rosso Fiorentino's Marriage of the Virgin (second chapel on right) one of the most sophisticated and elegant of all Mannerist masterpieces, the canon for what has been described as the stylish style (1523).

Brunelleschi's **Old Sacristy**, the funerary chapel of Cosimo il Vecchio's parents, is reached from the left transept. Donatello was responsible for most of the decoration (recently restored) and the impressive bronze doors (c1440), which Brunelleschi is said to have considered out of keeping with the measured elegance of his architecture. The altar in the sacristy chapel is modelled on the one in the baptistery and originally contained Brunelleschi's relief of the Sacrifice of Isaac, designed for the baptistery doors and now in the Bargello.

The left aisle gives access to a graceful 15th-century cloister and from there to the **Laurentian Library**, designed by Michelangelo in the 1520s to house the Medici collection of manuscripts. The wilful use of classical forms and breaking of classical rules creates a dramatic effect. The walls of the vestibule seem to be carved rather than built, with multiple layers of recession and projection and cramped pairs of massive columns. The staircase flows down from the library door in an irregular curving tongue. The library itself is much more conventional. Manuscripts are displayed on the desks.

The **Medici chapels** (the New Sacristy and the Cappella dei Principi) are entered from the far side of the church. Michelangelo's sacristy is cold and sombre, partly because the project was abandoned in the 1530s and many niches and sections of wall were left blank. The chapel was conceived as a memorial to Lorenzo il Magnifico and his brother Giuliano, with flanking tombs of two other members of the family, also called Lorenzo and Giuliano. Ironically Michelangelo completed only the side tombs, so the most famous monument to the Medici commemorates two of the family's less distinguished members. However, they are represented as generalised figures – one absorbed in thought, the other poised for vigorous action – and are no more than components of the cosmic allegorical scheme. Beneath the two so-called "captains", the muscular figures of Day and Night, Dawn and Dusk recline none too comfortably on the sarcophagus lids. On the entrance wall is a beautiful Madonna and Child (c1521), the only part of the main double tomb that Michelangelo achieved.

The **Cappella dei Principi** is a vast octagonal chamber opulently encrusted with coloured inlay, with the wall tombs of six Medici rulers from Cosimo I (d 1574) to Cosimo III (d 1723) in the corner niches. Planned by Vasari in the 1560s, the chapel was not begun until 1605 and not vaulted until the 19th century (the floor is even more recent). The original idea was that the chapel should open directly into the church; fortunately it does not.

☛ San Marco

The church of San Marco contains a characteristic but damaged altarpiece by Fra Bartolommeo and works by Florentine Mannerists of the late 16th century but is of no great interest. However, the convent next door, where Fra Angelico spent 10 years (1435–45), has been turned into a museum for the display of his work.

(*See Fra Angelico Museum*)

☛ Santa Maria del Cármine

The 15th-century church was almost entirely destroyed by fire in 1771 and replaced by the present uninteresting Baroque building; by good fortune the transept chapels were spared, including the famous Brancacci chapel, decorated with fresco scenes from the Life of St Peter by Masolino and Masaccio in the 1420s and completed by Filippino Lippi some 60 years later. Masaccio's part of the work has long been recognised as one of the greatest leaps forward in the history of western art and was studied by aspiring Florentine artists from Fra Angelico to Michelangelo (some of whose student drawings of the frescoes survive and who is said to have acquired his broken nose in an argument about their quality). Masaccio's most famous scenes, distillations of drama and gravity, are the Expulsion from Paradise, the Paying of the Tribute Money where, on Christ's instruction, Peter finds a coin in the mouth of a fish, and the Cripple Healed by St. Peter's Shadow. Filippino's work, full of portraits, is easily recognised on the lower section of both side walls. The Crucifixion of St Peter contains a portrait (in profile) of Botticelli.

Recently the frescoes have been under restoration and partly obscured by scaffolding.

☛ Santa Maria Maddalena dei Pazzi *(Borgo Pinti)*

Church of a former convent with chapels and cloister designed by Giuliano da Sangallo (c1490), but mainly visited for Perugino's fresco of the Crucifixion (1493-6) in the chapter house (reached via the cloister or crypt). The figures are split up into bays by a painted architecture but set against a unifying landscape of limpid beauty.

☛ Santa Maria Novella

Florence's main Dominican church, built in the 13th/14th centuries and much changed by Vasari in the late 16th century. The colourful marble façade is a very successful blend of styles, the main door and upper registers having been added to the half-finished Gothic façade by Alberti in the mid-15th century.

Inside the church (3rd chapel on left) is Masaccio's famous fresco of the Trinity, set in a classical painted architectural framework (c1425), one of the earliest examples in painting of careful perspective construction, exaggerated by a very low viewpoint.

The chancel is decorated with a series of frescoes by Ghirlandaio (1485-90), illustrating the Lives of Saint John the Baptist and the Virgin, but most interesting as a colourful evocation of Florentine life of the period, full of portraits. This was the artist's main project at the time of Michelangelo's apprenticeship to him and some scholars have sought to identify in various parts of the frescoes the youthful hand of a greater genius than Ghirlandaio's essentially descriptive and decorative one.

The decoration of the Filippo Strozzi chapel (right of the chancel) shows a very different approach to the filling of wall space, the work of Filippino Lippi (1485-1502) in his very personal, somewhat frenetic, late style. Larger scenes (from the Lives of St Philip and St John the Evangelist) are framed by illusionistic painted architecture with a wealth of classically-inspired ornament. Filippino also designed the stained glass window and the grisaille frescoes round it, full of complex neo-Platonic musical symbolism. Filippo Strozzi's delicately carved tomb is by Benedetto da Maiano (1491-93).

In the chapel to the left of the chancel is a wooden crucifix by Brunelleschi, said to have been intended as an example to Donatello of how the subject should be treated.

The Strozzi chapel (end of last transept) contains frescoes by Nardo di Cione (c1537) of the Last Judgement, Hell and Paradise, an overwhelming tumult of figures. The altarpiece (Christ and Saints) is the masterpiece of Nardo's more famous brother Andrea, known as Orcagna.

The sacristy houses a painted crucifix, possibly an early work by Giotto.

The Green Cloister is so-called because of the recently restored frescoes (executed in *terraverde*), a sequence of Old Testament subjects, including two bays by Paolo Uccello, one of the great masters of dramatic foreshortening. His image of the Flood (c1447) is a work of tremendous power.

The chapter-house or **Spanish Chapel** contains a famous series of tapestry-like frescoes by Andrea Bonaiuti (1365-7). This is a complex work, intimately tied up with the religious issues of the moment, which was one of deep social, economic and spiritual crisis. There are scenes from the Life (and death) of St Peter Martyr (entrance wall); the Road to Calvary, Crucifixion and Descent into Limbo (altar wall); the Apotheosis of St Thomas (left wall) and the Road to Salvation (right wall) including a picture of the cathedral with the dome that was still to be constructed, and black and white dogs ("*domini canes*") defending the faithful against the wolves of heresy.

☛ San Michele Visdomini

A small church near the cathedral, worth visiting for Pontormo's Holy Family with Saints (1518), a beautiful painting which shows a new note of excitement creeping into the calmly ordered world depicted by Fra Bartolommeo and Andrea del Sarto. The church is rather dark.

☛ San Miniato al Monte

A lovely Romanesque church built on a hillside commanding a wonderful panorama of the city. The coloured marble façade with its elegant geometric design was, like that of the baptistery, later thought to date from antiquity and inspired Renaissance architects. The eagle holding a bale of cloth on the pinnacle is the emblem of the cloth guild which looked after the building.

The dark interior is little altered; the open-framed wooden ceiling dates from the 14th century and some of the capitals are antique or Byzantine. Other notable features includ the inlaid marble floor with signs of the zodiac, oriental in inspiration; Michelozzo's beautiful Crucifix altar and tabernacle (1448); the ceiling by Luca della Robbia; the coloured marble pulpit in the chancel; the arcade of Roman columns round the apse framing windows of translucent marble, and, above, a 13th-century mosaic of the Virgin and St Minias, several times restored.

The chapel (1460-66) of the Cardinal of Portugal (off left nave), designed by Brunelleschi's pupil Manetti, is a harmonious ensemble of matching architecture, sculpture and painting with medallions by Luca della Robbia, the Cardinal's tomb by Antonio Rossellino and the altarpiece and frescoes by Baldovinetti.

In the sacristy are frescoes by Spinello Aretino (late 14th-century), of scenes from the life of St Benedict (including rolling naked among thorns to avoid temptation, flogging a monk tempted by the Devil in the guise of a monkey, and raising a monk crushed by the collapse of a wall).

☛ San Salvatore al Monte

A beautiful late 15th-century Franciscan church just below San Miniato.

☞ **San Salvi**
(*See excursions from Florence: Settignano*)
☞ **San Sepolcro** (*Piazza San Pancrazio; entrance in Via della Spada*)
A tiny barrel-vaulted chapel, just round the corner from the Palazzo Rucellai
and also the work of Alberti (1467). The funerary monument to Giovanni
Rucellai is an inlaid marble reproduction of the Sanctuary of the Holy
Sepulchre in Jerusalem, based on ancient descriptions.
☞ **Santo Spirito**
A large Augustinian church redesigned by Brunelleschi c1435, although not
finished until many decades after his death. It is one of the most harmonious
of Florentine churches. A novel feature was the continuation all round the
transepts and choir of the colonnades flanking the nave.

By Florentine standards the works of art in the church are not of
exceptional interest. In one of the central chapels of the right transept is
Filippino Lippo's beautiful Madonna and Child with Saints (c1488). Behind
the high altar are good paintings by Alessandro Allori (Christ and the
Woman taken in Adultery) and the Pisan artist, Aurelio Lomi. Several
paintings have recently been removed for restoration.

The sacristy was desgined by Giuliano da Sangallo (1488-96), with richly
decorated capitals.
☞ **Santa Trinita**
The building of the present church started in the mid-13th century, the
interior derives mainly from the 14th and the façade from the 16th.

The outstanding feature of the interior is the Sassetti chapel in the chancel,
decorated by Ghirlandaio (1479-86). The overall theme is the humanist idea
of Florence as the new Rome, reconciling pagan classical ideas with those of
Christianity. In the altarpiece of the Adoration of the Shepherds the manger
is a classical sarcophagus, and the decoration includes scenes from the lives
of Roman emperors. The frescoes illustrate the Life of Saint Francis, with
some scenes set in Florence and featuring portraits of well-known citizens.
The Raising of the Child shows the Piazza Santa Trinita, with the earlier
Romanesque church façade; the Confirmation of the Rule shows the Piazza
della Signoria with portraits of members of the Medici and Sassetti families.

The Bartolini chapel (4th on right, light inside) contains a beautiful
altarpiece of the Annunciation by Lorenzo Monaco and restored frescoes.
☞ **Chiostro dello Scalzo** (*Via Cavour 69*)
A beautiful series of grisaille murals depicting scenes from the Life of the
Baptist with a decorative framework of painted architecture and sculpture.
All but two of the scenes (by Franciabigio) were painted by Andrea del Sarto
between 1511 and 1526. A marked stylistic change is apparent in the scenes
painted last (the banquet, the beheading and Salome with the head of the
Baptist). The work was done for a brotherhood of St John whose members
went barefoot (*scalzo*) in procession.

Galleries, museums and palaces

*Most galleries and museums close at 2pm (1pm on Sundays and holidays)
and do not open at all on Mondays. However opening hours are sometimes
changed, and vary according to the season. Closure of rooms and whole
galleries for restoration is a fact of life. The best policy is to get an up-to-date
list of opening times at the tourist office on arrival.*

*The few museums open on Mondays include the Casa Buonarroti, the
Horne Museum and the Santa Croce museum (all in the Santa Croce area),
plus the cathedral museum (also open in the afternoons), the Palazzo Medici
Riccardi and the Palazzo Vecchio. They are closed on Tuesday or Wednesday
instead. The Uffizi and the Palazzo Vecchio are now open on weekdays until
7pm (but closed on Mondays and Wednesdays respectively).*

☛ Accademia

A museum which is small in size but enormous in impact and popularity, for
it houses some of Michelangelo's most famous and powerful sculptures. The
gigantic David (1501-4), originally on the Piazza della Signoria (where a copy
now stands), is often interpreted as a symbol of the vigorous Florentine
republic, ever-alert to the danger of tyranny. The later Medici rulers found
the statue easy enough to live with, so perhaps it should be understood as a
more general expression of fierce Florentine patriotism. When the 17ft statue
was finished, it took forty people four days to move it from near the cathedral
to the Piazza della Signoria.

The other statues by Michelangelo are four of the Slaves intended for the
tomb of pope Julius II in Rome; St Matthew (the only result of a commission
in 1504 for 12 apostles to adorn the cathedral crossing) and the Palestrina
Pietà, a late work whose authenticity is sometimes questioned. All these
statues are unfinished, and express with extraordinary power the artist's idea
of his own role as liberator of captive form from the block of raw material. As
so often in the work of Michelangelo, creation itself seems to be the subject.

There are several rooms devoted to Florentine gold ground paintings of the
13th and 14th centuries, some of outstanding quality, and to Renaissance
paintings, mostly of secondary importance but with works by Fra
Bartolommeo, Perugino and Botticelli, among others.

☛ Bargello (Museo Nazionale)

The main Florentine sculpture museum, its outstanding collection of
Renaissance masterpieces housed in a splendid medieval fortress. Built in the
mid-13th century as the town hall and residence of the chief magistrate, the
Bargello became a notorious place of imprisonment and summary execution,
and, in the 16th century, a police station. The beautiful internal courtyard is
adorned with crests of resident officials.

Downstairs is a marvellous and informative gallery of Florentine sculpture
in the 16th century including Michelangelo's drunken Bacchus (c1497), his
Pitti Tondo (Madonna, Child and St John, c1504), and Brutus (a glorification
of tyrannicide after the murder of Alessandro de' Medici, c1540); Cellini's
magnificent bronze bust of Cosimo de' Medici (1547), and bronze models for
his Perseus in the Piazza della Signoria; and Giambologna's famous Mercury
launched heavenward on a breath of wind (c1564), and Florence conquering
Pisa (or virtue conquering vice) – a typical exercise in spiralling composition
for a sculpture to be viewed from all sides (1570).

Upstairs, the highlights of the council chamber are the two bronze reliefs of the Sacrifice of Isaac, Brunelleschi's and Ghiberti's very different entries for the competition for the baptistery door commission (1401), and several masterpieces by Donatello including David (c1430), an exquisite, sensuous contrast to the spirit of Michelangelo's marble superman, and the noble St George, originally for the church of Orsanmichele (c1416). Adjacent rooms have very fine collections of decorative arts, notably ceramics and some beautiful early ivories.

On the second floor are several beautiful works by Verrocchio (Leonardo's master) including his bronze David, Francesco Laurana's bust of Battista Sforza and Antonio Pollaiuolo's straining Hercules and Antaeus, all dating from the last quarter of the 15th century. There is also a fine collection of small Renaissance bronzes.

☞ **Casa Buonarroti** (*Via Ghibellina 70*)

A small museum devoted to Michelangelo, in a house built by his nephew. The prize exhibits are the two earliest known works, The Battle of the Centaurs and the Madonna of the Stairs – both relief sculptures of the early 1490s, foreshadowing different aspects of Michelangelo's later work. A small wooden crucifix has been identified by many scholars as the one young Michelangelo is known to have carved as a present for the prior of Santo Spirito who had lent him a dissection room. There are sketches, facsimiles, portraits of Michelangelo and paintings by others working from his designs.

☞ **Cathedral Museum** (Museo dell' Opera del Duomo)

The office of works of the cathedral, founded at the end of the 13th century to administer and supervise the building, decoration and maintenance of the edifice, was moved to the present premises, designed by Brunelleschi, in the mid-15th century. Since the 19th century it has been a museum of works of art from the cathedral and its treasury. It has a magnificent collection of Florentine sculpture.

The most popular exhibit is Michelangelo's Pietà, a late work originally intended for the artist's own funerary chapel in Rome. The story goes that Michelangelo eventually gave up the work and smashed it in disgust at the poor quality of the block; a pupil pieced it together and finished the kneeling figure of the Magdalen.

Upstairs are the two beautifully decorated galleries, probably organ lofts but usually described as choir lofts (*cantorie*), executed in the 1430s by Donatello and Luca della Robbia. Donatello's frieze of exuberant dancing angels is surrounded by a wealth of elaborate decorative detail which was to prove very influential on later Renaissance artists. Della Robbia's more static loft is easier to see; the original relief panels, of music-making and singing angels, illustrations of the 150th psalm, are displayed below a reconstruction of the loft. In the same room are more sculptures by Donatello, vividly demonstrating his remarkable range of expressive power; these include a wooden Magdalen from the baptistery and two famous marble prophets from niches outside the campanile, probably Jeremiah and Habbakuk (nicknamed "*zuccone*" or fat-head), reported by Vasari to have been portraits of contemporary Florentines.

Next door are the original relief panels from the campanile. Most are the work of Andrea Pisano, but Giotto is said to have designed many and executed the first two of the Genesis series. There are interesting panels representing the liberal arts, sciences and professions. Two small rooms are devoted to Brunelleschi and the building of the cathedral dome; there are 15th-century wooden models of the dome, one in section, plus brick moulds and other items of building apparatus.

Two of the original panels of Ghiberti's baptistery doors are now displayed here.

☞ Fra Angelico Museum

The convent which Fra Angelico spent ten years (1435-45) decorating has been turned into a museum, forming a remarkable and fitting tribute to one of the greatest of all painters of devotional images. Angelico the blessed (Il Beato), is a favourite among visitors to Florence and buyers of Christmas cards the world over.

Outstanding among all the luminous masterpieces brought from Florentine churches is the linen-makers' guild altarpiece (1433), the Madonna and Child with 12 music-making angels, set in a marble frame designed by Ghiberti. The monumental figures of saints on the wings of the altarpiece show that Angelico was not just a pretty-face painter, but right up to date in his mastery of the latest developments in Florentine art.

Works by other artists include Ghirlandaio's Last Supper (a variant of the same subject in the Ognissanti), and an interesting unfinished panel of Madonna and Saints with St Anne, by Fra Bartolommeo (c1512).

At the head of the stairs leading up to the monks' dormitory is Angelico's famous Annunciation, set in a Renaissance loggia of monastic austerity. All the cells along the corridor are decorated with small frescoes; those by Fra Angelico (left of left-hand corridor) include another Annunciation. The prior's rooms are devoted to the memory of the reformist preacher Savonarola who was prior of San Marco from 1491 until hanged and burnt at the stake in 1498. On display are the remarkable portrait by his convert and fellow monk, Fra Bartolommeo, sermon notes, and the banner, said to be painted by Fra Angelico, which Savonarola carried round Florence with him.

As well as rebuilding the convent at the order of Cosimo il Vecchio, Michelozzo designed Europe's first public library. Illuminated manuscripts are displayed in this graceful, vaulted chamber, described by Kenneth Clark as "the Cavendish laboratory of humanism".

☞ Palazzo Davanzati (Museum of the old Florentine house)

A 14th-century town house preserved as a monument to the domestic architecture and lifestyle of early Renaissance Florence, and as such a fascinating complement to all the great works of art now displayed out of context. As well as paintings the contents include tapestries, lace, ceramics and painted chests (*cassoni*). As was usual, the kitchens are at the top of the house.

☞ Horne Museum (*Via dei Benci 6*)

A very attractive small museum of Renaissance paintings and artefacts, the collection of an English art historian, Herbert Percy Horne (1864-1916) and displayed in the 15th-century mansion which he faithfully restored and furnished. The paintings by Giotto, Dosso Dossi and Beccafumi are particularly lovely.

☞ Palazzo Medici-Riccardi

As designed by Michelozzo in the mid-15th century, Cosimo il Vecchio's palace was square and had an open loggia on each side of the street corner. The modest Cosimo eschewed the aristocratic fashion for giving most of the architectural emphasis to the first floor *(piano nobile)*.

The palace was the home of the Medici, and the heart of Renaissance Florence until duke Cosimo moved to the Palazzo Vecchio in 1540. Subsequently plundered, it now has few interesting contents except for the tiny chapel, sumptuously decorated with frescoes by Benozzo Gozzoli (1459/60). These show a long procession of the Magi, their retinues and exotic animals meandering through a delightful landscape, lovingly rendered and full of incidental detail, towards the altarpiece, a copy of Filippo Lippi's original Madonna, observed by ox and ass on the walls. Among countless Florentine portraits is the adolescent Lorenzo the Magnificent, the youngest Magus; in the crowd behind is Gozzoli, identified by a signature on his hat.

A separate entrance leads up to the *salone*, the ceiling decorated by Luca Giordano in the 1680s.

☛ **Palazzo Pitti**

Several museums, notably the magnificent Medici art collections, housed in a massively imposing palace on a slope south of the Arno.

The central block is the original palace, built in the mid-15th century by the vainglorious Luca Pitti, a rich merchant who, in contrast to the custom of the Medici, styled and situated his home as ostentatiously as possible. In 1549 the palace was sold to Eleanor of Toledo, wife of duke Cosimo, and for the next two centuries it was the Versailles of Florence, greatly extended and embellished not only to accommodate the family's growing art collection but also to serve as a setting for extravagant entertainments. Ammannati's courtyard, one of the masterpieces of 16th-century Florentine architecture, was flooded for naval battles and also hosted firework displays, jousts, opera and elaborate allegorical performances honouring the Medici and their guests. The park (Bóboli gardens) was decked out with statues and grottoes full of the clever conceits and the disordered garden architecture that was the fashion of the day, and court artists spent much of their time engaged in hydraulic engineering and devising ever more spectacular special effects for the various festivities.

The picture galleries were established in the 16th century, extended in the 17th and decorated with murals in the Roman Baroque style. The result is an art gallery (the Galleria Palatina) in a sumptuous context and still arranged like an old private collection with paintings filling the walls for decorative effect rather than sightseeing clarity, and not in any particular order. The Medici amassed paintings from many Italian and other European schools; the earliest works are from the High Renaissance. Most of the finest paintings are in the grand main reception rooms on the first floor, five of which have painted ceilings by Pietro da Cortona with allegorical subjects glorifying the Medici. The other twenty-odd rooms contain mostly smaller works, but certainly should not be ignored.

Selected masterpieces

Room 1 (Sala di Venere): Titian's The Concert (a very early work of much disputed authorship, c1510), "La Bella", and Pietro Aretino; two seascapes by Salvator Rosa and two contrasting landscapes by Rubens.

Room 2 (Apollo): Titian's "Duke of Norfolk", one of his greatest portraits (c1540).

Room 3 (Marte): Rubens' vast allegory of the Consequences of War (1638), and his Four Philosophers (c1611, including a self-portrait on the left); Titian's Cardinal Ippolito de' Medici in Hungarian Uniform (1533); Van

Dyck's Guido Bentivoglio, (c1623).

Room 4 (Giove): Andrea del Sarto's St John the Baptist (1523); Fra
Bartolommeo's Deposition, finished after his death in 1517 by Bugiardini;
Raphael's Veiled Woman (c1515), who isn't.

Room 5 (Saturno): works by Raphael including Madonna della Granduca
(c1504), portaits of Agnolo and Maddalena Doni (1506), and Madonna della
Seggiola (c1515), showing the development of the artist's style via the
influences of Perugino and Leonardo.

Room 6 (Iliade): Raphael's "La Gravida", a pregnant woman (c1506); two
Assumptions by Andrea del Sarto (1520's); Titian's Philip II of Spain.

Room 25 (Educazione di Giove): Caravaggio's Sleeping Cupid (1608); Allori's
gorgeous Judith with the Head of Holofernes (portraits of the artist, his
mistress and her mother; early 17th-century).

Room 29 (Stufa): the finest of Pietro da Cortona's murals, the Four Ages of
Man (1637-40).

The **Royal apartments** can also be visited; there are 18th-century French
tapestries and Medici portraits by northern artists.

The **Argenteria** is an exceptionally rich Medici collection of objets d'art
including gold and silver ware, cameos, ivories, pietra dura (marble inlay),
tapestries, porcelain, and Lorenzo the Magnificent's collection of antique
vases. The fine **Contini-Bonacossi** collection is mainly Italian paintings and
furniture, mostly rather earlier than those in the Galleria Palatina.

☞ Palazzo Vecchio

The town hall now as it was when first built at the end of the 13th century,
the Palazzo Vecchio is a great fortress at the heart of the city, its battlements
and tall watch tower dominating the Piazza della Signoria. Its changes of
name from Palazzo del Popolo to Palazzo della Signoria to Palazzo Ducale
and finally (when the Medici moved out to the Pitti) the Palazzo Vecchio sum
up the political history of Florence in the 14th, 15th and 16th centuries. Until
1985, the interior of the Palazzo Vecchio was of interest chiefly to those with a
special interest in history of late Renaissance decoration; now the collection
of works of art recovered since the war and displayed on the second floor
puts the Palazzo Vecchio well into the top ten sights.

The courtyard makes a charming contrast to the forbidding exterior. This is
less the result of Michelozzo's design (mid-15th century) than Vasari's efforts
to cheer it up for the wedding of Francesco I de' Medici in 1565. Verrocchio's
fountain was brought in from a Medici villa and the arcades decorated with
gilt stucco work.

The **Salone dei Cinquecento** is the great hall, built in 1496 to accommodate
the new Venetian-style council of 500 of Savonarola's constitution after the
expulsion of the Medici. In 1503 Michelangelo and Leonardo were
commissioned to decorate the walls with scenes of Florentine victories, a
famous rivalry that resulted in the two most influential works of art never to
be executed (the search for the early stages of Leonardo's Battle for the
Standard is still on). After the return of the Medici in 1512 the room became a
ducal chamber and the ceiling and walls were decorated by Vasari. The
outstanding feature of the room is Michelangelo's statue of Victory (c1526)
intended for the tomb of Julius II. The statue, a model of serpentine grace,
influenced Giambologna (among others); his model for Virtue (or Florence)
conquering Vice, conceived as a pendant for the Victory, stands opposite.

The little **Studiolo** of Francesco I, designed by Vasari, is a windowless chamber encrusted with small works of art like a casket. It is a much more appealing and characteristic Mannerist creation than the great halls. Set into the ceiling are portraits of Francesco's parents Cosimo I and Eleanor, by Bronzino, and there are mythological paintings around the walls and beautiful small bronzes, including an Apollo by Giambologna, set in niches.

From the **Quartiere di Leo X**, with Medici-related murals and a small chapel with paintings by Vasari, you continue to the second floor. Here is the **Quartiere degli Elementi**, recently furnished and with a remarkable collection of works of art recovered from abroad since the war. These include Roman statuary, early Florentine primitives with lovely Madonnas by Masolino and Masaccio and later Venetian paintings with works by Veronese and Tintoretto. The **Quartiere di Eleanor di Toledo** has also been re-arranged

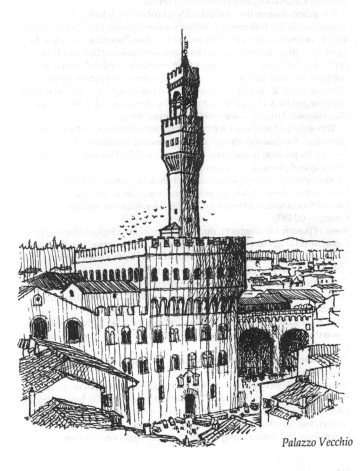

Palazzo Vecchio

241

and rooms are less bare than they used to be. They include a chapel beautifully decorated with mural paintings by Bronzino (1540-45), often shut.

The **Sala dei Gigli** (decorated with patterns of emblematic Florentine lilies) has patriotic frescoes by Ghirlandaio (c1485) with Florentine and Roman republican heroes, and a fine statue of the Baptist by Benedetto da Maiano (late 15th-century) over the door. Neighbouring rooms contain the original cherub from Verrocchio's fountain in the courtyard and Donatello's bronze Judith and Holofernes (c1455), originally designed as a fountain for the Medici palace, and a fascinating series of late 16th-century maps.

☛ Uffizi

A large and incomparably rich art gallery occupying one storey of a vast U-shaped building which was designed by Vasari in the late 16th century to accommodate the government offices (*uffici*). It is linked to the Pitti Palace by a long covered passage, the **Corridoio Vasariano**, which crosses over the Ponte Vecchio. The Corridoio is said to be open to visitors by prior appointment; as well as giving beautiful views over the city the corridor contains a fascinating collection of self-portraits.

The gallery houses the Medici family art collection, which was left to the Florentines in the 18th century, minus some sculptures (now in the Bargello) but plus some paintings recently brought in from Florentine churches. Its great strength is in works of the Florentine Renaissance (14th and 15th centuries), but there are also magnificent works from other Italian and foreign schools up to the 18th century. The sequence of the rooms (of which there are about 40) is a logical chronological one along the east wing towards the river and back along the west wing. The chronological order is broken by the octagonal Tribuna in the middle of the east wing.

Although the Uffizi does not compare in size with the world's major museums, the concentration of masterpieces and the tumult of people jostling for position is such that most people will find the gallery too much, mentally and physically, for a single visit.

Among scores of masterpieces, many of them important landmarks in the history of Renaissance art, the great treasures of the museum are:

Ground floor: a series of frescoes of famous Florentines by Andrea del Castagno (c1450).

Room 2 (Tuscan 13th century): three paintings of the Virgin enthroned by Cimabue (c1275), Duccio (c1285) and Giotto (c1330) grouped together as if to illustrate a lecture on the early Renaissance and Giotto's achievement.

Room 3 (Sienese 14th century): Simone Martini's Annunciation (1333).

Room 6 (the so-called International Gothic style of the early 15th century): Gentile da Fabriano's Adoration of the Magi (1423); Lorenzo Monaco's Coronation (1414) and Adoration of the Magi (c1422).

Room 7: Masaccio's Virgin and Child with St Anne (c1423), the figure of St Anne thought to be by Masolino; Domenico Veneziano's Madonna and Saints (c1445).

Room 8: several paintings by Filippo Lippi including a beautiful Virgin and Child with two angels (c1465).

Rooms 10/14: works by Botticelli, the most celebrated series in the gallery, including Primavera (c1478) and The Birth of Venus (c 1485), both elaborate allegories inspired by the pagan humanism of the court of Lorenzo de' Medici, and The Adoration of the Magi (c1474) including portraits of members of the Medici family and of the artist; Hugo van der Goes'

Adoration of the Shepherds (Portinari altarpiece, c1475) painted in Ghent for a Florentine church – some aspects of the work (the shepherds and the flowers) made a great impression on Florentine artists, as demonstrated by paintings hanging nearby.

Room 15: Leonardo da Vinci's unfinished Adoration of the Magi (1481), full of drama and incident and fascinating for students of Leonardo's working methods; Verrocchio's Baptism (c1470), famous for his pupil Leonardo's contribution of the left-hand angel.

Room 18: the Tribuna, built like a sanctuary for the worship of the most treasured Medici sculptures (including the celebrated Medici Venus, now thought to be a copy from the 1st century BC of a Greek original) displayed like devotional objects and surrounded by beautiful 16th-century court portraits (the best of them by Pontormo and Bronzino).

Room 20: Dürer, Adoration of the Magi (1504).

Room 21 (Venetian painting): Giovanni Bellini's Sacred Allegory (c1490)

Room 25 (West wing): Michelangelo's recently restored Holy Family, or Doni Tondo, (c1504), in its beautiful original frame; the central group, like a painted block of marble, seems to be a sculptor's manifesto. Apart from this, the meaning of many aspects of the painting, which is even more complex iconographically than it is formally, is unclear.

Room 26: Raphael's Madonna with the Goldfinch (1506) and group portrait of Leo X with two cardinals (1518).

Room 28: several works by Titian, notably the Venus of Urbino (1538).

Room 29: Parmigianino's supremely graceful masterpiece, the Long-Necked Madonna (c1535).

Room 43: Caravaggio's Head of Medusa and Bacchus, both early works of c1595.

Other sights

Florence has comparatively few outdoor sights. However the Bóboli gardens are open from dawn to dusk, and you can continue a walk up to the Forte di Belvedere.

☛ Bóboli gardens

A vast and beautiful park climbing the hill behind the Pitti Palace to the city's southern walls. As well as providing a welcome opportunity to break the intensive, exhausting and often stifling round of sightseeing, the gardens are themselves an interesting work of Renaissance art, created for Cosimo I in the second half of the 16th century and extended in the 17th. There are several ways in and out, so the Bóboli can be used as a thoroughfare.

Beside the Pitti Palace entrance is a fountain of Cosimo's dwarf astride a tortoise, a grotesque caricature of classical depictions of Neptune, by Cioli (1560). Nearby is Buontalenti's grotto, with a typically ambiguous pseudo-organic decor; Michelangelo's Slaves (casts of the originals in the Accademia) emerge from the rough cave walls. Practical joke devices to ensure that unwary visitors to the grotto got drenched are no longer active. In the furthest of three chambers is a beautiful statue of Venus by Giambologna (c1565). Another amusing rustic grotto (by Bandinelli) is slightly higher up on the same side of the gardens.

Other ornamental features of the gardens include an amphitheatre above the main courtyard, with an antique granite basin and an Egyptian obelisk, an 18th-century coffee house and a splendid long cypress avenue running down to a moated island (the Isolotto) with a monumental fountain and sculptures by Giambologna. At the top of the gardens is a small porcelain museum. There are good views over Florence and its rural surroundings from around here.

☛ **Forte di Belvedere**

A massive 16th-century bastion in the town walls (access from outside the Bóboli gardens). From the fort it is a beautiful walk round to San Miniato either along the best-preserved section of city walls as far the Porta San Miniato or by the more roundabout, rural and picturesque route of the Via San Leonardo and Viale Galileo.

Excursions from Florence

Fiésole is almost part of Florence and has several appealing hotels. The other excursions are within 10km of Florence and accessible by public transport; many other possible day-trips are described in the chapter on Tuscany. From April until the end of June, excursions by bus to see the gardens of various villas are organised by Agriturist (Piazza S. Firenze 3, Tel: 28.78.38); details are available from most travel agents and the tourist office.

CASTELLO

There are several Medici villas in the Castello neighbourhood (served by bus 28 from the station). Often the gardens are the most interesting part and the only part open to the public; check opening times before leaving.

Villa della Petraia, (re)built for cardinal Ferdinand de' Medici in the late 16th century, has an attractive park. **Villa di Castello**, home of the most important of the early Medici art patrons, Lorenzo di Pierfrancesco (Lorenzo the Magnificent's cousin), once housed Botticelli's Birth of Venus and Primavera, now in the Uffizi. In the mid-16th century duke Cosimo I, who was brought up at the villa and later retired there, had the gardens redesigned in the Mannerist style (like the Bóboli gardens). Although the highly elaborate project was never fully carried out, Vasari described the garden as the most magnificent in Europe. There remain a vast orangery and a grotto with pseudo-organic décor and animal sculptures, the work of Giambologna.

The bus continues to Sesto Fiorentino where the Baroque gardens of the mainly 17th-century **Villa Corsi** are worth visiting. With a car, you could also visit the villas at Careggi (between Castello and Florence) and, to the north, Trebbio and Cafaggiolo, all three modified for Cosimo il Vecchio by Michelozzo.

(For villas at Artimino and Poggio a Caiano see Tuscany chapter).

CERTOSA DI GALLUZZO

A vast Carthusian monastery (Certosa) above the main road, La Cassia (reached by bus 37 from the station or Porto Romana). The guided tour of the interior is mainly of interest for the series of frescoes of Scenes from the Passion painted by Pontormo in 1523-4 and much influenced by Dürer. Now detached from the great cloister, these are displayed, with a few other paintings, in the main hall. Most of the detail has been lost which underlines the highly unconventional design and gives the paintings a disturbing, almost abstract quality. In a chapel under the church are funerary monuments to members of the founding Acciaioli family.

FIÉSOLE

A small hill town (reached by bus 7) looking out over the city, much favoured as a place to live and stay, away from the bustle and heat of the city. Fiésole's foundation preceded that of Florence and until the early 12th century it dominated its lower and less defensible neighbour. The Via Vecchia Fiesolana climbs steeply to the town, passing San Domenico (see below) and Cosimo il Vecchio's villa, a favourite meeting place for Lorenzo the Magnificent's circle of poets and philosophers.

☛ **Archaeological Site**   A well-preserved **Roman theatre** (1st century BC) is used for summer performances, and there are remains of Roman baths, some Etruscan walls and a small museum.

☛ **Cathedral**   An 11th-century building with later enlargements (including a fortified bell tower from the early 13th century) and restoration. There's a fine Romanesque interior with some antique capitals and works by the 15th-century sculptor Mino da Fiésole (notably the tomb and altar in the Cappella Salutati on the right).

☛ **San Domenico**   A small church below the town, part of a convent where Fra Angelico first donned the habit and containing his Madonna with Saints (first chapel on left). In the chapter house (ring at the door to the right of the church) is his fresco of the Crucifixion, also c1425.

Five minutes' walk away, in an attractive riverside setting, is the isolated **Badia Fiesolana**, the original cathedral of Fiésole, now the European University. The delightful marble façade of the old Romanesque church is incorporated in the larger, blank one dating from the 15th-century rebuilding of the church for Cosimo il Vecchio. The very elegant Renaissance interior is rarely accessible, but it's worth ringing the bell.

SETTIGNANO

A less touristy hill village than Fiésole (reached by bus 10 from the station or Duomo), with a beautiful view of Florence from its peaceful Piazza Desiderio, named after Desiderio da Settignano, the most distinguished of a number of 15th-century sculptors who settled here. Nearby are the Villa Gamberaia and Villa i Tatti (which once belonged to the art historian Bernard Berenson and is now a research institute), both with beautiful gardens. Also on the bus route is the former Vallombrosan abbey of **San Salvi** (Via di San Salvi 16), with Andrea del Sarto's fresco of the Last Supper (1522), a graceful composition in which Christ identifies his betrayer by passing him the bread.

Hotels

ALBA
Via della Scala 22-38
50123 Firenze

£££
Open all year
Tel: (055) 211469

This old *palazzo*, close to the station, was entirely renovated in 1985. Formerly rather drab (like the street it stands on), it is now an immaculate small hotel, decorated with style and taste. There is nothing very Florentine about it but the hotel throughout is bright, cheerful and quiet. Bedrooms are cool, modern and double-glazed.

Facilities: *24 bedrooms (AC); lift*   **Credit/charge cards accepted:** *Visa*

ANNALENA
Via Romana 34
50125 Firenze

£££
Open all year
Tel: (055) 222402

This delightful little *pensione* stands in a quiet street not far from the Pitti Palace. It occupies two floors of a Medici palace which in its time has been a convent, a school for young ladies, a refuge for poor citizens, a gambling house and a home for refugees during the last war. The lofty beamed hall, with medieval-style furniture, is used as a lounge and breakfast is served in a small panelled room. Bedrooms are large and light with antiques and painted furniture. Some open onto a terrace overlooking a neighbouring garden.

Facilities: *20 bedrooms*   **Credit/charge cards accepted:** *Amex, Eurocard, Visa*

APRILE
Via della Scala 6
50123 Firenze

££
Open all year
Tel: (055) 216237

This handsome Medici mansion (on the same street as the Hotel Alba) has been renovated and converted into what is undoubtedly the most charming hotel in the station area. Original features have been preserved, such as *sgraffito* frescoes on the façade and the painted ceiling in the breakfast room. The bedrooms range from large rooms with painted furniture and moulded ceilings to much smaller rooms with modern utility furniture. There is a small and homely lounge/bar and a delightful tiled terrace.

Facilities: *29 bedrooms; lift*   **Credit/charge cards accepted:** *Amex, Eurocard, Visa*

ARIELE
Via Magenta 11
50123 Firenze

££
Open all year
Tel: (055) 211509

A fine old town house in a quiet back street, the Ariele has in the past been the residence of Napoleon's sister and the headquarters of various foreign consulates. Today it is a family-run *pensione*. The bedrooms are enormous –

some rather spartan and dark – with a motley collection of antique and modern furnishings. Downstairs rooms are homely and pleasantly cluttered. The salon, with gold flocked walls and brocade, opens out on to a small, shady garden of flower beds, palms and cypresses.

Facilities: *30 bedrooms; lift; garage* **Credit/charge cards accepted:** *none*

HERMITAGE £££
Vicolo Marzio 1   *Open all year*
50122 Firenze   *Tel: (055) 287216*

A few steps from the Arno and Ponte Vecchio this is one of the most central hotels in Florence. Views from its delightful roof-top terrace, where breakfast is served in summer, take in all the big city landmarks including the Duomo and Uffizi. Reception and breakfast rooms (on the 5th floor of the building) are small, intimate and typically Florentine. The bedrooms have all been redecorated recently. Riverside rooms are now double-glazed but the quietest rooms are still those at the back of the hotel, overlooking a small square. Very popular with British and Americans.

Facilities: *20 bedrooms; lift* **Credit/charge cards accepted:** *none*

KRAFT ££££
Via Solferino 2   *Open all year*
50123 Firenze   *Tel: (055) 284273*

A quiet location (about 20 minutes from the Duomo) and comfortable rooms are the main attractions of the Kraft. Public rooms are elegant and civilised, particularly the roof-top restaurant and its delightful terrace overlooking the city. The lounge and bar are combined in a high-ceilinged beamed room with leather seats and rugs on a tiled floor. Bedrooms are quiet and spacious and there's a choice of traditional and modern styles; all have spotless bathrooms. The roof-top pool is small but the views are superb.

Facilities: *70 bedrooms (AC); restaurant; lift; swimming pool* **Credit/charge cards accepted:** *Amex, Diners, Eurocard, Visa*

LOGGIATO DEI SERVITI £££
Piazza Santissima Annunziata 3   *Open all year*
50129 Firenze   *Tel: (055) 219165*

A lovely new hotel on one of Florence's finest squares. The building, a twin of Brunelleschi's famous Ospedale degli Innocenti opposite, has been sympathetically restored and elegantly furnished. Bedrooms are spacious, cool and, above all, quiet. Terracotta tiles, wrought-iron beds, pale plaster walls and Florentine and English antique furniture give a countrified feel to the rooms. There is an elegant small bar and a breakfast room.

Facilities: *19 bedrooms; lift; parking service* **Credit/charge cards accepted:** *Amex, Diners, Eurocard, Visa*

LUNGARNO ££££
Borgo San Jacopo 14 *Open all year*
50125 Firenze *Tel: (055) 264211*

Stylish and civilised, the Lungarno occupies both a modern building and medieval stone tower on the south bank of the Arno. Public rooms are quiet and comfortable with river views and furnished with floral sofas and armchairs, antiques and the owner's fine collection of 20th-century works of art (including a corridor of Cocteaus). Bedrooms are furnished with plush, warm fabrics and wall-to-wall carpeting, apart from the rooms in the tower which have old stone walls and rustic furniture – along with modern facilities. The best rooms have balconies overlooking the river.

Facilities: *71 bedrooms (AC); lift; garage* **Credit/charge cards accepted:** *Amex, Diners, Eurocard, Visa*

MONNA LISA ££££
Borgo Pinti 27 *Open all year*
50121 Firenze *Tel: (055) 2479751*

Occupying a Renaissance *palazzo* about five minutes from the Duomo, the Monna Lisa is a small, stylish and very sought-after hotel. The interior is strikingly handsome with vaulted, beamed or frescoed ceilings, antiques, polished tile floors and Renaissance paintings and sculptures which include Giambologna's first study for the Rape of the Sabines. An elegant *pietra serena* staircase leads to a variety of bedrooms – some large and civilised, overlooking the delightful courtyard and garden, others small and noisy on the roadside.

Facilities: *21 bedrooms (AC); parking* **Credit/charge cards:** *Amex, Diners, Eurocard, Visa*

PITTI PALACE ££
Via Barbadori 2 *Open all year*
50125 Firenze *Tel: (055) 282257*

Popular with British and Americans, the Pitti Palace is a small and inviting *pensione* just south of the Ponte Vecchio. The main rooms consist of a delightful small sitting room (the sort you might expect in a private home) and an L-shaped breakfast extension. There's a pretty roof garden/terrace with lovely views of the city. Reception has a good supply of guide books, lists of museum opening hours and so on, and the office is usually busy providing tourist information (in English). Bedrooms are slightly spartan (11 without private facilities) and the main drawback of the hotel is the noise, particularly for the rooms on the river side.

Facilities: *40 bedrooms; lift* **Credit/charge cards accepted:** *Amex, Visa*

PLAZA LUCCHESI

Lungarno della Zecca Vecchia 38
50122 Firenze

££££
Open all year
Tel: (055) 264141

Occupying a large 19th-century building, the Lucchesi lies on the banks of the Arno, about five minutes' walk from the Ponte Vecchio. The comforts and décor are what you might expect from a 4-star international hotel, but it is not without style or elegance. Bedrooms are essentially modern but retain some old-fashioned comforts. They are well equipped and have smart tiled bathrooms. There are good views of the Arno on one side and Santa Croce and the Duomo on the other.

Facilities: *100 bedrooms (AC); restaurant; lift; garage* **Credit/charge cards accepted:** *Amex, Diners, Eurocard, Visa*

RESIDENZA

Via Tornabuoni 8
50123 Firenze

££
Open all year
Tel: (055) 284197

A prime location and moderate prices are the main attractions of the Residenza. It occupies four floors of a 17th-century *palazzo* and the top rooms have terraces overlooking the terracotta roof-tops across the street. The main rooms are a mix of modern and old styles with rustic beams and traditional chintz combined with modern art and plush armchairs. Recent modernisations have not been entirely successful – the old rustic-style rooms are still the prettiest.

Facilities: *26 bedrooms; restaurant; lift* **Credit/charge cards accepted:** *Amex*

RIGATTI

Lungarno Generale Diaz 2
50122 Firenze

£
Open all year
Tel: (055) 213022

This charming family-run *pensione* occupies two floors of a 15th-century *palazzo* overlooking the Arno and close to Santa Croce and the Uffizi. It is about the nearest you will get to *A Room with a View*. The reception and huge sitting room are furnished with antiques, oil paintings, Florentine prints and carpets on woodblock floors. There's even a piano. Bedrooms vary from large and comfy to simple and tiny; about half have private facilities. Front rooms and the two terraces have fine views but are very noisy.

Facilities: *28 bedrooms; lift* **Credit/charge cards accepted:** *none*

Our price symbols

£	= you can expect to find a room for under £35
££	= you can expect to find a room for under £55
£££	= you can expect to find a room for under £75
££££	= you can expect to find a room for under £125
£££££	= you should expect to pay over £125 for a room

SILLA

££

Via de' Renai 5
50125 Firenze

Open all year
Tel: (055) 284810

A handsome old *palazzo* on the south side of the Arno (not too far from the action), the Silla is a reasonably priced small hotel. We have been unable to inspect the bedrooms but all have bath or shower and many of them overlook the Arno. One of the prettiest features of the hotel is the large terracotta paved terrace with huge white parasols and potted oleander. Reception rooms have recently been renovated and furnished with pretty painted furniture. The restaurant is in a simple trattoria style with red rush-seated chairs, brass pots and ceramics.

Facilities: *32 bedrooms; lift from 1st floor*   **Credit/charge cards accepted**: *Amex, Diners, Eurocard, Visa*

SPLENDOR

££

Via S. Gallo 30
50129 Firenze

Open all year
Tel: (055) 483427

Ten minutes north of the Duomo and very close to the church of San Marco, the Splendor is a quiet, congenial and reasonably-priced *pensione*. Public rooms still retain some of their original features such as the murals and the pink frescoed ceiling of the breakfast room; but they are rather dreary with incongruous modern additions. The prettiest area is the terrace with roses, creepers and terracotta pots of plants. Bedrooms are light and attractive with a combination of traditional and modern styles.

Facilities: *31 bedrooms; lift*   **Credit/charge cards accepted:** *none*

TORNABUONI BEACCI

££

Via Tornabuoni 3
50123 Firenze

Open all year
Tel: (055) 212645

Signora Beacci runs a comfortable *pensione* on the top three floors of a 14th-century *palazzo* on Florence's smartest shopping street. The best rooms are large, old-fashioned and quiet with parquet floors, rugs and traditional painted furniture. Others are more cramped and spartan. The wood-panelled dining room is slightly institutional but there is a delightful roof terrace where you can have breakfast or drinks.

Facilities: *32 bedrooms (AC); lift to third floor; restaurant; garage*   **Credit/charge cards accepted:** *Amex, Diners, Visa*

THE OUTSKIRTS OF FLORENCE

VILLA BELVEDERE   £££
Via Benedetto Castelli 3   *Closed Dec to Feb*
50124 Firenze   *Tel: (055) 222501*

Magnificent views and spotlessly clean rooms are the plus points of this
essentially modern hotel, on a hillside above the city. Front bedrooms are
bright and spacious with balconies; those without views at the back are
cheaper. Décor is spruce and modern throughout although there is the
occasional concession to Florentine character in the public rooms with
pictures of Tuscan landscapes and city landmarks. Breakfast and snack meals
are served in a bright, rather simple room with lovely views. The hotel is
family run and friendly; the garden is large and rambling with a pool and
tennis court.

Facilities: *27 bedrooms (AC); lift; swimming pool; tennis court; parking*   **Credit/
charge cards accepted:** *Amex*

VILLA LE RONDINI   £££
Via Bolognese Vecchia 224   *Open all year*
50139 Firenze   *Tel: (055) 400081*

This country hotel set in a large private estate 7km from Florence provides a
quiet and reasonably priced respite from the city. It's ideal in summer, with
its pool and tennis court. The villa is set in a typically Tuscan landscape,
surrounded by olive groves (you can buy home-made oil), vineyards and
cypresses and immaculate gardens. Public rooms consist of a rather sober
split-level lounge and a trattoria-style arched dining room. Bedrooms are
varied – some have lovely antiques and painted bedheads, others (including
those in the main annexe) are modern and pretty with mock beams. The
second annexe is a pleasantly shabby villa about half a mile from the main
building. The hotel is rather isolated and would probably suit only those with
cars, although there is a regular bus service into Florence

Facilities: *29 bedrooms (2 with AC); restaurant; swimming pool; tennis court;
riding; parking*   **Credit/charge cards accepted**: *Amex, Diners, Eurocard, Visa*

BENCISTÀ   ££
San Domenico   *Closed Nov to mid-March*
50014 Fiésole   *Tel: (055) 59163*

Set on a quiet hillside in spacious grounds of olive and orange groves, this
converted monastery, run as a *pensione* since 1926, makes a delightfully
peaceful base. There are lovely views from every angle, but particularly from
the restaurant and terrace which look down the hills to Florence. The main
rooms have all the charm and intimacy of a private country house – beams,
stone walls, fireplaces, bookshelves and beautiful 17th- and 18th-century

antiques. Bedrooms are solid and traditional, with period furniture. At 8pm
sharp a maid comes to turn back your sheets – and announce dinner. Half
board is obligatory.

Facilities: *35 bedrooms (18 with private bathroom); restaurant; parking*   **Credit/
charge cards accepted:** *none*

VILLA SAN MICHELE   £££££
Via di Doccia 4,   *Closed Nov to mid-March*
50014 Fiésole   *Tel: (055) 59451*

The most exclusive and expensive of Florentine hotels, the San Michele is a
converted monastery (said to have been designed by Michelangelo) with a
marvellous panorama of Florence. Rooms are understated and you pay for
studied rusticity and simple elegance rather than luxury. The restaurant is
particularly attractive with stone walls, immaculately laid tables and a fine
balcony whose arches frame sublime views of Florence. Some of the
bedrooms are sumptuous and ornate, others surprisingly simple (converted
monks' cells) but all have excellent new bathrooms. This is a very desirable
spot for those who can afford it, though the prices are hardly justifiable.

Facilities: *28 bedrooms (AC); restaurant; swimming pool (heated); parking; shuttle
bus service into Florence*   **Credit/charge cards accepted:** *Amex, Diners,
Eurocard, Visa*

TUSCANY & UMBRIA

❝*One lovely day succeeded another, the outlook was always upon cypresses and flowers and olive groves, every village church and contadino's cottage was part of the even texture of the landscape and nothing was vile*❞

ALAN MOOREHEAD

Introduction

For many British people Tuscany (and to a lesser extent its neighbour Umbria) represents the quintessence of Italy. The landscape is what Italy ought to look like: hummocky hills, fields of poppies, tailored vineyards and silvery olive groves, and isolated old farms and villas guarded by sentinel cypresses. Add a few medieval fortified hilltowns and the landscape looks just like the backdrop of a Sienese *trecento* painting. Agricultural methods have changed in the last twenty years; many vineyards have been industrialised, cash crops like sunflowers and tobacco have supplanted the traditional olive in some areas, and tractors have replaced white oxen. Yet the rural way of life prevails and there is a sense of continuity, and of harmony between man and nature, town and country. The human scale of the countryside is cosily reassuring to the northerner: as Nathaniel Hawthorne wrote in 1858 "I...wandered among some pleasant country lanes, bordered with hedges, and wearing an English aspect – at least, I could fancy so".

Yet this "typical" Tuscany is confined mainly to the heartland of the area, the wine-producing Chianti hills between Florence and Siena. There are several other well-defined areas of Tuscany, some quite different from the traditional picture. To the north-west of Florence and the Arno is the Garfagnana, the wooded foothills of the Apennines. The dominant feature of the coast beyond is the rugged chain of the Apuan Alps which forms a stark and jagged backdrop to the fertile plain of the Arno valley with its maize fields, lanes of pollarded trees and towns of green-shuttered houses. The mountains are streaked and veined with the white marble for which Carrara is famous; at first glance it looks like snow. The coastline (the Versilia) is flat and featureless with a series of monotonous resorts.

To the east of Florence stretching down to Arezzo is the Casentino, an area of mountains covered in thick woods of oak and chestnut. Often damp and cool, the woods provide a weekend respite for the Florentines who escape the heat of the Arno valley to go riding or look for wild mushrooms. Beyond the Chianti hills to the south-west are reddish metalliferous hills and the Maremma, once a malarial marsh, reclaimed in the 18th century as pastureland. The coast has little to offer except sandy beaches backed by pinewoods. The mineral-rich Tuscan archipelago and the promontory of Monte Argentario are more attractive for a beach holiday, but again there's nothing very typically Tuscan about them; in fact they've been part of Tuscany only since 1815. None of these areas has the cultural interest concentrated in and around Florence, Siena and Chianti.

Lauded as "the green heart of Italy" by the tourist office literature, landlocked Umbria is a gentle, tranquil landscape of verdant valleys and wooded hills. The central plain (*Piano degli Angeli*) is a patchwork of neat fields of cereals, sunflowers and tobacco, with haystacks still house-shaped or conical in the old-fashioned way.

Here and there an ancient abbey or monastery is a reminder that Umbria has been the birthplace of many saints, from Benedict, founder of western monasticism and patron saint of Europe (born at Norcia in 480) to Francis of Assisi and his disciple Clare (born in 1182 and 1194 respectively). The countryside is still recognisable in the frescoes of The Life of St Francis possibly painted by Giotto at Assisi and (nearly 200 years later) by Benozzo Gozzoli at Montefalco. Umbria is famous too for its lakes and fresh springs, praised since ancient times. Lake Trasimeno, scene of Hannibal's famous triumph against the Romans in 217BC, is not scenically memorable; as William Hazlitt wrote in 1826 "I have seen other lakes since, which have driven it out of my head". The lake often features in the misty landscapes of Perugino, Umbria's best-known painter who was born at nearby Perugia. The Fount of Clitumnus, where weeping willows and trembling poplars surround a small lake, is more romantic and evocative.

There is a harsher side to the serene Umbrian countryside. The east is earthquake-prone with remote, rugged mountains and damaged industrial towns. In the south, volcanic plateaux are geologically akin to neighbouring Lazio. The cities don't provide enough employment to keep younger people in the region and the population is declining. On the other hand, Umbria is popular with rich Romans who like to spend their weekends in the country. This is not a new phenomenon but the revival of a well-established Roman tradition. Pliny had a villa at Tifernum (now Città di Castello) where he liked to rusticate.

One of the chief charms of both Tuscany and Umbria is their medieval hill towns which often seem a natural more than a man-made feature of the landscape. In a sense they do indeed grow out of the countryside for the bricks are invariably from the surrounding soil be it limestone, sandstone or the red clay whose colour has become known as "burnt sienna" and "raw sienna". Many of these towns are of Etruscan origin; Volterra, Chiusi and Cortona are good examples, all with archaeological museums. The Romans left their mark too: theatres at Fiésole, Volterra, Gubbio and Spoleto, traces of villas on the islands, bridges and the odd bits of wall here and there. But the medieval townships with their defensive towers, their magisterial palaces and their loggias and markets belong mainly to the era of the communes.

From the 10th to the 13th centuries central Italy was ravaged by the power struggle between the pro-papal Guelphs and the Ghibellines who supported the emperor. Dante (a Guelph) moaned " Wretched country, look around your shores/On every coast, and then into your heart/And see if any part enjoys peace". The Guelphs, usually merchants and members of the middle class, built square battlements; the aristocratic Ghibellines built fancy fish-tailed ones. But it was not as clear-cut as that; loyalties were not always consistent and the conflict of the superpowers was often an excuse for more local quarrels between neighbouring towns and their chief families. In Umbria the medieval communes were nominally under papal rule but actually controlled by powerful local clans such as the

Baglioni in Perugia, the Trinci in Foligno and the Gabrielli in Gubbio. Even within one town there were rival factions. Temporary pragmatic alliances were continually being made; Perugia, for instance, sided with the Guelphs – except when the papacy was ailing or absent. The towns remained to a large degree independent until papal control was fully established in the 16th century. Most of the stout civic buildings in Umbrian towns date from that self-governing era.

In Tuscany separate city states evolved, each trying to establish a larger piece of the jigsaw than their neighbour. In the 11th and 12th centuries Pisa became a great maritime power and the characteristic striped marble churches were built wherever her influence extended – in Pistoia and Prato, Siena and Massa Maríttima, even in

---

Visiting Tuscany and Umbria

There are regular direct scheduled flights from London to Pisa (which gets heavily booked in summer). Rome (for Umbria) or Bologna (for Tuscany) are alternatives, with direct scheduled flights from London. Charter flights are also available, from London and some regional airports. The train journey from London to Pisa takes 24 hours; Motorail is available to Milan. Driving from London to Siena (about 1,000 miles) would take about 24 hours. It's worth considering staying a couple of nights en route in France. Buying petrol coupons in advance (see General Information chapter) could save you about £18.

Ferries for Elba leave from Piombino on the Tuscan coast. Bookings need to be made in advance – through Serena Holidays (UK agents for NAVARMA), 40-42 Kenway Road, London SW5, tel: 01-373 6548/49.

Both regions are well suited to a touring holiday; unlike in the flat areas of the north, the countryside itself is a major factor in the holiday. The area is well served by motorways, though tolls are expensive, but the historic centres of many towns are closed to traffic (except for residents), parking is invariably difficult, and one-way systems endlessly frustrating, so it's usually best to park outside the centre and explore on foot (unless you are staying at a hotel in the centre, when you can usually drive there and may be issued with a special parking permit). When making an excursion from one major town to another (eg Siena to Florence or Perugia) you might be better off taking the train.

To explore both Tuscany and Umbria in any depth (excluding Florence) would take about three weeks. Not only are there well-preserved medieval hill towns with plenty to see and some lovely countryside in between, but there's a wide choice of accommodation at all price levels. In Tuscany there are several comfortable country hotels with swimming pools; in high season a minimum stay of three days, generally on half-board terms, may be stipulated. It's worth considering a strategic base (near Siena, for example) and making daily excursions within a comfortable radius. From a hotel or villa in the Chianti you could easily visit Florence and many other parts of Tuscany by the day.

Another aspect of touring in Tuscany is the possibility of visiting vineyards and tasting their wines. The Strada del Chianti (Chianti wine route) is clearly marked by road signs and most of the larger estates welcome visitors and encourage visits to their enoteca to sample and buy their produce. Other parts of Tuscany and Umbria are less

---

Sardinia; inside Pisan sculptors carved intricate tombs and pulpits. In the 13th and 14th centuries Siena was the republic to be reckoned with and her prosperity was reflected in a period of artistic brilliance, with its roots in the Byzantine tradition. The still icon-like Madonnas of Duccio di Buoninsegna (d1318) began to break from convention; Simone Martini painted figures of a refined, Gothic elegance and even painted portraits; and the Lorenzetti brothers breathed life into these figures and painted landscape backgrounds that looked real.

In 1348 the Black Death wiped out over a third of the Tuscan population; an estimated 65,000 in Siena alone (including the Lorenzetti brothers). By 1434, the beginning of Medici rule in Florence, that city, solidly Guelph, had Arezzo, Pisa, Cortona,

---

well-organised for visitors.

Umbrian hotels tend to be more basic (mostly in towns) and the places of interest more widely scattered than in Tuscany, so you will probably want to move on every couple of days or so. Assisi is a good base for a few days; you could visit Gubbio and even Urbino, as well as southern Umbria. A good touring route is from Perugia via Assisi, Spoleto and Todi to Orvieto (you can then complete the cirle or continue north to Pisa or south to Rome on the motorway – a few hours' drive).

Tuscany is an excellent area for a self-catering holiday as many of the traditional villas and farmhouses can be rented by the week and several medieval castles have been converted into self-catering apartments. These can be booked through specialist agents, or by replying to small ads in the British national press. *(See also feature on Self-catering at the end of the chapter).*

Tour operators feature one- and two-week packages to coastal resorts (easily the most popular being Viareggio) and to Elba; and short breaks throughout the year to towns including Arezzo, Assisi, Lucca, Perugia, Pisa, Pistoia and – most popular of all – Siena. They also offer a wide variety of self-catering holidays. Special interest packages include art tours, riding and walking holidays, tours of gardens and villas, opera at Torre del Lago, and wine tours. Several companies organise pilgrimages to Assisi. For the smarter coastal resorts, including Punta Ala and Porto Santo Stefano, you will need to book independently. There are also relatively few packages to inland country hotels.

May and September are probably the ideal touring months, if sightseeing is your priority. The countryside is at its best in spring and early summer when the wild flowers are out and the grass is still green, but weather can be changeable and hotels may not fill their swimming pools until June. September can still be very hot and is good for the traditional jousting/crossbow festivals on the first and second Sundays of the month (Arezzo, Sansepolcro, respectively). High summer is fine if you have access to a swimming pool and plan only leisurely sightseeing trips (early in the morning or in the evening); you will probably need to take a siesta and anyway it is usually too hot to drive around comfortably in the afternoon. The Palio in Siena is held on July 2nd and August 16th. Summer is a good time for music-lovers; the international Festival of the Two Worlds (music and drama) at Spoleto is held in June and July and the Puccini opera festival at the open-air theatre at Torre del Lago is held in August.

Prato, Pistoia and Livorno under her belt. Proud Siena finally succumbed, with all her territories, in 1557. Lucca remained independent until 1847.

There is still a friendly (but serious) rivalry not only between the towns but between the various districts (*contrade*) of a single town, symbolised by annual festivals in medieval costume. Arezzo, Foligno and Sansepolcro are among the towns where there are annual jousting competitions (*giostre*). In Gubbio there's an archery display (Palio della Balestra) and the unique Corso dei Ceri. Siena, whose various *contrade* are symbolised by animals, is scene of the famous Palio, a horse race round the main piazza. This pageantry is not put on for the tourists; it is a more or less unselfconscious continuation of the medieval (and sometimes even earlier) traditions.

In the 15th century the focus of artistic and intellectual activity shifted to Florence where the cultural upheaval of the Renaissance was to have reverberations all over Europe. Inevitably Florence (and later Rome) became the magnet for Tuscan artists, although local schools of art persisted in centres such as Arezzo, Lucca and Siena. One of the few major artists who did not gravitate to Florence (although he trained there briefly) was Piero della Francesca, a native of Sansepolcro near Arezzo, who worked in that area and at the ducal court at Urbino. His mathematical mastery of perspective and his sense of volume and structure were far ahead of his time.

In Umbria the tradition of fresco painting (often the Lives of Saints) established by the Florentine Giotto at Assisi before 1306 culminated in Luca Signorelli's Last Judgement at Orvieto (1499). Pietro Vannucci, called Perugino, is the archetypal Umbrian painter, with his languid figures and landscapes. But, unlike his master Piero della Francesca or his pupil Raphael, he was not an innovator. The schools of art which grew up in the 15th century in Perugia and Orvieto (and to a lesser extent at Gubbio and Foligno) consist mainly of local painters influenced mainly by the Sienese school. Artistic developments in Florence reached Umbria only gradually, through artists such as Benozzo Gozzoli, Fra Angelico and Perugino who worked there.

Nor did Umbria produce any of the great medieval and Renaissance minds. These were Tuscan to a man, from Dante (whose Divine Comedy, in Tuscan dialect, is the basis for the modern Italian language) to the poets Petrarch and Boccaccio; from Politian, the humanist scholar and Galileo, the scientist and astronomer to that great all-rounder, Leonardo da Vinci. Machiavelli, a Florentine, retired to his Tuscan villa to write *The Prince* in 1513 and Michelangelo, born in the Casentino, bought an estate in Chianti in 1549. Vasari, the Renaissance art historian and artist, maintains that Michelangelo attributed his own genius to "the lively and subtle air one breathes around Arezzo".

The tradition of owning a country house in Tuscany or Umbria dates back to the Romans. While Pliny the Elder has left details of farming and wine-making methods, the letters of his nephew (the Younger) record details of a sumptuous villa and conversations with the servants. The tradition was revived in the 14th century when, according to the historian Villani, rich merchants bought feudal *castelli* as rural summer retreats. At the end of the 15th century Lorenzo the Magnificent had splendid country villas, inspired by those of ancient Rome, built near Florence. These were grand affairs with Renaissance decoration and fireplaces emblazoned with crests. The areas around Florence and Lucca still have the more palatial purpose-built villas; in the 19th century English aesthetes, aristocrats and expatriates favoured villas at Fiésole, Bellosguardo or Settignano. Tuscany became, in the words of Shelley, "a paradise of exiles". The conversion of roughstone villas and farmhouses is a more recent phenomenon, dating from the early 1960s when the *mezzadria* system (land in exchange for labour and a share in the profits) was abolished: farmers moved to the towns, leaving hundreds of abandoned farmhouses (*case coloniche*, roughly the equivalent of tied cottages in England, though invariably larger) for sale, especially in the Chianti area. Encouraged by the cheapness of these properties and the availability of local labour (also cheap) the British, Dutch, Americans and Swiss established cliquey colonies of expatriates and "Chiantishire" became the fashionable place to live. In the '70s the Germans jumped on the bandwagon. Now buyers have to go to Umbria to find a bargain.

Many of the recent changes have benefitted the holidaymaker. Roads have been dramatically improved. Villas and monasteries have been converted into comfortable hotels and equipped with swimming pools. Umbria has become a little more cosmopolitan with its annual international Festival of the Two Worlds at Spoleto and the ever-popular University for Foreigners at Perugia. Yet for the ordinary visitor the heart of Italy remains remarkably unspoilt. It provides an ideal combination of peaceful rural life with the opportunity for cultural forays, and, in the summer, the almost guaranteed sunshine which is as essential to the pale northerner as to the ripening grape.

Places to visit

AREZZO

An ancient city, lacking the immediate appeal of some of its Tuscan neighbours, but well worth a day's visit. The approaches are spoilt by modern development and once within the walls orientation is muddling with one-way streets, confusing signposting and parking problems. Most of the centre is post-war and there is nowhere pleasant to stay. However, the heart of the city, with its steep, winding streets, its picturesque shuttered medieval houses and Renaissance mansions and its fine, sloping Piazza Grande is reward enough. The paintings by Piero della Francesca in the church of San Francesco are the highlight of a visit to Arezzo and should not be missed; some of the other churches contain interesting paintings too. There's a regular antiques market in the Piazza Grande, also scene of the very colourful and impressive *Giostra del Saraceno* (jousting tournament) in September. Above the town is a large park with a Medici fortress.

☞ **Churches**   Apart from the Gothic San Francesco (see below), the chief churches of Arezzo are Santa Maria della Pieve, whose fine Romanesque façade has been under wraps for some years; San Domenico, with a crucifix by Cimabue, and, 1km from the centre of Arezzo, the lovely, porticoed Santa Maria delle Grazie. The cathedral has been much altered but is worth seeing.

☞ **Museum of medieval and modern art**   Housed in a vast 15th-century mansion. The upstairs rooms have been closed for some years, but there is early Aretine painting downstairs, with works by artists such as Spinello Aretino, follower of Giotto. Vasari's vast Feast of Ahasuerus hangs in the passage. There is a fine collection of ceramics.

☞ **San Francesco**   Piero della Francesca's celebrated frescoes illustrating the Legend of the True Cross, painted in the 1450s, are perhaps the chief reason for visiting Arezzo. The mastery of perspective conveyed through atmosphere, the most abstract treatment of the human form and marvellous realistic detail (especially the light) are remarkable. The narrative is complicated and a guide is essential. Other frescoes in the church, by local artists, are old-fashioned by comparison.

☞ **Vasari's house** (ring bell for custodian)   The home of Giorgio Vasari (1511-74), the painter, architect and chronicler of his artistic contemporaries. On an intimate scale (in contrast to his paintings), his house consists of a series of small rooms with vaulted, frescoed ceilings and a display of paintings by Mannerist artists.

ASSISI

A place of pilgrimage for hundreds of years, and architecturally scarcely changed since the Middle Ages, Assisi is beautifully sited on the slopes of Mount Subasio, with views over the *Piano degli Angeli* (Plain of Angels). Narrow, cobbled streets with steps and arches are lined with picturesque old houses, their balconies brimming with flowers. In the central square an ancient Roman temple rubs shoulders with civic buildings dating from the 13th century. The shops selling ceramics, cheap embroidered clothes and souvenirs and the bars offering "toasts" and "hamburgers" detract from the enchantment and contrast ironically with the non-materialistic lifestyle advocated by saint Francis. However, when the last coachload of daytrippers has gone and the shops are shut, Assisi regains some of its mystical tranquillity. The town is very well equipped with reasonably-priced hotels and makes a good base for exploring nearby Umbrian towns such as Perugia, Spello and Montefalco. The fort above Assisi is a good picnic place, with magnificent views, and there are some good walks up Mount Subasio.

☞ **Basilica of San Francesco**   The great basilica dedicated to saint Francis, in the beautiful pinky-grey stone characteristic of Assisi, dominates the town. The rather dark Lower Church is decorated by the greatest Italian painters of the 13th and 14th centuries – Cimabue, Simone Martini, Pietro and Ambrogio Lorenzetti. A crick in the neck and several 200 lire coins (for lighting) is the price you have to pay to see the marvellous paintings which cover the walls

Assisi, San Francesco

and ceiling. Especially fine are Simone Martini's frescoes of the Life of St
Martin and Lorenzetti's poignant almond-eyed Madonna of the Sunset (so
called because she seems to smile when lit by the rays of the setting sun). The
famous frescoes of the Life of St Francis which occupy the spacious Upper
Church are now attributed to an unknown master rather than, as before, to
Giotto. The solid forms, the simple narrative and the clarity of colour of these
exquisite scenes is very moving, their appeal universal (HV Morton has
described the church as "one of the world's largest and most beautiful picture
books", reminding us that it was decorated for the illiterate devout). The best
time to visit San Francesco – open all day from April to October – is early in
the morning (before the tourist coaches arrive) and in the afternoon (when
the light is better and the attractions of lunch and/or a siesta mean that it is
relatively uncrowded).

☛ **Santa Chiara**   A striking pink-and-white striped basilica dedicated to
saint Clare, the first Franciscan sister. The interior is austere and rather too
dark to admire the frescoes, by followers of Giotto.

☛ **San Rufino**   The lovely pale façade of the cathedral, dating from the 12th
century, has a beautiful rose window and Romanesque sculptures. The
surprisingly plain white interior is of a later date, and of relatively little
interest.

Excursions from Assisi

☞ Bevagna *(19km south)*

A pretty little country town in lovely countryside where saint
Francis is said to have preached to the birds. The Piazza della Libertà
has a stage-set feel with its fine old churches and consul's palace.

BEVAGNA
(*See Assisi*)

CARMIGNANO
A small town (*5km south-west of Poggio a Caiano*) worth visiting for Pontormo's Visitation (1530) in the church of San Michele. (*See also Prato*).

CASTIGLIONE DELLA PESCAIA
An old fishing port crowned by a castle and fortified wall; yachts now vie for space with the fleet of fishing boats and hotels have been built among the pine groves lining the beach.

CHIANTI
The unspoilt countryside between Florence and Siena constitutes most people's idea of Tuscany with its rolling hills, vineyards and

---

SAINT FRANCIS OF ASSISI

Once upon a time a frivolous dandy, Francesco Bernardone, renounced his lifestyle and gave his cloak to a beggar. Not content with this act of charity, he gave away all the rest of his possessions to live a life of utter poverty for three years. He was promptly denounced by his father, a rich businessman. Francesco believed that God had asked him to rebuild His church, the celestial city, and Francesco interpreted this literally, restoring abandoned churches, but also establishing a new kind of faith based on poverty and humility. His marriage to "Lady Poverty" is often depicted in paintings. In a medieval world rife with corruption and feudal factions, where religion was all pomp and dogma, the future saint advocated simple *joie de vivre* and love of thy neighbour, plus a strict adherence to the teachings of Christ. His most famous act was to preach to the birds, and ever since he has been associated with his love of animals and the natural world, and his belief that we are all creatures of God. His poems, the "Flowers" and the "Canticle to the Sun", have been widely translated and are sometimes read as prayers.

In 1210, Francesco dated to present to pope Innocent III a draft of his "Rule"; the pope then dreamt that he saw Francesco supporting the toppling basilica of the Lateran and promptly made him a monk. From then on the movement grew (with some opposition and internal conflicts), and the Franciscan order was officially founded in 1223. The following year, Francesco, praying at La Verna in Tuscany, received the stigmata (marks of Christ's wounds). He died in 1226, aged 44, on the spot near Assisi where the Baroque church of Santa Maria degli Angeli now stands. Soon afterwards, saint Francis of Assisi, the great communicator known as Alter Christus (Second Christ) was canonised; he is now the patron saint of Italy.

Two years after his death, work was begun on the basilica of San Francesco at Assisi, where the saint is buried. It was a simple shrine, an embodiment of Franciscan belief in poverty and humility. Several years later however, the chief Italian painters of the period were employed to decorate the upper church as a memorial to the saint, with frescoes of scenes from his life; later it was completed in French Gothic style, as if to illustrate the fact that a movement which had its roots in the gentle Umbrian countryside was to become international and thus compromised by its own success. Over seven hundred years later Assisi was acclaimed the world capital for peace, and was the site, in the summer of 1986, of an international ecumenical conference on the subject.

old villas and farmhouses. On the whole the towns are of little interest or beauty. However a tour might include **Greve**, an attractive town with a 17th-century arcaded square, **Volpaia**, a medieval hamlet, perfectly intact, and **Spaltenna** and **Badia a Coltibuono** where ancient abbeys have been converted into restaurants. For wine-lovers there are signs ("*strada del vino*") to estates where you can sample and buy chianti. There are several comfortable hotels in converted country villas with swimming pools, making the area an ideal base for exploring much of Tuscany. Although roads in the Chianti are winding and slow, the Florence/Rome motorway is easily accessible.

CARRARA

The only reason for visiting this otherwise dull town is to see the marble, renowned for its texture and purity since Roman times. You can visit the quarries and buy souvenirs at an on-site hut. At the Marina holiday-makers soak up the sun while lorries stack up with great slabs of marble at the adjoining port.

CHIUSI

An ancient town, worth including on the itinerary if you are interested in the Etruscans, who established a thriving city here in the 7th century BC. There is a fine **museum**, and, outside the town, interesting **tombs**.

CITTÀ DELLA PIEVE

A small hill town, birthplace of Perugino. There are works by him in the cathedral and the oratory of Santa Maria dei Bianchi.

CITTÀ DI CASTELLO

A dull industrial town near Perugia. The art gallery (pinacoteca) contains two early works by Raphael and paintings by Spinello Aretino and Luca Signorelli (St Sebastian, 1493).

COLLE DI VAL D'ELSA

A pretty medieval town in an imposing setting between Siena and San Gimignano. The fine gateway (Porta Nuova) leads up to the Via del Castello where there are interesting old houses and two small museums with Sienese school paintings.

CORTONA

One of Italy's most ancient cities, Cortona seems to spill down the slopes of Monte Sant' Egidio. Actually, it is a compact walled town with an austere historic centre and splendid views over the plain to Lake Trasimeno from the Piazza Garibaldi. There are attractive old medieval streets to wander around, often steep with shored-up old buildings, steps and arches. The medieval heart of the town consists of the Via Nazionale, the only level street in the town, lined with grocers and postcard shops, with mysterious alleys leading off it; and the Piazza della Repubblica, a picturesque jumble of medieval and Renaissance houses and civic buildings. Its focal point is the toytown Palazzo Civico (town hall). On Saturdays there's a market in the adjacent Piazza Signorelli. Cortona is not a jolly place; it has a quality of isolation and austerity more typical of Umbria than Tuscany.

☛ **Diocesan Museum**   Opposite the cathedral, in the church of the Gesù, is a small but important collection including paintings by the native Luca Signorelli (born 1450), a small collection of gold plate and works by Lorenzetti, Duccio di Boninsegna and Sassetta. The highlight is Fra Angelico's exquisite Annunciation; beside it is the predella of his Madonna and Saints (under restoration until 1988).

☛ **Museum of the Etruscan Academy**   Founded in 1727 and housed in a fine mansion with a medieval courtyard and external staircase. The huge hall contains the best of the collection: Etruscan votive figurines, paintings by Signorelli and Pietro da Cortona, and a 5th-century bronze oil lamp. There are also Egyptian mummies, a triptych by Bicci da Lorenzo with glowing colours, some 18th-century portraits, an important coin collection and works given by Gino Severini.

☛ **Santa Maria del Calcinaio**   A graceful Renaissance masterpiece impressively sited on the hillside overlooking the plain. It has a harmonious interior.

ELBA

A relatively unspoilt though not very beautiful island whose chief attractions are its beaches and clear waters. The landscape is mostly hilly with vines and olive groves; inland it is mountainous and thickly wooded with a few picturesque old villages. The coastline is deeply indented and rocky but there are some good sandy beaches. The chief things to see are connected with Napoleon's ten-month exile here (1814-1815), after his defeat by the allies at Leipzig. There are also scattered remains of Etruscan and Roman settlements, fortresses dating from the dominion of the Pisan republic (9th to 13th centuries) and some old churches and sanctuaries, but little of great interest. **Portoferraio**, the capital and main port of arrival, has a delightful walled old town with a main piazza shaded by plane trees. There are a few relics and mementoes in Napoleon's rather spartan house, the **Villa dei Mulini** (as well as at the **Villa di San Martino**, his summer residence, just outside Portoferraio).

The small resorts around the island are mostly geared to family beach life and there are plenty of campsites. The main resorts are on the west of the island. **Procchio** has the best choice of beach hotels. Nearby **Marciana Marina** has a small fishing harbour dominated by a Pisan watch-tower and a pleasant promenade with open-air cafés but only a pebbly beach. The pretty inland villages of **Poggio** and **Marciana** (with an archaeological museum) have narrow stepped alleyways and views over the vineyards and chestnut woods. There are plenty of signposted footpaths, and a cable-car from Marciana Alta to the top of Monte Capanne (1,019m). **Marina di Campo**, on the south coast, is an alternative resort, with a long beach and a small harbour.

On the east of the island, **Porto Azzurro** is a fashionable spot: there's a busy waterfront piazza with open air cafés, and sleek yachts line the harbour; but there's no decent beach and accommodation consists mainly of villas. **Rio Marina** is a small resort with a mineralogical museum, and, inland, several archaeological sites.

FIÉSOLE

(*see Florence chapter*)

FOLIGNO

A commercial town with a fine central piazza and cathedral. The Palazzo Trinci houses a disappointingly dull art gallery. Worth a passing visit but not a detour.

FORTE DEI MARMI

One of the smartest Tuscan beach resorts, attracting the more affluent Italian holidaymakers who own or rent villas in the pinewoods behind the resort. The pale grey sands are kept in immaculate condition, cleaned and raked daily and divided into neat concession areas.

GIANNUTRI

A tiny crescent-shaped island with ruins of a large patrician Roman villa. There are no hotels.

GIGLIO

A small rocky island where unspoilt scenery and good scuba-diving in clear waters attract regular day-trippers. **Campese** has become the main resort, with several hotels and a beach of coarse dark sand. **Giglio Porto** has more charm, but the beaches are some way from the harbour and hotels. **Giglio Castello** is the main town, a medieval village around the castle.

GROSSETO

The chief town of the Tuscan Maremma is mainly dull and modern, but the old core, preserved within hexagonal walls built by the Medici, is worth a brief visit. The cathedral (San Lorenzo) is Romanesque, but much restored.

☛ **Archaeological Museum**   A well-organised museum for antiquities from the Maremma area, notably the Etruscan cities of Roselle and Vetulonia. Upstairs is the Museum of Sacred Art (Museo Diocesano) with Sienese paintings.

GUBBIO

An isolated outpost of Umbria, well worth a special visit. Clinging to the slopes of the rugged Monte Ingino, Gubbio is dour of aspect, an almost perfect medieval entity with superbly preserved houses in greyish-pink stone and steep winding streets with wrought iron lamps. The atmosphere is appropriately sleepy; Gubbio seems locked in a time warp. The main street, **Via dei Consoli**, is lined with shops selling the colourful local ceramics as well as a bizarre selection of souvenir medieval weaponry. The focal point is the

Piazza della Signoria, a red-brick square borne up on stout arches and built into the hill, scene of the annual *Palio della Balestra*, a crossbow contest in medieval costume against the citizens of Sansepolcro. Above is the 15th-century **Ducal Palace**, with a lovely Renaissance courtyard. You can take a cablecar to the top of Monte San Ubaldo for panoramic views and the church of **Santa Maria Nuova** (with Ottaviano Nelli's masterpiece, the Madonna del Belvedere). At the bottom of the town is the Piazza 40 Martiri, a popular gravel park planted with trees and little grassy knolls with stone benches; nearby is **San Francesco**, an attractive old church with a recently restored cloister.

The *Corsa dei Ceri* is a mysterious Umbrian event, when men carrying the three *ceri* (wooden "candles" shaped like giant Christmas crackers) run through the streets and up Monte San Ubaldo on the saint's birthday, May 15th. Classical plays are performed in the **Roman Theatre** just outside the city walls from the second half of July to mid-August. Gubbio is a good base for an excursion to Urbino (*see separate entry*).

☞ **Consuls' Palace** A vast 14th-century edifice with battlements and a belfry. It contains a picture gallery of strictly local interest and the Eugubian tablets, among the earliest documents of Italian civilisation dating from about 2BC. For the amateur the chief reason for a visit is the balcony view over the jumbled terracotta tiled roofs to the hills beyond, with the Roman theatre clearly visible to the south.

LIVORNO

The second largest town in Tuscany, and a major Mediterranean port, Livorno (or Leghorn to the British) has almost nothing to offer the tourist, having been drastically bombed in the Second World War, and then hastily rebuilt. The original port was the concept of Cosimo de' Medici and a memorial to Ferdinand de' Medici (the Monumento dei Quattro Mori), dating from 1624, is all that survives of interest from this period. The fashionable quarter of Livorno lies around the public park of Villa Fabbricotti and the Viale Italia running due south along the seafront, with its luxury flats and villas and gardens of palms, pine and tamarisk.

LUCCA

Historically fiercely independent, Lucca is very different in appearance from most of its Tuscan neighbours and comparatively little visited. Ruskin, who came for ten days, recalled its charms for forty years. Within the walls the old town consists of narrow streets of Renaissance mansions with grid windows and green-shuttered houses, shady squares, statues, and Pisan Romanesque churches. Hilaire Belloc called it "the neatest, the regularest, the exactest, the most fly-in-amber little town in the world, with its uncrowded streets, its absurd fortifications, and its contented silent houses." Curiosities include the market square, on the site of the Roman amphitheatre – an oval almost enclosed by the walls of medieval houses – and the rosy-bricked Giunigi tower, sprouting trees. The main square, the Piazza Napoleone, is little more than a car park,

Lucca, San Michele al Foro

lined with pollarded plane trees and surrounded by imposing
19th-century buildings; the nearby Piazza San Michele is more
active, with smart cafés and shops in the streets leading off it. The
avenues along the old ramparts, with views over the meadows and
hills, are a popular place for shady walks. There are no really
attractive hotels in Lucca (even restaurants are quite hard to find)
but there are places to stay in the countryside nearby which are good
bases for visiting Pisa too. Olive oil is a speciality of Lucca. The
birthplace of Puccini, Lucca has an opera season in September; there
is also an opera festival at nearby Torre del Lago, where the
composer lived.

☛ **Giunigi Museum** (Museo Nazionale Villa Giunigi)   A good collection of
local painting and sculpture – including by Mateo Previtali, born in Lucca in
1435 – housed in a beautifully restored mansion dating from 1418.

☛ **National Gallery** (Museo e Pinacoteca Nazionale)   The 17th-century
Palazzo Mansi is worth visiting for its grand interior alone: several rooms
with fine contemporary furnishings and tapestries, and a lovely rococo
bedroom. The picture gallery is confined to four (duller) rooms but is an
interesting collection of 16th- and 17th-century works including Medici
portraits by Bronzino, a portrait of a boy by Pontormo and some Flemish

pictures. The collection was begun by Marie-Louise de Bourbon who was given Lucca as a duchy in 1819.

🖝 **San Frediano**   A bare, light, barn-like church with a lovely Romanesque font carved with scenes from the story of Moses and two rather worn tombs by Jacopo della Quercia. The glittery mosaics on the façade are restored.

🖝 **San Martino**   The exterior of the cathedral, with profuse carvings in the Pisan style dating from 1204, has been undergoing restoration for some years. The lofty, dark interior contains several treasures: a gilded Ghirlandaio in the sanctuary, a graceful Renaissance shrine containing the *Volto Santo* (a revered Crucifix mentioned in Dante's *Inferno*) and the exquisite marble tomb of Ilaria del Carretto, masterpiece of the Sienese sculptor Jacopo della Quercia.

🖝 **San Michele al Foro**   A striking Pisan Romanesque church with a heavily ornamented façade with tiers of decorated columns and animal motifs, surmounted by a statue of the Archangel Michael.

Excursions from Lucca

☞ **Barga** (*37km north*)
A medieval hill town in the Serchio valley, with superb views. The fine cathedral is mainly Romanesque, with some fine carving both inside (on the pulpit) and out. There is an opera festival here in July and August.

☞ **Villas outside Lucca**
The gardens of the Villa Reale at Marlia (*8km north-east*), home of Napoleon's sister Elisa who ruled Lucca from 1805-1814; the Villa Mansi at Segromigno (*10km north-east*) and the Villa Camigliano (*1km south*), with gardens by Le Nôtre, can all be visited. The Castello Garzoni at Collodi (*20km east*) is a 17th-century villa famous for its association with the creator of Pinocchio; the house and formal gardens are open to the public, but rather trippery.

MASSA MARÍTTIMA

The main feature of the old town is the attractive, gently sloping Piazza Garibaldi, surrounded by battlemented medieval houses built in great bricks of spongelike stone and dominated by the lovely 13th-century cathedral raised on a staircase plinth. The art gallery in the town hall is closed for restoration. Despite the name, the sea is about 20km away.

🖝 **Cathedral**   The interior is bare but graceful and light. There are faded frescoes, a Madonna with Saints possibly by Duccio, and a Romanesque font with Renaissance tabernacle.

MONTALCINO

A Tuscan hilltown with typical ingredients: churches with Sienese school frescoes, a couple of small museums, a Rocca (ruined castle) and medieval civic buildings as well as magnificent views over the countryside. Known chiefly for its wine, the celebrated Brunello, Montalcino is a pleasant, untouristy place. Nearby (*8km south*) is the fine Benedictine abbey of Sant' Antimo, a 12th-century church of earlier origin.

MONTEFALCO

Called "The Balcony of Umbria" (Ringhiera Umbra) for its 14th-century ramparts and panoramic views. Steep, narrow streets lead to a pretty circular piazza, arcaded and tree-lined. There are several churches with frescoes by Umbrian artists.

☛ **San Francesco**   The church of San Francesco has been converted into an art gallery/museum. The chapel frescoed by Benozzo Gozzoli with scenes from the life of St Francis is the highlight of a visit to Montefalco.

MONTE ARGENTARIO

The peninsula of Orbetello was once the island of Monte Argentario and as the narrow isthmus which links it to the Tuscan coast is mainly lagoon it still feels like an island. It has a rugged and beautiful coastline and there are splendid views from the summit of Monte Argentario (635m) and the panoramic road which encircles it. **Orbetello** itself is a small town on a narrow tongue of land between the lagoons. There are two fashionable resorts: **Port' Ercole**, which has no sandy beaches but a picturesque harbour with pastel-washed houses hugging the hillside above, and **Porto Santo Stefano** on a small headland on the northern coast, the port for ferries to Giglio and Giannutri. Monte Argentario is a favourite haunt of affluent weekending Romans who keep their yachts at Porto Santo Stefano.

MONTE OLIVETO MAGGIORE

(*See Siena*)

MONTEPULCIANO

A walled town with narrow, treacherously steep corridor streets leading up to the small but spacious Piazza Grande, surrounded by lovely old buildings with some pavement cafés. Henry James described Montepulciano as "not much else besides but perched and brown and queer and crooked, and noble withal". The nobility is chiefly in the handsome Renaissance mansions which line the main street and the Piazza Grande and in some splendid churches.

☛ **Cathedral**   The interior of the cathedral is bare but harmonious and contains a lovely triptych by Taddeo di Bartolo (1403).

☛ **Madonna di San Biagio**   A fine church, just outside the town walls, built in 1518-1545 to the designs of Sangallo the Elder, and considered to be his masterpiece.

MONTERIGGIONI

(*See Siena*)

NARNI

A walled Umbrian hill town with ugly modern outskirts. There are some austere medieval buildings, particularly in the **Piazza dei Priori**, and the deconsecrated church of **San Domenico** has a small collection of paintings (including an Annunciation by Benozzo Gozzoli) and sculpture. The bridge at Narni (the Roman Ponte Augusto) was the subject of the French painter Corot's most famous painting (1827).

ORBETELLO
(*See Monte Argentario*)

ORVIETO
Isolated high on a volcanic plateau, the façade of its cathedral visible from afar, Orvieto is magnificently sited. There are fine views over the Paglia valley from the town which is rather austere, with narrow, twisting cobbled streets leading to the mellowed old quarter overlooking the hills and volcanic rocks. The pride and joy of Orvieto are the cathedral and the local white wine.

☛ **Cathedral** The cathedral took over 300 years – and over 300 architects and artists – to complete. The façade, dating from the early 14th century, is decorated with multicoloured mosaics and beautiful sculptures by Lorenzo Maitani, illustrating scenes from the Old and New Testaments. They are quite easy to see and repay study. The lofty interior is rather dark and bare but the chancel is of great artistic interest. The frescoes illustrating the Last Judgement by Luca Signorelli are his most powerful work and were to influence Michelangelo. They date from 1499 when Signorelli was commissioned to finish the decoration of the Cappell Nuova, started over 50 years earlier by Fra Angelico. There are also some interesting roundels with scenes illustrating Dante.

☛ **Papal Palace** The gloomy Gothic palace displays works originally commissioned for the cathedral including a Madonna by Simone Martini, and an Annunciation group by Francesco Mochi.

☛ **Saint Patrick's Well** (Pozzo di San Patrizio) Constructed (1527-37) by Sangallo the Younger on the orders of pope Clement VII to provide water for the city in case of siege. It's an architectural curiosity with its two concentric spiral staircases cut 60m deep into the rock.

PERUGIA
The capital of Umbria is an acquired taste. The monotony of the industrialised suburbs, the steepness of the climb, the difficulty in parking – plus the forbidding walls and dour architecture – mean that first impressions are not always favourable. However the gaiety and elegance of the evening *passeggiata* on the Corso Vannucci should put you back in a relaxed mood. The street, lined with austere Gothic buildings, has smart clothes shops and pavement bars and is completely closed to traffic. In the evenings (especially Saturdays) there's a ceaseless stream of people strolling up and down the Corso. Everyone seems to be young and trendy (the youth element is accounted for by the University and the University for Foreigners). At the end of the Corso is the Piazza IV Novembre, dominated by the large **cathedral**, strikingly sober and plain. Here students sit on the steps overlooking the focal point of the square, the exquisitely graceful pink marble **Great Fountain** (Fontana Maggiore), its two tiers carved with narrative bas-reliefs. Opposite is the façade of the vast **Priors' Palace**, an austere battlemented building with Gothic mullioned windows and a graceful flight of steps.

Most of the main sights are within easy walking distance of (if not actually on) the Corso, Perugia's main street, and could be seen in one day. Daytime visitors should park in or around the Piazza dei Partigiani and then take the escalator up through the Rocca Paolina (Fortress) to the Piazza Italia, a sedate square at the east end of the Corso.

People staying in the centre can obtain a parking permit for a nearby street from their hotels on arrival. It's worth staying overnight (at least) to do justice to the city. You can explore the dark, winding, shallow-stepped lanes and mysterious – even sinister – arched alleys of the city. There are a number of interesting old **churches** outside the original walls of the city: the early Christian Sant' Angelo, the Gothic San Domenico whose monastery houses the National Archaeological Museum of Umbria, and San Pietro, a 10th-century basilica with various works of art inside.

☛ **Collegio del Cambio** (Moneychangers' Guild)   Two vaulted rooms with superb wood panelling and carving surviving from the mid-15th century. Perugino and his pupils frescoed the rooms between 1498 and 1500. Perugino's famous self-portrait shows a beefy face in strange contrast to the ethereal figures and sinuous draperies which he painted. Next door (same ticket) is the **Collegio della Mercanzia** (Chamber of Commerce) where guilds of merchants met to impose taxes and administer justice. The room is decorated with intricately carved geometric design panelling.

☛ **National Gallery of Umbria**   Like the two medieval guilds (see above) the National Gallery of Umbria is in the Priors' Palace, and entrance is from the side facing the Corso. The gallery contains a complete survey of Umbrian painting (with some Sienese and Florentine works too). Airily displayed in a series of over 20 rooms, it's an absorbing collection ranging from the beautiful to the merely intriguing (details of clothes, buildings etc). The highlight is the room containing Fra Angelico's Virgin and Child (1437) opposite Piero della Francesca's St Anthony altarpiece.

☛ **San Bernardino**   An exquisite Renaissance oratory by Agostino di Duccio. Lively figures in bas-relief decorate the façade.

Excursion from Perugia
☞ **Deruta** (*20km south*)
The old part of Deruta is minimal, though quite attractive; the long narrow Piazza dei Consoli, lined with shops, is more street than square. The major attraction for tourists is the ceramics industry, with many direct-sell factories along the Via Tiburtina.

PIENZA

A tiny and perfectly preserved example of Renaissance town planning. The rebuilding of the town was commissioned by pope Pius II in 1458 of the Florentine architect Bernardo Rossellini (who far exceeded his budget to glorify the birthplace of his benefactor). The buildings of the beautiful main piazza form a harmonious entity and there's one little bar from where you can enjoy the scenario (for stage set it is although there is seldom much action). Although Pienza is something of a ghost town (the centre is closed to traffic) there are some flourishing *alimentari* selling various wines (notably from nearby Montalcino), the local honey, herbs, *pecorino* (sheeps' cheese) and olive oil; tasting is encouraged.

☛ **Cathedral**   The perfect Renaissance exterior, based on the principles of Alberti, conceals an unusual interior modelled on the German hall churches which pope Pius II had seen on his travels, with some interesting paintings commissioned from Sienese artists. Pius II called his cathedral "the finest in all Italy".

☛ **Diocesan Museum**   Displayed in this small museum is a fantastic cope embroidered in England for Pius II: "[it] surely seems to excel all others in Christendom in its work and craftsmanship", he wrote.

☛ **Palazzo Piccolomini**   Inspired by a grander Florentine model and adapted to the scale of Pienza, the Palazzo Piccolomini has a graceful courtyard and splendid views from the loggia.

PISA

Once a powerful port and a maritime republic to rival Venice and Genoa, Pisa has always attracted foreign visitors, from oriental merchants to Romantic poets including Byron, Shelley, and the Brownings. The famous Leaning Tower and the airport (the closest to Florence) ensure a continuation of the tradition, despite the fact that Pisa, badly bombed in the Second World War, has little charm and no appealing hotels. There are, however, several fine churches notable for the characteristic striped Pisan façades with blind arches and carved colonnades – a formula seen on Pisan territory as far as Sardinia. The **Piazza dei Cavalieri**, originally the main square, is worth seeing for the church of Santo Stefano and the Palazzo dei Cavalieri, with its splendid *sgraffito* façade; both were designed by Vasari in the 16th century. But the chief glory of Pisa is still the so-called *Campo dei Miracoli*, comprising the tower, the baptistery, the cathedral, and the Campo Santo; as Dickens wrote: "The group of buildings, clustered on and about this verdant carpet, is perhaps the most remarkable and beautiful in the whole world". Not even the crowds, the snack stalls and the litter can entirely obliterate the beauty.

☛ **Baptistery**   Begun in 1152, but with later decorative additions (some now replaced by copies) by members of the famous Pisano family of sculptors, the baptistery is a cylindrical structure with a dome added in the 14th century. Nicola Pisano's pulpit (1260) was inspired by the classical sarcophagi in the cemetery.

☛ **Cathedral**   Begun in 1064 by a Byzantine Greek architect, but not completed until 1118, the cathedral is the major – and most influential – example of the Pisan style. The 16th-century bronze doors are very fine and Giovanni Pisano's pulpit (1302-11) is the highlight of the interior.

☛ **Cemetery** (Campo Santo)   Originally a cemetery for rich Pisan noblemen (with earth brought from the Holy Land), the Campo Santo has some splendid antique sarcophagi, sculptures and the remains of frescoes by Benozzo Gozzoli and others. Many of the treasures were destroyed or badly damaged by bombs in 1944, but preparatory drawings for the frescoes, displayed in a special museum (Museo delle Sinopie) give a clear idea of the original decoration and a fascinating insight into different techniques.

☛ **Leaning Tower** (Campanile)   Italy's premier tourist attraction is a white marble bell-tower with elegant arcading. The tower was probably already tilting when abandoned by the original architect in 1185; additions did not help and by the mid-16th century (as recorded by Vasari) it veered some 12 feet from the true. It now leans about 17 feet but is stable enough for thousands of tourists to experience the giddy sensation of a climb to the top – although it can be a dangerously slippery experience in wet weather. From here Galileo, a native of Pisa, conducted experiments on gravity. There are splendid views.

☛ **National Museum of St Matthew**   Important collection of Pisan sculpture and Tuscan painting, including a panel of St Paul by Masaccio and an altar-piece by Simone Martini, housed in a converted Benedictine monastery.

☛ **Santa Maria della Spina**   Tiny jewel of Pisan Gothic architecture.

PISTOIA

An interesting old town often unjustly left off the tourist itinerary, Pistoia is characterised by its pretty curving streets with green-shuttered houses and by its alleys with bracket lamps and colourful names (street of the white dog, madman's alley, lane of the beautiful women). At the centre of the city is a beautiful open square with a cathedral, baptistery, town hall and a pretty well. Behind it is the lively daily market, excellent for stocking up for picnics and full of atmosphere. The many churches, in Pisan Romanesque style, are often decorated with blue-and-white terracotta medallions and contain finely carved pulpits. The flat outskirts of the town are industrial (market gardens and wrought iron works) but to the north is the splendid scenery of the Apennines, ideal for summer excursions.

☛ **Cathedral**   The attraction of the cathedral is its setting, along with the octagonal Gothic baptistery, in the context of the Piazza. It has a lovely arcaded façade but a slightly disappointing interior. You have to pay the sacristan to see the celebrated silver altar (dark and behind railings).

☛ **Civic Museum**   A collection (mainly pictures) beautifully displayed in the great beamed halls of the medieval town hall. There are panel paintings from churches and convents in Pistoia but other Tuscan schools are also well represented and the collection spans several centuries. There's also a special section devoted to the sculptor Marino Marini (born Pistoia 1901). The ticket is valid for the Ospedale del Ceppo frieze too (see below).

☛ **Ospedale del Ceppo**   Above the arcades of this old hospital is a charming and very unusual ceramic frieze by the della Robbia family (or school). It's worth climbing the steps to the scaffolding platform for a closer look; the narrative detail, showing the Seven Acts of Mercy, is colourful (in both senses).

☛ **Sant' Andrea**   A fine Pisan Romanesque church with a lofty, bare basilican type interior. Giovanni Pisano's lovely pulpit, with a wealth of fine relief detail, is justly famous.

☛ **San Giovanni Fuorcivitas**   Another striped Pisan church, with a superbly carved pulpit, and a glazed terracotta Visitation by Luca della Robbia.

PRATO

A town famous for its textile industry since the Middle Ages, Prato is surrounded by sprawling suburbs, but has an interesting old centre. Within the city walls there are old cobbled streets with picturesque vistas and squares with distinctive striped churches. The slightly run-down feeling detracts from the appeal of Prato as a place to stay, but it's well worth an excursion (from Pistoia or Florence) for the paintings of Filippo Lippi alone.

☛ **Cathedral** The striking green-and-white striped exterior of the cathedral has an unusual outside pulpit designed by Donatello and Michelozzo (1428-38). The most exciting feature of the darkish interior are the frescoes by Filippo Lippi behind the high altar, begun in 1452. The scene depicting the Feast of Herod is famous for the enchantingly graceful Salome, like Botticelli's Venus come to life. The other frescoes, though dimly lit, are also worth looking at. Next to the cathedral is a small museum containing Donatello's original sculptures for the exterior pulpit, and other works of art connected with the cathedral.

☛ **City Art Gallery** (Galleria Comunale) The impressive brick Praetorian Palace houses a good collection of altarpieces by Tuscan artists (notably the Lippis) and some Neapolitan still lifes.

☛ **Santa Maria delle Carceri** Sangallo's exemplary church is slightly lost next to the very picturesque ruins of the old castle of Frederick II. The interior is a masterpiece of the early Renaissance.

Excursions from Prato

☞ **Villa Medicea, Poggio a Caiano** (*9km south-west*)
Lorenzo the Magnificent's splendid country house stands proudly on the edge of a busy little town, set in a park of fine old trees. The Villa Medicea, a Renaissance masterpiece by Giuliano da Sangallo, has recently been opened to the public after years of closure for restoration. There are superb frescoes in the entrance hall by Andrea del Sarto and Pontormo.

PUNTA ALA

A surprising luxury sports-oriented holiday playground spread over several miles of the wooded coastal strip north of the headland closing the wide bay south of Piombino (the Gulf of Follónica). A confusing network of roads and roundabouts links various residential complexes, the main one being the attractive, mostly private yacht harbour, others closer to the long sandy beach, which shelves very gently and has bars, showers and shaded car parks. There are hotels and lots of sports facilities, but no village.

SAN GIMIGNANO

With its medieval towers visible from afar, San Gimignano is a beguiling town, almost unchanged in appearance since the 14th century. Such is its popularity that there are enormous parking lots all around the town (the centre is closed to traffic) and a special co-operative to fix hotel and restaurant prices. The picturesque charm of the old streets and squares where swifts wheel from tower to tower is now threatened by a slightly trippery atmosphere. But there are some marvellous paintings to see and the churches and backstreets are seldom crowded. Hotels here, and in the surrounding countryside (with swimming pools), are excellent value and a good base for visiting Certaldo, Volterra and the Chianti.

☛ **Cathedral** (Collegiata/Duomo) The dark, Romanesque interior is

San Gimignano

decorated with interesting frescoes by Florentine and Sienese artists. The story of Ghirlandaio's Life of St Fina is the highlight and it's worth listening to the recorded commentary. Adjoining the cathedral are the Museum of Sacred Art and the Etruscan Museum.

☛ **Sant' Agostino**   Refreshingly secular in tone, Benozzo Gozzoli's frescoes of the Life of St Augustine are appealing for their fresh colours, clear narrative and vivid detail, especially in the faces. You can also visit the Renaissance cloisters, and buy postcards from a monk.

☛ **Town Hall and Picture Gallery** (Palazzo del Popolo)   The view from the top of the tower, the finely frescoed Council Chamber (Sala di Dante) with Lippo Memmi's Virgin Enthroned (Maestà, 1317), and the gallery (Museo Civico) are all worth seeing. In the gallery the rather comical fresco of a married couple sharing a bath attracts the most interest.

Excursions from San Gimignano

☞ **Certaldo** (*14km north*)
A hilltop village with restored medieval buildings including the Palazzo Pretorio, with frescoes and a small museum. The house of the poet Boccaccio (1313-75) can be visited on application to Signora Bianchi, Via delle Mura 1.

SAN MINIATO

A pretty town with attractive Renaissance buildings and unspoilt squares, exactly half-way between Pisa and Florence.

SANSEPOLCRO

Architecturally undistinguished, and geographically out on a limb, Sansepolcro is nevertheless worth including in the Tuscan itinerary for the paintings of its native artist Piero della Francesca.

☛ **Museum** In addition to old manuscripts, reliquaries and the works of local painters, the museum has a room devoted to Piero della Francesca. The famous Resurrection is the highlight; also here is his Madonna della Misericordia. The missing centrepiece of the triptych by Matteo di Giovanni is Piero's Baptism, now in London's National Gallery.

☛ **San Lorenzo** This otherwise uninteresting church contains a characteristically weird Deposition by Rosso Fiorentino (the church is usually locked but there may be someone around who has a key).

Excursions from Sansepolcro

☞ **Monterchi** (*17km south*)
Piero's lovely fresco of the Madonna del Parto (showing the pregnant Virgin Mary) is in the chapel of the cemetery.

SIENA

The Sienese consider themselves superior to the Florentines and many of the city's greatest monuments were built with this rivalry in mind. Siena's artistic and architectural heyday was in the 13th and 14th centuries before the upheaval of the Renaissance. The city has expanded considerably, and the outskirts are ugly, but within the original walls (almost intact) Siena has preserved its medieval character with narrow, dark and often steep streets lined with tall Gothic mansions in rosy-coloured brick. The focus of life is the fan-shaped **Piazza del Campo**, possibly the most beautiful square in Italy, although overcrowded in the tourist season. From the pavement bars and restaurants you can admire the herringbone pattern of the bricks, the lovely fountain, and the harmonious medieval architecture; and you can watch the world go by for hours. Twice a year the Campo is the scene of more frenzied activity: the traditonal Palio festival when the famous horse race (Corsa del Palio) is run around the piazza as a climax to a day of pageantry and rivalry between the various districts (*contrade*) of the city.

The main shopping street in Siena is the Via Banchi di Sopra, full of international big-name boutiques; it runs into the Via di Città with shops selling old prints and ceramics. You can buy the famous *panforte di Siena* almost everywhere, and ceramic plates and mugs depicting the emblematic animals of the *contrade* make an attractive souvenir. In addition to the main sights listed below which are all within a short walk of the Campo, there are some interesting **churches** (Sant' Agostino, Santa Caterina, San Domenico, San Francesco, Santa Maria dei Servi), with some important paintings of the Sienese school; they are rather scattered in the town and you need time and dedication to see them all.

☞ **Art Gallery** (Pinacoteca) A comprehensive and chronological survey of Sienese painting from the 13th-century artist Guido da Siena to the Mannerist Domenico Beccafumi (d1551), housed in the beautiful late Gothic Palazzo Buonsignori.

☞ **Baptistery** The most important feature of the dark interior is the font, decorated with bronze reliefs by Jacopo della Quercia, Ghiberti and Donatello.

☞ **Cathedral** "Nothing could be more Christian than the outlines of this noble church, and nothing more Moslem than the horizontal stripes of white and black marble with which it is built. As one looks at it, memories of other Gothic cathedrals are mingled with thoughts of Cairo, Damascus and Cordoba" (HV Morton). The dark interior of the cathedral is just as overpowering as its striking exterior. The wooden choir stalls, inlaid with designs of musical instruments, and the superb carved pulpit by Nicola Pisano should not be missed. Of the paintings, the highlight is the series of frescoes (1503-8) by Pintoricchio on the walls of the **Piccolomini Library**, illustrating scenes from the life of pope Pius II, one showing his visit to Britain and his reception by James I of Scotland. A recorded commentary is available. There are some lovely illuminated manuscripts on display too.

☞ **Cathedral Museum** (Museo dell'Opera del Duomo) A fine treasury, a select collection of Sienese primitives, and a good view from the top of the building are all overshadowed by the contents of the room devoted to Duccio's exquisite Maestà (1308-11). A reverential silence prevails.

☞ **Town Hall** (Palazzo Pubblico) The graceful Gothic town hall (still used as such) contains frescoed rooms open to the public as a museum. The most beautiful single work is Simone Martini's Maestà, the most famous the equestrian portrait of Guidoriccio da Fogliano, traditionally attributed to Simone Martini but now the focus of much art-historical controversy. For topographic interest and charming detail, Ambrogio Lorenzetti's frescoes illustrating Good and Bad Government are unrivalled. You can climb to the top of the tower for a dizzying bird's-eye view of the Piazza del Campo and the roofs of Siena.

Excursions from Siena

Most of Tuscany could be explored using Siena as a base; we include below only small places of relatively minor or specialist interest which you could visit on the way to or from Siena, or as part of an excursion.

☞ Monte Oliveto Maggiore (*36km south-east*)

The cloisters of the monastery contain marvellous frescoes by Signorelli and Sodoma (one of the last great painters of the Sienese school) depicting the life of St Benedict. The church has beautiful inlaid choir stalls.

☞ Monteriggioni (*14km north-west*)

This tiny hamlet was built by the Sienese as a fort against the Florentines. Its walls literally crown a hill ("Monterrigion di torri si corona" wrote Dante in his *Inferno*, Canto XXXI). The grandly named Piazza Roma contains a little church, a well and a couple of restaurants.

☞ **San Galgano** (*30km south-west on the road to Massa Maríttima*)
Tiny San Galgano boasts a superb ruined Cistercian abbey and a
Romanesque church with an oratory containing frescoes by
Ambrogio Lorenzetti.

SPELLO

The Roman walls and gateways, the picturesque narrow steeply
winding streets, cobbled, stepped and spanned by arches and
vaulting, are attractive enough, but an additional reason for visiting
Spello is for a single frescoed chapel in the church of Santa Maria
Maggiore.

☛ **Baglioni Chapel** After recent restoration the colours of Pintoricchio's
three frescoes are jewel-like. His love of detail, both decorative and
naturalistic, is almost Flemish, the self-portrait in the Annunciation is a
charming signature. The other subjects are the Nativity and Christ among
the Doctors.

SPOLETO

Built on a hill, Spoleto has a medieval centre where steep cobbled
lanes, spanned by arches and lit by lanterns, open out onto small
shady piazzas. Spoleto is off the main tourist beat and it is usually
quiet, except in the market square and the smart main shopping
street. However the annual Festival of the Two Worlds in July is an
international event and Spoleto has attracted a colony of artists.
Much of the action has shifted from the centre to the newer town
below where the only arresting feature is the huge Alexander Calder
sculpture outside the station. There are some fine Roman remains, a
dull provincial art gallery and quite a few churches – from Early
Christian (San Salvatore) and medieval (Santi Giovanni e Paolo, with
fragments of frescoes depicting the life of Thomas à Becket) to
Baroque (San Filippo).

☛ **Bridge of Towers** (Ponte delle Torri) Addison noted that the Bridge of
Towers, also called the Ponte Gattapone, was "not to be equalled for its
height by any other [aqueduct] in Europe". Built in the mid-13th century on
Roman foundations, it spans a fertile gorge which seems to spill down from
the ruins of the fortress (Rocca). The drop is particularly impressive viewed
from the footpath across the bridge.

☛ **Cathedral** A beautiful Romanesque exterior enlivened by a mosaic and
enhanced by its setting in a peaceful and unspoilt piazza, with a graceful
shallow flight of steps. The plain interior has frescoes by Filippo Lippi (not
his best) in the apse and by Pintorrichio in the Eroli chapel (you'll need to
find the custodian to show them to you).

☛ **San Pietro in Valle** On the portal of the lovely honey-coloured façade are
superb carvings, mostly depicting men struggling against beasts. The
carvings are among the finest in all Umbria yet the church, approached via an
unkempt, grassy flight of cobbled steps, is little visited. There is a spectacular
view of the Bridge of Towers (*see above*) from the Foligno-Terni road (S3)
below the church.

Excursions from Spoleto

☞ **Fount of Clitumnus** (*13km north*)

The famous source of the River Clitumnus (Fonti del Clitunno) forms a tiny lake of crystal clear water surrounded by trees. It was sacred to the Romans and much praised by the ancient poets, and later by Byron and the Italian Romantic poet Carducci. Now the road and a mock-rustic café spoil the atmosphere.

SELF-CATERING IN TUSCANY AND UMBRIA

"An airy villa with a loggia so that we can have meals outside, with just a few big rooms where we can receive our friends, and only a few bedrooms...Take care, also, with the cellars and store-rooms because the produce of this land is so plentiful" (16th-century architect's instructions).

Of course, you can go on a self-catering holiday anywhere in Italy; there are plenty of agents offering seaside flats and modern villas. However, no areas can compare with Tuscany and, to a lesser extent, Umbria for the appeal of their country villas. The archetypal Tuscan villa, or *casa colonica*, is a weathered, terracotta-tiled house with thick walls and large cool rooms, usually whitewashed, often with beamed ceilings and brick floors. Furniture is unpretentious but often antique: traditional oak chests, dressers and tables. Modernisation is usually limited to kitchen facilities and plumbing – you can expect a decent bathroom – but in many cases includes the addition of a private swimming pool and, sometimes, a tennis court. Maid service is usually part of the deal. A thoroughly comfortable holiday can thus be combined with an unrivalled base for sightseeing.

Below is a selection of agents and tour operators who can arrange self-catering holidays in farmhouses, typical country villas and even castles. Properties are normally rented by the week and travel arrangements including fly-drive packages can be booked.

Citalia, 50/51 Conduit Street, London W1R 9FB (tel: 01-434 3844); and Marco Polo House, 3/5 Lansdowne Road, Croydon, CR9 1LL (01-686 5533)

Chapter Travel, 102 St John's Wood Terrace, London NW8 6PL (tel: 01-586 9451). Chapter Travel are also agents for Cuendet.

Eurovillas, 36 East Street, Coggeshall, Essex CO6 1SH (tel: [0376] 61156)

Invitation to Tuscany, 24 Palmer Park Avenue, Reading, Berks RG6 1DN (tel: [0734] 67522)

Magic of Italy, 47 Shepherds Bush Green, London W12 8PS (tel: 01-743 9555). Magic of Italy are also agents for Solemar.

Perrymead Properties, 55 Perrymead Street, London SW6 35N (tel: 01-736 4592)

Vacanze in Italia, Bignor, nr Pulborough, West Sussex RH20 1QD (tel: [07987] 368)

Villas Italia, 93 Regent Street, London WS1R 7TF (tel: 01-439 8547)

Agriturist is an agent for self-catering accommodation and holidays on farms (Piazza S. Firenze 3, 50122 Florence; tel: [055] 287838; or, for Umbria, Via Tuderte 30, 06100 Perugia, tel: [075] 30174).

British owners of villas often advertise in national newspapers in this country. Bookings can be organised in English and payment made in sterling.

The Castello di Gargonza (Monte San Savino, 22km south-west of Arezzo) is a converted medieval village with twenty separate houses, each with self-catering facilities. See under *Hotels* in this chapter for more details.

*Todi, Santa Maria
della Consolazione*

TODI

The fine hillside setting of Todi can be seen for miles around, but it is
a small town and a passing visit of a few hours is all you need. The
views from the Piazza Garibaldi across a valley of fields to Monte
Martano are splendid.

☛ **Piazza del Popolo**   The main square, a perfect architectural ensemble, is
flanked by severe Gothic palaces: the crenellated Palazzo dei Priori (begun
1283) and the Palazzo del Capitano (1290-1300) with a monumental staircase
(the picture gallery inside is closed indefinitely for restoration). The focal
point is the wide flight of steps leading up to a bare Romanesque cathedral.

☛ **Santa Maria della Consolazione** *(just outside the town on the SS79 bis)*   A
very graceful Renaissance church inspired (possibly designed) by Bramante,
with a majestic and harmonious interior.

TREVI

One of Umbria's most picturesque hill towns. A small **art gallery**
(pinacoteca) contains works by Perugino, Lo Spagna and
Pintoricchio.

VIAREGGIO

Tuscany's largest and liveliest beach resort, with soft sands and a
busy seafront, is packed during the summer months. But it has
never been a pretty place. During a visit in 1921 Norman Douglas
dismissed Viareggio as "a town of heartrending monotony, the least
picturesque of all cities in the peninsula, the least Italian. It has not
even a central piazza!". Added to this singular shame, Douglas
described the inhabitants as "a shallow and rapacious breed who
fleece visitors during the summer weeks and live on the proceeds for
the rest of the year." Locals are still fleecing the tourists, particularly
on the beach where there are extortionate charges for hiring parasols
and deckchairs. Viareggio is, however, well placed for excursions to
towns like Lucca and Pisa (½ hour by train or bus) and boat trips to
the islands. The Lent Carnival is a famous four-week jamboree.

VINCI

The **museum** in the old castle is worth a visit to see working models of Leonardo's startlingly sophisticated designs (a helicopter, a machine gun, a loom etc). His putative birthplace is an old roughstone farmhouse amidst olive groves at nearby Anchiano.

VOLTERRA

Perched on an outcrop of volcanic rock, and surrounded by Etruscan and medieval walls, Volterra is somewhat grim and forbidding, at least from a distance. It has retained its medieval appearance almost intact and the central **Piazza dei Priori** must be one of the few squares in Italy with no pavement bars or cafés. It is something of a stage set and the only real action is on Saturday mornings when there's a market. Yet Volterra is not a complete backwater; the shops, many selling the traditional alabaster wares, are fashionable and thriving and there are plenty of lively backstreet *trattorie*. The huge Medici fortress (now a prison) which dominates the city is surrounded by a peaceful park.

Below the town are strange rippled hills and sheer sandstone cliffs known as **Le Balze** (the most dramatic view of this popular beauty spot is from a little track leading off the road to Pisa).

☛ **Art Gallery** (Galleria Pittorica/Pinacoteca)   A small collection in a lovely Renaissance palace (Palazzo Minucci-Solaini) with a pretty courtyard and small rooms with remains of frescoes. Rosso Fiorentino's masterpiece, a vivid, disturbing Deposition (1521) with an apparently putrid Christ, is the highlight. Light, colour and composition all serve to heighten the emotional impact of the painting. Ghirlandaio's The Redeemer is interesting for the beautiful local landscape detail.

☛ **Cathedral**   Solemn, stripey and cold, the interior of the cathedral has various interesting parts (Mino da Fiésole's tabernacle, polychrome crucifixion, Pisano pulpit and faint fragments of a Benozzo Gozzoli fresco) making up a confused whole. Opposite is a bare octagonal baptistery.

☛ **Guarnacci Museum**   Important collection of Etruscan art. with hundreds of funerary urns (DH Lawrence called them "ash-chests", which is a more accurate description).

☛ **Roman Theatre**   Seen from a walled street running above the site, the Roman theatre is very impressive although much restored.

Hotels

Artimino
PAGGERIA MEDICEA
Carmignano, 50042 Firenze

£££
Open all year
Tel: (055) 8718081

In a beautiful, unspoilt hilltop location 25km from Florence near the pretty hamlet of Artimino, this hotel is the former pages' quarters of the Medici villa known as 'La Ferdinanda', built in 1596. A cool, rustic elegance prevails in the large, beamed and thick-walled bedrooms which are sparsely furnished with provincial antique furniture. The chimney-pieces have been beautifully restored, and pristine shower rooms added. The lounge areas and bar are more modern (the hotel is sometimes used for conferences and sales promotions held at the Villa). The adjacent restaurant, *Biagio Pignatta*, is a sophisticated trattoria used by the hotel guests. There's a shop selling the produce of the estate, including its famous wines. An ideal base for visiting Pistoia, Prato and Florence as well as exploring this less well-known part of Tuscany.

Facilities: *37 bedrooms (AC); tennis courts; parking* **Credit/charge cards accepted:** *Amex, Diners, Eurocard, Visa*

Assisi
UMBRA
Vicolo degli Archi 6, 06081 Perugia

£
Closed mid-Nov to mid-Mar, except Xmas
Tel: (075) 812240

Easily the most appealing hotel in a town which has become very touristy. Run by the Laudenzi family since 1920, the Umbra is tucked away down a quiet alley off the main square, beyond a pretty walled garden. Bedrooms are mostly spacious and comfortable with old country furniture and some have lovely views over the countryside. There's a tiny but elegant lounge and a small terrace for sunbathing on the first floor. Regional specialities, including old recipes, are served in a light and elegant dining room or, in fine weather, on the pretty garden terrace, under the vines. The chef's speciality is *piccione alla ghiotta*, pigeon stuffed with ham, livers and herbs; if you choose this you are awarded a hand-painted ceramic plate (*piatto buon ricordo*). Half-board is not compulsory, but this is one of the best tables in Umbria. And all this charm, tranquillity and good eating is relatively cheap, especially by comparison with Tuscan prices.

Facilities: *27 bedrooms; restaurant (closed Tues)* **Credit/charge cards accepted:** *Amex, Diners, Eurocard, Visa*

Balbano
VILLA CASANOVA
55050 Nozzano

£
Closed Nov to Mar
Tel: (0583) 548429

A faded 18th-century *casa di campagna* in the hills between Lucca (10km) and Pisa, and a good, inexpensive base for exploring both towns, though not ideal for a long stay. Bedrooms are bare and simple, some with a certain rustic charm, others (on the top floor) very spartan. The restaurant, too, is a sensible, no-frills set-up, rather like a bistro with the day's menu written on a blackboard, gingham check tablecloths and flowers from the garden. There are rambling outbuildings and a terraced garden with fragrant shrubs and views over the valley; the swimming pool is not always in use.

Facilities: *40 bedrooms (including annexe); restaurant (closed lunch); lift; swimming pool; parking* **Credit/charge cards accepted:** *none*

Camaiore £
PERALTA *Closed Oct to mid-May*
55043 Lucca *Tel: (0584) 951230*

This is probably the most elusive hotel in Italy and it likes to remain that way. Bookings are normally made in England and without prior instructions you're unlikely to find this delightful spot in the hills above Viareggio. Formerly a hamlet whose livelihood centred on olives and chestnuts, Peralta is not so much a hotel as a cluster of converted buildings run on the lines of a house party. Guests eat and drink together, there's an English *cordon bleu* cook and the atmosphere is relaxed and congenial. Accommodation consists of rustic bedrooms with showers. In the main villa there are white stucco walls, open fireplaces, tiled floors, cushions on bamboo seats and benches and various games for wet days. It feels very isolated but there are beaches 20 minutes' drive away and Pisa and Lucca 45 minutes' away. It's also a lovely area for walking, with paths in every direction through the olive groves.

Facilities: *15 bedrooms; restaurant (closed Thurs); swimming pool; parking* **Credit/charge cards accepted:** *none* **UK reservations:** *Harrison Stanton and Haslam Ltd, 25 Studdridge Street, London SW6 3SL; tel: 01-736 5094.*

Campello sul Clitunno £
LE CASALINE *Open all year*
06042 Poreta di Spoleto *Tel: (0743) 520811*

Twelve km from Spoleto, near the Fonti del Clitunno, hymned by the ancient poets, this a a restaurant with rooms in a pretty, weathered old farmhouse surrounded by meadows and pine woods. It is a shambolic family-run place where no one takes any notice of you except at meal times. The chaotic atmosphere is replaced by a cool professionalism when the first guests arrive for dinner in the large, beamed trattoria, specialising in excellent charcoal-grilled meats. After dinner you retreat to a simple, rustic bedroom but there's no chance of breakfast before the staff arrive at 9am. For a quick getaway, it's as well to pay the bill the night before.

Facilities: *5 bedrooms; restaurant (closed Mon); parking* **Credit/charge cards accepted:** *Amex, Diners, Visa*

Castagneto Carducci £
LA TORRE *Open all year*
57022 Livorno *Tel: (0565) 775268*

A small, simple, cheap and very peaceful country hotel in an old rough-stone
house, beautifully set on a hill above the Tuscan coast between Livorno and
Grosseto, beside a ruined tower (mentioned in Dante's *Divine Comedy*). The
main building has the bedrooms, some with half-length baths and including
some triples and quads; there are no public rooms. The restaurant is in a
separate building and has boar on the walls and the menu, which also
includes good sausagey Tuscan *antipasto*. Breakfast can be taken on the
terrace, which has a slide and swing. Down at Marina di Castagneto there's a
long sandy beach and a vast children's playground.

Facilities: *11 bedrooms; restaurant (closed Mon); parking* **Credit/charge cards
accepted:** *Amex, Visa*

Elba £££
HERMITAGE *Closed Oct to Apr*
57037 Portoferraio *Tel: (0565) 969932*

The Hermitage consists of comfortable small cottages in pinewoods behind
the sandy bay of Biodola, 8km from Portoferraio. However, this is not the
hotel for a very private holiday, especially in high summer when there is
regular evening entertainment including a piano bar and beach barbecue.
Daytime activity revolves around the three swimming pools and six tennis
courts. Probably the best choice on Elba for a stay-put holiday – but not the
cheapest. The Biodola, under the same management, and with a longer
season, is a smaller, slightly cheaper alternative on the same bay.

Facilities: *110 bedrooms (AC in 66); restaurant; lift; swimming pools (heated);
tennis courts; parking* **Credit/charge cards accepted:** *Amex*

Gaiole in Chianti ££
CASTELLO DI SPALTENNA *Closed Nov to Mar*
53013 Siena *Tel: (0577) 749483*

This mellow stone building, solid and shuttered, built on a hill with sentinel
cypresses, is actually a 12th-century monastery attached to an even earlier
Romanesque church. As a hotel it offers just a few small, plain bedrooms;
most people come for the restaurant which is a huge vaulted hall complete
with a minstrel's gallery and roaring open fire. Simple Tuscan food like
crostini and charcoal-grilled meats, and *cantucci* dipped in *vin santo* are
served. At breakfast you can sample home-made honey and jam, a rare treat
in Italy. There's no bar as such, but a tranquil grassy courtyard where you
can sit in the evenings. An enchanting place for a couple of nights' stay.

Facilities: *7 bedrooms; restaurant (closed Mon, and Tues lunch); parking* **Credit/
charge cards accepted:** *Amex, Diners, Visa*

Greve in Chianti
GIOVANNI DA VERRAZZANO
Piazza Matteotti 28, 50022 Firenze

££
Closed Nov to Mar
Tel: (055) 853189

A good overnight touring stop in an area where it's hard to find reasonably-priced accommodation for less than three nights (especially at short notice). The hotel overlooks the market square and the statue of Verrazzano, the 16th-century discoverer of Manhattan (Amerigo Vespucci, who gave his name to America, was also born in Greve). Bedrooms are simply furnished with modern laminated units and shower rooms are basic; public rooms consist of a dark reception and bar and the trattoria itself. In an area of gorgeous countryside, many of the towns of the Chianti are rather disappointing; Greve, with its pretty triangular marketplace of green-shuttered buildings, is the exception. The verandah restaurant extension, with awning and potted plants, provides an admirable vantage point for the action below.

Facilities: *11 bedrooms; restaurant (closed Sun dinner and Mon)* **Credit/charge cards accepted:** *Amex, Diners*

Gubbio
BOSONE PALACE
Via XX settembre 22, 06024 Perugia

£
Closed Feb
Tel: (075) 9272008

Housed in an austere patrician villa with historic associations (one of the family had a sonnet dedicated to him by Petrarch and had Dante to stay) this is the classic place to stay in Gubbio: comfortable, traditional and cheap. It is also a good base for a day trip to Urbino, 60km away. The vast majority of the bedrooms are plain and sparely furnished in repro-rustic c1975 but there are also five attic rooms and several huge bedrooms with elaborate frescoed ceilings and lavish Renaissance furnishings – at no extra charge. There's no restaurant and the lounge and bar lack atmosphere, except for the breakfast room charmingly frescoed with *grotteschi*. There's an arrangement with a local restaurant, the *Taverna del Lupo* (closed Mon).

Facilities: *35 bedrooms; lift; garage* **Credit/charge cards accepted:** *Amex, Diners, Eurocard, Visa*

Monte San Savino
CASTELLO DI GARGONZA
52048 Arezzo

££
Closed Jan
Tel: (0575) 847021/53

The castle, owned by the family of Count Guicciardini, is in fact a walled medieval village where Dante is thought to have stayed in 1304. Within the walls are cobbled streets where little houses cluster for protection under the tower of the castle itself. These houses can be rented as self-catering properties by the week or used on a hotel basis (although bookings for one night may be refused). The restaurant, serving typical Tuscan food and wine from the estate, is just outside the walls. The houses have been sympathetically restored in typical Tuscan style, with the minimum of modern trappings. The grounds are extensive, with a lovely private garden. A swimming pool is planned.

Facilities: *40 bedrooms (in 20 separate houses); restaurant (closed Mon); parking* **Credit/charge cards accepted:** *Amex*

Orvieto ££££
LA BADIA *Closed Jan and Feb*
05019 Orvieto Scalo *Tel: (0763) 90359*

A converted Benedictine monastery in a beautiful situation looking up at Orvieto. The lovely buildings date from the 12th century. Rooms are averagely comfortable and traditionally furnished but surprisingly lacking in atmosphere. Food, too, can be institutional. Overall, however, the exceptional setting compensates for the shortcomings.

Facilities: *22 bedrooms (AC); restaurant (closed Wed); swimming pool; tennis courts; garage* **Credit/charge cards accepted:** *Amex, Eurocard, Visa*

Pancole £
LE RENAIE *Open all year*
53037 San Gimignano *Tel: (0577) 955044*

A few km north of San Gimignano, on the edge of a tiny village and in its own garden, this is a delightful and reasonably-priced hotel. One of Tuscany's few modern(ish) hotels, it has simple summery décor and furnishings (with a predominance of pink). Some bedrooms have private balconies where breakfast and even lunch can be served, and there's an elegant trattoria restaurant serving sound Tuscan cooking. A tranquil retreat from charming (but touristy) San Gimignano, and an equally good base for visiting Florence and Siena – with a swimming pool to come back to.

Facilities: *26 bedrooms; restaurant (closed Tues); swimming pool; parking* **Credit/ charge cards accepted:** *Amex, Diners, Eurocard, Visa*

Panzano in Chianti £££
VILLA LE BARONE *Closed Nov to Mar*
50020 Firenze *Tel: (055) 852215*

The Marchesa Viviani della Robbia, of the famous artist family, runs a most civilised country house retreat. More home than hotel, the villa has a series of calm, countrified rooms, with antique furniture, loose-covered sofas, books, and freshly-cut flowers. There's a low-key elegance that is, frankly, English. Half-board is compulsory but those wanting a degree of independence could stay in one of three annexes in converted old farm buildings. The pretty breakfast room has now been outgrown and there's a full scale restaurant in the old winery. The deliciously-sited swimming pool, with gorgeous Tuscan views, may weaken your resolve to spend the day sightseeing.

Facilities: *27 bedrooms (AC in several); restaurant; swimming pool; parking* **Credit/charge cards accepted:** *Amex*

Perugia   **£££**
LA ROSETTA   *Open all year*
Piazza Italia 19, 06100 Perugia   *Tel: (075) 20841*

La Rosetta is a large well-placed hotel, close to the sights and the shopping of
Perugia. Behind its vaguely Gothic, creeper-covered façade, set back from
the main Corso, is a hotel of patchy quality. The interior decoration is
unco-ordinated with an astonishing variety of styles, particularly in the
bedrooms which range from lofty, old-fashioned rooms with '50s furniture to
masculine rooms with clubby leather sofas, carpeted walls and built-in
furniture. Bathrooms range from brash to bizarre to beautiful. Public rooms
are drab with the exception of the cool vaulted restaurant, institutional in size
but serving sound Umbrian food at modest prices, popular with local
cognoscenti as well as hotel residents. You could try the *scaloppine alla perugina*,
escalopes with a chicken liver sauce; and there's a wider choice of desserts
than usual. In summer, dinner is served in the courtyard.

Facilities: *103 bedrooms; restaurant; lift; parking*   **Credit/charge cards accepted:**
Amex, Diners, Eurocard, Visa

Pistoia   **££**
IL CONVENTO   *Open all year*
Via San Quirico 33, 51100 Pistoia   *Tel: (0573) 452651*

In the hills above Pistoia, and about 5km east of the centre, a peaceful
whitewashed convent dating from 1800. Most of the character of the convent
has been preserved – from the high walls and the bare, cool public rooms
around a central courtyard to the tiny adjoining chapel. But bedrooms, plain,
whitewashed and rather small, are modernised and the bathrooms, almost
clinical in their cleanliness, have niceties such as bath foams and hairdriers
which the nuns would never have dreamt of. Especially attractive is the
restaurant, with several cosy little 'cells' for more intimate diners – or
families. A most tranquil place.

Facilities: *24 bedrooms; restaurant (closed Mon); swimming pool; parking*   **Credit/**
charge cards accepted: *Visa*

Porto Ercole   **£££££**
IL PELLICANO   *Closed Nov to Easter*
Cala dei Santi, 58018 Grossetto   *Tel: (0565) 833801*

A beautiful coastal setting and the comforts and atmosphere of a luxury
private villa makes this one of the most desirable and expensive places to stay
on the west coast of Italy. The accommodation consists of two- or
three-bedroomed villas, set on terraces and surrounded by gardens. Public
rooms in the main villas are beamed and decorated with pretty fabrics and
antiques and look on to the garden which leads down to the rocky coast.
There is no real beach but you can swim off the rocks or in a small pool.

Facilities: *34 bedrooms (AC); swimming pool (heated); tennis court; watersports;*
parking   **Credit/charge cards accepted:** *Amex, Diners, Visa*

Punta Ala
ALLELUJA
Via del Porto, 58040 Grosseto

£££££
Open all year
Tel: (0564) 922050

Punta Ala is a monopoly and its hotels are no doubt designed to complement rather than compete with each other, except in the sense that they are all very expensive. The Alleluja is an unobtrusive, low, plant-covered modern building set among spacious lawns and gardens with a pool and tennis court, and has the great advantage over the others of being within easy walking distance of the beach. The interior is simple but bright, comfortable and carpeted, with garden colours and lots of plants.

Facilities: *43 bedrooms (AC); restaurant; lift; swimming pool (heated); tennis court; parking* **Credit/charge cards accepted:** *Amex, Diners*

Radda in Chianti
PODERE TERRENO
53017 Siena

££
Closed Nov to Easter
Tel: (0577) 738312

A pretty old rough-stone *casa colonica* in the heart of the Chianti countryside between Radda and Volpaia (a perfect medieval village). It's not a hotel as such, but is run as a guesthouse by its charming young French owner, Sylvie Haniez. She and her English-speaking husband do all the cooking and guests sit together round a large refectory table in a delightful beamed living room with a huge open fireplace. Bedrooms (named after flowers and fruits) are whitewashed and prettily furnished with a mixture of rattan and old furniture, all with showers. Rooms are usually booked by the week.

Facilities: *5 bedrooms (+1 apartment); restaurant* **Credit/charge cards accepted:** *none*

Radda in Chianti
VILLA MIRANDA
53017 Siena

££
Open all year
Tel: (0577) 738021

A charming establishment run by a wily matriarchy, the Minucci family, since 1842. The *raison d'être* of the place is the restaurant (it is quite normal to arrive for lunch at 4pm), where delicious home-made food includes a legendary *ravioli*. Miranda (the grandmother) serves customers in the intoxicating shop where you can buy and sample wines, salamis and cheeses – including a superb chalky *pecorino*. Caterina and Alessandra cook and serve food in the cavernous trattoria. Since the 19th century this old inn has provided accommodation for travellers – originally a pallet of hay, now 22 attractive country bedrooms, each named rather than numbered. There are no public rooms to speak of; you enter the restaurant through the shop and the family's main room. The villa opposite has been converted to provide more bedrooms and a swimming pool to encourage longer stays.

Facilities: *35 bedrooms; restaurant; swimming pool; tennis court* **Credit/charge cards accepted:** *none*

Rigoli   **£**
VILLA CORLIANO   *Open all year*
56017 Pisa   *Tel: (050) 818193*

This superb villa is still in the hands of the family who bought the estate for
1,500 florins in 1448; its present owner, the Conte Ferdinando Agostino della
Seta, converted it to a hotel in 1980. It's about 10km from Pisa, set in a huge
park with a sweeping gravel drive. Inside, there's a frescoed *salone*, too
daunting to be comfortable but marvellous to look at. Bedrooms have some
original features – like frescoed ceilings – too, and are large but not luxurious.
Furniture is old rather than antique and the bathrooms are damp and
untiled – prehistoric compared with most villa conversions. There's a cool,
vaulted breakfast room but no restaurant. An aristocratic villa at less than
country house prices, well-placed for Pisa (including the airport) and Lucca.

Facilities: *17 bedrooms (only 6 with private facilities); parking*   **Credit/charge
cards accepted:** *Amex, Eurocard, Visa*

San Gregorio   **£**
CASTEL SAN GREGORIO   *Open all year*
06081 Assisi   *Tel: (075) 8038009*

Half-way between Perugia and Assisi, and a good base for visiting both
towns, the Castel San Gregorio is set in parkland overlooking the Plain of
Angels. It's a wisteria-covered miniature castle of indeterminate age,
apparently built from the ruins of the real Castel San Gregorio just up the
road, and a fairly eccentric establishment. Bedrooms, of which there are just
twelve, have either huge antique beds or quasi four-posters with curious
linen drapes of medieval inspiration. They vary considerably in size; some
have amusing circular bathrooms in the turrets. There's a cosy, elegant little
reading room. Throughout the décor is wintry – warm-toned felt walls and
carpets, plus raftered ceilings and dark period furniture. Meals are served at
a large dining table and guests left to get to know each other and overcome
language barriers; there is no menu and you are offered good, plain home
cooking and wine from the estate.

Facilities: *12 bedrooms; restaurant; parking*   **Credit/charge cards accepted:** *none*

San Gimignano   **£**
PESCILLE   *Open all year*
53037 Siena   *Tel: (0577) 940186*

A charming converted farmhouse just 3km from San Gimignano (of which
there is a classic view from the car park in front of the hotel). The hotel has
been simply decorated with great flair, and liberal use of natural materials:
oak and rattan furniture, terracotta floors and rush matting. Bedrooms at the
front have a marvellous view of San Gimignano; those at the back overlook
the gardens and vineyards. Old agricultural implements displayed on the
walls are a reminder that this is still part of a viable estate; the wine is sold at
the reception desk. Bedrooms are cool and stuccoed with fresh green-and-
white bathrooms. The lovely grassy garden is fairly wild, with the swimming

pool set apart in a partially walled area. There's now a smart new restaurant and lunches are served on the terrace. There's also an arrangement with the restaurant of the Bel Soggiorno hotel in San Gimignano (closed Mon) which serves excellent classic Tuscan dishes (like *pappardelle alla lepre*) at remarkably low prices.

Facilities: *32 bedrooms; restaurant; swimming pool; tennis court; parking* **Credit/ charge cards accepted:** *Amex, Diners, Eurocard, Visa*

Siena
CERTOSA DI MAGGIANO
Strada di Certosa 82, 53100 Siena

£££££
Closed mid-Nov to mid-Dec
Tel: (0577) 288180

The mellow, tranquil cloister of the oldest Carthusian monastery in Tuscany (built in 1314) is a fitting entrance to an immaculate hotel, exclusive in both size (5 bedrooms, 9 apartments) and price (ensuring a mainly trans-Atlantic clientele). The interior is decorated like an elegant country house with floral curtains and comfortable armchairs, antiques and paintings and vastly extravagant flower arrangements. Bathrooms are bright and modern. There's a clubby red library with leather studded wing chairs, card tables and a stereo system; the bar is no more than a discreet drinks cupboard. The dining room, a small vaulted room, is exquisite and rather intimate in scale; dining under the arcades overlooking the pool is more informal and relaxed. There's a peaceful garden with an English-style lawn, fruit trees, and views over the vineyards to Siena.

Facilities: *5 bedrooms (+9 suites); restaurant; lift; swimming pool (heated); tennis court; parking* **Credit/charge cards accepted:** *Amex, Diners, Visa*

Siena
PALAZZO RAVIZZA
Pian dei Mantellini 34, 53100 Siena

££
Open all year
Tel: (0577) 280462

A very traditional establishment which has been in the same family for around 200 years. It's in a 17th-century mansion about five minutes' walk from the Piazza del Campo and a stone's throw from the art gallery. Half *pensione*, half *palazzo*, it is old-fashioned but spacious with more than a hint of faded grandeur (family portraits, a private chapel, a grand piano). Most of the public rooms have a rather wintry-snug feeling with antique furnishings and little natural light, bedrooms too are lofty and large but dark. The saving grace is the quiet gravelled garden with lovely views over the countryside. A civilised retreat from the city and tourists, but probably nicest off-season when you are not tied to half-board in the sober, even institutional, dining room. Prices are realistic for people on a touring holiday.

Facilities: *28 bedrooms; restaurant (closed Nov to Mar); lift* **Credit/charge cards accepted:** *Amex, Diners, Eurocard, Visa*

Sinalunga
£££££
LOCANDA DELL' AMOROSA
Closed Jan and Feb
53048 Siena
Tel: (0577) 679497

A long, straight line of cypresses leads to a collection of lovely Renaissance buildings grouped round a gravelled courtyard. The old cowstalls house the excellent restaurant where, appropriately, Val di Chiana beef is the speciality. In the villa (1575) and outbuildings are the spacious, pleasant bedrooms whose sober rustic décor is enlivened with old prints and pretty fabrics. Modernisation is restricted to the bathrooms, all with baskets of soaps and sachets. The old tower has been converted to an apartment for four people. Within half an hour's drive of Arezzo and Siena, Pienza and Montepulciano, an exquisitely spoiling place to explore southern Tuscany and northern Umbria.

Facilities: *8 bedrooms; restaurant (closed Mon, and Tues lunch); parking* **Credit/charge cards accepted:** *Amex, Diners, Visa*

Spoleto
££
GATTAPONE
Open all year
Via del Ponte 6, 06049 Perugia
Tel: (0743) 36147

A small hotel in a perfect quiet position at the top of the town, between the castle and the magnificent old bridge (Gattapone was the architect) which is reserved for pedestrians and ideal for an evening stroll. The cathedral is also nearby and lit up at night. The Gattapone was a luxury building site when we visited, and work (to create a restaurant) is still in progress. Bedrooms are spacious and handsomely modernised, with marble, brass and dark wood. There is a plush leathery bar, strewn with art mags.

Facilities: *13 bedrooms (AC in 5)* **Credit/charge cards accepted:** *Amex, Diners, Eurocard, Visa*

Todi
££
BRAMANTE
Open all year
Via Orvietana 48, 06059 Perugia
Tel: (075) 8848381

Almost equidistant from Orvieto, Perugia, Assisi and Spoleto, the Bramante is named after the architect of the lovely Santa Maria della Consolazione, in whose shadow it lies. The hotel is smart and modern, but in the shell of an old (14th-century) stone-walled convent. The interior is cool and creamy, a very Italian juxtaposition of ancient and modern which is long on comfort but short on charm. It is used for conferences and banquets and facilities include a discothèque and congress room.

Facilities: *43 bedrooms (AC); restaurant (closed Mon); lift; tennis court; parking* **Credit/charge cards accepted:** *Amex, Diners, Eurocard*

Torgiano   **££££**
LE TRE VASELLE   *Open all year*
Via Garibaldi 48, 06089 Perugia   *Tel: (075) 982447*

A rather insignificant building in a side street of a hilltop Umbrian village
conceals one of the area's most comfortable hotels. The rooms are elegant
and spacious with antique furniture and works of art and an abundance of
fresh flowers. Meals are served on the terrace or in the dining room, which
serves delicious Umbrian specialities and Lungarotti wines. Torgiano is
known for its excellent wine museum – which is under the same ownership
as the hotel – so, not surprisingly, the cellars are well-stocked. Le Tre Vaselle
is not cheap, but it is an attractive alternative to staying in Perugia (15km)
and is a good choice for those who regard food and wine as a higher priority
than gardens and swimming pools.

Facilities: *48 bedrooms (AC); restaurant; lift; parking*   **Credit/charge cards
accepted:** *Amex, Diners, Eurocard, Visa*

Volterra   **£**
VILLA NENCINI   *Open all year*
Borgo Santo Stefano 55, 56048 Pisa   *Tel: (0588) 86386*

Just outside the medieval walls of Volterra, with fine views of the city and
hills (even the sea on a clear day) beyond, but within easy walking distance
of the centre, this is an attractive, neat, hotel in a restored 17th-century villa.
Bedrooms are light and spotless with simple pine furniture and white walls,
although a few are cramped in size. The three attic bedrooms, with sloping
pine ceilings, share a bathroom; the rest have private ones. There's no
restaurant but a good breakfast is served in the whitewashed and
brick-vaulted bar, hung with old French mezzotints of Tuscan towns.
Volterra's restaurants (many with characteristic pavement plinths for
outdoor dining) are within ten minutes' walk. Tables and chairs in the
garden obviate the need for a lounge on fine days. Very cheap for such a
convenient and attractive place.

Facilities: *14 bedrooms; parking*   **Credit/charge cards accepted:** *Eurocard*

ROME

*❝While stands the Coliseum, Rome shall stand;
When falls the Coliseum, Rome shall fall; And
when Rome falls – the World ❞*

LORD BYRON

Colosseum

Introduction

Ever since the era when all roads led there, Rome has been an idea
as well as a city: mother of civilisation, centre of power, source of
authority. Her earliest history is mixed with legend: Romulus the
shepherd-leader, fortifying the Palatine Hill; six more kings of Rome
including the Tarquin who raped Lucretia; Horatius at the bridge,
defending the city against exiled Tarquins and their Etruscan allies.
Five centuries BC the Romans rejected their kings and formed a
Republic. By 390BC they had conquered hostile neighbours –
Etruscans, Latins, Volscians. Then the Gauls arrived and destroyed
their city; the last legend of early Rome is the night attack on the
Capitol, thwarted by the cackling of Juno's sacred geese.

Less than a hundred years later the Romans had rebuilt their seat
of power and were challenging Greece and Carthage on their way to
winning the world. No enemy invaded their city again until the
Goths and Vandals, in the 5th century AD. Republic and Empire
spent the wealth of nations making Rome the finest capital the world
had ever known – richer than Athens, than Egypt, than Babylon.
Augustus, who "found it brick and left it marble", assembled there
most of the world's art treasures. For three centuries his successors
outdid each other in calculated effects to earn them adulation and
immortal memory. But by the 3rd century AD Rome was on the
defensive along every northern border, and in 271 Aurelian began a
wall around the city. The last great construction was to the glory of
God, not Constantine: in 326 he built the first basilica of St Peter.

The political supremacy of Empire dissolved in the Dark Ages, but
Rome through the presence of the popes was still the centre of
Western Christendom: the papacy acquired a unique blend of
spiritual and temporal power, rooted in Rome as the shrine of St
Peter. When, rich and corrupt, the papal court removed to Avignon
for the whole of the 14th century, Rome withered into the "rubbish
heap of history" mourned by Petrarch; while other Italian cities
flourished in the spring of the Renaissance, Rome was culturally
paralysed by the problems of the church.

A crumbling, depopulated medieval city was slowly restored with
the wealth brought by tens of thousands of 15th-century pilgrims,
and Rome approached a second age of supremacy. She herself
produced no great artists, but they came from Tuscany and Umbria
to decorate her churches under a succession of patron popes. For
Julius II, Michelangelo and Raphael laboured simultaneously in the
Vatican, and the new St Peter's got under way. In 1527 the city was
brutally invaded – a result of papal involvement in complicated
European politics and scant regard for the emerging Reformation in
Europe. The Sack of Rome symbolised the end of the optimism of
the Renaissance; Italy was to be dominated by the influence of Spain
for 150 years of repression and Inquisition. But Rome itself became
the European artistic capital of the 17th century. Counter-
reformation popes restored and rebuilt in swathes of town-
planning, and the triumphant swirl of Baroque style transformed

the city. The travertine stone of palatial façades became more dominant than Renaissance marble or medieval brick. A vast new basilica of St Peter – begun by Bramante, redesigned by Michelangelo and extended by Carlo Maderna – was completed inside by the architect, sculptor and painter Bernini; outside he built tall sweeping colonnades to unify the expanses of the piazza into a superb approach, his architectural masterpiece. The statues of saints fluttering stone draperies on the skyline, the central obelisk and splendid fountains are found repeated in settings only less magnificent all over Rome; scores of her churches were transformed by Bernini, his followers and his competitors into sumptuous visionary caverns.

The operatic richness of Baroque art was matched by the festivals and carnivals of an extravagant Baroque lifestyle – the papal equivalent of "bread and circuses". Through the 18th century Rome's residents were almost outnumbered by tourists and pilgrims, who wrote copious accounts of her splendours with only occasional complaints of her squalor. Impoverished Romans of all ranks made the most they could from *"Milordi pelabili clienti"* – "fleeceable customers" – who came to the city much as to a museum, for the evocative ruins of her classical past. The last great example of papal patronage of the arts was the purchase of ancient treasures up for sale to admiring foreigners, and their display in the Vatican's Museo Pio-Clementino.

Papal Rome – "a city misgoverned for centuries in the name of all that is sacred by a semi-divine priest-prince" – was not easily made the capital of a united Italy. After Napoleon's iconoclastic reforms, annexation of the Papal States and dismissal of "Citizen Pope", the status quo was restored with punitive repression. All over Italy revolution fermented, while a new generation of tourists fed their 19th-century Romanticism on the decay and corruption of the Eternal City. In every theory of Italian nationalism, from Gioberti's federation under the pope to Mazzini's free republic, Rome was its inevitable centre. But when a Kingdom of Italy was achieved its capital was first Turin, then Florence: the pope held Rome for nine years, protected by French troops as well as his spiritual authority. Forced in 1870 to concede the city, Pius IX issued excommunications all round and retired to the Vatican, whence no pope emerged for half a century.

Turin became Italy's biggest industrial centre; Florence remained an immaculate artistic showpiece; Rome simply grew. A population of 230,000 in 1870 reached a million by 1940 and is over three million today. The first invasion of state officialdom began a building boom, attracting a steady flood of immigrants from the countryside, whose poverty contrasted with new bureaucratic affluence. Planning was minimal, speculation avid and only briefly checked by collapse and bankruptcies in 1887. To foreign eyes Rome was vandalised anew, as office and apartment blocks, consulates and embassies, hotels and shops sprang up; new streets and whole new districts were developed. The final flourish of the 19th century was the enormous monument to Victor Emmanuel II in stupefying white marble; it remains the most visible building in the city.

The Fascist regime further "improved" the city centre; most controversial was the Via della Conciliazone to St Peter's, commemorating the Lateran Treaty with the pope. It was Mussolini who sponsored the enormous complexes of E.U.R (Esposizione Universale di Roma) south of Rome; post-war Rome is steadily covering with *Quartieri* and *Suburbi* the flat lands in all directions beyond the Aurelian Wall. Taking Fascism, war and terrorism into due account, the biggest impact of the 20th century on Rome has been its traffic. Buildings are threatened by its pollution and vibration, people more immediately under stress from noise, delays and the chariot-racing style of Roman drivers.

Traffic, crowds and southern summer heat apart, a first visit to Rome can be overpowering and discouraging. Guidebooks explain how much there is to see, how it takes planning and energy, how to select; they cannot convey how the scope and scale of it all assault the eye. The Baroque can repel taste trained on Gothic and Romanesque; mixed orgies of style can induce longings for the unity of Florence. Tourists of earlier times had fewer problems. One of the luckiest was Henry James in 1869, whose first day was ecstatic: "I went reeling and moaning through the streets in a fever of enjoyment. In the course of four or five hours I traversed almost the whole of Rome and got a glimpse of everything – the Forum, the Coliseum (stupendissimo!), the Pantheon, the Castle of St Angelo – all the Piazzas and ruins and monuments. The effect is something indescribable. For the first time I know what the picturesque is..... Even if I should leave Rome tonight I should feel that I have caught the keynote of its operation on the senses." On the other hand a combination of classical education and high Romantic expectation doomed Wordsworth to disappointment: "Is this, ye Gods, the Capitolean Hill?/Yon pretty steep in truth the fearful rock/Tarpeian named of yore?"

Two thousand years of construction and demolition have rather filled up the valleys between Rome's original Seven Hills and more. But the city still goes up and down a lot, in elevations too gentle for their title of Monte this and that but ideal for flights of steps, and there is a ring of natural viewpoints from which to get things in perspective. To the south, the ridge of the Aventine commands the whole panorama. From the gardens of the Janiculum, nearer and twice as high, Rome is revealed as many-coloured – overall ochre and sienna, blending russet and red brick, creamy travertine stone and blue-grey domes, the greens of pine and cyprus, the gleam of marble. Across the Tiber the high terrace of the Pincio Gardens is the traditional place to watch the sun set behind St Peter's dome and cupola. St Peter's roof – complete with coffee shop and post office – is a wonderful airy point of vantage; and the central views from the portico of the Victor Emmanuel Monument are splendid.

Exploring in the crowded streets and piazzas, even the non-specialist tourist tends to develop loyalties – statuphilia, fontomania. Fountains are very friendly affairs, sat on and dabbled in however grand, sculpture in close-up. Running water has inspired superb and inventive work, from the charming symmetry of the Fontana delle Tartarughe to the riotous assembly of the Trevi, or the *"Barcaccia"* – a gracefully sinking boat making the most of sluggish water pressure. Bernini's compositions include the heraldic bees of his Barberini pope alighting on a scallop shell, and his celebrated "Moor" and "Triton", realistic figures in a repertoire of nymphs and dolphins. Al fresco art regarded with passing affection is as much a Roman experience as solemn art inside the churches, where ritual and sanctity coexist with guided tours, or in the Vatican Museums where crowded miles of magnificence have colour-coded routes. St Peter's is annihilatingly solemn and magnificent. Everything inside the world's largest church is so proportionately enormous that size is only slowly apparent, as tiny human figures recede down the nave: under the dome comes the shock of tremendous space. Michelangelo's Pietà, in a side chapel, is the loveliest single object in a continuous immensity of mosaic and gilt.

The only antidote to Baroque is ancient Imperial. Today as in classical times Rome is governed from the Capitol, where the Senatorial Palace is flanked by museums in the Piazza del Campidoglio, a piece of Michelangelic town planning. Below is the Forum, an archaeologists' dream of a scrapyard which reconstructions suggest was always ugly. The Palatine, a much more complex riddle of a site going back to the Romulus legend of 753BC, has agreeable grassy gardens for picnic lunches. Close by, the Colosseum outranks all Rome's better-preserved arches and columns and temples. Until the mid-18th century it was despite universal admiration used regularly as a quarry; incomplete but set in order, it is massively evocative of gladiators, martyrs, beasts and 50,000 bloodthirsty spectators.

Around the silent ruins of Empire and the fixed shrines of the Church, modern Rome is a series of cross-currents. To the complexities of a cosmopolitan city have been added those of a national capital. State bureaucrats and diplomats, Vatican bureaucrats and diplomats, international bureaucrats and diplomats share space with local government, big business and the tourist industry. International bodies and academies swell the numbers of students, archaeologists, artists, historians, planners. In the 1950s and '60s the success of the Italian film industry brought American glamour to "Hollywood on the Tiber", and the glittering social life of filmstars, millionaires, writers and Italian aristocracy lit up the Via Veneto. By the time Fellini immortalised the party it had moved on to more private surroundings, but the legendary *dolce vita* still attracts evening crowds to the famous nightspots – Doney's, Harry's Bar, the Café de Paris. Romans swear that in the '80s there are only nonentities, whores and purse snatchers to be found in the Via Veneto, and that the social life of today reflects the swing in taste to politics. Yet a glow of *dolce vita* is part of everyone's memory of Rome. It has the rhythms of sun and siesta, the relaxed style which takes beauty for granted, and the animation of a theatre where the visiting crowds have always been an audience.

THE RENAISSANCE IN ROME

If it's true that you can't buy artistic talent, no one told pope Julius II, a Ligurian with a name (della Rovere) meaning oak, a personality to match, and a driving ambition to rival the achievements of an earlier Roman Julius. During his short tenure of the papal throne (1503-13) Julius transformed Rome from a political and cultural backwater into one of the leading players in the game of European power politics and the new creative focus, in place of Florence, of art in central Italy.

Considering the importance of religious art as a medium and of Antiquity as an inspiration, it is hardly surprising that the Renaissance found its full expression in Rome. The brief period (which ends with the city's sack at the hands of imperial troops in 1527) has been seen not only as the climax of the Renaissance but as the all-time zenith in the history of post-classical art. Raphael and Michelangelo set the standard for centuries of hero-worshipping artists.

In the absence of any great local artists Julius cast around for talent. This was not new: in the late 15th century pope Sixtus IV had brought in the best artists of the day – Botticelli, Perugino and others – to decorate the walls of his new chapel in the Vatican with frescoes. Beautiful as the results of this and other similar papal commissions are, they are not a new departure; the history of art would not be very different without them. Things changed under Julius II, partly because of the artists and the influence of ancient Rome on them, partly because Julius had the imagination ambition equal to their powers and inspired them to new heights of achievement.

The new dimension is monumentality. To Florentine grace is added weight, muscularity, a new interest in the nude and the expressive power of the idealised male body (as opposed to facial expression), and a preference for grand, simple forms over ornamental detail. Returning from Rome in 1514 the Florentine Fra Bartolommeo painted a St Sebastian to prove his mastery of the nude; women sinned at the sight of it, records Vasari. He also painted a St Mark "to show his mastery of large figures."

One result is that works are easily detached from their specific context and interpreted as general statements on the universal themes of life, to which Michelangelo's genius in particular was ideally suited. When asked why the princes commemorated in the Medici chapel in Florence were not represented by portraits, he replied that in a thousand years no one would care what these men looked like. In lesser hands, the generalised is not universal but vacuous.

In their attempt to breathe new life into the art of Antiquity artists were influenced by the expressive force of Hellenistic sculpture, especially the intensely emotional Laocoön, a statue from the 1st century BC known from Pliny's description and discovered in a Roman vineyard in 1506. Another key work was the Belvedere Torso, a fragment of a statue of Hercules from the same period which Michelangelo repeatedly studied and reconstructed in his own art (including the famous image of the Creation of Man on the Sistine Chapel ceiling). Both works are now in the Vatican museum.

Unafraid to tear down the old to make way for the new, Julius boldly decided to rebuild St Peter's. His architect Bramante's expressed aim was to place the Pantheon on top of the basilica of Constantine, a vast centralised domed structure on a scale to outdo the most famous and biggest of antique buildings. As a centrepiece Julius imagined his own tomb and called on Michelangelo to build it. The artist came up with a design for a free-standing monument with an architectural framework for reliefs and scores of statues. Perhaps fortunately, Julius's interest in the tomb, which would have kept Michelangelo fully occupied for decades, soon waned and much to the artist's disgust the project degenerated into a sequence of scaling-down compromises. The last version is in the Roman church of San Pietro in Vincoli, assembled by Michelangelo's pupils but including the famous Moses, a massive and magnificent fragment of the

THE RENAISSANCE IN ROME

original project and a striking indication of its impossibly ambitious scale.

Michelangelo referred to the project as a tragedy, but the ideas and forms of the tomb resurfaced in much of his later work; not only Moses and the various statues of slaves and prisoners directly related to the tomb, but also the Medici chapel in Florence and in a formal sense the ceiling of the Sistine chapel, the project on which Julius employed Michelangelo in 1508. Its scheme – painted scenes surrounded by an architectural framework inhabited by a population of prophets, sybils and beautiful naked males – is that of the tomb transposed onto a ceiling.

Rejecting assistance, Michelangelo painted the ceiling in a superhuman solo effort over four years. He wrote that his brush dropped a rich mosaic on his face all day long, and by the end he could read letters only by holding them above his head. In narrative terms the scenes run from the Separation of Light and Dark to the Drunkenness of Noah, but they were painted in reverse order and demand to be viewed and probably interpreted that way, as a spiritual journey towards the altar from the earthly prison to celestial liberation, with the Creation of Man its centrepiece and the Creation of Light its climax. The scenes and figures are depicted with growing energy and power as the artist/creator, who began the project an inexperienced and reluctant fresco painter, warmed to his task. The later prophets burst out of the painted architectural framework in which the earlier ones sit so calmly, and seem to prophesy the art of the future.

The Last Judgement on the end wall of the chapel was not painted by Michelangelo until much later (1536-41). Its sombre mood forms a striking contrast with the ceiling and seems to express both personal despair and the crisis of confidence brought about by the sack of Rome and a crescendo of religious dissent throughout Europe.

Raphael was recommended to the pope by his compatriot Bramante and came to Rome in 1508 to decorate a series of apartments now known simply as Raphael's rooms (Stanze). The finest of the frescoes are those in the library (Stanza della Segnatura), painted while Michelangelo was at work in the chapel just down the corridor. The suspicious Michelangelo had no affection for the young womaniser whom he accused of plagiarism. One artful borrowing was the late addition to one fresco of a figure, probably a portrait of Michelangelo, alone with his thoughts at the foot of the steps populated with more sociable groups of philosophers and mathematicians. The beautiful architectural setting for this scene (The School of Athens) probably comes closer to Bramante's plan for St Peter's than the building finally completed nearly a century later.

Raphael never ceased to experiment and the frescoes in the later Stanze combine a more weighty figure style, much influenced by Michelangelo, with more agitated composition. As the successful manager of a large workshop of specialist assistants, Raphael has kept art historians busy trying to identify the different hands at work in these frescoes and the other decorative projects and oil paintings he supervised, and to some extent participated in, until his early death in 1520.

In the less heroic, supremely civilised environment of Rome under Medici pope Leo X (1513-21), Raphael took a particular interest in archaeology and ancient Roman decorative painting, which he revived in a neo-classical style of great fidelity and inventiveness, probably taking a closer personal interest in such projects as painting a cardinal's bathroom in the new style than in much bigger projects. The fresco of Galatea in the Villa Farnesina is the masterpiece of this pagan side of Raphael's art, perhaps more appealing than his grand manner, at its most noble, graceful and influential in the set of tapestry designs (now in the Victoria and Albert museum) for the Sistine chapel.

Visiting Rome

There are daily scheduled flights (from London and Manchester) and regular charter flights (from London). Scheduled flights arrive at Fiumicino airport (30km); most charter flights at Ciampino (18km). Bus transport to the city centre is available from both. The train journey from London takes 24 hours; coach or car (with an overnight stop) considerably longer.

The best way to see Rome is on foot. Many of the most interesting sights are tucked away in the backstreets where traffic is restricted. Most sights are quite manageable from a fairly central hotel but the cobbled streets and hills take their toll. Bus services are frequent and efficient; you can get a map of routes from the tourist office. There's a flat fare; you buy tickets from newsstands, bars or tobacconists, enter the bus by the back door, and stamp your ticket in the machine. A weekly *abbonamento* or 3-day Roma Pass, available from the Azienda Tranvie Autobus Comunale (ATAC) booth on Piazza dei Cinquecento, is also valid on the underground (*metropolitana*). The underground system is limited, but it's swift, simple and usually uncrowded. Tickets are sold from machines in stations, or at newsstands.

Taxis wait at ranks in all main piazzas. There are supplements for luggage, for hiring after 10pm, and on Sundays and bank holidays. Drivers are entitled to charge double fares to the airports. Horse-drawn carriages (*carrozze*) congregate in the Piazza di Spagna; they are used only by tourists and you should bargain to fix a fare.

If you have a car, you should opt for a hotel with guarded (*custodito*) parking. There are plans to close more of the historic centre to traffic; already you need a permit for the streets round the Via del Corso (police in the piazza del Popolo regularly check motorists for permits). Driving requires snappy judgement and some bravado ("when in Rome..."). There's much hooting, overtaking, and cutting in and many drivers seem oblivious to red traffic lights. Car parks, though plentiful, are expensive.

Several companies offer almost identical tours of Rome and the surrounding area, from city sightseeing trips and papal audiences to evening tours of Tivoli (including dinner) and day trips to the Castelli Romani (nearby hill towns) or further afield to Etruscan sites and even other major cities. You can travel more cheaply by public transport; for information on out-of-town buses telephone Acotral (06-5798).

For the tourist, the most attractive area to stay in is medieval Rome, either side of the Via del Corso and within easy walking distance of many of the sights. There are plenty of small and relatively inexpensive hotels in this area, and to the west of the Via del Corso lie many of Rome's better restaurants and *trattorie*. The station area is cheaper but generally insalubrious, and most of the hotels on the Via Veneto are expensive and faded. The Aventine could suit people who want peace and quiet at a low cost; but they'll need to take buses (or, at night, cars) into the centre.

You can take a package tour to Rome by air for anything from two nights to two weeks. Over Easter, prices rocket to high-season level. Most tour operators use the larger hotels around the Via Veneto and the noisy Via Nazionale, and around the station. They generally offer a choice of grand old hotels or modern, purpose-built ones. Going independently is nearly always cheaper than taking a package if you choose a cheaper, more convenient (and probably more charming) place to stay; even staying at a grand hotel could work out cheaper if you opt for a charter flight.

There are advantages and disadvantages in visiting Rome at any time of year. In summer there are open-air concerts and opera performances at the ancient sites, but in August the city is deserted by everyone except tourists, and it is usually too hot for sightseeing. Spring can be lovely, with hot days and balmy evenings as early as May; September and early October are usually reliable. Winter temperatures and sunshine hours average well above those of London, but it can be chill, dull and damp.

Area by area guide

THE AVENTINE

The southernmost of Rome's original seven hills is now a sedate residential district, an oasis of peace above the hubbub of the city. Here faded villas bask behind high walls cascading with fragrant oleander, and activity is limited to the odd scurrying nun and the scratching of cicadas. The tranquillity is almost rural (but at dead of night there are car thieves about).

The classic approach to the Aventine is from the Piazza Bocca della Verità with its two charming little classical temples and the church of Santa Maria in Cosmedin. Near here Faustulus is said to have found Romulus and Remus. From the piazza you climb a narrow walled street to the lovely early basilica of Santa Sabina and from the quiet little Parco Savello you can look out over Trastevere to St Peter's. At the top of the hill is the delightful Piazza dei Cavalieri di Malta, designed by the 18th-century engraver Piranesi, with whimsical stone obelisks and trophies. However, the main attraction in this quiet little square is the view of St Peter's seen through a hole above the lock of the Knights' Priory, the dome framed by a pergola in the garden. This famous architectural conceit inevitably attracts tourist coaches and ice cream vans to an otherwise drowsy backwater. The other great view to be enjoyed from the Aventine is from the Piazzale Romolo e Remo where you can survey the vast desolate oval tract of the Circus Maximus, chariot-racing stadium of the Romans, with the impressive backdrop of the imperial palaces on the Palatine Hill. The Circus is now gravelled and surrounded by grass, and used mainly by youngsters playing football, but it's still very evocative and if you half-close your eyes you can hear the thunder of hooves and the cheering of 30,000 spectators.

Main roads surround the base of the hill; across the busy and boring Viale Aventino lies the Little Aventine, a more modern and less appealing residential area except for the much-restored early church of Santa Saba, with a Renaissance loggia containing sculptural fragments. Nearby is the Roman gateway of Porta San Paolo and beside it the monumental Pyramid of Caius Cestius, built in 12-11BC as the tomb of a Roman praetor. Just beyond is the Protestant Cemetery with its more recent tombs, notably that of Keats: "here lies one whose name was writ in water".

The Via Ostiense, a busy road out of the city, leads to the E.U.R., Mussolini's soulless garden suburb, completed in the 1950s.

Churches
Santa Maria in Cosmedin
Santa Sabina
San Paolo fuori le Mura

Hotels
Sant'Anselmo

TRASTEVERE

Traditionally compared with the Quartier Latin or Greenwich
Village, Trastevere (literally "across the Tiber") is considered the
Bohemian, radical district, its inhabitants something of a race apart,
at least in popular imagination. The Trasteverini stoutly claim to be
the only true descendants of the original Romans and, while it is
true that many who live on the right bank of the Tiber have done so
only for a couple of generations, this theory ignores the fact that in
the Middle Ages there was a sizeable community of oriental traders,
particularly Jews, in the area. The myth persists that it is only
recently that inhabitants of Trastevere have taken to crossing the
river at all.

The psychological gap is spanned in a matter of minutes by
one of several ancient bridges; the oldest, the Ponte Fabricio, and
the Ponte Cestio moor the ship-shaped Tiber Island to the bank.
First impressions of Trastevere may be disappointing; while many
people have preconceived notions of a quaint, Bohemian quarter full
of artists and poets, the reality is somewhat different. Trastevere is a
robust working class community and parts of it are dreary and traffic
choked. Its narrow streets have always been a haven for shady
characters and it is now notorious for drug addicts and petty
thieves, earning it the new nickname of "Trashtevere". Despite this
caveat there are indeed medieval lanes and piazzas and you can
search out local markets and surprising gardens, find hidden
cloisters and see Romanesque *campanili* soaring above the terracotta
roofscape. There are churches to be admired, backstreet *trattorie* and
osterie to be sampled. In the more touristy restaurants, such as those
on the picturesque Piazza dei Mercanti, menus are self-consciously
written in the Trastevere dialect. On Sunday mornings bargain
hunters flock to the Porta Portese flea market.

The heart of Trastevere is the pretty Piazza di Santa Maria in
Trastevere where from one of several pavement bars and restaurants
you can admire the glittering 12th-century mosaics on the façade of
the church. During the day the square with its dilapidated houses,
peeling posters and graffiti can be rather forlorn. Junkies often sit
round the fountain, muzzled dogs scrounge for scraps and boys
dribble a football in desultory fashion. But on fine evenings the
restaurants fill up, the mosaics are floodlit, and the atmosphere is
lively.

Beyond Trastevere, parallel to the Tiber, rises the Janiculum Hill
(Monte Gianicolo), a good place to walk off lunch. The park, laid out
with avenues of plane trees in the last century, is known chiefly for
its fine views and historical interest; here, in 1849, Garibaldi took his
heroic stand against the French. From the Piazza in front of San
Pietro in Montorio you can look out over Trastevere and the Palatine
and Aventine hills, as well as glimpse Bramante's exquisite
Tempietto. Further up there is a splendid panorama of the city. A
dignified equestrian statue of Garibaldi contrasts with that of his
wife, who (like some side-saddle cowboy) brandishes her pistol
while holding onto her baby. Busts of their followers line the paths.
The Gianicolo is particularly popular at weekends, when the Piazza

Garibaldi is crowded with young people, radios blaring and
motorbikes revving, leaving a trail of litter and discarded syringes.

Churches
Santa Cecilia in Trastevere
Santa Maria in Trastevere
San Pietro in Montorio and Tempietto

Galleries and museums
Corsini Gallery
Villa Farnesina

THE VATICAN AND AROUND

It was to commemorate the Lateran Treaty of 1929 which established
the Vatican City as a separate state that the ceremonial approach to
St Peter's, the Via della Conciliazione, was conceived. The ruthless
destruction of the medieval quarter of the Borgo to make way for it
has been much criticised and the rather dull architecture adds insult
to injury. Nevertheless, you cannot but be impressed by the majesty
of the prospect of Bernini's vast piazza, with its colonnaded, all-
embracing wings, and the great church beyond. It's particularly
awe-inspiring and beautiful early in the morning before the tourist
hordes arrive in the piazza and when Michelangelo's superb dome is
still half-shrouded in haze. And it's not only fervent Catholics who
are moved by the atmosphere generated when the Pope gives his
blessing to the crowd on Sundays at noon.

Most people are too busy scurrying round to the Vatican
Museums to explore the area around St Peter's, still known as the
Borgo (from the time when the whole district was divided into
Anglo-Saxon boroughs and hospices for pilgrims from the north).
Although the area in the immediate vicinity of the Vatican is full of
vans selling snacks and shops selling papal and other souvenirs,
there are some quiet narrow streets to the north, around Borgo Pio,
with a more genuine local character. Nearby is the massive brick
bulk of the Castel Sant' Angelo, originally mausoleum of the
Emperor Hadrian, later citadel, papal refuge and prison, now a
museum. However, the most impressive view is from the Ponte
Sant' Angelo, a bridge lined with marble statues of angels by Bernini
and his pupils. A less elevating sight is the neighbouring Palace of
Justice. The Romans consider it exceeds the Victor Emmanuel
Monument in ugliness and add the pejorative ending *"accio"* to its
name.

North and east of the Vatican City lies the quiet residential Prati
district. Although nothing remains of the meadows after which it is
named, this is a pleasant area of shabby, shuttered villas with
balconies and carved archways, overgrown gardens brimming with
flowers and courtyards with lofty date palms. There are blocks of
flats too, some modern, some 19th-century. The Via Cola di Rienzo,
a busy blossom-lined avenue with excellent shops, leads from the
Tiber to the Piazza Risorgimento, a vast square with palm trees,
criss-crossed by tramlines and pedestrian crossings, and lined with

pavement restaurants. From here the great bastion walls of the Vatican City lead to the entrance to the museums and the street is lined with souvenir stalls.

To the north-east of the Vatican are the residential districts of Trionfale (famous for its flower market) and Monte Mario.

Churches
St Peter's

Galleries and museums
Castel Sant' Angelo
Vatican Art Gallery
Vatican Museums

Hotels
Columbus
Gerber

CENTRAL ROME ...

The classic entry into Rome used to be through the triumphal arch of Porta Flaminia; this and the vast Piazza del Popolo were constantly being redesigned to make a fitting approach to the Eternal City. The Piazza del Popolo, once the site of the Roman Carnival and starting point for horse races down the mile-long Via del Corso, is still lively. Close to the graceful twin churches which flank the entrance to the Corso, fashionable bars with outside tables vie for custom (Rosati's scores highest on style, with prices to match). Traffic races round the ancient obelisk in the centre of the Piazza which once marked the turning point for races round the Circus Maximus. But there's also a sea of parked cars, for the area to the south is a restricted zone.

Beyond the Piazza the centre of Rome is split into two distinct halves by the Via del Corso, a lively shopping street whose narrow pavements overflow with pedestrians assuming precedence over such traffic as is allowed. In the evenings it becomes the scene of the jostling *passeggiata*, just like the *corso* of any other Italian town. However, beyond the arcaded Galleria, just over half way down, the traffic resumes and shops and bars give way to a vista of handsome but severe and blackened Renaissance *palazzi*, leading the eye inexorably to the dazzlingly white Monument to Victor Emmanuel II, nicknamed The Wedding Cake, or, by Italians, the Typewriter.

...WEST OF THE CORSO

The area to the west of the Corso stretches to the Tiber, comprising the original Campus Martius of ancient times. It's now a labyrinth of crooked lanes, many little changed since the Middle Ages, with here and there Renaissance and Baroque palaces and churches, squares and fountains. Long the centre of commercial Rome, it's probably still the most fascinating part, with literally layer upon layer of history (where else do you find the Stock Exchange built into the ruins of an ancient temple, a restaurant built into the ruins of Pompey's theatre, complete with Caesar's bloodstains, or a palace built into an ancient theatre?). Close to the Corso are the imposing Parliament buildings but beyond the atmosphere is more of village than capital city: small shops and workrooms, local street markets and little through traffic. The venerable Pantheon presides over a cheerful square with tables and chairs in the sun; although there's no longer a market in the portico of Classical Rome's best-preserved building, it's still very much taken for granted, part of everyday life. Nearby, the superb Piazza Navona, retaining the elliptical form of Domitian's stadium, is so enormous that it absorbs the crowds, and there's still a feeling of spaciousness. It's dominated by the lovely Baroque façade of Sant' Agnese, designed by Borromini (the inside is an anticlimax) and by Bernini's Fountain of the Four Rivers. Ochre-washed houses, their balconies crammed with flowerpots, form a backdrop to the scene below. From spring onwards, the action begins early in the afternoon when artists set up their easels and musicians serenade people taking leisurely lunches at pavement tables. There's no traffic noise but an almost constant chattering punctuated by pealing of church bells, jangling of *carrozze*, and intermittent muffled clapping of serenaders. But it's liveliest of all on balmy summer evenings when people meet at the Fountain just to wander round the piazza, or sample one of the famous chocolate *tartufi* at the Tre Scalini. Away from the magnet of the Piazza Navona, the little corner of old Rome between the Via dei Coronari, lined with expensive antique shops, and the busy Corso del Rinascimento, is one of the most charming, with lovely churches like Santa Maria della Pace and Sant' Ivo alla Sapienza hidden away in lost corners and courtyards. On the far side of the Pantheon are more narrow streets and churches more renowned for their contents than their exteriors, with the notable exception of Sant' Ignazio, on its charming rococo stage-set square.

At first sight the Corso Vittorio Emanuele, which bisects the district from the Tiber to the Piazza Venezia, has little to recommend it except as an efficient bus route. Nevertheless there are two fine Baroque churches, some superb Renaissance palaces (Palazzo della Cancelleria, Palazzo Massimo alle Colonne) and no less than three museums, all housed in old *palazzi*.

South of the Corso Vittorio Emanuele are more winding streets, often picturesquely named: street of the dark shops, street of the trunk-makers. There's also one superb straight one – the Via Giulia, lined with old Renaissance palaces and curious churches, perhaps the most prestigious address in the city. Nearby is the Palazzo Farnese, finest Renaissance palace in Rome, its severe façade dominating a square where Egyptian granite tubs from the Baths of Caracalla have been converted into fountains. In complete contrast is the neighbouring Campo dei Fiori, scene of executions from 1600 but now a lively market-place surrounded by picturesque, higgledy-piggledy houses. From here the Via dei Giubbonari, "street of the jerkin-makers", now full of trendy clothes shops, leads to the remains of the old Jewish ghetto close to the river and the Portico of Octavius which once served as a foyer for the ancient Theatre of Marcellus.

Ancient remains
Ara Pacis Augustae
Pantheon

Churches
Chiesa Nuova
Gesù
Sant' Agnese
Sant' Agostino
Sant' Andrea della Valle
Sant' Ignazio
Sant' Ivo della Sapienza
San Luigi dei Francesi
Santa Maria sopra Minerva
Santa Maria della Pace

Galleries and museums
Barracco Museum (Palazzo Piccola Farnesina)
Doria Pamphili Gallery (Palazzo Doria Pamphili)
Palazzo Venezia Museum
Rome Museum (Palazzo Braschi)
Spada Gallery (Palazzo Spada)

Hotels
Bologna
Cesari
Portoghesi
Raphael
Sole al Pantheon

…EAST OF THE CORSO

The area to the east of the Via del Corso has quite a different character from medieval or "Old Rome" on the other side. Since the late 16th century the Piazza di Spagna and the narrow streets leading off it have been the haunt of foreign tourists. It was here that the young noblemen on their Grand Tour left their carriages, here that English Romantic poets sought lodgings. In 1820 one writer could say of the Piazza di Spagna that it was "the focus of fashion and general resort of the English… a little less nasty than the other piazzas in Rome because the habits of the people are in some measure restrained by the presence of the English". Reminders of the Anglo-Saxon presence are the house in which Keats died in 1821 at the foot of the Spanish Steps and, on the other side, Babington's Tea Rooms, opened 75 years later, where you can still take tea and scones or even pay through the nose for *pasticcio di manzo* – shepherds' pie. The Caffe degli Inglesi, opposite, is now a bookshop but the Antico Caffe Greco, little changed since the 18th century, is as popular a meeting place as in the days when it was frequented by the great Romantic writers, artists and composers of the mid-19th century and the politicos of the 1870s. The charming Piazza di Spagna, with its exotic erect palms, its waiting carriages and curious

Spanish Steps

fountain (*"La Barcaccia"*) is still a mecca for tourists who congregate on the famous Spanish Steps. Here, among the flowerstalls and artists' easels, you can sit and watch the world go by without being fleeced. For the streets off the Piazza di Spagna are the most exclusive in the city, the old *palazzi* now housing jewellers' shops and boutiques, the whole area given over entirely to pedestrians. Via Condotti, directly opposite the Spanish Steps, is the most prohibitively exclusive of all.

The traffic-restricted shopping zone comes to a very abrupt end at the deafening Via del Tritone. Beyond it narrow lanes lead – unexpectedly – to Bernini's spectacular Trevi fountain, focal point of a small piazza. It's the backdrop for many a tourist photograph and receptacle of hundreds of coins thrown in each day as well as a popular evening rendezvous. Indeed its pouring pale green waters and dramatic figures, the extraordinary combination of natural and artificial, are perhaps best appreciated when floodlit at night; by day the souvenir stalls and clicking of cameras are distracting. Otherwise this is a quiet area except for the Piazza Santi Apostoli, often the focus of political rallies.

Churches
Trinità dei Monti

Galleries and museums
Accademia di San Luca
Colonna Gallery
Keats-Shelley Memorial

Hotels
Carriage
Fontana
Gregoriana
d'Inghilterra
Margutta
Mozart
Scalinata di Spagna
Trevi
Valadier

THE BORGHESE

Rome's most central (but only second largest) park is a skilfully landscaped refuge from the heat and hassle of the city. Although there's a certain amount of through traffic, the illusion is of rambling natural parkland, criss-crossed by avenues with the odd fountain, statue or classical temple. Romans come here at weekends to stroll among the umbrella pines, visit the zoo or learn to ride, as well as for the cultural attractions of its galleries and museums. Two of these are housed in Renaissance villas built as pleasure palaces by rich churchmen – the Villa Giulia of pope Julius III and the Villa Borghese built by cardinal Scipione Borghese and set in its own formal gardens. A third, the Villa Medici, now the French Academy, is often used for temporary exhibitions, but you can also visit the formal gardens – and admire the most exuberant façade – on Sunday mornings.

Forming part of the Borghese are the formal terraced gardens of the Pincio, conceived as part of Valadier's design for the harmonious Piazza del Popolo. The avenues, with their busts of Italian patriots (some with recently acquired broken noses) and their sublime sunset views, are a favourite with romantic strollers. A gradual climb leads past the austere façade of the Villa Medici to the Piazzale Trinità dei Monti at the top of the Spanish Steps. From here the Via Sistina leads down to Piazza Barberini, a noisy intersection graced by two lovely Bernini fountains. The broad avenue of the Via Veneto sweeps back up to the Borghese embracing in its loop the staid residential Ludovisi quarter. No longer the glamorous haunt of film stars, paparazzi and dilettanti, the Via Veneto is now tawdrily sedate, with lots of solid old hotels, shops and offices. The famous pavement bars and cafés, the flowerstalls and news-stands are still there to remind passers-by of the dolce vita of the '50s and '60s.

North-east of the Borghese, Via Flaminia leads past the Olympic village to the picturesque and ancient Milvio bridge, begun in the second century BC. To the north-west is the residential Parioli district and, due east, the Villa Torlonia area.

Churches
Santa Maria del Pópolo
Sant' Agnese fuori le Mura

Galleries and museums
Borghese Gallery
National Gallery of Modern Art
National Museum (Villa Giulia)

Hotels
Alexandra
Eden
Lord Byron
Residenza

THE BUSINESS AREA

The area between the Borghese and the station is the most citified part of Rome. The great busy streets which traverse it have names recalling the 19th century (Via XX Settembre, Via Nazionale, Via Cavour), while the narrower streets to the north-west, named after the different regions, remind one that it was here that the armies of a united Italy entered Rome in 1870. The focal point of the area is the vast Piazza della Repubblica, re-designed after the Unification.

But among the shops and airline offices, the ministries and embassies, the dour apartment blocks and the seedy *pensioni* there are echoes of an older Rome: the ruins of the Baths of Diocletian, a gateway designed by Michelangelo, and several Renaissance and Baroque churches. There are also some fine viewpoints from the Quirinal Hill. From the cramped but busy crossroads at the top of Via Quattro Fontane you can see roads leading to the Porta Pia (Michelangelo's gateway) and the obelisks in front of Santa Maria Maggiore, the Quirinal Palace and the church of Trinità dei Monti. From the vast cobbled space in front of the Quirinal Palace (once papal, now presidential, residence) you can look out over medieval Rome and see the dome of St Peter's, roughly at eye level, through a spiky screen of television aerials.

Churches
Sant' Andrea al Quirinale
San Carlo alle Quattro Fontane
Santa Maria degli Angeli
Santa Maria della Vittoria

Galleries and Museums
National Gallery of Art (Palazzo Barberini)
National Museum of Rome

Hotels
Villa del Parco

THE STATION AREA

The area in the immediate vicinity of the station has little to
recommend it, apart from the sleek, low Termini building itself.
Opposite, on the vast Piazza dei Cinquecento, stand serried ranks of
buses and scruffy stalls selling cheap bags and T-shirts. The streets
around are drably residential rather than sleazy but the Via Giolitti
and streets parallel to it are insalubrious, especially at night when
you are warned against pickpockets, drug addicts and drunks. The
only redeeming features of the area are the superb churches, mostly
with early Christian origins.

Churches
Santa Croce in Gerusalemme
Santa Maria Maggiore
San Giovanni Laterano
San Lorenzo fuori le Mura

Shopping

Antiques   The Via Giulia is lined with expensive antiques shops;
Via dei Coronari is cheaper but many of the items come from the
Portobello Road. Via del Babuino and Via Margutta are full of art
dealers and small galleries, but again much of the merchandise
comes from the London salerooms.

Books   For glossy artbooks you can't do better than Bocca on the
corner of Via delle Carrozze and Piazza di Spagna (a bookshop since
1866; before that the Caffe degli Inglesi). The Lion Bookshop on Via
del Babuino specialises in English books, but it can be more
expensive than Mondadori, Feltrinelli or Rizzoli who also have a fair
range. You can swap paperbacks at the Economy Book Center on
Piazza di Spagna and pick up remainders at the Libreria San
Silvestro on the Piazza San Silvestro. On Piazza Borghese are stalls
selling old books and prints, daily except Sunday.

Clothes   Most Italian designers, from Armani to Versace, specialise
in ready-to-wear. The most prestigious address for the big names is
Via dei Condotti, but the adjacent Via Borgognona, Via Frattina and
Via della Croce are almost as exclusive and the whole grid of streets
can be explored in the time it takes to walk up and down Bond
Street – without the traffic. For men as well as women all the smart
names are here – Cucci and Gucci, Battistoni and Valentino.

For cheap and cheerful clothes the best street is Via dei
Giubbonari (Street of the Jerkin-Makers). Look out for street stalls
selling lambswool jumpers and T-shirts. Silk lingerie is good value.
Via Sistina and Via Nazionale are cheaper than the area around the
Spanish Steps. The top end of Via Barberini and Largo di Santa
Susanna are especially good for mens' clothes. Silk ties are a bargain;
if you buy them from a stall make sure they really are silk.

Department stores   La Rinascente in Piazza Colonna is the smartest
department store; there are also branches of Coin, Upim and Standa;
but Romans tend to shop in small boutiques and markets.

Food   Franchi, on Via Cola di Rienzo, is arguably Rome's most mouth-watering delicatessen and next to it is Castroni, specialising in coffee and chocolates. There are plenty of other delicatessens, especially around the Campo dei Fiori, Rome's oldest market square. Apart from the market itself (fruit, vegetables and meat) there are some good general food shops, *alimentari*, and bakers. There are also numerous *pasticcerie* (cake shops); one of the best is da Angelo in Via della Croce.

Household goods   Linen and towels are smarter and better value than you find in London; good shops include Ellepi on Via della Croce and Frette on the Corso (also pretty lingerie). Croff Centro Casa is a modern household chain, selling attractive linens, ceramics and kitchenware with prices comparable to Habitat.

Leather   There are plenty of shoeshops scattered all over Rome (Via Cola di Rienzo has a good range). Styles tend to be on the conservative side, and there's not much choice between extremely expensive shops selling classic models and cheap shops where shoes are not built to last. You could be lucky at one of the markets (eg Via Sannio near San Giovanni in Laterano, or Vittorio Emanuele). Antuoni on Piazza del Esquilino has cheap mens' shoes (tasselled loafers) and womens' shoes in smart, casual styles and of reasonable quality. Bags and belts are not the bargain they are in Florence, but Anticoli in Piazzetta Mignanelli sells leatherware at factory prices and again it's worth trying the markets.

Markets   For anyone fascinated by food markets, Piazza Vittorio Emanuele is the one to see, with its pyramids of eggs and sacks of beans, its polished peppers and blankets of tripe, its meats of all descriptions (some beyond) and its busy vendors shouting, sharpening their knives and peeling their fruit. It also sells some clothes and household goods. The market on Campo dei Fiori is less claustrophobic and more picturesque, but despite its name it isn't the main market for flowers – this is the Mercato dei Fiori (Tuesdays only) on Via Trionfale. The chief flea market is at Porta Portese on Sunday mornings; the clothes are often older than the antiques. The market at Via Sannio is a weekday alternative.

Toys   Rome has several good toyshops; the Galleria San Carlo in the Corso, Regali in Via del Lavatore and the kiosk on Via di Ripetta. Al Sogno on the Piazza Navona specialises in cuddly animals – even ducks and dobermanns.

Wine   Trimani, in Via Goito, is Rome's most knowledgeable wine dealer. It's a rambling place, full of fascinating-looking bottles, with some good bargains at the cheap end.

THE VATICAN

The tiny state of the Vatican covers only just over 100 acres – about half of it gardens – and yet its spiritual and moral power is immeasurable, with an influence over the lives of some 800 million Catholics. The temporal power of the Papacy has dwindled from the enormous Papal States of the Renaissance down to the proverbial postage stamp which was agreed in the Lateran Treaty of 1929 when, for the first time, the Vatican became an independent sovereign state.

The Vatican has its own army, the Swiss Guards, with uniforms said to have been designed by Michelangelo, its own yellow and white flag and its own anthem, a march by Gounod composed for the coronation of Pius IX. It has a station and a heliport, its own stamps and coins, a printing press and even a prison. There is a duty-free petrol station and supermarket. About 700 citizens are entitled to a Vatican passport (although there are no border formalities). Recently the Vatican has come under criticism for shady financial dealings and allegations of corruption and waste. Romans joke that the letters SCV on licence-plates of Vatican-registered cars stands for "Se Cristo Vedesse" ("If Christ could see...")

Despite the present incumbent's relative accessibility, his helicopter and his Popemobile, an aura of mystique still surrounds the Papacy. The ritual of electing a new Pope is a case in point. A conclave of cardinals meets in the utmost secrecy in the Sistine chapel and two ballots are cast daily until there is a clear winner with a majority of 2/3 plus one. Ballot papers are burned after each vote and black smoke issuing from the chimney indicates an inconclusive vote. A white chemical added to the final papers gives the signal that a new Pope has been chosen; "Habemus Papam". The Pope's titles include Vicar of Christ, Successor of the Prince of the Apostles and Patriarch of the West.

The Vatican is one of the richest treasuries of art in the world. Yet many of the tourists in Rome, especially at Easter, are pilgrims to St Peter's, drawn to the Eternal City not by the ancient remains or the Baroque architecture but by their faith. On Sunday mornings, when the Pope is in residence, a huge crowd gathers for his address from the balcony of St Peter's. Audiences with the Pope, either in the Vatican or at Castel Gandolfo, his summer residence, can be arranged through travel agencies with the ease of booking a coach excursion.

☛ St Peter's

The original St Peter's was erected by the Emperor Constantine between 324 and 349. In its present form St Peter's, the largest Christian church in the world, dates from the early 1500s, when there were endless discussions of what form it should take and who should rebuild it. Ten architects (including Michelangelo and Bramante) and twice as many Popes were involved. A workforce comprising about 800 men raised the ancient obelisk in the centre of the piazza in 1586. To Carlo Maderno's Baroque façade Bernini added his splendid colonnades, designed to symbolise the embrace of the Church. The work was finished in 1667.

You can get a good view of the immense interior and of Michelangelo's dome by climbing the stairs to the gallery at its base. The focal point is the immense bronze canopy, the *baldacchino*, designed by Bernini for Urban VIII, its great columns buzzing with Barberini bees. Bronze for the baldacchino was taken from the Pantheon, prompting the famous contemporary quip "Quod non fecerunt barbari, fecerunt Barberini" (What the barbarians did not do, the Barberini did). Behind it is the exuberant Baroque **Chair of St Peter** (Cattedra Petri), also by Bernini, and the altar, flanked by splendid papal tombs, including that of Urban VIII by Bernini. Tucked away

THE VATICAN

behind glass in a side chapel is Michelangelo's supremely moving *Pietà*, his only signed work, sculpted when he was just 25. There are some splendid tombs and monuments (including one to the Stuarts) both in the church itself, in the Treasury (Pollaiolo's tomb of Sixtus IV) and in the Vatican grottoes. Visit the grottoes last as the exit is outside St Peter's. First take the lift (small charge) to the roof for angels'-eye views of the Piazza below (and even better ones on a clear day from the lantern, over 500 steps up).

Special permission is required to visit the Vatican Necropolis and the tomb of St Peter, discovered in 1940; apply at the Tourist Office (*Ufficio Scavi*).

☛ **Vatican Gardens**
The Information Office (on the left of the steps leading to St Peter's) organises guided tours of the gardens.

☛ **Vatican Museums**
A half-hourly shuttle bus runs from the Information Office on the Piazza San Pietro through the gardens to the Vatican Museums. In addition to several museums, much of the Vatican Palace (begun during the Middle Ages and altered and enlarged by successive Popes) is open to the public, notably the Sistine Chapel and Raphael's Stanze (Rooms), for most people the highlights of a visit.

The Museums cover a daunting area; it is estimated that a comprehensive visit would entail a 4½ hour walk and the brochure advises the visitor "to proceed at a slow and regular pace and not attempt the desperate undertaking of trying to absorb every detail of every section in a single day." With this *caveat* in mind, the authorities have devised a one-way system with four colour-coded itineraries of varied duration. In the entrance hall there's an illuminated chart indicating which rooms are closed.

It makes sense to break the "rules" and visit the **Pinacoteca** (gallery) first as so much of the collection is from the early Renaissance. Ideally, see the Raphael Stanze and Sistine Chapel as a separate visit.

Rooms 1 and 2: Early gold-ground tripychs (including Giotto)
Room 3: International Gothic and Florentine painters of the Renaissance, including Filippo Lippi's Coronation of the Virgin and paintings by Fra Angelico
Room 4: Mellozzo da Forli's frescoes for the apse of SS Apostoli and the famous portrait of Sixtus V
Room 6: Carlo Crivelli's strange Virgin and Child (1482) and Pietà, with a stylised expression of grief
Room 7: Works by Umbrian artists, notably Perugino, master of Raphael, and Pinturicchio
Room 8: Three great works by Raphael, including his Transfiguration, unfinished when he died in 1520
Room 9: Leonardo's monochrome St Jerome
Room 11: Mannerist painters including Vasari (The Stoning of St Stephen)
Room 12: Caravaggio's Deposition, and works by his French and Bolognese followers
Room 15: Sir Thomas Lawrence's portrait of George IV
There is a tiny room of Russian, Greek and Slav icons and Bernini's plaster casts for St Peter's.

All visitors to the Sistine Chapel automatically pass through the galleries of tapestries and frescoed maps but you need to take tour C or D to see Raphael's famous Stanze first.

THE VATICAN

Raphael's four **Stanze** were painted (mainly between 1508 and 1514) for Julius II as private apartments. The most important room is the Stanza della Segnatura (the Pope's study or "signing room") with frescoes of the School of Athens (the triumph of philosophy) and the Disputation (the triumph of religion), both masterpieces of High Renaissance art. Nearby (also tours C and D only) are the **Chapel of Nicholas V**, frescoed by Fra Angelico and Benozzo Gozzoli (1448-50) and the **Borgia Apartments** decorated by Pintoricchio (1492-5).

The **Sistine Chapel**, used for the most solemn ceremonies and papal elections, was built between 1475 and 1481 by Sixtus IV who commissioned Tuscan and Umbrian artists to decorate the walls. It was over twenty years later that Pope Julius II persuaded Michelangelo to tackle the ceiling.

"All the world hastened to behold this marvel and was overwhelmed, speechless with astonishment", wrote Vasari of the **Sistine Ceiling**. Now visitors can once again see the ceiling in its pristine state, cleaned of the grime of over 450 years (but also, say some scholars, of subtle light and shade effects). The vault itself was completed in just two years (1510-1512), with Michelangelo stretched on scaffolding at a paintbrush's length from the ceiling. The monumental grandeur of the whole concept cannot fail to impress. It is a complex work, parts of it tied up with Neoplatonist philosophy and, in the *ignudi* (male nudes) and the sublime Creation of Adam (first scene but painted last), the Renaissance idea of divine perfection incarnated in man.

The incredibly powerful vision of The Last Judgement was begun in 1533, after the Sack of Rome had all but devastated Papal morale and the confident ideals of the Renaissance. The work was immediately controversial and in the 1560s Pope Paul IV ordered a cleaning-up campaign of what he described as "a stew of nudes": draperies were strategically applied. Later, a total whitewash was narrowly averted.

In contrast to Michelangelo's monumental, muscular figures are the anecdotal wall paintings of Botticelli, Perugino, Ghirlandaio and others, all dating from the reign of Sixtus IV in the early 1480s. The Donation of the Keys, by Perugino, is particularly beautiful.

After the Sistine Chapel the **Apostolic Libraries** are an anti-climax for the average visitor, but there are lovely views over the well-groomed gardens.

The highlights of the **Pio-Clementino Museum** are the Belvedere Torso and the Laocoön, both famous classical statues which were very influential on Renaissance artists. This museum can be visited at the end of the tour, or with the Pinacoteca.

Other museums, of lesser and/or specialist interest include the Chiaramonti, Etruscan and Egyptian museums, the Gregoriano Profano and Pio Cristiano museums, and the missionary/ethnological and historical museums. It is advisable to adjust your itinerary to satisfy particular interests and to skip other sections.

The Vatican Museums are open on Mondays (and free on the last Sunday in the month).

Arms of popes Gregory IX, Urban VIII, Gregory XIII and Innocent XII

Sightseeing

"A man may spend many months at Rome and yet have something of note to see every day"
(John Raymond "An itinerary contayning a voyage made through Italy in the yeare 1646 and 1647", 1648)

Ancient remains

Some of Rome's greatest monuments are often invisible under protective scaffolding for months, even years, at a time for repairs and restoration. The self-contained area of the Forum is the greatest concentration of classical remains in the city (and subject to an entrance fee). Beyond the city walls is the Appian Way (Via Appia Antica) where the Catacombs, early Christian burial chambers, can be visited on guided tours. The list below is selective; there are also ancient churches (see under Churches below), walls, bridges, sewers and city gates. (See also the section on excursions from Rome, at the end of this chapter.)

Most archaeological sites are open from 9am until dusk. The Formum and Palatine are open on Mondays. Other monuments may be closed in the afternoon.

☞ **Ara Pacis Augustae** (Altar of Augustan Peace)
The most important monument of the Augustan Age, dating from 13BC, has been reassembled from fragments (and copies of fragments) and protected from the 20th century by a great glass box. The narrative reliefs and decorative detail are fascinating. Nearby is the overgrown **Mausoleum of Augustus**.

☞ **Baths of Caracalla**
Not so much a public baths, more of a Roman leisure centre. The baths, dating from AD212, were once equipped with a library, gallery, sports facilities and central heating. Little remains of the once lavish interior, except some fragments of the mosaic floors, but the massive brick ruins now form a romantic backdrop for open air opera performances in summer.

☞ **Baths of Diocletian**
The remains of Rome's largest public baths have been incorporated into a church (**Santa Maria degli Angeli**, designed by Michelangelo) and a museum (**Museo Nazionale**).

☞ **Castel Sant' Angelo**
Originally built as a mausoleum to the Emperor Hadrian in AD135-9, the Castel Sant' Angelo was later fortified and used by the popes. It contains apartments with fine Renaissance frescoes and furnishings and a collection of arms and armour (*see under Museums below*).

☞ **Colosseum**
Bloodthirsty Romans have been replaced by ravaging tourist hordes but the largest of the classical amphitheatres (AD80), blackened and pockmarked by time, remains incredibly impressive. During the Renaissance the Colosseum was used as a quarry for building materials and by the 19th century it had become a picturesque, overgrown ruin. Now restored, it has until recently been a giant traffic roundabout.

☛ The Forum (Foro Romano)

The remains of the political, religious and commercial hub of ancient Rome is an extensive and complex site and to make sense of it you need a good plan. It is also helpful to see the overall layout from the viewpoint at the top of the Via del Campidoglio (or from the Palatine hill) before entering from the Via dei Fori Imperiali. The most interesting and important remains, listed as an anti-clockwise tour, are as follows:

Temple of Antoninus and Faustina   Erected by the emperor Antoninus in AD141 in honour of his dead wife, it was later converted into a church and given a Baroque façade.

Curia (Senate House)   Now an austere brick building (sometimes used for exhibitions), the Curia was originally faced with marble. The present building dates from the 3rd century.

Arch of Septimus Severus   Built in 203 to commemorate the victories of the emperor over the Parthians.

Temple of Castor and Pollux   All that remains of this temple (dating from 5BC) are three beautiful columns held together by the remains of an architrave.

Temple of Vesta   Adjoining the remains of the Temple of Vesta is the **House of the Vestal Virgins**; the courtyard and pools are still visible.

Basilica of Maxentius   Parallel to the Sacred Way, only one triple-vaulted aisle of the Basilica remains of this grandiose 4th-century building, the shell now used for summer concerts.

Arch of Titus   A triumphal arch erected after the death of the emperor Titus in AD81. It commemorates his capture of Jerusalem.

From here you can proceed to the Colosseum or the Palatine (*see separate entries*).

☛ Imperial Forums

Opposite the main (Roman) Forum are the ruins of others built by later emperors, including Caesar, Vespasian and Augustus. The most interesting ruins (for the non-specialist) are those of **Trajan's Forum** (Foro di Traiano) with the remains of a market and **Trajan's column**, a masterpiece of classical art celebrating the emperor's military victories.

☛ Palatine

Most celebrated of the seven hills of Rome, the Palatine was inhabited during the Iron Age (several huts remain) and was, according to legend, where Romulus founded the city. Later it became a residential area of the Republican city, counting Catullus and Cicero among its inhabitants. The emperor Domitian (AD81-96) transformed it into an imperial palace and later emperors extended it, but it then fell into ruin. Excavations began in the 18th century; there is little to see but the atmosphere is romantic and there are some peaceful picnic spots. The lovely **Farnese gardens**, laid out in the mid-16th century by cardinal Alexander Farnese, nephew of pope Paul III, are worth visiting. Nearby is **Livia's House**, one of the more significant ruins, probably once part of the home of the emperor Augustus.

☛ Pantheon

Despite damage, unworthy "improvements" and plundering of materials, the Pantheon remains the best-preserved building of classical times. The majestic domed interior seems to echo with age and the visual impact of its pure proportions – lit by a shaft of light from an opening in the dome – make the detail (tombs, pictures) seem irrelevant.

Churches

Below is a selection of the most attractive of Rome's numerous churches, covering a span of some 2,000 years, from Early Christian to the Baroque. Churches outside the walls (fuori le mura) are listed together at the end.

Churches are normally open from about 7am to about 7pm, but closed at midday for up to four hours. Opening hours vary and times are usually posted on doors. It is usually in order to visit churches during a service – use your discretion.

It is essential to take a stock of L100 and L200 coins to light paintings – many are barely visible in natural light.

Concerts are held in some churches (advertised on posters).

☛ Gesù
A famous and much-copied Counter-Reformation church with characteristic scrolls on the façade (1575). The opulent painted ceiling (masterpiece of GB Gaulli) and the chapel of St Ignatius Loyola are Baroque extravaganzas.

☛ Sant' Agostino
The façade of Sant' Agostino, one of the earliest Renaissance churches in Rome, is now drab and the interior has been spoilt by later decoration. However, the church is worth visiting for Caravággio's moving Madonna of the Pilgrims (1605), considered very shocking when it was painted – primarily because of the pilgrim's bare, dirty feet.

☛ Sant' Andrea al Quirinale
An ornate oval church with a typically Baroque exploitation of natural light sources. It is usually considered to be Bernini's theatrical answer to Borromini's San Carlo alle Quattro Fontane up the road.

☛ Sant' Andrea della Valle
Sant' Andrea's blackened but graceful façade, with plants sprouting from the cornice, is typically Baroque. Behind it is a great hall of a church, bathed in yellow-gold light and almost secular in its opulence, with a magnificent dome by Lanfranco (1621-25). Puccini set the first act of *Tosca* here.

☛ San Carlo alle Quattro Fontane
A *virtuoso* performance by Borromini, completed in the year of his death, 1667. Although the church is diminutive ("San Carlino"), Borromini's style is by no means cramped. The Four Fountains crossroads which gives the church its name was part of a scheme of Sixtus V (1585-90) to link the major basilicas by straight roads.

☛ Santa Cecilia in Trastevere
A dignified 18th-century church (of ancient origin) set in a pretty rose garden. The *campanile* and portico are all that remain from the 12th century. Inside is a chilling statue of the martyred saint whose body was discovered in 1599 (and sketched by the artist, Stefano Maderno). Santa Cecilia is the patron saint of music and the church is sometimes used for concerts.

☛ San Clemente
An ancient basilica, rebuilt in 1108 (over a 4th-century basilica which can still be visited). Inside there are superb mosaics, and, in the chapel of St Catherine lovely frescoes by Masolino (c1430).

☛ Santa Croce in Gerusalemme
The church built by the Emperor Constantine to house a relic of the True

Cross was almost totally rebuilt in the 18th century, leaving a Gothic belltower. There are some beautiful Renaissance mosaics in St Helen's chapel.

☛ San Francesco a Ripa

A 13th-century church on the sight of a hospice where saint Francis of Assisi stayed in 1219. It contains Bernini's statue of the swooning Blessed Ludovica Albertoni.

☛ San Giovanni in Laterano

The cathedral church of Rome – and therefore the world – is of ancient origin and history but the present exterior dates from the 18th century. Inside it is suitably majestic and solemn, but the beautiful, peaceful cloisters are perhaps more inspiring to the soul.

☛ Sant' Ignazio

In a graceful rococo piazza, Sant' Ignazio looks like part of a stage set. Nothing prepares you for the scale of the interior with Pozzo's fantastic *trompe l'oeil* dome and ceiling painting representing the glorious ascent of St Ignatius to Paradise (1684).

☛ Sant' Ivo alla Sapienza

Framed by the courtyard of the former University (*sapienza* means wisdom), Sant' Ivo shows Borromini at his most creative. The ground plan was inspired by the bee, emblem of the Barberini family. The façade of gently moulded curves, with its spiralling dome, is chastly echoed inside (ask the custodian of the State Archives to let you in).

☛ San Luigi dei Francesi

The French national church, dating from the 16th century, is worth seeing primarily for Caravággio's wonderfully vivid paintings of the Life of St Matthew in the Contarelli chapel. It is essential to light the paintings. There is also a series of frescoes by Domenichino, illustrating the life of St Cecilia.

☛ Santa Maria d'Aracoeli

On the summit of the Capitoline hill and approached by a steep flight of over 100 steps, the church is outwardly austere. The rich interior contains lovely frescoes of the Life of San Bernardino by Pinturicchio (c1485). The venerated "Santo Bambino", a wooden figure said to be carved from the Tree of Gethsemane, is kept in a chapel near the sanctuary (where letters addressed to him from all over the world are displayed).

☛ Santa Maria in Cosmedin

A Romanesque church with a dark but impressive interior (pavement, paschal candlestick, fresco fragments, mosaic in the sacristy). Byzantine mass is held on Sunday mornings. In the simple brick arcade is the *Bocca della Verità* (Mouth of Truth), a gaping stone mask which, according to legend, will bite off the right hand of a liar. Plenty of tourists enjoy the challenge.

☛ Santa Maria Maggiore

Crowning the Esquiline Hill is one of the great basilicas of Rome. The majestic interior includes superb Byzantine mosaics (hard to see without binoculars), and florid Baroque chapels. The ceiling is said to have been gilded with the first gold to arrive from the New World.

☛ Santa Maria sopra Minerva

In a colourfully over-restored Gothic interior are some beautiful chapels with tombs and monuments from the Gothic to the Baroque periods, and other works of art. Notable is the Carafa chapel (right transept) frescoed by Filippino Lippi with lovely imaginary landscapes and pale but vivid colours

(1489-1493). Nearby is a beautiful 13th-century mosaic of the Madonna and Child.

☛ Santa Maria della Pace

A sadly dilapidated but charming little church, lost in a picturesque corner behind the Piazza Navona. The façade is by Pietro da Cortona. Apply to 5, Vicolo dell' Arco to see the cold interior with Raphael's Sibyls, via Bramante's elegant cloister.

☛ Santa Maria del Pópolo

An early Renaissance church, dating from the 1470s. Inside (first chapel on right) is a delicate fresco by Pintoricchio of The Adoration, a nice contrast to Caravággio's dramatic masterpieces of the Crucifixion of St Peter and the Conversion of St Paul, painted in 1601 (Cerasi chapel, near the main altar). The Chigi chapel (left transept) was designed by Raphael, the choir by Bramante (with frescoes by Pintoricchio and two magnificent tombs by Andrea Sansovino).

☛ Santa Maria in Trastevere

Gorgeous mosaics, both inside and out, are the main reason for visiting this basilica, a place of worship since the 3rd century, but dating mainly from the 12th. The mosaics in the apse, by Byzantine craftsmen, are the earliest; those of the chancel, by Pietro Cavallini, date from the late 13th century.

☛ Santa Maria della Vittoria

The interior of this comparatively conservative 17th-century church is High Baroque in its opulence. The showpiece is Bernini's most sensuous (some would say sensual) marble group, The Ecstasy of St Teresa (1652), showing the saint pierced by the arrow of Divine Love, while members of the Cornaro family look on as if in boxes at the theatre.

☛ St Peter's

(See The Vatican, page 312)

☛ San Pietro in Montorio

This church has some interesting tombs and frescoes, including (first chapel on right) a Flagellation by Sebastiano del Piombo (1518). In the courtyard Bramante's perfectly proportioned *tempietto* (1502), one of the most exquisite buildings of the Renaissance, marks the supposed site of saint Peter's crucifixion.

☛ San Pietro in Vincoli

The chains of saint Peter, displayed in a casket under the high altar, wouldn't deter a bicycle thief. More impressive is Michelangelo's powerful statue of Moses, which with the subsidiary figures of Rachel and Leah was part of a grand project for the tomb of Julius II which occupied Michelangelo for some 40 years but was never completed.

☛ Santa Sabina

A huge and peaceful 5th-century basilica, considered the finest of its kind in Rome. In the vestibule are carved panelled doors over 1,500 years old – the depiction of the Crucifixion (top left) is one of the earliest extant representations of the subject.

☛ Trinità dei Monti

The focal point of the Spanish Steps, this outwardly charming church has a rather dull and dark interior with paintings of which Daniele da Volterra's Deposition (1541), considered by Poussin the third greatest painting in the world, is the best.

Churches outside the walls (fuori le mura)

☛ Sant' Agnese (Via Nomentana)

In 304 a young Christian girl called Agnes refused to marry the prefect's son and was exposed in a public place of ill repute, probably the Piazza Navona. The loose tresses of a miraculous crop of hair preserved her modesty and the flames of a fire lit to burn her recoiled to consume the incendiaries. A sword proved more effective, and the young martyr was buried here, north-east of the city; a basilica was soon erected over her tomb. The present church, reached by descending a long staircase where a near contemporary inscription tells the story of the martyrdom, dates from the 7th century and has undergone only cosmetic changes since then. In the midst of the later decoration is a Byzantine mosaic featuring St Agnes in Byzantine costume with the sword of her martyrdom at her feet. She is flanked by the popes who sponsored church building work in her honour.

There are guided tours of a network of catacombs (3rd-century) with well preserved but empty funerary niches.

☛ Santa Costanza (next door to Sant' Agnese)

The circular mausoleum of two daughters of emperor Constantine, one of whom (Constantia) was cured of leprosy while asleep beside the tomb of saint Agnes and built the first church of Sant' Agnese. The mausoleum was later transformed into a church (and dedicated to saint Costanza, someone else altogether) but has kept much of its very beautiful 4th-century mosaic decoration, although the dome mosaics are lost. The vault's apparently pagan scenes and their delightful decorative borders may have a Christian significance. The mosaics in the lateral niches are probably slightly later work, and are more obviously Christian in content.

☛ San Lorenzo

A pilgrimage basilica built over the tomb of saint Lawrence who was martyred here, toasted on an iron grate, in 258. The original 4th-century church was much altered and enlarged in later centuries and is now an intriguing amalgam of different buildings. The most major restructuring was in the 13th century, when the 6th-century church was reorientated from west to east and became the raised choir of a new larger building; the present nave, façade, portico and campanile date from this period. There are beautiful works of art from various periods (antique and medieval) in the portico and both sections of the church, including good examples of Cosmatesque inlay work and pavement. The mosaic over the triumphal arch (originally opening onto the old church's choir) shows Christ blessing with saints and the 6th-century pope Pelagius offering his church.

☛ San Paolo (Via Ostiense)

One of the great Roman pilgrimage basilicas, built in the 4th century on the site of the tomb of saint Paul, martyred near here under Nero, and famous as one of the most sumptuously decorated of all Roman churches until destroyed by fire in 1823, after which it was completely rebuilt. The surroundings and exterior of the basilica are equally ugly, but the grand 5-aisled interior is still tremendously impressive and has some beautiful works of art: the canopy over the high altar and saint Paul's tomb, by Arnolfo di Cambio (late 13th-century); restored 13th-century mosaics in the apse; a magnificent Romanesque candlestick in the right transept; and Rome's most delightful cloister, a rose garden surrounded by 13th-century arcades with intricately carved columns and brilliant mosaics.

Trevi fountain

Galleries and museums

State galleries and museums are usually open from 9am-2pm, daily except Mondays, and Sundays (when most close at 1pm). Privately owned galleries have different opening hours (and days). It is essential to ask the tourist office for the current list of opening hours as these are often changed at short notice. As a general guide, we give the main exceptions to the above times under each entry. This includes additional opening times (eg some state museums open late two evenings a week). The Keats-Shelley Memorial, the Vatican museums and the Villa Farnesina are open on Mondays.

☛ Accademia di San Luca
Recently re-opened after several years' closure, this is a varied collection of paintings from the 15th century onwards, mainly, but not exclusively, Italian.

☛ Barracco Museum
A small, specialised collection of ancient sculpture, Egyptian, Assyrian and Greek as well as Roman, housed in a Renaissance palace, the Piccola Farnesina (much restored in the 19th century).

☞ Borghese Gallery and Museum

The Borghese Gallery is closed indefinitely for restoration, but the Museum (ground floor, sculpture collection) is open to limited numbers of visitors. The Villa Borghese was built in 1613 for the high-living patron of the arts, Cardinal Scipione Borghese. Although much of his sculpture collection was sold in 1807 by Pauline Bonaparte's husband (and is now in the Louvre), Bernini's remarkable statue groups remain and are the chief glory of the Borghese Museum. His Apollo and Daphne (1622-25) is the ultimate Baroque statue: a masterpiece of frozen action with the moment of truth encapsulated for ever. The picture collection consists mainly of Renaissance works, with masterpieces by Florentine and Venetian artists, notably Bronzino, Correggio (Danäe) and Titian (Sacred and Profane Love). There are also great works by Caravággio and Raphael (The Deposition).

☞ Capitoline Museums

Contained in twin palaces overlooking Michelangelo's Piazza del Campidoglio, these form what is probably the oldest private collection in the world, founded in 1471. The **Museum of the Palazzo dei Conservatori** contains rooms full of sculpture, notably the Etruscan "she-wolf" and the "spinario" (Boy with a Thorn in his Foot). The **Pinacoteca** is a very fine collection of paintings (mainly 16th- to 18th-century) displayed in a majestic suite of furnished rooms. Venetian paintings include an early Titian (The Baptism of Christ) and works by Bellini and Veronese. Pietro da Cortona's dramatic Rape of the Sabine Women (1629) is perhaps the most memorable picture, and a good example of Baroque painting on a smallish scale.

Opposite, on the left of the piazza, is the Palazzo Nuovo containing the **Capitoline Museum**, devoted entirely to sculpture. Here the highlights are Roman copies of Greek sculptures, the Capitoline Venus and the Dying Gaul. There's a room with 64 busts of Roman Emperors – a sort of rogues' gallery or early Madame Tussaud's (*also open Saturday nights 7pm-11.30pm*).

☞ Castel Sant' Angelo

An important museum for anyone interested in Renaissance decoration or arms and armour, the Castel Sant' Angelo is (roughly speaking) Rome's equivalent to the Tower of London, although with a much longer history. On the second floor are the fine apartments of Clement VII, with paintings by Tuscan and North Italian artists and rooms displaying weaponry from prehistoric times to the 18th century. On the third (top) floor are the Papal Apartments, with Renaissance furniture, tapestries and paintings, superb carved or painted ceilings and stucco decoration and frescoes, notably by Perino del Vaga. Paintings include Lorenzo Lotto's St Jerome and works by the Ferrarese painter Dosso Dossi.

☞ Colonna Gallery

A private collection sumptuously displayed in a series of rooms, notably the opulent Great Hall, with ceiling paintings glorifying Marcantonio Colonna, victor of Lepanto. Mostly 17th- and 18th-century, with a Venetian emphasis. (*Open Saturday mornings only*)

☞ Corsini Gallery (Galleria Nazionale)

This fine collection now belongs to the State but is still displayed in the Palazzo Corsini, built for the Cardinal Corsini who acquired the nucleus of the collection in the mid-18th century. Mainly Italian Baroque art, including important works of the Neapolitan and Bolognese schools, but with some Dutch and Flemish works too.

🖝 Doria Pamphili Gallery
A fabulous collection, in the exuberantly decorated palace of one of Rome's
most famous noble families. The paintings include Caravággio's Flight into
Egypt and Velasquez's portrait of the Pamphili pope, Innocent X (1650).
Guided tours of the apartments are worthwhile (although in Italian), for the
superb furnishings, tapestries and paintings by Sano di Pietro, Filippo Lippi,
Bronzino and others. (*Open Tuesdays, Fridays and weekends only, 10am-1pm*)

🖝 Keats-Shelley Memorial
The house where Keats died in 1821 is something of a shrine, with portraits,
mementoes, manuscripts, books and drawings, all meticulously labelled.
The library atmosphere is in striking contrast to the jollity of the Spanish
Steps below, but opposite is another place of pilgrimage for the English –
Babingtons tea rooms. (*Also open weekday afternoons but closed weekends*)

🖝 Museum of Modern Art
A huge and well-organised collection. There are works remarkable for their
sheer size or for their subject matter (statue of Edward Jenner vaccinating a
child) but the most appealing are the portraits – Boldini's flamboyant women
(Marchese Casati in a flurry of peacock feathers and tulle) and Medardo
Rosso's ephemeral, shadowy Donna Velata. The collection includes blatantly
derivative Italian impressionists.

🖝 Museum of Roman Civilisation
The history of ancient Rome illustrated with models; good schoolroom stuff.
(*See excursions: E.U.R*)

🖝 Napoleonic Museum
Founded by a descendant of the Bonapartes, a fascinating and wide-ranging
collection, with jewellery and dresses, Empire furniture, and portraits by
David and Winterhalter.

🖝 National Gallery (Palazzo Barberini)
A visit to Italy's National Gallery (misleadingly called *d'arte antica*) can be
disappointing. It is not as rich as you might expect and it is under constant
re-arrangement; whole rooms may be shut at any time. On the first floor
is the *salone* with Pietro da Cortona's ceiling (1633-39), a masterpiece of
illusionistic perspective glorifying the Barberini family. Highlights of the
picture collection are Raphael's portrait of his mistress, La Fornarina, and
Caravággio's Judith and Holofernes. Flemish and French artists are also
represented. The decorative arts section includes some exquisite rococo
interiors.

🖝 National Museum (Villa Giulia)
The twin delights of a charming Renaissance villa, built as a papal country
retreat, and one of the most important collections of Etruscan art in the
world. The highlight of the collection, at least for amateurs, is the 6th-century
terracotta sarcophagus of a husband and wife, illustrating the Etruscan belief
in life after death.

🖝 National Museum of Rome
The ruins of the Baths of Diocletion form a suitable context for this vast
archaeological collection. Statues line – almost litter – the cloister while inside
three rooms with exquisite fragments and Roman mosaics and frescoes
discovered only in the last century are on view. The other rooms have been
closed for re-organisation for several years.

🖝 Palazzo Venezia Museum
A palace used by popes, Napoleon and Mussolini and now for art

exhibitions. There are several rooms with original Renaissance decoration and displays of ceramics, sculpture, tapestries etc.

☛ **Rome Museum** (Palazzo Braschi)

The history and life of the city illustrated in paintings, prints and even a railway carriage, built in 1858 for pope Pius IX.

☛ **Spada Gallery**

The small collection of 16th- and 17th-century paintings is hung in the original setting; four rooms of a patrician palace bought by cardinal Spada in 1632. Paintings include the cardinal's portraits, by Guido Reni and Guercino. From the courtyard you can glimpse Borromini's enchanting *trompe l'oeil* colonnade.

☛ **Vatican Museums**

(*See The Vatican, page 313*)

☛ **Villa Farnesina**

An archetypal Renaissance palace built for the Chigi family, by the Sienese painter/architect Baldassare Peruzzi. It is set in lovely gardens close to the Tiber. The interior is famous for the frescoed loggia designed partly by Raphael, although only the magnificent Galatea (1514) in the adjoining room is by his own hand. Upstairs is the bedroom with Il Sodoma's masterpiece, a fresco depicting the Marriage of Alexander and Roxana. (*Also open Mondays.*)

Excursions from Rome

ALBAN HILLS (CASTELLI ROMANI)

A round trip to the Alban hills (*about 100km*) can be a pleasant day out from Rome although the various towns, called *castelli romani* because they were fortified in the Middle Ages, are less picturesque than they sound. Most were damaged during the Second World War and are spoilt by post-war building. **Frascati** (*20km south-east*), famous for its association with the eponymous wine, is disappointingly short of charming piazzas lined with bars, but it is worth seeing the superb Aldobrandini villa, set in magnificent formal terraced gardens. Most of **Grottaferrata** is a charmless suburban sprawl, but there's an interesting fortified abbey (dating from the 11th century) and, just outside the town, at least one good hotel. The perfectly circular and steep-sided **Lake Nemi** is surrounded by market gardens, and the little town of Nemi, perched high above the lake, is famous for its strawberries; almost every bar offers them by the plateful in season. From Nemi you can continue to **Velletri** (not, strictly speaking, one of the Castelli Romani) where the cathedral and chapter museum are worth seeing, or return to Rome via **Lake Albano** and **Castel Gandolfo**, a rather trippery small town where the pope has his summer residence. In July and August there are excursions from Rome for the pope's traditional Sunday morning blessing.

E.U.R.

The E.U.R. (Esposizione Universale di Roma – *about 6km south-west of the centre*) is a district conceived by Mussolini as a monument to the glory of Rome. Work stopped during the war but the project was later revived and completed for the 1960 Olympic Games (Nervi's Palazzo dello Sport). It is a strangely lifeless suburb of broad boulevards and stark white buildings. There are museums devoted to medieval art, Italian folklore, prehistory and ethnography (Museo Luigi Pigorini) and Roman civilisation (a didactic museum consisting entirely of models and reconstructions). The E.U.R can be reached in about 15 minutes by underground.

OSTIA

The ruins of Ostia, main port of Rome until the 2nd century AD, can be visited by public transport (*24km south-west*, about half an hour from the centre by bus, train or underground). There are also some afternoon tours from Rome. For those with hired cars, a visit combines well with departures from Fiumicino airport. However, the site is extensive and you need several hours to cover the ground thoroughly (park near the museum for quicker access to the most interesting parts). In many ways, Ostia is a site for scholars, lacking the evocative atmosphere of the Villa Adriana at Tivoli or the miraculous state of preservation of Pompeii or Herculaneum. However, the remains give a better idea than anything in Rome itself of ordinary everyday life, and of the architecture which even now lies buried under the city. Umbrella pines and cypresses lend the site a certain melancholy beauty. In the small town of Ostia Antica (not to be confused with the modern Ostia Lido) is a fine castle built in 1486 for Giuliano della Rovere (later pope Julius II), set in an unspoilt piazza.

TIVOLI

A classic day trip from Rome (*30km east*), Tivoli is an attractive little town with pleasant outdoor bars and restaurants close to the famous beauty spot of the Villa Gregoriana. The main attractions, however, are the remains of Hadrian's Villa (Villa Adriana) and the gardens of the Villa d'Este, both open all day except Mondays. There are half day and evening excursions from Rome to Tivoli and the Villa d'Este but you need to go independently to see the Villa Adriana, which is 6km from Tivoli itself.

☛ **Villa Adriana**

The remains of the cultured emperor Hadrian's sumptuous pleasure palace, built in the 2nd century AD, are still remarkably evocative. A model displayed near the car park gives a good indication of the original appearance and vast scale of this villa with its buildings inspired by Hadrian's travels to the remoter corners of the Empire. The so-called Maritime Theatre (an elegant circular room with a tiny island) and the Canopus (a canal with a graceful colonnade, inspired by a temple Hadrian saw in Egypt) are particularly enchanting but the whole site is awe-inspiringly romantic (and seldom over-crowded). Many of the artefacts found here over the years are in collections in Rome and elsewhere; only less important finds are displayed in the museum.

☛ **Villa d'Este**

The splendid, formal garden created in the 1570s for cardinal Ippolito d'Este (a son of Lucrezia Borgia) is one of the great gardens of Europe, and has influenced the design of many others. Its chief glories are the exuberant fountains, arranged in terraces descending from the villa. These include the Organ Fountain, whose hydraulic mechanism originally played "music", the semi-circular Ovetta fountain (you can walk behind the curtain of water) and the picturesque Avenue of a Hundred Fountains, where scores of sculptures spout water. The fountains are floodlit at night from April to October (there are organised evening excursions from Rome). The interior of the villa is worth visiting for its frescoed rooms and a small, but good picture collection, in need of some cleaning and restoration.

☛ **Villa Gregoriana**

A picturesque park, overlooked by Roman temples. Terraces offer splendid views of the famous waterfalls; the spectacular Cascata Grande was created in 1835 by pope Gregory XVI who had the natural flow of the River Aniene diverted to a drop of some 160 metres.

Hotels

ALEXANDRA   £££
Via Vittorio Veneto 18   *Open all year*
00187 Roma   *Tel: (06) 461943*

The Via Veneto is not what it was but the Alexandra seems impervious to changes in fashion. It's redolent not so much of '50s glamour but of a bygone age of simple comforts. Piecemeal redecoration has been respectful of this; plainly painted walls, quietly patterned loose covers on comfy old armchairs and framed sepia photographs of 19th-century Rome. There's a charming, if rather noisy, Liberty sitting room with period furniture and potted palms; another, chintzier, one; and a breakfast room with more than a hint of art nouveau (and boiled eggs for breakfast!).

Facilities: *45 bedrooms; lift*   **Credit/charge cards accepted:** *Amex, Diners, Eurocard, Visa*   **Metro:** *Barberini*

BOLOGNA   £££
Via Santa Chiara 4a   *Open all year*
00186 Roma   *Tel: (06) 6568951*

A large hotel close to the Pantheon, run with considerable style by the Grifoni family for several generations. The private house atmosphere belies the size. Calm prevails in the coolly classical entrance hall and the gracious drawing room and adjoining *salottino* furnished with pieces collected by the owner's mother. The smart little bar is almost oriental in its simplicity. But bedrooms are less elegant and simply furnished (hence the relatively low price and official category). You can breakfast in one of two classically-inspired rooms, or (as it's not included in the room rate) at the nearby Bar Sant' Eustachio, famed for the excellence of its coffee.

Facilities: *117 bedrooms; lift*   **Credit/charge cards accepted:** *none*

CARRIAGE   ££
Via delle Carrozze 36   *Open all year*
00187 Roma   *Tel: (06) 6793152*

In a street where English noblemen once parked their carriages (hence the name), this hotel is now in a traffic-restricted and thus fairly quiet, although central, area. The spacious bedrooms are English in style with light flowery wallpaper and old stripped pine and painted furniture. Desks in all the rooms make up for the lack of a lounge as such and most people choose to have their breakfast on a tray rather than in the rather dark downstairs bar. A peaceful – and practical – place to stay.

Facilities: *28 bedrooms (AC in 10); lift*   **Credit/charge cards accepted:** *Amex, Diners, Eurocard, Visa*   **Metro:** *Piazza di Spagna*

CESÀRI   ££
Via di Pietra 89a   *Open all year*
00186 Roma   *Tel: (06) 6792386*

Down a quietish alley off the Corso, close to Piranesi's favourite Temple of Neptune and the lovely church of Sant' Ignazio, this family-run hotel has been in existence since the early 18th century. Distinguished guests have included Mazzini, Garibaldi and Stendhal but the hotel remains a modest establishment without pretensions. The bedrooms are large and high-ceilinged with simple furnishings and bathrooms which range from large, light and old-fashioned to boxy, efficient little shower cubicles (and some, cheaper, have no facilities). There's a small TV room and bar but breakfast is served in the bedrooms (as it isn't included in the room rate you could always patronise one of the local bars in the street). Excellent value and friendly atmosphere.

Facilities: *50 bedrooms; lift*   **Credit/charge cards accepted:** *Amex, Diners, Eurocard, Visa*

COLUMBUS   £££
Via della Conciliazione 33   *Open all year*
00913 Roma   *Tel: (06) 564874*

About as close to the centre of the Roman Catholic universe as you could hope to be, the Columbus is housed in a 15th-century *palazzo* built by a cardinal of the della Rovere family. Converted into a hotel in 1950, the hotel retains many of its medieval features: vast halls and a superb frescoed gallery partly attributed to Pintorrichio. However the atmosphere is monastic (monks were moved here when their palace was destroyed to make way for Bernini's colonnades in 1655) – especially in the wide bare corridors and solemnly stylish bedrooms, of which a third have only basins. There's a walled terrace garden. Not super-central, but ideal for people who want more than an overnight base, and reasonably priced.

Facilities: *120 bedrooms; restaurant; lift; parking* **Credit/charge cards accepted:** *Amex, Diners, Eurocard, Visa*

DIPLOMATIC

££££
Via Vittoria Colonna 28   Open all year
00193 Roma   Tel: (06) 6799389

The main attraction of the Diplomatic is its cheerful restaurant and pretty patio, shaded by greenery and huge umbrellas. It's one of the few hotels in Rome where you can enjoy not only an alfresco breakfast, but a fresh *antipasto* buffet lunch or a reasonably priced set dinner. Bedrooms are small and charmless with mod cons such as hairdriers in the bathrooms. Although on the "wrong" side of the Tiber, in immediately dull surroundings, the Diplomatic is only a short distance from the Vatican and the Piazza del Popolo. A well-run hotel under the same management as the Valadier.

Facilities: *50 bedrooms (AC); restaurant; lift* **Credit/charge cards accepted:** *Amex, Diners, Eurocard, Visa*

EDEN

£££££
Via Ludovisi 49   Open all year
00187 Roma   Tel: (06) 4742401

In the smart Ludovisi quarter (with Mayfair prices to match), the Eden is one of Rome's most famous hotels, long the haunt of politicians. It is comfortable rather than ultra-luxurious but a lot less stuffy than others in this class. The breathtaking panorama from the fifth floor restaurant and bar (with charming terrace) detracts from the need for a little refurbishment, and the best bedrooms have been stylishly redecorated. In the comfortable public rooms rare Etruscan finds are nonchalantly displayed.

Facilities: *120 bedrooms (AC); restaurant; lift; parking* **Credit/charge cards accepted:** *Amex*

FONTANA

£££
Piazza di Trevi 96   Open all year
00187 Roma   Tel: (06) 6786113

The price you pay for a view over Rome's most fabulous fountain is high, in terms of decibels as well as *lire*. The hotel, a converted monastery, actually predates the fountain by several hundred years, but there's little evidence of this inside. Rooms are small, some cell-like, and the flowery wallpaper can be oppressive. Picture-window views from the bar/breakfast room compete with the chequer-board décor. In the wee small hours, when the crowds have dispersed, you can hear the coins being vacuumed from the fountain.

Facilities: *28 bedrooms (AC); lift; free parking permit* **Credit/charge cards accepted:** *Amex, Diners, Visa*

GERBER

Via degli Scipioni 241
00192 Roma

££
Open all year
Tel: (06) 3595148

A small, modern hotel in a residential and shopping area north of the Vatican. Spacious, flowery bedrooms in warm tones are comfortable enough, baths and showers neat. Public rooms are not conducive to lingering but there's a roof terrace for sunbathing (with deckchairs and shower) and a little paved garden too. It's reasonably quiet, conveniently close to public transport, and cheap.

Facilities: *28 bedrooms; lift; parking* **Credit/charge cards accepted:** *Amex, Diners, Eurocard, Visa* **Metro:** *Lepanto*

GREGORIANA

Via Gregoriana 18
00187 Roma

££££
Open all year
Tel: (06) 6794269

In a quiet street of shuttered *palazzi* close to the top of the Spanish steps, the interior of the Gregoriana comes as a surprise. From the orientally-inspired reception lobby, you step into a lift papered with art nouveau tendrils, out onto a landing with black satin walls and leopardskin cushions.... Bedrooms (where breakfast is brought on trays) are mercifully spacious and uncluttered, with strong accents of colour in carpets and lacquered furnishings, bathrooms refreshingly flowery. Sophistication on a small scale; book early to avoid disappointment.

Facilities: *19 bedrooms (AC); lift* **Credit/charge cards accepted:** *none* **Metro:** *Piazza di Spagna*

D'INGHILTERRA

Via Bocca di Leone 14
00187 Roma

£££££
Open all year
Tel: (06) 672161

Within spitting distance of Balenciaga, the d'Inghilterra occupies a prime shopping (or window-shopping) position although that is unlikely to have been its attraction for the king of Portugal, Henry James or Mendelssohn. A 19th-century hotel which lives up to its name, with a series of small rooms en suite, each like an elegant private drawing room both in scale (intimate) and furnishings (tasteful), and with a clubby bar hung with Morland engravings and hunting scenes. Bedrooms too, could be in an English country house: most large and comfortable. Some bathrooms are super smart marble affairs, others average. No restaurant but a charming breakfast room frescoed like a classical garden. A most civilised retreat.

Facilities: *102 bedrooms (AC); lift; parking* **Credit/charge cards accepted:** *Amex, Diners, Eurocard, Visa* **Metro:** *Piazza di Spagna*

INTERNAZIONALE
Via Sistina 79
00187 Roma

££££
Open all year
Tel: (06) 6793047

An elegant and expensive small hotel which rivals its more prestigious
neighbours, and appeals to the same conventional tastes. Flowers are
artificial, as is the Empire style furniture, and the gothic staircase is
unashamedly 19th century. But the overall atmosphere of a private house has
a certain appeal, bedrooms are large (noisy on the front) and bathrooms have
been smartly rejuvenated.

Facilities: *38 bedrooms (AC); lift*   **Credit/charge cards accepted:** *Amex, Diners,
Eurocard, Visa*   **Metro:** *Piazza di Spagna*

LORD BYRON
Via G. de Notaris 5
00197 Roma

£££££
Open all year
Tel: (06) 3609541

Outrageously expensive for a non-central hotel which doesn't even have a
garden to speak of. But the Lord Byron earns its place in the luxury category.
Everything from the perfectly plumped cushions to the pristine marble
bathrooms looks untouched and unsullied. Bedrooms vary in size and
decorative appeal but all are calm and immaculate. There's a summery
restaurant which dares to call itself "Le Jardin".

Facilities: *50 bedrooms (AC); restaurant (closed Sun); lift; parking*
Credit/charge cards accepted: *Amex, Diners, Eurocard, Visa*

MARGUTTA
Via Laurina 34
00187 Roma

££
Open all year
Tel: (06) 3614193

The three Papi brothers run a modest small hotel in a narrow, cobbled street
of antique restorers and *alimentari*. It's cheap by any standards, and very
central. For a small supplement (and if you book well in advance – Signor
Papi described it as an "eternal lottery"') you could choose one of the doubles
on the top floor which share a sunny roof-terrace, laden with roses. These
attic rooms (hot in summer) have a rustic, cottagey charm with beamed
ceilings and old furniture. Other rooms, including the small breakfast room,
are less special but pleasant and individual in feel, and spotlessly kept. Noise
is mainly of hammering and sawing, plus the odd delivery van, for this is a
traffic-restricted zone.

Facilities: *25 bedrooms; lift*   **Credit/charge cards accepted:** *Amex, Diners,
Eurocard, Visa*   **Metro:** *Flaminio/Piazza di Spagna*

MOZART
Via dei Greci 23b
00187 Roma

£££
Open all year
Tel: (06) 6788923

On the corner of the Via del Corso, in a street of picture framers, bookbinders and interior decorators, the Mozart can be noisy. First impressions are favourable; there's an atmosphere of understated elegance, a happy combination of rustic tiles and whitewash and discreet silk stripes. Bedrooms and passages aren't quite as new, but neat with muted colourschemes and brass bedheads. Beds and bathrooms are not for giants. There's no lounge as such but the reception area has a bar, sofas, magazines and even smart headed writing paper. There's a basement breakfast room. Calm and civilised – but do request a quiet bedroom.

Facilities: *31 bedrooms (AC); lift; free parking permit* **Credit/charge cards accepted:** *Amex, Diners, Eurocard, Visa* **Metro:** *Piazza di Spagna*

PORTOGHESI
Via dei Portoghesi 1
00186 Roma

££
Open all year
Tel: (06) 6564231

Tucked away next to Sant' Antonio dei Portoghesi in a narrow street north of Piazza Navona, this hotel is still officially on Portuguese territory. Until three years ago it had been owned by the same family for 150 years; standards have been maintained and the new management is friendly and helpful. Although bedrooms are quite small (with a high proportion of singles) and basically furnished, all have trouser presses and the majority have nice brightly tiled bathrooms. It's quiet enough at night although sawing and drilling in the local workshops could disturb your siesta. Breakfast is served in a freshly stuccoed room with rustic tiles and mellow brick ceiling, all whiteness and light, or on a pretty roof terrace from which you can almost touch the cupola of Sant' Antonio. There is no lounge or bar, but you can buy cold drinks. Excellent value for money, although a short walk from any public transport.

Facilities: *27 bedrooms (AC in 23); lift* **Credit/charge cards accepted:** *Visa*

RAPHAEL
Largo Febo 2
00186 Roma

££££
Open all year
Tel: (06) 650881

Behind a creeper-clad façade on a fairly quiet little piazza, close to Piazza Navona. The reception area and adjacent lounge and bar are strewn with a curious miscellany of antique pieces, but the atmosphere is airily informal. Table lamps, oil paintings and antique carved dressers make the large basement restaurant cosily uninstitutional. Bedrooms are quite small and plain with a mixture of old and new furniture, bathrooms not to the highest standard (but towelling bathrobes add a touch of luxury).

Facilities: *85 bedrooms (AC); restaurant (closed weekends); lift* **Credit/charge cards accepted:** *Amex, Diners, Visa*

LA RESIDENZA ££££

Via Emilia 22
00187 Roma

Open all year
Tel: (06) 460789

Close to the Via Veneto and the American Embassy, this renovated villa is set back from a dull street, but stands out with its flashy flagpoles. Inside it has been stylishly refurbished with rattan and regency stripe, polished parquet (or marble) and rugs everywhere, antiques and oil paintings. But artificial lighting is required even during the day. Bedrooms are international in style with no frills but plenty of mod cons; several have small terraces. A buffet breakfast is a feature of this elegantly cosmopolitan small hotel.

Facilities: *27 bedrooms (AC); lift; parking*   **Credit/charge cards accepted:** *none*   **Metro:** *Barberini*

SANT' ANSELMO ££

Piazza Sant' Anselmo 2
00153 Roma

Open all year
Tel: (06) 573547

Almost audible tranquillity is the reward for those who choose to stay in the Aventine, a smart residential area of detached villas where the air is heavy with the scent of oleander. The most attractive of the handful of hotels in the area, the Sant' Anselmo feels more like a private house than a hotel. Inside all is light and elegant with cool marble floors and summery colours. The bright little breakfast room/bar opens out onto a charming terrace, and below it a little garden with a rose pergola and fountains. Bedrooms range from light attic rooms with nursery type white furniture and accents of primary colours to high-ceilinged, more traditionally furnished rooms with embroidered bedcovers and prettily painted doors. All have pristine bathrooms. There's a trattoria and a bus stop close by, but you could feel stranded without a car.

Facilities: *45 bedrooms*   **Credit/charge cards accepted:** *Amex*

SCALINATA DI SPAGNA £££

Piazza Trinità dei Monti 17
00187 Roma

Open all year
Tel: (06) 6793006

A pretty little classical villa on the piazza – little more than a taxi rank – at the top of the Spanish steps. The brass plaque on the door reads "your home in Rome" and indeed the interior of this small *pensione* is homely to a fault. Bedrooms are very large and mostly quite drably decorated and furnished. Minibars and trouserpresses have been installed. The best rooms have french windows onto the brick terrace where breakfast is served in fine weather among tubs of greenery and yesterday's sheets hanging out to air. Otherwise it's in a little front parlour. Expensive for this type of accommodation, but a superb location and views.

Facilities: *14 bedrooms*   **Credit/charge cards accepted:** *none*   **Metro:** *Piazza di Spagna*

SOLE £££ but shown as ££

SOLE ££
Piazza della Rotonda 63 *Open all year*
00186 Roma *Tel: (06) 6780441*

When Ariosto stayed here in 1513 this old inn had already been going some sixteen years. But it's dwarfed in antiquity by the venerable Pantheon which it overlooks – and you pay over the odds for the classic location. Bedrooms are large and high-ceilinged, slightly shabby but pleasant overall with quite nice little shower rooms. The cavernous breakfast room on the first floor is brocaded and hushed, the lounge dim but with a certain charm. Rooms overlooking the Pantheon are air-conditioned but you can't shut out the noise (chatter rather than traffic) from the piazza below.

Facilities: *31 bedrooms (AC in some); lift* **Credit/charge cards accepted:** *Amex, Diners, Eurocard*

TREVI ££
Vicolo del Babuccio 20 *Open all year*
00187 Roma *Tel: (06) 6789563*

Hidden in a quiet little alley close to the Trevi Fountain, this simple hotel is under the same management as the Fontana. Although used chiefly as the overflow from its sister hotel, the Trevi shouldn't be written off as the poor relation. A pretty floral décor prevails in the carpeted bedrooms, while the reception is unpretentiously stylish – plain walls, matt terracotta tiles and black lacquer desk and bar. Guests are asked to use the breakfast room at the Fontana. A good cheap hotel but a bit cramped for a long stay.

Facilities: *21 bedrooms; lift;* **Credit/charge cards accepted:** *Amex, Diners, Eurocard, Visa*

VALADIER ££££
Via della Fontanella 15 *Open all year*
00187 Roma *Tel: (06) 3610592*

Once a "house of ill-repute", the Valadier is now eminently respectable and enjoys a fairly quiet location close to the Piazza del Popolo (whose architect it is named after). At the time of going to press the hotel was undergoing extensive redecoration; it promises to be very sophisticated.

Facilities: *40 bedrooms (AC); restaurant; lift* **Credit/charge cards accepted:** *Amex, Diners, Eurocard, Visa* **Metro:** *Piazza di Spagna/Flaminio*

VILLA BORGHESE £££
Via Pinciana 31 *Open all year*
00198 Roma *Tel: (06) 8440105*

The novelist Alberto Moravia once lived in this town house overlooking the gardens of the Villa Borghese. Even today it is more like a private house than a hotel. Bedrooms are mostly spacious and individual in feel, the only consistent factor being the rather incongruous Indian silk screen prints.

Bathrooms are neat modern additions, but overall the atmosphere is of faded
gentility. The public rooms are cosy and rather charming with loose-covered
sofas and armchairs, paintings and antiques. The summery breakfast room,
with its wicker, floral-cushioned chairs, opens onto a terrace. Not central; a
good choice for those with cars.

Facilities: *30 bedrooms*   **Credit/charge cards accepted:** *Amex, Diners, Visa*

VILLA DEL PARCO   £££
Via Nomentana 110   *Open all year*
00161 Roma   *Tel: (06) 864115*

A delightful family-run hotel, until recently classed as a *pensione*, whose main
disadvantage is its distance from the centre (about 15 minutes by bus). It is
well set back from the noisy Via Nomentana, close to the park of Villa
Torlonia. The welcoming interior is furnished in country-house style with
well-puffed sofas, oil paintings and antiques. Passages are hung with old
prints of Rome and fresh flowers abound. Bedrooms tend to be large and
comfortable, some pretty and appealing, some plain. The cool (basement)
sitting room, bar and breakfast room have a tranquil rural charm – breakfast
is also served on the patio in front of the entrance in summer.

Facilities: *24 bedrooms (AC); parking*   **Credit/charge cards accepted:** *Amex,
Visa*

THE OUTSKIRTS OF ROME

Grottaferrata   ££
VILLA FIORIO   *Open all year*
Viale Dusmet 25, 00046 Roma   *Tel: (06) 9459276*

Grottaferrata is surrounded by a race-track of a one-way ring road, and this
fine old villa is neither totally peaceful nor easy to spot (beside the road from
Frascati). It is worth finding though, set among lush gardens with a cool
terrace and a good kidney-shaped pool, and generally successful in the
difficult combination of authentic antique splendour and modern hotel
comfort. This is a popular place for evenings out of the capital and wedding
parties; the atmosphere is quite formal and food is surprisingly good. Some
bedrooms share a terrace of their own. The hotel's location is convenient for
suburban sightseeing (the Castelli Romani) and for the charter flight airport
(Ciampino). It's about 25km from the centre of Rome.

Facilities: *20 bedrooms; restaurant; swimming pool (heated); parking*   **Credit/
charge cards accepted:** *Amex, Diners, Visa*

CENTRAL ITALY

Rome is the only capital city I know which has retained the Middle Ages on its doorstep

HV MORTON

Civita Castellana

CENTRAL ITALY

Introduction

This is a bits and pieces area: that part of Italy which is further north than the south and further south than the north and the Tuscan and Umbrian centre; the area around Rome, you might think, and not give it a second thought. You would be wrong. The very dissimilar regions grouped together in this chapter do not individually or together count among the great highlights of Italian tourism, but that itself is part of their appeal, and there is no shortage of fine scenery, historic and sightseeing interest and even some coastline that is both beautiful and sandy.

Modern Rome's influence on its surrounding countryside does not extend far. There are Sunday afternoon resorts in the hills south-east of the city, there are a few unattractive Roman beach resorts north and south of the mouth of the Tiber and there are one or two Roman ski resorts in the mountains. But most of mountainous Abruzzi is wild and empty and most of Roman Lazio is rural, peaceful and provincial. On the Adriatic side of the mountains, a small area between the high peaks and a long sandy coastline contains some of Italy's most attractive country, interesting but uncluttered by mass tourism, mountainous but not inaccessible, busy and civilised but unscarred by heavy industry.

HV Morton's reference to the Middle Ages on the doorstep of Rome was to Abruzzi, home of the highest mountains in peninsular Italy (that is, excluding the Alps and Mount Etna), a notoriously wild, primitive and unruly region of wolves, witches and snake charmers, in its traditions and superstitions not so much medieval as pre-Christian. In a country obsessed with the division between civilised, wealth-creating north and depressed, idle south, it is natural to assume that the further south you go the more remote and undiscovered Italy becomes. Not so: Abruzzi is wilderness Italy at its wildest. There are peaks of nearly 10,000 feet, bears, eagles and chamois. The scenery is more beautiful than Calabria's, the region is less distant and easier to combine with others for a touring holiday.

It would be stretching a point to suggest that the mountains of Abruzzi can rival the Alps in their appeal either to winter or summer visitors. In few places is the landscape exciting in the way the Alps can be (the Gran Sasso and the Maiella are the most impressive massifs) and it entirely lacks the element of glaciers and snowy peaks in summer. The Abruzzi National Park itself is mostly wooded, and its beauty lies more in its freedom from the influence of man than in scenic grandeur.

Inevitably, Abruzzi has shared in the development that has brought all the most remote and notoriously primitive corners of Italy into the twentieth century. Travelling around the region you are unlikely to wonder whether you have been transported five hundred yeas into the past and you will no longer encounter the curiosity that might greet a visitor from another planet. The snake-men of Cocullo and the old woman of Scanno in their traditional costumes are now well-used to tourists and television cameras and will talk to you about football, just like locals everywhere else in Italy.

Many fascinating things Abruzzi may no longer be. It remains a very peaceful and beautiful mountain region well worth exploring and offering a striking change from the culture trail of northern central Italy. Its southern neighbour Molise, only recently given the status of a region of its own, shares Abruzzi's tranquillity but not the beauty of its landscape, except in the Matese mountains north-east of Naples where the peaks give huge views across Italy, from Adriatic to Tyrrheian seas. Except for a few quiet ruins of ancient cities, Molise is like most of inland southern Italy: dull.

On the western side of the Apennines, Lazio (ancient Latium) has several different faces. North of Rome it shares the characteristics of Umbria, with towns of volcanic stone, lakes in old craters and eroded hills of soft tufa stone bringing down old villages as they crumble; and of the coastal part of Tuscany, with an uninteresting flat coastline and quiet medieval towns which make well-known Tuscan beauty spots like San Gimignano seem twee and touristy. "Corneto possesses little interest save to those who love to dwell with the past", wrote George Dennis over a century ago in his splendid guide to this part of Italy. He was quite right. As our nostalgia grows and places where it is possible to dwell with the past become fewer and fewer, the few such as Corneto (which we now call Tarquinia) become more and more appealing.

Northern Lazio is southern Etruria, and its greatest treasures are the excavated zones where the Etruscans lived and, more to the point, where they buried their dead. Although the tombs have been emptied of their movable treasures (the Villa Giulia in Rome and archaeological museum in Florence can fill the gaps admirably), enough remains at the burial grounds at Cervéteri and Tarquinia and several other smaller rural sites to fascinate expert and non-specialist alike. If you come into the second category, you will probably find these cities of the dead more impressive than the museums and their contents drily presented out of context; also that what you learn about the Etruscans will endear them to you and give you an appetite to know more.

South of Rome lies the flat Pontine plain, once the Pontine marshes, favourite hunting grounds of sporting Romans. This swampy and unhealthy area remained without any significant human population until finally drained, irrigated and cleared of malaria in the 1930s. A small part of it has been preserved as national park, a monument to the old marshes and their wildlife, but the area now consists mainly of uninteresting new towns and beach resorts redeemed by long empty stretches of beach and sand dunes, very little built up. The hills looking out over the plain are dotted with small towns, many of them with a longer history than Rome and full of fragmentary ancient buildings half buried in a maze of twisting medieval alleys.

On one such hill commanding the main road south or, as it happened in winter 1943-4, north, is the great monastery mountain of Cassino, medieval home of the Benedictine order. The might of its fortifications and its strategic position made Monte Cassino the natural point where the Allied advance on Rome found its crisis. The monastery fell under intensive bombing and many thousands of soldiers fell among the ruins and on the devastated mountainsides. The buildings have been beautifully reconstructed and the human sacrifice commemorated with war cemeteries. Another name most familiar as a Second World War battlefield is Ánzio, where American and British forces landed in 1944 and where they remained hemmed in for long months before being able to form a united front across the peninsula. Ánzio has risen again and is a busy town and beach resort, inevitably without much charm.

On the Adriatic side of the Apennines, the very name of the Marches (Marche) tells of the area's transitional position in history, a buffer zone of petty states whose rulers benefited from their strategic location between the lands of empire and papacy, selling their loyalty for what amounted in practice to independence. One of these states, San Marino, is independent to this day. Although nominally under papal control from the early Middle Ages, the

---

Visiting Central Italy

Rome is the obvious gateway to Lazio and Abruzzi; for details of travel, see the Rome chapter. The Marches are equally accessible from Venice and other Adriatic airports (Rimini, Ancona) used by tour operators offering package holidays on the Adriatic coast, one of Italy's busiest holiday regions. There are very few packages to other areas covered by this chapter (Tyrrhenian coast and islands, and the interior).

The Adriatic has the usual seaside season, July and August. Outside these months the facilities on the concession beaches may not be available. The northern resorts (around Rimini) are the most widely available through British operators, and livelier in June and September. These are also the resorts best placed for excursions, of which many are laid on. The Adriatic coast is a busy through route. The hills south of Ancona (the Conero Riviera) have some good peaceful hotels ideal for a quiet stopover near the motorway. The area's main music festivals are at Pesaro, home of Rossini, in August/September; and Macerata (open-air opera) in July.

North of Rome the coast of Lazio has neither busy nor atttractive resorts, but there are beaches, some of them black sand. The coast between Anzio and Gaeta is more of a holiday area, with busy modern resorts around Monte Circeo and Anzio/Nettuno, mainly used by Romans. Sabaudia has vast expanses of dunes; Sperlonga stands out as an unusually picturesque and undeveloped old village with excellent beaches. Gaeta and Terracina are much more urban but also combine old-town charm and resort liveliness. Ponza is a fashionable little island resort off this part of the coast.

The attraction of inland Lazio is the old towns north of Rome, by no means only of interest to etruscologists and easily combined with a tour of Tuscany and Umbria. Rome is no place to use as a base for excursions and since, as everyone knows, all roads lead to the eternal city, it is hard to tour the area around it. But this hilly area has a number of beautiful old rural retreats, including some of Italy's most famous fountain-filled gardens, notably at Tivoli (described in the Rome chapter) and around Viterbo. All these places are very busy at week-ends.

Abruzzi and Molise is a high mountain area with a mountain climate and beautiful mountain flowers in May and June. Winter is long but the wintersports season is short, and the skiing is strictly for Romans. There are few summer resorts in the mountains as there are in the Alps; Scanno, Pescocostanzo and Pescasséroli are the main ones.

Marches are cut off from Rome by the Apennines and the region's main communications now and in the past are along the coast (with Venice) and by sea.

The Adriatic coast from the Po delta to the Gargano peninsula does not change much in character from region to region. Although naturally attractive – an enormous extent of sand backed by fertile hills and taller mountains – it is now very far from beautiful, blotted by an interminable and only occasionally interrupted sprawl of styleless beach resorts and suffering from railway and motorway running the length of the coast. The main interruption is just south of Ancona, where a beautiful hilly promontory provides an oasis of peace and pebble beaches in the middle of the long urban sandscape. There is an enormous amount of beach but almost all the coast is easily accessible and built up and there are more than enough crowds to go round. Some of the resorts have grown up from old and in several cases interesting towns, others are entirely new. The difference is not always immediately obvious. Even in the old resorts the accommodation consists of modern hotel blocks, mostly far from the town centre but well placed for access to a sandy, gently-shelving beach with concession areas offering watersports facilities, bars and changing rooms in the high season summer months. One or two of the old towns (such as Pésaro and Fano), have kept some of their old-town character, but the larger ones (Rimini and Pescara) have become dominated by mass beach holiday tourism to such an extent that it would be perverse to visit them for any other purpose. Many of the resorts are proud of their colourful carnival celebrations and stage various cultural events in high season. For those who want to combine sun and sand with some sightseeing, the northern resorts are very well placed for interesting day-trips – Verona, Venice, Ravenna, Urbino, San Marino. Possible excursions from the coast of Abruzzi and Molise include fewer famous sights but more beautiful mountain country and some attractively unspoilt country towns.

Strike inland from this monotonous coast and you will discover a charming hill region of little old country towns empty of tourists and full of traditionally-minded craftsmen and small-scale local industries; for once modern Italy seems to have found the right balance between depressed idleness and modernisation. If what appeals to you about Italy is the quiet, warm variety of the rural economy, the scenes of country life that could be taken from a medieval tapestry or book of hours, the Marches will do as well as the hills of Tuscany and Umbria. In few places is there much to see, but there are one or two exceptions, notably Urbino, which combines the charm of an old country market town with the sightseeing interest of one the great centres of Renaissance art and culture. Wander around salmon-coloured Urbino and you will discover that not only is the most perfectly Tuscan-looking town in the Marches, but so too is the most perfectly Tuscan-looking landscape.

One good reason to tour the local musuems of the Marches (especially Recanati, Loreto and Jesi) is the art of Lorenzo Lotto, a taste acquired by many when Venice came to the Royal Academy a few years ago. Lotto was an itinerant artist of great piety and with a very personal vision who in the course of a long life travelled repeatedly in the Marches painting altarpieces for monasteries and town churches, before settling down to spend his last years in the religious community at Loreto. More than most artists of the time Lotto defies categorisation, his art showing a vast range of influences without ever being slavish or repetitive.

Places to visit

ANAGNI

An old hill town and former papal residence. At the end of the long narrow main street is a splendid collection of medieval buildings including the Romanesque **cathedral**, from the side wall of which a statue of pope Boniface VIII looks out over the square. Boniface was the victim of scandalous treatment in 1303 when an agent of the king of France hit him in the face and locked him up in his palace at Anagni. The cathedral is well set and has a fine campanile, but its great treasure is the decoration of the crypt, with mosaic pavement and a series of very Byzantine-looking 13th-century frescoes.

The nearby town of **Alatri** (*about 25km east*) has a remarkable series of pre-Roman walls and a very well-preserved citadel with massive gateways (4th-century BC). **Casamari** (*14km south-east of Alatri*) is an unspoilt Cistercian monastery, mostly from the 13th century.

ANCONA

It is said that Ancona, one of the big sea ports of the Adriatic coast, turns its back on the rest of the Marches. The tourist can return the snub without fear of missing much. The regional capital is a big, ugly, dirty industrial port whose recent history is a depressing chronicle of destruction. Having been flattened by some 160 Allied bombing raids in 1943-4, the city was shaken by a violent earthquake in 1972 and much of the old centre is abandoned and desolate. Ancona means elbow: not because of the treatment it receives from travellers, but a description of its splendid setting on a promontory at the northern tip of the Cónero mountain massif, a rare knobbly joint in the straight, sandy Adriatic coast. On a fine day Ancona's inhabitants can see the sun rise from the sea and disappear into it.

☛ **Cathedral** (San Ciriaco)   Proudly set high above the port, this is a splendid domed, cruciform Romanesque church mostly dating from the 11th and 12th centuries when an older basilica on the site was transformed. A handsome pair of lions support the pillars of the main doorway. The view from the terrace includes a triumphal arch (Arco di Traiano) set up beside the port in AD115, commemorating its construction under Trajan.

☛ **Monte Cónero**   This 572m mountain forces rail and motorway inland south of Ancona, and provides some beautiful scenery with white cliffs, bright pebble beaches and brilliant turquoise water.

☛ **Museum** (Pinacoteca, Via Pizzecolli)   Paintings ancient and modern

include works by Crivelli, Lotto and Andrea del Sarto.
☞ **Santa Maria della Piazza** Romanesque church with a richly decorated but very dirty façade, shown off to no advantage in a dingy part of the old town by the port.

Excursions from Ancona
☞ **Portonovo and Sirolo** (*13km and 20km south-east*)
On the Riviera del Cónero, Portonovo is a popular local resort area, although scarcely a village, where a very picturesque Romanesque church (mid-11th century) stands near the beach in someone's back garden. A Napoleonic fort has been converted into a waterside hotel. Further south, Sirolo is more villagey, with a good beach and some seasonal cafés below the resort.

ÁNZIO
Not much that is old or attractive remains of ancient Antium, a favourite ancient Roman resort much praised by Cicero (who had a villa there) and the birthplace of Caligula and Nero. In its day Antium's Temple of Fortune rivalled Palestrina's in size and magnificence. There are scanty remains, partly underwater, of Nero's villa where many famous sculptures including the Apollo Belvedere were found in the Renaissance.

The town, which had been abandoned in the Middle Ages and rebuilt in the 17th century, was largely destroyed after the Allied landing (22nd January 1944) when for four months the Anzio bridgehead was cut off from the rest of the Allied front.

Modern Ánzio has a lively and colourful fishing and yacht harbour with waterside restaurants; the modern beach resort now merges with **Nettuno**, which has a Renaissance fortress and some old streets. There is a war museum at the American cemetery at Nettuno, and an English war cemetery on the Albano road out of Ánzio.

L'ÁQUILA
The capital of Abruzzi is a big town on a hill, itself overshadowed by the surrounding mountains, the highest in central Italy and snowy for much of the year.

Although old and interesting, the city is a severe one, with streets of tall grey Baroque palaces, business hotels and a broad but otherwise unremarkable main square. L'Áquila has suffered much from earthquakes, worst of all in 1703. With one exception the main monuments are more imposing than attractive.

In the early Middle Ages L'Áquila emerged as the most important of scores of local strongholds, and under the encouragement of emperor Frederick II all their populations came together in a new imperial city, a buttress against papal encroachments into the lands of the Regnum. There are said to have been 99 of these fortresses and 99 churches in L'Áquila. These figures are an overestimate, but the town bell is tolled 99 times every evening and there are 99 spouts in a splendid late 13th-century fountain (the **Fontana delle 99 Cannelle**) which survives inside the town walls near the station.

☛ **Castle** A massive 16th-century fortress of no great decorative quality at
the top of the town, surrounded by an empty moat and public gardens. Its
walls (30 feet thick) enclose the main regional museum of Abruzzo art and
archaeology (**Museo Nazionale**), including a large selection of provincial art
(the medieval section is the most interesting) and a mammoth's skeleton
found locally.

☛ **San Bernardino** The city's big church, on a busy square and
commanding a magnificent view out over the mountains to the south. The
Franciscan Bernardino of Siena, one of the most famous and most tirelessly
itinerant of medieval preachers, died at L'Áquila in 1444. The church was
erected in his memory in the second half of the 15th century, except for the
façade (1527), a wall of no little historical importance according to the art
experts. You are more likely to be delighted by the beautiful tombs (both by
the local artist Silvestro d'Aquila) of Saint Bernardino (in a funerary chapel
off the right aisle; c1505) and Maria Pereira, the Spanish wife of a powerful
local lord (on the left wall of choir; 1496). There are good terracotta sculptures
in the second and third chapels on the right, by Andrea della Robbia and
Silvestro d'Aquila respectively. Most of the richly-decorated Baroque interior
dates from after the 1703 earthquake, which brought down ceiling and dome.

☛ **Santa Maria di Collemaggio** A beautiful late 13th-century church on its own to the south-east of town. The façade has splendid rose windows and geometric patterns of pink and white marble, repeated on the floor inside. The interior is bare and simple (except for the Baroque choir and transept), with some interesting frescoes and a fine series of 17th-century paintings of the life of St Celestine by Andreas Ruthart, a northern painter of hunting scenes who became a Celestine monk. His art was little affected by the conversion.

The saint in question is the unfortunate hermit Pietro Angeleri or da Morrone who was persuaded ("with respectful force", is the chronicler's well-judged phrase) to abandon the mountainous solitude of his retreat near Sulmona and his preferred modest apparel (a muleskin) in favour of the papal tiara. Seated on a donkey led by two of the most powerful European rulers, Charles of Anjou and Charles of Hungary, Pietro arrived at L'Aquila and was crowned pope Celestine V at this church in 1294. A good man, Celestine was a very bad pope and after five months his letter of resignation was gratefully received.

Excursions from L'Áquila
☞ **Gran Sasso**
The highest mountain in the Apennines (2,912m). Near the entrance to the motorway toll tunnel through the mountain (towards Téramo), the old walled village of **Assergi** has some simple accommodation and a 12th- to 15th-century church picturesquely set on a rock above the river. A road climbs to the bottom station of the Gran Sasso cable-car (*21km*) which rises over the steep slopes of the southern wall of the mountain massif to a shoddy hotel/refuge on a shoulder at the foot of the impressive dolomitic peaks collectively known as the Gran Sasso, its shadowy crevices flecked with snow even in high summer. There are ski-lifts around the top of the cable-car (2,130m), but the place is mainly of interest to climbers in summer and ski mountaineers in winter. In 1943 the cable-car brought the overthrown Mussolini (who is reported to have been very nervous about its safety) to the hotel, which he described no doubt inaccurately as the world's highest prison. He spent two weeks eagerly awaiting the first snows and a chance to get his skis on, before being whisked off in a bold rescue by a commando force of Nazi airmen. A new cable-car is currently under construction.

Even if you are unperturbed by cable-cars, the best way to enjoy the magnificent scenery is by car: the road continues past the lift station and makes the ascent much less directly, via the vast high plateau called **Campo Imperatore** (*39km*) where cattle and horses roam free in a landscape of Patagonian breadth and splendour. In spring the plain is carpeted with alpine flowers. A few shepherds live in rough shacks and follow their flocks round the pastures.

From Campo Imperatore the road continues over a pass and down through a no less beautiful but more familiar mountain landscape dotted with old hill villages. **Castel del Monte** (*63km*) and **Santo Stefano di Sessanio** (*77km*) are well worth a walkabout. The second belonged to the Medici in the 16th century; the family shield with its six balls is much in evidence.

☞ **Bominaco** (*29km south-east*)
A tiny hill village south of the L'Áquila/Sulmona road, easily
combined with a visit to Campo Imperatore. A large fortified
monastery was dismantled in the 15th century, leaving the castle a
picturesque ruin but fortunately sparing the two beautiful churches
nearby. If you are in luck, the key-holder will be at the café. If not,
you will be tantalised by post cards showing the 13th-century
frescoes covering the interior of the smaller church (scenes from the
Lives of Christ and St Peregrine, and a calendar of the diocese of
Valva, now Corfinio). The larger church of Santa Maria is a beautiful
11th-century building with good carving outside and a splendid
pulpit (dated 1180) and Easter candlestick.

ÁSCOLI PICENO

Large provincial capital set at a river junction on the Via Salaria
(so-called because of the transport of salt from the Adriatic to Rome),
beneath steep hills. The outskirts are unprepossessing but the old,
greyish pink centre of town, enclosed by the two rivers, is one of the
most handsome and interesting in the region and the **Piazza del
Popolo** one of the most charming of all Italian town squares. An
unusual variety of buildings – the beautiful south wall of the Gothic
church of San Francesco, arcaded Renaissance buildings with
decorative battlements, a Liberty-style café and the imposing façade
of the town hall (13th- to 16th-century) – surround a lively social
forum always full of mothers parading their babies, children on
bikes, old men passing the time of day, and busier citizens hurrying
here and there. On the first Sunday in August Áscoli has a jousting
competition with a parade in Renaissance costume on the square.

It is well worth wandering round the narrow streets of the old
quarter between the Piazza V. Basso, where the picturesque little
Romanesque church of San Vincenzo e Anastasio has an unusual
squared façade, and the Tronto. A Roman bridge (Ponte di Solestà)
is still in use.

The **cathedral** is a building of no great distinction except for the
beautiful altarpiece by Crivelli (1473) in a chapel on the right. The
octagonal 12th-century baptistery forms a traffic island beside the
church.

ATILIA

Archaeological site of the Roman town of Saepinum, beside the
main Isernia to Benevento road south of Campobasso. After
Saepinum was sacked in the 9th century its inhabitants decamped to
a safer position on a nearby hillside, the present unremarkable
village of **Sepino**.

Excavation of a small theatre is still in progress, but there is plenty
else to see: a forum with columns, roads, town walls and gateways
(notably the north-western Porta di Boiano, with elegant sculptures
and inscription commemorating the town's fortification at the
expense of imperial princes Tiberius and Drusus in AD4). A small
museum is open in the mornings.

Interesting though the archaeology is, the most memorable aspect of the place is the vivid impression it gives of what it must have been like to visit Italy's famous ancient sites two hundred years ago. There are no fences or ticket offices, and not many visitors. The old high street is still used by shepherds taking their flocks on the annual migration from plains to high pastures, as it has been for nearly 2,000 years, according to another inscription on a gateway. A small farm community still lives among, and indeed in, the ruins and there is no obvious distinction between ancient and modern buildings, nor between a man's dual role as site caretaker/guide/museum keeper and subsistence farmer. Roman pillars support the rough fabric of an 18th-century farm building, mangy dogs lie in the shade of raised temple pavements, a few untidy vines hang behind the columns of the forum. Timeless is a word that springs to mind.

BRACCIANO

A small town beside the volcanic lake of the same name, a popular Roman recreation zone at weekends. The town is dominated by the round towers of the impressive 15th-century **Castello Orsini Odescalchi**, still inhabited and reported to be unpredictable in its opening hours. The interior has good frescoes and furniture (not original but in keeping).

CASTELLI ROMANI

(*See Rome chapter*)

CERVÉTERI

A small town on a low hill a few miles inland north of Rome, famous for its Etruscan burial grounds, which rank alongside Tarquínia (*see separate entry*) as the most important to have been discovered.

At the height of its power (8th to 5th centuries BC) Etruscan Caere was one of the largest and most brilliant cities of the Mediterranean, with close trading and artistic links with Greece. Its decline set in after the destruction of its main port Pyrgi in 384 at the hands of Dionysius of Syracuse, and in 354 Caere submitted to Rome. Malaria and Saracen raids persuaded its medieval inhabitants to abandon the city and old Caere became known as just that, Caere Vetere. Most of the movable contents of the tombs are in the great museums of the world (Rome, Florence, Paris, London) but there is a small and well-presented **Etruscan museum** (vases, sculptures and photographs of local sites) in a 16th-century palace at the top of the town, surrounded by an impressive collection of fortified medieval buildings.

☞ **Banditaccia necropolis** This is the main monumental zone of the vast area of burial grounds surrounding Cervéteri, reached by a rough road leading west from the town centre. Guided by an itinerary of arrows, you wander the streets of a silent funeral town of large, tuftily overgrown funeral mounds, visiting the tombs that are open. As at many of the archaeological sites of southern Etruria, the peaceful rural setting contributes greatly to the elegiac beauty of the place. Compared with those at Tarquínia, the tombs are impressive structures, the most elaborate being complete houses with entrance halls and funerary "bedrooms", and with very varied decoration ▷

THE ETRUSCANS

Remarkably little is known about the origins, life style or language of a people who dominated central Italy for several centuries before yielding in the 4th century BC to the military machine that was Rome. The Etruscans left no literature and the large number but very limited variety of surviving inscriptions gives only a very incomplete understanding of their language, although the alphabet, based on south Italian Greek, is easily deciphered. Etruscan grammars produced in Roman times have all disappeared and so too have Etruscan histories such as the one assembled by the scholarly emperor Claudius. Some ancient historians report that the Etruscans came from the middle east, others that they were native to central Italy. The debate has never conclusively been settled.

In their home territory between the Arno and the Tiber the Etruscans formed independent city states in the early centuries of the first millennium BC. They grew rich from trade in local metals and developed a taste for jewels, pots and works of art from Greece and the eastern Mediterranean, brought to them by Greek and Phoenician traders. They adopted many eastern customs and beliefs, including a special interest in interpreting divine intentions from the weather and from examination of the liver, and developed their own artistic styles, much influenced by Greek art but with a preference for stylised and even abstract decorative form. The twelve main Etruscan cities convened for an annual religious festival near Lake Bolsena and occasionally elected an overall leader in response to threat from outside, but were essentially independent and often rival powers, at least until they came under Roman control. One of the most striking things about the burial grounds, at Cervéteri and Tarquínia for example, is how totally unlike each other they are.

At the height of their power the Etruscans controlled large areas south of Rome and in the Po valley, Rome itself being ruled by the Etruscan Tarquin dynasty for most of the 6th century. In the 5th century they lost ground on all sides and after long wars Rome eventually established control over Etruria by the middle of the 4th century. Under Rome many of the Etruscan cities continued to flourish, and in its institutions, customs, art and superstition Rome absorbed many aspects of Etruscan civilisation.

Etruscan houses and temples were built of perishable materials, and have perished. What survives and forms the basis of most of our knowledge of the Etruscans is a wealth of tombs almost as great as the poverty of what remains in all other fields. Even allowing for the fact that we are scarcely likely to get anything other than a seriously unbalanced view of a people by exclusive study of its graveyards, it is clear that the Etruscans attached unusual importance to the way they honoured their dead. They constructed elaborate networks of monumental underground chambers for them, decorated the rooms with beams, chairs carved from the rock, relief carvings, beautiful *objets d'art* and paintings of joyous celebration that have left an irresistible vision of a people who believed firmly in pleasure.

Greek and Roman writers have confirmed this view of the Etruscans, reporting that the girls thought nothing of taking up prostitution to raise a dowry, that few women knew for certain who had fathered their children, and that twice a day men and women sat down together (this was what seemed most irregular to the Roman males, who admitted only courtesans to their parties) to luxurious banquets attended by naked servants. The truth was no doubt less wildly bacchanalian, but this half-imagined fantasy of an uninhibited, free-living people whose idea of the hereafter was an eternal knees-up has great charm. DH Lawrence for one found that the Etruscans fitted his philosophy perfectly. The more they drank and danced, the less they wore, and the more they lavished their tombs with phallic symbols, the more Lawrence admired

THE ETRUSCANS

them for their naturalness and physical enthusiasms. Lawrence toured Etruscan burial grounds and declared that "of all the people that ever rose up in Italy, the Romans were surely the most un-Italian. Because a fool kills a nightingale with a stone, is he therefore greater than the nightingale? Rome fell and the Roman phenomenon with it. Italy today is far more Etruscan in its pulse than Roman".

The familiar reclining tomb sculptures and lively portrait busts of late Etruscan art were profoundly influential on Roman and later art. From earlier centuries (6th and 5th BC) Etruscan painters have left very beautiful wall paintings, a speciality of Tarquínia and still best seen there. On the walls of these dank vaults the Etruscans live on in scenes not of obscure mythology but of everyday life, with a preference for dancing and drinking in a framework of pure decorative invention. Many of the paintings have deteriorated since the tombs were opened, but they still convey with remarkable vigour and beauty the spirit that thrilled Lawrence: "the big long hands thrown out and dancing to the very ends of their fingers, a dance that surges from within, like a current in the sea".

☞ **Main Etruscan sights:**
Museums and burial grounds at **Tarquinia** and **Cervéteri**; burial grounds at **Nórchia**, and **Castel d'Asso** (both near Viterbo); museums in **Rome** (Villa Giulia), **Florence** (archaeological museum), **Volterra** and **Chiusi**.

including simulated roof beams, chairs and capitals carved in the stone. By far the most interesting, but unfortunately often closed, is the Tomb of the Low Reliefs, decorated with relief carvings of domestic utensils and pets taken straight from everyday Etruscan life. Originally the tombs contained vases, sculpture and jewellery, providing the dead very literally with a comfortable home for an enjoyable life to come after the tombs were sealed up. Tomb design varied down those centuries when the Banditaccia received the Etruscan dead. The early ones (8th-century) are simple wells and ditches. In later centuries mounds of earth were heaped on top of the tombs, which themselves became gradually more elaborate underground chambers (or hypogea). The mounds ceased to be added in the 4th century. Guidebooks and leaflets of varying explanatory depth are on sale at the entrance.

CHIETI

Abruzzi provincial capital of no great distinction, but with a good **archaeological museum**, including a famous statue of a remarkably curvaceous warrior (6th-century BC), from Capestrano.

CIVITA CASTELLANA

A very ancient hill town near the motorway north of Rome, in an impressive landscape of sharply cut gorges and tufa hills. In the 3rd century BC the Romans moved the inhabitants from their easily defended position down to a new town (**Falerii Novi**) on the plain below, 6km east. In the difficult times of the 8th century the old site was recolonised, and the so-called new town stands as a fascinating overgrown ruin, with an exceptionally well-preserved triangle of town walls and fortifications. Inside one gateway is a ruined 12th-century church.

In Civita, the **cathedral** has a beautiful Romanesque façade, its simple forms contrasting with the colurful mosaic decoration of the porch, one of the finest examples of the work of several generations of the Roman Cosmati family, who have given their name to this art form. The **Rocca** is a splendid example of a Renaissance fortress, built in the late 15th and early 16th centuries for popes Alexander VI and Julius II and inhabited by Cesare Borgia, whose features are perhaps to be recognised in the relief of Christ in the courtyard. The octagonal tower and inner courtyards are the work of the elder Antonio da Sangallo. The castle now has a small museum of local archaeology.

FABRIANO

Hill town near the Umbrian/Marches border, with a handsome central Piazza del Comune, where the fountain and imposing Palazzo del Podestà date from the mid-13th century. The art gallery (**Pinacoteca**) has a good collection of works by local medieval artists, not including Gentile da Fabriano.

Excursion from Fabriano
☞ **Grotta di Frassasi** (*14km north*)
Towards Jesi, in an impressive landscape of limestone gorges, is this long network of caves with spectacular rock formations (guided

tours). Among the spa buildings near the entrance is the unusual-looking 11th-century church of **San Vittore delle Chiuse**.

FANO

A large town and beach resort south of Pésaro famous for its carnival celebrations (a parade of allegorical carts) and its good beaches, one sandy, the other stony.

The old town south of a canal has kept its rectilinear Roman plan, a section of Roman walls and a town gateway (**Arco di Augusto**) erected in 2AD. On the wall beside the very elaborate Renaissance doorway of the adjacent church of San Michele is a relief showing the arch as it looked before Federico da Montefeltro's siege army blew the attic storey off in 1463. Stones from the arch were used for the church and the elegant loggia on the town side of it. The main square (Piazza XX Settembre) is overlooked by the imposing Palazzo della Ragione (1299; the tower is modern). The neighbouring Palazzo Malatesta (15th- to 16th-century) houses an interesting and varied small museum (archaeology, coins and paintings). Two beautiful 15th-century tombs of members of the Malatesta family are in the porch of the nearby former church of San Francesco, of which little else survives.

Between the railway (which runs alongside the old town and the fortications of the 15th-century Malatesta castle) and the sea is a large area of modern resort development, extending a long way north and south of Fano. The sandy beach north of the canal and port is the smaller of the two and gets very crowded.

Apart from Fano, the main focus of the long ribbon of coastal development between Ancona and Pésaro is **Senigallia**, laid out in a similar way to Fano with the town centre (of no great beauty or interest) set back from the sea and separated from it by road, railway and a zone of modern hotels and other holiday-related development.

FERMO

A lively hill town a few miles inland north of Áscoli Piceno, with splendid views from the gardens near the cathedral at the top of the town. The **cathedral** is an interesting building with a lop-sided medieval façade and campanile, and miscellaneous fragments from earlier buildings inside (redecorated in the late 18th century), including early Christian sacrophagi and a 5th-century mosaic pavement.

☛ **Palazzo del Commune** This Renaissance building houses a good art gallery (Pinacoteca) with a beautiful early work by Rubens (Adoration of the Shepherds, 1608) and a series of small paintings of the Life of St Lucy by the 15th-century Venetian artist Jacobello del Fiore.

FOSSANOVA

A handsome and well-preserved late 12th-century abbey and cloister on the edge of the Pontine plain near Priverno, as pure an example of Cistercian architecture as you will find in the order's native Burgundy. Suppressed by Napoleon in 1812, the church was used as

a stable for herds of buffalo and suffered much less damage and
alteration than if it had been appropriated for human use.

GAETA

A big town and naval port beautifully situated on a mountainous
promontory at the southern tip of a sweeping sheltered bay. On the
flat isthmus is the lively modern resort area Sérapo, with big hotels
and a wide, sandy south-facing beach. Old Gaeta is on the
promontory, separated from Sérapo by the 500ft Monte Orlando.
Near the waterfront, the cathedral has a fine 12th- to 13th-century
campanile incorporating many classical fragments, and an Easter
candlestick from the same period decorated with relief scenes from
the lives of St Erasmus and Christ. Behind the cathedral a fascinating
maze of tumbledown medieval alleys and staircases climbs steeply
to the citadel, a naturally impregnable fortress (fortifications from
the 13th to 16th centuries), where Bourbon resistance to the forces of
Italian unity came to an end after a three month siege in February
1861. From the top of the town there are splendid views across the
bay and out to sea over sheer cliffs.

A road climbs through attractive gardens on the lee side of **Monte
Orlando**, also accessible by steep paths up from the old town and
Sérapo. On top stands a broad stumpy Roman tower, the tomb of
one of Julius Caesar's most successful generals, Lucius Plancus
(22BC). Ancient fortifications line the rocks above Sérapo beach; at
the end of them the cliffs are split by clefts said to have been caused
by the earthquake when Christ died. From a sanctuary, a staircase
leads down into the central of these clefts.

There are good beaches and several comfortable isolated hotels
along the rocky coast between Gaeta and Sperlonga (*see separate
entry*).

JESI

A large town on a hill above the river Esino, about 10 miles upstream
from its mouth near Ancona. Jesi was the birthplace of one of the
gigantic achievers of medieval Europe, Frederick II of Hohenstaufen
(1194-1250), administrator, legislator, scientist and warlord: the
Renaissance universal man two centuries ahead of his time. An
impressive section of the 14th-century fortifications stands intact on
the north-eastern edge of the old town.

☞ **Palazzo della Signoria** The elegant 15th- to 16th-century building
contains a museum distinguished by several paintings by Lotto, including
one of his great masterpieces, an altarpiece (1532) depicting the story of St
Lucy, whose misfortunes included being tied up and dragged along by a
team of bulls.

LAKE BOLSENA

The largest of Italy's volcanic lakes (over 40km round), surrounded
by a ring of low, fertile hills. **Capodimonte** is the most picturesque of
the waterside villages, set on a promontory with an octagonal
16th-century castle looking out over the lake and its two small
islands. There is a black sand beach with trees, pedaloes and a good

fish restaurant. The water smells slightly sulphurous, but is rich in fish. Its eels were singled out for special praise by Dante (*Purgatorio XXIV*).

A good viewpoint over the lake is the terrace at nearby **Montefiascone**, a small town famous for the name of its white wine, Est! Est! Est!, and the story behind it. A thirsty travelling prelate, Johannes Fugger (or Jo Fuk as he is named on his tomb), asked his servant to mark "Est" on his itinerary wherever good wine was to be found. Beside Montefiascone the servant wrote Est! Est! Est!; Fugger duly overindulged, and died. The story is told, or at least hinted at, in Latin on Fugger's tombstone in the right-hand corner of lower **San Flaviano**, an interesting two-storied Romanesque church.

Excursion from Lake Bolsena

☞ **Civita di Bagnoregio** (*2km from Bagnoregio, between Montefiascone and Orvieto*).
A dilapidated and largely abandoned old hill village gradually being undermined by the erosion of its foundation of soft tufa rock, and only accessible by footbridge. All around, the erosion of similar hills has produced a weirdly beautiful landscape.

LORETO

One of the most famous pilgrimage towns of Europe, which grew up in the 15th and 16th centuries when the story was put about that an old sanctuary, recorded since the 12th century, was the room where the Annunciation had taken place. According to the legend the Holy House had been miraculously translated from Nazareth first to Dalmatia in 1291 and from there to a laurel grove (whence Loreto) near Recanati during the night of 9th December 1294. Loreto has the cheap religious knick-knack industry without which no pilgrimage town would be complete, but is well worth visiting for sightseeing reasons, the monumental precinct of basilica and apostolic palace being most impressive. The main pilgrimages are on festivals to do with the Virgin: March 25, August 15, September 8, December 8. In celebration of the Translation fires are lit all over the region on the night of 9th December.

☛ **Basilica and Apostolic Palace**   Building work began in the late 15th century and many of the leading architects and artists of the time were employed. Bramante designed the great L-shaped apostolic palace (early 16th-century) and the beautiful marble shell enclosing the Holy House itself, a small chamber in the middle of the basilica. This casing is decorated with powerful Michelangelesque figures of prophets and sybils, scenes from the Life of the Virgin and one depicting the Translation of the House. Inside the chamber are some blackened medieval frescoes and miscellaneous hanging relics. The two round sacristies on the south side of the basilica have beautiful late 15th-century frescoes by Melozzo da Forlì and Signorelli.

There are good late 16th-century reliefs on the bronze doors of the main façade; the bronze statue of Sixtus V dates from the same period. The onion-topped campanile is an 18th-century addition. It is worth wandering round the back of the church, which is incorporated into the brickwork of the town's handsome 16th-century fortifications, and onto the terrace for a good view of the surrounding countryside.

The **museum** in the apostolic palace is interestingly varied, with 17th-century Brussels tapestries after Raphael's designs and a room with a number of late paintings by Lotto, who spent the last years of a spiritually very troubled old age as a lay brother at Loreto and died there in 1556. These include powerful images of saints Christopher, Roch and Sebastian and of Christ and the Adulteress, and the remarkable and perhaps unfinished Presentation in the Temple, Lotto's last work. The altar has human feet.

MACERATA

A hill town and provincial capital south-west of Ancona. The centre is old, still partly walled and not short of charm, and there are some churches and a museum of minor interest. The vast neo-classical arena (**Sferisterio**) was built in the 19th century for the local handball game (*pallone al bracciale*, not unlike Basque pelota), and hosted the first national championship in 1936 as well as horse races and bull-fights. It is now used for concerts and drama, with an opera festival every summer (July and August).

THE MATESE

The long mountain massif dividing Campania from Molise reaches a peak of 2,050m, the Monte Miletto. Of all the mountain areas of southern Italy the Matese is about the most beautiful, yet very little visited. Its varied landscape of lakes, high plateaux and thickly wooded valleys can be easily sampled from the road over the mountains from Vinchiaturo (on the Molise side) past Guardiaregia to the high Lago di Matese, near the watershed, and from there down either towards Venafro or Piedimonte d'Alife (in Campania). Women in several of the small villages (Letino, Gallo, Guardiaregia) still wear traditional costume. The mountains are porous and riddled with caves; the most interesting to visit are near Letino (Grotte delle Lete).

A beautiful road climbs south from the Isernia to Benevento road near Boiano past San Massimo to the Rifugio Jezzi (1,430m), a good starting point for stiff hikes up to the two main peaks.

MONTE CASSINO

One of the world's most famous monasteries was destroyed, and not for the first time, during the three-month battle of Cassino in early 1944 when its setting on a mountain 1,500 feet above the town of Cassino made it one of the key points in the German defensive line blocking the Allies' advance on Rome. The abbey has been faithfully and beautifully rebuilt, as was, and is well worth visiting. The place has the double sanctity of one of the great holy places of Christendom and one of the great war memorials of Europe, and great care is taken to save it from becoming just another tourist attraction. Entrance is free and unguided; decorous dress is required and picnics are forbidden near the monastery, which closes for three hours at midday. Quite apart from the interest of the monuments, the scenery at the top and the views from the coach-wide road up to it are splendid.

Monte Cassino was founded by saint Benedict in the 6th century and its monks are credited with keeping the embers of civilisation aglow through the Dark Ages, as well as spreading the faith to such distant corners of Europe as Britain (saint Augustine). A terrible earthquake in 1349 brought it to the ground and the buildings that crumbled beneath hundreds of tons of Allied explosives on the 15th February 1944 and during the ensuing battle dated mostly from the 16th to 18th centuries.

A series of spacious classical cloisters and courtyards leads to the vast and ornate Baroque church, where no attempt has been made to recreate Giordano's original painted decoration. The museum has a beautiful collection of religious manuscripts, some paintings of relatively minor interest and a large number of photographs of the abbey and surrounding landscape before, during and after the battle. You wonder how the mountain itself survived such an onslaught.

There are several war cemeteries on the mountain and at its feet, commemorating the losses of many different nations (including New Zealand and Poland) in the battle. The modern town of Cassino, which was also destroyed, is not interesting.

MONTEFIASCONE

(*See Lake Bolsena*)

NÓRCHIA

Lonely rural site of an Etruscan necropolis reached by rough road from Vetralla (*10km south-west of Viterbo*). The rock wall of an overgrown gorge glows honey-coloured in the late sun and is pitted like a comb with rock-cut tombs from the 4th and 3rd centuries BC. Clambering round the steep paths and rock ledges, it is hard to make much sense out of the place but it is very impressive in an unspecific way, and there are clear signs of temple-like architectural features (including figures carved in relief) round the entrances to some of the tombs. Ruins of a medieval castle and church complete the romantic beauty of the scene.

NORMA

An old village spectacularly perched high on an eroded mountainside above the Pontine plain, best seen from below, near the romantic-looking swampy ruin of the medieval town of **Ninfa**, abandoned in the 17th century because of malaria. Ninfa is very occasionally open to the public but, if passing through, you will probably have to be content with a view of it from the road. The local long-horned cattle are awesome beasts but rarely aggressive.

Just outside Norma (about 10 minutes' walk, not well signed) are the ruins of ancient **Norba**, including some remains of temples and walls from the 4th century BC. The site commands a beautiful view. (*See also Sermoneta*)

PALESTRINA

A small town facing southwards from a steep hillside east of Rome, famous for the 16th-century composer of religious music named after his home town, and the vast Temple of Fortune, one of the largest and most famous of all Roman temples, much of its ruins laid bare by bombing during the Second World War. Access to the large terraced area of ruins, with niches and chapels in the hillside, is from the top of the town opposite the 17th-century **Palazzo Barberini**. This fine palace has been in a state of some disarray lately but its archaeological museum remains open; its contents include a very helpful model reconstruction of the temple and a magnificent mosaic of the Flooding of the Nile (1st century BC), with scores of small scenes full of exotic and entertaining detail.

PÉSARO

A big town on the Adriatic coast with a moderately attractive and interesting old centre, mostly dating from the 16th century when Pésaro replaced Urbino as the preferred ducal residence and regional capital, and a large area of fairly typical Adriatic beach resort development filling the space between old town and the sea. The centre of the town is the handsome Piazza del Popolo, where the 15th- and 16th-century ducal palace overlooks a 17th-century fountain. The impressive **Rocca Costanza** was built by Luciano Laurana, architect of the Urbino ducal palace, in the late 15th century. Originally part of the town walls, it is now a prison. Pésaro is the home town of the composer Rossini (1782-1868); it has a conservatory of music, frequent concerts and an annual opera festival in August. In the 16th and 17th centuries Pésaro was a famous centre of majolica (tin-glazed earthenware) manufacture.
➥ **Civic Museum** (Via Toschi Mosca, near the cathedral) The ceramic collection here is one of the finest in Italy. The other great treasure of the museum is Giovanni Bellini's Pésaro altarpiece (c1475), in its splendid original frame. The main scene is the Coronation of the Virgin, with the fortifications of Gradara visible in the background. The small scenes round the frame are well worth studying.

Excursions from Pésaro

☞ **Imperiale** (*5km north-west by the minor coast road towards Gabicce*)
A beautifully decorated summer villa built for Pesaro's rulers Alessandro Sforza (late 14th century) and Francesco Maria della Rovere (mid-16th century). Visits can be organised through the tourist office.

☞ **Gradara** (*14km north-west*)
A beautifully preserved small fortified town on a hill beside the main road north of Pésaro, an extremely popular target for outings from the seaside resorts in the Rimini area. You have been warned. The sentry walk round the battlements is still practicable and open to visitors. At the top of the town stands the castle, built in the 13th century and restored in the 15th. Tours of the interior reveal a courtyard, armoury, torture chamber, and some medievally furnished rooms including one alleged to have been the setting in about 1285 of the famous murder of the young lovers Francesca da

Polenta (more palatably known as Francesca da Rimini) and Paolo Malatesta at the hands of the vile Gianciotto Malatesta the Lame (his brother and her husband), as recounted by Dante (*Inferno V*) and countless more recent retailers of Gothic romantic tragedy.
(*See also Urbino; San Marino*)

PESCARA

The biggest and busiest town of Abruzzi and one of the big resorts on the Adriatic coast. None of which should persuade you to break a journey there, although there are plenty of modern hotels and over five miles of uninterrupted sand stretching north of the main river estuary where the city has grown up. Pescara's great pride is having given birth to Gabriele D'Annunzio (1863-1938) celebrated poet, playwright, patriot and popular hero of pre-Fascist Italy, no less ardent in his advocacy of war than of voluptuous liberation, and prodigiously energetic in his personal pursuit of both.

In a colourful career that included a solo flight to drop pamphlets over enemy Vienna, the most remarkable exploit was when D'Annunzio, unhappy with the decisions taken at the end of the First World War concerning the Italian frontier, assembled his own army of so-called legionnaires (including Mussolini), occupied Fiume and ruled it, first as part of Italy then independently, for over a year. After this great adventure, which did much to influence the ideas and style of Fascist Italy, he retired to a villa (the Vittoriale) at Gardone Riviera beside Lake Garda. This is a much better place to visit for a flavour of D'Annunzio's excessive style than the house where he was born in Pescara, although this is open to the public.

PESCASSÉROLI

An old village among woods in a high valley at the heart of the **Abruzzi National Park** and its main resort. There is a small museum and information centre, and hotels and chalets dotted around the open slopes near the village, which offer good skiing in winter. The Park covers about 300 sq km of mostly wooded, wild rather than spectacular mountain country. There are bears, wolves and chamois apparently more closely related to the Pyrenean than the Alpine variety.

Excursions from Pescasséroli

☞ **Circular driving tour** (*about 120km*)
The long tour over the Passo del Diavolo takes you to Pescina on the edge of what used to be the **Fucine Lake**, now the Fucine flats, irrigated and intensively cultivated. The shallow lake had no natural outlet and regularly caused floods. In AD52 Claudius and Messalina presided over the ceremonial opening of a drainage tunnel, with a nautical battle that turned the water of the lake red before the outlet was opened. The system did not work well, and the lake was not effectively drained until the 19th century, when an enterprising banker took the job on in exchange for ownership of the land. On the road east towards Sulmona, **Cocullo** is one of the Abruzzo villages famous for its snake charmers (*serpari*) and their festival in

early May. In celebrations derived from pagan ritual, snakes are draped round the statue of St Dominic and paraded round town. The return route passes through some very impressive rocky gorges to **Scanno** (*see separate entry*) and back into the park up the beautiful Sangro valley. There is a small zoo at **Castel di Sangro**.

PESCOCOSTANZO

A village high (nearly 1,400m) up in the wild country south of Sulmona, near the **Piano delle Cinquemiglia**, a long (5 ½ miles, actually), narrow, empty, treeless pass/plateau notorious for its brigandage and its winter storms, which claimed for victims 300 Venetian soldiers in February 1528 and 500 Germans 13 months later.

Pescocostanzo is by no means the simple shepherds' village you might expect to find in such rough country, but a substantial, handsome and dignified place known for its craftsmanship in wood, metal and lace. The paving of the streets is patterned, and elegant iron balconies grace a few houses. The main church (Collegiata) is also built on a grand scale, with a lavish coffered wooden ceiling (17th- and 18th-century) and an elaborately wrought iron screen closing off the choir (c1700). People use the village as a base for walking in summer and skiing (mainly cross-country) in winter.

The main road towards the Adriatic passes through some splendid scenery around **Fara San Martino**, at the foot of the impressive cliffs of the Maiella, one of the great massifs of the Apennines.

PONZA

The largest and most popular of a small group of islands off the Tyrrhenian coast, about 20 miles from Monte Circeo and accessible from Naples, Formia, Terracina and, in summer, Ánzio. All the islands are volcanic in origin.

Ponza is about 5 miles long and between 200 yards and a mile wide. Its main village (Ponza) is a pretty fishing port of pink and white houses, full of life early in the morning when the catch is unloaded. There are some good, mostly pebble beaches, but few are easily accessible: most of the coast consists of tall cliffs of golden tufa rock. The best way to enjoy the island is by yacht, and many smart Italians do.

There are organised boat trips from Ponza to the other islands. The inhabited ones are Ventotene, with its notorious prison islet of Santo Stefano (whose visitors included former president Pertini), now abandoned and overgrown; and Palmarola, a favourite stopover for birds on their spring migration (March to May). Uninhabited Zannone is now part of the Circeo national park and solely of interest to naturalists. As well as migrant birds it has its own species of lizards, butterflies and spiders, and a few mouflons introduced from Sardinia in 1922.

RECANATI

A lively red-brick town on a hill looking down over Loreto's towers and the Adriatic, Recanati was the home of the poet and philosophical writer Giacomo Leopardi (1798-1837), one of the great figures of Italian literature. Deformed and unhealthy, Leopardi lost himself (and eventually his sight) in tireless study from a very young age. His most famous poetry is the expression of despair. A local of lesser stature but perhaps wider international fame is the great tenor Beniamino Gigli (1890-1955).

☞ **Palazzo Comunale** The museum in the town hall has a section devoted to Gigli, with old opera costumes and photographs and an accompaniment of piped arias (and the television, if there is football for the attendant to watch, as there usually is). There is also a room with two of Lorenzo Lotto's greatest masterpieces, an early altarpiece (Madonna and Saints, 1508) brilliant in colour but sombre in mood, and the artist's most popular version of the Annunciation (1528), known here as the Madonna del Gatto after the cat which, like its mistress, reacts with terror to the intrusion of archangel and God, who seems on the point of diving in from a cloud. The painting is full of delightful domestic detail and shows better than any other of Lotto's works his remarkable ability to breathe humanity into the conventional themes of religious art.

RIETI

Attractive old town north-east of Rome, at the foot of the capital's local ski mountain Monte Terminillo. Rieti was known in the early Renaissance for the expertise of its goldsmiths and there are good examples of their work in the cathedral treasury and the town museum. At the nearby monastery of Fonte Colombo (*5km south-west*) saint Francis fasted for forty days and had an operation for a cataract.

SABAUDIA

One of the new towns created in the 1930s when the Pontine marshes were drained, on the edge of a lagoon separated from the sea by a long range of sand dunes and a road, with good beaches and no development along the shore itself.

To the south of the lagoon the wooded **Monte Circeo** rises nearly 2,000 feet above sea and plain, an impressive isolated landmark (once it was an island) and the legendary home of the sorceress Circe. On the slopes above the resort of **San Felice Circeo** are some ruins of an ancient acropolis from the 4th century BC. Boat trips from San Felice visit some of the dozens of caves in the cliffs at the foot of the mountain, one called the grotto of Circe. In another a 70,000 year-old Neanderthal skull was found.

San Felice, Sabaudia and Monte Circeo are now included in a small national park, created to preserve the rich wildlife of the area before it was drained and civilised.

SAN CLEMENTE A CASÁURIA

A 12th-century Cistercian monastery church in an unattractive roadside situation beside the Rome/Pescara motorway near Torre dei Pásseri, north of Sulmona. The church is most famous for the sculptural decoration of the porch and around the central bronze

doorway; you need to be admitted (9am till 3pm) to see even this.
The finest works of art inside the church are the pulpit and
candlestick. The crypt dates from the 9th century. Apart from the
church, the monastery was destroyed by earthquake in 1348 and not
restored.

SAN MARINO

The world's smallest republic is an interesting relic of the
independent communal style of medieval Italian government, ruled
by captains elected for 6-month periods, councils of 60 and 10, and
law officers brought in from outside. Women got the vote in 1959.
San Marino covers 24 square miles, on the slopes and surroundings
of Monte Titano (739m) which provided a Dalmatian stone mason
and companions with a refuge from persecution by the emperor
Diocletian in about AD300. The independence of the mountain
stronghold was recognised in the 9th century and has been
preserved ever since. Only a few miles inland from Rimini and
nearby resorts, San Marino is a very popular day-trip target and
makes as good a living out of the knick-knack and ceramics industry
as it does from stamps. It also receives money from Italy not to
produce tobacco. The main sight to see is the triple citadel of San
Marino itself, an impressive landmark on top of the mountain with
fortifications dating from the 13th to 16th centuries. The main
commercial centre is the lower town of Borgomaggiore.

SCANNO

A beautiful cobbled village on a mountainous spur in the heart of the
Abruzzi mountains near but not beside a lake of the same name,
which reminded Edward Lear of Wastwater in Cumberland.

Scanno is famous above all for the colourful local costumes of its
womenfolk. Like so much that is folklorish, the costumes more or
less died out after the war but have lately been revived. Whether out
of genuine pride in origins or in dutiful recognition of the
commercial potential of being seen sitting spinning in doorways and
wearing traditional costumes (mainly turban-like headgear), this is
what the old women do.

There is some skiing at Scanno in winter, and plenty of
accommodation, most of it beside the water or along the road
between village and lake.

There are splendid drives in the area, to Sulmona through tight
rocky gorges, and in the other direction over an open grassy pass
towards Villetta Barrea and the National Park.
(*See also Pescasséroli*)

SEPINO

(*See Atilia*)

SERMONETA

A very picturesque walled medieval village in a similar position to
that of Norma (*see separate entry*). Its impressive castle has a
13th-century keep and Renaissance fortifications; the cathedral has a

painting of the Virgin holding Sermoneta on her lap, by Benozzo
Gozzoli (late 15th century).

SPERLONGA

A casually fashionable resort and one of the most beautiful old
villages on the Italian coast, on a rocky outcrop looking down over
the sandy coast between Rome and Naples. Its sandy charm was
exploited by pleasure-seeking Romans, including the emperor
Tiberius, who customised seaside caves (*speluncae*) to accommodate
their dubious entertainments.

On the night of 5th August 1534 the infamous Algerian pirate
Kaireddin Barbarossa landed at Sperlonga on a mission to kidnap
the beautiful Julia Gonzaga, then resident at Fondi, for the harem of
the Ottoman Sultan Suleiman the Magnificent. Julia managed to
escape to the mountains leaving the empty-handed Barbarossa to
vent his frustration on the unfortunate town and inhabitants of
Fondi.

Considering its rare attractions, Sperlonga is remarkably peaceful,
although not exactly undiscovered. With its narrow, whitewashed
and vaulted alleys lined with poky tourist shops and bars, the old
upper town would not be out of place in the Cyclades. Children play
in the shadows and narrow openings give sudden plunging views
over the sea. There are staircases down on both sides, to a splendid
crescent beach (with some concession areas and bars) on one side
and the new town on the other, where a row of modest hotels lines
the shore. Between the two is a small fishing harbour.

☛ **Tiberius' Villa, Grotto and Museum**   This lies about 1km south of
town, accessible only from the main road. Athough its existence was no
secret, the site was not excavated until after the Second World War, when it
turned up some remarkable treasures, now on display in the museum. They
include fragments from three massive sculptural groups of scenes from the
Odyssey, one of them (Ulysses attacked by the monsters of Scilla) signed by
the three Rhodian sculptors of the Laocoön (*see Rome chapter, The Renaissance*),
active in the 1st century BC. As well as these gigantic and tremendously
powerful works, the museum has some very beautiful smaller sculptures.

Excavated foundations of the villa among the olives surround the
museum. The cave itself opens onto the beach; decorated with glass mosaics
as well as sculptures, it served Tiberius as a banqueting hall and his enemies
as a place for attempted assassination. Huge blocks of stone fell from the
ceiling onto the assembled company, but bodyguard Sejanus hurled himself
across the imperial person in protection. Neither was hurt and nor was any
harm done to the bodyguard's career. In front of the grotto is a series of
artificial pools, where most of the sculptural fragments were found. Among
them, intriguingly, was a crocodile's skull.

SUBIACO

A small town in the hills east of Rome, and saint Benedict's chosen
base before Cassino. Benedict's own monastery (*monastero di San
Benedetto, 2km east*) now consists of 13th- and 14th-century buildings
which cling perilously to a rough rock face, a thoroughly convincing
setting for a hermit's lair. A series of rooms and staircases make up

the upper and lower churches, which are decorated with a variety of frescoes from the 12th to 16th centuries. One chapel has what is said to be the earliest portrait of St Francis, from before his canonisation and without halo or stigmata. The lower chambers have a very lively series of scenes from the life of St Benedict. One scene shows the holy man in the grotto (Sacro Speco) where he spent three years and which you visit at the foot of the stairs. Benedict's twin sister Scolastica founded another monastery nearby (*monastero di Santa Scolastica*): a solid group of warm brick buildings beneath a handsome Romanesque campanile. There are three cloisters, visited in order of increasing age: Renaissance, Gothic and Romanesque.

SULMONA

A lively and, by local standards, attractive and interesting town at the heart of mountainous Abruzzi. Sulmona is a town of historical parts. In 43BC it gave birth to Ovid. In the Middle Ages it was famous for the virtuoso creations of the local goldsmiths; now its confectioners enjoy a reputation for similar, albeit more transitory, wizardry. And it was the chosen retreat of the 13th-century hermit Pietro Angeleri, also known as Peter of Morrone after the mountain north of town where he lived in rough solitude until persuaded in 1294 to occupy the papal throne as Celestine V. The monastery he founded is now used as a prison; a rough path leads on up to ruins of an ancient temple, known locally as Ovid's villa.

Despite having been a repeated earthquake victim, Sulmona has kept plenty of old buildings. The finest of them is the façade of the **Annunziata** palace and church, on the main Corso Ovidio. Most of the decoration of the façade dates from the 15th and early 16th centuries, and Gothic and Renaissance styles mingle around the doorways below and windows above. Between them runs a decorative frieze with sacred and profane scenes entwined in its vegetable forms. One of the most spectacular sweet shops in town is next door. Only a very sweet tooth could bring itself to crunch into these delicately-arranged sprays of sugared almond flowers.

The wide market square is overlooked by some 20 arches of a 13th-century aqueduct.

TARQUÍNIA

The first dominant Etruscan city power before being rivalled by Caere (Cervéteri), Tarquínia provided Rome with a ruling dynasty from 616BC until 510BC, when Tarquin the Proud was expelled from a Rome outraged by his assault on the virtue of Lucretia. The site of the ancient city was abandoned for a hill nearer the sea in the early Middle Ages, the new town being known as Corneto until 1922. The burial grounds have produced some of the greatest treasures of Etruscan art, including a unique series of tombs decorated with frescoes, an invaluable source of information about Etruscan life and culture and in many cases extremely beautiful.

Tarquínia is one of the most picturesque old towns in central Italy: in the north-western corner of town the effect of the tall, windowless towers (of which over a dozen stand intact), solid medieval walls and massive fortifications is almost undiluted by modern buildings. Inside the walls of the citadel, the 12th-century church of **Santa Maria di Castello** has decorative mosaic inlay round the main doorway. The hill drops sharply away below the walls on this side, giving a splendid view over a quiet, steep-sided valley and open hills beyond.

A couple of miles away, the undistinguished but serviceable resort of **Lido di Tarquinia** has plenty of sand and a variety of accommodation.

☛ **Museo Nazionale** (Piazza Cavour) On the main square, this 15th-century palace of no great beauty houses an excellent museum, mainly devoted to Etruscan art with a rich collection of sarcophagi and vases and a very famous terracotta group of winged horses (4th-century BC) from a temple at the ancient city. The second floor, where a room contains reconstructions of five of the painted tombs (with the original paintings) for which Tarquinia is most famous, has been closed for some years.

☛ **Etruscan necropolis** The land between the ancient and modern cities of Tarquinia, beside the Viterbo road, is a vast tract of burial grounds. Some of this area has been excavated and the rest serves as a rich vein of illicit supply for the auction rooms of the world, energetically and very profitably exploited by local amateur archaeologists, more accurately known as tomb robbers. Among the thousands of underground tombs so far officially uncovered about 150 are painted, and about 20 of these are well preserved. In the utterly unspectacular setting of a rough field dotted with what look like public convenience shacks (the entrances to the tombs), you are admitted to about half a dozen of the painted tombs; attendants are present but uncommunicative. The necropolis was used from the 7th century BC until the Roman period, but most of the painted tombs now open to the public date from the 6th and 5th centuries, the period when the art of Etruscan fresco painting is generally thought to have been been at its finest. Apart from one scene from Greek mythology (in the early Tomb of the Bulls), the walls are decorated with a delightful range of genre scenes conveying a picture of Etruscan life lived for pure pleasure, their expectation of the hereafter: banquets with naked servants, dancing and hunting scenes, and the simple delight a man takes in the cultivation of his back garden. The tombs are damp; avoid leaning on the hand rails.

TÉRAMO

Large and not very attractive provincial capital in northern Abruzzi, with some remains of a Roman theatre and, in the interesting 13th- and 14th-century **cathedral**, two beautiful works of art: the silver altar front by Niccolo da Guardiagrele and the polyptych (Coronation of the Virgin) by Jacobello da Fiore, both from the mid-15th century.

TERRACINA

A large, mostly modern and unattractive coastal town and resort with an old quarter set back at the foot of Monte Sant' Angelo, which drops down to the sea on the eastern edge of the town. The Naples road (the Appian Way) passes through a Roman cutting over a hundred feet deep, as indicated by the Roman numbers inscribed in the rock. The **cathedral** is built on the foundation of a Roman temple, some of which is still visible, as is other Roman masonry nearby. The portico has antique columns supported by medieval animals, and a beautiful 12th-century mosaic frieze. Inside, a section of mosaic pavement, an Easter candlestick and pulpit all date from the 12th and 13th centuries.

From the heart of the old town it is a stiff walk up to the hilltop site of the ancient acropolis (Anxur), past houses in the fabric of the medieval town walls whose sentry walk is still used for access. The reward is impressive ruins of temple and fortifications, and a splendid view of the coast, Monte Circeo and, in clear weather, Mount Vesuvius, the Ponza islands and Ischia. There is also a road up the hill.

TIVOLI

(*See Rome chapter*)

TUSCÁNIA

There are few visions of rural Italy to compare with the one savoured by the local loving couples who gather at sunset on the lawns at the feet of the old walls of Tuscánia, looking east. A tranquil landscape rolls away behind a foreground hillock crowned by a group of golden medieval buildings that catch the dying rays to great effect. The great church on the hill (San Pietro) and another like it nearby are the main reasons for a visit to Tuscánia, but the town itself also has plenty of rough medieval charm and much of its fortified walls still stands. Tuscánia was first Etruscan, then Roman, and came under papal control in the early 14th century. An angry pope Boniface VIII changed its name to Toscanella in a bizarre punishment for rebellion; the old name was readopted in 1911. The town was severely damaged and 30 of its inhabitants killed by an earthquake in February 1971; most of the damaged area has now been restored.

☛ **San Pietro**   A vast and substantially unaltered 8th-century church crowning the site of the Etruscan acropolis outside town. The façade, a later addition from the late 12th and early 13th centuries, has beautiful decoration of carved white marble, including an Etruscan relief of a dancing man to the left of the rose window. The massively simple interior includes a mosaic floor, the work of Roman artists, and a number of Etruscan funerary sculptures with heavy-bellied figures in characteristic post-prandial mode. There are some remains of frescoes in the choir, and an interesting variety of pillars (many of them Roman) in the crypt. To appreciate the full beauty of this church, leave the car at the bottom of the hill and walk up. Buildings beside the church include the old bishop's palace and some excavations of the Etruscan and Roman site.

☛ **Santa Maria Maggiore**   At the foot of the same hill and beside a road junction, this church lacks the beauty of San Pietro's setting but it has equally beautiful marble carving on the façade, also from the late 12th century. The interior, reconstructed at the same time, includes a more than usually gruesome 14th-century fresco of the Last Judgement over the chancel arch.

URBINO

Of all the towns of central Italy outside Tuscany and Umbria, Urbino is the most irresistibly magnetic to travellers on a Renaissance tour; and of all places in whatever province, it is perhaps Urbino that fits most perfectly our idea of what a Renaissance art city should be. Even more than Siena, it is what many visitors expect of Florence but do not find. The very name seems to indicate some ideal of town life at its most civilised, and the idea is not far wrong. Appropriately enough, one of its treasures is a Renaissance painting of just such an ideal. It also gave birth, in 1483, to the artist known as the supreme interpreter of ideal beauty, Raphael, son of local court artist Giovanni Santi.

Urbino is a monument to one man: not Raphael, who left for Perugia in his mid-teens, but Federico da Montefeltro (1410-83), bastard younger son of the local ruling family who turned out to be the most brilliant military leader, most enlightened ruler and most cultivated patron of the arts and scholarship of the 15th century: the ideal Renaissance prince. In his days, wrote Baldassare Castiglione in the *Book of the Courtier*, he was the light of all Italy. And his court, wrote Kenneth Clark rather more recently, was one of the high water marks of western civilisation. Federico was invited to take control of Urbino in 1444 after the townsfolk had done away with his loathsome half brother Oddantonio, who made a habit of borrowing other men's wives. Federico made a fortune out of fighting, and winning, battles for other people, spent his fortune making Urbino beautiful and filling its libraries with rare books, and kept it free from war. "In the common calamities of the wars of Italy it remained for a season without any at all" (Castiglione again).

It could not last. Federico's son Guidobaldo promised well but was immobilised by gout before he was 20 and was perhaps not surprisingly unsuccessful in most of his military adventures. Urbino came under the della Rovere and Medici families and in 1631 Rome took direct control. Federico's great treasures, notably the library he valued more highly than any painting or palace, were removed to the Vatican.

Decline into unimportance meant that little happened to change the face of Urbino; the old centre, built entirely of salmon-coloured brick, contains few buildings more recent than Federico's vast palace which still looks directly out over a quiet ochre and green landscape of small, sharp hills of olive, vine and cypress. A town of university and other institutes, Urbino has not forgotten its past role as a place of intellectual pursuits. It is not a large town and apart from the Ducal Palace its sights are of minor interest: a few hours are enough.

☞ **Ducal Palace** (National Gallery of the Marches)   Not a palace but a city in the form of a palace, is Castiglione's fair summary of a vast complex of Renaissance building, the work of some of the finest architects and decorators of the period. The Dalmatian architect Luciano Laurana, whom Federico engaged in 1468, usually takes most of the credit. Laurana's greatest achievements are the main courtyard and the narrow west front, a famous

Urbino, Ducal Palace

landmark with its two slender round towers soaring like minarets above the town and countryside. The main entrance to the palace is on the other side, near the cathedral, a low winged façade behind which is Laurana's beautiful courtyard, its lower arches surmounted by a long inscription glorifying Federico. The spacious rooms of the palace have richly decorated fireplaces and doors and on their walls hang the museum's paintings, which include one portrait by Raphael and two great masterpieces by Piero della Francesca: the haunting Flagellation, a painting that has launched many an erudite art historian into stormy seas of speculative interpretation, and a typically classical-looking Madonna. A famous portrait, probably by Berruguete, shows the Renaissance prince Federico in full armour in his study, one hand on a sword, the other between the pages of a book, and with his son at his side.

Among so many beautiful rooms it is easy to miss the staircase from room 10 (first floor) which leads to Federico's chapel (beautiful views from the balcony). Tucked away nearby is his study, its walls decorated with remarkable wooden inlay thought to have been designed by Botticelli; it depicts arms, books, musical instruments, and a portrait of the duke.

☛ **Other sights** **Raphael's house** is an ordinary Renaissance dwelling with a fresco Madonna claimed to be a juvenile work of the master. The **cathedral** (mostly late 15th-century, but with a much later neo-classical façade) has a number of good paintings, the best of them by Federico Barocci (mid-16th-century). A delightful series of 15th-century frescoes (Crucifixion, Life of the Baptist) covers the interior of the **Oratorio di San Giovanni**, below the ducal palace (Via Barocci); the neighbouring **Oratorio di San Giuseppe** has a beautiful stucco Nativity (early 16th-century).

VITERBO

A big town north of Rome, historically prominent as the favourite papal residence in the 12th and 13th centuries (when Rome was uninhabitably violent), and the setting for the marathon conclave of 1268 which resulted in the election of Gregory X after nearly three years of indecision. The cardinals found themselves unable to agree until the town ruler locked them in, cut the food supply and took the roof off the building. After all this, Gregory X survived only one month in office. The papal connection was severed in 1280 when townsfolk rudely burst into the cathedral during conclave and arrested two cardinals. The people were excommunicated and for nearly a century no pope set foot in Viterbo; its position as a power independent of Rome declined rapidly.

Viterbo is made of a dark volcanic stone which makes the medieval walled centre severe and almost claustrophobic. Despite this and heavy bombing in the last war much of the old town is harmoniously old and extremely picturesque, especially around the **Via San Pellegrino**, which runs up from the Porta San Pietro to the Piazza San Lorenzo on the site of the old acropolis. There is illumination after dark and a well-signed walking itinerary round this old quarter, with its towers, fountains, vaulted streets and many houses with external staircases. The Corso Italia is very lively in the early evening.

The effect of the monumental **Piazza San Lorenzo** with its splendid 13th-century Papal Palace has lately been rather spoilt by scaffolding, making it difficult to enjoy the full beauty of the terrace and views out over the surrounding hills. Apart from the 16th-century façade, the **cathedral** is an impressive Romanesque building; the wooden ceiling is a post-war replacement of the original. The beautiful campanile dates from the 14th century.

Two other fine Romanesque churches are **Santa Maria Nuova** (just off Via San Lorenzo) and **Santo Sisto** (beside Porta Romana). At the north of the walled town, **San Francesco** contains the beautiful tomb of pope Adrian V who died at Viterbo in 1276. In this town famous for the beauty of its fountains, the finest is the 13th-century **Fontana Grande**, on the square of the same name.

☛ **Museum** This is outside the walls to the east, in convent buildings beside the church of Santa Maria della Verità (with good 15th-century frescoes). The museum has a collection of Etruscan works of art and interesting paintings including works by Salvator Rosa and the 15th-century local artist Pastura, otherwise known as Antonio da Viterbo; but the pride of Viterbo, one of the greatest masterpieces (Pietà) by Michelangelo's disciple and collaborator Sebastiano del Piombo, is temporarily absent.

Excursions from Viterbo

☞ **Bagnaia** (*5km east*)

The road from Viterbo passes the beautiful Renaissance church and cloister of **Santa Maria della Quercia**. Bagnaia is famous for the formal gardens of the **Villa Lante**, not one villa but two small pavilions built by Vignola in the late 16th century. The guided tour is long-winded, obligatory and only in Italian. Apart from an elaborate system of fountains and watercourses, a prominent decorative feature of gardens and architecture is the use of the emblems of the three families connected with the villa: Montalto (a jelly-like mountain with a star), Gambara (a prawn) and della Rovere (a lion). The tour includes the interior of one of the pavilions, decorated with attractive frescoes and French landscape paintings.

☞ **Castel d'Asso** (*10km south-west*)

A ruined 15th-century castle above the site of a large Etruscan necropolis, with rock tombs similar to but earlier than those at Nórchia, with decorated façades and inscriptions. The easiest way to reach the site is via the old Roman spa, Bagni da Viterbo, signed from the Viterbo to Tuscánia road.

☞ **Caprarola** (*15km south-east*)

Hillside village dominated by the **Villa Farnese** built (1559-75) by Vignola for cardinal Alessandro Farnese, using the plan (a pentagon with circular courtyard) of an earlier fortress. The magnificent interior decoration is very well preserved and includes *trompe l'oeil* architecture with dwarfs in doorways, beautiful landscapes round the staircase, a room entirely decorated with maps, another (Sala degli Angeli) with a remarkable echo if you stand in the middle. The guide is uncommunicative and you see very little of the gardens.

Nearby is the volcanic **Lago di Vico**, surrounded by steep wooded slopes including the conical Monte Vénere, an island until the lake was partly drained in the 16th century. According to the legend Hercules came looking for the nymphs Melissa and Amalthea, nurses of Zeus. On being invited to give a display of strength, he thrust his sword into the ground, challenging anyone to pull it out. He alone could do so, and from the hole sprang the lake waters.

☞ **Bomarzo** (*19km north-east*)

It is interesting to know that they had monster parks in the 16th century, and fun to visit one of the best-preserved examples of the genre, built in 1552 by Vicino Orsini in a wooded valley below the hilltop palace and village of Bomarzo. Close to the motorway and Rome, the park pulls in the Sunday masses (despite a high entrance charge) and teems with people kicking footballs around, listening to radios, and posing for wedding photos in the gaping orifice of some monstrous sculpture. There is a leaning house, an elephant toying with a Roman soldier and many more exotic and fanciful beasts. As works of art they are undistinguished, and as monsters they are unlikely to impress a child of the 1980s. A few real animals are on display caged near the entrance.

Hotels

L'Áquila
GRAND E DEL PARCO
Corso Federico II 74, 67100 L'Áquila

££
Open all year
Tel: (0862) 20248

L'Áquila is a big town and regional capital and most of its hotels are business-oriented. This is the most attractive of them, recently refurbished to a fairly high standard of comfort and some style, not too noisy despite being on a busy cross-roads, and with good views from many bedrooms over public gardens and beautiful mountain scenery beyond.

Facilities: *40 bedrooms; restaurant; lift*   **Credit/charge cards accepted:** *none*

Pescassèroli
CRISTIANIA
67032 L'Áquila

££
Open all year
Tel (0863) 91395

A delightful wooden chalet with painted shutters, a roaring fire, stuffed birds, rustic furniture and colourful bedspreads, in a peaceful open setting at the foot of Pescassèroli's ski slopes deep in the national park. The management herself warns that dining arrangements are "not quite like a restaurant, but you do have some choice". Out here in remotest Abruzzi you might expect to escape English and American voices, but you probably won't: the place is a favourite escape for Rome-based supra-nationals, especially the FAO crowd. It was full when we turned up in September and, considering how far you would have to travel to find a more welcoming mountain hotel, we were more disappointed than surprised.

Facilities: *12 bedrooms; restaurant; parking*   **Credit/charge cards accepted:** *none*

Portonovo
EMILIA
60020 Ancona

££
Closed Nov to Feb
Tel: (0775) 801117

As the chalky promontory that forces the motorway inland south of Ancona provides welcome relief from the general style of the Adriatic coast, so the Emilia does from the norm of Adriatic coast hotels. It is a low-slung modern building high above the sea, partly built into the hillside. Bedrooms are simple (showers only) and small, but many have balconies and sea views and the rest of the hotel is bright and comfortable, with plants and beautiful modern paintings. Lawns and a splendid 30-metre pool are well kept, and the food in the simple, tiled dining room is excellent, fishy and expensive. Friendly family management.

Facilities: *30 bedrooms; restaurant; lift; swimming pool; tennis court; parking*   **Credit/charge cards accepted:** *none*

Portonovo   ££
FORTINO NAPOLEONICO   *Open all year*
Via Poggio 166, 60020 Ancona   *Tel: (071) 801124*

If the Emilia turns you away, this may provide an entertaining, albeit rather gimmicky, alternative of particular appeal to those worried about Italy's reputation for more or less petty crime at the expense of tourists. Down by the water's edge at Portonovo, an interesting low, clover-shaped fortress has been converted into a most unusual hotel, complete with ornamental cannons. In many ways, the fortified style is less than ideal in a seaside hotel: bedrooms look out over the internal courtyard rather than the sea. The central "keep" has become a fine vaulted sitting room, but the dining room is a bit institutional.

Facilities: *30 bedrooms; restaurant; parking*   **Credit/charge cards accepted:** *Amex, Diners, Visa*

Urbino   £
RAFFAELLO   *Open all year*
Via Santa Margherita 38/40, 61029 Pesaro e Urbino   *Tel: (0722) 4784*

When in doubt in Italy, it is a sound principle to head for the hotel named after the local artist. In Urbino there is no outstandingly attractive accommodation, but the Raffaello will do: a clean, simple and inexpensive billet at the peaceful heart of the old town (as the larger hotels, including the Piero della Francesca, are not), without a restaurant, which is no hardship. The alley where it stands near the Via Raffaello is too narrow for cars, but the hotel is ideally placed for exploration of the town on foot.

Facilities: *16 bedrooms*   **Credit/charge cards accepted:** *none*

Viterbo   £
LEON D'ORO   *Closed Christmas to Feb*
Via della Cava 36, 01100 Viterbo   *Tel: (0761) 31012*

The charm of Viterbo is its old town centre, and the Leon d'Oro is about the best of the hotels inside the walls, one of several in the same street between the northern gateway (the Porta Fiorentina) and the Corso Italia, which swarms with life in the early evening. It is a straightforward comfortable town hotel, with a large sitting room and a small breakfast bar downstairs, and the considerable attraction of an indoor garage. Rooms on the street side are a bit noisy.

Facilities: *44 bedrooms; restaurant; lift; garage*   **Credit/charge cards accepted:** *Amex, Diners, Visa*

NAPLES &
CAMPANIA

*❝It is hard to say whether the view is more
pleasing from the singularity of many of the
objects, or from the incredible variety of the
whole . . . Nature seems to have formed this
coast in her more capricious mood❞*

PATRICK BRYDONE

Positano

Introduction

"I sha'nt go to Naples" Lord Byron wrote home in 1817, "It is but the second best sea view and I have seen the first and third, viz. Constantinople and Lisbon". Only lordly self-confidence could skip so high-ranking an item on the itinerary. The Gulf of Naples was *de rigueur*, the southern climax of the Grand Tour, combining art and classical associations, scenery and interesting physical phenomena in a climate much pleasanter than Rome's. The seething street life of Naples itself was an added fascination – squalid humanity obtruding well beyond the limits of a picturesque background and compelling reactions of pity and terror. But the incomparable beauty of the bay justified even "See Naples and die". It remains hardly diminished by pollution, industrial zones and modern city sprawl, a vast curve of blue in a dramatic shoreline beginning at the island of Ischia, completed by Capri, dominated by Mount Vesuvius in the middle. The volcano's habitual plume of smoke used to be the finishing touch in paintings and photogaphs, but it dwindled and disappeared after the last eruption in 1944. On the southern side of the Sorrento peninsula, the Amalfi coast is equally celebrated for its wildly picturesque, cliff-clinging towns and villages, of which Positano is the most extreme example.

The world-famous sites and sights of Campania are all within easy reach of its world-famous coastline; it is for this splendid combination that millions of tourists arrive each year. Beaches are thin, few and not the point – though a quieter seaside holiday is possible further south along the rocky Cilento coast. Inland of Naples the region has fertile agricultural plains, then its share of the Apennines' rolling foothills and bleak central spine. It's not very rewarding or hospitable touring country. Villages and towns are much rebuilt after the ravages of the Second World War and in many areas after earthquake damage: few have much charm. Rather than leisurely exploration, a swift excursion along a motorway is the best way to visit isolated remnants of inland history such as Benevento's well-preserved Roman arch, or the newly-restored Carthusian monastery far south at Padula.

The modern difference between rich north and poor south is an inversion of Italy's early civilisation. The north was an unknown area of primitive tribes when Sicily and the southern mainland made up Magna Graecia, greater Greece. The new town Neapolis swallowed up an earlier Greek colony called Parthenope after a mythical siren – a name revived (as in "Parthenopean Republic") whenever poetry or history required a resounding title. Greek cities vanished under ubiquitous Roman building, but at Paestum on the gulf of Salerno three superb Doric temples remain from the ancient settlement Poseidonia.

The Romans' favourite place for rest and relaxation was the north headland of the bay of Naples. Baia, now mostly land-slipped under the sea, was an opulent holiday playground of palaces and entertainment and innumerable baths – the ruined "temples" visible today are elaborate spa facilities. Every Roman notable visited, and the richest built villas. The emperor Tiberius died here after ten years' notorious retirement on Capri. Not far inland a volcanic area (the Phlegrean Fields) provided hot springs in the eerily convincing landscape of myth and epic; the ancient Cumaean Sybil had a real cave – gloomy Lake Avernus was believably the entrance to Hades described by Homer and the Roman poet Virgil. Although in the reign of Augustus it was transformed as a naval base, a superstitious half-belief lingered on for centuries. Modern tourists experience more of a *frisson* walking over the Solfatara, a volcanic crater of continuous small-scale activity.

The major first eruption of Vesuvius in AD79 which destroyed Pompeii and Herculaneum came – in spite of a preliminary earthquake – as a complete surprise to the Romans, who knew the volcano only as a mountain of particularly fertile slopes. The amazingly detailed picture of life in antiquity revealed by excavations in the 18th century prompted Goethe to remark that "there have been many disasters in this world, but few which have given so much delight to posterity". For all travellers of classical education and lively imagination, a trip up Vesuvius to stare into the crater became more than ever an imperative. Shelley wrote a haunted account, Ruskin declared the volcanic power of destruction "if not the personality of an Evil Spirit, at all events the permitted symbol of evil, unredeemed". But Goethe had already expressed the emotional sum: "The Terrible beside the Beautiful, the Beautiful beside the Terrible, cancel one another out and produce a feeling of indifference. The Neapolitan would certainly be a different creature if he did not feel himself wedged between God and the Devil". However fatalistically oppressed by this and other extremes, Neapolitans display not indifference but enormous energy, now as in Lady Blessington's description of 1823: "The lower classes of Naples observe no medium between the slumber of exhaustion and the fever of excitement... Their conversation, no matter on what topic, is carried on with an animation and gesticulation unknown to us. Their friendly salutations might, by a stranger, be mistaken for the commencement of a quarrel, so vehement and loud are their exclamations, and their disagreements are conducted with a fiery wrath which reminds one that they belong to a land in whose volcanic nature they strongly participate". Volcanic associations seemed to many observers the only explanation for the vitality of the Neapolitan slums, whose overcrowded squalor was so shameful a contrast to the public brilliance with which the city welcomed the world.

For six hundred years, with only brief interruptions until the Unification of Italy in 1860, Naples was a royal capital. All Italy south of the papal states was *Il Regno*, a realm "protected by salt water on three sides and holy water on the fourth" said its longest-reigning monarch. The kingdom later called "The Two Sicilies" was established in 1137 by the Normans who ruled it from Palermo. In successive medieval power struggles it became Hohenstaufen, Angevin and Aragonese; a French king lost its island half after the rebellion in 1282 called the Sicilian Vespers. Transferring the capital, the Anjou dynasty first made Naples splendid; but the more rigid, isolated Aragonese regime of the 15th century largely excluded her from the creative spirit of the Renaissance. While in other parts of Italy wealth and power were balanced among cities and princes, the devitalised south emptied its resources only into Naples, to support an absolute and feudal monarch in luxury. Under Alfonso "The Magnanimous", the survivors of an Abruzzi earthquake were compelled to go on paying the taxes of the dead. His sinister successor Ferdinand I eliminated rebellious barons by murder and liked to keep about him the bodies of his enemies, embalmed and fully dressed.

In 1503 there began two centuries of direct rule from Spain. Naples housed the Viceroy's court and state bureaucracy, backed by a naval and military presence; culture and etiquette finally drew everyone of blood, wealth or influence to live there. Through the 16th century and half the 17th, Naples' population grew until it was the biggest metropolis in Europe; other capital cities outstripped it only after a virulent outbreak of plague in 1656 killed 60% of its inhabitants. In search of work, a constant stream of immigrants poured in from the countryside. Grandiose public building – and vast green spaces – reduced the area available for the mass of the population, and the city centre took on the aspect we still see today: houses six storeys high, crammed into the narrow streets first laid out by the Greeks, so dark and airless at ground level that the business of living moved outdoors into the noisy littered alleys strung with washing, the only home of thousands of beggars. In the same teeming quarters the many churches have interiors most extravagantly rich. Under the Spanish impetus of the Counter-Reformation, art finally flourished: Neapolitan Baroque expressed itself in virtuoso sculpture, intricately decorative stonework, and the dramatic religious painting of the 17th-century Naples school, inspired by Caravaggio and Ribera.

When in the 18th century yet another foreign viceroy – Austria's – was succeeded by the Bourbon dynasty that became Naples' own, the city with all its problems enjoyed a cultural and social heyday. The magnificent Teatro San Carlo was built, and a superb new museum took the best of the excavated treasures from Pompeii and Herculaneum. A Frenchman in 1739 found in Naples "the only city in Italy which really feels like a capital… a Court which is a proper Court and a glittering one at that… the same busy and lively atmsophere one finds in Paris or London and which does not even exist in Rome". Europe's crowned heads and Grand Tourists, musicians and *literati* visited in droves, and the British were particularly welcome in the brilliant years while Sir William Hamilton was ambassador. But the revelry was interrupted by French invasions, in 1797 (the "Parthenopean Republic") and 1806 (Napoleon's imperial representatives). After the Bourbons' second return from exile in Sicily in 1815 their local popularity – and their kingdom's relative prosperity, compared with other Italian states – no longer prevented horrified criticism of their regime in Naples. ▷

Visiting Naples and Campania

There are scheduled and charter flights from London to Naples, and by air is the most practical way to go – the train journey takes 30 hours and a second-class return costs rather more than a charter flight. Local transport (train, bus and boat) is good, and a car no great advantage in this area. The only fast road through Campania is the Autostrada del Sole, which links Naples and Salerno; the coast road is so tortuous that drivers can't afford to enjoy the spectacular scenery.

Hydrofoils and steamers ply between Naples and Sorrento and the islands (in summer, only island residents can take cars across to Capri and Ischia).

Many organised excursions are available from the resorts around Sorrento and Amalfi, including to Naples, Pompeii and Vesuvius, Herculaneum, Paestum, Salerno, Caserta and Montecassino. There are also excursions to and from Capri and Ischia and coach and boat trips along the coast. The choice is more limited from resorts south of Salerno (day trips to Paestum are the exception). You can also get local buses between the towns and a high-speed suburban railway, the Circumvesuviana, runs from Naples to Sorrento via Herculaneum and Pompeii.

Naples does not make a good base as its hotels are generally intolerably noisy, lacking in character or charm, and often insalubrious. But if you want to do the city justice it's worth staying a night or two (bear in mind that everything of interest, except churches, is shut on Mondays). The most pleasant hotels are in Mergellina, at the edge of the bay; the cheapest in and around the Piazza Garibaldi.

Getting around Naples can be something of a nightmare. It is not a city you can easily cover on foot; some of the most appealing parts are well out of the centre. Buses and trams are overcrowded, and for long distances the underground is a more pleasant alternative. There are four funicular railways, the most useful of which goes from Via Toledo to the Vomero quarter (Certosa di San Martino and Villa Floridiana). Getting up by car is virtually impossible unless you know Naples backwards.

There is plenty of hotel accommodation along the coast south of Naples; it's necessary to book well ahead in summer. Many of the hotels have swimming pools, important in an area where beaches are generally poor or dirty. There are several fairly basic campsites in attractive settings on the Sorrento peninsula. Sorrento (a large traditional cliff-top resort) and Positano (a small, chic and charming hillside resort) make good bases; for a relaxing and mainly stay-put holiday with opportunities for watersports, you might choose the islands of Capri or Ischia. Capri is also chic and charming; the most elegant (and surprisingly quiet) hotels are villas in Capri town itself. Ischia, more beach-orientated, has several lively purpose-built resorts, many with spa facilities.

There is a large selection of tour operators offering hotel and self-catering holidays by air to the resorts along the Bay of Naples, the Sorrento peninsula, the Gulf of Salerno, and Capri and Ischia – nearly all for 7 or 14 nights. Sorrento is easily the most popular resort, with a range of nearly 50 hotels offered (coach and rail packages are available too). A few companies (including opera specialists) offer city breaks to Naples. Occasionally, Naples and the surrounding area is included in art tours by coach.

Despite sea breezes, in high summer Naples is intensely hot and smog frequently shrouds the glorious panorama from the city's hill tops. For ten days in early September the city is taken over in the revelry of the colourful Piedigrotta festival. If you want to concentrate on the museums, March to May is probably the best time to visit the city. Coastal resorts are crowded in July and August, but there is plenty of entertainment including local festivals. The islands suffer from day-trippers as well as holiday-makers; June is probably the best month to go, avoiding peak prices and the risk of rain in September. Resort hotels generally close from about October to Easter.

Most quoted was Gladstone's damning "negation of God, erected into a system of government".

In 1860 the Risorgimento movement towards a reformed and united Italy culminated in the victorious arrival of Garibaldi in Naples. The royal capital and principal Italian city became – virtually overnight – a disadvantaged provincial backwater. After an epidemic of cholera in 1884, measures for rebuilding were speeded up, but improvements over the next 50 years were almost nullified by wholesale damage in the Second World War. Haphazard and illegal postwar building so altered the appearance of Naples that a state enquiry in 1971 called it "blindly transforming the ancient and marvellous capital of the Mediterranean into the present most uninhabitable provincial capital in Italy". In 1980, the earthquake which destroyed whole villages in Campania badly shook the city centre: unsafe streets and a wave of refugees were simultaneous new setbacks to the dream of civic order. Along the gulf coast and on the inland plains the industrial and commercial enterprises – oil refineries, cement works, aircraft and automobile assembly plants and food-processing factories – are state-owned attempts to improve the economy, but private industrialists of any size are reluctant to invest in an area where it seems eternally impossible to be efficient. Naples in the 1980s continues to suffer from over-population, chronic unemployment and poverty. One plague from which it is free is mass tourism: the city once full of foreigners, still a major treasurehouse of culture, is now appreciated only by the most intrepid Italophiles.

Places to visit

AMALFI

Before the Norman conquest of the south, Amalfi was a wealthy trading republic ruled by her own doge. One of her navigators is credited with inventing the compass, and the *Tavole Amalfitane* set a famous code of maritime law. The city's rapid decline, from the 12th century, was emphasised by the subsidence under the sea of a large part of it, in 1343. The most striking thing about Amalfi today is its setting – view it from a boat if you can. The town stands in a deep valley on a coastline of jagged cliffs and hilltop watch towers. Pastel-washed houses, villas, cupolas and campaniles cling to the cliffs above the bay, interspersed with terraces of vines. Seen from the sea its beauty seems unspoilt, but its streets are overrun with souvenir shops and the beaches are crowded strips of grey sand and pebbles, backed by tourist-orientated cafés. Amalfi, which used to be a favourite wintering haunt among Victorians and Edwardians, is still popular with the British, either as a package holiday resort or a stop-off place for local excursions. The hotels are mainly out of the centre of town, some high up in the rock face with lovely views.

The older part of Amalfi has a distinctly Moorish flavour, particularly the covered streets and steps leading off the main street.

Walk a few minutes inland and you come to the Valle dei Mulini, named after the watermills where paper was once manufactured and now a valley of lemon trees where you'll be served fresh lemon juice on rustic benches in the shady groves.

☛ **Cathedral** (Sant' Andrea) A handsome blend of Saracen, Romanesque and Lombard-Norman features with a (much-restored) striped façade approached by a fine flight of steps. The bronze doors, made in Constantinople in 1066, are remarkable. Inside, elaborate 19th-century mosaics decorate the narrow bays and the pair of ancient pulpits. The cloisters and dome of the belltower are in Arab style and date from the 13th century.

Excursions from Amalfi

☞ **Emerald Grotto** (4km west)
A grotto with remarkable stalagmitic formations in the emerald waters. It can be approached by stairs or a lift, or the sea.

☞ **Atrani** (1km east)
A pretty village worth visiting for the churches of San Salvatore (with handsome 12th-century bronze doors) and La Maddalena.

BAIA

A seaside village with very little left of imperial Rome's most prestigious holiday centre: pillaged by Saracens and made uninhabitable by malaria, most of its deserted palaces finally disappeared beneath the sea through gradual land slippage. Behind the present town excavated remains include the octagonal temple of Diana and the spa complexes called the Temples of Venus and Mercury – they're poorly signed and difficult to locate. Statues found here and in the harbour have gone to the National Archaeological Museum at Naples.
(*See also Phlegrean Fields*)

BENEVENTO

An important ancient city on the Appian Way, originally called Maleventum, but renamed in 268 BC when it became a Roman colony. The ugly post-war sprawl all but engulfs a compact old centre with mysterious cobbled streets and remains of the oldest Lombard walls in Europe. Hotels and restaurants are few, and basic.

☛ **Roman Theatre** One of the largest Roman theatres still existing, built in the reign of the emperor Hadrian and enlarged by Caracalla. The site has been spoilt by development.

☛ **Santa Sophia** A tiny church dating from 762, situated on a pretty cobbled piazza. It has a carved portal and a plain domed interior.
In the cloister is the small **Samnite Museum** (Museo Sannio) where Grecian vases from Caudium and fragments of Egyptian sculptures from Domitian's Temple of Isis are the star exhibits.

☛ **Trajan's Arch** A dignified and very well preserved monument to the "optimus princeps" erected in AD114, with scenes glorifying Trajan's career sculpted in relief. The arch is at its most impressive when floodlit.

Capri

CAPRI

The little island of Capri has always been something of a paradise for pleasure-seekers, and among the first to be captivated by its beauty were the Romans. Augustus visited Capri on his return to Italy from his victory over Anthony and Cleopatra; instantly taken by its beauty, he exchanged the island for Ischia which was already in his possession. Tiberius was also inspired by the place and spent the last years of his life here (AD26-37) – a decade of crime and depravity according to the malicious pens of Suetonius and Tacitus. Tiberius built 12 villas on Capri; fragments survive and local guides will tell you with great relish that he kept a different mistress in each one. The Marquis de Sade (intrigued by the perversions of Tiberius) was an early visitor. The island became particularly popular in the 19th century, partly due to the appeal of the Blue Grotto which was known to the Romans, but (although locals claimed to have known its whereabouts for years) was officially "discovered" only in 1826. More recently Capri has attracted writers and artists, Russian revolutionaries and film-stars – from Gorky to Gracie Fields.

Capri is still beautiful; the precipitous coastline of deep coves and grottoes and weirdly-shaped rocks, and the luxuriant gardens and panoramic views are superb. But the dreamy remote quality described by 19th-century writers is harder to find; parts of the island are now crushed under the weight of mass tourism. Go in high season and you'll arrive at the main port (Marina Grande) to an onslaught of touts and swarming hordes of day-trippers. The few beaches that exist are small, pebbly, and very crowded (although if you scramble down the cliffside you can find a few unspoilt coves). Capri is also one of the most expensive places in Italy.

The centre of **Capri** town is small, chic and quaint with little white houses, cobbled passageways and smart boutiques. Inevitably it has become overcrowded and overcommercialised. The focal point is the little piazza where wealthier tourists sit and sip cocktails. Less sophisticated is the resort of **Anacapri**, on the high eastern plateau of the island, reached by a panoramic road of dizzy hairpin bends (10 minutes by bus, or about 45 minutes on foot). There's another spectacular panoramic view from **Monte Solaro**, reached by cable-car from Piazza Vittoria.

☛ **Blue Grotto** (Grotta Azzurra)   Capri's biggest money-spinner is perhaps an overrated experience. Tourist-laden motorboats ply from the Marina Grande to the grotto (you can also take a bus or walk from Anacapri). At the entrance, greedy "fishermen" demand an extra fee for transferral to their (smaller) boats which glide into the fluorescent blue depths, lit by sunlight passing through seawater.

☛ **Villa Jovis** (45 minutes' walk from Capri)   Although the overgrown ruins hardly suffice to evoke the grandeur of the largest palace of Tiberius, there are glorious views over the cliffs from the belvedere whence, according to legend, he threw his enemies. The steep path from the centre of Capri town is pleasantly quiet and devoid of tourists.

☛ **Villa San Michele** (5 minutes' walk from Anacapri)   The enchanting home of Axel Munthe, the Swedish author and physician, with the ancient sculpture and antique furniture he collected.

CAPUA

Present-day Capua grew up in the Middle Ages a few miles from the ancient city of the same name (now Santa Maria Capua Vetere), which stood vulnerably in the middle of an open plain. The more defensible site repeatedly failed to deter attackers, including Cesare Borgia who broke a truce in 1501 and massacred 5,000 Capuans (the town bells still toll on the 24th July in commemoration of the event). Many of the buildings, including the Norman fortress and the cathedral's 9th-century campanile, show the signs of widespread appropriation of stones from the buildings of ancient Capua, mainly the great amphitheatre. Seven busts of divine figures are incorporated in the façade of the 16th-century town hall.

☛ **Museo Campano** (Museum of Campania)   This museum gives a good idea of the large scale and lavish style of the ancient city and its temples, and has an excellent archaeological collection of local finds, including a remarkable series of tufa statues of the temple of Dea Matuta (a fertility goddess). The medieval section has equally fine sculptures from a castle built by Frederick II in 1239, later demolished.

Excursions from Capua

☞ **Santa Maria Capua Vetere** (*5km south-east*)

Ancient Capua, first an Etruscan then a Samnite city, was famous as the largest and richest city in southern Italy. An uneasy alliance with Rome in the 4th century BC ended with revolt in 216 when the Capuans turned to Hannibal, perhaps hoping to supplant Rome with Carthaginian help. All the vigour of Carthage was sapped by the notoriously luxurious Capuan life style, and its treachery cost the city dear. Although no longer a great power, Capua remained a rich city throughout the imperial age, with a six-mile perimeter, dozens of temples and a famous gladiatorial school even in the 4th century AD. The **amphitheatre** is a magnificent ruin, second in size to the Colosseum in Rome. Although used as a source of building material for nearly a thousand years it remains most impressive. Two of the external arches on the western side still have their divine heads (June and Ceres) in place, part of the same series as those in the museum and on the town hall façade in Capua. The gardens beside the amphitheatre are filled with sculptural bits; the mosaic pavement dates from the 2nd century AD. The guardian of the site may be persuaded to conduct you to the interesting **Mithraeum** (Mitreo), a 3rd-century underground sanctuary with frescoes of themes from the Persian Mithraic religion, a popular rival faith to Christianity. The warrior-god Mithras is seen killing a bull.

Ancient Capua was destroyed by Saracens in the 9th century, abandoned and renamed in the Middle Ages after the surviving cathedral. Santa Maria Capua Vetere is now once again a larger town than modern Capua.

☞ **Sant' Angelo in Formis** (*4km east*)

A very fine Romanesque basilica built on the site of a temple and using its floor, with a dated inscription from 74BC. There are many antique columns and 11th- and 12th-century Byzantine-style frescoes inside the church and in the porch.

CASERTA

Caserta, now little more than a suburb of Naples, is visited chiefly for the massive **Royal Palace** (Palazzo Reale) which dominates the town. Built by Vanvitelli (from 1752-1774) for the first Bourbon kings of Naples with the intention of rivalling Versailles, the palace is larger than the royal residences of the most powerful European countries of the time. The approach from the Caserta Sud motorway turn-off is the most impressive and was originally part of a design, influenced by Bernini's colonnade at St Peter's, for a vast piazza, focal point of a new capital city which was never realised. The State Apartments, approached via a monumental staircase, are richly stuccoed and gorgeously decorated but most of the furniture has been removed. More impressive is the vast formal park with a vista to a great waterfall (Cascata Grande) tumbling down from the hills. It's worth the half-hour walk (or quicker pony trap or bicycle ride) to see the fountains with the Baroque statue groups of Actaeon and his hounds and Diana bathing.

Excursions from Caserta

☞ **Casertavecchia** (*10km north-east*)

The perfect antidote to the grandeur of the Royal Palace at Caserta, this is a tiny medieval village where narrow alleys of polished cobbles lead to a small enclosed square dominated by the façade of the Romanesque cathedral. There are several rather charming restaurants, some with shady gardens.

(*See also Capua*)

CUMAE

This was one of the most ancient and important Greek settlements in Italy – a sophisticated centre of Hellenic civilisation. Today it is wild, overgrown and deserted apart from the handful of tourists who come to admire the views and the scattered excavations of the Acropolis: the Temple of Apollo and the Temple of Jupiter are little more than foundations. The **Cave of the Cumaean Sibyl**, excavated as late as 1932, is better preserved: a long tunnel cut in distinctive trapezoid shape leads to the chamber where she spoke her echoing prophesies to the Greeks who came to consult the Oracle – and to Aeneas, hero of Virgil's epic Roman poem.

(*See also Phlegrean Fields*)

HERCULANEUM (ERCOLANO)

Named after Hercules by its original Greek settlers, Herculaneum came under complete Roman rule in 89BC. It developed into a quiet residential town without forum or amphitheatre, more affluent but much less lively than its big commercial neighbour Pompeii. The eruption of Vesuvius in AD79 destroyed both cities, but the people of Herculaneum had time to evacuate their town, which was then submerged in molten lava to a depth of over 60 feet, preserving rows of houses more than one storey high. The hard and deep covering of tufa-like volcanic debris (and the fact that the modern town of Resina was built over part of the ancient town) has made excavation far more arduous than at Pompeii, but the details, hewn out of solid rock, are quite remarkable: frescoes, mosaics, sculptures and even woodwork such as beams, beds, window frames and sliding doors – albeit in a blackened charcoal state.

The first discoveries were made in 1709 by workers sinking a shaft for a well: marble statues were dispersed among various museums during the Austrian occupation. The restored king of Naples instigated more exploration in 1738 – ten years before work began at Pompeii – collecting considerable treasures of sculpture and papyrus manuscripts. More systematic excavations begun in 1927 still continue.

The remains of Herculaneum give you a very good idea of the comfortable style of life its citizens enjoyed. However, it takes a good deal of imagination to visualise the original seaside resort. The villas once overlooked the sea but the coastline has altered so that the ruins are now well back from the water, on the edge of an unprepossessing town. Most houses are locked up – ask a guard to let you in or join the tail end of a group being guided round.

☛ Among the highlights are:

House of the Mosaic Atrium   Luxurious house with mosaic-paved atrium and terrace overlooking the sea.

House of the Deer   Decorated with frescoes and paintings, and two sculptured groups of stags at bay.

House with the Wooden Trellis (Opus Craticum)   The only surviving example of wood and plaster construction: plebeian shop and two flats, with upper floor complete.

House of the Wooden Partition   Beautifully preserved two-storey façade; inside, a partly preserved wooden partition and the charred remains of a bed.

House of the Neptune and Amphitrite Mosaic   House and well-preserved shop with the original wooden shelves; mosaics depicting Neptune and Amphitrite in the inner court.

Baths   Well-planned Roman baths, divided into men's and women's sections; various wall paintings and mosaic floors.

ISCHIA

While Capri has long been a haunt of the British and Americans, Ischia is almost entirely geared to the German market. It is the largest of the Neapolitan islands – about twice the size of Capri – and the main attractions are good sandy beaches, numerous thermal establishments and an abundance of hot springs which have evolved from the island's volcanic past. Therapeutic sands, mud baths, massages and thermal waters are all part of the package. Luxury hotels have their own spa equipment; alternatively you can get free treatment at the beach of Maronti where tourists wallow up to their necks in the hot volcanic mud.

The island is fertile and hilly, with vineyards carpeting the slopes of the dominant Monte Epomeo. There are hills covered in wild flowers, pinewoods and chestnut groves, and a rugged and varied coastline. You can quite easily escape to quiet corners – there are unspoilt hillside villages and secluded beaches. **Porto d'Ischia** is the main hub of tourism, with the greatest concentration of hotels, boutiques, restaurants and nightclubs, plus the attraction of a long beach and active little harbour. Beyond it lies the more local little fishing town of **Ischia Ponte**. On a high rock approached by a causeway is the **Castello d'Ischia**, an Aragonese castle with a cathedral and a convent (in the gruesome crypt are the skeletons of long-deceased abbesses). Apart from a few churches, there is nothing else to see on Ischia.

Resorts best known for hot spring spas and thermal treatments are **Casamicciola Terme**, a sprawling, low-lying complex of modern hotels which would barely be recognised by Henrik Ibsen who lived and wrote here, and the grander **Lacco Ameno**. Smaller and rather more charming is the village of **Forio** with pastel-washed houses clustering around a circular watchtower, and **Sant' Angelo** with a central piazza.

NAPLES (NAPOLI)

People tend to love or loathe Naples. It's a city of extraordinary vitality and theatricality in a beautiful natural setting, with plenty to offer the keen sightseer. It is also a filthy, raucous port of dilapidated buildings and squalid backstreets with screeching hawkers and urchin pickpockets. The romantic image of a city of song with a perennially festive atmosphere is now a misconception; street musicians and spontaneous Neapolitan refrains have been replaced by international pop music blaring from tapes sold at roadside stalls. The casual visitor may find the streets downright dirty and the volatile, energetic Neapolitans merely noisy.

Undoubtedly the most beautiful feature of the city is its setting. Seen from the sea on a fine day, its buildings rise up against a dramatic backdrop of vivid blue sky and steep volcanic hills dominated, to the east, by Mount Vesuvius. At close quarters it is a chaotic urban sprawl with its ugly dockyards and oily waters. Even the finer streets in the centre are not very pleasing aesthetically, being an unsatisfactory hybrid of building styles. Yet while few single structures stand out as architectural masterpieces, many of the city's palaces, museums and churches contain exceptionally rich works of art.

The heart of ancient Naples is known as **Spaccanapoli**; the street which "splits" Naples and gives the district its name is the Via Roma. Off this street, and its continuation, Via Toledo, are the steep, dark and densely populated alleys which are so characteristic of the city. Lofty, tottering houses, mouldering palaces, blackened churches and hole-in-the wall workshops line the streets and washing is strung between the windows.

Due south of Via Toledo, on the bay, lies the old village of **Santa Lucia**, still one of the more picturesque areas of Naples although its attractions as a fishermen's quarter have diminished in the face of yacht clubs and tourist waterside restaurants. Linked to the mainland by a causeway looms the forbidding hulk of the Castel dell'Ovo ("Egg Castle"), a Norman fortress. To the north stretches the Villa Comunale, a large and rather seedy public park with an aquarium, cafés and snack vans and tree-lined paths. Beyond it is the district of **Mergellina**, a good area to stay with fine views over the bay and hydrofoil services to the islands. **Posillipo** (from a Greek word meaning "that which soothes pain") is a fashionable residential quarter on the promontory separating the Bay of Pozzuoli from the Bay of Naples. There are villas, lush gardens and lovely views of the Bay below.

On the hill behind Spaccanapoli is the sprawling residential quarter of **Vomero** which provides a quiet respite from the city centre (to which it is linked by funicular). On a clear day there are sweeping views of the city and bay below. The massive Castel Sant' Elmo, for centuries crucial to the city's defence, dominates the area; just below stands the Carthusian Monastery of San Martino with, to the west, the spacious park of the Villa Floridiana.

Naples

Main sights

With the notable exception of the palace at Capodimonte, some 4km north of the centre just inside the ring road, all the main sights are in Spaccanapoli or Vomero.

☛ **Capodimonte Palace, Museum and National Galleries** The 18th-century palace of the Bourbons, surrounded by a vast park, contains important collections of works of art. The National Gallery (second floor) is a wide-ranging, well-organised collection with fine examples from all the main Italian schools. The nucleus of the collection was amassed by the Farnese family. Among the most noteworthy paintings are Simone Martini's St Louis of Toulouse (1317), Masaccio's Crucifixion (1426), a charming and very characteristic Madonna and Child by Botticelli, Giovanni Bellini's Transfiguration and Caravaggio's Flagellation. A room devoted to Titian includes two famous works of the 1540s, his Danäe and the portrait of Pope Paul III with his nephews. The Flemish works include Brueghel's well-known Parable of the Blind (1568).

On the first floor are the Royal Apartments with important collections of ceramics, ivories, armour and 19th-century paintings.

☞ **Certosa di San Martino** A Carthusian monastery founded in the 14th century but reconstructed in the 17th century in Baroque style. It houses a museum devoted to the history of the kingdom of Naples with naval and folklore sections; costumes, carriages and immaculate crib scenes with tiny terracotta figures (one scene so small that it's set in an eggshell). The extremely ornate church has a rich collection of Baroque paintings. Elaborate white marble cloisters surround peaceful gardens.

☞ **National Archaeological Museum** One of the most important museums in Europe containing priceless collections of classical sculptures, frescoes, paintings, mosaics and other works of art, representing the most important periods of ancient civilisation. Outstanding are the Graeco-Roman sculptures from the Farnese collection, including extraordinarily realistic portrait busts, and mosaics from Pompeii, Herculaneum and neighbouring regions. The huge Farnese Bull was carved from a single block of marble and restored by Michelangelo; superb Greek and Roman copies of famous statues include the Javelin Thrower, the graceful Venus Callipyge and the Farnese Hercules bulging with exaggerated muscles. The mosaics and murals still at Pompeii today pale in comparison with those now kept in the museum which are outstandingly beautiful.

Other sights

☞ **Castel Nuovo** The austere castle of the Angevin rulers, rebuilt by the Aragonese who added the turrets and the fine Renaissance triumphal arch which adorns the entrance. The marble reliefs commemorate the defeat of the French and king Alfonso I's triumphant entry into Naples in 1443.

☞ **Cathedral** A huge Gothic church dedicated to San Gennaro, the patron saint of Naples. The façade is 19th century and bears little resemblance to the original design although the central portal survives from the 15th century. The chapel of San Gennaro, which houses precious reliquaries containing the blood of the saint, was decorated by the rival Baroque artists, Domenichino and Lanfranco, both from northern Italy.

☞ **Gesù Nuovo** A Jesuit church dating from the end of the 16th century. Behind the unusual façade of patterned stonework is an extravagant Baroque interior, with extensive coloured marble and marquetry. Francesco Solimena's fresco of the Expulsion of Heliodorus (1725) is on the entrance wall.

☞ **Royal Palace** (Palazzo Reale) A large and forbidding building designed by Domenico Fontana (1600), with statues set in niches depicting eight Neapolitan kings. The royal apartments feature lavish High Baroque and Imperial décor with painted ceilings, massive chandeliers and mirrors, tapestries, marble floors, and paintings of the Neapolitan school.

☞ **Sant' Anna dei Lombardi** One of the city's richest collections of Renaissance decoration and sculpture with monuments, tombs and reliefs by Tuscan artists in several chapels.

☞ **Santa Chiara** An austere Gothic church built by Robert the Wise, king of Naples in the early 14th century. It was badly bombed in the Second World War but has been restored; the sepulchre of King Robert (1343) was salvaged and lies behind the high altar. The beautiful majolica-tiled cloisters of the adjacent convent surround rustic gardens – a peaceful enclave in the city centre. In 1986, during restoration financed by the designer Mario Valentino, 16th-century frescoes were discovered (under later ones) on the walls of the convent. They are highly imaginative and vivid.

☛ **San Lorenzo Maggiore**   The finest Gothic church in Naples, San Lorenzo was begun by French architects under the patronage of Charles I of Anjou. It has been much restored, but the original choir, with an elegant polygonal apse, survives. There are some fine tombs.

☛ **Additional sights**   The museums of Villa Pignatelli (works of art and furnishings), Villa Floridiana (European ceramics) and Palazzo Cuomo (Filangieri Museum of arms, painting and sculpture) are worth seeing if you have more than a day or two in Naples. There are many churches, in addition to those listed above, which have interesting Gothic and Renaissance tombs and frescoes, and paintings of Neapolitan Baroque artists such as Massimo Stanzione and Solimena.

PADULA

The **Certosa** (Carthusian Monastery) of San Lorenzo, recently restored after over a century of neglect, is remarkable for its sheer size and for its magnificent Baroque decoration and worth a detour to see. It is about 100km south-east of Salerno, close to the Sala Consolina motorway exit. Founded in 1306, the monastery is a vast complex which grew and was embellished over the centuries until it was suppressed in 1866. The most beautiful features are the Great Cloister (begun 1583), the choir stalls (15th and 16th centuries) and the polychrome altar in the church, and Gaetano Barba's magnificent oval staircase (18th century). The Certosa, famous as the place where Charles V and his entourage feasted on a 1,000-egg omelette in 1535, is now used for cultural exhibitions relating to the region.
(*See also Teggiano*)

PAESTUM

The strongest reason for heading south of the Sorrento peninsula is a visit to the ruins of Paestum, 40km south of Salerno: a lonely, silent and desolate plain where three great Doric temples stand solemnly among herbs and wild flowers, against a backdrop of jagged mountains. The Greek city (Poseidonia) was taken over by local Lucanians, who in turn came under Roman rule. Malaria gradually depopulated the community, and after the Saracen attacks of the 9th century Paestum became completely deserted and overgrown. Untouched by medieval history, it was rediscovered during the building of the 18th-century carriage road. The Paestum that Goethe described in 1787 is more or less what you can expect today: "The country grew more and more flat and desolate, the houses rare, the cultivation sparser. In the distance appeared some huge quadrilateral masses, and when we finally reached them, we were at first uncertain whether we were driving through rocks or ruins. Then we recognized what they were, the remains of temples, monuments to a once glorious city.....At first sight they excited nothing but stupefaction. I found myself in a world which was completely strange to me....Reproductions give a false impression; architectural designs make them look more elegant and drawings in perspective more ponderous than they really are. It is only by walking through them and round them that one can attune one's life

Paestum

to theirs and experience the emotional effect which the architect intended."

Of the three temples, the largest and best preserved is the **Temple of Poseidon** (Roman Neptune), a supreme architectural masterpiece, standing roofless but otherwise intact. The nearby **Basilica of Hera** (Roman Juno) is the oldest of the Doric temples, dating from 565BC. The third temple, confusingly called the **Temple of Ceres** (it was in fact dedicated to Athena), is one of the earliest examples of the blending of Doric and Ionic orders. Two of its Ionic capitals are preserved in the local museum. Roman ruins include a forum and amphitheatre, but neither are as impressive as the temples. In the **Museum** are sculptures, painted pots, terracottas and very early tomb paintings, most notable of which is the delightful Tomb of the Diver, a very rare example of Greek painting, which was (with other tomb frescoes) uncovered by a farmer in 1969. In July and August there is a season of drama, music and ballet at Paestum.

Paestum resort, well out of sight of the temples, is little more than a sprawl of hotels and campsites, set in a flat landscape of artichoke fields. The grazing buffaloes produce the mozzarella cheese sold by the roadside and served in local restaurants.
(*See also Velia*)

PALINURO

A popular resort on a spectacular headland of the Cilento coast, named after Palinurus, Ulysses' helmsman. There are some spectacular grottoes and unspoilt coves and sandy beaches, accessible only from the sea. The area is excellent for scuba diving.

THE PHLEGREAN FIELDS (CAMPI FLEGREI)

The volcanic area north-west of Naples including Cumae, Baia and Pozzuoli (*see separate entries*). Here the contrast between the delightful coastline and the desolate inland territory of lakes and

craters formed the Greeks' conception of heaven and hell. The
Romans regarded the area with superstitious respect, and Virgil's
account in the Aeneid elaborated on Homer's in the Odyssey. The
"fields of fire" emit steam and noxious gases, and until the
beginning of this century it was the practice to demonstrate the two
feet of carbon dioxide in one of the caverns by throwing in a dog,
which died, Mark Twain reported, in a minute and a half.

The entrance to the Underworld was said to be located at **Lake
Avernus**; this did not prevent Agrippa turning the lake into a naval
base (linked to the sea by canal, long vanished). Although it never
regained its classical forested gloom, Lake Avernus is strangely
beautiful from afar. The most interesting feature of this distinctive
(though not exactly attractive) landscape is the **Solfatara** near
Pozzuoli, a low-lying volcano thought to have erupted last in 1198.
Its huge crater is hot and hollow under the foot and jets of steam and
sulphurous vapour (*fumarole*) perform at intervals.

POMPEII

No visit to Campania would be complete without seeing Pompeii,
the Roman city which died so abruptly in the first eruption of Mount
Vesuvius, and you don't need to be a connoisseur of classical
antiquity to enjoy it. For most people the interesting part is picturing
the everyday life that went on 2,000 years ago from the details that
remain: the bakeries with kneading machines and ovens, some still
containing loaves of bread; the kitchens with pots and pans; the
marble shop counters; the paintings and frescoes in even the
humblest abodes; the graffiti scratched in red chalk or charcoal
which include announcements of gladiatorial combats, election
notices, lists of market days, exchanges of lovers, quotes from Virgil.
The most poignant details are the Pompeiians themselves, recreated
in plaster casts from the imprints their bodies made in the ashes – a
woman clutching a jar of treasures, a girl burying her head in her
mother's breast. Excavation, both here and at Herculaneum, has
provided a unique source of information about many aspects of
social, economic, religious and political life in the Graeco-Roman
world.

Pompeii had been a local port since the 6th century BC, in the
hands of various peoples; by 200BC its culture was completely
Greek. Like some other cities of the south, Pompeii held out against
Rome and was not completely subjugated until after the Social War
(80BC) when a colony of Roman veterans was established there
under Publius Sulla, nephew of the Roman general. The earliest
houses date from the First Samnite period (4th-3rd centuries BC) but
the most luxurious residences were built during the Second Samnite
period (200-80BC) when trade was flourishing. The House of the
Faun for example has two main rooms, four dining rooms, two large
gardens, mosaic floors and frescoed walls.

In AD63 an earthquake severely damaged both Pompeii and
Herculaneum and the cities were still suffering from the disaster
when the final devastation struck in AD79 (see account under entry
for Vesuvius), burying Pompeii under 23 feet of volcanic debris.

Pompeii

Although ruins of Pompeii were first found in the 1ate 16th century by an architect tunnelling under the hill to build a water channel, the full extent of the buried city was not discovered until 1748. The excavations made a huge impact throughout Europe, starting a fashion for antiquity and and stimulating the neoclassical style among artists and architects. Much of the earliest digging was by disrespectful treasure hunters, and in 1860 random digging was brought to a halt and systematic excavation was enforced. By the early 1970s about three-quarters of the city had been excavated.

Pompeii is still undergoing restoration and there are many closed doors – more, since the 1980 earthquake – but even taking this into account, there's an enormous amount to see. The site has a certain monotony as there are a great many little streets. "Crowded and rectilinear... like a row of bathing huts" said Rose Macaulay. The most popular features are the brothels and Pompeiian pornography (much of it kept under lock and key but readily opened by tip-seeking guards). It is advisable to get a detailed guidebook – or a guide, with whom you agree a price before you start. Avoid the midday heat – there's very little shade.

☞ Among the highlights are:

House of Mysteries   The finest wall paintings, showing lifesize figures performing the mysterious Dionysiac rites which though prohibited were still widely practised in the 1st century BC.

House of Menander   An elegant residence where great hoards of silver were discovered (now in Naples Archaeological Museum); richly decorated with paintings and mosaics.

House of the Vettii   A typical luxury patrician villa with impressive murals and gardens. The Vettii brothers dealt in agricultural produce, and a series of paintings shows cherubs picking and pressing grapes, and selling the wine.

House of the Faun   One of the biggest villas, with well-preserved decoration; named after a celebrated little bronze statue – in Naples, but a copy *in situ*.

Stabian Baths (Terme Stabiane)   The city's largest public baths, a hugh complex including swimming pool, plunge baths, dressing rooms. Fine stucco decoration preserved in the men's section.

Forum   The focal point of Pompeiian life; central square and public meeting place where transactions were made and judgements proclaimed.

POSITANO

"Positano bites deep. It is a dream place that isn't quite real when you are there and becomes beckoningly real after you have gone" wrote John Steinbeck in the 1950s. Although the dream element can rapidly be dispelled by the throngs of tourists in high summer, Positano is indeed picturesque. Moorish-style houses are packed tightly on a steep terraced hillside above a small bay with a majolica-domed church and a small beach with fishing boats. There is just one narrow street through the town and a maze of steep staircases and narrow alleys (" You do not walk to visit a friend, you either climb or slide" wrote Steinbeck). Terraces festooned with bougainvillaea and streets flanked with cafés and boutiques selling gaily coloured dresses give the whole place something of a festive air. Steps lead down to a small grey beach and the canopied restaurants that cluster around it. For the local boats the richest catch these days is tourists taking coastal trips.

Positano prospered in the Middle Ages as part of the Maritime Republic of Amalfi – medieval towers can still be seen along the shoreline – and in the 18th century under the Bourbons, when a trading fleet again filled the harbour. The end of Bourbon rule in 1860 marked the start of Positano's decline; tourists who ventured here in the later 19th century found no more than a village of farmers and fishermen. In the 1930s, when it could still be described as a quiet fishing village, Positano became a colony for artists and writers, otherwise known as "the poor man's Capri". Today it's the richer tourists and celebrities that live or stay here (Franco Zeffirelli has a villa), but thanks to restrained tourist development and a far from flashy atmosphere, it has retained its charm.

POZZUOLI

West of Naples on its own bay, modern Pozzuoli (home town of Sophia Loren) is busy and industrial. Ancient Puteoli was the Romans' chief Mediterranean trading port, civilised and wealthy, but not much has survived. The coastline of this volcanic area has been rearranged over the centuries by the local phenomenon of "slow earthquakes", and the Roman harbour has disappeared under the sea. Near the modern port in a waterfront park the so-called **Temple of Serapis** (in fact it was an elegant market hall) stands in a shallow seawater pool, its three remaining marble columns bearing evidence of much deeper submersion.

☛ **Amphitheatre** Discovered during the construction of the Rome-Naples express railway in 1926, Pozzuoli's amphitheatre was built in the 1st century AD to hold 40,000 spectators; you still get a splendid impression of its size. The substructure of corridors and cells is particularly well preserved. (*See also Phlegrean Fields*)

PROCIDA

Small, unexploited and very Italian, the island of Procida is distinctly run-down, with few hotels, and nothing much to do apart from look at the fishermen's houses or wander around the vaguely Byzantine but very battered centre.

RAVELLO

One of the loveliest places on this lovely coast, Ravello is set high on the mountainside above Amalfi ("closer to the sky than it is to the seashore", wrote André Gide). The views, encompassing miles of rugged coastline, are superb. Ravello began as a wealthy offshoot of the Amalfian Maritime Republic, later gained independence and its own bishop, and had a period of splendid prosperity in the 13th century. It's a small and intimate town of rustic streets and stairways, Moorish palaces and monasteries and romantic villas with hanging gardens. There are several appealing hotels in old palaces and converted monasteries.

☛ **Cathedral** (San Pantaleone) Dominating the central piazza, a hybrid structure whose outstanding features are the 13th-century campanile and the bronze doors (1179) with 54 panels depicting Old Testament scenes, usually protected by wooden doors. Inside is a pulpit with glorious Byzantine mosaics and richly carved cornices and capitals.

☛ **Palazzo Rufolo** A palatial Moorish-style villa, begun in the 11th century, whose distinguished residents included pope Hadrian IV and Charles of Anjou. Boccaccio was so charmed by the place that he used it as the setting for one of his lewd tales, and in 1880 Wagner conceived the idea of the magic garden in *Parsifal* through the inspiration of the villa's exotic gardens. A Wagner festival is held here in July.

☛ **Villa Cimbrone** Ravello's other famous gardens belong to the Villa Cimbrone, a mansion restored by an eccentric Englishman at the end of the 19th century. Today the gardens are pleasantly rambling and shambolic, with battered statues and an unforgettable panorama of the Bay of Salerno from the clifftop **Belvedere Cimbrone**.

SALERNO

An ancient city which was capital of the kingdom of Naples under
the Normans and became famous for its school of medicine in
medieval times, Salerno is now little more than a frenetic modern
city. Subject to countless invasions and a very heavy battering in the
Second World War, the old quarter is reduced to a few narrow
sloping streets but with sufficient architectural details decorating
doorways and houses to give you some idea of medieval Salerno.
The best examples are along the Via dei Mercanti.

☞ **Cathedral**   A Norman cathedral, altered in the 18th century. It retains its
original aspect with a courtyard (atrium) with antique columns from
Paestum. Particularly fine are the bronze doors, cast in Constantinople in
1099. The inside suffered at the hands of restorers after severe earthquake
damage in 1688 and is somewhat drab, apart from the splendid pulpits
decorated with mosaics and supported by beautifully carved granite
columns. There are some interesting tombs and mosaics, and the cathedral
museum has a remarkable 12th-century ivory altar front.

SANTA MARIA DI CASTELLABATE

An attractive small fishing harbour and low-key resort which makes
a good base for exploring Paestum, Velia and the rocky Cilento
coast. Simple hotel accommodation can be found in the village and a
better-equipped hotel a short bus ride away. There is a small sandy
beach, a 16th-century castle (converted into self-catering
apartments) and a Romanesque church.

SORRENTO

Sorrento's praises have been sung since Antiquity – from Homer to
the Romantic writers and poets of the 19th century. Sorrento was an
important Roman resort, popular with the hedonist élite for its
wines, mild climate, and carefree atmosphere. During the 18th and
19th centuries it was again a prestigious resort where aristocrats and
Bourbon princes spent a leisurely life in palatial villas and the
Romantic poets enthused about the sunsets. Today the face of
Sorrento has changed, and only the package tour brochures wax
lyrical about the resort itself. Nothing, however, has changed
Sorrento's most striking feature – the spectacular setting, perched
high on a cliff surrounded by citrus groves and with sweeping views
of the Bay of Naples and the dark cone of Mount Vesuvius that
looms above. According to legend, it was sailing past Sorrento that
Odysseus had himself tied to the mast of his ship to resist the lure of
those deadly enchantresses, the Sirens.

Sorrento is now a booming package-holiday resort. But despite
the unsightly building development of the 1960s and the traffic, it
still has a certain old-fashioned charm. Take away the souvenirs and
signs in English (80% of its summer visitors are British) and the
centre is still distinctly Italian, with a decayed 19th-century dignity.
Streets and alleys are crammed with tiny shops selling locally made
lace, marquetry and *Capodimonte* porcelain, and pavements are lined
with lively cafés and bars. Along the main shopping street, the
Corso d' Italia, even a double-glazed hotel room won't ensure a

good night's sleep. The best bet is one of the old-fashioned cliffside establishments surrounded by semi-tropical gardens and suspended high above the sea. Lifts take bathers down to the tiny strips of volcanic sand – barely wide enough for a line or two of parasols – and a succession of wooden platforms on stilts which are the only bathing facilities that Sorrento can offer.

Although there is little to see in Sorrento there is a wide range of boat and coach excursions.

☛ **Correale Museum**   A collection ranging from Greek and Roman sculptures to manuscripts of the celebrated poet Tasso (born in Sorrento in 1544) and Neapolitan paintings, furniture and porcelain, housed in an 18th-century palace.

☛ **San Francesco**   A Baroque church with delightful 14th-century cloisters.

Excursions from Sorrento

☛ **Sorrento peninsula**
Vico Equense (*15km north-east*), Massa Lubrense (*8km south-west*), a sleepy town with hotels isolated on vine-clad hillsides above a small harbour, and Sant' Agata (*8km south*) are all small resorts with interesting churches and splendid views. You can continue to Positano and Amalfi (*see separate entries*. The drive is spectacular.

TEGGIANO

A well-preserved old town interesting for its Romanesque and Gothic churches built on the still-visible remains of ancient pagan temples, for its 16th-century palaces and the cathedral and castle, both of the 13th century but later rebuilt.
(*See also Padula*).

VELIA

The ruins of Velia can be seen as an excursion of about 30km from Palinuro or Santa Maria di Castellabate (*see separate entries*) or combined with a visit to Paestum (*20km north*). The ancient Greek city (Elea) was an important trade link between Reggio and Etruria, and there was a flourishing school of philosophy there. The site is divided into three areas: the southern quarter (with the agora), the northern quarter, and the acropolis; a visit takes about an hour.

VESUVIUS

The massive purple pyramid of Mount Vesuvius looms over the entire Bay of Naples – "a peak of hell rising out of Paradise" as Goethe put it. The famous eruption of AD79 stands out in history as one of the world's most horrifying natural disasters. A vivid eyewitness report is preserved in two letters written by Pliny the Younger, nephew of the Elder Pliny who died in the eruption: "We had scarce stepped out of the path, when darkness overspread us, not like that of a cloudy night, or when there is no moon, but of a room when it is shut up, and all the lights extinguished. Nothing then was to be heard but the shrieks of women, the screams of children, and the cries of men; some calling for their children, others for their parents, others for their husbands, and only distinguishing each other by their voices; one lamenting his own fate, another that of his family; some wishing to die, from the very fear of dying; some lifting their hand to the gods; but the greater part imagining that the last and eternal night was come, which was to destroy both the gods and the world together."

Vesuvius has erupted sporadically since. In 1631 over 3,000 people were killed when streams of lava poured out of the crater, flowing towards the sea, and the skies were darkened for days. The last major eruption was in 1906 when the top of the cone fell into the crater and a massive cloud of ashes loomed above. Wide streams of lava gushed down and the streets of Naples were buried in ash. The whole region east of Vesuvius was devastated, with the loss of over 100 lives. The most recent eruption, in 1944, closed the main fissure and altered the shape of the crater.

The crater is a dramatic sight, and worth the journey (unless you suffer from vertigo; there is no protection from the dizzy 1,000 foot drop). The ascent of Vesuvius takes you through an extraordinary variety of landscapes. Orchards and vines flourish on the fertile volcanic soil of the lower slopes (where bars serve the distinctively flavoured local wine, Lacrima Cristi); higher up, copses of oak and chestnut give way to undulating plateaux covered with broom. Still higher, on the slopes of the great cone, the landscape becomes dramatically barren with black and spiky lumps of lava among the patches of broom and laurel. Before the eruption of 1631, after a long period of inactivity, there were forests in the crater and three lakes where cattle used to drink. But volcanic gases have killed vegetation in and around the crater.

The last part of the journey has to be done on foot (the chair lift has ceased to function), and although stout shoes are essential the walk need deter none but the frail or elderly. There are two approaches to the summit. The main route starts on the west side and involves three or four hours (return) easy walking through strange bare scenery. The other approach, from the toll road to the south, is followed by a steep walk to the crater (45 minutes return). Whichever route you take you will be charged at the top for "a compulsory guide" despite the fact that there is usually no guide available and you are likely to walk round the crater on your own.

Hotels

Amalfi   £££
CAPPUCCINI CONVENTO   *Open all year*
Via Annunziatella 46, 84011 Salerno   *Tel: (089) 871008*

A beautifully converted medieval convent in the hills above Amalfi. A lift
takes you slowly and somewhat precariously up the steep hillside to a
wooded setting of terraces and gardens of lilac and bougainvillaea. Where
possible the structure of the old convent has been preserved. The monks'
cells are now elegant superbly furnished bedrooms and the cloisters –
highlight of the hotel – are virtually intact. Public rooms are cool and quiet,
furnished with antiques. A delightful balustraded terrace commands fine
views of Amalfi and the coast and there is a small private beach.

Facilities: *49 bedrooms; restaurant; lift; parking*   **Credit/charge cards accepted:**
Diners

Amalfi   ££
LUNA CONVENTO   *Open all year*
Via P. Comite 19, 84011 Salerno   *Tel: (089) 871002*

Five minutes uphill from the centre of Amalfi, this converted 13th-century
convent (where saint Francis of Assisi stayed in 1220) has superb sea and
town views. Bedrooms – some traditional with antiques and chintz, others
modern – are built round beautiful Byzantine cloisters where breakfast is
served. There are two restaurants, one across the road in an old watchtower
with a terrace overlooking the sea. This is also the setting for the somewhat
incongruous discothèque. Below is the hotel's swimming pool and a rocky
beach.

Facilities: *45 bedrooms; restaurant; lift; swimming pool; parking*   **Credit/charge
cards accepted:** *Amex, Diners, Eurocard, Visa*

Capri   ££££
LUNA   *Closed Nov to mid-April*
Viale Matteotti 3, 80073 Capri   *Tel: (081) 8370432*

Away from the centre, looking over the sea and south side of the island, the
Luna is one of the less pretentious first-class hotels of Capri, quiet and
civilised. The furnishings are traditional (parts are rather old-fashioned) and
most of the bedrooms have sea-view terraces. A path lined by pergolas leads
through subtropical gardens to a good-sized pool, one side of which borders
the ruins of the *Certosa* (Carthusian monastery).

Facilities: *48 bedrooms (AC); restaurant; swimming pool*   **Credit/charge cards
accepted:** *Amex, Diners, Eurocard, Visa*

Capri
VILLA KRUPP
Viale Matteotti 12, 80073 Capri

££
Open all year
Tel: (081) 8370362

Set in the Augustus Gardens on a hillside above the town of Capri, this tiny hotel has lovely views of the island. Bedrooms are spacious and bright. The only public area is a terrace where breakfast can be taken. From 1908 to 1910 the villa was the residence of Lenin; Gorky stayed here, and his desk is now part of the furniture.

Facilities: *12 bedrooms*   **Credit/charge cards accepted:** *none*

Capri
VILLA SARAH
Via Tiberio 3a, 80073 Capri

££
Closed Nov to March
Tel: (081) 8370689

One of the quietest hotels on the island, the Villa Sarah is well out of Capri centre, up a steepish path which leads eventually to Villa Jovis. It is a small and spotlessly clean hotel with light, airy rooms and a homely atmosphere. There is no lounge or restaurant, just a simple whitewashed breakfast room.

Facilities: *24 bedrooms*   **Credit/charge cards accepted:** *Amex*

Ischia
IL MONASTERO
Castello Aragonese, 80070 Ischia Ponte

£
Closed Nov to March
Tel: (081) 992435

Converted from a 15th-century monastery, this small *pensione* has a remarkable setting below the ruins of the Aragonese castle. A bridge links the castle with the main island of Ischia. The monks' cells are simple but pretty bedrooms, half of which open out onto the terrace, and the old monks' hall is a rustic dining room with fine sea views and a terrace. A delightful place to stay, very reasonably priced.

Facilities: *15 bedrooms; restaurant (breakfast and dinner only)*   **Credit/charge cards accepted:** *none*

Ischia
SAN MICHELE
80070 Sant' Angelo

££
Closed Nov to March
Tel: (081) 999276

Set on a hill above the resort of Sant' Angelo, the San Michele is a modern hotel surrounded by gardens and terraces shaded by pines. There's a very attractive pool and thermal treatment on site. Bedrooms are clean, modern and bright, all with private bathroom and many with balconies and lovely sea views. There's a trattoria-style restaurant and a carpeted bar with relaxing armchairs and a terrace. A winding path takes you down the hill to the centre of the resort.

Facilities: *56 bedrooms; restaurant; swimming pool (heated); thermal treatment*   **Credit/charge cards accepted:** *none*

Positano   ££
L'ANCORA   *Closed Oct to March*
Via C. Colombo 36, 84017 Salerno   *Tel: (089) 875318*

This is a small, modest and (by Positano standards) reasonably priced
family-run hotel, the main feature of which is its superb setting on the
hillside. Public rooms have vinyl furniture but are cool and crisp; bedrooms
are traditional and spotlessly clean with tiled floors. The terrace, where meals
are taken, has lovely views of the bay and a canopy of vegetation provides
shade. Guests may use the swimming pool of a nearby hotel.

Facilities: *18 bedrooms (AC in 4); restaurant; parking*   **Credit/charge cards
accepted:** *Amex, Diners, Visa*

Positano   ££
CASA ALBERTINA   *Open all year*
Via della Tavolozza 4, 84017 Salerno   *Tel: (089) 875143*

Like most of the hotels and houses of Positano, the Casa Albertina clings to
the steep terraced hillside and overlooks the beach and bay. You have to
climb up several flights of steps to get there but it's well worth the effort. It is
quiet and charming with the homely atmosphere that you might expect from
a small family-run hotel. Bedrooms are prettily furnished in traditional style
and all have terraces where meals can be served. Downstairs the rooms are
small and intimate; weather permitting, meals are taken on the terrace, with
a splendid view of the sea.

Facilities: *21 bedrooms (AC in some); restaurant; lift;*   **Credit/charge cards
accepted:** *Amex, Diners*

Positano   ££
MIRAMARE   *Open all year*
Via Trara Genoino, 84017 Salerno   *Tel: (089) 875002*

Occupying a stunning site above the bay and beach, the Miramare is a
delightful small hotel converted from old fishermens' houses. Bedrooms
retain their original structure and all have private terraces. The vaulted,
whitewashed public rooms have been elegantly furnished with antiques. The
dining room, enhanced by the views, is particularly attractive.

Facilities: *18 bedrooms; restaurant; parking*   **Credit/charge cards accepted:**
Amex

Our price symbols

£   = you can expect to find a room for under £35
££   = you can expect to find a room for under £55
£££   = you can expect to find a room for under £75
££££ = you can expect to find a room for under £125
£££££ = you should expect to pay over £125 for a room

Positano
SAN PIETRO
Via Laurito 2, 84017 Salerno

£££££
Closed Nov to early April
Tel: (089) 875454

There is no expense spared in this lap of luxury at the eastern end of Positano. The hotel sits on a cliff about a mile from the centre and all its rooms have balconies with glorious views across the bay. Cool elegance prevails throughout; there are several comfortable sitting areas with high quality reproduction antiques and an abundance of lush green plants. Bedrooms are fresh, light and very inviting with large comfortable bathrooms. Below the hotel there is a private beach and a bar, reached by lift.

Facilities: *60 bedrooms (AC); restaurant; lift; swimming pool; tennis court; parking* **Credit/charge cards accepted:** *Amex, Diners, Eurocard, Visa*

Ravello
CARUSO BELVEDERE
Via Toro 52, 84010 Salerno

££
Closed Feb
Tel: (089) 857111

This 13th-century *palazzo* was turned into a small hotel in 1903 and has been in the same family since then. It is an oasis of peace with rambling gardens, terraces and a famous belvedere overlooking the coast. In summer meals are served outside. There are open fireplaces, stone columns, oil paintings and an atmosphere of slightly faded grandeur. Bedrooms are comfortable and old-fashioned, some with tiled verandahs.

Facilities: *24 bedrooms; restaurant* **Credit/charge cards accepted:** *Amex*

Ravello
PALUMBO
Via Toro 28, 84010 Salerno

££££
Open all year
Tel: (089) 857244

Converted from an aristocrat's exotic hilltop *palazzo*, the Palumbo has the splendid views and total tranquillity enjoyed by Ravello's other hotels. In addition it is beautifully preserved and furnished. It has been run by the same Swiss family for over a century; early guests included Wagner and Greig, DH Lawrence and EM Forster. Comfortable public rooms focus on a 13th-century Moorish courtyard. Bedrooms (7 in annexe) are white, cool and elegant; and there's a quiet, inviting atmosphere throughout the hotel. Several terraces and the garden all make the most of the coastal views of the Gulf of Salerno.

Facilities: *20 bedrooms (AC); restaurant; parking* **Credit/charge cards accepted:** *Amex, Diners, Eurocard, Visa*

Ravello £
PARSIFAL
Via G. D'Anna 5, 84010 Salerno

Closed mid-Oct to March
Tel: (089) 857144

This old monastery (founded by the barefoot monks of saint Augustin in 1288) was converted to a simple hotel in 1946 and named in honour of Wagner whose *Parsifal* was said to have been inspired by the gardens of nearby Villa Rufolo. Its rooms are delightfully quiet and there are magnificent views of the Amalfi coast. Bedrooms are simple, clean and adequate. Meals are served on a balustraded terrace with fine views.

Facilities: *19 bedrooms; restaurant; parking* **Credit/charge cards accepted:** *Amex, Diners, Eurocard, Visa*

San Marco di Castellabate ££
CASTELSANDRA
84071 Salerno

Closed mid-Oct to March
Tel: (0974) 966021

An isolated hotel in a lovely situation above the bay and surrounded by luxuriant gardens. This is a large hotel, sometimes used for conferences, and it suffers from a slightly impersonal atmosphere and a not always well co-ordinated décor. All bedrooms have terraces; superior doubles and suites are more spacious and more appealingly decorated. There is a minibus service to the sandy beach at Santa Maria, about 4km away. A good base for visiting Paestum, but not recommended for long stays, or in August.

Facilities: *125 bedrooms (AC in some); restaurant; swimming pools; tennis courts; parking* **Credit/charge cards accepted:** *Amex, Diners, Visa*

Sorrento ££
BELLEVUE SYRENE
Via Marina Grande 1, 80067 Napoli

Open all year
Tel: (081) 8781024

This splendid 18th-century pile stands on a cliff-top very close to the centre of Sorrento, with a lift down to a sunbathing jetty and tiny black beach. Inside it's rather like a rambling mansion, with fine furniture, paintings and marble floors contributing to an air of faded elegance. Bedrooms are also slightly faded and full of character, many of them (like the restaurant and terrace) enjoying unbroken views across the bay to Mount Vesuvius. The worst rooms are those in the annexe at the back of the hotel.

Facilities: *50 bedrooms; restaurant; lift; parking* **Credit/charge cards accepted:** *Amex, Diners, Eurocard, Visa*

Sorrento
TRAMONTANO
Via Vittoria Veneto 1, 80067 Napoli

£££
Open all year
Tel: (081) 8781940

This large, imposing hotel occupies a prime site, set right on the cliff in
central Sorrento. Public rooms are cool, comfortable and spacious and the
restaurant, salon and terrace have superb views across the bay. Bedrooms
are large and light with antiques, about half overlooking the sea. Despite a
central location, it's very peaceful. A lift takes guests down to a jetty and thin
strip of sand.

Facilities: *110 bedrooms; restaurant; lift; swimming pool; parking*   **Credit/charge
cards accepted:** *Amex, Diners, Visa*

Torre del Greco
SAKURA
Via de Nicola 28, 80059 Napoli

££
Open all year
Tel: (081) 8815202

If you want a peaceful, cool, comfortable hotel with a pool, ideally placed for
excursions to (in order of proximity) Vesuvius, Herculaneum, Naples
(14km), Pompeii and the Sorrentine peninsula, the Sakura leads a small and
undistinguished field. A low modern block tucked away in the woods that
clothe the fertile lower slopes of the dormant volcano, the hotel is fairly
expensive, not much to look at and short of character; simplicity of furniture
and decoration is taken almost to the point of austerity. Breakfast was
uninspired and accompanied by rock music. But the hotel's attractions are
powerful, and include long views of the Bay of Naples (over the shanty
coastal sprawl of Herculaneum and Torre del Greco) and down to Sorrento.
The pool is large and has a bar, but is open only from June to August, and is
not exclusively reserved for hotel guests. You pay to swim. The hotel is not in
Torre del Greco, but beside the road which leads up Vesuvius from the
Ercolano motorway exit south of Naples.

Facilities: *72 bedrooms (AC); restaurant; lift; swimming pool; parking*   **Credit/
charge cards accepted:** *Amex, Diners, Eurocard, Visa*

THE SOUTH

*❝We have now entered upon a part of Italy
which is behind-hand in civilisation to a degree
which will only be credible to those who have
tried it❞*

AUGUSTUS HARE

Molfetta, San Corrado

Introduction

Everybody knows that Italy is boot-shaped, yet comparatively few tourists take much interest in its mountainous toe, poised to kick Sicily, its (paradoxically flat) stiletto heel, or the dramatic scenery of its spur – let alone the boring old instep.

It is not really fair to blame the present-day tourist for lack of initiative; this is a part of Italy until recently neglected and still often ignored by other Italians. It is a harsh land, mainly mountainous, prone to earthquakes and therefore poor. Malaria is a scourge eradicated only since the last war. Day to day existence has almost always been a struggle.

Yet the south draws those who have had enough of so-called civilisation, and of fellow tourists. One of the earliest English travellers south of Naples was Thomas Hoby who travelled through Calabria in the mid-16th century "both to have a sight of the countrey and also to absent myself for a while owt of Englishmenne's companie for the tung's sake" – a sentiment which might be shared nowadays. Although you are unlikely to be "stared at like men dropt from the sky", like George Berkeley and his tutor who ventured out of the standard Grand Tour circuit in the late 18th century, your arrival in a remote mountain village will still generate some surprised interest, plus a degree of incomprehension – for such places have little to offer in the way of organised hospitality or things to see. The three southern regions of Apulia, Basilicata and Calabria do however have a great deal of scenic and cultural variety.

Apulia (Puglia) is mostly flat and fertile apart from the spectacular scenery of the Gargano peninsula (the spur of Italy's boot), where dramatic limestone cliffs plunge into a turquoise sea and the interior is thickly wooded. Just inland is the Tavoliere (tableland), a vast often parched plain of wheatfields, surrounded by hills. Tobacco, olives and vines are the chief crops of the Murge plateau between the spur and the heel (which is properly called the Salentine peninsula). There are no rivers and the rainfall is low; almost all the water comes from Basilicata. Although it requires a fertile imagination to envisage the famous Roman battles on the plains of Apulia, much remains as testimony to a history of continuous invasion and occupation. Some of the coastal towns consist of flat-topped whitewashed houses with external staircases which are of almost Biblical appearance, and certainly more typical of Greece or Northern Africa than Italy. The Normans left their mark with a series of remarkable cathedrals (*see page 407*), whose design often shows features of Byzantine or Arab origin (there were Sicilian Moslems living in Apulia at the time, and there were endless Saracen invasions). Frederick II (1197-1250), the most enlightened ruler of his age, left a number of splendid castles as did his Angevin successors who ruled Southern Italy from Naples until the 16th century. Peculiar to Apulia are the curious *trulli* houses (*see page 414*) of the Itrian valley between Alberobello and Martina Franca. Baroque architecture is one of the surprises of the Salentine peninsula.

Neighbouring Basilicata (ancient Lucania) is over 90% mountain, barren, poor and earthquake-prone (the most recent tremor in July 1986 caused a landslide which killed 8 people). The earthquakes of 1851 and 1930 destroyed much of interest in the area around Melfi, first capital of the Normans. Towns are remote and difficult of access and the only areas of real natural beauty are the Basento valley and the narrow strip of western coast around Maratea – spectacularly beautiful but geographically more akin to Calabria than Basilicata. Monte Vulture, an extinct volcano near Melfi, dominates Basilicata, and the lakes nearby are popular with local tourists. The southern coast, the instep of Italy, once boasted two of the great cities of Magna Graecia, Metapontum and Siris; but apart from the coast, Basilicata was almost by-passed by history. Today, many would agree with Augustus Hare who wrote "Only those who have plenty of time to spare and courage to face something more than discomfort will find interest in the classic sites and the remains of old Greek cities along the coast". Until recently malarial swamps, the beaches of this coast are sandy and backed by pinewoods but with no appealing resorts.

Calabria, with around 600 kilometres of coastline, is overall 92% mountain, with peaks reaching over 2,000 metres. In spring you could ski in the mountains of the Sila and swim in the Ionian sea a few hours later. At its narrowest point – 30km – there are spectacular views of both the Tyrrhenian and Ionian seas. Here in 71BC the Roman consul Crassus erected a barrier to stop Spartacus' army marching up the peninsula; it worked. Calabria has traditionally been seen as a pathway to the richer and more strategic Sicily; Alaric, king of the Visigoths, was on his way to attack Sicily when he died at Cosenza.

The west coast is unattractively built-up between Praia a Mare and Amantea with a string of unexceptional resorts and virtually no counter-attractions, save the odd almost deserted hill-village behind. From the Gulf of Sant' Eufemia to Reggio the scenery becomes more dramatic and the resorts and beaches more appealing: the Tropea peninsula is easily the most attractive area to stay on the Calabrian coast. The beautiful mountain hinterland is probably best appreciated from the motorway and a few excursion drives; roads, paths and villages are sparse. The east coast is for the most part barren, windswept and desolate. Little remains of the great cities of Magna Graecia – except in the wonderful national museum at Reggio. In the centre (the ball of the foot) is the Sila, a vast mountain plateau with man-made lakes, alpine meadows and forests. In the so-called Greek – actually Albanian – towns on the edge of the Sila (which date not from the days of Magna Graecia, but a medieval migration) language and customs are still based on Greek. A feature of the Calabrian coastline is the occasional Aragonese castle, symbol of direct Spanish rule from 1559 to 1713 which brought religious bigotry and heavy taxation.

Traditionally, Italy stops at Naples (if not Rome) for most tourists. The earliest travellers found the deep south far from idyllic. First there was the danger of brigands, or as Crauford Tait Ramage put it (mildly) in the 1820s "it is harassing to be constantly in the expectation of being either robbed or murdered". This problem was largely eliminated by a military campaign in the 1860s. A hundred years later kidnapping became common, but like the Sicilian Mafia, the Calabrian N'drangheta ("honoured society") has no grudge against tourists. Then there was the accommodation, or rather lack of it, which Hare summed up thus "civilisation may be said to cease altogether at Salerno". In those days the inns were so filthy that travellers relied on personal contacts when possible ("A stay at Melfi is only endurable if the visitor is provided with an order from Prince Doria to stay at the castle"). Nowadays, hotels are reasonably comfortable, at least for a touring holiday, and cheaper than those in the north.

One of the compensations for the early travellers, which is more or less lost today, was the study of a civilisation with its roots in pre-classical times. Ramage, one of the more eccentric visitors to the south, sub-titled his account of his rambles in Southern Italy in 1828 *Wanderings in Search of its Ancient Remains and Modern Superstitions*. He noted belief in miracles, witchcraft and the evil eye. Over a

Visiting the South

There are daily scheduled flights from London to Bari (with a stop at Rome), but cheap tickets are not available. You might as well fly on a PEX or APEX ticket to Naples and drive from there. Charter flights are available from London to Naples, Bari, Brindisi and Lamezia Terme.

Unless you opt for a stay-put holiday with the odd excursion, you will need a car. Rail networks and bus communications are poor and it is not really practicable to rely on public transport unless you have unlimited time and patience. If you drive from the UK, it's worth buying petrol coupons in advance (*see General Information chapter*).

Apulia is well-suited to a touring holiday (a week or so); there's scenic variety, architectural and historic interest and enough attractive places to stay. The Gargano peninsula, Polignano and Alberobello all make good bases for a couple of nights or so. If you fly to Naples you could complete a round trip by returning on the motorway via Potenza, or you could extend a holiday to include Calabria (allow at least two weeks).

Calabria is not as suitable for a touring holiday. The scenery is spectacular – so spectacular that driving anywhere takes ages unless you're on the A3 motorway which runs the length of Calabria to Reggio. The Salerno to Reggio stretch is toll-free so there's no advantage in using the crowded coast roads or tortuous inland roads unless you have to. Places to stay in Calabria are concentrated along the west coast, much of which is separated from the motorway by mountains (and from the sea by the railway line). Unless you are happy to stay put (and there are few appealing resorts north of Amantea), you should choose a resort close to the motorway. Tropea, a charming old town away from the railway, is one of the best resorts. The Tropea peninsula also has the most dramatic coastline, the best beaches and the most scenic hinterland. Resorts on the east coast of Calabria and the ball of the foot are few and far between and beaches are bleak. An attractive alternative is Maratea, on the west coast of Basilicata hundred years later Carlo Levi, a political prisoner interned in Basilicata, found religion there was still almost pagan; the peasants believed in the double nature of everything and saw the Madonna as a fierce goddess who had to be appeased. Levi's own housekeeper was considered a witch. Even now parts of the South are still backward; marriages are often arranged, the traditional vendettas are inherited and revered images may be punished if they do not grant favours. But for the average tourist, glimpses of the past will be restricted to the occasional peasant woman carrying things on her head and outmoded agricultural practices. Local costume is still worn, but only for festivals. You may hear unintelligible dialects in some of the remoter areas, or notice the practice of the Greek orthodox religion in the east of Calabria. But the overall impression is of an area which has been dragged abruptly into the 20th century about fifty years late.

Italy's Mezzogiorno has almost nothing in common with its Gallic namesake, the Midi, the rich south of France. It is poor, almost traditionally neglected and a thorn in the flesh of a modern European country. It is, in short, a problem. The poverty of the south is not merely financial; the Italians describe it more aptly as

---

north of Calabria, with good, though expensive, hotels.

The south (beyond the Neapolitan Riviera) is still not really geared to international tourism. There are few organised excursions, except from package tour hotels. Most hotels were purpose-built during the last 20 years and designed for family holidays. There is an increasing number of holiday villages with optional self-catering. In resort hotels you may be expected to stay for at least a week on half-board terms in July or August. Camping is concentrated mostly on the northern part of the Gargano peninsula and on the west coast of Calabria.

A few tour operators offer package holidays by air to the far south of Italy. Self-catering holidays outnumber hotel holidays. The most popular areas for tour operators are the west coast of Calabria or, in Apulia, on the Gargano peninsula or near Alberobello (both inland and on the coast). Art tours are sometimes offered: usually two-week tours of Apulia with Campania.

The tourist season does not begin until about May (some hotels are shut from November to March). In July and August resorts are packed with Italians and inland towns virtually deserted; one of the few attractions of a holiday at this time is the Itria Festival of opera, concerts and recitals at Martina Franca. May, June and September are the best months from the point of view of weather (not excessively hot) and ease of booking hotels. Prices are cheaper and half-board terms not usually obligatory.

It's worth bearing in mind that everything tends to happen much later in the south (with correspondingly later closing times for museums etc); for instance shops often don't open till 9.30 am, lunch is around 1.30pm and dinner is served around 9.30pm (earlier in hotels); it is usually acceptable to arrive in a restaurant as late as midnight. However, the siesta is taken seriously, especially in summer; even bars may be shut for the afternoon until about 5pm and museums and churches are invariably closed. The only sensible thing to do is to take a siesta too.

miseria and until recently it was chronic. Much of this misery was due to the immense size of the great farms (*latifondi*) which were worked in gangs under an overseer, and to the absenteeism of the landlords. Poor living conditions and malnutrition led to mass emigration, leaving female-dominated societies. Malaria was prevalent well into the 20th century and Carlo Levi diagnosed trachoma, black fever and dysentery in Basilicata in the 1930s.

Until recently the population was virtually uneducated; Crauford Tait Ramage noted "the government seems well satisfied that ignorance should be the predominating feature of the people...Everything is done to repress their energies and to keep their minds in an obscure twilight". A hundred years later the situation was the same: "The people from Rome prefer us to stay like beasts" complains one of Levi's *contadini* (peasants) in *Christ stopped at Eboli*. Carlo Levi portrays the State, through the eyes of the downtrodden peasants, as just another foreign overlord who imposes taxes, demands unsuitable crops and denies the existence of malaria as mere fiction. Rome becomes an evil deity in their world of magic and miracles, witchcraft and superstition.

Since the formation in 1950 of the *Cassa per il Mezzogiorno*, a government fund for the development of the south, much has been done to bridge the gap and bring the most backward areas of Italy into the 20th century, breaking down the mentality of thousands of years of inertia and submission. The problem had been recognised by political writers at the time of the Unification, but it was an intellectual debate. Not until Carlo Levi published *Cristo* in 1945 was the South forced into the consciousness of the ordinary Italian, who had by now had enough of Fascism. Charity and paternalism would not do; the problem had to be attacked at the roots.

Agricultural reform included the expropriation of many large estates and their division into smallholdings, mechanisation, irrigation, reforestation and the draining of marshes. Piecemeal industrialisation produced vast steel and petrochemical plants, nicknamed "the cathedrals in the desert", and large northern companies were given tax incentives to move south. Controlled emigration – 60,000 people left Calabria between 1950 and 1970, double that figure left Basilicata in 1970 alone – meant more employment. Living conditions improved dramatically – running water became available to most households, hospitals and schools were built and the government evacuated the notorious *sassi* (inhabited caves) at Matera (*see page 414*). Eighteen thousand miles of road were laid and the Autostrada del Sole was extended to Reggio, and, in 1970, linked to Potenza, capital of remote Basilicata. There were concerted efforts to encourage tourism, mostly concentrated along the west coast of Calabria. In short, communications were improved at every level.

But, a quarter of a century later, there are still problems. The EEC is a threat to agriculture with Greece, Spain and Portugal providing hot competition on European markets. The '70s' oil slump put paid to the success of some of the more ambitious industrial projects, which have generated previously unknown pollution. The exodus to the north has been reduced to a trickle as people return, disillusioned and unemployed. And the vocational training and universities have resulted in a well-qualified population with not enough white-collar jobs (the south has double the national rate of unemployment). The resources of the *Cassa* have slipped into northern pockets or been used by unscrupulous politicians for their own power; useless construction projects have created employment – and won votes. Finally, and fundamentally, the patient, fatalistic southerner is still reliant on forces outside and above for progress.

What then is the attraction of the South for the visitor today? For those familiar with Tuscany, the major cities and the Neapolitan Riviera it is refreshing to find untamed, unvisited mountain areas and abandoned beaches. Calabria has the wildest scenery, and cheaper, less crowded beach resorts than elsewhere on the coast. Apulia, undoubtedly, has the most variety and interest from the artistic point of view and is well-suited to a touring holiday, with an optional extension to parts of Basilicata. It also has the glorious coastal scenery of the Gargano peninsula. Sooner or later, every true Italophile should visit the South, if only to put the rest in perspective.

Places to visit

ALBEROBELLO

The *zona monumentale* of Alberobello is composed almost entirely of over 1,000 immaculately whitewashed *trulli (see page 414)*. Alberobello is picturesque, verging on cute, with pony traps and rustic-style wooden signs. *Trullo* shops sell souvenirs and local wines and almond milk (tastings offered). You can stay in a *trullo* hotel (or pray in a *trullo* church) and there's an interesting little museum devoted to these strange dwellings, and the lifestyle of the people who lived in them (all documentation in Italian).

Excursions from Alberobello
☞ **Castellana Grotte** (*15km north-west*)
Don't let the dullness of the town itself, or the very trippery area around the entrance to the caves 2km away, put you off visiting these spectacular grottoes. They're remarkable chiefly for the huge size of the first cavern (discovered 1938) and the splendour of the last, the *caverna bianca*, which with its stalactites like icicles of cream has recently been voted by the cave cognoscenti the most beautiful in the world. There are 1- and 2-hour tours but the short tour does not include the last cave, undoubtedly the highlight of a visit. Take sensible shoes; it's a 3km walk.
(See also Martina Franca)

ALTAMURA
(See opposite page)

BARI
A busy port with broad, straight streets and a sweeping esplanade leading to a labyrinthine medieval town on the promontory. Once a Byzantine stronghold, Bari has always had strong trading links with the Eastern Mediterranean and the narrow alleys of the old town seem more Arab or Greek than Italian. Augustus Hare thought that old Bari had "all the characteristics of the meanest parts of Naples". Women while away the day sitting on chairs outside their houses, urchins dribble footballs down the echoing streets. In this context, the Norman cathedral comes as a surprise. "Fish-famous Barium" still lives up to Horace's epithet and there are a few bustling *trattorie* close to the old castle where you can sample the day's catch.

☛ **Archaeological Museum** Local finds include Hellenistic vases, Roman glass and jewellery and neolithic flints. Fascinating stuff, dowdily displayed. Closed Sunday.

☛ **Art Gallery** A well-arranged collection illustrating chronologically the history of Apulian art, from early icon-like paintings (including works by Greek and Cretan painters who came to the Adriatic after the fall of Constantinople in 1453) to the Renaissance influences of the early 1500s, and from the patronage of Venetian artists for prestige to the dominance of Neapolitan art. 19th- and 20th-century local-born artists are represented too.

☛ **Basilica of St Nicholas** *(See opposite page)*

BARLETTA
A busy and often traffic-clogged port with a handsome bleached castle (closed for restoration) and the Colossus, a bronze statue of a Byzantine emperor, more remarkable for its size (over 5m high) and age (over 1,500 years old) than aesthetic qualities. There are several quite interesting old churches, including the cathedral, which, grimy and defaced by graffiti, is rather a hotch-potch of styles.

BISCEGLIE
(See opposite page)

BITONTO
A small town with a beautiful cathedral, blackened with age and sprouting vegetation, charmingly situated in the walled corner of a little piazza.
(See opposite page)

BRINDISI
The ancient port of Brundisium was visited by Horace and Cicero, and Virgil died here in 57BC. Now the main ferry port for Greece, Brindisi lacks the charm of Bari although there are some interesting old churches. Once used as a naval base by the Romans and the Crusaders, it is now teeming with backpackers. A Roman column marks the end of the Appian Way.

ROMANESQUE CHURCHES OF APULIA

The Norman occupation of Apulia in the 11th century brought French influences to both architecture and sculpture, and there were strong links with Sicily (another Norman conquest). But there were other influences from abroad: Bari was the main port of embarkation for the crusades, and tales of far-off lands may have reached the local sculptors who included lions and elephants in their decoration of churches. Vestiges of Byzantine influence too remained, both in the ground plan and in sculptural detail, the latter often inspired by the great bronze doors at Monte Sant' Angelo (*see separate entry*) which were actually brought from Constantinople. The result is a unique series of cathedrals and the adoption of the blanket term "Apulian Romanesque". The typical Apulian Romanesque church has a majestic façade, usually divided into three by pilasters, its central doorway with an elaborately carved portal, often with a rose window above; scenes from the Life of Christ are typical subject matter. The pattern is Norman, the interpretation local. The sides are decorated with blind arcading or a gallery, often with a frieze or a row of corbels supporting the eaves – a Norman feature often with Byzantine or even Saracenic inspiration (wavy abstract patterns). Inside, look for elaborately carved pulpits and bishops' thrones, often the most original products of the Apulian sculptor's chisel, with naturalistic detail often used symbolically.

Castel del Monte, with its fine 13th-century castle, makes an ideal base for a day's round trip. You would start at **Canosa** where the externally undistinguished San Sabino has the oldest bishop's throne in Apulia. It was carved for Bishop Ursone by the 11th-century sculptor Romualdo and has been compared to an Islamic chess piece; the animal carvings show traces of Arab influence. Also part of the cathedral is the Tomb of Bohemond, son of Robert Guiscard, who died in 1111. This simple mausoleum, the earliest Norman tomb in southern Italy, has magnificent bronze doors showing Mohammedan/Saracen inspiration in the finely wrought decoration. The cathedrals of **Barletta** and **Trani**, based on the model of San Nicola at Bari, are worth seeing; Trani's has a more attractive setting (*see separate entry*) and was recently restored and stripped of 19th-century decoration. The beautiful bronze doors are by Barisano of Trani (1175-9) who also made the doors of the cathedrals at Ravello and at Monreale in Sicily. Further down the coast is **Bisceglie**, with a cathedral dating from 1073 (much altered, with a lovely 13th-century façade) and the church of Santa Margherita (1197). At **Molfetta** the Duomo Vecchio (or San Corrado), begun in 1150, is one of the most unusual examples of the style with a Byzantine groundplan, blind arcading of Saracen inspiration, and the lion supports usually associated with the Lombard style which may well have derived from Apulia. The prototype for many so-called Apulian Romanesque cathedrals (including that of Bari itself) is the basilica of San Nicola at **Bari**, a fine pilgrimage church founded when the relics of saint Nicholas were brought back from Asia Minor in 1087 by local sailors. The figurative and decorative carving of the exterior combines Arabic, Byzantine and classical influences, but the masterpiece of Apulian sculpture is the magnificent episcopal throne inside the church. The cathedral at **Bitonto** seems strangely forgotten but is one of the most beautiful in Apulia, a late (1200) example of the Romanesque style. Its façade boasts a superb carved portal, the lofty interior a womens' gallery and a fine pulpit dating from 1229 with an intriguing relief panel, thought to show Frederick II with one of his wives and his two sons. From Bitonto you could make a detour to **Altamura** whose cathedral (constructed on the orders of Frederick II but much altered after an earthquake in 1316) has a superb carved rose window and perhaps the finest portal in Apulia, its sculptures illustrating biblical stories. Or you could return to Castel del Monte via the cathedral at **Ruvo**, also with richly ornamented portals.

CANOSA

A remote Apulian town with some scattered Roman remains and an interesting cathedral. *(See previous page)*

CASTEL DEL MONTE

Dominating the landscape for miles around, Frederick II's perfectly octagonal hunting lodge, stronghold and retreat has given its name to a scattering of houses (including two places to stay or eat) and to the local wine. The Emperor (considered by his contemporaries to be *"Stupor Mundi"*, the wonder of the world) may have designed the castle himself, possibly to represent the eight-sided crown of the Holy Roman Empire. You have to furnish the interior with your imagination (add Frederick himself, poring over his treatise on falconry); a sunset stroll when the castle is closed may be more rewarding.

Excursions from Castel del Monte

☞ **Andria** (*17km north*)
A town of narrow alleys on a plan of concentric circles, characterised by the tall belltowers of its churches. Two of Frederick II's wives (including Isabel Plantagenet, daughter of Henry III) are buried in the cathedral.

☞ **Romanesque churches of Apulia** *(See previous page)*

CATANZARO

Since 1971 the capital of Calabria, Catanzaro is a town whose "manifold charms" (Norman Douglas) have been swamped by expansion and modernisation. There are several churches of above average interest (the tiny church of the **Osservanza** contains a lovely sculpture by Antonello Gagini) and a small **archaeological museum** in the public gardens of the Villa Trieste. There are several adequate hotels. The Lido (*8km south*) with its palm-tree lined square, has improved since Norman Douglas described it as "an unappetising spot; a sordid agglomeration of houses... ankle-deep dust, swarms of flies..." but it is a rather bleak part of the Calabrian coast.

Excursions from Catanzaro

☞ **Taverna** (*25km north*)
The painter Mattia Preti, known as *"Il Cavaliere Calabrese"*, was born here in 1613 and there are examples of his work in the churches of San Domenico, Santa Barbara and San Nicola.
(See also Sila Massif)

COSENZA

On the edge of the Sila and at the confluence of the Crati and Busento rivers (where Alaric the Visigoth is said to have been buried), Cosenza is divided into two parts: the dull new town spreading over the plain and, on the far side of the river, the old town, sprawling down the slopes below a ruined castle. The narrow, steep streets of the old town are picturesque and there is a beautiful cathedral, consecrated in 1222 in the presence of Frederick II (the extraordinary Byzantine cross he donated can be seen on application to the Marriage Office). There are no hotels in the old town, but there is adequate accommodation in the newer part.

CROTONE

Ancient Croton, famed for its philosophers and Olympic athletes, is now an industrial eyesore. Augustus Hare wrote "it is impossible to imagine a place of more God-forsaken aspect than Cotrone" (sic) and went on to describe its two inns as "very miserable" and "quite wretched"; 100 years later it still isn't a good place to stay.

GALLIPOLI

Gallipoli consists of an old town on a promontory, dominated by a castle, and a newer town with modern resort hotels. None of it really lives up to its name (the Greek Kallipolis, beautiful city) although the cathedral is worth visiting.

THE GARGANO PENINSULA

One of Italy's most ravishingly beautiful areas, discovered, but not wrecked, by tourism. The coastline is stupendous: craggy bleached limestone cliffs, pale sandy beaches, grottoes and rocky coves with crystal clear turquoise waters. The perfect contrast to this dazzling scenery (and indeed to the heat) is the thickly wooded interior, the primeval *Foresta Umbra* where the light barely penetrates the trees. In addition to natural beauty, the Gargano has some attractive old towns. **Péschici**, perched high above the sea, has a certain charm (the rather dull hotels are concentrated below, at sea level, but there are rooms for rent in the town). The picturesque old quarter of **Vieste** with its whitewashed houses, stepped alleys and balconies brimming with flowers and festooned with washing is totally unspoilt (although the same cannot be said of the coastline either side of the main part of the town with its endless holiday villages and campsites, used mainly by German tourists). Inland are two places of pilgrimage: the dreary town of **San Giovanni Rotondo**, home of the remarkable Padre Pio (d1969) who claimed to have received the stigmata, and – more appealing – the village of **Monte Sant' Angelo**, dramatically perched on a ridge crowned by a massive ruined castle.

☛ **Sanctuary of St Michael**   An ancient and much-revered church in a grotto supposedly consecrated by the Archangel himself, who appeared to Norman knights returning from the Holy Land in the 11th century. If you pass the first test – people wearing shorts are turned away – you descend some 86 steps to the vast natural cave which contains little except an indifferent statue of St Michael. Its doors, however, are remarkable: panels of bronze bas-reliefs, the figures outlined in silver, believed to have been cast in Constantinople.

Monte Sant' Angelo is approached on twisting roads through rugged terrain from the attractive little resort of **Mattinata** or from **Manfredónia**, a sprawling town which is long on history but short on charm.

Excursions from the Gargano Peninsula

☞ Churches

Overlooking the vast, parched Tavoliere Plain is the lovely little
church of **San Leonardo di Siponto** (locked except on Sundays) with
an exquisite carved doorway combining northern (Lombard, Pisan)
and eastern (Byzantine and Saracen) influences. **Santa Maria di
Siponto** (Sipontum was a Roman town which no longer exists) is
more difficult to find, a strange square church barely glimpsed from
the road. From here you could drive to Lucera and Troia (see below),
by-passing Foggia, which, practically destroyed by an earthquake in
1731, is laid out in grandiose 19th-century style and has little charm.

☞ Grottoes

There is no better way to explore the coast of the Gargano than by
boat, and most hotels can organise this for you. The loveliest stretch
is south of **Pugnochiuso** but there are also grottoes near **Péschici**
(organised excursions of the whole coast leave from the harbour).
Some of the grottoes are spectacular natural formations (with
fanciful names), others merely pretty, with translucent blue-green
waters. If you hire a boat and start early you could even bag yourself
a private beach (the smaller the beach the greater your territorial
rights).

☞ Lucera and Troia

Lucera is a modern industrial town with an old walled centre whose
narrow balconied streets of decrepit, even derelict, houses, have a
certain charm. Crumbling pastel-painted houses surround a
particularly lively and picturesque market square. There are some
Roman remains, a small museum and a cathedral built by Charles II
of Anjou in 1300, but little to detain the visitor for long. Above the
town brood the remains of the huge fortress built by Frederick II,
once defended, according to some historians, by Saracen raiders
recruited from Sicily by the Emperor who allowed them to practice
their religion freely. **Troia**, spread on the summit of a long, low hill,
consists essentially of one long, cobbled main street with flower-
bedecked balconies. Its remarkable cathedral is a successful fusion of
different styles: Pisan in architectural origin, it has Lombard
sculptures on the façade and an intricately fretted rose window of
Saracen inspiration. Its bronze doors, dating from the early 12th
century, are the work of Oderisius of Benevento. Inside, an eagle
lectern is incorporated into a finely-carved raised pulpit (*ambo*).

☞ Trémiti Islands *:20km north)*

In summer steamers to the Trémiti islands leave daily from
Mandredonia, Vieste and Péschici. The trip from Péschici takes
nearly 2 hours. There's also a daily hydrofoil service from Rodi
Gargánico which takes 45 minutes.

These islands are also called the *Isole Diomedes*, after the legend
that they were created by Diomedes when he flung boulders into the
sea to mark the limits of his new kingdom on the Gargano
peninsula. They have traditionally been a place of exile; Caesar

Augustus banished his granddaughter to San Domino for her promiscuity, Charlemagne's father-in-law, accused of conspiracy, was also exiled there. The islands were used as a penal colony from the late 18th century until 1860 and the convent of San Nicola was a prison from 1926 to 1945.

San Domino, the largest island (about 4 sq km), is also the most beautiful with a marvellous coastline of steep cliffs and limestone grottoes and the only sandy beach of the archipelago (Cala delle Arene). There are three hotels and a campsite (most in pine woods).

San Nicola, rugged and covered in *macchia* (scrub), has a rather desolate appearance, but the town itself is of some historic interest. The traditional fishermens' houses are characteristic. The abbey church of **Santa Maria a Mare**, founded by the Benedictines in 1045 but later much altered, has an important Renaissance doorway and interesting interior.

Caprara is uninhabited; so is **Pianosa**, only accessible by private boat.

GERACE

A sleepy isolated hill town with an impressive but precarious setting on crumbly, brownish cliffs with splendid views. A steep climb up narrow streets leads to a cobbled piazza dominated by the cathedral, the largest in Calabria. Above it is the imposing Norman castle: Edward Lear, who visited Gerace in 1817, wrote "Each rock, shrine and building at Gerace seems arranged and coloured on purpose for artists, and the union of lines formed by nature and art is perfectly delicious."

☛ **Cathedral**   A lovely Norman cathedral founded by Robert Guiscard in 1045 and later enlarged and restored by Frederick II in 1222, only to be severely damaged in the earthquake of 1783. The main features of the pale, bare interior are the antique columns (probably from the temple at nearby Locri) and beautiful wall tombs.

☛ **Other churches**   San Francesco, recently restored, is a Romanesque church with a fine portal showing Saracenic influence; inside is a tomb in late Pisan style and a high altar with remarkable marble inlay. The church of San Giovanello is Byzantine-Norman.

GROTTAGLIE

A remote Apulian town famous (locally) for its ceramics. The workshops are concentrated in a small quarter in the shadow of the old castle, their flat roofs often used for an array of terracotta pots. Designs are mostly fairly simple. The **Chiesa Matrice** has a fine Apulian Romanesque portal.

LECCE

In a land of stout Norman castles and restrained Romanesque churches, the city of Lecce comes as a glorious surprise. The flamboyant decorative style known as "Lecce Baroque" came into being in the mid-17th century and flourished (literally) for about sixty years. Aided by the softness of the local limestone, the stonemasons let their chisels run wild. Balconies are held up by

Lecce, Baroque window

grinning caryatids, classical columns are festooned with foliage, window frames laden with swags of fruit, while doorways drip with trophies and crests. The centre of the city is compact and can be explored easily on foot; lose yourself in the streets around Piazza Sant' Oronzo and you will see not only the more famous churches and palaces, but many others, equally delightful. The main sights are floodlit at night and it's worth staying overnight to wander round in the evening, and maybe to see the church of **Santi Nicola e Cataldo** (Norman church with a Baroque façade) and the **Provincial Museum**, which are (like the majority of hotels) close to the old city walls, and not within easy walking distance of the centre.

☛ **Piazza del Duomo** A showcase square, at its most theatrical when floodlit (concerts and ballets are performed here in July). It comprises the **cathedral** (which collapsed shortly after the architect, Zimbalo, finished it and had to be rebuilt) and the **seminary**, a much lovelier building by Zimbalo's pupil Giuseppe Cino, as well as the elegant **Bishop's Palace**.

☛ **Provincial Museum** A collection of finds relating to the Salentine peninsula (including a vast number of Greek vases), plus a picture gallery containing a few early Venetian triptychs and Byzantine Madonnas, but mostly works by local Baroque painters. Closed Saturday.

☛ **Santa Chiara** Recently restored, this church is "Lecce Baroque" at its most excessive. The **Governor's Palace**, once the Celestine convent and until recently home of the Provincial Museum, adjoins the church but offers little visual relief.

LOCRI

The excavations of ancient Locri, oldest of the Greek cities of
southern Italy, lie about 3km from the seaside town of the same
name. The ruins are extensive and include walls, the remains of
temples and a Graeco-Roman theatre. There are some finds housed
in the antiquarium, but the majority are in the National Museum at
Reggio.
(*See also Tropea*)

LUCERA

(*See excursions from Gargano Peninsula*)

MANDURIA

Necropoli and megalithic walls survive from the early Messapian
city (5th – 3rd centuries BC) and there is a fine cathedral (basically
Romanesque, with 16th- and 17th-century additions).

MARATEA

The most attractive resort on the Tyrrhenian coast south of
Campania, Maratea is in the short but spectacular strip of coast
which is part of Basilicata. The Marina di Maratea is a popular
stretch of coarse greyish sand. More appealing are the pretty little
port with good restaurants, the residential area (Maratea Inferiore)
with villas and hotels, and the medieval town (Maratea Superiore or
Castello), now abandoned but with superb views over the Gulf of
Policastro. The summit of Monte San Biagio, with its modern statue
of the Redeemer, is another splendid viewpoint – but the beauty of
the area is threatened by a vast new hotel complex.

From Maratea you could comfortably do a day trip to the Sila
Massif (*see separate entry*).

MARTINA FRANCA

One of the South's best-kept secrets (even Augustus Hare and HV
Morton, who covered the rest of Apulia in astonishing detail, appear
to have missed it). The charm of Martina Franca lies in its graceful
18th-century town houses, mostly white-stuccoed but with Baroque
doorways and windows, bulging wrought-iron balconies and
elegant bracket streetlamps. There's a Ducal Palace (possibly
designed by Bernini, with 18th-century frescoes inside), a handful of
Baroque churches and a panoramic view over the Itrian valley.
Wander up the steps and through the arches of the narrow streets at
siesta time and you will have the place virtually to yourself, like
some abandoned stage set. But Martina (called "Franca" because it
enjoyed immunity from tax under Philip of Anjou) is known locally
for its heady white wine and for the annual Festival of the Itrian
Valley (mostly opera, some concerts and recitals) which takes place
at the end of July.

There are two simple hotels with swimming pools in the newer
part of the town.
(*See also Trulli, next page*)

TRULLI

A *trullo* is a circular single-storey hut, built of drystone blocks with a conical roof of overlapping slates. The *trulli* are confined to a relatively small area of Apulia, the Valle d'Itria, between Locorotondo and Martina Franca. On this fertile and prosperous plain, among the vines, olives and almonds and little allotments divided by drystone walls, hundreds of *trulli* are dotted, or huddled in picturesque groups, some smartly plastered and whitewashed with neat gardens, others tumbledown and abandoned. The greatest concentration of *trulli* is at **Alberobello** (*see separate entry*).

The origins of these simple dwellings are unknown. Some sources maintain that the original *trulli* were built by Byzantine monks as early as the 8th century, others that they were primitive tombs and that the different symbols on the pinnacles, and painted on the roofs, have magic, Christian or pagan significance. Comparisons have been made with similar constructions in Syria and with the dome-shaped graves at Mycenae and with the *nuraghi* of Sardinia. However, some experts think the explanation is more simple – they were built from the early 16th century by shepherds and farmers with stones cleared from the fields. There is also a theory that the ancient building style was revived in the 17th century to thwart the tax collectors of the Kingdom of the Two Sicilies; houses could be dismantled quickly and later rebuilt. Recently, houses have been built in *trullo* form using modern construction methods.

MASSAFRA

The most impressive of several small towns (Laterza, Castellaneta – birthplace of Rudolph Valentino – and Gravina) built over a deep ravine with cave churches nearby. The new and old towns (called Borgo and Terra) are dramatically split by the great divide, and there are troglodyte dwellings and some 28 grotto churches and crypts with the remains of Byzantine frescoes; the most important and best-preserved include the churches of San Antonio Abate, La Candelora and the Madonna della Scala.

MATERA

An extraordinary and little-visited town in a spectacular position. A honeycomb of houses and caves known as *i sassi* (the rocks) is cut in tiers into the side of a steep ravine, and connected by a labyrinth of alleys and staircases. In his famous novel *Christ stopped at Eboli* Carlo Levi recounts how his sister visited Matera (in the 1930s) and found "children naked or clothed only in rags with wrinkled faces like old men, reduced to skeletons by hunger"; they were suffering from trachoma, malaria and dysentery as well as the mysterious "black fever". Conditions were appalling, most families living in one room with their animals. Most of the *sassi* were evacuated in 1974, though a few in the Sasso Barisano, below the cathedral, are still inhabited. Local boys now offer tours of the abandoned and crumbling houses, the churches and the Albanian quarter for a small fee (often "foreign coins" for their collections). Tours can also be arranged through the provincial tourist board.

In contrast to the picturesque squalor of the abandoned *sassi* there are some splendid and unusual churches, including the Angevin Gothic church of **San Francesco** (with part of a polyptych by the 15th-century Venetian artist, Bartolomeo Vivarini).

☛ **Cathedral**   In Apulian Romanesque style, the handsome golden stone cathedral has a fine rose window and portals. The interior has some interesting works of art and access to the small church of **Santa Maria di Costantinopoli**. There are good views of the Sasso Barisano district from the belvedere.

☛ **Rock churches** (*chiese rupestre*)   There are some 130 rock churches in and around Matera, dating from the 11th century but sometimes disguised by later façades. **Santa Maria di Idris** (in the Sasso Caveoso district) is carved out of Monte Errone and has typical wall paintings. **San Pietro Barisano** (in the Sasso Barisano) is partly carved out of the rock, has a 17th-century appearance but dates back to the 12th century.

METAPONTO

One of the great city states of Magna Graecia, Metapontum was founded in the 7th or 8th century BC but later destroyed. Pythagoras is said to have died here. Finds from the city displayed in the **antiquarium** and the remains of a Doric temple called the **Tavole Palatine** are worth seeing – about 3km inland from the Lido, a small resort. There are also remains of another temple and a theatre.

MOLFETTA

A pretty harbour town with a lovely Romanesque cathedral (San Corrado or Duomo Vecchio – *see page 407)*. The picturesque jumble of domes and twin bell-towers are best seen from the side facing the sea. Behind the cathedral is a maze of old houses shored up with great wooden beams across the alleys. The Baroque cathedral (Santa Maria Assunta) and the church of San Bernardino are also worth visiting.

MONTE SANT' ANGELO

(*See Gargano peninsula*)

OSTUNI

Ostuni dominates a featureless plain, its jumbled pyramid of chalk-white houses with their flat roofs giving the town an Arab, almost biblical appearance. There are some fine Baroque buildings including the cathedral in the old town, but it's not worth a major detour.

ÓTRANTO

An attractive small port, still little known to tourists, with an exotic air provided by the square white houses and palm trees and the Aragonese castle. Most English people who have heard of it associate Ótranto vaguely with Horace Walpole; in fact he called his novel *The Castle of Ótranto* because he thought the name "sonorous" – he never went there. The very picturesque main street, charming and not yet spoilt by souvenir shops, opens out onto a promenade along the seafront, backed by immensely thick defensive walls. Here, every year, the citizens of Ótranto gather in a moving ceremony to mark the wholesale slaughter of their ancestors by the Turks in 1480. Some 800 survivors of the siege were offered mercy if they embraced the Moslem faith; this they refused and they were duly despatched, along with their executioner who was so impressed by their steadfastness that he announced an untimely conversion to the Christian faith.

☞ **Cathedral** Prettily situated on a triangular piazza, the cathedral, founded under the Normans, has a lovely Renaissance rose-window and a Baroque portal. Inside, a superb mosaic pavement depicts biblical and mythological scenes, including a representation of King Arthur.

☞ **San Pietro** A charming little Byzantine church, with a Greek-cross plan and faded frescoes.

Excursions from Ótranto

☞ **Grottoes** (*16km south*)
Within easy reach of Ótranto are the seductively named **Zinzulusa** grottoes (long queues in August). Not nearly as beautiful as those of Castellana (*see Alberobello*), they are meandering, and smell of damp. Their interest is chiefly zoological as they are home to a unique (but almost invisible) species of crustacea. From the mouth of the grotto "Antonio" offers boat trips to the "azure" and "dovecote" grottoes. There are others in the area, notably the **Romanelli** grottoes.

☞ **Santa Maria di Leuca** (*27km south*)
Having got this far south, few will resist the temptation to visit the Italian Land's End. It's an attractive drive from Ótranto; a wild and barren shoreline with spits of land jutting into the sea and ruined watchtowers (around Porto Badisco where Aeneas landed) gives way to a dramatic corniche running through small resorts riviera-like in their luxuriance. In high season traffic can be nose-to-tail, but at any time drivers would do well to watch out for Italian kamikazes rather than straining their eyes for the coast of Albania. Santa Maria di Leuca itself is a small natural harbour with a town straggling behind. The southernmost point is a rocky promontory with a lighthouse, souvenir stalls and piped music.

PIZZO

A small seaside resort with rocky bathing, convenient for the airport at Lamezia Terme, about 35km north. The town is dominated by the

Aragonese castle of 1486 where Murat, ex-king of Naples, was shot dead in 1815; it's now a youth hostel.
(*See also Tropea*)

POTENZA

The capital of Italy's poorest and remotest region, Basilicata, is a straggling eyesore, spilt over several hills above the Basento valley. There are some interesting churches, but all have been partly rebuilt after earthquake damage; the most recent was in 1980.

PRAIA A MARE

A small resort with simple accommodation. There are boat trips to the grottoes on the island of Dino, opposite the town. Behind Praia, the rugged little villages of Tortura and Aieta are worth visiting.

REGGIO DI CALABRIA

Already rebuilt after an earthquake in 1783, Reggio was virtually demolished (and some 5,000 inhabitants killed) by that of 1908 which also destroyed Messina. In 1943 Reggio suffered further damage, from bombs, and it is now almost entirely modern, with wide, straight streets and low, boxy buildings. The city has a pleasant airy feel and a mild climate which facilitates the growth of exotic plants (Reggio has the monopoly on the export of bergamot, used for perfume). Despite the reversals of both history and nature, remnants of the original Greek walls and a Roman bath survive near the elegant palm-lined Lungomare (seaside promenade). The chief reason for visiting Reggio, apart from access to Sicily, is the wonderful museum which brings to life the lost cities of Magna Graecia of which Reggio, then Rhegion or Rhegium, was one of the greatest. There are splendid views across the Straits of Messina to Mount Etna and inland to the Aspromonte mountains. There are hydrofoil and ferry services to Messina (15-50 minutes) and the Aeolian islands (*see Sicily chapter*). Reggio has adequate hotel accommodation.

☛ **National Museum** A superb collection of antiquities from the cities of Magna Graecia, notably Locri. Finds include vases, weapons, jewellery, a fine collection of coins and some important bronze and marble statues. The undisputed highlight of the museum is the pair of statues called the Riace bronzes, found off Riace on the Ionian coast in 1972 and first displayed, after restoration, in 1980. They are thought to be the work of Phidias and/or Polyclites, Greek sculptors of the 5th century BC. There are also sections devoted to prehistory and the Middle Ages. The picture collection includes two small paintings by Antonello da Messina and a work by Mattia Preti (1613-99), a Calabrian-born painter who achieved fame in Naples and Rome.

Excursions from Reggio
☞ **The Aspromonte Mountains** (*35km*)
The drive to the modest resort of Gambarie (1,300m) offers panoramic views and ascends through beech and pine forests. From Gambarie a chairlift and a stiff four-hour walk take you to the summit of Montalto (1,956m).

☞**Messina and Taormina**
(*See Sicily chapter*)

ROSSANO

A hill town on the edge of the Sila which was an important centre of
Byzantine culture between the 8th and 11th centuries. Relics include
a small church, **San Marco**, built in the 10th century. Rossano's
greatest treasure, kept in a small museum in the Archbishop's
Palace, is the **Purple Codex**, a precious illuminated gospel dating
from the 6th century.

RUVO DI PUGLIA

In addition to a fine Norman Apulian-Romanesque cathedral with
rich sculptural decoration, Ruvo boasts a famous collection of
ancient Greek terracotta vases in the Palazzo Jatta.

SCILLA

A fishing village with a small harbour, a good sandy beach and a
picturesque residential quarter, the Chianalea. The rock Scylla, the
dread crag of Homer's *Odyssey* ("Fell Scylla rises, in her fury roars,
At once six mouths expands, at once six men devours") dominates
the small harbour town, crowned by a castle (now a youth hostel).
There are fine views of Sicily across the narrowest point of the Straits
of Messina, where lurked Charybdis, the legendary whirlpool.

SERRA SAN BRUNO

A remote and severe-looking mountain village, with characteristic
iron-balconied houses and some grey provincial Baroque churches
with good woodcarvings inside. The famous (but much modernised)
old Carthusian monastery (only men may enter the precincts) is just
outside the town.
(*See also Tropea*)

THE SILA MASSIF

A vast plateau, over 1,000m above sea level, with mountains,
forests, pastureland and lakes, and chalet-style accommodation. The
northernmost part is known as the **Sila Greca** because of the Greek
Orthodox Albanian colonies there (an estimated 200,000 at the
beginning of this century). There are some interesting small towns
worth visiting for their churches, including **Acri**, **San Demetrio
Corone** and **Rossano**, once capital of Calabria (*see separate entry*).

The **Sila Grande**, the central part of the area, is dominated by the
highest peak, Monte Botte Donato (1,928m). To the south of it lies
the **Sila Piccola** where Lake Ampollino, fringed with pines against a
mountain backdrop, is the chief attraction. The hilltop village of
Santa Severina has some good examples of Byzantine and Norman
architecture and **Taverna** is of artistic interest (*see Catanzaro*).

Apart from the main road (via San Giovanni in Fiore) traversing
the plateau, roads are twisting and often steep. The chief resorts are
Lorica in a pretty wooded area on the shore of **Lake Arvo** in the Sila
Grande, and **Villaggio Mancuso** and **Villaggio Racisi** in the Sila

Piccola; all offer basic chalet-style accommodation. The whole area is too vast for a day trip but expeditions can be made from **Cosenza** (Sila Greca or Grande) and **Catanzaro** (Sila Piccola).

The appeal of the Sila is overrated from the British point of view; it doesn't offer the kind of holiday that you would come to Italy, and especially southern Italy, for. There is far more spectacular scenery in the Alps and Dolomites. Although it provides a nice contrast to the coast, cooler weather cannot be guaranteed especially in the more exposed areas, which are parched in summer.

STILO

An attractive village of narrow streets and higgledy-piggledy terracotta-tiled houses, built on the rocky slopes of Monte Consolino. The main reason for visiting Stilo is to see the tiny brick **Cattolica**, an early Christian church in Byzantine style (similar to churches in Armenia and Georgia). The cruciform interior contains the remains of Byzantine frescoes. There are several other churches worth seeing too.
(See also Tropea)

Stilo, Cattolica

TÁRANTO

A large industrial city with huge 19th-century buildings, wide
streets and spacious palm-lined squares, and an enormous port. The
old town, reached via a swing bridge, is dirty and dilapidated and
despite the fish market and Aragonese castle, not very picturesque.
On balance, Táranto is a place to by-pass on holiday, although for
archaeological interest the museum is second only to that of Naples.
☛ National Museum   A very fine collection of Greek sculptures, Roman
mosaics, Tarantine ceramics and some lovely and delicate gold jewellery,
with exquisitely wrought leaf decoration. The whole of the second floor is
shut indefinitely.

TRANI

The most appealing of the Adriatic ports in Apulia. A long avenue of
19th-century buildings leads past the old quarter where washing
flaps from balconies, to the harbour lined with a jumble of
pale-painted houses and filled with jolly boats. But the most striking
sight is the splendid cathedral, in a spacious square comprising the
Swabian castle and handsome palaces dating from the 15th century,
the whole sun-bleached ensemble suspended between a sky and a
sea that vie for blueness. The cathedral, approached by an unusual
double staircase, has a superbly carved portal and windows with
Saracenic and Moorish influences. Inside it's narrow and lofty with
two tiers and a beamed ceiling, very light but much restored. Below
is a crypt with a forest of pillars and a lower church adorned with
14th- and 15th-century frescoes whose colours are still quite strong.
You could happily spend a day pottering around Trani's old
churches, but there's nowhere appealing to stay.

TROIA

(See excursions from the Gargano peninsula

TROPEA

A pretty fishing port with a picturesque old town perched on a cliff.
There is a good beach of coarse sand, simple seaside accommodation
and a lively atmosphere (good shops and restaurants). There are
some fine old palaces in the narrow streets of the old town, and
several churches including a Norman cathedral. The peninsula of
Tropea has several other towns worth visiting (*see separate entries on
Pizzo, Vibo Valentia*), and the area makes a good base for visiting the
interior of Calabria. There are camping sites, hotels and villages
along the coast, notably at **Parghelia**, **Capo Vaticano** and **Gioia
Tauro**.

Excursions from the Tropea Peninsula
☞ **Mountain scenery, churches and ancient remains**
A round trip via Serra San Bruno, Stilo and Gerace (*see separate
entries*) would involve a fairly arduous drive of about 150 miles,
through some spectacular wild scenery and over mountain passes
with some superb views. Keen archaeologists could include the
ruins of ancient Greek cities at Locri (*see separate entry*) and Caulonia.

VALLE D'ITRIA
(See page 414 and Martina Franca)

VIBO VALENTIA

A seaside resort on the peninsula of Tropea, with some artistic interest. The vast Baroque cathedral (Collegiata) contains sculptures by the Gagini family. Several other churches were rebuilt after earthquakes in the 17th and 18th centuries and are worth seeing for their Baroque paintings and sculptures. There are some excavated remains of the ancient city of Hipponium (mostly temples and walls) and a good **archaeological museum**. Material from the site was used to build the medieval castle.
(See also Tropea)

Hotels

Alberobello   **£££**
DEI TRULLI   *Closed Nov to mid-March*
Via Cadore 32, 70001 Bari   *Tel: (080) 721130*

The delights of Alberobello itself could pall after a day or so, but this hotel, secluded in its own grounds, is an excellent base for visiting other parts of Apulia. It also offers you the opportunity to stay in your very own *trullo*; each has an entrance hall, one or two bedrooms (each with bath or shower) and a small sitting room. Conversions have been sensitive and uncontrived, the rooms simply whitewashed, with plain country furnishings. The trattoria-style restaurant and space-age *trullo* bar are in a separate building with a pleasant gravelled courtyard in front. The swimming-pool area has been slightly neglected, but all in all this is a most appealing place.

Facilities: *20 "trulli" (90 beds); restaurant; swimming pool; parking*   **Credit/charge cards accepted:** *Amex*

Castel del Monte   **£**
OSTELLO DI FEDERICO   *Closed Nov*
70031 Andria   *Tel: (0883) 83043*

In the shadow of Frederick II's famous castle, this modern low stone "hostelry" built into the slope of the hill caters mainly for passing trade and locals who come to the large restaurant or the pizzeria. The bedrooms, whitewashed and furnished with country antiques are, as far as the management is concerned, of secondary importance (breakfast comes a poor third in their order of priorities). But for anyone on a touring holiday of Apulia this is a charming base for a couple of nights.

Facilities: *7 bedrooms; restaurant (closed Mon and Aug except pizzeria); parking*   **Credit/charge cards accepted:** *none*

Castel del Monte
PARCO VECCHIA MASSERIA
70031 Andria

££
Closed Jan and Feb
Tel: (0883) 81529

An attractive alternative to the Ostello di Federico. Although not so strategically placed (down a rough drive about 1km from the castle), it does have the benefit of its own, rather scrubby, grounds and swimming pool, without the casual trade of the Ostello. Bedrooms, in two separate annexes, are spartan, but the barn-like restaurant is more countrified. Packet pasta and plain charcoal-grilled meats are the order of the day; well-prepared, but unexciting.

Facilities: *23 bedrooms; restaurant (closed Wed); swimming pool; tennis court; parking* **Credit/charge cards accepted:** *none*

Cetraro
GRAND HOTEL SAN MICHELE
87022 Cosenza

£££
Closed Nov
Tel: (0982) 91012

Mercifully secluded from the string of coastal resorts, the San Michele is a completely self-contained oasis of civilisation in a former monastery. It has been restored to its former elegance after a period of neglect. The lounge is large but with the atmosphere and furnishings of a private drawing-room. The restaurant, slightly institutional in atmosphere, serves excellent food with a local emphasis, and wine from the hotel's own estate. One of the main attractions is the pool, surrounded by luxuriant semi-tropical vegetation and romantically lit at night, on a raised terrace overlooking the sea. There is also a small pebbly private beach, reached by lift. If you tire of relaxing you could always take one of the excursions organised by the hotel (to unspecified 'Historical Centers', the Sila, and the Aeolian islands off Sicily).

Facilities: *73 bedrooms (AC); restaurant; lift; swimming pool; tennis court; golf course (5 hole); parking* **Credit/charge cards accepted:** *Amex, Diners, Visa*

Lecce
RISORGIMENTO
Via Imperatore Augusto 19, 73100 Lecce

££
Open all year
Tel: (0832) 42125

On the site of a 16th-century inn, this hotel is now housed in a fine early 19th-century palace in a central but fairly quiet street. The hotel's heyday was around 1900 when it was a famous meeting-place of politicians; it's still resolutely traditional, if rather shabby. The rather oppressive felt-walled bedrooms are relieved by positively Mediterranean bathrooms. Food in the fusty dining room is surprisingly good; service willing but unprofessional, at least in August. More conveniently situated, smaller and cheaper than its competitors.

Facilities: *57 bedrooms (AC); restaurant; lift* **Credit/charge cards accepted:** *Amex, Diners, Eurocard, Visa*

Maratea
SANTAVENERE
85040 Fiumicello di Santa Venere (Potenza)

££££££
Closed Oct to May
Tel: (0973) 876910

This is a very elegant and comfortable hotel, far and away the most civilised in Basilicata or, indeed, neighbouring Calabria. It is secluded in its own grounds, with a small private jetty and stony beach. There's a peaceful, light sitting room, more country house than hotel, with flowery loose-covered armchairs and 18th-century oil paintings. Bedrooms are furnished mainly with antiques and have terraces overlooking the sea or gardens. The only disappointment here is the food which is above average but very overpriced.

Facilities: *44 bedrooms (AC); restaurant; swimming pool; tennis court; parking*
Credit/charge cards accepted: *Amex, Diners, Visa*

Mattinata
ALBA DEL GARGANO
Corso Matino 102, 71030 Foggia

££
Open all year
Tel: (0884) 4771

On the edge of a lively but unspoilt little resort, this is a small family-run hotel well-placed for seeing the best of the Gargano. Traffic is restricted at night so any noise will be from itinerant ice-cream eaters and strolling Italians, many of whom will pop into the bar as one of their pitstops. In good weather you can drink out on the pavement terrace, dine in the courtyard and ask the owner to take you out in his motorboat to see the grottoes. But there are few comforts for off-season travellers; the public rooms lack atmosphere. Standard pine and stucco bedrooms are entirely adequate, and some have small balconies. The only drawback is that the beach (with a stretch reserved for hotel guests) is a short bus ride away; perhaps that's why both resort and beach are relatively unspoilt.

Facilities: *40 bedrooms; restaurant (closed Tues from Oct to May); parking*
Credit/charge cards accepted: *Visa*

Ótranto
ALBANIA
Via San Francesco di Paola 10, 73028 Lecce

£
Open all year
Tel: (0836) 81183

A small new hotel built in local style, spotless and Swiss-run. All freshness and light, the rooms are airy and uncluttered, furnished Habitat-style. The restaurant serves local specialities, particularly seafood. The hotel organises boat trips along the coast.

Facilities: *10 bedrooms; restaurant (closed Wed except July and Aug)* **Credit/charge cards accepted:** *Visa*

Polignano a Mare ££
GROTTA PALAZZESE *Open all year*
Via Narciso 59, 70044 Bari *Tel: (080) 740261*

An unimposing whitewashed building down a narrow side-street of similar
houses hides one of Italy's most unusual and spectacular hotels. Built into
the rock, with a sheer drop to the sea, the hotel has a splendid restaurant
overlooking the inside of the grotto (floodlit at night) after which it is named.
It would be a sin not to eat seafood here, a superb *antipasto di mare*, potato
gnocchi with a delicate lobster sauce, fish grilled over charcoal... The very
professional waiters will give advice. Accompanied by Donna Marzia (a
lovely blonde wine who improves with age) a candlelit evening here is
romanticissimo. Bedrooms are on the small side but the lounge and bar are
cool and comfortable, and furnished like a country villa. Hitherto one of the
South's best-kept secrets, but the nearest beach is 3km away.

Facilities: *14 bedrooms (AC); restaurant* **Credit/charge cards accepted:** *Amex,
Diners, Eurocard, Visa*

Scalea ££
DE ROSE *Open all year*
Lungomare Ajnella, 87029 Cosenza *Tel: (0985) 20273*

On the edge of a very popular resort, but in a relatively secluded position,
and with reasonably swift access to the all-important motorway which runs
the length of Calabria, the de Rose offers a kind of '70s sophistication but has
little atmosphere. Activities are organised for Italians rather than foreign
tourists, but watersports and excursions are available. Rooms are spacious
and coolly stylish. A salt-water swimming pool on a terrace overlooking a
beach of fine shingle is perhaps the main attraction. Above average for a
stretch of coast lacking in decent hotels.

Facilities: *66 bedrooms (AC); restaurant; lift; swimming pool; tennis court;
parking* **Credit/charge cards accepted:** *Amex, Diners*

Vieste del Gargano ££
SEGGIO *Closed Nov to Feb*
Via Veste 7, 71019 Foggia *Tel: (0884) 78123*

The recently converted 17th-century town hall (*'seggio'*) is at the heart of the
old town of Vieste, a picturesque warren of narrow whitewashed streets.
Inside it is now modern ski-chalet style and homely with few facilities, but
smashing sea views. It's a friendly, family-run establishment, one of very
few in the area not catering for mass tourism. You can park your car in the
tiny piazza – but how you manage to get it there is another matter. Good
value for a night or two's stopover on a touring holiday, off season.

Facilities: *22 bedrooms; restaurant* **Credit/charge cards accepted:** *Amex,
Diners, Eurocard*

SICILY

*❝For Sicily is by no means a beautiful island,
but a very ugly island with a few exquisitely
beautiful spots in it❞*
AUGUSTUS HARE

Taormina

Introduction

Sicily, as they say in all the books and all the brochures, is a land of paradox and contrasts; so striking and picturesque are they that the island lends itself irresistibly to descriptive hyperbole and sweeping summaries, making it sound like the Mediterranean island that is all things to all tourists. Scented citrus groves beneath a snow-capped, smouldering volcano; sandy crescent beaches in the shadow of palm trees and in the lee of a majestic Norman cathedral decorated with Byzantine mosaics; a cliff-top medieval town on the site of an ancient sanctuary, with views of Africa; city street markets more than coincidentally tinged with the flavour of an Arab souk; Greek temple columns supporting the fabric of a Baroque cathedral. Such is the magic of Sicily, say the guides, that everything is possible, even a Mediterranean island holiday with the cultural interest of visits to Rome, Athens and Ravenna. Gaze into a bubbling volcanic crater one day, bathe from volcanic rock beaches the next; take in a play in the most beautifully set of all ancient theatres in the evening, and the next day.... a valley of Greek temples perhaps, or the miraculously preserved mosaics of a Roman emperor's hunting villa, or a mint-condition 18th-century town of golden symmetry and reasonableness.

It all sounds too good to be true, and in many ways Sicily is incredibly, embarrassingly rich in interest. It can be disconcerting for those who like to be able to immerse themselves in a period and go to Greece for their antiquity, Ravenna for their mosaics, and Rome for their Baroque façades, to find everything thrown together in a glorious shambles and to be transported from one continent to another in a few paces, or merely at the turn of a head. But that is Sicily, microcosm island almost exactly half way between Gibraltar and Suez, at the centre of the sea that is called the centre of the world; island between east and west, Europe and Africa. It has undoubtedly been the victim of its position, but posterity is the beneficiary. There is nothing false about the claims made about the quality and diversity of the island's appeal to the sightseer; it could hardly be exaggerated.

What can be overstated is the suitability of Sicily to island holidaymakers who rank sightseeing lower on their list of priorities than unwinding, away from people, noise and traffic, whose excursions are from beach to restaurant and back, whose cultural involvement goes no further than a good book by day and a spot of local dancing by night. Although there are a couple of resorts that do cater for this kind of holiday, they do not fit very happily into their role, and there is no escaping the fact that for a quiet, convenient and comfortable beach holiday, Sicily is not the place to choose (although the Aeolian islands, also covered in this chapter, may be). It is the largest Mediterranean island, and its population of 5 million (one Italian in ten is a Sicilian) is larger and denser than most other Italian regions. The island's population has always been concentrated on the coast, and is becoming ever more so as development money is put into the industrialisation of coastal cities rather than agriculture. Not all round the coast, but along most of two of the three sides, the northern and eastern ones (or Tyrrhenian and Ionian). Unfortunately these are the mountainous coasts of greatest natural beauty. These days the legendary beauty of the coastal scenery around Palermo or between Catania and Taormina is not easy to enjoy without blinkers, and the disappointment tends to be all the more acute after reading the fulsome tributes of past travellers. These coasts are the main axes of communication from the tips of the island to Messina and the mainland, and as well as being heavily built up for long stretches they carry motorway and railway, the latter in many places restricting access to the sea. Good beaches along the coast are few, and the few that there are suffer from severe overcrowding and filth, especially the ones within easy range of Palermo, Catania, Messina and Syracuse, which accounts for most of the coast between Trápani and Syracuse, the long way round. The south coast is drier, flatter, emptier and sandier; it isn't at all crowded, except with coaches around Agrigento, and isn't spoilt, except by earthquakes around Castelvetrano. But good beaches are disappointingly few, and attractive beach resorts are even fewer.

Like Southern Italy as a whole, Sicily is poor; not as poor as it was, but still poor. Unlike most of Southern Italy, the poverty encountered on the coastal tourist trail is not rural but urban; so it does not consist of rough peasants goading lazy mules with thistles, but of purpose-built slums littering the coast near Palermo and shanty towns along the city's inland periphery. The discovery of oil and the building of large refineries around Syracuse and Catania brought prosperity to south-eastern Sicily, but needless to say this hasn't made the coast any more attractive to the visitor.

Once expectations of a remote island idyll have been banished, there can be no complaint about Sicily's fascination, uniquely varied among Mediterranean islands. A tour of its long coastline offers never (well, hardly ever) a dull moment. The landscape itself is monumentally dramatic around Mount Etna, standing two miles up in the Sicilian sky, keeping snow well into summer, and dominating much of the Ionian coast. Its foothills are made of ancient lava flows where the ground is so densely fruitful (mainly citrus groves and vineyards) as to be almost claustrophobic. New lava scars the greenery in bare dark tongues where it has flowed, and black rocks thrown down by eruptions stand along the coast. To the north, the Sicilian coast of the Strait of Messina and the long Tyrrhenian coast are backed by less high but still impressive mountains, framing long bays of celebrated beauty. The hills of the quiet south-eastern corner of the island, with their nut trees, rough-stone walls and honey-coloured towns, compose the most restful and charming of Sicilian landscapes.

Huge expanses of rolling hills of the interior are given over as they have been for at least two thousand years to the growing of wheat, a desert of fertility, to use Goethe's phrase. Vineyards and olive groves along the sandy south coast and in the west give variety and colour to the agricultural landscape. The fact that Sicily's fame has always been its prodigious fertility may seem puzzling, for the present state of the island (except around Etna) belies any such suggestion. It is not that standards have changed; the island has been the victim of consistently bad husbandry, the effects of which are now irreversible. The soil has been exhausted by centuries of over-cultivation of wheat, a tradition started by the Romans and intensified this century with Mussolini's short-sighted *"battaglia del grano"*. In the early Middle Ages Arab occupiers of the island encouraged irrigation; no later rulers continued the work and the gradual deforestation of the island, which once abounded in game, to a point where now less than 1% of it is wooded has contributed to the ruin of the soil and changed the climate. Catania's rainfall declined by over a third during the course of the 19th century. Now the soil is so poor that when it does rain, as it does torrentially in autumn and winter, the moisture floods straight down to the sea, overfilling wide river beds (*fiumari*) for a short period before these dry up again. Landslides are commonplace and the land yields less now than it did in Roman times.

Sicily's great source of fascination is the range and quality of monuments that illustrate the island's complicated history and testify to its great importance in the Mediterranean world. Sicily's strategic position at the centre of the Mediterranean and its natural wealth (the result of limestone and lava) made it a great temptation for every Mediterranean power. In the 8th century BC Greek expansionists established settlements on the east coast, many of which grew into prosperous cities and powerful political forces, Syracuse for many centuries being the rival of Athens and for 1,500 years the pre-eminent city in Sicily.

At the end of the first Punic War in 241BC Sicily became the first Roman province. Roman rule did little to change the ethnic character of the island but did considerable damage to the land itself by casting the island into a role of imperial granary. With the notable exception of the magnificent mosaics of the 4th-century Roman hunting villa at Casale, near Piazza Armerina, the Romans took away much more from Sicily than they contributed to it. One influence in the other direction, according to Livy, was that the statues and other works of art taken from Syracuse to Rome by Marcellus started the fashion for Greek art.

The split between East and West, between the area of Greek influence and the area unaffected by it, has been a very important division throughout Sicily's history. Long after the archaic period Eastern Sicily remained very Greek in character and religious practice. In the seventh century AD Syracuse was the capital of the Byzantine Empire for a short time. Arab control of the island (from the mid-9th to the mid-11th century) did not prevent its Christian inhabitants from continuing to live there in safety, and when Norman adventurers of the Hauteville family were entrusted by the Pope with the mission of conquering Sicily for Christendom and themselves, they found an island where Greeks and Arabs co-existed without losing the separateness of their ways of life.

The story of the Normans in Sicily is one of the most extraordinary and vividly illustrated episodes in medieval history. It is the story of a long century of enchantment when Norman mercenary adventurers were apparently charmed by their Eden-like surroundings to such an extent that they sank, or rather ascended, into a spirit of religious and racial tolerance which made possible a unique flowering of art where Byzantine, Islamic and western European traditions coexist in a strangely harmonious way. Whether or not the art is worth more than the sum of its parts, it is a fascinating phenomenon and the parts are exquisite. Sicily in the 12th century enjoyed peace at a time when peace was no more conspicuous a feature of European life than were racial harmony and cooperation in government, the arts and scholarship. Undoubtedly all this was the personal achievement of a succession of remarkably intelligent and energetic rulers, who surrounded themselves with Byzantine and Greek advisors, scholars and artists, and lived in a style more oriental than European. Their buildings remain, exact illustrations of the spirit of the time, eloquent enough to convince the most sceptical that Sicily's Golden Age is not just a romantic invention; one notable example is the chapel of the Royal Palace in Palermo, where the conventional Latin architecture is clothed with the brilliant raiment of Byzantine mosaics, and crowned by a purely Arab wooden honeycomb ceiling of marvellous intricacy.

The art is an art of palace chapels, exotic royal pleasure domes and great cathedrals more than it is popular art or an art which flourished in small rural churches. No doubt the racial harmony was also a feature of court life rather than everyday life. For a few generations, the Hautevilles' outstanding vigour and military prowess were not diminished by a life of lotus-eating languor in an easy-going society. When the leadership fell into less exceptional hands, the fragility of the cohesion of Norman Sicily soon became all too apparent.

After the Norman period Sicily was never to be an important kingdom again, and rarely saw its rulers. Frederick II of Hohenstaufen (nicknamed *Stupor Mundi* and one of the most fascinating characters of medieval history) established a new, absolute, Roman-style authority; his legacy to the island is no more than a few forbidding royal fortresses. With papal support a French prince, Charles of Anjou, took Southern Italy and Sicily from Frederick's heirs, but the French and their methods were so loathsome as to provoke even the normally apathetic Sicilians to revolt, no doubt encouraged by Charles's Spanish and Byzantine enemies. The dramatic story is told of how the insulting attentions of a soldier called Drouet towards a Sicilian woman on her way to vespers on Easter Monday 1282 sparked off a massacre throughout the city. French men, women, children and churchmen, and any stranger unable to get his tongue convincingly round the word *"ciciri"* were all slaughtered. This revolt against French rule became known as the Sicilian Vespers. In a few weeks the French were evicted from the island, and after a brief flirtation with ideas of communal independence the Sicilians offered their crown to Aragon, a claimant through marriage to a Hohenstaufen princess.

This was the beginning of a period, only briefly interrupted, of nearly 600 years of Spanish rule – a period of social stagnation and economic decline for which the absentee Spanish rulers are often blamed but which probably have more to do with the refusal of the Sicilian landowning aristocracy to contemplate any change to an inefficient, inequitable, fossilised feudalism and the absence of any other social or ruling force capable of forcing change upon the barons.

Problems included non-existent communications (no roads and no navigable river) and the lack of any effective control over the island's interior, combined with the attitudes of the aristocracy who considered agriculture far too ignoble a pursuit to merit their interest, and busied themselves with buying rank and showing it off. The extent of the snobbish Sicilians' obsession with protocol surprised even the stylish Spanish: the streets of Palermo were often blocked by head-on confrontations of carriages, neither of whose occupants was able to make way for the other.

The display impressed many visitors, just as the lavishness of the reconstruction of towns in the south-east after the 1693 earthquakes seems to indicate a prosperous island. Any travellers who ventured

Visiting Sicily

There are daily scheduled flights – involving a stop at Rome or Milan – from London to Palermo and Catania; cheap PEX fares are available. Charter flights go direct from London to Palermo and Catania. Italian State Railways have a Motorail service to Villa San Giovanni (from where ferries operate to Messina, 35mins); there is another car ferry (50mins) and a hydrofoil from Reggio di Calabria. Other ferries from the mainland operate from Genoa (23 hours), Livorno or Naples (10 hours) to Palermo.

Driving in Sicily presents no particular difficulties, except in and around Palermo where route finding is complicated. Main roads are good but often very slow at weekends and in summer, notably around Palermo and north of Catania. There are motorways along much of the northern and eastern coasts with a toll-free stretch across the island from Palermo to Catania (less than three hours by coach). The ancient sites of Segesta and Selinunte are close to a motorway linking Palermo to the west and south coasts. It is thus possible to see most of the island's major sights on day trips (albeit long and exhausting ones) from a single base. There are daily car ferries and hydrofoils to the Aeolian islands in high season from Milazzo and Messina (and to the less attractive Egadi islands, from Trapani).

Organised coach tours with guides play a more important part in Sicilian tourism than in that of any other region. Local travel agents run day trips from the major resorts (Cefalù and Taormina) to the major cities and sights, notably Palermo from Cefalù and Mount Etna from Taormina. Travelling by public transport is a slower but cheaper alternative; regional bus services are generally better than train. Bus services in the main cities are also efficient. Horse-drawn carriages can be hired in Palermo (pay by the hour and bargain with the driver first). Taxis are scarce and you may need to telephone for one.

Although Sicily has attracted travellers since the 18th century, there are no long-established resorts, with the exception of Taormina. The result is a scattering of hotels around the main centres of interest, much of it very simple and adding little to the delight of touring Sicily. Taormina, with some excellent and relatively peaceful hotels, has much in common with the traditional resorts of the Neapolitan Riviera, but across the island, with an armed guard, as Brydone did, discovered the reality: "deserted fields, barren wilderness, oppressed peasants, and lazy, lying, lecherous monks. The poor inhabitants appear to be more than half starved".

The long period of Spanish rule influenced the style of behaviour in fashionable society, but in terms of art and architecture the Spanish influence was not very important, except in the late Middle Ages: the so-called Catalan Gothic style of the 14th and 15th centuries can be seen in much of the exterior of Palermo cathedral. Architects and artists employed in the 17th and 18th centuries were Italians trained in Italy, and Sicilian Baroque is best understood as a provincial Italian development, in places heavy and uninteresting but at its best (church architecture in Syracuse, Ragusa and Módica, Serpotta's stucco decorations in Palermo chapels, and the marble inlay decoration of several Palermo churches) exuberant and highly individual.

Brief periods of Italian and Austrian rule followed the extinction of the Spanish Hapsburg line in 1700; in 1734 the Spanish Bourbons were welcomed back. In 1798 and 1806 Napoleon's Italian campaigns forced the Bourbon king Ferdinand and queen Maria

it has outgrown its hill top and its role as an exotic, exclusive hideaway. The cramped development of the coast nearby (Giardini-Naxos and Letojanni) is unappealing. Cefalù has become an important package destination but most of the hotels are some kilometres from the attractive old town itself. Sicilians have their own resorts which get extremely crowded in summer and have fewer hotels. The smartest and liveliest is Mondello, a good base for visiting Palermo, but not for a whole holiday. There are smaller and more relaxing resorts around the south-east coast (Fontane Bianche and Marina di Ragusa) and on the north-west tip (San Vito lo Capo).

Hotel standards are generally disappointing, except in Taormina. In towns and resorts they tend to be large, modern and lacking in charm. There is a token grand old hotel in several cities, but it is usually rather run-down.

Tour operators inevitably concentrate on Cefalù and Taormina, offering holidays by air for 7 or 14 nights, some as two-centre holidays. Palermo and Agrigento are the only places of any cultural interest offered, and only Taormina and Palermo are offered for winter breaks. Sicily is a special favourite with tour operators offering art and archaeology tours – cheaper operators as well as specialist art tour companies; they are usually between October and May, and last one week.

The great heat of the midsummer months and the coastal traffic make touring by car and tramping round the sights uncomfortable. The Aeolian islands are more suitable for holidays in July or August although naturally hotels should be booked well in advance. April and May are ideal months to visit Sicily: prices are lower than in high season, the countryside is at its most beautiful – still green and with a profusion of wild flowers – and there is still snow on Etna. There are local spring festivals in many villages; if you go at Easter, you may be lucky enough to see some spectacular Holy Week pageantry. However, although the weather may seem pleasantly warm, hotels often don't fill their swimming pools until June. In summer there are open-air performances and festivals of classical drama, music, ballet and opera. Winter may be wet but is usually mild; Palermo, like Taormina, was once a fashionable winter watering place and is well worth considering for a snatched off-season break.

Carolina reluctantly to take refuge in Palermo along with their entourage which included Sir William and Lady Hamilton and frequently Lord Nelson, who joined the ranks of absentee Sicilian landlords when he was made Duke of Bronte. The British invested heavily to keep Sicily out of French control, and their large military presence gave them effective control of the island. In 1812 the king was forced to agree to the independence of Sicily with a liberal British-style constitution. This proved quite unworkable and lapsed once the Napoleonic threat and the British army had disappeared. Sicily reverted to being a neglected and increasingly oppressed outpost of Bourbon Naples.

The existence of armed squads in rural Sicily and increasing evidence of popular unrest in the towns encouraged Garibaldi to use Sicily as the platform for his ambition to bring about the unification of Italy. He landed at Marsala in 1860 and against all military odds the opportunistic gamble paid off, his own charisma perhaps supplying the necessary ingredient for one of Sicily's few eruptions of briefly concerted revolt against the occupying power, characterised by barbaric cruelty. After a heroic victory over Neapolitan forces at Calatafimi, Garibaldi's Thousand took a day off to visit the famous Greek temple at Segesta before moving on Palermo, which fell to them after three days of street fighting.

Government from Piedmont, under Victor Emmanuel and Prime Minister Cavour, did nothing for Sicily. Its old role of providing grain for others, in this case the industrial north, was considered quite satisfactory. The most positive development was large-scale emigration around the turn of the century, changing attitudes and causing a labour shortage in Sicily. Mussolini contented himself with renaming a few towns and villages and boosting short-term grain yield in his campaign for national self-sufficiency. In contrast to Fascist policy elsewhere, very little was done here to improve conditions by public works programmes, and a report in 1940 found most of Sicily's roads unusable and half the peasants living in one-room huts with their animals. Mussolini did act with suitable vigour to improve security, and claimed to have cut the murder rate from ten a day to three a week. The achievement was reversed when the Allied forces used the connections of expatriate *mafiosi* to assist their invasion of the island in 1943, and rewarded them with positions of authority. The island fell after five weeks of fighting, fiercest in the towns around Etna. Palermo also suffered widespread bomb damage.

In 1946 Sicily was given a large measure of autonomy and a generous subsidy to make up for previous deprivation. An even greater economic boost came with the development of a petro-chemical industry in the '50s when oil and gas were found in eastern Sicily, much of which now seems busy and prosperous compared with southern Italy as a whole. In the west progress and industrialisation has been much slower, mainly because of the persistent influence of the Mafia, now at last publicly acknowledged to be Sicily's greatest problem.

Places to visit

AEOLIAN ISLANDS

A remarkably varied and beautiful archipelago of seven small
volcanic islands in the Tyrrhenean sea north of Sicily, named after
the God Aeolus who kept the winds imprisoned in his cave at
Strómboli and gave a bagful of adverse ones to the visiting
Odysseus. The area is indeed one of violent and unpredictable
winds. The islands, particularly Lípari and Panarea, are increasingly
fashionable among well-to-do Italians with and without yachts, but
are still very quiet by the standards of Mediterranean tourism. They
represent many people's ideal – the tranquillity, natural beauty and
climate of a small and remote Greek island, without either the
deprivations in terms of food and accommodation (standards are
higher than the Sicilian average), or the presence of large numbers
of shoestring travellers. Beaches mostly consist of volcanic sand –
black lava or white pumice.

Access is shortest and most frequent from Milazzo, but there are
also services (boat and hydrofoil) from Naples, Messina and
Palermo. From Milazzo it takes about 2 hours to Lípari by boat, ¾
hour by hydrofoil. Cars are allowed only on Salina and Lípari, and
are not really necessary (car, moped and bicycle hire can be arranged
on Lípari). There are frequent ferry and hydrofoil services between
the islands.

Lípari is the largest (about 4 miles by 3) and liveliest of the islands
and the main holiday destination. Lípari town is the resort, a
delightful little port with a walled acropolis where excavations have
been exceptionally fruitful, yielding evidence (layers of pottery) of
continuous occupation from the 4th millenium BC. There is a very
good archaeological museum beside the cathedral.

Away from the little town there are mountains to climb, hot
springs and bright white hillsides and beaches of pumice streaked
with black and red obsidian. This volcanic glass was much prized for
making sharp tools before the use of metals and Lípari obsidian has
been found in Spain and France.

The island of **Strómboli** is the world's most active volcano, which
erupts almost constantly, providing evening spectators with an
unforgettable firework display. Lava flows down only one side of
the mountain, and the active crater is several hundred feet below the
3,000-foot summit of the cone. It is a stiff 3-hour climb to the top
(guides are available, but the paths are marked). An alternative
viewpoint is the observatory on the northern tip of the island, about
half an hour's walk from the village (from which there are no views
of the eruptions), but perhaps the best and certainly the least
arduous way to admire the spectacle is an evening boat trip.
Strómboli has only a few hundred inhabitants, but the main village
(made up of two hamlets of San Bartolo and San Vincenzo) has
hotels and restaurants and there is a good black beach nearby. The
eastern slopes of the island volcano are green and fertile and

produce excellent wine.

Vulcano is another active volcanic island, the nearest to the Sicilian coast. The main community consists of the two ports (Porto di Levante and Porto Ponente) either side of the isthmus linking the island and Vulcanello, a cone which emerged in 183BC. Around the ports are hot pools used for therapeutic baths and the sea fizzes with sulphurous vapours. From the port it is a difficult and dangerously exposed walk of about an hour to the island's main crater (Fossa), an impressively desolate landscape with all the signs and smells of volcanic activity. Most of the hotels and restaurants are at the pleasure port (Porto Ponente).

Tiny **Panarea** has spectacular formations of volcanic rock on the island. There are several good hotels in San Pietro. **Salina** is a larger island (about 2 miles by 3), but busier with producing sweet white wine (malvasia) than tourism. **Filicudi** and **Alicudi** are small and remote islands at the western end of the archipelago, not much visited except by snorkellers and divers who love the clear waters and the lobsters.

AGRIGENTO

One of the leading Greek colonies in Sicily, the only one to rival the power, wealth and artistic achievement of Syracuse. Agrigento's **Valley of Temples** is the most important archaeological site on the island, and is so rich in well-preserved monuments that it is of as much interest to the casual temple-spotter as it is to the serious student of Greek civilisation, but it is easy to be disenchanted by the coach parks and cafeteria right at the heart of the sacred zone, and by the sweet-papers showered like confetti along the way up to the Temple of Concord. For a close inspection and full appreciation of the many ingredients of the ruins, a detailed guide is recommended. To explore the large area fully takes about a day. The temples stand on a wide shelf between the modern town and the sea. The area is seen at its best at the end of the day and from the belvedere on the edge of the Piazza Pirandello.

Akragas was founded by Greeks from Gela and Rhodes in 581 BC, and ruled from 571 to 556 by Phalaris, known to posterity (probably without justification) as the man who delighted in roasting those unlucky enough to displease him, in a huge bronze bull which was so designed that the howls of the victims bellowed forth convincingly like the raging of an angry bull. One of the first into the pot was the designer of the infernal device. This was said to be the only good deed Phalaris ever did. In later centuries Akragas was a much more civilised and very properous city of as many of 200,000 inhabitants. Its Golden Age began with the benevolent Theron, who married his daughter to Gelon of Syracuse; in alliance the two powers trounced the Carthaginians at Himera in 480, and prisoners were used in the building of the **Temple of Olympian Zeus**, one of the largest and most revolutionary of Greek temples, which was probably never finished. As well as being the victim of earthquakes, it was reduced more systematically to rubble by quarrying for suitable material for harbour walls at Porto Empédocle, the outlet for

Agrigento's sulphur and potash industries. As a result there isn't much left to admire except the vast ground plan and, as a further aid to appreciation of the scale of the construction, a reassembly of blocks into one of the giant figures (telamones) originally built into the walls between the columns, supporting the architrave.

Of the various other temples in a less complete state of ruination, the outstanding one is the Doric **Temple of Concord** (5th century BC), which is one of the most intact of all Greek temples, thanks to its having been converted into a Christian church. Beyond it, the **Temple of Juno** or **Hera Lacinia** (like the temple of Concord its name is a misnomer) stands at the top of a particularly vivid example of Sicilian soil erosion.

The briefest of visits should include the excellent **archaeological museum** which stands beside the road down from the town to the area of the temples. As well as many beautiful sculptures and vases, it contains a reconstruction of the Temple of Olympian Zeus with a standing telamone. Beside the museum is the interesting church of **San Nicola**, built in the 13th century but incorporating many classical features, and the so-called **Comitium**, a recently-excavated assembly area (2nd century BC) like a small, shallow theatre.

Modern Agrigento crowns the ridge to the north of the Valley of Temples, the site of the Greek Acropolis. The most interesting monument is the 13th-century Cistercian convent of **Santo Spirito**, whose inmates specialise in making (and selling) sweets. Its church contains a series of stuccoes by Serpotta (late 17th-century). The old town has a tatty medieval charm but is ringed by shoddy new buildings, some of which collapsed in a recent landslide. This also severely damaged the cathedral, a now dilapidated building of many architectural styles. Its archives include a handwritten letter from the devil.

The sorry state of modern Agrigento and its province makes a sad contrast with the celebrated wealth of Akragas, exceptional even by ancient Sicilian standards and founded on its olives, wine, corn, sulphur and the famous local breed of race horses. The playwright Luigi Pirandello grew up in the district in the late 19th century and left a vivid evocation of its depressed state and the misery of the time of mass emigration. A brief tour of the countryside north of Agrigento will give some flavour of rural Sicily, very different from the busy coastal strip. To an Italian the name Canicattì, a market town 20 miles north-east of Agrigento, means what we understand by Timbuctoo.

BAGHERIA
(See excursions from Palermo)

CALTAGIRONE
A large, hilly and attractive old town between Gela and Piazza Armerina. The main industry and tourist attraction is pottery: there are numerous displays of finished work (not cheap) in shops around the town and several factories open their doors obligingly to show tourists real potters at work. Ceramic tiles are a favourite feature of

the local architectural style and the church façades and staircases covered in these tiles, although not always models of decorative restraint, certainly make Caltagirone a colourful contrast to most Sicilian towns.

CASALE

Perhaps the greatest, and certainly the most easily enjoyable, treasure of Roman Sicily is the recently-excavated ruin (if the word can be applied to so wonderfully preserved a collection of works of art) of a lavishly decorated villa tucked away in a wooded hollow a few miles south-west of Piazza Armerina. It was constructed on a very large scale and in a manner that indicates great wealth and an even greater concern to show it off; on the basis of the internal evidence of the mosaics, the villa is generally thought to have been conceived at the end of the 3rd century as a hunting lodge for Maximian, Emperor from 286 to 305. It is often referred to as the Villa Imperiale, or less speculatively Filosofiana (after the name of the nearest Roman settlement). The buildings were occupied until the 12th century, when much was destroyed. At a later date the ruins were buried by a landslide and although their existence was known, a thorough campaign of excavation was not undertaken until 1950.

Little of the decorated walls and none of the vaulting survives but the layout of the villa, a complicated arrangement of four linked groups of buildings, is clearly defined. Much of the site is covered by translucent plastic domes erected to protect the mosaics and perhaps to convey some idea of the shape of the villa. They have the effect of making the place look rather like a garden centre.

What remains is a remarkable collection of mosaic pavements, covering the floors of nearly all the fifty-odd rooms, including the various bathroooms and lavatories, whose exceptional sumptuousness is held to be evidence of the villa's imperial status. The mosaics, probably the work of African artists, deal with a wide variety of mythological, descriptive and more simply decorative subjects (including a few non-figurative geometric designs). The quality is consistently very high, with the exception of one of the most well-known scenes, a row of ten girls in bikinis doing gym and playing ball. This remarkably contemporary-looking scene is a slightly later addition. The most fascinating mosaics are the two devoted to hunting. One ("The Small Hunt") depicts a series of countryside hunting scenes, perhaps set in the neighbourhood of the villa. "The Large Hunt" fills a 200-foot corridor and deals with the capture of wild animals in Africa and Asia (represented by allegorical figures at either end of the composition) and their transport back from these far corners of the Empire to Rome (for circus entertainment). No less beautiful is the series of mosaics dealing with the Labours of Hercules in the main dining room.

The mosaics at Casale are not universally admired. Lawrence Durrell, preferring to think of the villa as "just the home of the local Onassis", writes it off as "a rather ordinary aesthetic experience" produced by "interior decorators with a sense of grandiose banality, a sense of the expensively commonplace". Certainly there is something questionable about mosaic pavements that can be seen to their full advantage only from galleries running some height above them (as are now in place). However, another writer identifies an impressionistic rendering of three-dimensionality "surely designed to have its full impact when trodden upon". It is not possible to test this interesting theory.

CATÁNIA

Sicily's second city in size (nearly half a million inhabitants) and first in economic importance, Catánia is now the main international airport on the island and many visitors' point of arrival and departure. The city centre is almost entirely the creation of the eighteenth century, and the student of provincial Baroque architecture will find many things to look at and a few to admire. Contemporaries heralded Catánia as one of the most beautiful cities in Europe; the verdict of posterity has been more qualified enthusiasm, and, for the lay tourist, Catánia is not a very appealing place. Despite having good hotels and restaurants, it is too big and too difficult to negotiate by car to be a good touring base, its own sights are of secondary interest, and the port and seafront area is unpleasantly industrial. Nearby, the lower slopes of Mount Etna are outstandingly fertile, producing two crops of citrus fruit each year instead of the normal one; but a rather less attractive by-product of the volcano is the sulphur industry which makes some of the surroundings of Catania smelly and dirty. Catánia's most unattractive feature is the use throughout of dark grey lava stone, which makes the city look as dirty as dingiest Palermo, which it isn't.

The city was founded in 729BC by Greeks from Naxos and later became an important Roman port. Its history until the end of the seventeenth century almost rivals that of Messina as a woeful catalogue of pillage and earthquakes. Etna physically dominates the city and achieved the most thorough demolition job: in 1669 a violent rupture of the side of the mountain unleashed a torrent of lava that flowed over the 60-foot city walls and pushed the coastline a quarter of a mile out to sea. The job of reconstruction was not far advanced when the great earthquakes of 1693 swallowed up the city; only 2,000 of the 24,000 inhabitants survived. Apart from small excavated sites in the town centre (a Roman theatre and amphitheatre) there are very few pre-1693 buildings in Catánia – the main exception being the 13th-century Castello Ursino fortress where the earlier lava flow is visible, like a petrified moat; three Norman apses of the cathedral also survive.

The buildings around the main cathedral square are not particularly distinguished, but it is an impressive open space with an amusing central fountain (a grinning antique lava elephant supports an Egyptian obelisk) and a long perspective up the Via Etnea towards the volcano. The Via Crociferi which climbs parallel to the Via Etnea is lined by some of the finest of Catania's elaborate Baroque façades, including one house that spans the street.

☛ **Cathedral (Duomo)**   Some foundations (column bases) of the Norman cathedral are uncovered inside and there are some interesting tombs, including that of Vincenzo Bellini, the operatic composer (of Norma and La Sonnambula) who was born in Catania in 1801.

☛ **San Nicolò**   One of Catánia's great landmarks, a mammoth (or perhaps more appropriately white elephant) domed church whose eerie emptiness exaggerates the size of the largest church in Sicily, begun immediately after the earthquake and abandoned incomplete a century later. An interesting feature is the meridian line on the floor telling the date from the position of a shaft of light shining through the roof in the middle of the day. The neighbouring buildings, now occupied by schools, originally made up one of the largest, richest and most famous of Benedictine convents and are well worth exploring.

☛ **Museums**   The vaulted chambers of the Castello Ursino house a large and varied municipal museum with an archaeological collection, paintings and other local objects of antiquarian interest. Bellini's house, near the Greek theatre on the Piazza San Francesco, is where the composer was born.

☛ **The coast north of Catánia**   This is continuously built up, a string of suburban sea resorts (including Acitrezza and Acireale) which get extremely crowded at weekends. The shore consists of black lava rocks apparently strewn at random and providing some dramatic scenery and rocky bathing.

CEFALÙ

A very picturesque fishing port and small town, tightly packed into the space between an imposing rocky headland and the sea and dominated by the magnificent Norman cathedral – one of the most beautiful buildings in Sicily. Recently Cefalù has become one of the most popular package tour resorts on the island, mainly because of two attributes, either one of which is rare in Sicily and which in combination are almost unique. It is a lively and attractive place; and it has a fairly good beach (brochure photographers have ways of making it look bigger and better than it is). Hotel accommodation consists mainly of new blocks along the coast; this may be a great disappointment for those who discover that their base for a week is further than an evening stroll from the town, but it does mean that the tourist boom has not spoilt the look of old Cefalù.

The tight grid of old streets between the palmy cathedral square and the sea is free from traffic and very pleasant wandering territory in the early evening. The narrow backstreets have a more authentic atmosphere, with washing strung up and plenty of old locals in doorways and on balconies, watching the tourists watch them. Round the fishing harbour, where a few boats bear witness to the old superstition of painting eyes on the bows, buttressed houses drop down to the stony waterside. There are cafés here as well as on the cathedral square; do not expect to hear much Italian spoken.

Steps and a steep path make it possible to climb the rock for splendid views along the coast; there are some remains of a prehistoric settlement.

☛ **Cathedral**   Founded in 1131 by Roger II who landed gratefully at Cefalù after near-disaster at sea. The cathedral is built on a fairly conventional Latin plan, no doubt because control of the work was entrusted to Augustinian

Cefalù

monks whom Roger imported from the continent. The east end and
decoration were soon completed (in 1148) and in these lies the distinction of
the building. The great landmark is the twin-towered west end, not finished
until 1240, but built in a perfectly fitting, sobre and massive Romanesque
manner. Inside, the nave has interesting features – antique columns spanned
by slender pointed arches betraying Islamic influence, and some of the
original 13th-century vaulting beams bearing Saracenic decorative motifs –
but the visitor's attention is instantly engaged by the magnetic power and
simple beauty of the mosaic of Christ Pantocrator (blessing with one hand
and holding a Bible open at the words "I am the light of the world" in Latin
and Greek), which occupies the conch of the apse, masterfully exploiting the
shape of the vault. This work, in the purest Byzantine style, is the earliest of
its kind on the island and is the acknowledged masterpiece of Sicilian mosaic
art. The central figure of Christ is surrounded by mosaics of a hierarchy of
madonna, archangels and apostles. It is well worth walking round the
cathedral to admire the architecture of the east end.

☛ **Lavatoio** A very ancient public washplace, known in antiquity, used and
decorated in the Arab period, and still operational.

☛ **Museo Madralisca** A collection of local archaeological finds, lifted above
the mass of local museums by a beautiful portrait of a man, by Antonello da
Messina (late 15th-century).

439

ENNA

Provincial capital and historically the most important town of the
Sicilian interior, Enna is the target of most tourists' single incursion
from the coastal tour. Although not a very charming, beautiful or
characteristically Sicilian town, nor a particularly interesting one to
visit, Enna's setting is magnificent – on a high crest between two
spurs, dominating vast cereal-growing plains. Enna was the key
stronghold in central Sicily, and many generations of fortifiers have
added to its formidable natural defensive qualities. The impressive
castle that stands at the eastern end of the town is called the **Castello
Lombardo**, but is mostly the work of the Hohenstaufen Emperor
Frederick II in the 13th century, and of the Aragonese ruler of the
same name in the 14th. Several towers remain, and give enormous
views. The hill town seen on the other side of the motorway is
Calascibetta.

The **cathedral** was rebuilt in the 16th century in a strange mixture
of styles; the façade is Gothic in form but Baroque in idiom and the
nave is flanked by thick black Corinthian columns supporting Gothic
arches and standing on bases carved with grotesque figures and
monsters. The rich cathedral treasure is housed in the nearby **Alessi
museum**.

Excursions from Enna

☞ Hill towns and fortresses

Enna is a good base for exploring the little known interior of the
island. **Calascibetta** (*3km north*) has a more run-down charm than
Enna, and there are many other towns in the province with a similar
appeal. Guidebooks tend to show aerial photographs of these hill
towns, and rarely do they look so beautiful when seen from the
ground. Among the most interesting are **Nicosia** (*44km north-east*),
Troina (*77km north-east*), the highest town on the island, and
Centuripe (*67km east*), whose remarkable situation on a high saddle
earned it the misfortune of being the stronghold the Germans chose
to defend most tenaciously against the Allied attack in 1943. Near
Nicosia, the castle ruins above **Sperlinga** bear an inscription
commemorating its non-participation, alone on the island, in the
anti-French revolt known as the Sicilian Vespers (1282).

☞ Lake Pergusa (*12km south-east*)

The still, sulphurous waters of this little lake are surrounded by a
race track and there is a cluster of ugly modern hotel buildings
nearby. These, combined with the odorous emanations from the
water and its popularity with water skiers, take much of the pleasure
out of a visit to a place with an important place in legend. It was here
that Hades surfaced from the underworld to abduct Persephone,
daughter of the corn goddess Demeter, while the girl was idling by
the lake. Preoccupied by the search for her daughter, Demeter let
the earth go to ruin, until Zeus struck a compromise solution,
allowing Persephone to divide her time between Sicily for one half of
the year when the earth would bear fruit, and the underworld for

the other half when the earth would be barren.
(*See also Piazza Armerina; Casale*)

ERACLEA MINOA

Archaeological site between Sciacca and Agrigento in a beautiful
setting on low and unstable cliffs above one of Sicily's best and least
crowded beaches, backed by pines and eucalyptus. There is not
much development: just campers, a few villas and a shanty
supermarket among the trees.

Little is known about the origins of the town, although both parts
of its name have fed speculation. It is recorded as having been
settled by Greeks from Selinus in the 6th century BC and suffered
greatly from its borderline location between Selinus and Akragas
and between Greeks or Romans and Carthaginians. It was
abandoned suddenly and totally in the 1st century BC, perhaps as a
result of landslide. On the edge of the partly excavated ruins of the
town, much of which has slipped into the sea, is a theatre (4th
century BC) and remains of walls built in the same manner as the
ones at Gela. There is a small museum at the entrance to the site.

ÉRICE

Of all the sacred sites in Sicily, the shrine of love goddess
Astarte/Aphrodite/Venus on Mount Eryx is the one that acts most
powerfully on the imagination of the mythologically-minded tourist
(it has to, for there is almost nothing left from antiquity except some
splendid cyclopean walls). What remains is a small, grey, walled
and fortified medieval town, huddled on the top of an isolated,
windswept mountain over 2,000 feet above the coast near Trápani.
The views in all directions are enormous and it is said that on a clear
day scouts on the watchtower of Érice could count the ships leaving
Tunis. Obviously such a place was no less important strategically
than it was as a holy shrine and the mountain was much fought
over, particularly by the Romans and Carthaginians.

The magic of Érice resides in its remarkable aerial setting and
changing coastal views from the ascent road which snakes
laboriously up the mountainside from Trápani. Not only does Erice
seem to be suspended somewhere between earth, sea and air, it also
appears to have been by-passed by several centuries, having
declined in importance after the Middle Ages, since which time
there has been little new building. There are not many cars within
the walls, the stone is uniformly grey, there are no gardens, and the
dark garb of the inhabitants does nothing to relieve the monochrome
effect, which adds to the overall impression of unreality.

Apart from the pleasure of wandering around the village and
looking out from it, there are few specific sights of interest. The old
walls, parts of them dating from the 5th century BC, are best
admired at the northern end of town, around the Porta Spada. The
Chiesa Madre (14th and 15th centuries), near the Porta Trápani, is
the largest and most interesting of Érice's medieval churches. There
is a small museum with some fragments found locally, including a
head of Aphrodite (4th century BC).

MOUNT ETNA

"When we asked the cavaliere about climbing Etna, he refused even to discuss an enterprise which was so hazardous, especially at this time of year. 'Most foreign visitors are too apt to consider the ascent a trifling affair. But we, who are near neighbours of the mountain are content if we reach the summit twice or thrice in a lifetime, for we never attempt it except under ideal conditions. If you will follow my advice ride early tomorrow morning to the foot of Monte Rosso: you will enjoy the most magnificent view and at the same time see the place where the lava of 1669 poured down on our unfortunate city. If you are wise you will let others tell you about the rest'." (Goethe; May 1787).

Mount Etna is far and away the biggest thing in Sicily. Being what it is, very much alive, statistics about its size and shape can only be provisional, but for the last few centuries the rim of its central crater has stood at about 3,000m, nearly double the height of any other Sicilian mountain, and to travel around the base of the mountain requires a journey of some 140km. Its vast mass is the dominant feature of the landscape of central and south-eastern Sicily; the great cone climbs so gently that it's hard to take the mountain seriously when you view it from far away across the island, from Enna for example, about 60km away. Only the tell-tale pall of smoke confirms the identification of what might otherwise be a rather undistinguished broad hill, much closer at hand and much less high.

Etna is Europe's largest volcano, and has erupted about 130 times over the last 25 centuries; it shows no signs of retiring from active volcanic service, nor of allowing any observable pattern to be read into its capricious behaviour. The last few decades have been a period of more than usually intense activity – most recently throughout the first half of 1983 – and surprising though this may seem, Etna in eruption is an even greater tourist attraction than Etna temporarily quiescent. Hundreds of thousands of people flock to watch the evening fireworks, and to see the glowing tongue of lava inching down the slopes.

Extremely destructive eruptions are very rare. In most cases the lava flows slowly, so that even if the eruption is large enough or low enough (most eruptions do not issue from the central crater) to affect the inhabited lower slopes, the damage is to property not individuals. Only a handful of people have lost their lives this century, and most of those were in an unlucky group of tourists swallowed up near the summit in 1979, like Empedocles who, according to legend, threw himself into the crater in the hope of persuading everyone, by disappearing, that he was a God. (The truth came out in the form of one of his golden sandals, ejected by the volcano). Considering the fame of the story, it has to be counted immortality of a sort.

There have been a few occasions when the mountain has literally split its side and lava has gushed down to the sea, burying whatever it did not carry before it. In 1669 lava 2km wide flowed over the 60ft walls of Catánia, engulfed the city and filled most of the harbour. The lava took eight years to cool. The real danger though is earthquakes, and although they may be associated with eruptions, the immediate neighbourhood of Etna is no more dangerous than the rest of Sicily. In 1908 Messina was demolished by an earthquake centred on the Straits, and 80,000 lives were lost, a bitter irony considering that the people of Messina were the proud possessor of an autograph letter from the Virgin Mary, sent from Jerusalem on Sunday 26th June AD42 and promising the city protection for ever. In January 1968, south-western Sicily was the victim, and the signs of damage are still evident.

The greatest natural disaster of all came only a few years after Etna's great eruption of 1669, in 1693, when south-eastern Sicily was devastated by an upheaval centred on

MOUNT ETNA

the Val de Noto. At 10pm on the 7th January "Mount Aetna began to utter those hideous roarings that seldom but usher in some tragedy of the nature of what followed. Loud bellowings continued until the 9th when at about 12 o'clock they began to cease or rather fall lower. Within an hour after, the inhabitants of Catánia began to perceive a shaking under them for about 3 minutes. This did little other hurt than affright the people and give them fears of some further hurt... During the 3 minutes that this shake continued and an hour before there was not the least noise from Mount Aetna, but within a minute after the shake was over not only did the noise redouble infinitely more terrible than it had been before, but the whole top of the mountain appeared in flames. The horridest shake of all fell out on the 11th, and affected the whole island. Fishermen in the bay of Catánia saw the city sink down with the noise as it were of some thousand pieces of Great Ordnance discharged at once. Some minutes thereafter to the eastward near where the city stood there rose up a little mountain which lifting itself up several times a considerable height sunk at least likewise out of their sight.

In the place where Catánia stood appears now at a distance a great lake with some great heaps of rubbish appearing here and there above the water. Before and for some minutes after the earthquake Mount Aetna appeared more than ever in flames... but a few minutes after Catánia was swallowed up... neither were flames to be seen nor the least noise to be heard for 5 or 6 hours. And then the mountain began to roar and throw out flames again more duskish and smoky than at any time before."

Modica had been swallowed up on the 9th, without a survivor. Noto was completely destroyed on the 11th. In place of Scicli "there is now a stinking pool of water; a part of the steeple of San Salvatore stands above the water. Noone was saved." At the other end of the island, the dome above the high altar of Monreale cathedral collapsed. "Sicily, that was one of the beautiful'st, richest and fruitful'st lands in the world, is now a heap of rubbish and a continued desolation".

The wealth that Etna has bestowed is the fertility of the volcanic soil. Its lower slopes are intensively cultivated, and are said to support a denser population than any other non-industrial region of the world. Up to about 500m there are citrus groves, above them vines and olives flourish to about 1,300m, and there are thick woods and scrub up to about 2,000m, broken up in many places by swathes of recent lava and sprouting scores of subsidiary cones and craters among the vegetation. Above are only hostile bare slopes of dark lava, not pleasant to look at or walk on. In winter Etna is snowy and some of its slopes are equipped for skiing; on the less sunny upper slopes the snow lasts well into the summer.

Visiting Etna has been complicated by recent eruptions. The road up to the Rifugio Sapienza (1,881m) from Nicolosi was cut by the 1983 lava flow, and although Sapienza itself is still accessible by road from Zafferana, the Etna cable-car (whose top section has been out of action since 1971) was not working at all when we last visited. The less widely publicised northern approach to and route up Etna has not been affected. From a cluster of huts and cafés at the top of beautiful pinewoods near Mareneve rugged minibuses take tourists up to 3,000m, leaving a relatively short walk up to the crater, conditions permitting. The trip takes about 3 hours, and costs about 30,000 lire. Excursions by night can be arranged; the lava in the crater glows, and the beauty of sunrise viewed from the top of the mountain, which might be the top of the world, is celebrated. Private vehicles are not allowed to attempt the track, and would-be independent hikers are strongly advised to take advice before setting off. When conditions are considered relatively safe, the rim of the crater is easily reached with no more specialised equipment than a pair of stout shoes and some warm clothes.

GELA

An important Greek colony, now a major oil refining town on the sandy south coast. The hinterland is a fertile (but scenically uninteresting) agricultural plain which brought wealth to Gela long before the dicovery of oil. Modern Gela is not prepossessing; many tourists can resist the pull of its one great sightseeing attraction, the most perfectly preserved section of Greek defensive wall in existence, on Capo Soprano at the western end of town. These walls were built at the end of the 4th century BC by Timoleon of Syracuse. Gela was destroyed in the Roman period and little remains to be seen apart from the walls, which escaped destruction by virtue of being submerged in a sand dune, as they remained until 1948.

☛ **Museum**   Near the site of the old acropolis, finds from Gela and other nearby archeological sites are well displayed. Geloan artists of the 6th and 5th centuries were famed for their terracotta work and sculpture, and non-archaeologists will be pleased to discover that the museum contains beautiful works of art and not just interesting fragments.

GIARDINI-NAXOS

Forming a long narrow sprawl of modern hotel development and filling the very limited space available along the shore below Taormina lies the resort area of Giardini-Naxos, Mazzarò and Letojanni. The two identifiable resorts (Giardini-Naxos and Letojanni) stretch along their strips of coarse sand and shingle beach and are separated by the rocky Capo Taormina; Mazzarò consists of little more than hotels, including some relatively secluded ones with their own coves. The main road which used to pass through has been relieved by the motorway, but is still very often blocked solid and blaring with impatient horns. Of the two resorts, Giardini is marginally the livelier and less ugly.

MARSALA

A busy commercial town on the south-west corner of the island, originally a Carthaginian port (Lilybaeum) and deriving its current name from the Arab period (Marsa Ali means harbour of God). In the later Middle Ages Marsala became the frequent victim of African-based pirate raids and Trápani gradually became the more important trading port for all except wine, for which Marsala has been famous for over 2,000 years. The present character of marsala wine and the international trade in it owe much to British merchant families. In 1773 John Woodhouse shipped 60 oak barrels of marsala wine to England, having added a dose of alcohol to ensure that the wine would not suffer from its long journey. The end product was a rich, golden fortified wine, greatly appreciated in Britain. Other British families (Ingham and Whitaker) followed; the British firms were later taken over by the Italian Florio (now part of Cinzano), but expatriate families remained involved in the wine business and the names are still prominent. Several of the wine firms in Marsala open their establishments to tourists in the mornings; Florio offers tours and tastings.

Vineyards (mostly owned by small-scale proprietors) throughout south-western Sicily produce today's wine, which is classified Fino, Superiore or Vergine depending on the quality of the ingredients and the length of the ageing process, which, in the case of a Marsala Vergine, is likely to be about 10 years and may be as long as 30. The wine is usually sweetened by the addition of an evaporated must (*vino cotto*) but not all marsala is treacle sweet: variations are signalled either by the words secco, demi-sec or dolce, or, in the case of Superiore, by the letters SOM (Superior Old Marsala) or GD (Garibaldi Dolce). The strength of Marsala varies between 15% and 20% by volume, export wines usually being stronger than those for Italian consumption.

Marsala's setting has fine defensive qualities and it was an important port and stronghold in antiquity. Carthaginians settled there at the beginning of the 4th century BC and the town was the only place in Sicily to resist Pyrrhus in his attempt to establish Greek control over the whole island in 276. After a ten year siege Lilybaeum yielded to Rome in 241BC. There has been some excavation of the cape where the ancient town was situated, but for the moment there is not a lot to see apart from the hulk of a Punic warship (3rd century BC), found off the coast nearby. It is the only known ship of this period.

Present-day Marsala is a pleasant enough town, with a handsome arcaded square in front of the Baroque cathedral and some adequate hotels (quite a rarity in this part of Sicily).
(*See also Motya*)

MESSINA

A large and, by Sicilian standards, prosperous city and busy port on the Sicilian side of the eponymous strait, only a few miles from the mainland – reached in under half an hour by ferry, less by hydrofoil. Messina is often considered to be a mainland town out of place on the island because of the ease of communications across the water and the steep mountains that rise up behind the town, cutting it off from the rest of Sicily.

The first impression given by the town is unprepossessing, although the setting is splendid. Messina has been the victim of a succession of disasters almost without equal in history, and its featureless architecture is designed to resist the inevitable onslaught of earthquakes. Buildings are low and widely spaced; the large public buildings, where a ponderous classical style has been employed, look particularly ill-proportioned.

Down the centuries there have been plagues (Messina was The Plague's port of disembarkation in western Europe, in 1347), bombardments and earthquakes, adding an element of irony to the local tradition that the Madonna herself wrote a letter to the Messinese promising eternal protection. The letter (written in Jerusalem and dated Sunday June 26th AD42) was preserved in the cathedral, and most Messinese had Letterio or Letteria as one of their names in memory of this promising epistle. If the custom has died out, the Messinese can hardly be accused of being ungrateful. The greatest calamity of all was an earthquake that demolished the city in the early hours of December 28th 1908, when nearly everyone was in bed. This massive upheaval brought about a two-foot change in the water level of the coast, sent a 20-foot tidal wave crashing along the coast of Calabria, and accounted for an estimated 84,000 lives in and around Messina during a two-month period of shaking.

One benefit of all the destruction (most recently at the hands of American bombers in 1943) and the earthquake risk is that the town is open and spacious. The harbour is deep and safe and the Strait has always been busy despite the legendary perils of its waters, guarded on the Sicilian side by the whirlpool of Charybdis and on the Calabrian by a six-headed monster based on the rock Scylla. Currents in the Strait are indeed exceptionally strong, and the rocky Sicilian coast may have been more dangerous before earthquakes changed its complexion. The Strait is rich in fish including some very rare deep-water species, specimens of which occasionally appear on the surface turned inside out by the force of depressurisation. Among the pleasures of a ferry crossing is the sight of the swordfish (*spada*) fishing boats travelling at great speed and carrying out something more like a whale hunt than the customary line-dangling or trawling exercise. In pleasing symmetry, the boat seems to be fashioned in the image of its valuable quarry, with the main fisherman, who brandishes a great harpoon, perched far in front of the body of the boat on a long, sword-like prow. On a high crow's nest another member of the team scans the water for signs of fish and shouts instructions both to the man at the wheel of the boat and to the harpoonist. Needless to say, catching a swordfish by this method is no mean achievement, and traditionally the successful fisherman is allowed by his cooperative team to keep a kilo of meat from each victim. A *spada* can weigh over a hundred kilos, so the system is less extravagant than it sounds.

Even without the disturbing knowledge that this is one of the most accident-prone places in the world, few tourists would choose to spend much time in Messina. It is not a bathing resort and its hotels are modern and ordinary. The two main sights are well worth a brief visit.

☞ **Cathedral** A repro medieval cathedral, but a very good one. The original (late 12th century) was built by the Normans whose invasion of Sicily started at Messina. There is some fine Gothic carving round the main doorway, and the interior is grand and harmonious with a painted wooden ceiling and a polished marble floor. The main curiosity is the less convincing imitation Gothic bell-tower on the square, with an intricate mechanical astrological clock. The best display of its complex clockwork pageantry is at midday. The tower can be climbed, for good views of the coast.

☞ **Museum** (Museo Nazionale) A very rich collection whose great treasures are a beautiful Madonna by Francesco Laurana (late 15th-century), and a polyptych of the Madonna and Child painted in 1478 by Sicily's greatest artist and one of the great masters of the early Renaissance, Antonello da Messina. Despite damage, there is plenty of lovingly-rendered detail. The museum also has two paintings by Caravaggio, painted in 1609 for local churches.

MONDELLO

The seaside resort suburb of Palermo, set on a beautiful small rocky bay between the mountainous hills of Monte Pellegrino and Monte Gallo. Onto the old fishing village has grown a residential area with quiet villas, a yacht-club, and a broad, well-kept concession beach. There are more hotels and restaurants than anywhere else in western Sicily, and many visitors to Palermo will welcome the chance, especially in summer, to escape to the relative calm and comfort of Mondello. Driving into the centre of Palermo (or anywhere else) from Mondello is tortuous and slow; buses don't beat the traffic, but they do know where they're going.

☛ **Palazzina Cinese** The main road into Palermo runs through the large park of La Favorita, laid out by Ferdinand IV in 1799, when the French invasion forced him to flee Naples for a few years. At the same time the very entertaining Palazzina Cinese was built in the fashionable chinoiserie style as a suburban retreat for Queen Maria Carolina. It has been well restored and includes a set of English prints given to the king and queen by Lord Nelson, who spent much of his time nearby with Sir William (or more often Emma) Hamilton. The inside is by no means all oriental in inspiration: there is a Turkish room and a hall beautifully decorated in the neo-classical "Pompeiian" style. Also in the park is the **Museo Pitrè**, an interesting museum devoted to Sicilian customs, costumes, and folk art, including puppets and painted carts – now rarely seen in Sicily.

MONREALE

A small hill town commanding fine views down over the Conca d'Oro and the Bay of Palermo. Monreale owes its fame to the great Norman cathedral and cloister, founded in 1174 by William II as the seat of an archbishopric to rival the power of Palermo's archbishop Walter of the Mill, and completed with exceptional speed in about ten years. The walls of the vast interior are clothed with a glittering series of mosaics, the largest surface area of figurative mosaic in any church, and very lively and graceful in the detail and design of the individual scenes. In the main apse the figure of Christ blessing dominates a host of archangels and saints, including the recently slain Thomas Becket (right of the main window), a somewhat mysterious inclusion in a cathedral founded by Henry II's son-in-law. The mosaics on the walls of the nave make a sequence of stories from the Old Testament, and those round the choir and aisles illustrate the New Testament. Two mosaics flanking the main arch in the transept, directly above the thrones of king and archbishop, show king William being crowned by Christ and offering the cathedral to the Virgin. The mosaics are easier to admire than most of the others in Sicily, mainly because the light is good. It is interesting to compare the mosaic scenes with the same ones carved in relief on the cathedral's bronze doors, those at the west end signed by Bonanno of Pisa (1186).

The columns of the nave are antique and the floor and lower section of the walls are decorated with beautiful patterns of marble inlay.

The cathedral cloister is as delightful as the interior of the great church is dazzling. Pairs of slender columns are inlaid with mosaic and surmounted by hundreds of intricately carved capitals of great beauty and remarkably varied inspiration. Many of the Biblical scenes extend across both halves of a pair of capitals; the Annunciation is a particularly successful example. Another repeats the image of king William offering his cathedral to the Virgin.

The cathedral's exterior is relatively dull, except for the east end, decorated with interlacing arcades and geometric patterns, adding an Islamic touch echoed in the narrow pointed arches of the cloister.

MORGANTINA

Archaeological site in a remote rural setting a few miles north east of the medieval village of Aidone, near Piazza Armerina. The city was settled in the early 6th century BC by Greeks who coexisted for a period with native Sikel inhabitants until the city was destroyed, probably in the uprising led by the Sikel Ducetius. It was recolonised by Siracusan Greeks in the 4th century BC and most of the visible remains date from the ensuing period of Morgantina's greatest prosperity. There is a small theatre, an unusually designed agora on two levels and some residential houses with mosaics.

MOTYA (MOZIA)

Archaeological site on a small, round island (San Pantaleo) about half a mile offshore in a lagoon north of Marsala. Motya was settled by the Phoenicians and used between the 8th century BC and the beginning of the 4th as one of their main trading bases in Sicily. Defences were erected in the 6th century and reinforced at the end of the 5th. In 397 the town was besieged by Dionysius of Syracuse, with ballistas and siege towers as high as the many-storied defences. After a long and desperate struggle Motya, which had been abandoned by the Carthaginian fleet, was destroyed and its Greek inhabitants crucified. It was resettled again but was no longer important, the Carthaginians preferring Marsala (Lilybaeum) as a naval base.

To the archaeological interest of a visit is added the simple pleasure of being ferried in a little boat across the shallow waters and wandering around a peaceful island, covered with pines, cacti, vines and tomato fields, together with a few pebble mosaics and remains of old wells, walls and an artificial harbour. The site was excavated by a member of the wine-producing Whitaker family and there is a small Whitaker museum near the landing place, where some local finds are on display. Probably because they needed more space for burials, the Carthaginians built a causeway from the northern side of the island to Birgi, and although this is now submerged under a few feet of water, it is still used for transporting grapes to the Sicilian mainland in high carts.

NOTO

If the measured grace and harmony of the 18th century are made manifest in the architecture of any Italian town, it is Noto, not far from the coast south of Syracuse. After the earthquake in 1693 a new town was built a few miles east of the site of the old (Noto Antica) whose ruins were abandoned. New Noto was constructed on a simple grid across a gentle hillside. The arrangement is in no way monotonous, thanks to the use of sloping squares crowned with churches, to break up the main streets, which run across the hillside, and to provide broad, monumental vistas. Many of the palace façades lining the narrow streets running up the hill are elaborately decorated with great fantasy; the carved animals and grotesque figures supporting the balconies of the **Palazzo Villadorata** (Via Nicolaci) are particularly famous. The beauty of Noto resides more in the overall effect (especially when the late sun reveals the full radiance of the golden stone) than in individual monuments. An exception is the church of the **Crocifisso**, which contains a beautiful Madonna by Francesco Laurana (1471). The Romanesque lions beside the doorway were salvaged from Noto Antica. The favourite place for lolling around is the Piazza 16 Maggio.

(*See also Ragusa*)

PALERMO

Although no longer economically the most important city on the island, Palermo has been its capital since the period of Arab control. In the early Middle Ages, when Arab, Norman and Hohenstaufen rulers held court there, it was one of the most prosperous, and artistically and intellectually one of the most brilliant cities in the Mediterranean, a melting-pot for Latin, Byzantine and Islamic cultures, where the presence of Arab and Greek scholars attracted others from all over western Europe. Much remains from this period, especially the Norman part of it, making Palermo one of the most fascinating cities in Italy, lesser in interest only than Rome, Florence and Venice.

It is not just in the style and quantity of individual monuments (most typically the exotic hanging gardens of date palms in the cloister of San Giovanni degli Eremiti, where slender columns frame glimpses of little red Islamic domes) that Palermo recalls more than anywhere else the dazzling glory and semi-oriental style of the century of Norman rule. The style of the modern city and its way of life also seem less European than anywhere else in Italy – the coffee is thicker and the sherbets sweeter, and there is more than a hint of Eastern promise in the colourful labyrinth of street markets and the shanty suburbs. The traveller might think himself in Tangier or Fez, and if it is not standard practice to haggle over the price of a swordfish steak in the market, it certainly is if you plan to use one of the horse and trap taxis. A rather less appealing way in which Palermo smacks of the near Orient is its deserved reputation for lawlessness. The Mafia has always been a western Sicilian phenomenon, and has become centred on Palermo, fountainhead of island patronage, and other towns along the north-west coast. The streets of the capital have been the setting for a bloody crisis brought about by a campaign of unprecedented vigour from the state to which the *mafiosi* have responded in the only way they know.

Palermo's setting is one of legendary beauty which the modern sprawl of the city has done a lot to spoil. The wide bay is framed by a horseshoe of mountains which once enclosed a lush vale of citrus groves, the famous Conca d'Oro (Golden Conch). Here the exotic pleasure palaces built for the Norman rulers and their harems were "strung round the hills like pearls around the throat of a woman", in the words of the 12th-century traveller Ibn Jubair. These days the waterfront and hinterland hills are less than enchanting, and excursions from the city centre are complicated by tortuous, poorly

THE MAFIA

Sicily's most famous export is the rat-a-tat of sub-machine gunfire in deserted Chicago warehouses; the double-breasted gangsters of the Mob, imposing their own primitive order with their own system of rough justice in the backstreet jungle land where only the fittest and the luckiest survive. The films always start back in the homeland with touching scenes of rural piety and close-knit family life, formative influences on the honourable thieves in their future lives across the ocean.

"He who neither speaks, nor sees, nor hears, lives in peace for a hundred years", a Sicilian prison wall graffito, sums up the principle of *omertà* which is the key ingredient of a *mafioso* outlook on life and one of the main reasons why the Mafia has proved so stubbornly ineradicable. It also sums up the modern reality that although the origins of *omertà* may have something to do with a code of honour, the reasons for non-cooperation have much more to do with simple fear. People do not speak, or did not do so until very recently, because there is no one to whom they could speak in absolute certainty that they were not speaking to someone with Mafia connections. Secrecy and silence fuels fear, and Mafia justice has a reputation for crossing oceans and breaking effortlessly into the securest of prisons to silence traitors.

The *mafioso* outlook is the product of centuries of rule by foreign powers unable to guarantee law and order. Until well into this century the interior of Sicily was little known and hardly policed at all. Travel was difficult, dangerous and rarely undertaken. Justice was administered locally with no chance of appeal, and the way it was administered rarely inspired any respect for the idea or forces of law. The peasants' only alternative to accepting the economic terms dictated to them was to take to the hills and a life of brigandage. The landowners made their own provision for the defence of their property and their dependents.

Most of the landowning class spent most of its time far from its estates and rented them out to entrepreneurial foremen (*gabellotti*) who became sources of local patronage. The *gabellotti* were able to extort favourable terms from the peasantry by intimidation (protection rackets), and used the same methods to dictate terms to the landowners. This sort of arrangement is vividly portrayed in Lampedusa's *The Leopard*, which deals with the Risorgimento period (1860).

Although in the 19th century the Mafia was identified with the cause of freedom from foreign rule, this was incidental. Its nature is anti-progressive, both socially and economically, and it has always been the enemy of industrialisation. It depended on pockets being lined with rake-offs from agricultural yield, which kept agricultural prices high and the rural populace poor. The break-up and sale of the old feudal estates only confirmed the *gabellotti* in their power, for they were the agents of sale, and became landowners and businessmen themselves. It suited them that the island stagnated economically as an agrarian province of the industrial north, and it suited the politicians of the industrial north that the island's votes could be bought easily and cheaply. The signed one-way systems through the slums and heavy traffic. The Norman palaces and their gardens are mostly run down and suburban (although restoration has at last been started).

The centre of Palermo, for all its grimy, crumbling dereliction, is fascinating. If the most remarkable monuments are those dating from the Norman period, the style of central Palermo is mainly Baroque. In the early seventeenth century the maze of central streets was rationalised by the creation of two main axes (now the Via Maqueda and Corso Vittorio Emanuele) intersecting at the Piazza

THE MAFIA

Mafia became part of the political and legal establishment to such an extent that no will to cleanse the system of its influence could be carried through, not at least by means of the normal legal or democratic processes.

Mussolini had no need for votes, no respect for normal legal processes and was set on achieving good publicity. He declared war on the Mafia, arresting and imprisoning on the basis of the slightest suspicion. The campaign enjoyed some success, although the large-scale arrests may have served only to strengthen the position of a few *cosche* (Mafia clans) at the expense of their rivals, and thus reduce the cause of sectarian violence (and improve the statistics) without solving the problem. The Mafia re-established control of the island after the Allies used its connections to assist the invasion of Sicily in 1943. The granting of considerable autonomy to Sicily in 1946 was in one respect a step backwards: renewed efforts to purge the island have been frustrated by the fact that the judges and politicians are Sicilians, and the police has been little more than the instrument of gang rivalry, weakening one or another *cosca* just as the Fascists did.

Since the War the Mafia, re-imported from America, has changed character. The context of Mafia activity is now urban and the stakes are much higher: diversion of money destined for urban redevelopment and big international contraband business, most notoriously hard drugs. Palermo is reputed to be the world's most important heroin refinery, a rather inglorious resurrection of the island's role as the trading crossroads of the ancient world. The conflicts between generations within Mafia *cosche* about the differing styles of business have been the subject of plenty of romanticised drama, although it is unlikely that many members of the honoured society, old or young, lose much sleep worrying about the morality of trafficking in drugs. They may be more concerned that, by entering these new fields of activity, the Mafia has condemned itself to war against society (and not just Italian society), rather than exploitation of it from within. It has lost credibility by undermining what little honourable basis there may have been left to the concept of *omertà*, and it has given powerful reinforcement to its opponents in their attempts to loosen tongues. The Mafia used to be a state of mind and inseparable from the social order; now it is just organised crime.

It is often claimed that the old order did at least guarantee order, albeit unfounded in law. Many are the stories of visitors being surprised to discover that items which had gone missing were mysteriously restored to them once the loss was known to anyone of any influence. The safety of Sicilian streets is no longer conspicuous, and Palermo is one of the worst places for two-man teams of bag-snatchers on Vespas. Nevertheless Mafia violence is of a very different nature from acts of political terrorism or bandit kidnappings in other regions: its targets are specific, and the casual tourist in Sicily has no reason to be alarmed by the impressive murder rate (especially in Palermo).

Vigliena or **Quattro Canti**, a noble crossroads decorated with symbolic Baroque statuary that is almost impossible to admire because of the dirt and the traffic. These streets and the more recently created Via Roma are invaluable navigational aids. During the 17th century the Sicilian aristocracy deserted its lands in favour of court life in Palermo and the size of the nobility multiplied under the Spanish policy of resorting to sale of titles as a major source of revenue. Hundreds of more or less palatial town houses were built to accommodate the new Palermitani in a style appropriate to their status. Their dilapidated façades, with cracks papered over by layer upon layer of posters and black-bordered death notices, line the streets of the city, and their cart-wide doorways occasionally allow glimpses of dark courtyards where weeds take root and scooters rust.

One of the most vivid and at times disconcerting impressions left by a wander around central Palermo is the sudden transition achieved in a few paces. One moment you are milling along a wide street full of traffic and tourists and lined by Baroque buildings and modern shops; the next you are lost in the dark, narrow alleys of slumland relieved only by the spaces cleared by the bombs of 1943, where the proverbial urchins play football among the piles of rubbish and wait for a promising car to be left unattended for a few minutes. There seem to be no smart or poor areas; everywhere shoulders are rubbed. Nowhere exemplifies this better than Palermo's traditional grand hotel, the **Villa Igiea**, a relic from the turn of the century when Palermo was an elegant wintering spot. The hotel, well worth visiting for its art nouveau décor and old photos of rich and royal Edwardian visitors, stands in a very seedy part of town on the edge of the harbour. Work is being done to upgrade its sea front with the building of a marina.

Like Sicily as a whole, only more so, Palermo can be a richly rewarding place to visit, but is hardly a relaxing or charming one. A summer visit is likely to be more enjoyable if you can get out in the evening; the nearby seaside resort of Mondello is the obvious choice for a place to stay, although commuting to Palermo by car is not recommended. For winter visits there are several comfortable business-style hotels in the centre.

No visit to Palermo is complete without some exploration of the street markets and the seeking out of a puppet show. The most entertaining market is the Vucciria, a teeming hubbub of stalls filling the streets around Piazza Garafello, near the church of San Domenico. It was in this quarter that the Gagini family of sculptors had their workshop. The puppet shows are traditional popular street entertainment which survive without having had to be resurrected by folklore enthusiasts. The shows are usually naïve versions of the crusading epics with white knights clanking on, engaging a vastly superior number of black knights in noisy and brutal battle from which a single white hero invariably emerges victorious. That at least is the gist; you are unlikely to understand more unless you have a thorough mastery of local dialect.

Main sights:

☛ **Cathedral**   Founded in the late 12th century by Palermo's English archbishop Walter of the Mill (Gualtiero Offamílio) who is reported to have attained office "less by election than by violent intrusion", the cathedral was an amalgam of Norman and Gothic styles even before the late 18th century, when the interior was completely reworked and the exterior no less emphatically transformed by the additon of a dome. The main doorway is on the southern side – a beautiful Gothic porch which includes a column with an inscription from the Koran, perhaps taken from an earlier mosque on the site. The sober grey interior is a stark contrast to the golden and mostly medieval exterior. The main interest is the collection of six royal tombs on the left of the main entrance; two of them have marble canopies inlaid with glittering mosaic. The great king Roger II's tomb is here but the workmanship on it is not particularly fine – the tomb was made up quickly after his death and the one he had intended for himself stayed at his chosen resting place (Cefalù), empty. It found its way to Palermo in 1213 because Frederick II had selected it for himself; this is the finest and most elaborate of the tombs. The cathedral also contains a number of charming works by the various members of the Gagini family of 16th-century sculptors. The greatest of them, Antonello Gagini (1478-1536), executed the cathedral's high altar; this was broken up and many fragments decorate chapels and nave pillars round the cathedral. There is work by his two sons in the north transept. In the chapel beside the north transept is a Madonna by Francesco Laurana. It is well worth walking round the outside of the cathedral to admire the Norman east end and the beautiful Gothic decoration of the twin-towered west end.

☛ **Gesù** (Jesuit church, often known as Casa Professa)   The main alternative to Santa Caterina for those seeking Baroque marble inlay decoration, here dating from the late 17th century. The overall effect of the inlay, stuccoes and frescoes is, as it was intended to be, overwhelming.

☛ **The Martorana**   This small church is an extraordinary and ill-assorted mixture of Baroque and Arab-Norman elements. The former include the façade, so there is no chance to assess the merit of Ibn Jubair's verdict (1184) that it was the most beautiful work in the world. Of the original church the splendid bell-tower survives, as do some of the most charming of all Sicilian mosaics decorating the vaults of the central section of the church, which was originally built on a Greek cross plan. Among the scenes surrounding the dome (Christ attended by strangely contorted archangels) are particularly beautiful representations of the Nativity and the Death of the Virgin. The entrance preserves two interesting mosaic panels among the later reconstruction; both of them contain lively and very individual portraits of two of the most important figures in the history of Norman Sicily. One, a famous anti-papal propaganda image, shows Roger II being crowned by Christ; the other panel, poorly restored in places, shows George of Antioch at the feet of the Virgin who holds a scroll inscribed with an intercession on his behalf.

☛ **National Archaeological Museum**   One of the richest collections of Greek and Roman antiquities in Italy and an essential complement to visits to the main classical sites on the island. The greatest treasures are the famous sculptures from the temples of Selinus (Selinunte), showing the stylistic development from the so-called archaic period (early 6th century BC) to the classical style of the early 5th century.

☛ **National Gallery of Sicily** Housed in the beautiful Palazzo Abatellis, built in the last decade of the 15th century in the Catalan-Gothic style, this large museum contains a few works of the very highest quality. The Triumph of Death fresco (mid-15th century) is a terrifying apocalyptic vision. The masterpieces of two of the most enjoyable of early Renaissance artists are Francesco Laurana's portrait bust traditionally called Eleanor of Aragon, and Antonello da Messina's breathtaking portrait of the Virgin surprised at her reading by the Angel of the Annunciation. Few would dispute that this is the most beautiful object in Sicily. Another great treasure is the Flemish Jan Gossaert's Malvagna Triptych (c1520), showing the Virgin and Child with angels and saints, set in a painted architectural screen of astonishing Late Gothic intricacy.

☛ **Norman Palace** (Palazzo dei Normanni) HQ of Norman rule and still the seat of Sicilian government. The palace is a vast, outwardly unadorned building beside one of Palermo's few public gardens. The guided tour of many uninteresting government rooms is worth putting up with because it also includes the so-called Roger's Room (Sala di Re Ruggero), decorated with some of the most instantly enjoyable (although not so easily comprehensible) of all Norman mosaics, which almost certainly date from the late Norman period, after Roger II's death in 1154. Here more than in most places the idea of cross-fertilisation, so often used as a neat summary of the art of the Norman period, is appropriate.

The royal chapel (**Cappella Palatina**) is the highlight of a visit to the palace and for many people one of the highlights of a visit to Sicily. You don't have to do the guided tour to visit the chapel, but you must cover shoulders and knees. The chapel (accessible from the first floor of the main palace courtyard) was founded by Roger II in 1130. He employed Byzantine artists to fill the walls with mosaics, and Arab ones to create an intricate wooden honeycomb ceiling in the purest Muslim tradition (except that they painted on it figurative human scenes, difficult to admire without binoculars). The floor and lower part of the walls are covered by patterned mosaic inlay, and such is the richness of the overall effect that entering the chapel is like stepping into a jewel-encrusted casket. Apart from some areas of clumsy restoration, the finest mosaics are those in the dome and choir (Christ blessing, saints and patriarchs, scenes from the Life of Christ), in the purest Byzantine manner and dating from the time of Roger (1140s). The less formalised scenes (Lives of St Paul and St Peter) on the walls of the aisles and the less interesting Old Testament cycle in the nave are probably the work of local artists of a slightly later period, and suggest that work on the chapel was not finished until the 13th century. Beside the pulpit stands a beautifully carved 15-foot candlestick, probably presented by the archbishop of Palermo in 1151.

☛ **Piazza Pretória** A monumental square near the Quattro Canti designed to accommodate a large and elaborate late 16th-century fountain, originally intended for a Florentine villa but exported to Palermo in 1574 in 644 pieces. The host of mannered statues of nymphs and river gods and the monstrous water-spouting beasts make an impressive and interesting work although not a very harmonious one.

☛ **San Cataldo** The next-door church to the Martorana, a simple cube topped by three little red domes and flanked by palms, is one of the characteristic images of Norman Sicily. The interior, rarely accessible, is as simple as the exterior. There are some beautiful antique capitals.

☛ **Santa Caterina**   A large, late 16th-century church on Piazza Bellini, often closed but worth checking, especially on Sunday morning. The interior constitutes the best preserved and most brilliant example of the technique of coloured marble inlay mosaic, which was one of the features of Sicilian Baroque art. This style of decoration, dating here from the early 18th century, evolved to include relief as well as coloured patterns, and this is used to dramatic effect. One of the pillar base medallions illustrates the story of Jonah – the whale's mouth gapes cavernously and the ship includes wire rigging.

☛ **San Giovanni degli Eremiti** (St John of the Hermits)   An exquisite red-domed Arab-Norman church and cloister near the Norman palace, on the site of a mosque which had succeeded an earlier monastery, and of which some remains are visible. At the time of its foundation by King Roger in 1142, this was the wealthiest monastery in Sicily. Now the place is deconsecrated and stands as an evocative memorial to the period. Its little domes protrude like luscious fruit above the date palms and figs in the cloister and few religious establishments seem more hedonistic in spirit. The church's setting in a particularly shabby part of town heightens the enjoyment of this oasis of seclusion.

San Giovanni degli Eremiti

☛ **Serpotta's Oratories**   The work of Giacomo Serpotta (1656-1732), the great master of stucco decoration, is best seen in three oratory chapels, annexes to the churches of **Santa Zita, San Lorenzo** (via Immacolatella) and **San Doménico** (via Bambinai). In Serpotta's hands simple square chambers are transformed into theatres of irresistible grace and gaiety. His art is at its most exuberant in the oratory of the Rosary of Santa Zita, whose walls literally overflow with a multitude of cherubs playing with scrolls, garlands, swags of fruit and military trophies. On the end wall they hold up a curtain and a framed relief of the Battle of Lepanto, where Catholic victory was decided by the intervention of the Madonna of the Rosary. There is more discipline in the decoration of the San Lorenzo oratory where scenes tell the lives of saint Lawrence and saint Francis. An altarpiece by Caravággio has been stolen. In the San Doménico oratory Serpotta's work was more circumscribed by an existing series of paintings (including Van Dyck's beautiful Virgin of the Rosary altarpiece). Serpotta filled the spaces with beautiful stucco statues.

Suburban sites

☛ **Catacombs** (Convento dei Cappuccini, Via dei Cipressi, near the Monreale road)   One of the most lively burial places it will be your macabre good fortune to visit. This old convent on the edge of town used to be the place to be seen, dead or alive, and in the dusty, white-washed basement corridors noble Palermitani of centuries past (until 1881) occupy niches or shelves according to their status. Many are no more than bones, but others stand in their faded glad-rags, disturbingly well-preserved; skin has dried to the skulls in nightmarishly twisted leather grimaces. When Brydone visited the place in the late 18th century, he found that "it is a common thing to make choice of their nich, and to try if their body fits it, that no alterations may be necessary; and sometimes by way of voluntary penance they accustom themselves to stand for hours in these niches".

☛ **Monte Pellegrino**   The celebrated 2,000ft golden mountain that drops steeply into the sea to the west of Palermo and shelters the city and its famous bay. At the summit is a massive statue of St Rosália, patron saint of Palermo. The road up passes her cave sanctuary, now a chapel with Baroque façade, containing her tomb. A major pilgrimage takes place here on July 11th – 15th. The mountain has a small colony of peregrine falcons, and hawk-eyed observers may catch a glimpse of one plummeting down beside the rock. Egg-snatching is apparently a serious problem.

☛ **Santo Spirito dei Vespri**   At the cemetery of Sant' Orsola (Via dei Vespri) on the southern edge of Palermo. This simple Norman church was founded for the austere Cistercian order by Walter of the Mill in 1173. The exterior is beautifully decorated with interlacing arches of various materials. The rebellion known as the Sicilian Vespers began here in 1282.

☛ **La Zisa**   On the western edge of the city, not far from the Piazza Principe di Camporeale. The finest of the Norman kings' exotic pleasure palaces in the lush surroundings of Palermo, La Zisa was built by William I and II in the second half of the 12th century, and takes its name from the Arabic "Aziz", the splendid. After many alterations and centuries of neglect, La Zisa is being restored. The interior contains a beautiful frieze of mosaic decoration with peacocks and hunters and a stone honeycomb ceiling.

(See also Mondello; Monreale; Solunto)

Excursions from Palermo

☞ **Bagheria**
When a 19th-century visitor described Bagheria as the Richmond of Palermo, the comparison between the two genteel metropolitan outposts was no doubt apt. Now Bagheria has become just another of Palermo's dirty suburban neighbours; its onetime pre-eminence and the mouldering hulks of its famous aristocratic villas make its current state all the more depressing.

According to the same anonymous lady traveller, the palaces were used during the periods of spring and autumn freshness, the Sicilians preferring to retire during the summer heat to the narrow streets of their capital for shade, passing the long day in drowsy siesta. Most are now in varying stages of dereliction and only two are open to the public. One is the notorious **Villa Palagonia**, built by one Prince of Palagonia in the early 18th century and later adorned by his eccentric grandson with a grotesque array of monstrous sculptures (said to be caricatures of his wife's lovers) along the walls of the courtyard. The place was a tourist attraction even in the 18th century, when Goethe and Brydone recorded their visits to the villa.

Another traveller of the same period, Swinburne, wrote sanctimoniously of this "avenue of pandaemonium" that, thanks to the soft and perishable nature of the stone, "we need be under no apprehensions of this collection passing to posterity as a monument to the taste of the eighteenth century". He would be distressed to learn that the villa does survive and so does a representative sample of the monsters outside. The state of the building is lamentable and, if the interior is safe, it does not look it. Restoration is planned.

The nearby **Villa Valguarnera**, the acknowledged architectural masterpiece of the Bagheria villas, is also open. Its terrace commands a celebrated view over the Bay of Solunto.

☞ **Piana degli Albanesi** (*24km south-west*)
The main Albanian settlement on the island, whose inhabitants still speak a Greek dialect, practise a kind of Greek unorthodoxy, and dress up in picturesque costume for special events and religious festivals. None of these things make Piana a particularly interesting place for a casual visit except on feast days, but the beauty of the drive up through the hills of the Conca d'Oro above Palermo itself justifies the excursion.

PIAZZA ARMERINA

A handsome old golden town which repays more attention than most tourists, intent on the nearby Roman villa at Casale, devote to it. A Baroque cathedral with a gleaming green dome crowns one hill and dominates the town. The church contains a beautiful painted crucifix (1485) and a venerated icon, the Madonna delle Vittorie, brought into view only when the event is celebrated, with great pageantry, on the 13th and 14th August each year. There are other fine Baroque buildings around the cathedral and various churches of interest in and around the town, some of them dilapidated.
(*See also Casale; Morgantina*)

RAGUSA

The main town of the south-eastern corner of Sicily, and the centre of the local oil business. The town is dramatically set on a two-humped ridge in a faulty landscape of steeply-cut valleys. The old town, Ibla, linked to prosperous, businessman's Ragusa by a narrow isthmus, is untouched by development. Exploring Ibla is one of the greatest treats of the Baroque south-east. There are delightful gardens beyond the old church of **San Giorgio Vecchio**, giving splendid views of the old town stacked up on its small spur, and of the surrounding landscape. At the top of Ibla stands its former cathedral, plain **San Giorgio** since the two parts of town merged in 1926. Far from being plain, the façade of San Giorgio, designed by Rosario Gagliardi in the 1740s, is a masterpiece of graceful, swelling rhythms embellished with a measured abundance of decorative swirls and frills, and most advantageously displayed high up on a platform above an obliquely set, wedge-shaped, sloping, palm-lined, cobbled piazza; no Baroque church could ask for more. San Giorgio is lit up in the evening, to magical effect. By comparison, the new town's **cathedral**, which dates from the earliest years of post-earthquake reconstruction in the 1690s, seems ponderous and earthbound. There is a good **archaeological museum** near the cathedral, and a number of Baroque palaces also in the vicinity, built long and low in case of earthquakes.

There are hotels in the new town, some of them comfortable and modern by Sicilian standards, although not very attractive. Ibla is unspoilt almost to the point of being lifeless, and has few shops, restaurants or hotels.

Excursions from Ragusa

☞ **Coastal resorts in the south-east**
In summer the Ragusans migrate to their local seaside resort **Marina di Ragusa** south of the town. Like Ragusa itself, it is a surprisingly prosperous resort. Being almost exclusively patronised by locals, it consists mainly of holiday homes and flats, and alternates between extremes of crowding (for a couple of summer months and at weekends) and emptiness. The beach is sandy and better than most on the island. There are other, less cheerful villages with good beaches in the neighbourhood (**Pozzallo's** has a cleaning machine!) and a few simple hotels.

☞ **Baroque towns**
Several towns near Ragusa were more or less totally reconstructed in the local Baroque style, often unhelpfully described as Spanish in character. The countryside is delightful and the towns benefit greatly from the warm golden colour of the local stone, which contrasts very favourably with the uniform blackness of the lava towns around Etna. **Scicli** (*24km south*) was one of the hardest hit of all the south-eastern towns in January 1693. "In place of the town there is now a stinking pool with a part of the steeple of S Salvator standing above the water. No one was saved", wrote an observer. The Scicli that rose again after the waters subsided is a fascinating

Ragusa, San Giorgio

little town, little visited. It lacks the symmetry of Noto (*see separate entry*) but has one or two beautiful church façades (notably San Bartolomeo) and some bizarrely adorned palaces, the most remarkable of them (Palazzo Beneventano) now an ironmonger's shop. The spirit of the decorative detail here seems medieval. There are ruins of medieval fortifications on the hill that dominates the town. **Módica**'s situation along the floor of a gorge (*15km south-east*) is hardly less dramatic than Ragusa's. There are many beautiful golden façades along the lively, palm-lined main street, but the town's finest building is the church of San Giorgio, beside the road that leads steeply up to the upper town (Módica Alta), but preferably approached by a long staircase from the bottom. Although not improved by the later addition of the upper register, the façade is majestic; like the slightly later San Giorgio in Ragusa Ibla, it was the work of Gagliardi.

Other towns with individual Baroque buildings of interest are **Comiso**, and **Vittoria** (*20km and 29km west*). Neither town is particularly appealing, partly because of their setting in rather featureless agricultural country on the edge of the plain of Gela. (*See also Noto*)

RANDAZZO

An attractive old town on the northern side of Etna and built almost
entirely of black lava, Randazzo is visually much enlivened by the
use of white limestone for decorative contrast in the church
architecture (the campanile of San Martino is a particularly beautiful
example). It is the nearest town to the main crater and a tongue of
lava from the most recent major eruption cuts through the
cultivations on the edge of town, stopping just short of the road.
Despite its proximity to the source of so much destruction Randazzo
suffered little until 1943 when Allied bombing seriously disfigured
its medieval complexion. Among many picturesque and interesting
old buildings, the main church is Santa Maria, originally built in the
13th century but much changed since, notably by the addition of a
dome at the beginning of the 19th century.

SCIACCA

A peaceful but rather dull spa town on the south coast. The thermal
properties of the sulphurous local springs were appreciated by the
Greeks of Selinunte (said to be the earliest Greek spa) and by the
Romans who referred to Sciacca as Thermae Selinuntinae. The spa
business means no shortage of somewhat institutional hotel
accommodation but some development is under way to make
Sciacca into a more up-to-date and lively resort.

The most interesting buildings are at the western entrance to the
partly walled town: these include the fortified 16th-century gateway
and the nearby churches of Santa Margherita, whose north doorway
was sculpted by Francesco Laurana (late 15th century), and the
Carmine, its façade a curious mixture of Baroque below and Gothic
above (including the rose window).

Excursions from Sciacca

☞ **Caltabellotta** (*about 20km north-east*)
The road to this spectacular village climbs rapidly through the
cultivations of the coastal strip into a wild and barren mountainous
landscape. It's a moodily atmospheric place with crumbling
medieval ruins of church and castle among the rocky crags which
crown the narrow streets and staircases of the inhabited village and
give dramatic, plunging views. Much of the damage is the result of
the 1968 earthquake.

SCOPELLO

A small fishing village near Castellamare del Golfo on the
promontory that encloses the Gulf of Castellamare to the west. The
village has a small stony beach and there are other rocky coves
nearby. At weekends the area is a magnet for inhabitants of
Castellamare and other towns of the urban north-west coast, and the
village and approach road are quite unable to cope with the influx.
There is more beach space and some simple accommodation at the
quiet resort village of **San Vito lo Capo** on the tip of the promontory.

Segesta

SEGESTA

Perhaps the most eloquent of all classical sites in Sicily, despite being one of the few not to benefit from a coastal setting. Segesta was an important town but there is little more to the present archaeological site than a Doric temple and a theatre, dating from the 5th and 3rd centuries BC respectively. These two beautiful monuments stand apart on separate hilltops in a quiet, open, stony landscape, still wonderfully empty despite the recent intrusion of a motorway. There is a minimum of tourist clutter (just a café between the two hills). If the lonely, rough-hewn grandeur of the unfinished, yet somehow perfectly unfinished, temple and the broad splendour of the setting of the theatre do not in some way stir the soul, then it is fair to assume that you need not trouble yourself with classical sightseeing anywhere.

The ancient town of Segesta, set on Monte Barbaro (where the theatre is), was one of the main settlements of the Elymians, a little understood race who occupied much of north-western Sicily at the time of early Greek and Phoenician settlements. Subsequently the town and the people became Hellenized, but had to switch allegiance frequently between Carthaginians and Greeks to ensure survival; a constant rival was the neighbouring Greek colony of Selinus. In 307BC Agathocles, tyrant of Syracuse, sacked the city, torturing and killing thousands of inhabitants and selling others into slavery. He repopulated the place, and during the next century the theatre was built. Segesta changed allegiance a few more times before betraying its Carthaginian garrison and giving itself to Rome, under whose dominion it flourished. It was finally destroyed, in the 10th century.

Apart from the lack of a roof, features of the temple that reflect its unfinished state include the bosses on the steps (used for lifting the stones into position), unfluted columns and the absence of stones filling in the spaces between their bases. Romantic notions that the temple was never intended to be more finished than it is are certainly misguided.

SELINUNTE

One of the most important Greek colonies in Sicily and one of its most interesting archaeological sites. There is something appealing about a place that took its name (Selinus) from the local abundance of wild celery, and the ancient city, set on an unspectacular stretch of sandy southern coastline not far from Castelvetrano, has a peaceful charm of its own. There is a small modern beach colony (Marinella) nearby, but this does not compromise the tranquillity of the ruined ancient city.

Selinus was settled by Greeks from near Syracuse in the mid-7th century; it is clear from excavation that the site had much earlier been occupied by Phoenicians. The westernmost Greek city on the island and not easily defensible, its great prosperity and artistic vitality resulted from peaceful trade with Africa and the eastern Mediterranean. A surprise attack by Carthage in 409 BC found Selinus incapable of defending itself, and the town was taken and sacked before help could arrive. It never regained its former importance.

The city was built on three low hills separated by two small rivers (one of them now extinct) and their harbours. The eastern hill is occupied by the ruins of three great temples, the second by the acropolis, with more temples (and now a museum) inside its defences and the site of the residential city outside them. To the west of the river Modione is a large burial area with an early sanctuary which has been particularly fruitful for the archaeologists. The temples are referred to by letters. Many beautiful sculptures from them are preserved in the Palermo archaeological museum.

The most impressive ruins are those on the eastern hill, and the most impressive thing about them is their ruinousness. Whereas in many places archaeologically inexpert visitors may feel frustration at the lack of easily comprehensible structures, here the massive chaos of enormous, piled-up blocks of temple G conveys with extraordinary vividness the destructive power of the forces that brought down this immense edifice, unfinished after over a century of construction work, in a matter of seconds. For it is quite obvious that these ruins do not tell the usual story of sack and pillage, depopulation, neglect and piecemeal theft of sculptures and blocks of stone for other building projects. This lot came down with an almighty thump, and without Samson or an atomic bomb no human force could have done the job. It was, no doubt, an earthquake; probably about one thousand years after the city was abandoned in the 1st century BC. Temple G was huge, second in size to the Temple of Zeus at Agrigento. Construction probably started in the sixth century BC, and was evidently not finished when Carthaginians took and sacked the city in 409 (many of the columns were left unfluted). The columns were nearly 50 feet high and made up of drums weighing as much as 100 tons each. The colonnades of Temple E on the eastern hill have been reconstructed, as has a smaller part of temple C on the Acropolis. Built in the early 6th century, this is the earliest of the Selinuntine temples. On the eastern side of the acropolis hill is a large section of defensive wall, tiered like a very steep, wide staircase.

Stone for the building of Selinus came from the **Rocche di Cusa** quarries (*12km along the coast north-west of Selinus, most easily reached from Campobello di Mazara*). They were clearly suddenly abandoned, probably in 409BC when the city came under threat of Carthaginian attack. Huge drums for Temple G were left on the quarry site ready for transport and others abandoned beside the road to Selinus, where they remain. Half-cut blocks and evidence of the quarrying techniques can be seen in the quarry walls.

SOLUNTO

Archaeological site of a town founded in the mid-4th century BC on the slopes of a beautiful headland west of Palermo. A large area has been uncovered, revealing a grid of streets and a number of interesting pavements and frescoes, mostly Roman. The main appeal is the beautiful setting and views along the coast towards Cefalù; the Aeolian Islands are sometimes visible. Rather than taking the most direct road to or from Palermo, it is well worth driving all the way round the promontory which divides the bays of Palermo and Solunto.

SYRACUSE (SIRACUSA)

One of the great powers of the Ancient World, and the most important city in Sicily from the early 5th century BC until the Arabs took and wrecked it in AD878. The pre-eminence of Syracuse started with the achievements of Gelon of Gela who, in alliance with Theron of Akragas, defeated the Carthaginians in 480 and thereby established himself as the most powerful individual in the Mediterranean and Syracuse, his chosen capital, as its foremost city. This position was maintained until the alliance with Rome was unwisely broken in favour of Carthage in 215. The ensuing long Roman siege (213 to 211) was marked by the ingenuity of Archimedes in producing mechanical devices to foil the enemy, including mirrors and magnifying lenses to blind them and perhaps even burn their boats. Eventually the city was taken and Archimedes run through (against the express command of the Roman general Marcellus) while reading at his desk. Under Roman rule Syracuse lost importance but its wealth and art treasures attracted visitors even after the notorious Roman governor Verres had done what he could to remove all objects of value. Syracuse did not recover from its destruction in the 9th century and its sorry dereliction provoked much thought among the historico-moralising travellers of the 18th and 19th centuries. When Brydone arrived in 1770 he found that "this proud city that once vied with Rome itself" (Athens would have been more to the point) "is now reduced to a heap of rubbish, for what remains of it deserves not the name of a city. The inhabitants are so overrun with the itch that we begin to be extremely well-satisfied that we could not procure beds".

This century Syracuse has enjoyed something of a revival, and it is now a rapidly expanding modern town, almost as big if nowhere near so powerful as it was in its heyday, and much less dilapidated than many other Sicilian towns. There is clean accommodation and lots to see, including a very extensive and interesting archaeological zone (Neapolis) which has been somewhat impinged upon lately by the expansion of the town.

The heart of the old city is the crumbling Ortygia, an island linked to the modern city on the mainland by two small bridges, and separating Syracuse's two harbours, the large to the south and the small to the north. Ortygia has participated little in the recent growth and modernisation of the city and it is a picturesquely run-down backwater, underpopulated but full of tourists, who come to see the town's main sights (other than the archaeological zone) and also a fashionable recreational and shopping zone for well-to-do Syracusans. The tree-lined Foro Italico on the large harbour front is a popular evening promenade with cafés and restaurants, expensive yachts and beautiful sunset views. Nearby is the famous **Arethusa Fountain**, now a dirty duck pond. Originally a valuable source of fresh water for the island, it was thought to be a resurgence of a river that disappeared underground at Olympia. After sacrifices at Olympia, it is said, the waters of Arethusa rose tinged with blood for several days. The medieval fortress on the end of the island, built by Frederick II in the 13th century, is used as a barracks and not open to visitors; the best view of it is from the sea.

☛ **Archaeological museum** (Museo Nazionale)   One of Sicily's richest museums, now on Ortygia and awaiting rehousing on the mainland. There is an enormous amount of fragmentary material from pre-Greek Sicilian civilisations, much of it of limited interest to non-specialists, and an exceptional collection of pottery and sculpture from Greek and Roman periods. Greek Syracuse was the origin of what is often referred to as the most beautiful coinage ever minted. The museum's coin collection is celebrated, but not always accessible.

☛ **Catacombs**   The most interesting of several areas of early Christian catacombs are entered near the church of San Giovanni, built over the **crypt of St Marcian**, first bishop of Syracuse and martyred in AD254. The crypt (access from the church) contains an altar where saint Paul is said to have preached and a pillar against which Marcian is said to have been flogged. The adjoining network of catacombs was used until the 6th century; the niches are empty.

☛ **Neapolis**   A very extensive archaeological zone on the inland side of the city. The setting is no longer either peaceful or particularly beautiful and the area is always swarming with people and surrounded by souvenir sellers and touts for pony trap rides. The main elements of the site are an enormous and very well-preserved **Greek theatre** cut out of the rock (mostly 3rd century BC); a **Roman amphitheatre** (2nd-century AD), also mostly intact; the base of a huge sacrificial altar (**Hieron's Altar**, also 3rd century BC); and a large area of **quarries** (*latomie*) used for the building of the ancient city and, more famously, as open-air prisons for up to 7,000 captives during the war with Athens (413BC). There was neither shade from the heat nor shelter from the cold, and the daily ration was a glass of water and half a pint of corn. These quarries are now colourful gardens and make an enjoyable walk; the great popular attraction is the so-called **Ear of Dionysius**, a man-made, tall, arched cavern with remarkable acoustics. These and the existence of a small opening in the roof gave rise to the idea that Dionysius designed the cave as a means of eavesdropping on his captives, but its true purpose is unclear. The theatre is the setting for biennial drama festivals in early summer. The high gangway near the top of the theatre bears inscriptions to Zeus, king Hieron and his wife and daughter-in-law. The beauty of the view over the great harbour from its tiers has been compromised by urban sprawl and a screen of trees.

☞ **Piazza del Duomo** (Ortygia)   One of the most beautiful squares in Sicily, irregular in shape and flanked by a harmonious variety of Baroque buildings including the remarkable **cathedral**. In the early 18th century a splendid new façade was added to the church, a 7th-century conversion of a Doric temple, making this building as characteristic of eastern Sicily as the very different church of the Martorana in Palermo is of the west. The Greek columns still stand, supporting the nave and the fabric of the walls of the cathedral (as can be seen from the street running alongside its north wall, where medieval battlements have replaced the entablature). Cicero left a famous description of the sumptuous original decoration of the temple. Its walls were painted with battle scenes and heroic portraits, it had doors of gold and ivory and on the roof stood a huge statue of the goddess Athena carrying a golden shield which flashed in the sun like a beacon for distant ships. Now the interior of the cathedral is impressively bare; the beamed roof, rough piers and patterned marble floor all reinforce the impression of a living Greek temple. It is well worth wandering inside the beautiful courtyard of **Palazzo Beneventano** (late 18th-century) opposite the cathedral.

Excursions from Syracuse

☞ **Fontane Bianche** (*12km south*)
Not so much an excursion as a possible base for those who want to mix sightseeing with pleasure, a small seaside resort which serves Syracusan week-enders and reflects the relative prosperity of the modern city. There is not much of a community, mainly comfortable villas with gardens, and one or two small hotels. The resort is young, crowded and lively in summer, with a windsurf school and some disco-life. There is a campsite, not well placed for the beach.

☞ **Castello Eurialo** (*9km north-west*)
A network of Greek fortifications on the western end of the Epipolae ridge, a key position for the defence of Syracuse against attack from the interior. Originally built by Dionysius I in the 5th century BC, the fort was subsequently altered and much of what remains is thought to date from the 3rd century BC; Archimedes may have been involved in its construction. The fortress was never finished, and surrendered to the Roman Marcellus without a struggle in 212BC.

☞ **Fonte Ciane** (*7km south-west; leave Syracuse on Canicattini road*)
The source of the little river Ciane, which runs into the great harbour south of Syracuse (passing the scanty ruins of a Greek temple near its mouth), is celebrated as the only place in Europe where papyrus grows wild, and for its possible connection with the legendary rape of Persephone (Ciane was a nymph in Persephone's entourage).

☞ **Palazzolo Acréide** (*43km west*)

An attractive but in no way exceptional old town near the site of
Akrai, one of the earliest Syracusan settlements (7th century BC).
Although often omitted from itineraries of Sicily's important sites, it
is well worth a visit, even for non-specialists. There is a small Greek
theatre (3rd-century BC) and quarries with recesses originally
occupied by commemorative plaques and offerings, and chambers
used for burial in the early Christian and Byzantine periods and later
turned into Arab dwellings. The "Panorama Road" above the town
skirts the acropolis and gives splendid views including a honeycomb
cliff used as a Greek necropolis. The custodian can give access to an
unusual series of twelve sculptures of the goddess Cybele (3rd-
century BC); ask for "*i santoni*".

☞ **Pantálica** (*53km west, reached via Floridia and Ferla*)

The most important prehistoric site on the island, a huge necropolis
of some 5,000 rock tombs from the 13th to the 8th centuries BC. The
wide limestone plateau was first occupied as a retreat from coastal
trading settlements in the face of external threat, and became a very
large Sikel town usually identified with ancient Hybla. Abandoned
at about the time of the foundation of Syracuse, Pantalica once more
served as a place of refuge from barbarian raids in the 5th and 6th
centuries AD, when the tombs were used as dwellings.

TAORMINA

One of the most famous beauty spots in the world, and the only
place in Sicily which is a major international resort and which lives
off tourism. In these ways its atmosphere is closer to the picturesque
resorts of the Amalfi coast than it is to the rest of Sicily. Like them it
is an excellent base for excursions, except in midsummer and at
weekends when the coastal traffic is often so bad that the shortest
excursions may take hours.

Taormina's uniquely privileged position makes it the royal box in
one of the grandest of nature's theatres, the capabilities of which
were exploited by the Greeks and Romans who built a theatre in a
perfect setting. The resort stands perched on the lower of a
descending series of crags nearly a thousand feet above the coast,
where railway line, coast roads and traffic are very uncomfortably
jammed between cliff and water. Taormina's growth has been
limited by geography, and recently the coastline below has turned
into a long stretch of tourist development, more convenient for
beach-lovers but without the charm of the old hill-village, now a
hill-town.

There are wonderful views in all directions, by day and night. To
the north the mountainous Sicilian coast converges with the dark
hills of Calabria across the water, and to the south stands Mount
Etna, seen from just the right height and at just the right distance for
appreciation of the overall coastal composition of which the volcano
is the towering centrepiece. It nearly always puffs intermittently like
an indolent pipe-smoker. By day the smoke darkens any fluffy white
cloud; by night the coastline and inshore waters twinkle into the

distance as if with phosphorescence, and the most fortunate spectators are treated to a display of fireworks from the volcano.

The resort is surrounded by a very narrow one-way circuit where pedestrians and frustrated motorists vie for priority. Parking is usually extremely difficult, and tourists passing through Taormina for a quick visit should consider leaving the car down below at Mazzaro and catching the cable-car up and down. (The cable-car doesn't run late enough in the evening for this to be practical for a night out).

The centre of the old village is a maze of steep, narrow streets, mostly reserved for pedestrians; it is still very charming in a restored and stagey way, with colourful window boxes, outdoor cafés on the small squares and a cheerful abundance of tourist shops. Painted pottery is the main speciality. Evenings are lively with bars and discothèques as well as lots of restaurants. There are regular evening performances in the Graeco-Roman theatre, which is much more Roman than Graeco. There are many restored medieval buildings as well as plenty of foolish pastiches; but with the exception of the theatre and its famous view of Etna framed by its ruined arches and columns, Taormina is not so much a place for seeing sights as for milling around in the throng and unwinding in what is by Sicilian standards a very sophisticated resort, not unlike Mykonos with its mixture of residual, slightly off-beat elegance and brash mass tourism. Taormina attracted Allied bombs in 1943; more recently it has suffered, inevitably, from the advent of package tours and the building of large new hotels and anonymous noisy night-spots to accommodate and entertain them. Those who knew Taormina in its quieter days say that the place has been spoilt beyond recognition, but first-time visitors are less likely to be appalled, for most of the spoiling has happened down by the shore. There are still small, friendly, and very individual villa hotels with steep terraced gardens looking out over the coast, little affected by the turn of touristic events, and where it is easy to enjoy an easy life of idleness in an enchanting setting just as more leisured generations of travellers used to do (DH Lawrence is their most famous representative).

Excursions from Taormina

☞ **Naxos** (*7km south*)

The first Greek settlement on Sicily (about 750BC) on Capo Schiso, a promontory south of Taormina and closing the bay of Giardini. Naxos never became a city of importance and, having backed the wrong side during the Athenian war, was destroyed in 403BC by Dionysius of Syracuse. The archaeological site is not yet a particularly interesting one.

☞**Gole dell' Alcantara** (*about 15km west*)

An impressive rocky canyon on the course of the river Alcántara which, unlike most Sicilian rivers, is not dry in summer. This is a pretty place for sunbathing and cool picnics, but is a standard coach trip from Taormina and nearby beach resorts and gets accordingly crowded. The visit can be fitted into an excursion to the north-eastern slopes of Etna and Randazzo (*see separate entries*). There are splendid pine woods between the lava-cobbled town of **Lingualossa** (*37km south-west*) and **Mareneve**, a modest base camp for winter skiing and summer coach rides up to Etna's main crater. The road back from Lingualossa gives beautiful views of the setting of Taormina.

☞ **Santi Pietro e Paolo** (*19km north*)

A beautiful, isolated Norman church among lemon groves beside the usually dry river Agrò whose bed joins the sea between Forza d'Agrò and Santa Teresa di Riva. The church, which is not well signed, can be reached either from Sávoca or Scifi, or by driving up the river bed. (If the river is in spate, use the Sávoca approach). Built for Greek monks in the early 12th century, the church bears a dedicatory inscription in Greek from 1172. The exterior is decorated with colourful patterns of brick, limestone and lava; inside, a honeycomb dome reveals Arab influence. The building is kept closed, but there may be someone around who has a key.

(*See also Mount Etna; Randazzo; Giardini-Naxos*)

TÉRMINI IMERESE

A dull coastal town founded by the Carthaginians after the destruction of Mimera at the end of the 5th century BC, and an important spa from Roman times on. Termini's waters are good for arthritis and for the production of prestige-quality pasta. There is not much to see in the town but it is well worth driving up into the hills south of Termini for the coastal views and to explore **Cáccamo**, a steeply pitched old village dominated by the towers and battlements of a magnificent castle, most of it medieval.

TÍNDARI

Remains of an ancient city on a beautiful headland west of Milazzo, the site of its acropolis now dominated by a vast and gaudy modern pilgrimage basilica which has the rare distinction, shared with Sacré-Coeur in Paris, of being uglier than the cheap plastic replicas of itself that fill the souvenir stalls outside. The object of veneration is a Black Virgin, clothed in white, on display inside the church.

Tyndaris was a late Greek colony, founded by Syracuse in the early 4th century as a defence against possible Carthaginian attack from the north. Some of the Greek walls and a monumental gateway are visible from the road leading up to the basilica. The excavated site of the Greek and later Roman city includes a small theatre looking out to sea, now once again used for performances, and the so-called Basilica, a monumental gateway and vaulted passage dating from the 1st century BC.

TRÁPANI

A large port at the foot of Mount Érice, important in ancient and medieval times as a trading post between Europe and Africa, and still used by ferries to and from Sardinia and Tunis (the frequent presence of Arabs hawking goods or simply hanging around on the

dusty quayside contributes to the rather middle-eastern
atmosphere). Most of the local maritime activity is now connected
with tuna fishing and salt industries. Trápani was severely damaged
by bombs in the Second World War and much of the town is new
and unattractive. The unspoilt old part of town occupies the
blade-shaped tongue of land between sea and harbour (where a
fortress is now used as a prison). Trápani has numerous moderately
interesting sights (mostly churches along the regular grid of streets
near the harbour) but no individual building of outstanding interest
and, pleasant as it is, is not worth a major detour. Sightseers
determined to do it justice should not omit the **museum** (Museo
Pedoli), attractively housed in a convent with a fine medieval and
Baroque church, on the inland outskirts of town.

The **Egadi Islands**, served by hydrofoil from Trápani, are mainly
of interest to fishermen.

Hotels

Agrigento ££
VILLA ATHENA *Open all year*
Via dei Templi 33, 92100 Agrigento *Tel: (0922) 23833*

A perfectly sited hotel overlooking the astonishing Valley of Temples which
you will have come to Agrigento to see. It is a handsome 18th century villa
which was converted to a hotel in 1972; the decoration is somewhat worn.
Some bedrooms open onto a terracotta terrace overlooking the Temple of
Concord, where breakfast can be served.The drawbacks of the hotel – there is
no lounge, for instance – are compensated for by the situation and the lovely
garden with a pleasant pool area. The restaurant, under a separate roof, is
popular with locals, especially at Sunday lunch.

Facilities: *41 bedrooms (AC); restaurant; swimming pool* **Credit/charge cards
accepted:** *none*

Erice ££
MODERNO *Open all year*
Via Vittorio Emanuele 67, 91016 Trapani *Tel: (0932) 869300*

A friendly owner-managed hotel in the charming old hilltop town of Erice.
Apart from pine furniture there is nothing particularly modern about it, but it
is neat and well-kept and has a cosy atmosphere. There is an elegant
parquet-floored dining room and a terrace for drinks. A good base for a night
or two on a touring holiday; Segesta is 40km away.

Facilities: *40 bedrooms; restaurant; lift; garage* **Credit/charge cards accepted:**
Amex, Diners, Visa

Giardini Naxos
ARATHENA ROCKS
Via Calcide Eubea 55, 98035 Messina

££
Closed Nov to Mar
Tel: (0942) 51349

A charming hotel in a secluded position at the edge of the busy little resort of
Giardini Naxos. It is family-run and to a great extent retains the atmosphere
of a private home; there are comfortable sitting rooms with loose covered
armchairs, antique furniture and vases of gladioli and lilies and, in the
bedrooms, furniture painted in traditional style by the manager's wife. The
dining room is a cool trattoria where traditional Sicilian cooking is adapted to
today's lighter appetite.

Facilities: *52 bedrooms; restaurant; lift; swimming pool; tennis court; parking*
Credit/charge cards accepted: *Amex, Diners, Visa*

Palermo
VILLA IGIEA
Salita Belmonte 43, 90100 Palermo

££££
Open all year
Tel: (091) 543744

A castellated villa built at the turn of the century as a watering hole for the
nobility, now an oasis in the suburban sprawl of Palermo. Rooms are
enormous, and very grand, with the original art nouveau decoration. Sepia
photographs recall the good old days before the shipyards had encroached
on the views. Although the air is heavy with nostalgia, this is still a very
civilised and comfortable place to stay; the gardens and pool are splendid
and only the cooking is a disappointment.

Facilities: *118 bedrooms (AC); restaurant; lift; swimming pool; tennis court;
parking* **Credit/charge cards accepted:** *Amex, Diners, Eurocard, Visa*

Syracuse
VILLA POLITI
Via M. Politi Laudien 2, 96100 Siracusa

££
Open all year
Tel: (0931) 32100

Another grand old hotel, sadly past its prime, but with considerably more
charm than its modern counterparts. The villa is dilapidated and the interior
in need of redecoration, but there is a good swimming pool.

Facilities: *90 bedrooms (AC); restaurant; lift; swimming pool; tennis court;
parking* **Credit/charge cards accepted:** Amex, Diners, Eurocard, Visa

---

Our price symbols

£   = you can expect to find a room for under £35
££   = you can expect to find a room for under £55
£££   = you can expect to find a room for under £75
££££   = you can expect to find a room for under £125
£££££ = you should expect to pay over £125 for a room

Taormina   £££££
SAN DOMENICO PALACE   *Open all year*
Piazza San Domenico 5, 98039 Messina   Tel: (0942) 23701

Secluded in its own gardens below the tourist hubbub of Taormina, this is
Taormina's grandest hotel, originally a monastery. Inside it is very large and
grand, but rather gloomy and eccentric; the public rooms are filled with
antique furniture and paintings, but they're predominantly brown and dark.
By contrast the glassed-in courtyard, with its palms and a little wall trailing
with bougainvillea, is enchanting. So too are the glorious terraced gardens,
brimming with heavily-scented flowers in summer, and overlooking the sea
and, to the left, the Greek theatre. The pool is in a rather cramped area, near
the road. The bedrooms, which we have not been able to inspect, are the
original monks' cells.

Facilities: *117 bedrooms (AC); restaurant; lift; swimming pool (heated); tennis court;
parking*   **Credit/charge cards accepted:** *Amex, Diners, Eurocard, Visa*

Taormina   ££
TIMÉO   *Closed Nov to Mar*
Via Teatro Greco 59   Tel: (0942) 23801

A quiet, civilised hotel next to the entrance to the Greek Temple, and with
beautiful views from the restaurant terrace. At the time of going to press the
hotel was closed for extensive redecorations which should be completed by
spring 1988.

Facilities: *50 bedrooms; restaurant; lift; parking*   **Credit/charge cards accepted:**
Amex, Diners, Eurocard, Visa

Taormina   ££
VILLA BELVEDERE   *Closed mid-Nov to March*
Via Bagnoli Croce 79, 98039 Messina   Tel: (0942) 23791

One of the cheaper hotels in Taormina, the Belvedere is small, friendly and
civilised. It lies close to the public gardens just out of the centre. It is a family
enterprise, run by a French husband and Italian wife. Bedrooms are simply
furnished but the majority have magnificent views across the bay: the best
are the ground floor rooms with large terraces; the worst are the few noisy
rooms at the back of the hotel which are best avoided altogether. There are
two little salons and an attractive breakfast room with pillars and white
arches. The garden leads down to a small heated pool with its own bar.

Facilities: *36 bedrooms; swimming pool (heated); parking (limited)*   **Credit/charge
cards accepted:** *Eurocard, Visa*

Taormina　　　　　　　　　　　　　　　　　　　　££
VILLA PARADISO　　　　　　　　　　　*Closed Nov to mid-Dec*
Via Roma 2, 98039 Messina　　　　　　　*Tel: (0942) 23921*

Not unlike the Villa Belvedere, but a bit more comfortable, the Paradiso is a
white creeper-clad villa which also enjoys superb views of the bay and Etna.
It's also very close to the centre of town. Various small salons are furnished
in the style of a private villa with white arches, elegant seating and an
interesting collection of watercolours. The taverna style restaurant overlooks
the bay. Bedrooms at the back are a bit noisy but the majority are quiet and
comfortable with separate sitting areas and reproduction antiques or painted
furniture. There is free use of the tennis court in the public gardens opposite,
and a private bus to the beach.

Facilities: *33 bedrooms (AC); restaurant; lift*　　**Credit/charge cards accepted:**
Amex, Diners, Eurocard, Visa

Taormina　　　　　　　　　　　　　　　　　　　　£££
VILLA SANT' ANDREA　　　　　　　　　　*Closed Nov to Mar*
Via Nazionale 137, 98030 Mazzarò　　　　*Tel: (0942) 23125*

The Villa Sant' Andrea was converted into a hotel by its English owners in
1950 and it combines the best of Italian style with a slightly English country
house atmosphere; the blend of fresh modern fabrics and antiques is very
successful. Bedrooms are comfortable and pleasantly unfussy. The emphasis
is on the restaurants, both a stone's throw from the beach. The main
restaurant, Oliviero's, is cool and predominantly white with good quality
rattan furniture and fresh floral curtains. There is a shaded terrace for
outdoor dining, and lovely gardens lead down to a small pebbly beach where
the hotel provides deck-chairs and sun umbrellas.

Facilities: *36 bedrooms + annexe with 14 bedrooms (AC); restaurant*　　**Credit/
charge cards accepted:** *Amex, Diners, Eurocard, Visa*

SARDINIA

❝Sardinia, which is like nowhere. Sardinia,
which has no history, no date, no race, no
offering. Let it be Sardinia❞
DH LAWRENCE

Porto Rafael

Introduction

Living at Taormina in early 1921, DH Lawrence quite suddenly and quite simply felt the need for a change. It was a toss-up between Spain and Sardinia, Sardinia won the toss, and le ménage Lawrence set off without further ado for the island "outside the circuit of civilisation". The idea of a holiday destination which is "like nowhere" (not like nowhere else, but like nowhere) has stayed with Sardinia; it strikes a chord with many a holidaymaker fed up with the sightseeing trail and fed up with brochures and guide books that force-feed history and culture, telling of battles where there are ploughed fields and open hillsides, telling of architecture where there are places of human worship, and rating the beauty of a landscape on an arid arithmetical scale. Perhaps the most famous thing about Sardinia is what Lawrence wrote about the town of Nuoro, namely that there is "nothing to see. Sights are an irritating bore. I am sick of things....". How can those who want nothing more than to find "a place in the sun" fail to warm to such a promise (especially when this particular nowhere has a reputation as one of the most stylish and luxurious places in the Mediterranean to do nothing)?

Lawrence's idea of Sardinia is characteristically overstated. The island has a race, a language and even a culture very much its own, it has its history and for the last 500 years it has been no more cut off from the circuit of civilisation than any other Mediterranean island. All the same, the impression he has left of the island is still more right than it is wrong, despite important changes to the Sardinian style of life since the War. The contrast between the two major Italian islands, very similar in size (Sicily is a few square miles larger), could hardly be greater. Sardinians are few in number (about 1 ½ million), and their island is on of the most sparsely populated regions of Italy. Much of the coast remains deserted or inaccessible and there are only short stretches of coastal road or railway. Apart from Cágliari and Sássari (which account for a quarter of the island's population) there are no big towns, and the pattern of settlement is large, widely spread inland villages with few isolated dwellings between them. The result is that the most enduring memory of travelling around the large island is one of emptiness and space. But the greatest contrast of all, and the reason why a visit to Sardinia is of a quite different nature from visits to most other Italian regions, is that there is little to see (and what there is has not much to do with Italy).

The history of Sardinia, the Mediterranean island furthest from any mainland, is one of isolation. For over two thousand years it has not mattered very much to anyone (except Nelson, who considered it to be the key to control of the western Mediterranean and who tried to persuade the king of Sardinia to sell his island to the British for £500,000) and it has been little touched by the currents of European civilisation – artistic, economic, social or political. Deprived in many ways, it has also been untainted. As on many remote islands, things have survived which evolution has elsewhere consigned to history. In other places these things are wildlife, like Australia's egg-laying mammals and marsupials. Sardinia has its own animals, including wild sheep or mouflons, white donkeys and flocks of wild horses so shy and so remote in choice of habitat that little is known about them (no carcass has ever been found). But the most interesting survivals are the Sards, whose dialects, clothes, customs and even physical type make the island the ethnographic. museum of the Mediterranean.

Great fascination lies in the knowledge that the race has its roots in a prehistoric culture that was certainly among the most individual and vigorous in the Mediterranean world before Sardinia suffered invasion from Carthage in the 6th century BC. Not much is known about the people, but they left behind them thousands of conical, tower-like dwellings and fortresses (*nuraghi*) and some interesting works of art. In the face of invasion, military defeat and partial colonisation, the Sards retreated inland and in the remote, mountainous country of the interior of the island nothing happened for century upon century to change the stock or the way of life of a people who can reasonably be looked upon as the direct descendants of the *nuraghi*-builders. These people of the Barbágia region south of Núoro are a race of shepherds: Sardinia's sheep population of 2.5 million accounts for one third of the Italian total and in the Barbágia sheep outnumber people eight to one. The men spend months on end alone with their flocks, following them around the high country and down into the plains to the west in autumn, living off bread and ricotta, making cheese individually in makeshift factories, and leaving their families grouped together in large villages. The dialects retain many archaisms, including the use of *domus* instead of the Italian *casa* and *andamus* instead of *andiamo*. Items of clothing, including the male's stocking cap and jerkin, and musical instruments have undergone no evolution since pre-Roman times. Sards often use a "th" sound instead of s or z (Sássari is pronounced thathari) and any map shows use of j, k, and x, all absent from the Italian alphabet. Needless to say, the shepherds are not very communicative and not many of us would find it illuminating if they were. Their folklore is rich and includes many strange, primitive customs attending marriage, birth and death. The shepherds, who have plenty of time for contemplation and composition, maintain a strong poetic tradition, stage rural competitions in impromptu recitation, and are given to outbursts of spontaneous wailing song. The easiest way to gain some flavour of Sardinian folklore is to attend one of the many local festivals, some of which attract pilgrims from all over the island in a great gathering of the clans with all the colourful variety of local costumes on display. Many of the religious festivals are accompanied by undisguised remnants of pagan ritual and all are followed by plenty of simple celebratory singing, dancing, eating and drinking.

The subtitle "unknown island" has become one of the clichés of Sardinian tourist promotion. That there is an island people and an island way of life to get to know is not in question. What is more

doubtful in these days of convenience holidays close to home and
easy access to the most distant corners of the world is whether many
people have the time and the desire, or committed curiosity,
undoubtedly required to come to discover much about an island
which may seem rather dull compared with the Far East, South
America or even Turkey. It was different in the old days, before
travel was redefined by Baedeker and all his descendants; when
folklore was real and when such matters as the temperament of the
local men and the characteristic dress and beauty (or otherwise) of
the local women were a source of endless fascination for travellers.
Not only did these things have some meaning, but it was also much
easier than it is now to find out what local life was all about; in fact, it
was impossible to travel and not find out about it. Murray's
Handbook (to Corsica and Sardinia) advised that "In Sardinia inns
are the exception, for we cannot dignify with such an appellation the
houses without doors and windows and without any other
refreshment than some bad wine, which the wayfarer will find in
the principal villages". In these circumstances, the wayfarer was
strongly advised to travel with letters of introduction provided by
the British consul in Genoa and, thus armed, he travelled straight to
the heart of island life. Nowadays, while much of the island is still
without inns worthy of the appellation, the Sards are no longer in
the habit of taking travellers into their homes, which does not make
things easy for the curious wayfarer.

It is interesting that, for all his delight in the "open, manly and
downright" nature of the Sards, with their stocking-cap a flag of
obstinate resistance to the "cosmopolitanism and internationalism"
of the big world, the Lawrences stayed only six days on the island
and were well-pleased to get back to the mainland and then to the
"loveliness of the tall coasts" of Sicily. The 200-odd pages devoted to
this brief excursion leave a strong impression that the writer enjoyed
the writing a good deal more than the travel. Sórgono, which they
had approached with keen anticipation, turned out to be rather
over-simple even for a man of Lawrence's rough and ready tastes.
They found no sanitation, had trouble locating a fire (it was
February) and a meal, and they were downright shocked by the
"degenerate aborigines" who used the unlit streets for their
ablutions. They could hardly leave fast enough, and even Núoro
detained them less than 24 hours. So much for the nobility of the
savage, the joy of nothing to see and the contempt for the
Baedeker/Michelin mentality.

Similarly, much of Sardinian scenery makes better reading than
prolonged viewing from inside a car. After Italy, "almost always
dramatic, and perhaps invariably romantic", Sardinia is indeed
"another thing. Much wider, much more ordinary, not up-and-
down at all, but running away into the distance". It is indeed "like
liberty itself after the peaky confinement of Sicily", but scenery is not
life: liberty is not everything, and most of us can have too much of a
good thing. Once thickly wooded, Sardinia is no longer so, and large
tracts of the interior are clothed with waist-high macchia – a
near-impenetrable mixed vegetation of thickly-intertwined herbs

and shrubs, sweetly fragrant and colourful in spring, but not so delightful in high summer when the prevailing countryside smell is the smell of fire, burning or burnt out.

As it happens, Sardinia is far from flat, and there are landscapes of wild, sweeping splendour in the Gennargentu mountains south of Núoro; but even in these parts moments of drama are rare and Sardinia cannot compare with neighbouring Corsica for mountain spectacle and varied scenic interest. The shepherds' villages are mostly unpicturesque, their architectural style being unadorned and now characterised by half-finished new houses bristling with the structural rods of storeys to be built when the postman brings the next bundle of savings sent back from abroad.

The trouble is that the island is big (three times Corsica's size) and journeys are infrequently punctuated by points of interest; a touring holiday may seem quite a slog with little prospect of a reward, in the form of friendly hotel and restaurant, at the end of a long day's driving. In order to appeal as a whole, Sardinia ought to be a lot smaller, like a medium-sized Greek island.

As it is, Sardinia does appeal greatly and has developed its own distinct style of Mediterranean tourism. That style has little to do with the real life of the island, for the tourist development is confined to exploiting the potential of Sardinia's one thousand miles of mostly empty coast. Most consumers of Sardinian holidays stay in a new coastal resort and the nearest they get to discovering the unknown island is going on an organised picnic excursion into the hills where some Sard dons a local costume and roasts a wild pig on a spit, preferably without setting fire to the macchia in the course of the proceedings. The coast is well-suited to development, being empty, unpolluted and in many places sandy, but the lack of many existing villages or roads has made development expensive and slow, and large areas are still almost untouched. There are no very large resorts and crowded beaches are rare even in August. The weather is good enough for a six-month summer season and the breezes excellent for sailing.

The flagship of Sardinian tourism is the Costa Smeralda, a small strip of the wild and fragmented north-east coast which was bought by a private development consortium and turned from nothing into an exclusive holiday area with luxury hotels, watered golf courses and holiday villages built around some of the best-equipped yacht marinas in the Mediterranean. Great care was taken to avoid the uglier aspects of development, including overcrowding, and the general style is such that luxury resort masquerades as simple Mediterranean coastal village. One of the most distinctive features of the Costa Smeralda is that everything is expensive.

The Costa Smeralda accounts for only a tiny part of the Sardinian coast and the process of developing its great potential has only begun. On either side of the Costa Smeralda are areas of less exclusive and less carefully stylish new resorts, with cheaper accommodation and a greater emphasis on beaches and nightlife and less on marinas. Very different in style is the old town and beach-resort suburb of Alghero, the only long-established resort on the island and the main British destination. Elsewhere tourism is limited to a few local resorts south of Olbia and east of Cágliari, and new self-contained projects at various points along the south coast. Much of the east coast is inaccessible from the interior and offers sailors no anchorage. The west coast is slightly more hospitable, but even here there are vast areas of emptiness, including long stretches of magnificent beach reached by rough, slow roads. In Sardinia there is still no shortage of places, and sandy beaches, that are like nowhere. Some of these places are luxury hotels with all sorts of sports facilities; others are quite undeveloped.

Not all of the interior of Sardinia is wild and mountainous

Visiting Sardinia

There are daily scheduled flights to Alghero and Cágliari but all involve a stop at Milan or Rome and the cheaper fares (PEX, APEX) are not available. You can, however, fly to Rome on a PEX or APEX ticket and then take a domestic/internal flight (with reductions for families). Charter flights go direct from London to Alghero, Cágliari and Olbia.

There are regular overnight ferries from Genoa, Livorna and Civitavecchia. All go to Olbia; those from Genoa and Livorna also go to Porto Torres, and those from Genoa and Civitavecchia also go to Cágliari. In addition there is a summer service from Civitavecchia to Golfo Aranci (on the Costa Smeralda) and from Naples to Cágliari. It is essential to book tickets; in peak season demand for car spaces and sleeping quarters is very heavy. But summer queues are notorious and there have been stories of high season bookings not being honoured for the sailing booked. Serena Holidays (40-42 Kenway Road, London SW5, tel: 01-373 6548) are the UK agents for the Tirrenia Line (most services); and CIT (50 Conduit Street, London W1, tel: 01-434 3844) for the Italian State Railways' car ferry from Civitavecchia to Golfo Aranci.

If you do take your own car to Sardinia, you probably won't do enough driving for petrol coupons to be a worthwhile investment. There are no motorways on Sardinia, but roads are generally good except in remote areas, such as the Gennargentu mountains. Detours to beaches can be long and tiring, and petrol stations are fairly few and far between (especially in the south-east) and close as early as 11.30am. In addition many inland signposts are shot out, and in the south-east tourist development around the coast has meant new roads not yet on maps. The main through routes (Cágliari to Porto Torres via Oristano and Sássari, and Cágliari to Olbia via Oristano and Núoro) are, however, fast and surprisingly empty, partly because there is comparatively little to see on the island and most holiday-makers tend to stay put and limit themselves to local excursions from their resorts. But if you do want to do a quick tour of the island a week is just about adequate to sample the different aspects of its landscape and so the modest amount of required sightseeing. Sardinia is too large (about 70 by 170 miles) to explore from a single base.

Typical organised excursions from Alghero or the Costa Smeralda are day trips to the Gennargentu mountains or Corsica and visits to nearby grottoes, boat trips to La Maddelena and Caprera and evening barbecue excursions. It is difficult to organise excursions by public transport, especially to nuraghic sites and the Pisan churches near Sássari, and it could be worth hiring a car for a day or two if you want to be independent. Also, there is no public transport on the Costa Smeralda. There are regular car ferries to the islands off the north coast, and also to Corsica (these, too, should be booked in advance – Serena Holidays (see above) are agents for Corsica Ferries). Bus services link the main towns and serve the remoter rural areas – but these

shepherd country: in all senses the island is divided by a line
running approximately north/south. To the west of the division the
land is agricultural and the ethnic stock has been diluted by foreign
settlement (mainly Pisan, Genoese and Spanish). There are fertile
plains between Cágliari and Oristano (the Campidano), vineyards
and olive groves covering large areas of the north-west and
producing some good, strong wines, and mining in the south-west.
Large areas of the notoriously unhealthy and swampy coast have
been cleared of their malaria, properly irrigated and given over to
varied agriculture, including rice, citrus fruit and artichokes. Large
refineries and petro-chemical plants have been set up near Cágliari

services are not geared to tourists and are subject to seasonal variations (they may be
reduced, for instance, during school holidays, even in high season). The train service is
more limited and slower than the bus system and gives no access to the coast except at
the main ports. However, the narrow-guage branch line from Cágliari to Sorgono and
Arbatax runs through the scenic Barbagia (Gennargentu).

None of the provincial capitals makes a good base, although Cágliari and Sássari are
worth visiting. Alghero is a good traditional choice, with a pleasant old town and
slightly old-fashioned hotels on good beaches. At the opposite end of the scale (and of
the north coast) is the Costa Smeralda, catering for the international jet-set, with
rustic-style hotels at Caribbean prices. In between are the resorts of Santa Teresa di
Gallura and Baia Sardinia, with attractive hotels and good beaches; Baia Sardinia is the
better choice if you want a bright nightlife, too. Porto Rafael has the most attractive
self-catering accommodation. There is much development in the south, but on the
whole resorts there have less to offer (isolated areas of new self-catering
development). The quality of hotels in Sardinia is generally high, especially by
comparison with much of the mainland coast, and some hotels are in the luxury
category. Most good hotels have swimming pools and many have tennis courts.
However, accommodation in towns, even in Cágliari, is dull. Most self-catering is in
large developments and holiday villages with central facilities. Campsites vary from
spacious, well-designed sites in attractive beach settings to cramped and untidy ones
with few facilities. Camping is best on the east coast, around Budoni and San Teodoro.
The area is becoming increasingly popular, especially with Germans, but is still very
quiet by Mediterranean standards.

For the purpose of escaping to Sardinia to do nothing more than wind down on a
beach (to which the island is ideally suited), the package holiday is the obvious route.
Several tour operators offer one- or two-week packages by air, with self-catering or
hotel accommodation. Alghero is the cheapest and most-used resort; packages to the
Costa Smeralda, though not cheap, are less expensive than going independently. Some
operators offer combined holidays with Corsica and Sicily, or golfing, tennis and sailing
holidays.

From May to September, Sardinia's weather is reliably hot, dry and sunny. If you have
to take a holiday in July or August, Sardinia is ideal for sunbathing, swimming or sailing
as beaches are uncrowded and there is usually a sea breeze. From October to
December there are heavy, thundery rainstorms although temperatures remain warm.
Winter on the coasts is mild but there is snow in the mountains. By early spring
temperatures climb steadily but the countryside is still green; it's a good time to tour
the island. At Easter there are traditional festivals in the villages; for a full display of
Sardinian costumes you should try to see the Sagra di Sant' Efisio in Cágliari (May 1st)
or the Cavalcata Sarda at Sássari (last Sunday in May).

and Porto Torres.

Malaria has been Sardinia's greatest scourge throughout history, certainly as powerful as geography and any external attack in persuading Sardinians to neglect their coastline until very recently, and in disenchanting outside visitors. In the 1920s 80% of the island was considered to be malarial, and Sards made up nearly half of all Italian cases of the sickness. Pomponius Mela wrote that the island was almost as pestiferous as it was fertile, and the Romans were content to have as little to do with it as they could manage while ensuring that it produced large quantities of grain. Another of its famed hazards was a poisonous parsley-like plant (perhaps ranunculus sceleratus, or celery-leaved crowfoot) which brought on facial convulsions like laughter, followed by death, in any who ate it, prompting Homer to use the term Sardonian, or as we would say sardonic, for bitter laughter that is not what it seems.

The anopheles mosquito has at last succumbed to the DDT treatment and few worry about the sardonic danger of marsh grazing. One remaining scourge is the lawlessness of the shepherd society, one of the less attractive aspects of its primitive state. The people are proud never to have been conquered and have no respect for outsiders (as they consider Italians to be) and their rules. There are similarities with the Sicilian Mafia in the conditions that have given rise to the problem and in the difficulty of securing any popular cooperation with efforts to control it. There are equally important differences, reflecting a simpler social and economic structure and perhaps the more straightforward and individualistic nature of the Sards. The traditional crime is simple theft, usually of livestock, often aggravated by murderous vendettas. Rather than rely on police help, the Sards look after themselves by organising their own groups to patrol the hills and compensate each other for losses, and they settle their own scores – so that in the statistics crime and punishment become crime and crime. More recently kidnapping has become fashionable as an even easier way to get rich than rustling, and perhaps associated with feelings of resentment at the way nothing has been done to give the Sards a share of the fruits of the island's luxury tourist development. Certainly in some areas outsiders are not made to feel immediately welcome. Notorious bandit villages in the middle of ideal hide-out country are Orune, north of Núoro, and Orgósolo to the south. During the first half of this century Orgósolo (population 4,000) averaged one murder every two months and one lesser crime every week, despite a massive police presence reaching a ratio of one policeman for five inhabitants in the 1950s. In an attempt to bring some new prosperity to the interior a new industrial town has been set up at Ottana, near Núoro, with a target population of 40,000.

Places to visit

ALGHERO

Sardinia's third town in size and its most important fishing port and tourist resort, with a traditional popularity among the British that goes back further than the most recent vogue for Sardinian holidays. The combination of walled medieval town and nearby beach resort, with a reasonable number of interesting excursions in the neighbourhood, distinguishes Alghero from other Sardinian resorts. It is less smart and up-to-date, but has the attraction of age and the greater one of real life. Judged on their own merits Alghero the old town is more distinguished than Alghero the beach resort. The town is the leading lobster port of Italy; coral is another local speciality and Alghero sardines are said to be of the highest quality.

The Algherese are proud of the fact that their real life is not at all Sardinian but Catalan. Having been founded in the early 12th century by the Dorias of Genoa and named after the local abundance of seaweed, Alghero was taken by the Aragonese in the mid-14th century after a naval battle in Porto Conte. The Algherese proved to be awkward subjects and at the end of the century they were all exiled and the town repopulated with Catalans. Laws were passed forbidding outsiders to enter the town armed or in groups of more than ten, and obliging them to leave town every evening at the sound of a trumpet. Catalans were given monopoly rights over the local fishing and the town became known as Barceloneta. Not surprisingly there has never been much love lost between the Algherese and other Sards, especially those from nearby Sássari, and the ethnic individuality of the town was not diluted. Until recently the local fishermen spoke an archaic Catalan, and bilingual naming of streets and monuments is maintained with an almost pedantic care. The fishing industry is one sign of Catalan rather than Sardinian character. Visitors in the last century discerned less industrious Spanish traits in the local people. The 19th-century traveller Walter Tyndale wrote of their pompous vanity and of a society "formal and vapid with a graft of Italian manners without the polish which characterises the best society of both countries". Earlier, Nelson had written of his astonishment at the "listless inactivity of the inhabitants and generally lethargic aspect of the town, its guns honeycombed for want of paint. For want of active commerce the grass grows on the street".

The old town occupies a promontory, and is surrounded by beautiful old walls and bastions, constructed in the 14th and 15th centuries. Its streets are cobbled, the stone is golden and the town houses handsome and substantial. The **cathedral** retains the beautifully decorated octagonal bell-tower and one doorway (both at the back of the church) from the original 16th-century building, but is otherwise uninteresting. Rather than seeing any specific sights, one wanders round old Alghero enjoying it. There are tourist shops, bars and restaurants with menus in English, but the place is by no means overrun. The Piazza Sulis is the focus of evening life.

The modern tourist development of the resort exists on both sides of the old town and harbour. The smarter hotels, several of them with their own small private beaches, are to the south. The main beach extends northward beside the road to Porto Conte, and there are campsites and cheaper hotels beside the road and railway. Much of this noisy, scruffy sector is further than a stroll from the old town.

Excursions from Alghero

☞ **Fertilia** (*6km north*)
New town founded in 1936 on the edge of a large area of agricultural redevelopment, and populated with refugees from Istria (part of Italy ceded to Yugoslavia). Typical of its period, the architectural style is decidedly overweight. Nearby are sandy beaches with accommodation and, beside the road towards Porto Conte, remains of a fortified *nuraghic* village (Nuraghe Palmavera).

☞ **Porto Conte** (*13km north-west*)
The Roman Portus Nympharum, a magnificent natural harbour sheltered by two rocky promontories. There are a few quiet hotels among the trees beside the weedy water on the eastern side of the bay, and another in a splendid but windy situation beside the old lighthouse (now a nightclub) on the point. The more exposed western promontory is **Capo Cáccia**, an imposing mountainous mass of reddish limestone, its weather-beaten cliffs rising some 600 feet from the sea. There is a road along its sheltered side and up to the top, where a long staircase (over 600 steps) now leads down to the famous **Grotta di Nettuno**, previously only accessible by sea, still the most enjoyable and least exhausting way to visit the grotto. Boat trips lasting about three hours are organised twice a day from Alghero provided the sea is calm. This is the most spectacular of Sardinian grottoes, a beautiful natural architecture of stalagmites and 'tites reflected in the clear waters of a lake. The boat trip includes other nearby caves. The Neptune cave has been known for centuries, and was equipped with lights by Admiral Smyth in 1824. Tyndale reported that it was inaccessible 300 days a year, but was lucky. He was reminded of Wells chapter house, Christ Church Oxford and the Alhambra, and found visiting the grotto equal in magnificence to a night on Mount Vesuvius during one of the great eruptions of the century (19th) when the principal and nine minor craters were pouring forth their fiery wrath.

☞ **Argentiera** (*38km north-west*)
An abandoned and atmospheric silver mining town founded in Roman times, with fine coastal views.

ARBATAX

A small village on a bay providing a rare anchorage on the southern half of the east coast. There is a long beach beneath red cliffs and some simple accommodation.

BARÚMINI

Village 60km north of Cágliari near the most important *nuraghic* site on the island.
(See Prehistory, page 487)

BOSA

A small town in the fertile valley of Sardinia's only navigable river, the Temo, a short distance from its mouth (Bosa Marina). Bosa is overlooked by the ruins of a 13th-century Genoese castle, a short walk up from the cathedral. The only other building of interest is the church of San Pietro (11th- to 13th- century), about a mile to the south-east. The architecture is attractively rough and simple and the farmyard surroundings add to its charm. It was previously part of a Cistercian monastery.

Until recently famous as one of the most unhealthy places on an unhealthy island, Bosa is now known for its lace, leather and sweet malvasia wine. There is some fishing activity, and boats are moored along the town's green river banks.

Bosa Marina is a smelly little place with a litter-prone beach, a sailboarding school, and not many tourists from further abroad than Bosa. The new road to Alghero (37km) hugs the rocky coast, giving beautiful views but no access to beaches.

CÁGLIARI

Sardinia's capital and main port, and the only place on the island with the atmosphere of a modern city. Its history is long and mostly undistinguished. Having been much favoured as a wide and safe port by Phoenicians, Carthaginians and Romans, Cágliari attracted Arab attacks in the early Middle Ages and resisted with courage and success. Independence ended in the 13th century when the city came under first Pisan and later Aragonese control. Several centuries of Spanish rule finished ingloriously in 1708 when the city yielded to a small Austro/British naval force without a fight. In order to save the Spanish viceroy some embarrassment the British admiral was persuaded to deliver a small bombardment after the city had surrendered so as not to give the impression of too easy a victory.

Although life ticks over faster than elsewhere on the island, Cágliari is not exactly frenetic. It suffered severe bomb damage in 1943 but the heart of the old city retains plenty of picturesque, run-down charm. This old part of town (Castello) is set on a hill climbing steeply above the harbour front, within and immediately surrounding the walls of an old citadel originally build by Cágliari's Pisan occupiers in the 13th century. Although it is possible to drive up to Castello, its tortuous streets and staircases are best explored on foot, starting from the Piazza Costituzione. A terrace at the top of the staircase gives splendid views over coast, city and sea; reciprocally, the sight of the citadel above the arcaded buildings of the busy, tree-lined harbour frontage presents the sailor with the most handsome view of Cágliari.

Until the end of the 19th century the city did not extend beyond the immediate surroundings of the citadel, and there is little that is particularly interesting or attractive about the rest of the city, which now covers a large area. The parallel Via Roma and Via Sardegna by the harbour are popular for idling, eating and drinking. The Via Garibaldi, running north from the main Piazza Costituzione, is the smartest part of town for clothes shopping, and other nearby shops sell Sardinian textiles, jewellery and other handicraft.

The coast to the west is dominated by gleaming refineries and a new industrial port; to the east lie Cágliari's beaches, starting with a long stretch of sandy suburban lido (**Poetto**). Cágliari is flanked by numerous *stagni*, swampy areas once occupied by rivers and in many cases below sea level. Those which have not been turned into salt-pans are much favoured by fishermen and migrant bird life, including flamingoes.

One of the great events of the Sardinian year is the Sacra di Sant' Efisio, a pilgrimage festival lasting from the 1st to the 4th of May, celebrating the delivery of Cágliari from plague in the 17th century, attributed to the influence of a Roman general, Christian convert and martyr. A procession accompanies a statue of the saint to and from the chapel on the site of his martyrdom at Nora (38km from Cágliari). For spectators the great interest of the event is the variety of costumes from all corners of the island.

Main sights in the old town (Castello)

☛ **Archaeological museum**   The best museum on the island for an appreciation of Nuraghic civilisation, although the standard of presentation and explanation is not the highest. The great interest of the museum is the collection of bronze statuettes, the largest in existence.

☛ **Cathedral** (Santa Cecilia)   The original features of the Pisan Romanesque building are the 12th-century pulpits (hand-me-downs from Pisa cathedral) near the main entrance, the four lions on the steps outside, the bell tower and transept doorways. The façade is modern (in a Romanesque style), the interior mostly Baroque. The vaulted sacristy gives access to a small museum housing the cathedral treasure, including a triptych by Flemish Renaissance artist Gerard David. This is said to have been stolen from the pope's bedroom during the sack of Rome by a Spanish mercenary blessed with a good eye and the good fortune to survive a stormy shipwreck near Cágliari on his way home. The painting also survived and he presented it to the cathedral in grateful repentance.

Other sights

☛ **Basilica of San Saturnino**   A beautiful domed, cruciform 5th-century church, meticulously restored after bomb damage in 1943. The church commemorates the martyrdom on this spot of the early Christian Saturnus, Cágliari's patron.

☛ **Roman Amphitheatre**   Built, or rather carved out of the rock, in the 3rd century AD, on the north-western slopes of the citadel. Theatre performances are often held here.

CALA GONONE

A small seaside village near Dorgali, reached dramatically by a road which drops steeply from a tunnel through the mountain. Looking up at the forbidding wall of grey rock, it is not hard to understand why few places along this eastern coastline are accessible. Neither the beach nor the style of the recent development of the village as a resort is particularly inviting, but Cala Gonone has scarcity value and the added attraction of a boat trip and guided tour of the nearby **Grotta del Bue Marino** named after its colony of seals, the last in the Mediterranean. The seals are only occasionally visible, but one has been carved in the cliff nearby. There is plenty of natural sculpture to admire in the rock forms of the cavernous halls and tunnels making up the tour, eerie effects of reflection in the dark waters, and often impressive bellowing of the sea crashing around the rocks below. The trip usually takes place twice a day, and lasts about two hours including the boat rides.

CAMPIDANO

The wide plain running between Cágliari and Oristano, separating the mineral-rich mountains of the south-western corner (the Iglesiente) from the wilds of the Barbágia. The Campidano is now the most fertile part of the island, and one of the least interesting to see. Sometimes referred to as the Prato Africano, it features houses of sun-baked mud and straw, some of them whitewashed, and cactus hedges.

CAPRERA

(See La Maddalena)

CARLOFORTE

(See San Pietro)

CASTELSARDO

An impressively-situated fortress village, small resort and fishing port (famous for its lobsters) on a rocky promontory in the middle of the north coast. Its changes of name tell its history: from the early 12th century it was Castel Genovese, from the mid-15th Castel Aragonese, and since the mid-18th (when Sardinia passed into the hands of the house of Savoy) Castelsardo. There are a few scraps of beach near the fishing harbour at the foot of the steep rock, but the main tourist attraction is the area of narrow cobbled streets around the severe fortress on top, and the beautiful views of the rocks and beaches along the north coast. Shops sell the basketwork (dwarf palm is the raw material) which is a local speciality, and there are usually people working at it in front of their houses. The **cathedral** contains a beautiful 15th-century painting of the Virgin and Child by an artist known only as the Castelsardo master.

Excursions from Castelsardo
☞ **Elephant Rock** *(6km south-east)*   ▷ page 488

PREHISTORY

Writings about Sardinia rarely omit two observations about the island. The first is how appropriate it is (for an island where folklore involves so much dressing up) that the one Italian word "costume" carries both meanings of custom and costume, a point which could presumably be made with equal validity about the English and their habits. The other is the paradox that the most interesting period of Sardinian history is the period about which least is known. This is another way of saying that the most interesting period of Sardinian history is its prehistory, of which our understanding is by definition limited. It is not simply that the rest of Sardinia's history is so boring: before being stopped in its tracks by invasion and conquest during the first millennium BC, Sardinia's native civilisation was highly developed and individual. Unfortunately writing was not its strong suit, and the information given by ancient writers (mainly Greek) about the history of Sardinia and the origins of its people is unconvincing.

Man reached remote Sardinia relatively late, probably at the end of the 3rd millennium BC. There is no firm evidence of Phoenician settlement earlier than the end of the 9th century and only the most imprecise certainty of some earlier contact, or shared inheritance, with other Mediterranean peoples. The island may have been the home of the mysterious warlike sea people called Shardana, referred to in Egyptian writings of 1,400 to 1,200 BC as being people from Mediterranean islands; alternatively some of the Shardana may have ended up on Sardinia and given their name to it. A Sardinian tribe called the Balari may have settled on the Balearics; or perhaps the Balari were Balearic people who settled on Sardinia. There is a story that Nora was founded by an Iberian king Norax, and there are obvious similarities between that name and the ancient name for Majorca (Nura) and the monuments which have given their name to the Nuraghic civilisation.

Archaeologists have studied sacred wells, rock tombs known as witches' houses (*domus de janas*), collective burial monuments known as giants' tombs (*tombe di giganti*) and standing stones. They have yielded some secrets about the people of the 2nd millennium BC and their ways of worship. Building techniques show a gradual development culminating in the island's most distinctive monument and one of the characteristic features of the Sardinian countryside, the *nuraghe*, in its simplest form a conical tower built of massive stone blocks. The builders surrounded each completed ring of stones with earth before rolling up blocks for the next layer, ending up with a buried building which was finally stripped of its earth casing. No mortar was used and the *nuraghi* were either slab-roofed or vaulted. Similar structures, although less numerous and less elaborate, are to be found on the Balearics and on Corsica, and there are similarities with the Mycenean vaulted tholos chambers.

Nuraghi were built over a long period from about 1,400 to 300 BC, and vary greatly in function and complexity, with fortresses, watchtowers and simple dwellings all conforming to the same basic structural pattern. The main stimuli to development were the economic and cultural ones of peaceful Phoenician settlement (8th century), bringing trade and wealth and the first exploitation of Sardinia's mining resources, followed by invasion and war with Carthage (6th century) when the nuraghe developed into a more complicated structure designed to resist sieges, battering rams and other offensive missiles. The towers became central keeps of large fortified areas, with high entrances reached only by portable ladders and discontinuous staircases in the dim interiors designed to confuse intruders. Later *nuraghi* were built after the Sards succumbed and retreated to the more remote regions of central and eastern Sardinia outside Carthaginian and Roman control, and were used as places of refuge and bases for guerilla warfare.

PREHISTORY

There are some 7,000 *nuraghi* on the islands, most densely concentrated in a diagonal band across the island from south to north-west, in the areas around Sássari, Alghero, Macomer, and north of Cágliari. Among the thousands, two are outstanding in size and in having been thoroughly, although certainly not exhaustively, excavated. At both sites there is sometimes a guide on hand to illuminate and explain, but often there is not; it is always worth carrying a torch when visiting *nuraghi*. Part of their charm is their roughness and the lack of attention they have received from restorers, fencers in, labellers and ticket collectors; overgrown, dilapidated and in many cases still buried, the stumpy towers are part of the Sardinian landscape.

Su Nuraxi, just outside the village of **Barúmini** 60km north of Cágliari, was probably the most important Nuraghic settlement on the island. In the middle of a wide plain stands a tall central tower thought to date from the 14th or 15th century BC, originally 50 feet and three storeys high. Over the course of the following centuries a village of small houses grew up near the tower, which was itself modified to improve its defensive strength by the addition of outer walls and extra towers, no doubt following wars between different Sard powers. These defences were not good enough to resist Carthaginian attack in the mid-6th century and Su Nuraxi was laid low. It was recolonised and partly rebuilt soon after, and occupied until Roman times. The ruins lay buried until floods in 1949 washed earth away to uncover unmistakable signs of an important and extensive area of ruins. Now the foundations have been laid bare, and from the terrace of the truncated tower the plan of the settlement can be admired, along with the quiet beauty of the dusty plain, flanked by *nuraghe*-shaped hills, no doubt with many a prehistoric secret waiting to be uncovered.

Unlike Su Nuraxi, the monumental **Nuraghe Sant' Antine**, the most important of many ruins on a plain near **Torralba** south of Sássari, has long been known as the greatest of all the *nuraghi*, a favourite symbol of island pride and independence. Its two-storey central tower stands 50ft above a triangular bastion whose corner towers are linked by a curtain wall with galleries. Inside the courtyard is a well and in the central tower are vaulted chambers, corridors and a staircase. The construction dates from the 9th to 7th centuries.

Other large *nuraghi* include Santa Barbara, about a mile north-east of Macomer, Losa, just outside Abbasanta, and Serra Orrios, between Núoro and Dorgáli.

Even the best-preserved *nuraghe* leaves a lot to the imagination of the visitor. A good way to fuel the imagination is to visit the museums in Cágliari and/or Sássari which contain the best collections of material unearthed by study of *nuraghi* and other prehistoric sites. The most appealing and distinctive feature of Nuraghic culture is the art of small bronze statuettes, a fine collection of which is in the Cágliari museum; the subjects vary from simple shepherds and musicians to warriors, chiefs and supernatural figures.

▷ A remarkable and not too fancifully named rock beside the road, with prehistoric burial chambers known as witches' houses (*domus de janas*), their walls showing some signs of carved decoration.

☞ Romanesque churches

Two of the isolated Pisan Romanesque churches that characterise northern Sardinia are **Nostra Signora de Tergu** (*about 5km south*), beside the rough road from the coast west of Castelsardo to Nulvi, and **San Pietro di Simbranos**, (*about 21km south-east*) near Bulzi.

☞ Beaches

There are several excellent and usually empty sandy beaches accessible from the impressive coast road between Castelsardo and Santa Teresa di Gallura (*70km north-east*). **Badesi Mare** has an enormous beach and a campsite, but not much of a resort. **Isola Rossa** has a few hotels and restaurants and beaches each side of a promontory of pink rocks and islets. Even in high season these places are very peaceful.

COSTA SMERALDA

The most famous and exclusive name in Mediterranean tourism, a fascinating exercise in sensitive, respectful development, perhaps demonstrating that property development is far too important to be left to property developers. In the early '60s a group of wealthy individuals including the Aga Khan bought a very thin strip of the remote, deserted and unproductive north-eastern corner of Sardinia, about 35 miles of very indented coast with stiff breezes, rocky capes, sheltered coves and sandy beaches – a sailing holidaymaker's paradise. The new landowners formed a consortium and set very strict rules governing the way the land could be developed: cables were to lie underground, only a small proportion of each plot of land could be built upon, and vegetation disturbed by building work had to be replaced. The result is a landscape that, superficially at least, seems very undisturbed. Small villas and villa-style hotels stand among the native coastal vegetation beneath an impressive wall of grey mountainous hills rising steeply behind the green coast. It has been an expensive dream to realise and accordingly it is an expensive place for a holiday. There is only one resort, **Porto Cervo**, its focus a large yacht marina in a wide, sheltered cove. On the slopes above the harbour are grouped a maze of colourful little villas, stylish shopping precincts, a sports club and a modern church with an El Greco donated by one of the Costa Smeralda's noble patrons. Cars are kept at bay, of course, and this is not a beach resort. The rest of the coast, which stretches from near Baja Sardinia on the Gulf of Arzachena in the north to the Gulf of Cugnana in the south, consists of isolated hotels and colonies of villas with their own well-equipped beaches.

The idea that there is anything remotely natural about turning this wild stretch of coast into a luxury playground is pretty far-fetched and the care to achieve an organic style (which extends to the use of inscribed rough stone signposts) may seem precious, and the results contrived and stagey. Certainly this is the style of the famous Cala di Volpe hotel, a fantasy castle with private moorings for the guests and a lush golf course next door. The hotel is the only large-scale component of the Costa Smeralda and, inevitably, it has been given over to expensive package tourism and Americanised. There are other more secluded and discreetly luxurious hotels which have not gone the same way (notably the Pitrizza, at Liscia di Vacca near the northern boundary).

The Costa Smeralda occupies a very small area of even this corner of Sardinia's thousand-mile coastline. To drive from one end to the other takes only a few minutes (the road is much straighter than the coast). On either side of its boundaries is a spin-off area of new resorts, created without the same self-imposed constraints; although they look messy and blatant compared with the Costa Smeralda, they provide slightly less expensive, livelier holidays for people more interested in beaches, watersports and discothèques than yachts and hot and cold running asses' milk. **Baia Sardinia** and **Portisco** are good new resorts in this style, just outside the perimeters of the Costa Smeralda.

GALLURA

The island's granite north-eastern corner, its beautiful rocky and indented coastline neglected until the tourist boom of recent decades. The main development has been the Costa Smeralda, the name of a business venture controlling a small section of the coast but which is often used to refer to the whole area between Olbia and Santa Teresa di Gallura.

The main resort to the west of the Gulf of Arzachena is **Santa Teresa di Gallura**, a dull village near the windswept northern tip of mainland Sardinia, with a 16th-century Spanish tower commanding splendid views of the white cliffs of Corsica about ten miles away. Santa Teresa stands on a hill with a large and growing number of hotels above a sheltered sandy town beach on one side, and on the other a sheltered inlet and port with ferry services to Bonifacio in Corsica and La Maddalena. Around Santa Teresa there are beautiful rocky bays with larger and better beaches and some modern tourist development, notably on the bay of **Santa Reparata**, beside the granite **Capo Testa**, a promontory joined to land by a sandy isthmus and used as a quarry by the Romans and Pisans, supplying granite columns for the Pantheon and the cathedral at Pisa. Blocks of abandoned work in progress can be seen lying around on the shore. The trip across the strait of Bonifacio to Corsica takes about an hour, and is recommended.

Palau is a quiet little port facing the island and town of La Maddalena, with frequent ferry services and inviting restaurants by the quayside. There is a long sandy beach. Nearby is **Porto Rafael**, a very picturesque and exclusive holiday village created around a charming arcaded piazza with boutiques, bar, restaurants, yacht-club and discothèque. The villas, let out to self-caterers, are purpose-built in traditional Sardinian style and overlook a sandy bay with its own jetty.

The most spectacular of all the many beautiful rock formations of this stretch of coast is the figure of a bear, hollowed out and carved by the wind on the **Capo d'Orso**, a few miles east of Palau. From the cape there are beautiful views over the La Maddalena archipelago.

Arzachena is a quiet, not very touristy village in pleasantly fertile agricultural surroundings; the long, narrow Gulf of Arzachena seems more like a river estuary than sea.

(Resorts east of Arzachena are described in the entry for the Costa Smeralda)

GENNARGENTU MOUNTAINS

The highest peaks of the island are in the Barbágia, south of Núoro. The mountains themselves are not spectacular, climbing steadily to just over 1,800m (**Paunta la Marmora** is the highest at 1,834m) and exploring is more a matter of hiking than climbing. Forests of chestnut and oak give way to open ground above the tree-line; wildlife includes a few dozen remaining mouflons (wild mountain sheep), boar and vultures. Snow lies until May and in winter skiers take to the slopes of **Bruncu Spina** near **Fonni**, the highest village in Sardinia (1,000m). Like those of most local villages, its inhabitants are shepherds whose males leave home with their flocks to spend six months a year down in the Campidano. **Aritzo** is another attractive village with accommodation, and is a good base for walkers. One of the biggest of the local festivals in the region is at Ollolai on August 24th.

One of the best ways to see the mountain region is by train: the narrow-gauge lines from Cágliari to Sorgono and Arbatax pass through some of the most remote and beautiful of Sardinian landscapes.

IGLÉSIAS

The main town of the mountainous south-west and the centre of Sardinia's mining industry. Considering this, Iglésias is surprisingly pleasant, with tall, balconied houses, cobbled streets and a number of fine medieval churches (to which the town owes its name). Most of the church building went on in the 13th century when the Pisans revived the mines, neglected since Roman times. The cathedral has a simple 13th-century façade; the interior was updated in the 16th century. There is a mineralogical museum.

The most important minerals are lead, zinc and silver. Coal was discovered near the coast in the late 19th century and a new mining town, Carbónia, founded in 1940. The coal industry is now in decline and most of the pits disused, but the mining of metals continues to thrive, Sardinia producing 80% of Italy's lead and zinc. The biggest mines are at **Monteponi**, just outside Iglésias on the way to Carbónia, and **Montevecchio**, in the hills west of Gúspini.

LA MADDALENA AND CAPRERA

La Maddalena is a small island just off the Gallura coast, reached by ferry from Palau and linked to neighbouring Caprera island by causeway and bridge. It has an important naval base and a town of nearly 10,000 inhabitants and is piled up on the hillside facing Sardinia. The Agincourt Sound, as the anchorage between the islands and Sardinian mainland was then known, was considered by Nelson to be the finest man o' war harbour in Europe and was the base for his fleet for 15 months before a hurried departure on 20th January 1805 in the pursuit of the French which was to end at Trafalgar. During all the time Nelson was there he never set foot on Sardinia, which was neutral. Some sailors did venture ashore for wooding and watering, however; as an anti-malaria precaution they were supplied with two gills of wine or one gill of spirits per day, to be mixed with Peruvian bark. In fact, the islands were much less unhealthy than most of Sardinia and Nelson's men suffered no illness at all.

La Maddalena has good beaches, especially round its northern coast, and is a popular holiday destination in its own right as well being a favourite day trip by boat from the resorts along the Gallura coast.

Caprera is about the same size as La Maddalena but is little inhabited except for a colony of Club Mediterranée huts. The island was Garibaldi's home for over twenty years before his death in 1882. His simple house, the Casa Bianca, can be visited, and contains old photographs and other mementoes, including the famous red shirt and the bed of the father of Italian unity. His grave is a simple granite slab with a constant naval guard in attendance. Beside it are several other tombs of members of Garibaldi's large and confusing family, including his youngest daughter Clelia, who lived on Caprera until her death in 1957.

MAMOIADA

A shepherd village south of Núoro famous for the pagan hunting ritual (men dressed up in sheepskins with wooden masks and strings of bells) of its pre-Lent festival; the villagers take their act to Sássari for the Cavalcata Sarda. They strike camp around the church of San Cósimo (just outside Mamoiada) for another important festival over the days leading up to September 27th.

NORA

Important archaeological site of a Phoenician, Punic and Roman colony in a beautiful setting on the south coast near Pula, west of Cágliari. The narrow promontory with harbours on either side is a typical Phoenician choice. The Romans established themselves at Nora in 238BC and made it their most important military base on the island. A large area has been excavated, uncovering elements of both Punic and Roman cities, including a Punic temple, Roman mosaics and a theatre where performances are often staged in summer. At the neck of the promontory is the 11th-century chapel of Sant' Efisio which stars once a year, at the beginning of May, in the great festival of the same name (*described under Cagliari entry*). The façade of the church is not original.

NÚORO

Capital of the Sardinian interior, Núoro stands at the heart of the region of the island least contaminated by outside influence, where Sardinian life survives at its most Sard. The Romans subjected central Sardinia with considerable difficulty, and their name for its inhabitants (*barbaricini*) survives in the present name of the wildest mountain area, La Barbágia. In later periods the *barbaricini* were left undisturbed, and their dialect remains the closest to Latin of any in the Mediterranean. Núoro is spectacularly set on a 1,500ft granite plateau with mountain views to the south, but there is not much else to see; Núoro would not be the essential Sardinian town if there were. It is now a provincial capital and has become a dull-looking town of mostly modern buildings. In the ordinary course of events few people wear colourful traditional costumes, although as always there are plenty of women in black, some of them with coloured headdress. The most lavish costumes, and not only from Núoro, are brought out for the great local festival, the Sacra del Redentore on 29th August, when a procession makes its way up to **Monte Ortobene** (907m), five miles from town. Even at other times the mountain is a popular excursion, with oak woods ideal for picnics, and restaurants near the large statue of the Redeemer on the summit.

There is a good **costume museum** on the hill of Sant' Onofrio on the southern edge of town.

OLBIA

A large and busy ferry port (services to Civitavecchia, Livorno and Genoa) of some 20,000 inhabitants. As in Porto Torres, the only exception to its general lack of appeal is a large Romanesque church, in this case San Simplicio, an appropriate name for a building of unadorned elegance. The Gulf of Olbia is dominated by the massive **Isola Tavolara**, a table mountain rising nearly 2,000ft from the sea. Apart from a few houses on the spit of land at its western tip, Tavolara is deserted. Some ferry services use the smaller port of **Golfo Aranci** on the northern tip of the Gulf of Olbia. It lacks appeal as a beach resort.

Excursions from Olbia

☞ **Coastal resorts south of Olbia**

There are several small local resort communities and clusters of villas on the sandy lagoons and inlets south of Olbia. Beyond **San Teodoro** (*27km south*), a lively village, there are stretches of pinewoods along the shore and a number of small but growing resorts, which cater very well for campers, many of them German. The landscape is one of the most pleasing in Sardinia: small-scale cultivations, vines, cows and eucalyptus trees set against a contrastingly rugged mountain background. **Santa Calletta** (*65km south*) is a small coastal village with a beach, some accommodation and not much tourism. South of Siniscola, where the main road heads inland to Núoro, the mountains take over and access to the sea is less and less frequent. **Santa Lucia** (*65km south*) has a good beach and campsites, and there are more beaches and a fertile landscape around the Cedrino estuary near **Orosei**(*93km south*).

ORGÓSOLO

A notorious bandit village deep in the wild Sopramonte hill country south of Núoro, the heart of the Sardinian heartland. Orgósolo's reputation was made by a 15-year vendetta between two families, sparked off by their rival claims to the accumulated property of a successful thief who died without heirs in 1903. Their bloody rivalry is commemorated by a vigorous series of street wall paintings which contribute to a somewhat sinister and unwelcoming atmosphere. One does not feel like hanging around. There is nothing much to see: the ways of the shepherd folk may be primitive, but the village has no particular rustic charm. There are scores of unfinished new buildings telling of an unsteady flow of remittances from expatriate family members.

The road to Oliena is rough and slow but gives a vivid impression of the desolate splendour of these scrub-covered hills, where the untamed shepherds roam undisturbed with their flocks.

ORISTANO

Provincial capital and agricultural market town, a few miles inland from the west coast at the northern end of the productive Campidano plain. Although not much of a tourist centre, Oristano is a pleasant place to spend some time wandering around the old streets of the centre and enjoying the lively evening atmosphere under the palm trees on the Piazza Roma, a welcome contrast to the institutional nature of Oristano's local beach resort (**Marina di Torre**

Grande). On the square stands one of two towers to survive from Oristano's 13th-century fortifications. The town's main shopping street (Corso Umberto) leads down to the Piazza Eleanora, named after the town's great heroine, who is also commemorated by a statue. Oristano was the capital of Arborea, one of the four self-governing provinces (*giudicati*) of medieval Sardinia. Eleanor of Arborea took over its leadership in 1383 and defended the independence of Arborea from Aragonese control with such skill and energy, both diplomatic and military, that she is inevitably compared to Joan of Arc. Arborea's independence did not long survive her, but her work as an enlightened legislator was soon adopted as the basis for the whole island's legal code until 1860.

Oristano's main festival takes place at the beginning of Lent. As well as jousts and other trials of horsemanship, there is much singing and dancing. There is also a festival at Torre Grande on August 14/15th.

Oristano is the centre of the area of production of Vernaccia, Sardinia's most famous wine. It is white and extremely strong.

Excursions from Oristano

☞ **Santa Giusta** (*3km south*)

A beautiful Romanesque church, originally a cathedral and built on a larger scale than most of the island's medieval churches, unflatteringly but conveniently set beside the main road. The nave's wooden vault is supported by an interesting variety of granite and marble columns, some of them borrowed from nearby classical sites.

☞ **Sinis Peninsula** (*10km north-west*)

The sandy spit of land closing the gulf of Oristano to the north was the site of the Phoenician, Punic and Roman city of **Tharros**, finally abandoned in favour of Oristano in the 11th century because of its vulnerability to pirate attack. There is a 16th-century tower and some excavated ruins, including identifiable roads, on the shore but much of the ancient remains are underwater. Take a mask and enjoy the perfect archaeological experience. The beach is good and attracts rough campers; locals have shanty beach houses made of reedy thatch. The little domed church of **San Giovanni in Sinis** dates partly from the 5th century, partly from the 11th. Little **San Salvatore** looks more like an encampment than a village, and with reason: the inhabitants of Cabras move in once a year (in early September) for a festival. At other times a ghost village, it has been used for a spaghetti western, which explains the Wild West Saloon on the dusty square. Underneath the church is a very ancient sanctuary with traces of Punic, Arab and Greek inscriptions and Roman wall paintings. The custodian may be reluctant to open up for small numbers. **Cabras** is a large fishing village on the edge of one of the many lagoons (*stagni*) along the coast near Oristano. They still use flat-bottomed boats made of reeds, unchanged since antiquity. One method of fishing, a tamer version of the tunny-harvest (*mattanza*), consists of staking out the *stagni* and driving the fish into a corner with nets and barriers of reeds, until there is such a density of fish that men can wade through plucking them out by hand.

☞ **Arborea** (*10km south*)
The area south of Oristano was the main element of the Fascists' Sardinian agricultural redevelopment programme. The Tirso was dammed, a vast tract of marshy coast was drained and irrigated, hundreds of new farms were created for settlers from north-eastern Italy, and the town of Mussolinia was founded in 1928. Now named Arborea, it will win no prizes for architectural merit or inventiveness, but the area as a whole is interesting to see. There is dairy farming, rice, tobacco, vineyards and rows of eucalyptus trees.

☞ **Marina di Arbus** (*70km south*)
A magnificent stretch of empty beach and dunes reached by a long, beautiful drive through mountains and small mining communities from Arbus, between Iglésias and Oristano. The coast has been named Costa Verde and is scheduled for development, but for the moment there is little there except a few shacks (including a restaurant).

PALAU
(*See Gallura*)

PORTO CERVO
(*See Costa Smeralda*)

PORTO RAFAEL
(*See Gallura*)

PORTO TORRES
A busy ferry port (the main one for the Genoa link) flanked by refineries and without charm. The only redeeming features are a Roman bridge over the river on the way out to Stintino and the vast and beautiful 11th-century basilica of **San Gavino**, formerly the cathedral. The crypt, occasionally accessible, contains Roman sarcophagi whose contents include the remains of three local martyrs, Roman convert Gavinus among them, beheaded in 300AD. There is a colourful memorial to the event in the main church. The precinct of the church consists of very primitive, windowless cell houses.

There are plenty of beaches on the outskirts of Porto Torres; **Platamona Lido** has trees as well as sand and is a popular resort for the inhabitants of both Porto Torres and Sássari; it is one of the few places on the Sardinian coast which suffers from crowds.

SAN PIETRO

Island off the south-west coast, reached by ferry from Calasetta on
Sant' Antíoco or Porto Vesme, near Porto Scuso on the Sardinian
mainland. The main interest of the rocky island is its history and its
tunny fishing. In 1737 Genoese inhabitants of the Tunisian island of
Tabarca appealed to king Carlo Emanuele of Sardinia to be allowed
to settle on San Pietro because of the dangerous conditions under
which they lived. Their request was granted but things did not
improve much, as San Pietro bacame the frequent victim of slave
raids as Tabarca had been before. The inhabitants of the single town,
Carloforte, still speak a Genoese dialect and are now mainly
occupied with tunny fishing, for which the waters between Sant'
Antioco, San Pietro and Porto Scuso are the most important in
Sardinia.

Shoals of tunny pass through these waters during the early
summer on their way to the Black Sea. Fishermen spend weeks
laying down a complicated system of net barriers which channel the
fish into a dead-end of netting, the so-called *camera della morte*. When
the head fisherman observes through a glass-bottomed boat that the
chamber is sufficiently full of fish the entrance to the underwater
chamber is closed and the tunny hauled out of the water, thrashing
wildly in a foam of sea and blood as the fishermen spear them one
by one. A fish may be as much as ten feet long, so the *mattanza*, as
the slaughter is called, is not without danger for the fishermen. The
mattanza takes place two or three times each year between May and
July and can be observed at Porto Scuso as well as Carloforte and
Calasetta.

Carloforte is an attractive and colourful little port with a few small
hotels and fish restaurants. Boat trips round the island can be
organised; the best beaches are on the western side.

SANTA CATERINA PITTINURI

Pleasant, quiet new resort between Oristano and Bosa. An
important port in ancient times, there are a few Carthaginian and
Roman remains and an acropolis.

SANTA MARGERITA DI PULA

A general name for the area of holiday development that extends to
the south-west of the small town of Pula, interesting only for the
ruins of Nora (*see separate entry*). Santa Margerita has no real centre,
but consists of self-contained units including campsites, the Forte
holiday village, and hotels including the most luxurious and
expensive ones outside the Costa Smeralda. The coast is sandy, the
water clear, and there are pinewoods in many places.

SANT' ANTÍOCO

Not quite an island because it's linked to the south-west coast by a
narrow causeway, where an old Roman track is visible beside the
road. Two stones beside the road are known as monk and nun,
turned to stone when fleeing to live together on Sant' Antíoco. The

first greeting to the island is a large industrial port. The town of Sant'
Antíoco itself is not particularly interesting, although there are
excavations of the ancient Phoenician and Roman city. The
12th-century church in the upper town was built on top of early
Christian catacombs, which can be visited, and contains the relics of
the African Antiochus whom the Romans were unable to kill even
by total immersion in boiling pitch and susbsequent dumping at sea.
He floated to the island and converted its people.

Most of the island is given over to vineyards. There are beaches
and some holiday development along the west coast of the island
and around the bright little port of **Calasetta**, where ferries make the
short crossing to the island of San Pietro.
(See also San Pietro)

SANTA TERESA DI GALLURA
(See Gallura)

SÁSSARI

The main city of northern Sardinia, only half the size of Cágliari but
several times larger than any other of the island towns. Like several
other inland towns Sássari grew up in the early Middle Ages when
barbarian and Arab raids, culminating in this case with the sack of
Porto Torres at the hands of the Genoese in 1166, persuaded coastal
inhabitants to retreat from the sea. The city stands on a high plateau
which falls away impressively to the south, where the Cágliari road
descends in a sweeping series of hairpins.

Sássari is not much of a sightseer's town and it is in no way a
holiday resort. It is just an attractively busy place to observe
Sardinian town life, at its most animated on the main square in the
evening. This is the **Piazza d'Italia**, open and imposing although of
no great architectural merit. It is well worth exploring the narrow
north-west of the square. The busy Corso Vittorio Emanuele bisects
the old town and is the main shopping street. Nearby is the
cathedral, mostly dating from the 15th century, except for the
façade, which is Baroque. On the southern side of the old town are
public gardens with an exhibition hall displaying Sardinian
handicraft. There is a special biennial handicraft exhibition
coinciding with the Cavalcata Sarda festival on Ascension Day, one
of the island's great folklore gatherings, with costumed participants
from all over Sardinia. Another brilliantly colourful procession takes
place on 14th August, with huge candles borne round the town in
thanksgiving for deliverance from plague.

☛ **Sanna Museum** (Via Roma, on the eastern side of town)   This is well
arranged and contains a large number of prehistoric and classical fragments
along with some helpful reconstructions of Nuraghic and earlier sites. There
is also an excellent ethnographic section, with local cloths, costumes,
ceramics, looms and furniture; and a small section of paintings.

Santissima Trinità di Saccárgia

Excursions from Sássari
☞ Romanesque churches

An excursion to see the Romanesque churches in the peaceful
countryside east of Sássari is much more rewarding than plodding
round the mostly uninteresting town churches. The most
picturesque church on the island is **Santissima Trinità di Saccárgia**
(*17km south-east*), a beautiful example of the decorative Pisan style,
with bands of black and white stone across the façade and tall
bell-tower, and other colourful geometric designs in medallions
above the porch, where there are amusing animal carvings on the
capitals. The church and some overgrown outbuildings are all that
remain of an abbey, founded in the early 12th century by the local
ruler in gratitude for his wife's fertility, which had been revealed to
her at this place. There are 13th-century frescos inside, but the
church is usually closed. Other beautiful churches of the same
period in the neighbourhood (all close to the Sássari-Ozieri-Olbia
road) are, from west to east: **San Michele di Salvenero** (on a hill
overlooking the Saccárgia church), **Santa Maria del Regno** in Ardara
(*27km south-east*), and **Sant' Antíoco di Bisárcio**, splendidly set
(despite some very ugly modern block buildings below it) on a rocky
hillock, and easily spotted from the main road north-west of Ozieri.

The church crawl is not complete without a southward detour to visit San Pietro di Sorres. (*See Torralba*)

STINTINO

A lively little yacht harbour and fishing port near the north-western tip of Sardinia, founded at the end of the 19th century by refugees from the nearby island of **Asinara**, which was taken over by the government for use as a penal colony. There are excellent beaches (**La Pelosa**) between the village and the cape, with some new holiday development.

Stintino is the main tunny-fishing centre in northern Sardinia. There is no set date for the slaughters (*mattanze: see San Pietro*), which take place several times a year in spring and early summer.

THARROS

(*See Oristano*)

TORRALBA

Village beside the main Sássari to Macomer road, notable for the density of *nuraghi* in the neighbourhood (including the *nuraghe* Sant' Antine: *see Prehistory, page 487*) and the beautiful church of **San Pietro di Sorres**, prominently set on a high ledge above Bonnánaro. The church was built by Benedictines in the late 12th century as part of a large monastery, recently restored and reinhabited (which makes the church easier to enter than many in the Sardinian countryside). Church and neighbouring buildings are decoratively constructed with black and white (basalt and limestone) bands, repeated in the columns of the nave. Geometric patterns in the blind arcades of the façade add colour and a jewelled refinement to the simple architecture.

VILLASIMIUS

A small village on the beautiful south-eastern corner of Sardinia which is by-passed by main roads but increasingly attracting the attention of tourism developers. Villasimius itself is not so much a resort as a place near the coast where holidaymakers in modern colonies of villas and flats come for provisions. Most of the new development consists of villas and campsites on the previously deserted sandy coast north of Villasimius, the recently christened Costa Rei. Beaches are excellent.

The road between Villasimius and Cágliari is a tortuous and most beautiful one, hugging the mountainous coast and giving occasional access to small coves, some of them with hotels and villas for the inhabitants of Cágliari who come out to these beaches at weekends.

Hotels

Alghero
CALABONA
07041 Sassari

££
Closed Nov to March
Tel: (079) 975728

None of Alghero's hotels has much charm, but this one, a mile from the centre, is good of its kind. It's a three-storey arcaded block in Mediterranean style, with a large pool and a small rocky beach. All the bedrooms have terraces – those facing on to the open courtyard are the nicest, but also the noisiest (there is a disco one or two evenings a week).

Facilities: *113 bedrooms (AC); restaurant; lift; swimming pool; parking* **Credit/charge cards accepted:** *Amex, Diners, Eurocard, Visa*

Baia Sardinia
BISACCIA
07021 Arzachena

£££
Closed Nov to March
Tel: (0789) 99002

Although built in the '60s, La Bisaccia has mellowed gracefully and enjoys a prime position above the beach. The public areas are airy and spacious with white stucco walls and cane furniture; particularly attractive is the restaurant with a terrace overlooking the sea where barbecues are sometimes served. Bedrooms are cool and simple, though not always big, and in the same rustic style; all have balconies. There are also several small villa-apartments, ideal for families, and an annexe. An attractive hotel with a lively atmosphere and super views.

Facilities: *110 bedrooms; restaurant; lift; swimming pool* **Credit/charge cards accepted:** *Amex, Diners, Eurocard, Visa*

Oliena
SU GOLOGONE
08025 Nuoro

£
Closed Nov
Tel: (0784) 287512

A low whitewashed villa partly camouflaged by flowering shrubs, in the rugged interior of Sardinia, about 8km east of the mountain village of Oliena. The hotel is simply furnished in rustic style with Sardinian paintings and sculpture. The vast dining room and lovely courtyard cater for far more than just hotel guests and Su Gologone is to be avoided at weekends. But the food is excellent, and typically Sardinian; salamis and roast suckling pig are always on offer and there may be little choice. On our last visit the pool was not in use.

Facilities: *33 bedrooms; restaurant; swimming pool; tennis court; riding; parking* **Credit/charge cards accepted:** *Amex, Eurocard, Visa*

Porto Cervo £££
BALOCCO *Closed mid-Oct to March*
07020 Costa Smeralda Tel: (0789) 91555

Just above Porto Cervo, at Liscia di Vacca, the Balocco offers bed and breakfast accommodation at a sensible price. It is a simple stuccoed villa with a luxuriant sub-tropical garden and a pretty kidney-shaped pool (and a smaller one for children). The best feature of the bedrooms is the individual terraces, where an above-average breakfast can be brought to you.

Facilities: *31 bedrooms (AC); swimming pool; parking* **Credit/charge cards accepted:** *Amex, Diners, Visa*

Porto Cervo £££££
PITRIZZA *Closed Oct to mid-May*
07020 Costa Smeralda Tel: (0789) 92000

An utterly exclusive little hotel, elegant yet informal. Bedrooms are in six individual villas with private terraces in the 4-acre grounds overlooking a lovely private beach. There is a lounge – more like a private drawing room – a restaurant and a piano bar in the main villa.

Facilities: *28 bedrooms (AC); restaurant; swimming pool; parking* **Credit/charge cards accepted:** *Amex, Diners, Eurocard, Visa*

Porto Cervo £££££
ROMAZZINO *Closed mid-Oct to mid-May*
07020 Costa Smeralda Tel: (0789) 96020

A self-contained luxury resort, the Romazzino is less pretentious than some of the other hotels in the Costa Smeralda group but built in similar Mediterranean style. It is secluded in its own immaculately-kept gardens leading to a private beach of coarse, pale sand and clear waters. The interior is prettily and freshly decorated and furnished in summery Sardinian style. There's a freshwater pool with a barbecue and bar and the hotel offers waterskiing and windsurfing lessons and boat rental (at a price).

Facilities: *99 bedrooms (AC); restaurant; lift; swimming pool; tennis court; shuttle service to Pevero golf club; parking* **Credit/charge cards accepted:** *Amex, Diners, Eurocard, Visa*

Our price symbols

£ = you can expect to find a room for under £35
££ = you can expect to find a room for under £55
£££ = you can expect to find a room for under £75
££££ = you can expect to find a room for under £125
£££££ = you should expect to pay over £125 for a room

Santa Margherita di Pula
IS MORUS
09010 Pula

£££££
Closed Nov to March
Tel: (070) 921424

Easily the most comfortable hotel for miles around, the Is Morus is a civilised oasis about half an hour's drive south-west of Cagliari. The villa is surrounded by pinewoods and eucalyptus trees, with a garden of oleander and frangipani. The interior is calm and cool with white walls and a combination of elegant modern and rustic Sardinian furniture. All bedrooms have terraces overlooking the sea where there is a private beach with loungers and parasols and facilities for watersports.

Facilities: *85 bedrooms; restaurant; swimming pool; tennis court; shuttle service to Is Molas golf club; parking* **Credit/charge cards accepted:** *Amex, Diners, Eurocard, Visa*

Santa Teresa Gallura
SHARDANA
Baia Santa Reparata, 07028 Sassari

££
Closed Oct to May
Tel: (0789) 754031

If you want the comforts and lifestyle of the Costa Smeralda without the jetset people and prices, the Shardana is a good choice. Accommodation is in small stuccoed villas ranged in terraces in Moorish-Mediterranean style. The restaurant and piano bar are in a separate villa, and there is a bar at the pool for snacks and drinks. Watersports can be arranged from the hotel. A good place to unwind for a few days, but perhaps too isolated for a longer stay.

Facilities: *51 bedrooms; restaurant; swimming pool; tennis court; parking* **Credit/charge cards accepted:** *Amex*

GENERAL
INFORMATION

Travel

Motoring
*Driving licence; Insurance; Petrol and coupons; Route planning;
Crossing the Channel; Motorail; Driving regulations; Accidents and
breakdowns; Car hire; Motorways; Parking; Road signs; Speed
limits; Useful words and phrases; Driving in Italy – a personal view;
Useful addresses*

Air

Bus

Rail

Sea

Accommodation

Hotels

Camping and caravanning

Self-catering

Package holidays

Recommended books

*Hotels and restaurants; Guidebooks: whole country; Guidebooks:
series; General; Art; Food and wine; Travellers before 1900; Regional
guides and literature: Lakes and mountains, Venice, Northern cities,
Liguria, Florence, Tuscancy and Umbria, Rome, Central Italy,
Naples and Campania, The South, Sicily, Sardinia, Islands*

Maps

General information

*Medical care; Changing money; Booking a hotel; Opening hours;
Public holidays; Beaches and bathing; Restaurants; Telephoning;
Tipping; Tourist information offices*

Festivals and events

Weather

Glossaries

Art and architecture; Food

Travel

MOTORING

Driving licence

A British driving licence must be accompanied by a standard form of translation, obtainable (free) from Automobile Association (AA) and Royal Automobile Club (RAC) centres, tour operators specialising in Italy, CIT's motoring department at Croydon and the Italian State Tourist Office. If yours is the pink, EEC-format licence now issued by the DVLC to new drivers and in any circumstance requiring a replacement, it is officially accepted in Italy without the translation. In practice it still simplifies matters to have one.

Insurance

You will need ordinary travel insurance to cover you for things like loss of your possessions and medical expenses (*see Medical Insurance in the General Information section below*); you may want to insure against breakdowns (*see below*); and you will probably also want to buy special motor insurance to cover you for accidental damage to your car or other cars (or people).

Your ordinary UK motor insurance policy automatically gives you the legal minimum cover for Italy, but this legal minimum is usually much less than the cover which you have at home. To extend your normal cover, you need a Green Card (international motor insurance certificate); contact your own insurer for this, well ahead of your trip.

Breakdown insurance – called "vehicle security" or "vehicle protection" – is designed to protect you from some of the expense and inconvenience which can result from a major car breakdown. If your car is out of action, policies have provisions for either accommodating you while it's being repaired or continuing your holiday by other means. Some policies cover other risks such as illness and car theft. The four policies used by most respondents to a survey of 3,700 members of the Consumers' Association who had taken their car abroad were AA 5-star, Europ Assistance, RAC Travellers Bond and Caravan Club Red Pennant (members only).

None of the policies covers the cost of spare parts and you may have to pay a labour charge. Minor problems can be most conveniently and swiftly solved locally, without recourse to breakdown insurance facilities.

(*See also Accidents and breakdowns*)

Petrol and coupons

In the form of coupons and vouchers, the Italian authorities offer reductions in the cost of petrol (15%) and motorway tolls to foreign tourists taking their own cars into Italy. You may buy one of four different and quite complex "Packages", covering the north, centre, south, and far south plus Sicily or Sardinia; purchasers are also entitled to a free breakdown service from the Italian motoring organisation ACI. The outlay is considerable, and only worthwhile if you drive long distances within Italy. Advantages are heavily weighted: maximum possible savings in northern Italy would be about £25, in the far south about £80.

The AA and RAC issue helpful explanatory leaflets, and the Packages are most readily available from AA and RAC centres including UK port offices. They can be sold only to personal callers presenting passport and vehicle registration document. It is possible to arrange a refund on unused petrol coupons, either at the frontier as you leave Italy or at the point where you bought them.

Italy has two grades of petrol. Benzina Normale should not be put in cars used to UK four-star: buy Benzina Super. Petrol stations are normally closed for lunch between about 12.30pm and 3pm, except on motorways (24-hour service). Credit cards are rarely accepted for payment. Garages other than the main filling station chains may not accept petrol coupons.

Route planning

The quickest route from the Channel to Italy is via Calais, Basel and the St Gotthard Tunnel. You can get detailed information on this or any desired route from the motoring organisations. The AA has discontinued its European Through-Route Maps and now offers a computerised service for £3.75 to members, £6.75 to non-members: available through any of its centres, or write to head office. Motorways are free in Belgium and Germany; you pay tolls throughout France and Italy and on a few motorways (including the Brenner Autobahn) in Austria; Switzerland levies an annual tax on anyone using any of the Swiss motorway network, and requires display of a sticker. You can buy it at the Swiss frontier, or at AA and RAC offices in the UK.

Crossing the Channel

The shortest Channel ferry routes, and the most convenient for driving direct to Italy, are those from Dover/Folkestone to Calais/ Boulogne. They take from 1 to 1¾ hours; hovercraft from Dover (more expensive) only half an hour. Other crossings to France take considerably longer. Dover to Oostende (3¾ hours) or to Zeebrugge (4 hours) are suitable choices if you want to avoid French motorway tolls and drive through Belgium, Germany, and Austria or Switzerland. If you live in south-east England you might opt for the cheapest ferry – Sally Line, Ramsgate to Dunkerque, 2½ hours. On the popular short routes prices don't vary much between operators (Sealink, Townsend Thoresen) but the time of sailing and the season make substantial differences to the cost.

Motorail

You can put your car on French motorail from Boulogne to Milan. The service operates between May and mid-September. It takes 15 hours, arriving early in the morning. The Italian motorail service south from Milan leaves in the evening. Destinations served from Milan include Rome, Bari, Brindisi and (for ferries to Sicily) Villa San Giovanni, near Reggio di Calabria; other departure points are Turin,

Genoa, Bologna and Bolzano.

British Rail can book the French motorail service; CIT can help with the Italian, but it has to be by written application (including a deposit) at least two months in advance.

Driving regulations

The minimum age for driving a car in Italy is 18 (21 if the car is capable of more than 112mph/180kph). A GB nationality plate, an interior and a left-hand exterior rear-view mirror are compulsory. You must carry a red warning triangle, and you must not carry petrol in cans. Seatbelts, soon to be compulsory, are strongly advised, and children should travel in rear seats.

You drive on the right, and (unless a sign indicates otherwise) give priority to traffic approaching from the right. Vehicles meeting and both wishing to turn left must pass in front of each other, not behind as during a right turn in the UK. Sounding your horn is prohibited in towns of any size but compulsory outside built-up areas in any situation where you need to give warning of your approach. In tunnels (however well lit) you must use dipped headlights. For many offences there are on-the-spot fines.

Speed limits in built up areas: 50kph (31mph); on country roads: 100kph (62mph) for cars from 900-1300cc, 110 kph (68mph) for cars over 1300cc; motorways: 130kph (80mph) for cars from 900-1300cc, 140kph (87mph) for cars over 1300cc. You are fined on the spot and heavily for speeding (if you choose to pay later, you'll pay a third more).

Accidents and breakdowns

The emergency telephone for police, fire and ambulance is 113. Telephones on motorways are 2km apart, and sometimes have separate call buttons for technical and medical assistance. If an accident (*incidente*) involves injury it is obligatory to summon medical assistance and to inform the police. If you need help with a breakdown (*guasto*) on an ordinary road dial 116, the emergency number for English-speaking assistance round the clock, and the nearest office of the ACI (Italian Automobile Association) will be alerted. If you can't move your car off the road you must place your red warning triangle at least 50 yards behind it, whether or not you have hazard warning lights.

The ACI breakdown service (ACI staff on motorways, repair garages on other roads) is available to visiting motorists but must be paid for – *see Insurance*. If however you have bought petrol coupons, production of the *Carta Carburante Touristica* (tourist fuel card) which comes with the package entitles you to free use of the service, and in some cases free use of a replacement car.

If your breakdown is not total but you need a spare part, the ACI can help you find a dealer for your car. ACI branches are listed, with telephone numbers, in the official Tourist Office handbook. Garages (and breakdown services) are mentioned in the gazetteer sections of the Michelin Red Guide *Italia* and the AA *Travellers' Guide to Europe*.

Car hire
Major car rental companies (including Avis, Europcar and Hertz) have offices in airports, city centres, towns and resorts. You can arrange to collect the car in one place and leave it in another at no extra charge (provided the company has an office there). Small local firms offer cheaper rates but cars can only be booked locally and may have to be returned to the same office. It is well worth booking your car in advance, from the UK. Hiring when you arrive, even from the cheaper firms, can cost twice as much. Car hire is also readily available through tour operators in conjunction with a flight, a villa or a hotel package.

Motorways
The motorway network is extensive, particularly in the north, and covers about 6,000km/3,700 miles. Motorways (*autostrada*) are numbered from A1 (Milan to Rome) to A31. Motorway access signs are highlighted in green, rather than blue as in the UK and most other European countries.

A toll is payable on most stretches; you take a ticket from an automatic dispenser and the toll is calculated when you leave the motorway (or, in some cases, at intermediate stages) according to vehicle size and distance. On some sections a flat fare is charged; you pay when you enter the motorway. Tolls are fairly expensive: the journey from Milan to Rome would cost about £20 (L38,450/ L39,800) for a 4-door saloon. Motorway toll vouchers are available to motorists taking an Italian petrol coupon package (*see above*). Motorway tunnels through the mountains from France and Switzerland cost about £13 (L26,000) one-way. You'll need cash – credit cards are not accepted.

Parking
Parking is forbidden in the usual situations which apply in the UK (main roads, close to bus stops, etc) but the fines for offences are higher. Particularly avoid parking in a *zona verde* (green zone) or *zona rimozione* (removal zone), from both of which your car will be towed away, to be retrieved only at great inconvenience and expense. Cities have authorised parking lots where you pay by the hour, and sometimes meters. In most there is a *zona disco* or blue zone, where vehicles can park up to the local time limit if they display a disc, obtainable from petrol stations.

Road signs
Accendere i fari/le luci (in galleria) switch on headlights (in the tunnel)
Caduta massi falling rocks
Curva/volta pericolosa dangerous bend
Divieto di sosta/sorpasso no overtaking
Incrocio crossroads
Lavori in corso road works
Passaggio a livello level crossing
Rallentare slow down
Senso unico/vietato one-way only/no entry

Sosta autorizzata parking permitted (followed by indication of times)
Sosta vietata no parking
Uscita exit or turn-off
Vietato ingresso veicoli no entry for vehicles
Vietato transito autocarri no entry for heavy vehicles

Useful words and phrases
Petrol *benzina*; diesel *gasolio*
Fill the tank, please *faccia il pieno, per favore*
Check the oil/tyres, please *controlli l'olio/i pneumatici, per favore*
Discharged battery *batteria a scarico*
Oil/water leak *fuga d'olio/fuoruscita d'acqua*
Puncture *foratura*
Carburettor *carburatore*; distributor *distributore*; fuses *i fusibili*; spark plug *candele*

Something is wrong with *Qualcosa non va*
..the engine *nel motore*; the clutch *nella frizione*; the gearbox *nella scatola cambio*; the brakes *ai freni*; the steering *allo sterzo*; the suspension *nella sospensione*; the drive-shaft *nel'albero di transmissione*

Driving in Italy – a personal view
Italian regionalism is most obvious on the road. In the north they drive fast cars impatiently. In the south they drive slow cars erratically. In the centre – Rome and Naples – they drive with a terrifying combination of speed, aggression and impulsiveness. Throughout the country they drive competitively and inconsiderately, in other words badly (regardless of their speed of reaction and mastery of the controls). The further south you go, the more the horn is used; in Sicily it is rarely silent, and you soon learn the difference between the toot of self-advertisement (always advisable before overtaking) and the long blast of anger. The rule about not hornblowing in town is loudly derided, and it is a matter of civic pride to a Neapolitan (and to a lesser extent Roman) driver to take up the challenge of a red traffic light like a bull.

The main problems of Italian motorway driving are steering a middle course on a two-lane carriageway between Fiat 500s in one lane and turbo-charged Maseratis in the other, poorly signed exits, and entrances without accelerating lanes. Overtaking on the inside is commonplace and it is very difficult, even at high speed, to keep your distance: a gap is an invitation. On rural by-roads slow-moving or stationary farm vehicles are to be anticipated round every corner. A roadside shrine is the surest warning of a dangerous corner.

Italians (except policemen) are not outraged by unconventional manoeuvres, such as main-road U-turns. Romans like nothing better than to dodge queues by driving along tram-lines. An attempt to follow their example may be embarrassing if your exit is blocked. Do not leave anything of value visible in a parked car. If possible lock the petrol cap and take the radio/tape deck out. It is a wise precaution to ask for specific amounts of petrol rather than a fill-up.

Useful addresses

ITALIAN STATE TOURIST OFFICE (ENIT)
I Princes Street, London W I R 8AY. Tel: 01-408 1254

CIT/CITALIA (Head Office, including Motoring Department)
Marco Polo House, 3 Lansdowne Road, Croydon CR9 I LL. Tel: 01-686 0777
CIT/CITALIA (London Office) and ITALIAN STATE RAILWAYS
50 Conduit Street, London W I R 9FB. Tel: 01-434 3844

Automobile Association (Head Office)
Fanum House, Basing View, Basingstoke, Hants RG21 2EA. Tel: (0256) 20123

Royal Automobile Club (Head Office)
RAC House, Lansdowne Road, Croydon CR9 2JA. Tel: 01-686 2525

ACI (Head Office)
Via Marsala 8, 00185 Roma. 24-hour assistance tel: Rome (06) 4212

AIR

The Italian airports with regular, direct scheduled flights from London are Bologna, Genoa, Milan, Naples, Pisa, Rome, Turin and Venice. You can also fly direct from Manchester to Milan and Rome, and from Birmingham and Glasgow to Milan. Regular UK charter flights also go to these cities.

Italian airports with scheduled services (some seasonal) from London via Milan or Rome are Alghero, Bari, Cágliari, Catánia and Palermo. UK charter flights (some seasonal) also go to these airports.

Other Italian airports used by UK charter flights (some seasonal) include Ancona, Bérgamo, Brindisi, Lamezia Terme, Olbia, Pescara, Rimini, Treviso, Trieste and Verona.

The cheapest scheduled fare is a Super APEX (advance purchase fare). Only a limited number of seats on specified flights are sold at these prices. Booking must be completed two to four weeks before departure, and the length of stay is limited. There are penalties for altering or cancelling a booking. PEX fares do not require advance booking, but there are similar restrictions on how long you stay, and penalties for altering or cancelling.

Charter fares are chiefly sold via tour operators' "flight only" brochures, available from travel agents. There may be some restriction on your stay – a minimum week and a maximum month is common. Sometimes tour operators' "charter" fares are for blocks of seats on scheduled flights: these are not necessarily cheaper than APEX or PEX, but have less restrictive booking conditions.

Specialists in flights to Italy include Citalia (tel: 01-686 5533); Ciao Travel (tel: 01-629 2677); Pegasus (tel: 01-373 6055) and Pilgrim-Air (tel: 01-637 5311/5333). These offer a variety of charter and cheap scheduled fares with or without car hire in Italy.

Italy has a good network of internal air services. On domestic flights there are family reductions (90% for children under 2, 50% from 2 to 12, 30% from 12 to 22) and up to 30% discount on night flights and weekend return tickets.

BUS

National Express Eurolines (Victoria Coach Station, London SW1; tel: 01-730 0202) runs a coach service to Rome via Dover, Paris, Aosta, Turin, Milan, Venice, Bologna and Florence.

In Italy, country buses are run by various privately-owned local companies. Buses are most useful in remote rural areas; otherwise trains provide a more efficient service.

RAIL

British Rail and their agents issue tickets from London to main Italian stations covering travel across the Channel by boat, jetfoil or hovercraft and sleeping cars from the continental port. Book well in advance of your trip. First class sleeping compartments are single or double, second class three-berth. Cheaper couchettes (adaptable seats, no washbasins) may be available in either class. You can break your journey at stations *en route* if you wish. Services and fares are described in British Rail's destination leaflet for Italy, available from main stations or by post (send s.a.e) from the European Rail Travel Centre, PO Box 303, Victoria Station, London SW1V 1JY.

The super-luxurious alternative is to take the Orient Express: Pullman carriages from London, special accommodation on the ferry and the stylish original train from Boulogne to Venice, by a leisurely route through France and Switzerland. Details and bookings from Venice Simplon-Orient-Express Ltd., 20 Upper Ground, London SE1 9PF, tel: 01-928 6000.

Tickets for travel within Italy can be bought in the UK from branches of Thomas Cook (and any travel agent who keeps a stock) and from Italian State Railways, CIT, 50 Conduit Street, London W1R 9FB (tel: 01-434 3844). From CIT (and main Italian stations) you can buy reduced-fare tickets intended for foreign tourists. The *Biglietto turistico libera circulazione* (rover ticket), valid for 8, 15, 21 or 30 days, allows unlimited travel. The *Biglietto chilometrico*, valid for 3,000km over up to twenty journeys, is a two-month railpass which can be shared by up to five people. Other reductions (family, day returns) can be obtained in Italy.

Italian State Railways operate a comprehensive network of services with trains classified according to speed. Europe's luxury expresses are now organised as the EuroCity network, and between Italy's main cities the fastest travel is by the InterCity (IC) trains. On these a *Rapido* supplement (up to 30% of the fare on first or – when available – second class) is compulsory on ordinary tickets: not on the rover ticket. A seat reservation (small charge) is sometimes compulsory, always advisable, and easily arranged at the station. Non-supplement trains are *Espresso*, *Diretto* and *Locale* in descending order of speed and increasing number of stops.

Train travel in Italy is still relatively cheap: it's worth paying the *Rapido* supplement (and/or travelling first class) for speed and comfort. Italians make full use of their 16,000km network and trains can be very crowded, reaching saturation point around the national holiday of the Assumption, August 15th. British Rail has an office in Milan: Via Pirelli 11, 20124 Milan, tel: (02) 6552297.

SEA

(*See Visiting sections in area chapters for details of ferry services to the islands*). For details of regulations for private craft, contact the Italian State Tourist Office (1 Princes Street, London W1R 8AY).

Accommodation

HOTELS

Hotels in Italy now have a system of official star ratings: 5★ equals the former De Luxe category, and 1★ the former 4th class. *Pensioni* are now rated as 3★, 2★ and 1★ hotels instead of having their own overlapping system. They are seldom "boarding houses" and often comfortable small hotels; meals, apart from breakfast, are seldom obligatory and indeed may not be available. *Locande*, "inns", are generally a very basic 1★ – though any hotel may use the name and one in Venice is 3★.

For each category a price range is fixed by law, but the range varies according to region and location – Venice and Capri have Italy's most expensive accommodation overall.

Prices are quoted per room, rather than per person, except where half-board applies. On Tourist Office lists, official hotel prices include service, sojourn tax and VAT. Breakfast (prices for this are not officially regulated) is quoted separately. However, in practice, breakfast is likely to be included in room rates quoted by hotels and you should stipulate at the time of booking if you don't wish to take it. You may be charged extra for air conditioning. The words *con bagno* may mean "with bathroom" (even if this has only a shower) or "with bath".

Seasonal price differences vary from area to area, resort to resort and even hotel to hotel. In city hotels, which are usually open all year, lower rates are generally offered only in winter, if at all. In coastal or lake resorts, where hotels may be open only half the year, July and August are generally treated as high season, with maximum prices, and often an obligation to stay a minimum of three nights on half-board terms. May, June and September are generally considered mid-season, except in extremely popular areas such as the coastal resorts of Campania where high-season rates (and minimum-stay/half-board stipulations) apply.

Some regional hotel lists, with official prices, are available from the Italian State Tourist Office (1 Princes Street, London W1R 8AY). In Italy, regional and local tourist boards can supply lists of hotels; a few – in major cities, at mainline railway terminals – have a booking service.

CAMPING AND CARAVANNING

There are around 2,000 campsites in Italy, concentrated mainly along the coasts and lakeshores. There is no official grading system, and although many have attractive settings (frequently in pine woods or on terraces above the sea) pitches are often far too close together. For a list of campsites accepting reservations and a rating of their facilities, write to Centro Internazionale Prenotazioni Campeggio, Casella Postale 23, Florence, or visit their office at exit 19 on the Autostrada del Sole, 14km north-west of Florence. The Touring Club Italiano publishes an annual directory of all the campsites in Italy, *Campeggi e Villaggi Turistici in Italia*, available in Italian bookshops; an abridged list with location map is available (free) from the Italian State Tourist Office in London.

SELF-CATERING

There are plenty of modern purpose-built villas and apartments in seaside resorts, particularly along the Adriatic coast (mainly purpose-built apartments) and the islands of Sardinia and Sicily (apartments, villas and holiday villages). For the British, Tuscany is a particularly popular area, with a wide variety of properties, including old villas and farmhouses.

Inclusive self-catering holidays are offered by specialist tour operators (see Package Holidays below). Accommodation can also be arranged independently through a letting agency. The largest are Interhome (tel: 01-891 1294) with properties all over Italy; and Cuendet, through its UK agents Perrymead Properties (tel: 01-736 4592) and Chapter Travel (tel: 01-586 9451), concentrating on Tuscany and Umbria. The Italian organisation *Agriturist* (Corso V. Emanuele, 101 Rome; tel: 06-656241) can supply details of cottages to rent in all regions.

PACKAGE HOLIDAYS

Lots of tour operators offer packages which include travel (by air, coach, rail or car) and stay-put accommodation (in hotels, self-catering villas, or on campsites); or car, coach or rail touring holidays with or without booked accommodation. A comprehensive list of tour operators offering inclusive air, coach and rail holidays, special interest holidays including art and architecture tours, and self-catering holidays can be obtained from the Italian State Tourist Office, 1 Princes Street, London W1R 8AY. Summer and winter lists are compiled each year.

Three main specialist companies offer holidays all over Italy: Citalia (CIT), tel: 01-686 5533; Magic of Italy, tel: 01-743 9555; and Pegasus, tel: 01-370 6851.

Recommended books

Hotels and Restaurants

The red Michelin guide *Italia* is useful for practical information; it lists a range of hotels and restaurants in all areas, gives an indication of price, and contains maps (including very useful city maps) to help you find them. Facilities and judgements are given in symbol form which gives little impression of what a place is like.

The hefty *Guida d'Italia* (Espresso; in Italian) errs on the side of too much detail for restaurants – but very little for hotels. Restaurants are awarded marks out of 20; we found judgements prejudiced in favour of expense-account restaurants of little tourist appeal. *I Ristoranti di Veronelli* (Mondadori) is more concise. There is no descriptive country-wide restaurant guide in English which we can recommend.

Guidebooks: whole country
Michelin Traveller's Guide to *Italy* with separate volume for *Rome*
Phaidon cultural guide to *Italy* with separate volumes for *Florence and Tuscany, Rome and Latium*

Guidebooks: series
American Express Guides to *Venice; Florence and Tuscany; Rome* (Mitchell Beazley). Lively readable reliable guides with practical information including restaurant and hotel recommendations for the (relatively few) areas they cover
Berlitz Guides to *Venice*; the *Italian Riviera*; the *Italian Adriatic; Florence; Rome; Sicily*. Pocket guides with lots of photos, most useful for coastal areas not covered by many other guides
Blue Guides to *Venice; Northern Italy from the Alps to Rome; Florence; Rome and environs; Southern Italy from Rome to Calabria; Sicily* (A & C Black). The most scholarly and comprehensive guides, covering the whole country in great detail
Companion Guides to *Venice; Florence* and *Rome* (Collins). More anecdotal than the rest, they make good bedtime or armchair reading and give a feel of the various city areas with suggested walks

General:
John Haycraft, *Italian Labyrinth* (Penguin)
Peter Nichols, *Italia Italia* (Macmillan; out of print)
John Julius Norwich, *The Italian World* (Thames & Hudson)
David Willey, *Italians* (BBC Publications)

Art
Mitchell Beazley's Traveller's Guides to Art, Helen Langdon, *Italy*
Pelican Style and Civilisation series, especially: Michael Levey, *Early Renaissance*; Michael Levey, *High Renaissance*; John Shearman, *Mannerism* (all Penguin)
TW Potter, *Roman Italy* (British Museum Publications)
Thames & Hudson History of Art series, especially: Alastair Smart, *The Renaissance and Mannerism in Italy* (Thames & Hudson)
(*See also individual areas, below*)

Food and Wine
Burton Anderson, *Vino* (Papermac)
Elizabeth David, *Italian Food* (Penguin)
Susan Grossman, *Self-catering in Italy* (Christopher Helm)
Spike and Charmian Hughes, *The Pocket Guide to Italian Food and Wine* (Xanadu Publications)

Travellers before 1900
Charles Dickens, *Pictures from Italy* (Granville Publishing)
Goethe, *Italian Journey* (Penguin)
Henry James, *Italian Hours* (Century)
Tobias Smollett, *Travels through France and Italy* (OUP)
Stendhal, *Rome, Naples and Florence* (John Calder)

Regional guides/literature
Lakes and Mountains
Samuel Butler, *Alps and Sanctuaries of Piedmont and the Canton Ticino* (Sutton)
Umberto Eco, *The Name of the Rose* (Picador)
Reginald Farrer, *The Dolomites* (Cadogan Books)
Alessandro Manzoni, *The Betrothed* (Penguin)

Venice
Milton Grundy, *Venice, an anthology guide* (A & C Black)
Peter Lauritzen, *Venice Preserved* (Michael Joseph)
JG Links, *Venice for Pleasure* (Bodley Head)
Giulio Lorenzetti, *Venice and its Lagoon* (Edizioni Linz)
Thomas Mann, *Death in Venice* (Penguin)
Daphne du Maurier, *Don't Look Now and Other Stories* (Penguin)
James Morris, *Venice* (Faber)
John Julius Norwich, *A History of Venice* (Penguin)
John Steer, *A Concise History of Venetian Painting* (Thames & Hudson)
Johannes Wilde, *Venetian Art from Bellini to Titian* (OUP)

Northern Cities
HV Morton, *A Traveller in Italy* (Methuen)
Iris Origo, *The Last Attachment* (John Murray). The story of Byron's love affair in Ravenna with Teresa Guiccioli
Stendhal, *The Charterhouse of Parma* (Penguin)
Edith Templeton, *The Surprise of Cremona* (Methuen)

Florence
Harold Acton and Edward Chaney, *Florence, a Travellers' Companion* (Constable)
EM Forster, *A Room with a View* (Penguin)
Christopher Hibbert, *The Rise and Fall of the House of Medici* (Penguin)
Mary McCarthy, *The Stones of Florence and Venice Observed* (Penguin)
Rupert Scott, *Florence Explored* (Bodley Head)

Tuscany and Umbria
Raymond Flower, *Chianti* (Croom Helm)
EM Forster, *Where Angels Fear to Tread* (Penguin)
Olive Hamilton, *The Divine Country* (Deutsch)
Iris Origo, *The Merchant of Prato* (Penguin); *War in Val d'Orcia* (Century)
Laura Raison, *Tuscany, an Anthology* (Cadogan Books)
Christopher and Jean Serpell, *The Travellers' Guide to Elba and the Tuscan Archipelago* (Jonathan Cape)

Rome
Edward Gibbon, *The Decline and Fall of the Roman Empire* (Penguin)
Christopher Hibbert, *Rome, the Biography of a City* (Viking)
Alberto Moravia, novels eg *The Woman of Rome* (Secker & Warburg)
HV Morton, *A Traveller in Rome* (Methuen)
David Willey, *Welcome to Rome* (Collins)

Central Italy
Baldesar Castiglione, *The Book of the Courtier* (Penguin)
Oliver Knox, *From Rome to San Marino, a Walk in the Steps of Garibaldi* (Collins)
DH Lawrence, *Etruscan Places* (Penguin, with *Sea and Sardinia)*
Daphne du Maurier, *The Flight of the Falcon* (Penguin)

Naples and Campania
Norman Douglas, *Siren Land* (Penguin)
Flora Fraser, *Beloved Emma* (Weidenfeld & Nicholson). A biography of Lady Hamilton
Axel Munthe, *The Story of San Michele* (Mayflower). About Capri
Desmond Seward, *Naples, a Travellers' Companion* (Constable)

The South
Norman Douglas, *Old Calabria* (Century)
George Gissing, *By the Ionian Sea* (Century)
Carlo Levi, *Christ stopped at Eboli* (Penguin)
HV Morton, *A Traveller in Southern Italy* (Methuen)

Sicily
Vincent Cronin, *The Golden Honeycomb* (Granada)
Lawrence Durrell, *Sicilian Carousel* (Penguin)
Margaret Guido, *Sicily, an archaeological guide* (Faber)
Christopher Kininmouth, *Travellers' Guide to Sicily* (Jonathan Cape)
Richard Payne Knight, *Expedition into Sicily* (British Museum Pubs)
Giuseppe di Lampedusa, *The Leopard* (Fontana)
John Julius Norwich, *The Kingdom in the Sun* (Fontana) and *The Normans in the South* (Solitaire)
Steven Runciman, *The Sicilian Vespers* (Cambridge University Press)
Giovanni Verga, *The House by the Medlar Tree* (Dedalus)
Paul Watkins, *See Sicily* (Format)

Sardinia
Grazia Deledda, novels eg *After the Divorce* (Quartet); *The Woman and the Priest* (Dedalus)
Margaret Guido, *Sardinia* (Thames & Hudson)
T & B Holme and B Ghirardelli, *Travellers' Guide to Sardinia* (Jonathan Cape)
Russell King, *Sardinia* (David & Charles)
DH Lawrence, *Sea and Sardinia* (Penguin, with *Etruscan Places*)

Islands
Dana Facaros and Michael Pauls, *Italian Islands* (Cadogan Books)

Maps

Whole country

For general planning and an overall picture of the country, several maps showing all Italy on one sheet are available in Britain. Which you choose probably depends on which you like the look of – one man's fascinating detail is another's confusing clutter. *Bartholomew's* (1:1,250,000) is clear and basic. *AA/Baedeker* (1:750,000) and particularly *Roger Lascelles/RV* give more information, but both have a predominantly orange colour style which makes them rather difficult to read. At 1:1,000,000 (about 16 miles to the inch) *Hallwag* and *RAC* look cooler and clearer, and *Kümmerley + Frey* has the most detailed road and touring information. *Michelin* is good all round – durable in spite of its thinner paper, easy to handle, giving very clear and accurate road information except when the solid yellow blob marking a large town obscures through-routes (the maps are designed to be used with the town plans of their Red Guide).

Half the country

For route planning and main-road motoring a map showing all the north or all the south of Italy will often suffice, provided the boundary suits you. *Freytag & Berndt* produce a double-sided single sheet (1:650,000) which is excellent for navigation if you like the use of colour and the strong mountain effect. On two sheets with overlap, *Kümmerley + Frey* (1:500,000) again has the most detailed road and touring information, and *Touring Club Italiano (TCI)*, Italy's major cartographic publisher, produce a very accurate and beautifully drawn map (1:800,000) with some useful city inserts.

Smaller areas

For local journeys and exploring minor roads, *TCI*'s series of 15 overlapping sheets at 1:200,000 (about three miles to the inch) gives clear and excellent coverage of the Italian regions. You can also buy these maps in road atlas form: three volumes cover the north, the centre and the south. Also available in Britain are "tourist area" maps at scales from 1:100,000 (the Lakes) to 1:35,000 (the Sorrento peninsula), published in Italy with varying amounts of tourist information, sometimes multi-lingual. For the Dolomites there are motoring and walking maps at 1:50,000 and 1:25,000.

Cities

City and town plans are available in England: Hallwag for instance publish Rome, Florence and Venice, and Italian publishers (FMB, LAC, Tabacco, Verdesi) cover all sizeable towns and resorts. They vary in clarity, ease of use and amount of information and are not necessarily up to date. It's probably better to make a choice after arriving in Italy; a free tourist office map may be entirely adequate. The Michelin Red Guide, produced annually, contains small but accurate town plans for cities and major towns (good on one-way systems) to help you drive through or locate a hotel.

General information

Medical care

Under the EEC reciprocal health agreement, British visitors can obtain all medical and dental services available to Italians. Before leaving you need to get the *Medical costs abroad* leaflet (no SA30) from your local Department of Health and Social Security (DHSS) or a travel agent and to complete the form (CM1) in the middle of the leaflet. The DHSS will then send you form E111 which you should take with you when you go abroad. If you are ill you should, if possible, take your form E111 to the Local Health Unit (*Unita Sanitoria Locale*) before you seek treatment, otherwise you may have to pay part of the costs. Full details on what to do will be issued with the E111.

The E111 does not cover all medical expenses and it is advisable to take out separate medical insurance anyway for full cover. Only holiday insurance schemes and private patients plans cover the cost of returning to the UK in the event of illness while abroad. Check you have adequate cover if you already belong to a private patients plan.

The Italian *farmacia* (chemist) is normally open only during shopping hours but a sign should be posted in the window indicating nearby chemists open at night, in the afternoon and on Sundays (these are also listed in the telephone directory). You have to pay a standard charge for prescribed medicines.

Changing money

For rough calculations, £1 = 2,000 *lire*. The Italian government has announced plans to knock three noughts off the *lira*, adopting *centesimi* as subdivisions, but the *lira nuova* is so far only agreed in principle.

Before you go, buy some Italian currency: the exchange rates are usually more favourable in the UK than in Italy. The maximum you are allowed to import into Italy (or buy from a UK bank) is L400,000.

Sterling travellers' cheques are better than *lire* ones (you can get *lire* cheques only from Italian banks here, and cashing them in Italy can be a problem). When changing travellers' cheques, there is a flat-rate commission of about L1,000-L3,000 per transaction, so it doesn't pay to cash very small amounts.

A Eurocheque card allows you to cash up to £100 per day; Eurocheques can often be used to pay bills in hotels, shops and restaurants. Each cheque is guaranteed up to the equivalent of £100. The cost varies among UK banks: £3.50 to £5 per year for the card, plus 1.6% commission and a small handling charge on each cheque used.

In Italian banks queues are usually long and opening hours short. You can also change money in tourist offices and *bureaux de change* (look for *cambio* sign). Many hotels will exchange travellers' cheques, but their rates tend to be very poor.

Major credit cards (Eurocard and Visa) and charge cards

(American Express and Diners' Club) are widely accepted in hotels, restaurants and smarter shops in cities and tourist resorts. They are not accepted at petrol stations and it is unwise to rely on this method of payment in country areas.

Booking a hotel
It is simplest to telephone a hotel to make a booking, especially if you are not sure about up-to-date prices; most hotel staff at least understand basic English and many speak it fluently. Hotels may require you to send a deposit (*deposito* or *caparra*) in confirmation of your booking; send either a bankers' draft or an ordinary bank cheque written out in *lire*. If you choose to write, you could follow this example:

The Management,
LA DIREZIONE,
Hotel (name)
ALBERGO......

Dear Sirs,
EGREGI SIGNORI,

I would like to book a double room with bath/shower (single room without bath) from...........to...........inclusive
VORREI PRENOTARE UNA CAMERA DOPPIA CON BAGNO/
DOCCIA (CAMERA SINGOLA SENZA BAGNO)
DA..........AL..........compreso

I/We would like breakfast only/half board/full board
VORREI/VORREMMO SOLO COLAZIONE/MEZZA PENSIONE/
PENSIONE COMPLETA

Please would you send me a copy of your brochure/price list
VI PREGO DI INVIARMI UNA COPIA DEL VOSTRO DEPLIANT/
TARIFFARIO

Awaiting your confirmation, I remain yours faithfully
IN ATTESA DI VOSTRA CONFERMA, PORGO CORDIALI SALUTI

Other useful words and phrases:
a double room (one bed) *una camera matrimoniale*
a twin-bedded room *una camera a due letti*
air conditioning *aria condizionata*
an extra bed *un letto supplementare*
a child's bed *un letto da bambino*
a cot *una culla*
front/back room *camera sul davanti/dietro*
lake/sea view *vista sul lago/mare*
terrace *terrazza*

Opening hours

As a general rule, almost everything – churches, shops, banks, offices, petrol stations and some museums – closes at lunchtime, often for several hours.

Banks   Banks are open from 8.30am to 1.20pm, and often for one hour in the afternoon (usually from 2.45pm or 3pm to 3.45pm or 4pm). They are closed on Saturday and Sunday and on public holidays, but money can be changed at *bureaux de change* in main railway stations and airports.

Museums, galleries and sites   Opening hours vary considerably throughout the country, and according to the season, and it is essential to check times locally when you arrive. As a very general rule, state museums are normally open from 9am to 2pm (Sundays to 1pm), and closed on Mondays. Other museums and galleries often have different hours. Archaeological sites are usually open until dusk.

Shops   Shops are generally open from 8.30am or 9am to 1pm and from 3.30pm or 4pm to 7.30pm or 8pm, with some variations in the north – notably Venice and Milan, where the lunch break is shorter and shops close earlier. They are closed on Sunday and usually on one afternoon a week, not necessarily Saturday. Early closing for most shops is on Monday but for food shops it is usually Wednesday or Thursday. Shops in tourist resorts are sometimes open all day, six days a week. Italians tend to do their shopping in the cool of the evening; this is good for tourists, too, as many sights are closed.

Public holidays

Banks, offices, shops and some museums are closed on the following days: **New Year's Day** January 1st; **Epiphany** January 6th; **Liberation Day** April 25th; **Easter Monday**; **Liberation Day** April 25th; **Labour Day** May 1st; **Republic Day** June 2nd; **Assumption** (Ferragosto) August 15th; **All Saints** (Ognissanti) November 1st; **Immaculate Conception** December 8th; **Christmas Day** December 25th; **St Stephen's Day** December 26th.

Beaches and bathing

There is normally a charge for the use of beach umbrellas, cabins and deck-chairs. This varies from resort to resort and according to the season; L6,000 (£3) per day for all the facilities is about average. Beach facilities are not always included in hotel or package-holiday prices; it's worth checking when you book. There is usually at least one non-paying public section between the concession areas, and the five metres of sand nearest to the sea on any beach are public territory.

In July and August you can hire boats or pedaloes in most resorts but only the larger resorts offer a full range of sailing, waterskiing, boardsailing and scuba-diving.

Restaurants

The most expensive type is the *ristorante*, with long elegant menus in the window, sometimes in more than one language. Then there are all manner of *trattorie*, middle-range restaurants which often display a set-price *menu turistico*. The latter are not necessarily good value: undiscerning tourists are commonly served dull food, poorly cooked. Cheapest and often most interesting is the *osteria*, which can be very simple and family-run. Here the available menu may not be written down at all but reeled off in Italian. Lack of much choice is often a good sign.

Cover charges (per person) vary according to the category of the restaurant, and a service charge of 12%-15% of the total is added to your bill except where a fixed price or tourist menu is indicated. You are required by law to retain your receipt (*ricevuta fiscale*), and may later be asked to produce it as part of a spot-check. All restaurants have to close on one day a week.

Telephoning
Telephone calls can be made from most bars (look out for the special dial symbol); for older payphones you will need *gettoni* (metal tokens) which you can buy at the cash-till for 200 *lire*. For local calls you simply dial the number; for calls to another area there is a prefix. For local directory enquiries, dial 12; operator 13; emergencies 113 (ambulance/fire/police). Long-distance and international calls can be made from the offices of SIP (Società Italiana Posta/Telefoni – pronounced "seep") in major towns; you queue to book a cabin and pay afterwards (all S.I.P. offices have telephone directories for the whole of Italy).

For calls to the UK, dial 00, wait for a tone change, then dial 44 followed by the UK area code (omitting the first 0) then the number.

When calling Italy from Britain, dial 010 39 followed by the local area code (but omit the initial 0) then the number.

Tipping
In restaurants and bars it is customary to leave waiters a tip for satisfactory service, although a service charge is normally included in the bill. Cinema usherettes and hotel porters also expect small tips (L500 per suitcase is reasonable). It is also polite to tip the garageman who cleans your windscreen although gratuities are seldom solicited. Taxi drivers expect about 10%.

Tourist Information Offices
The Italian State Tourist Office, 1 Princes Street, London W1R 8AY, telephone (01) 408 1254 can supply additional information. Their office is open from Monday to Friday, 9.30am to 5.30pm.

In Italy the Italian State Tourist Office (*Ente Nazionale per il Turismo* or ENIT) provides information on the whole country. There are also regional tourist boards (*Ente Provinciale per il Turismo* or EPT) in each of the 95 provincial capitals, with branches at airports, railway stations, ports and on motorways. In addition small towns and resorts have their own local tourist office (*Azienda di soggiorno* or *Pro Loco*). All can advise on accommodation, opening hours, restaurants, local events, transport etc. and provide free brochures, hotel lists, timetables and maps.

Festivals and events

January
Piana degli Albanesi: Epiphany celebration (Byzantine) (6th)
Rome: Epiphany fair on Piazza Navona (5th-6th)

February
Agrigento: Almond blossom festival
Venice: Carnival (week before Lent)
Viareggio: Carnival (week before Lent)

March/April
Easter Celebration of Holy Week throughout Italy. On Easter
Sunday in Florence: Scoppio del Carro (explosion of the cart)
Oristano: Sa Sartiglia (first week in March)

May
Assisi: Calendimaggio (first week)
Bari: Sagra di San Nicola (7th-8th)
Cagliari: Sagra di Sant' Efisio (1st)
Gubbio: Festa dei Ceri (15th);
Palio dei Balestrieri (last Sunday)
Massa Marittima: Joust of the Falcon (20th or next Sunday)
Sassari: Cavalcata Sarda (last Sunday)
Venice: Vogalonga (a Sunday)

June
Florence: Gioco del Calcio (24th and 28th);
Festa di San Giovanni with fireworks display (24th)
Genoa: Festa di San Giovanni (24th)
Pisa: Regatta of San Ranieri (16th-17th)
Gioco del Ponte (28th)

July
Pistoia: Joust of the Bear (25th)
Rome: Festa de' Noiantri (16th-24th)
Siena: Palio (2nd)
Venice: Il Redentore (third Sunday)

August
Ascoli Piceno: Joust of the Quintana (first Sunday)
Feltre: Palio (first weekend)
Lavagna: Torta dei Fieschi (14th)
Massa Marittima: Joust of the Falcon (second Sunday)
Nuoro: Festival of the Redeemer (29th)
Piazza Armerina: Palio dei Normanni (13th-15th)
Siena: Palio (16th)
Ventimiglia: Regatta (9th-10th)

September
Arezzo: Joust of the Saracen (first Sunday)

Asti: Palio (third Sunday)
Florence: Festa delle Rificolone (7th and 8th)
Foligno: Joust of the Quintana (second Sunday)
Lucca: Holy Cross celebrations (14th)
Marostica: Human chess game (even years; second weekend)
Naples: Piedigrotta (first 10 days of month)
Sansepolcro: Palio dei Balestrieri (second Sunday)
Venice: Regatta (first Sunday)
Viterbo: Macchina of Santa Rosa procession (3rd)

October
Alba: Joust of the Hundred Towers (first Sunday)

November
Venice: Festa della Salute (21st)

December
Advent and Christmas celebrations, fairs, cribs in churches

Weather

Italy stretches 745 miles from the major climactic boundary of the
Alps to the latitudes of North Africa. Broadly speaking, its northern
plain, though not landlocked, has the "Continental" climate of hot
summers and cold winters, while its southern peninsula has the
transitional "Mediterranean" climate controlled by subtropical
anticyclones in summer and temperate westerly airstreams in
winter.

Northern lakes and mountains
Italy's Alpine border has its own climate of change and contrast,
according to height as well as season. In winter the mountains are
often sunny in settled anticyclonic conditions, while down in the
valleys fog and frost can linger all day. In summer, the situation is
reversed: cloud and thundery showers affect the heights while the
valleys, and particularly the Italian Lakes, stay warm and sunny. A
week free of cloud and showers is rare, and thunderstorms can
occur in any month; on a motoring holiday you can take advantage
of the very local variations, keeping to the lee side of mountains to
escape the squalls. Between the opening of the Alpine passes (April,
in a cold year) and their closure by fresh snow (October) the summer
season at the main holiday resorts is generally warm, often brilliant,
but endlessly changeable. Much depends on the prevailing wind.
Occasionally the Alps produce the phenomenon called a *föhn* (fall)
wind, a strong airstream forced up over the peaks to descend again
dry and gaining heat, raising valley temperatures quite dramatically
and bringing days of clear weather. A *föhn* is good news for tourists,
but has a bad reputation among locals for causing both avalanches
and migraines.

Coasts

Around the long central ridge of the Apennine mountains lie 4,632 miles of Italian coastline; weather differences between west and east coasts are most marked in the north in winter, diminishing to virtually nothing in the far south in summer. In the northern Adriatic, winter and spring temperatures are at times brought low by the *bora*, a strong cold wind from the high Yugoslav plateau. The Ligurian coast is mild in winter, protected by the curve of the Alps from the cold *mistral* of France's Rhône valley (which occasionally has enough momentum to become the *maestrale* and take a sweeping curve across Sardinia and Sicily). Another contribution to the year-round lush vegetation of the Italian Riviera has given to meteorology the term "Gulf of Genoa depression", produced here by unstable cool air crossing warm sea in the lee of the Alps; a "Genoa low" brings a week or more of exceptionally intense rain showers. In the northern Adriatic, the coast warms up swiftly in late spring and has high summer temperatures a degree or two above Liguria's; they drop abruptly in October. Long dry periods are punctuated by summer storms – especially around Venice – which keep the rainfall averages rather higher than Genoa's.

South of Rome, higher temperatures on the west coast occur chiefly during a bout of the sirocco, a thoroughly unpleasant wind bringing dust and oppressive heat from the Saharan desert. The prevailing summer pattern, all round the Tyrrhenian, Ionian and southern Adriatic shores, is one of local sea breezes – a much more welcome phenomenon with a decisive effect on coastal temperature and humidity. By the afternoon of a sunny day, cooler air at sea level is drawn in over the more rapidly heated land, and if it cools down enough at night a corresponding land breeze blows offshore towards dawn. If the land is low-lying, sea breezes can travel a long way – Rome, 20 miles from the coast, sometimes benefits from the *ponentino* – but southern Italy's coastline is more often close to mountain slopes. Highest seaside temperatures of all – and uncompromising zeros in summer rain statistics – are found in Sicily and Sardinia. Throughout southern Italy the siesta habit helps to cope with searing midday sun and sleeplessly hot nights, from mid-May to mid-October. By September, the temperature of Mediterranean seawater is higher than the average air temperature in Britain.

Sunshine and rainfall in coastal cities

	APRIL		MAY		JUNE		JULY		AUG		SEPT	
Genoa	48	8	51	7	56	5	65	4	62	5	53	6
Venice	44	9	52	8	54	8	64	7	60	7	53	5
Rimini	39	8	51	7	56	7	63	4	63	5	53	6
Naples	51	8	56	7	60	4	69	2	70	3	63	5
Trapani	59	6	65	3	67	2	79	0	76	2	70	3
Bournemouth	45	9	45	10	47	8	43	7	46	9	39	10
	Sun	Rain	Sun	Rain	Sun	Rain	Sun	Rain	Sun	Rain	Sun	Rain

Sun = bright sunshine, percentage of daylight hours
Rain = average no. of days it rains (1.0mm or more)

Cities

Winter sightseeing, relatively uncrowded, can be very pleasant provided ideas of "sunny Italy" are not exaggerated. December is the dullest month everywhere and January the coldest, but temperatures are comparable with an English spring in Florence, Rome, Naples and Palermo, which get twice as much sunshine as London. Though on average it rains on almost as many days, Italian rain tends to be torrential and soon over rather than drizzly and prolonged, and museum-hopping is an excellent way of taking shelter. Italy's northern cities are another matter. From Turin to Venice, the "Continental" climate (which in summer produces abundant vines on the hillslopes and rice in the Po valley) is uncharitable in winter. Freezing fog is common in the Lombardy plain as cold air from central Europe descends through the mountain passes. Venice on the coast, though still colder than London, has much more winter sunshine than the inland cities: February, the month of Carnival, is often particularly dry and bright here while central and southern Italian cities have their wettest weeks.

The Mediterranean spring is an indecisive affair – from March to May there are false starts of summery weather. In north Italy March temperatures climb rapidly out of their winter extremes but the difference is less marked in the south, where mild and changeable weather brings the countryside to its greenest. City sightseeing is popular everywhere in a season too unreliable for seaside holidays; Rome of course fills up to capacity for Easter.

By April to May, temperatures in Florence catch up with those of Rome and Naples further south. Enclosed in its ring of hills Florence stays hot and humid all summer, simmering like a cauldron at midday through June, July and August, with little relief at night. Rome can be equally uncomfortable; Naples does benefit from sea breezes. In the northern cities as temperatures climb the arrival of a thunderstorm can be welcome – spectacular, often refreshing, and not too prolonged – but such relief is rarer in the south.

September can be the best month for cities: it's less fiercely hot, the crowds have not yet deserted the beaches and the school term has begun. Weather is much more reliably calm than in spring, the mellow sunlight at its most flattering and the nights cooling down. Early October is equally good, but the later the date, the greater the gamble. Around the 20th there is an observed, regular drop in pressure in the Mediterranean and, say meteorologists, "the probability of receiving rain in any five-day period increases dramatically" as the first cold fronts move over the still-warm sea.

By November, northern Italy is cooling as rapidly as in spring it warmed up; Venice has its wettest month, and inland cities their first fogs; sunshine percentages plummet. Florence too cools down and cloud collects in its hills, but Rome and the south stay sunnier and drier – Sicily in particular often has fine November weather, like the best sort of British autumn, with only an occasional heavy rainshower.

Average daily maximum temperature (°C) in cities

	J	F	M	A	M	J	J	A	S	O	N	D
Venice	5.5	7.6	11.8	16.5	21.0	24.7	27.2	26.8	23.8	18.5	11.8	7.5
Florence	9.0	11.0	14.4	18.8	23.2	27.0	30.0	29.5	25.7	20.3	14.0	10.6
Rome	11.1	12.6	15.2	18.8	23.4	27.6	30.4	29.8	26.3	21.5	16.1	12.6
Naples	11.7	12.6	14.8	18.2	22.2	26.3	29.1	29.0	26.0	21.7	17.0	13.6
Palermo	15.8	16.4	17.4	20.0	23.6	27.0	29.7	30.0	28.2	25.0	21.4	17.7
London	6.3	6.9	10.1	13.3	16.7	20.3	21.8	21.4	18.5	14.2	10.1	7.3

Glossary 1
Art and architecture

altar-piece work of art placed above the altar

antique Greek and Roman art

badia Benedictine abbey

ambo pulpit in early Christian church

amphora large Greek or Roman two-handed vessel

apsidal chapel chapel located off the apse at the end of the church, behind the choir

architrave horizontal frame above a door

archivolt moulded architrave around arch

atlantes male figures used as supporting pillars

atrium central court of Roman house

baldacchino canopy supported or suspended over an altar

basilica aisled church with no transepts

bottega artist's studio; pupils/assistants under his direction

campanile bell-tower, usually detached

camposanto cemetery

cartoon full-size drawing as design for painting or tapestry

caryatids female figures used as supporting pillars

cassone decorated chest

certosa Carthusian abbey

chiaroscuro treatment of light and shade in painting

cosmati work (cosmatesque) style of mosaic decoration named after 12th-century Roman family of specialist artists

cupola dome; ceiling of dome

diptych work of art consisting of two panels

duomo cathedral

faience decorated earthenware and porcelain still manufactured in, among other places, Faenza (Marches)

fresco method of painting in watercolour laid on wall or ceiling before plaster is dry

fresco secco painting on dry plaster with pigments suspended in water

graffito/sgraffito decoration (or defacement) by scratches through plaster

greek cross cross with all four arms of equal length

grisaille monochrome painting, often imitation sculpture or relief

grotesque Renaissance decorative style, including animal and human forms interwoven with vegetation, in imitation of ancient Roman painting (from grottoes)

hypogeum underground chamber, usually for burial of Etruscan dead

iconostasis screen bearing icons and separating the sanctuary from the nave

intarsia/tarsia mosaic woodwork

latin cross plain cross with lowest arm longer than the other three

loggia open-sided gallery, arcade or balcony

lunette semi-circular space in dome or ceiling, decorated with a painting or relief

maestà depiction of Madonna and Child enthroned in majesty

majolica Italian Renaissance (and modern) earthenware with coloured ornamentation on opaque white glaze

mandorla almond-shaped lozenge of light surrounding figure (usually the Virgin) in a religious painting

museo dell' opera museum attached to an important church containing works of art and other items belonging to it. Nothing to do with opera

narthex vestibule of an early Christian church

pala large painted altar-piece

palazzo dignified and important building; mansion or palace

palombino fine-grained white marble

pendentive intersection of dome by two adjacent arches springing from supporting columns

peristyle court, cloister or space surrounded by row of columns

pietà picture or sculpture of the Virgin Mary holding the dead body of Christ on her lap

pietra dura hard or semi-precious stones, often used in the form of mosaics

pietra serena blue-grey stone used for decorative effect in Florentine architecture

polyptych work of art consisting of four or more panels

predella painting or panel, usually in sections, attached below altar-piece or on raised shelf behind

putto cherub

sacra conversazione literally, Holy Conversation: painting of the Madonna and saints as a group

scuola Venetian lay brotherhood dedicated to charitable works

sfumato literally, smoky effect. Depiction of hazy atmosphere blurring outline in painting; one of Leonardo da Vinci's specialities

stucco plaster or cement used for coating wall surfaces or moulding into architectural decorations

tempera egg-based paint, the usual medium for easel paintings until oil became widespread in the Renaissance

tessera small cube of marble or glass used in mosaic

thermae Greek or Roman public baths

tondo round painting or relief

triptych painting or tablet in three sections, particularly altar-piece

trompe l'oeil literally 'deceives the eye'; illusionistic decoration, often painted architecture

tympanum (carved) space between lintel and arch of doorway

villa country residence; country estate in Roman times

trecento the 14th century (1300s)

quattrocento the 15th century (1400s)

cinquecento the 16th century (1500s)

Glossary 2
Food

abbacchio baby lamb
Abbruzzese, all' with red peppers
acciughe anchovies
acquacotta Tuscan vegetable broth
affettati misti sliced cold meats
affumicato smoked
agliata, all' with a garlic sauce
aglio garlic
agnello lamb
agnol(ott)i meat-filled pasta
agoni freshwater shad (herring family)
agro sour
aguglia garfish
albicocche apricots
alici anchovies
alloro bay leaves
alosa shad (herring family)
amaretti macaroons
amatriciana, all' with tomato and bacon sauce
ananas pineapple
anguilla eel
anguria watermelon
anellini tiny pasta rings
animelle sweetbreads
anitra duck
anolini (in brodo) small ravioli (in broth)
antipasto hors d'oeuvre
antipasto genovese broad beans, salami and Sardo cheese
aragosta crayfish, rock lobster
arancini breadcrumbed rice balls containing veal and peas
arancia orange
aringhe herrings
àrista roast loin or saddle of pork
arrabbiata, all' with tomato, bacon and hot pepper sauce
arrosto roast
arselle baby clams
asparagi asparagus
astaco river crayfish

baccalà dried salt cod

bagna cauda garlic and anchovy dip
barbabietola beetroot
basilico basil
bavette (alla trasteverina) ribbon pasta (with tuna, tomatoes, anchovies and mushroom sauce)
beccaccia woodcock
beccaccino snipe
beccafichi small birds
bianco, in boiled or plain
bianco white
bigne doughnuts, beignets
bigoli buckwheat pasta, like spaghetti (Venice)
bisato eel (Venetian dialect)
biscotti biscuits
bistecca (al sangue, a puntino, ben cotta) steak usually rib (rare, medium, well-done)
bocconcini veal, ham and cheese 'mouthfuls'
bocconotti sweet pastries filled with aromatic jam
boldrò angler fish
bollito boiled
bolliti misti mixed boiled meats
bolognese, alla with meat sauce or with ham and cheese
bomba di riso pigeons baked with rice, speciality of Parma
bombolone doughnut
bongo-bongo profiteroles
boraggine borage
boreto fish chowder (Grado)
boscaiola, alla with aubergines, tomatoes and mushrooms
bottar(i)ga dried grey mullet roe
bracciolette veal rolls
brace, alla cooked over live embers
braciola (di maiale) (pork) chop
braciolette ripiene stuffed veal rolls
bracioline cutlets
branzino sea bass, pike or perch
brasato braised
bresaola dried salt beef
brodetto (Adriatic) fish soup

brodo broth
bruschetta garlic toast
bucatini small pasta tubes
budino mousse; pudding
bue beef
burridà Genoese or Sardinian fish stew
burro butter
busecca thick vegetable and tripe soup or stew
busecchina chestnuts stewed in white wine, milk and cream
buttariga see bottar(i)ga

cacciagione game
cacciucco (alla livornese) (Tuscan) fish soup
calamar(ett)i (baby) squid
calzone pizza dough pasty stuffed with ham and cheese
camoscio chamois
canestrelli small clams or scallops
canestrini tiny pasta shells
cannelloni large pasta tubes, usually stuffed and baked
cannoli Sicilian pastry horns
cannolicchi short pasta tubes (Sicily)
canocchie shrimps
caparozzoli raw sea truffles
capelli d'angelo 'angel's hair' pasta
capesante scallops
capitone eel
capocollo cured pork
caponata rich vegetable dish with capers, aubergine, tomato, olives, oil
capone gurnard (fish)
cappe various types of bivalve mollusc
cappelletti stuffed pasta hats
capperi capers
cappon magro Genoese fish salad with vegetables and garlic sauce
caprese Capri style; mozzarella and tomato salad
capretto kid
capriata vegetable stew
capriolo roe-deer
carbonara, alla (spaghetti) with bacon, egg, cream and Parmesan
carbonata beef in red wine
carciofi globe artichokes

cardi cockles; cardoons
carne suina pork
carote carrots
carpa carp
carpaccio slivers of raw fillet beef with oil, lemon and Parmesan
carpionato; carpione, in marinated
carre rib or loin
carta da musica Sardinia bread, eaten with oil and salt
cartoccio, all' cooked in paper
casa, di house speciality
casalinga home-made
casarecchi Sicilian type of pasta
casonsei stuffed pasta rings (Bergamo)
cassata sponge cake or ice-cream with candied fruits
cassoeula Milanese pork and vegetable stew
cassola Sardinian fish stew
castagnaccio chestnut cake
castagne chestnuts
cavalucci Sienese biscuits
cavolett(in)i Brussels sprouts
cavolfiore cauliflower
cavolo cabbage
ceci chick peas
cèfalo grey mullet
cenci alla fiorentina fried twists of pastry
cerignole giant green olives
cervella brains
cervo venison
cetriolini gherkins
cetriolo cucumber
chele claws
chifferotti small curved pasta tubes
cialde wafer or waffle
cicoria chicory
cieche baby eels
ciliegie cherries
cima Genoese stuffed veal roll
cima di rape turnip tops
cinghiale wild boar
cipolla onion
ciuppin Livornese fish soup
cocomero watermelon
coda alla vaccinara braised oxtail
coda di rospo angler-fish (tail)
composta stewed fruit

conchiglietti shell-shaped pasta
condiggion; condijon mixed
vegetable salad
coniglio rabbit
contorni vegetables
controfiletto sirloin steak
copate Sienese nougat wafers
coppa pork salami, brawn or meat
loaf; ice cream 'coupe'
coratella lungs, heart, liver and/or
intestines
cosciotto (di agnello) leg (of lamb)
costa (di maiale) (pork) chop or rib
costata (di bue) rib (of beef),
entrecote steak
co(s)toletta cutlet or chop
co(s)toletta alla Milanese
breadcrumbed veal cutlet
cotechino pork sausage
cotto cooked
cozze mussels
crema custard; cream soup
crescione watercress
crespelle, crespolini pancakes
creste di Gallo pasta coxcombs
crostata tart, flan
crostini 'croutons', often with
capers, anchovies or chicken livers
crudo raw
culatello type of Parma ham
culingiones Sardinian ravioli
cuore heart

datteri dates
datteri di mare clams ('sea dates')
dentice fish similar to bream
diavola, alla with peppery sauce
dital(in)i tiny pasta tubes
dolce dessert; sweet
dorata golden brown; gilt-head (fish)
dragoncello tarragon

fagiano pheasant
fagioli beans (haricot)
fagioli all'uccelletto stew with
beans, tomatoes, sausages, sage,
garlic
fagiolini runner or French beans
falsomagro (farsumagru) Sicilian
veal roll with hard-boiled egg,
cheese and spices

faraona guinea-fowl
farcito stuffed
fare, da to order
farfalle pasta bows, 'butterflies'
fasoeil al furn oven-baked beans
fave (al guanciale) broad beans
(with onion and bacon)
fegato (alla veneziana) liver (with
onions)
ferri, ai charcoal-grilled
fesa (di vitello) leg (of veal)
fett(in)a (small) slice
fettuccine Roman ribbon pasta
fettunta see bruschetta
fichi (mandorlati) (dried) figs
filetti breasts (poultry)
filetto (Casanova) fillet steak (with
brandy and Marsala)
finanziera with truffles, marsala,
sweetbreads, mushrooms
finocchio fennel
finocchiona Florentine salami with
fennel
fiori di zucca fried marrow flowers
fitascetta onion bread ring
focaccia savoury bread or pizza
focaccia di vitello veal rissoles
fonduta cheese fondue
formaggio cheese
forno, al baked
fracosta rib (of beef)
fragol(in)e (wild) strawberries
fragoline di mare tiny squids
fresco fresh; cold
fricco del Friuli potato omelette
fritole Venetian fritters with raisins,
pine kernels and lemon
frittata omelette
frittata con gli zoccoli omelette with
pieces of bacon
frittata genovese spinach omelette
frittelle fritters
fritto fried
fritto misto mixed fry in batter
(meat/vegetables/seafood)
frutti di mare seafood
fugazza Venetian sweet with orange
peel, cloves, ginger, almonds and
vanilla
funghi (porcini) (boletus)
mushrooms

fusilli pasta twists

gallina boiling fowl
gamberetti shrimps
gamberi large prawns
garagoli type of shellfish
garofalato Roman stew with wine and cloves
gelato ice-cream
gianchetti tiny fish fry
ginepro juniper
girello steak
gnocchi small potato, semolina or maize flour dumplings
gnumerieddi Apulian lamb sausages
granatina syrup of pomegranate
grance(v)ole Adriatic spider crabs
granchio crab
granita grainy water ice
gratinato baked with butter and Parmesan or (fish) garlic and herbs
griglia, alla grilled
grissini breadsticks
grongo conger eel
guanciale pig's cheek bacon

insalata salad
involtini skewered, rolled, stuffed meat – usually veal
iota bean soup with turnips or sauerkraut and pork rind

lamponi raspberries
lasagne flat pasta baked in layers with meat filling
latte milk
lattuga lettuce
lauro see alloro
legumi vegetables
lenticchie lentils
lepre (alla montanaro) hare (stewed with pine nuts and sultanas)
less(at)o boiled
licurdia Calabrian onion soup
lingua tongue
linguine ribbon pasta, usually with clam, tomato and parsley sauce
lombata loin or fillet
lombata di maiale pork tenderloin
lombatine chops or entrecote
lombo loin

lonza cured fillet of pork
lucanega see luganega
luccio pike
luganega pork sausage or salami
lumache snails; pasta shells
lumache alla Milanese snails with oil, anchovies and garlic

maccheroni alla chitarra macaroni with hot peppers (Abruzzi)
macedonia fruit salad
maggiorana sweet marjoram
magro, di with light vegetable stuffing
maiale pork
malfatti baked gnocchi
malloreddus Sardinian gnocchetti
maltagliati short pasta tubes
mandilli di sea 'silk handkerchiefs', dialect name for kind of pasta
mandorle almonds
maniche pasta tubes ('sleeves')
mantecato salt cod purée; soft ice cream
manzo beef
marinara, alla with seafood
marmora striped bream
marroni chestnuts
marsoni small fish
mascarpone cream cheese, similar to 'fromage blanc'
mazzancolle very large prawns
medaglioni medallions, rounds
mela apple
melacotogna quince
melanzane aubergines
menta (romana) (pepper)mint
mentuccia peppermint
merluzzo cod
messicani stuffed veal rolls
mezzemaniche short pasta 'sleeves'
miele honey
migliaccio pie (can be savoury or sweet)
Milanese, alla (usually) cooked in breadcrumbs
minestra soup
minestre in brodo pasta in broth
minestrone soup with vegetables and pasta or rice
mirtilli bilberries

mirto myrtle
missoltitt grilled and marinated lake sardines
misto mixed
molecche soft shelled crabs
mondeghili beef and cheese rissoles
monte bianco chestnut purée with cream
montone mutton
more blackberries
morene lampreys, murry
mormora see marmora
morseddu Calabrian giblet stew
mortadella Bolognese pork sausage
mostarda pickle
mozzarella in carrozza cheese sandwich dipped in egg and fried
muggine grey mullet
mugnaia, alla 'meunière', fried in butter with lemon juice and parsley
muscolo shin of beef; mussel
mustica tiny eels with peppers

nasello hake
'ncapriata boiled bean purée
nero black
nocciole hazelnuts
noci (wal)nuts
nodino veal chop

oca goose
olivette veal rolls
ombrina Mediterranean fish similar to bass
orata gilt-head bream
orecchiette little pasta 'ears'
ortaggi vegetables
ortiche nettles
ortolana, all' with vegetables
osso buco stew of veal marrowbone
ostriche oysters

padella frying pan
paggello Spanish bream
paglia e fieno green and white tagliatelle ('straw and hay')
pagliacci concave pasta circles
pagliata intestines
paillard thin grilled steak
palombacce wood pigeons
palombo kind of dogfish

pan speziale spiced bread
pan'unto see bruschetta.
panata bread soup
pancetta lightly salted belly pork
pane bread
pane frattau baked bread, egg, cheese and tomato dish from Sardinia
panettone Milanese cake with dried fruit
panforte Sienese spiced cake
panna (montata) (whipped) cream
pansoti type of ravioli, stuffed with ricotta, egg, herbs and walnut sauce
panzanella Tuscan bread salad
panzarotti deep-fried cheese and ham pasties
paparot spinach soup
pappardelle (con la lepre) ribbon pasta (with hare sauce)
Parmigiana, alla Parma style, usually with Parmesan cheese
passatelli (in brodo) vermicelli-like breadcrumb, cheese and egg mixture (in broth)
passato underdone; sieved
pasta e fagioli thick pasta, bean and pork soup
pasta frolla short pastry
pasta sfoglia flaky pastry
pasticcio pie
pastine small rice-like pasta grains
pastissada stew (Venetian dialect)
patate potatoes
pearà Veronese sauce made with breadcrumbs, bone marrow, cheese and stock
penne pasta 'quills'
peoci mussels (Venetian dialect)
pepe pepper
peperata Veronese sauce
peperonata sweet peppers and tomatoes stewed with onions and garlic
peperoncini chillies
peperoni sweet peppers
pere pears
pernice partridge
pescatrice angler fish
pesce (pronounced peshay) fish
pesce di spada see pescespada

pesce persico perch
pesce prete stargazer (fish)
pescespada swordfish
pesche (pronounced peskay)
peaches
pesciolini whitebait
pesto basil sauce (Genoa) with pine
kernels and Parmesan
petto di pollo boned chicken breast
pezzato lamb stew
piadina type of pizza
piccagge type of pasta from Liguria
piccante with a piquant sauce
piccata thin veal escalope
piccione pigeon
piedini di maiale pig's trotters
pi(g)noli pine kernels
pip(ett)e (short) curved pasta tubes
piselli peas
pizza capricciosa Chef's special
pizza
pizza Margherita with tomatoes,
anchovies, mozzarella and basil
pizza napoletana with tomatoes,
mozzarella, anchovies and oregano
pizza quattro stagioni with four
seasonal sections, including seafood
pizza rustica pie with onions,
tomatoes, anchovies and olives
pizzaiola, alla with tomato and
garlic or marjoram
pizzoccherri kind of pasta with
potatoes, cabbage and cheese
pol(i)p(ett)o squid or octopus
polenta boiled maize
pollame poultry
poll(astrin)o (spring) chicken
pollo alla padovana chicken
fricassée
pollo in porchetta chicken stuffed
with ham
pollo sorpresa Chicken Kiev
polpette rissoles or meatballs
polpettone meat (or fish) roll
pomodori tomatoes
pompelmo grapefruit
porceddu Sardinian suckling pig
porchetta roast suckling pig
porri leeks
potacchio, in with garlic, rosemary,
parsley, white wine

poveracci ink fish
prezzemolo parsley
prosciutto ham
prugne plums
punta di vitello stuffed roast breast
of veal
puttanesca, alla with fiery garlic,
anchovy and hot pepper sauce

quaglie quails
quagliette small pieces of meat on
skewers

rabarbaro rhubarb
radicchio bitter red chicory from the
Veneto
rafano horseradish
ragu meat sauce
rana pescatrice see pescatrice
rane (in guazzetto) frogs' legs (in
butter and white wine)
rape turnips
ravanelli radishes
razza skate
reginette frilled pasta strips
ribes nero blackcurrants
ribollita Florentine bean and
vegetable soup
ricchi e poveri beans and caviar
ricci sea-urchins
ricciarelli a Tuscan almond paste
confection
ricotta soft sheeps' cheese
rigatoni short, thick pasta tubes
ripieno stuffed
risi e bisi thick rice and pea soup
from the Veneto
riso al salto fried leftover rice
riso giallo saffron rice
risotto rice dish with strict regional
variations
risotto in Capro Roman risotto with
lamb (Venice)
risotto alla certosina risotto with
shrimps, peas and mushrooms
risotto alla finanziera chicken liver
risotto
risotto di magro risotto with
vegetables or fish
risotto alla Milanese creamy saffron
risotto

risotto alla pilota risotto with sausages and onions

risotto primavera risotto with fresh vegetables or (Parma) chicken livers

risotto al puntal risotto with a pork chop

risotto alla Rossini risotto with funghi porcini, eggs and Parmesan

risotto alla sbirraglia Venetian chicken risotto

risotto di secole Venetian beef or veal risotto

ristretto clear soup; concentrated

rognoni kidneys

rombo turbot

rombo liscio brill

rosmarino rosemary

rospo angler fish

rosso red

rostin negaa Milanese dish of veal in white wine

rotelle pasta wheels

sagne chine Calabrian lasagne with cheese, artichokes and meatballs

salamoia, alla pickled

sale salt

salmi, in in a rich red wine sauce

salsa sauce

salsa verde herb sauce served with boiled meats

salsiccia sausage

saltimbocca alla romana veal and ham (rolls) with sage

salvia sage

San Pietro John Dory (fish)

saor Venetian sweet and sour sauce

sard(ell)e sardines

sardenara kind of pizza with sardines, tomatoes and olives

sartu di riso Neapolitan rice pie with meat, mushrooms, tomatoes and cheese

sbrisolana crumbly cake from Mantua

scalopp(in)a veal escalope

scaloppa alla Milanese fried breadcrumbed escalope of veal

scampi Adriatic prawns

scapece, a marinated

schiacciate see focaccia

sciule piene stuffed onions

scorfano scorpion fish, used in soups

scottadito grilled cutlets

scrippelle 'mbusse Abruzzese pancakes

sebadas Sardinian ricotta-filled pastries

sedano celery

selvaggina game, usually venison

semifreddo ice-cream dessert

senape mustard

seppie cuttlefish

serpentaria see dragoncello

sfogio sole (Venetian dialect)

sfogliatelle flaky pastry cases filled with ricotta and candied fruit

sformato kind of souffle

sgombro mackerel

siciliana, alla usually with capers, tomatoes, anchovies, olives, onions, red peppers, herbs

sogliola sole

sopa soup (Venetian dialect)

sopa coada substantial pigeon soup from the Veneto

sottoaceti pickled vegetables

spannocchi corn-on-the-cob

spezzatino stew

spezzato chopped small, diced

spiedini kebabs

spiedo, allo cooked on the spit

spigola sea bass

spinaci spinach

spuma mousse

spuntino snack

squadro monkfish

starna partridge

stellette, stelline pasta stars

stoccafisso dried cod

storione sturgeon

stracciatella clear soup with egg; chocolate chip ice-cream

stracotto beef stew (veal stew in Florence)

strangolapreti/strozzapreti Roman gnocchi, 'prieststranglers'

stufatino Roman beef stew or Florentine veal stew

stufato stew(ed)

succo juice

sugo gravy, sauce
suppli (al telefono) fried savoury rice balls (with hot stringy cheese)
susine plums

tacchino turkey
taccula roast thrushes or blackbirds, Sardinian speciality
tagliarini; tagliolini thin tagliatelle
tagliatelle ribbon pasta
taralli Sicilian doughnuts
tartaruga turtle
tartufata meat sauce with truffles
tartufi truffles
tartufi di mare; tartufoli small clams
tartufo icecream in chocolate shell (or sauce)
telline cockles (Tuscan dialect)
temoli grayling (fish)
teneroni end of rib with breast meat
testa head
tiella pie (Lazio and Apulia)
timballo kind of (pasta) pie
timo thyme
tinca tench
tiramisu 'pick-me-up', liqueur-soaked sponge dessert
tonnarelle type of tagliatelle
tonnato with a tuna fish sauce
tonnellini match-like noodles
tonno tuna
torrone nougat
torta flan, tart
torta tarentina potato pizza
torta verde Ligurian spinach pie
tortelli (di erbette) kind of ravioli (with spinach and ricotta stuffing)
tortellini small stuffed pasta rings
tortiera, in baked
tortiglione almond cake
tortiglioni pasta tubes
tortino kind of omelette, usually with vegetables; croquettes
totani squid
trenette (al pesto) flat pasta (with 'pesto' sauce)
trifolato sliced
triglia red mullet
trippa tripe
troffie small, light potato dumplings
trota (salmonata) (salmon) trout

uccelletti small (roast) birds
uccelli scappati thin skewered pieces of meat with sage
umido, in steamed
uova affogate poached eggs
uova bazzotte soft-boiled eggs
uova al tegame baked eggs
uova in camicia poached eggs
uova in padella fried eggs
uova mollette boiled eggs
uova sode hard-boiled eggs
uova stracciate/strapazzate scrambled eggs
uva grapes
uva passa raisins
uvetta sultanas

valdostana, alla with mountain cheese and ham
vellutata creamy soup
verdura vegetables
vermicelli (version of) spaghetti
verza Savoy cabbage
vincisgrassi lasagne dish with rich chicken liver, sausage and mushroom sauce
vitello veal
vitello alla genovese veal with white wine and artichokes
vitello tonnato cold veal in tunny sauce
vitellone young beef
vongole clams

zaba(gl)ione whipped egg yolks, sugar and marsala
zampone boiled stuffed pig's trotters
zenzero ginger
zimino Genoese fish stew
ziminu Sardinian fish stew
zite large pasta tubes
zucca pumpkin, marrow
zucchini courgettes
zuppa soup
zuppa alla romana lettuce soup
zuppa cuata Sardinian dish with eggs, tomato and bread
zuppa inglese trifle
zuppa pavese clear soup with a poached egg and fried bread

MAPS

The maps on the following pages are designed to help situate most of the places mentioned in the text.

The numbers on this key map refer to our area chapters, as indicated below.
The maps on the following pages do not show any chapter boundaries.

1 **Lakes and Mountains**
2 **Venice**
3 **Northern Cities**
4 **Liguria**
5 **Florence**
6 **Tuscany and Umbria**
7 **Rome**
8 **Central Italy**
9 **Naples and Campania**
10 **The South**
11 **Sicily**
12 **Sardinia**

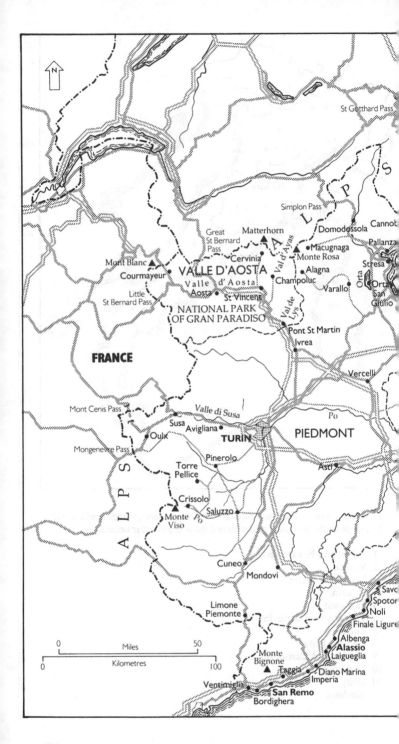

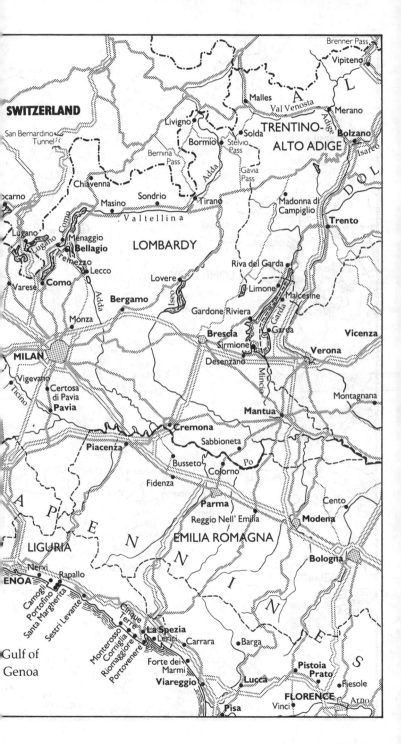

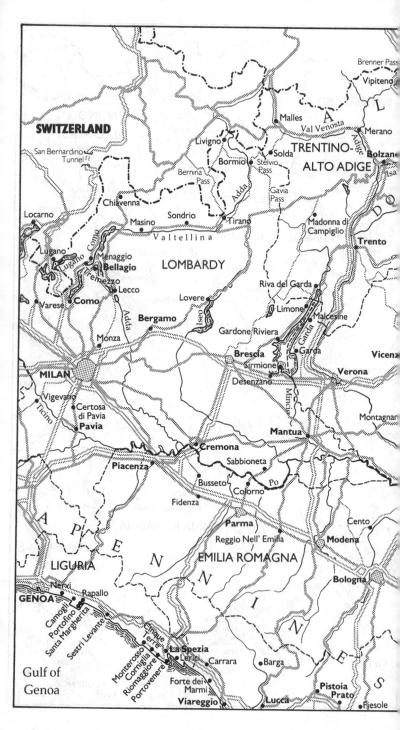

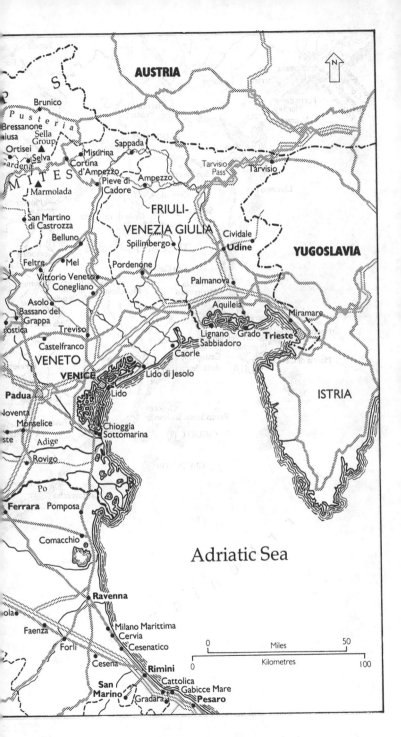

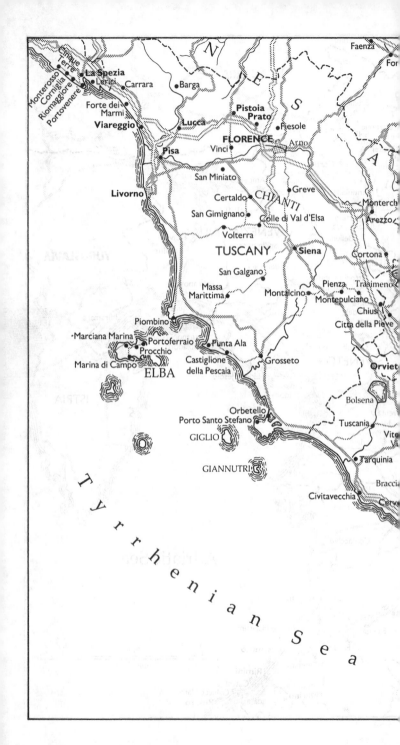

Milano Marittima
Cervia
Cesenatico
Rimini
Cattolica
Gabicce Mare
Gradara **Pesaro**
Fano
Urbino
Senigallia
MARCHES
Ancona
Jesi
epolcro
ta di Castello
Fabriano
Gubbio
Loreto
Recanati
Macerata
ugia
Fermo
Assisi
Spello
ruta
Foligno
Bevagna
Montefalco
Trevi
UMBRIA
Todi
Spoleto
Ascoli Piceno
San Benedetto del Tronto
Alba Adriatica
Giulianova
Narni
Terni
Teramo
Silvi
Montesilvano
Pescara
aprarola
Rieti
Tiber
▲ Gran Sasso
Civita Castellana
L'Aquila
Bominaco
Chieti
ABRUZZI
Sulmona
Tivoli
NATIONAL PARK
OF
ABRUZZI
Scanno
Pescocostanzo
Subiaco
Pescasseroli
ME
Frascati Palestrina
Anagni
MOLISE
Ostia
Nemi
Castel
Gandolfo
Velletri
stia
Monte
Cassino
LAZIO
Norma
Sermoneta
Campobasso
Vinchiaturo
Anzio
Fossanova
THE MATESE
Volturno
Terracina
Sperlonga
Sabaudia
Gaeta
Benevento
Capua
Santa Maria Capua Vetere
Casertavecchia
Caserta
CAMPANIA

0   Miles   50
0   Kilometres   100

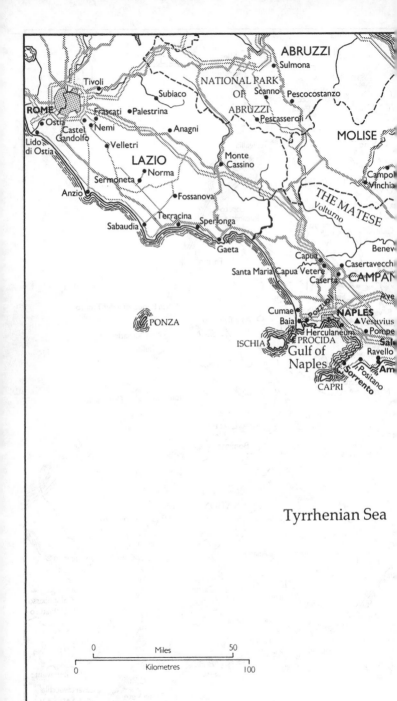

ABRUZZI

Sulmona

NATIONAL PARK
Tivoli
Subiaco   OF   Scanno
Pescocostanzo

ROME   Frascati Palestrina   ABRUZZI   Pescasseroli

Ostia   Nemi   MOLISE

Castel   Anagni
Gandolfo
Lido   Campo
di Ostia   Velletri   Vinchia
                         Monte
        LAZIO   Cassino   THE MATESE

        Norma   Volturno
Sermoneta

Anzio   Fossanova

        Terracina   Benev
Sabaudia   Sperlonga
                                        Capua
                    Gaeta   Casertavecch
                            Santa Maria Capua Vetere   CAMPAN
                                            Caserta
                                                        Ave

                                    Cumae   Pozzuoli NAPLES
                            PONZA   Baia   ▲Vesuvius
                                            Herculaneum Pompe
                            ISCHIA   PROCIDA   Sal
                                        Gulf of   Ravello
                                        Naples   Am
                                                   Positano
                                        CAPRI   Sorrento

                        Tyrrhenian Sea

            0   Miles   50
            0   Kilometres   100

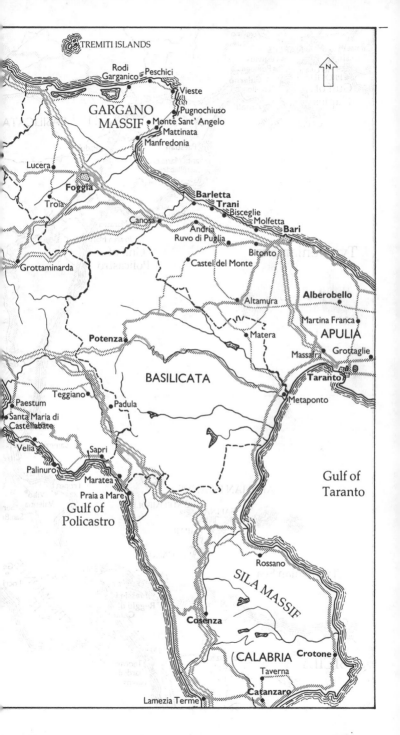

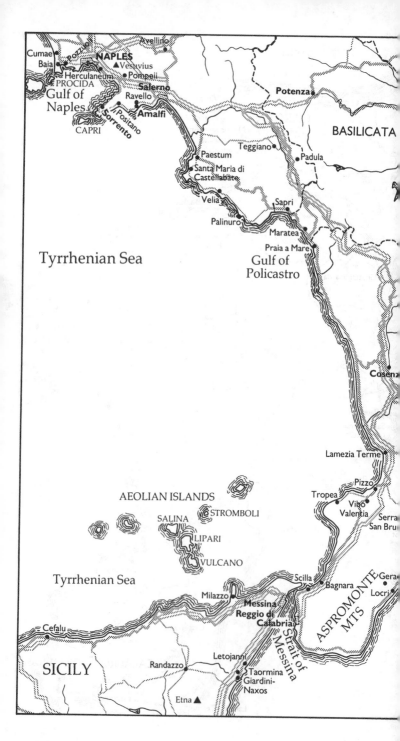

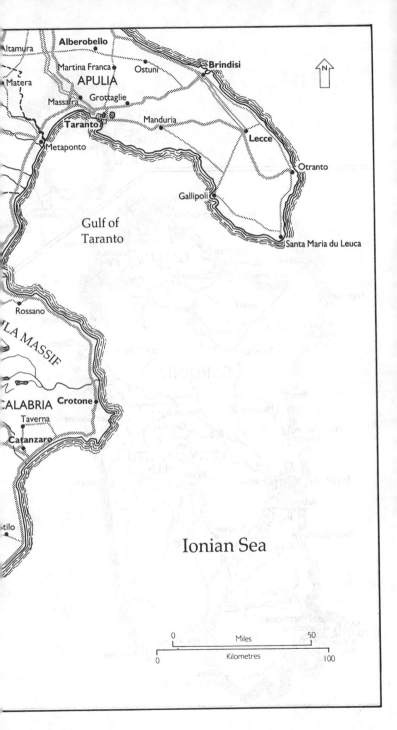

Altamura

Alberobello

Martina Franca • • Ostuni
APULIA

Brindisi

Matera

Massafra • • Grottaglie

Taranto

• Manduria

Lecce

Metaponto

• Otranto

Gallipoli

Gulf of
Taranto

Santa Maria du Leuca

Rossano

'LA MASSIF

CALABRIA **Crotone** •

Taverna

Catanzaro

Ionian Sea

tilo

```
0              Miles        50
├──────┼──────┼──────┤
0              Kilometres        100
```

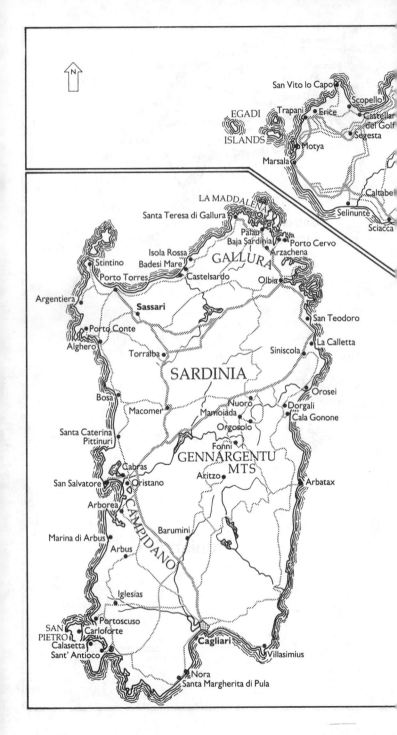

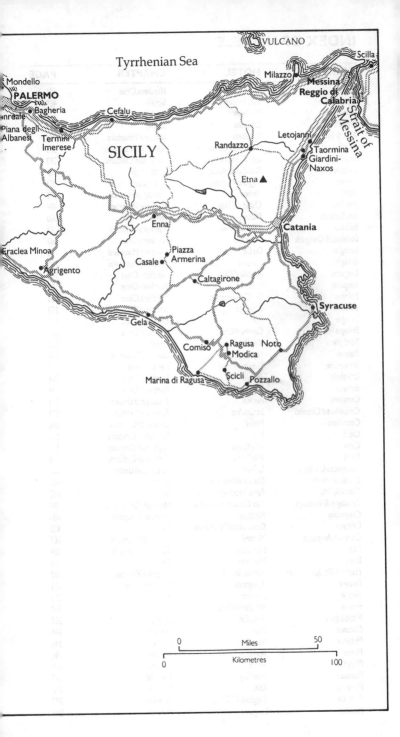

INDEX OF HOTELS

INDEX

Hotel reports

The report form on the following page may be used to endorse or
criticise an existing entry or to nominate a hotel that you feel
deserves inclusion in the next edition of the *Guide*, or in an issue of
Holiday Which? magazine. There's no need to restrict yourself to the
form, but all nominations should include your name and address,
the name and location of the hotel, when you stayed there and for
how long.

There is no need to give details of prices or number of rooms and
facilities, as all nominated hotels will be inspected by the *Holiday
Which?* team. We are anxious to find out from readers details of
food, service and atmosphere, and should also be grateful for any
brochures and menus.

To: *The Holiday Which? Guide to Italy*

Freepost, London WC2N 4BR

NOTE No stamps needed in UK, but letters posted outside the UK should be addressed
to 14 Buckingham Street, London WC2N 6DS and stamped normally. It is not our policy
to publish names of readers who recommend a new hotel or criticise an existing entry.
Unless asked not to, we shall assume that we may publish extracts from any report
either in the *Guide* or in the magazine *Holiday Which?*

Name of hotel ....

Address ....

....

Date of most recent visit ....

Duration of visit ....

Report:

(Continue overleaf if you wish or use separate sheet)

Signed ....

Name and address (CAPITALS PLEASE) ....

....